with MyEconLab

- **Real-Time Data Analysis Exercises**—Using current macro data to help students understand the impact of changes in economic variables, Real-Time Data Analysis Exercises communicate directly with the Federal Reserve Bank of St. Louis's FRED® site and update as new data are available.

- **Current News Exercises**—Every week, current microeconomic and macroeconomic news stories, with accompanying exercises, are posted to MyEconLab. Assignable and auto-graded, these multi-part exercises ask students to recognize and apply economic concepts to real-world events.

- **Experiments**—Flexible, easy-to-assign, auto-graded, and available in Single and Multiplayer versions, Experiments in MyEconLab make learning fun and engaging.

- **Reporting Dashboard**—View, analyze, and report learning outcomes clearly and easily. Available via the Gradebook and fully mobile-ready, the Reporting Dashboard presents student performance data at the class, section, and program levels in an accessible, visual manner.

- **LMS Integration**—Link from any LMS platform to access assignments, rosters, and resources, and synchronize MyLab grades with your LMS gradebook. For students, new direct, single sign-on provides access to all the personalized learning MyLab resources that make studying more efficient and effective.

- **Mobile Ready**—Students and instructors can access multimedia resources and complete assessments right at their fingertips, on any mobile device.

PEARSON

THE ECONOMICS OF
MONEY, BANKING, AND
FINANCIAL MARKETS

The Pearson Series in Economics

Abel/Bernanke/Croushore
Macroeconomics*

Acemoglu/Laibson/List
Economics*

Bade/Parkin
Foundations of Economics*

Berck/Helfand
The Economics of the Environment

Bierman/Fernandez
Game Theory with Economic Applications

Blanchard
Macroeconomics*

Blau/Ferber/Winkler
The Economics of Women, Men, and Work

Boardman/Greenberg/Vining/Weimer
Cost-Benefit Analysis

Boyer
Principles of Transportation Economics

Branson
Macroeconomic Theory and Policy

Bruce
Public Finance and the American Economy

Carlton/Perloff
Modern Industrial Organization

Case/Fair/Oster
Principles of Economics*

Chapman
*Environmental Economics: Theory,
Application, and Policy*

Cooter/Ulen
Law & Economics

Daniels/VanHoose
*International Monetary & Financial
Economics*

Downs
An Economic Theory of Democracy

Ehrenberg/Smith
Modern Labor Economics

Farnham
Economics for Managers

Folland/Goodman/Stano
The Economics of Health and Health Care

Fort
Sports Economics

Froyen
Macroeconomics

Fusfeld
The Age of the Economist

Gerber
International Economics*

González-Rivera
Forecasting for Economics and Business

Gordon
Macroeconomics*

Greene
Econometric Analysis

Gregory
Essentials of Economics

Gregory/Stuart
*Russian and Soviet Economic Performance
and Structure*

Hartwick/Olewiler
The Economics of Natural Resource Use

Heilbroner/Milberg
The Making of the Economic Society

Heyne/Boettke/Prychitko
The Economic Way of Thinking

Holt
Markets, Games, and Strategic Behavior

Hubbard/O'Brien
Economics*
Money, Banking, and the Financial System*

Hubbard/O'Brien/Rafferty
Macroeconomics*

Hughes/Cain
American Economic History

Husted/Melvin
International Economics

Jehle/Reny
Advanced Microeconomic Theory

Johnson-Lans
A Health Economics Primer

Keat/Young/Erfle
Managerial Economics

Klein
Mathematical Methods for Economics

Krugman/Obstfeld/Melitz
International Economics: Theory & Policy*

Laidler
The Demand for Money

Leeds/von Allmen
The Economics of Sports

Leeds/von Allmen/Schiming
Economics*

Lynn
*Economic Development: Theory and
Practice for a Divided World*

Miller
Economics Today*
Understanding Modern Economics

Miller/Benjamin
The Economics of Macro Issues

Miller/Benjamin/North
The Economics of Public Issues

Mills/Hamilton
Urban Economics

Mishkin
*The Economics of Money, Banking, and
Financial Markets**

*The Economics of Money, Banking, and
Financial Markets, Business School Edition**
Macroeconomics: Policy and Practice*

Murray
Econometrics: A Modern Introduction

O'Sullivan/Sheffrin/Perez
Economics: Principles, Applications and Tools*

Parkin
Economics*

Perloff
Microeconomics*
*Microeconomics: Theory and Applications
with Calculus**

Perloff/Brander
Managerial Economics and Strategy*

Phelps
Health Economics

Pindyck/Rubinfeld
Microeconomics*

Riddell/Shackelford/Stamos/Schneider
*Economics: A Tool for Critically Understanding
Society*

Roberts
*The Choice: A Fable of Free Trade and
Protection*

Roland
Development Economics

Scherer
*Industry Structure, Strategy, and Public
Policy*

Schiller
*The Economics of Poverty and
Discrimination*

Sherman
Market Regulation

Stock/Watson
Introduction to Econometrics

Studenmund
Using Econometrics: A Practical Guide

Tietenberg/Lewis
*Environmental and Natural Resource
Economics*
Environmental Economics and Policy

Todaro/Smith
Economic Development

Waldman/Jensen
*Industrial Organization: Theory and
Practice*

Walters/Walters/Appel/Callahan/
Centanni/Maex/O'Neill
*Econversations: Today's Students Discuss
Today's Issues*

Weil
Economic Growth

Williamson
Macroeconomics

*denotes MyEconLab titles   Visit www.myeconlab.com to learn more.

THE ECONOMICS OF
MONEY, BANKING, AND FINANCIAL MARKETS

Eleventh Edition

Frederic S. Mishkin
Columbia University

PEARSON

Boston   Columbus   Indianapolis   New York   San Francisco   Hoboken
Amsterdam   Cape Town   Dubai   London   Madrid   Milan   Munich   Paris   Montreal   Toronto
Delhi   Mexico City   Sao Paulo   Sydney   Hong Kong   Seoul   Singapore   Taipei   Tokyo

Vice President, Business Publishing: Donna
    Battista
Acquisitions Editor: Christina Masturzo
Editorial Assistant: Christine Mallon
Vice President, Product Marketing: Maggie Moylan
Director of Marketing, Digital Services and Products:
    Jeanette Koskinas
Senior Product Marketing Manager: Alison Haskins
Executive Field Marketing Manager: Lori DeShazo
Senior Strategic Marketing Manager: Erin Gardner
Team Lead, Program Management: Ashley Santora
Program Manager: Carolyn Philips
Team Lead, Project Management: Jeff Holcomb
Project Manager: Alison Kalil
Supplements Project Manager: Andra Skaalrud
Operations Specialist: Carol Melville
Creative Director: Blair Brown
Art Director: Jon Boylan

Vice President, Director of Digital Strategy and
    Assessment: Paul Gentile
Manager of Learning Applications: Paul DeLuca
Digital Editor: Denise Clinton
Director, Digital Studio: Sacha Laustsen
Digital Studio Manager: Diane Lombardo
Digital Studio Project Manager: Melissa Honig
Digital Content Team Lead: Noel Lotz
Digital Content Project Lead: Courtney Kamauf
Full-Service Project Management, Composition,
    and Interior Design: Cenveo® Publisher
    Services
Cover Designer: Jonathan Boylan
Cover Art: Photodisc/Getty Images; E+/Getty Images;
    Digital Vision/Getty Images; Kushch Dmitry/
    Shutterstock; Image Source/Corbis
Printer/Binder: R.R. Donnelley/Willard
Cover Printer: R.R. Donnelley/Willard

Library of Congress Cataloging-in-Publication Data

Mishkin, Frederic S.
  The economics of money, banking, and financial markets / Frederic S. Mishkin, Columbia University. – Eleventh edition.
  pages cm
Includes index.
ISBN 978-0-13-383679-0 – ISBN 0-13-383679-7
  1. Finance. 2. Money. 3. Banks and banking. I. Title.
HG173.M632 2016
332–dc23

                              2014041906

10 9 8 7 6 5 4 3 2 1

ISBN 10: 0-13-383679-7
ISBN 13: 978-0-13-383679-0

To Sally

Brief Contents

Chapters on the Web

Contents in Detail

PART 2   Financial Markets   63

CHAPTER 4
The Meaning of Interest Rates   64

CHAPTER 4 WEB APPENDIX
Measuring Interest-Rate Risk: Duration

Go to the Companion Website, http://www.pearsonhighered.com/mishkin

CHAPTER 5
The Behavior of Interest Rates   85

CHAPTER 5 WEB APPENDIX 1
Models of Asset Pricing
Go to the Companion Website, http://www.pearsonhighered.com/mishkin

CHAPTER 5 WEB APPENDIX 2
Applying the Asset Market Approach to a Commodity Market: The Case of Gold
Go to the Companion Website, http://www.pearsonhighered.com/mishkin

CHAPTER 5 WEB APPENDIX 3
Loanable Funds Framework
Go to the Companion Website, http://www.pearsonhighered.com/mishkin

CHAPTER 6
The Risk and Term Structure of Interest Rates 116

CHAPTER 7
The Stock Market, the Theory of Rational Expectations, and the Efficient Market Hypothesis 140

CHAPTER 7 WEB APPENDIX
Evidence on the Efficient Market Hypothesis
Go to the Companion Website, http://www.pearsonhighered.com/mishkin

---

PART 3   **Financial Institutions   161**

CHAPTER 8
An Economic Analysis of Financial Structure   162

PART 4   Central Banking and the Conduct of Monetary Policy   291

CHAPTER 14 WEB APPENDIX 1
The Fed's Balance Sheet and the Monetary Base
Go to the Companion Website, http://www.pearsonhighered.com/mishkin

CHAPTER 14 WEB APPENDIX 2
The M2 Money Multiplier
Go to the Companion Website, http://www.pearsonhighered.com/mishkin

CHAPTER 14 WEB APPENDIX 3
Explaining the Behavior of the Currency Ratio
Go to the Companion Website, http://www.pearsonhighered.com/mishkin

CHAPTER 14 WEB APPENDIX 4
The Great Depression Bank Panics, 1930–1933, and the Money Supply
Go to the Companion Website, http://www.pearsonhighered.com/mishkin

CHAPTER 15
Tools of Monetary Policy   341

CHAPTER 16
The Conduct of Monetary Policy: Strategy and Tactics 366

CHAPTER 18
The International Financial System 427

PART 6   Monetary Theory   455

CHAPTER 21
The Monetary Policy and Aggregate Demand Curves 494

CHAPTER 22
Aggregate Demand and Supply Analysis 509

CHAPTER 22 WEB APPENDIX 1
The Effects of Macroeconomic Shocks on Asset Prices
Go to the Companion Website, http://www.pearsonhighered.com/mishkin

CHAPTER 22 WEB APPENDIX 2
Aggregate Demand and Supply: A Numerical Example
Go to the Companion Website, http://www.pearsonhighered.com/mishkin

CHAPTER 22 WEB APPENDIX 3
The Algebra of the Aggregate Demand and Supply Model
Go to the Companion Website, http://www.pearsonhighered.com/mishkin

CHAPTER 22 WEB APPENDIX 4
The Taylor Principle and Inflation
Go to the Companion Website, http://www.pearsonhighered.com/mishkin

CHAPTER 25 WEB APPENDIX
Evaluating Empirical Evidence: The Debate Over the Importance of Money in Economic Fluctuations
Go to the Companion Website, http://www.pearsonhighered.com/mishkin

Contents on the Web

The following chapters are available on our Companion Website at http://www.pearsonhighered.com/mishkin.

WEB CHAPTER 1
Financial Crises in Emerging Market Economies   **W-1**

WEB CHAPTER 4
Financial Derivatives   W-1

HALLMARKS

Although this text has undergone a major revision, it retains the basic hallmarks that have made it the best-selling textbook on money and banking over the past ten editions:

- A unifying, analytic framework that uses a few basic economic principles to organize students' thinking about the structure of financial markets, the foreign exchange markets, financial institution management, and the role of monetary policy in the economy
- A careful, step-by-step development of economic models (the approach used in the best principles of economics textbooks), which makes it easier for students to learn
- The complete integration of an international perspective throughout the text
- A thoroughly up-to-date treatment of the latest developments in monetary theory
- A special feature called "Following the Financial News," included to encourage reading of a financial newspaper
- An applications-oriented perspective with numerous applications and special-topic boxes that increase students' interest by showing them how to apply theory to real-world examples

WHAT'S NEW IN THE ELEVENTH EDITION

In addition to the expected updating of all data through 2014 whenever possible, there is major new material in every part of the text.

MyEconLab

Enhanced Pearson e-text with Mini-Lecture Videos: A New Way of Learning

The Enhanced Pearson e-text in MyEconLab for the eleventh edition is available online from MyEconLab textbook resources. Instructors and students can highlight the text, bookmark, search the glossary, and take notes. More importantly, the enhanced Pearson e-text provides a new way of learning that is particularly geared to today's students. Not only will students be able to read the material in the textbook, but by a simple click on an icon they will be able to watch over 120 mini-lecture videos presented by the author, one for every figure in the text. For analytic figures, these mini-lectures build up each graph step-by-step and explain the intuition necessary to fully understand the theory behind the graph. For data figures, the mini-lectures highlight the key data points that are of greatest interest. The mini-lectures are an invaluable study tool for students who typically learn better when they see and hear economic analysis rather than read it.

Real-Time Data

A high percentage of the in-text data figures are labeled *MyEconLab Real-Time Data*. For these figures, students can see the latest data in the enhanced Pearson e-text, using the Federal Reserve Bank of St. Louis's FRED database. In addition, the new edition of the text includes a whole new class of problems that involve real-time data analysis. These problems, marked with 🌐, ask the student to download data from the Federal

Reserve Bank of St. Louis FRED website and then use the data to answer questions about current issues in macroeconomics.

In MyEconLab, these easy-to-assign and automatically graded Real-Time Data Analysis exercises communicate directly with the FRED site, so that students see updated data every time new data is posted by FRED. Thus the Real-Time Data Analysis exercises offer a no-fuss solution for instructors who want to make the most current data a central part of their macroeconomics course. These exercises will not only help students understand macroeconomics better but will also enable them to see the real-world relevance of their studies.

The Business School Edition: A More Finance-Oriented Approach

I am pleased to continue providing two versions of *The Economics of Money, Banking, and Financial Markets*. While both versions contain the core chapters that all professors want to cover, *The Economics of Money, Banking, and Financial Markets*, Business School Edition, presents a more finance-oriented approach—an approach more commonly taught in business schools, but also one that some professors in economics departments prefer when teaching their money and banking courses. The Business School Edition includes chapters on nonbank finance, financial derivatives, and conflicts of interest in the financial industry. The Business School Edition omits the chapters on the *IS* curve and the monetary policy and aggregate demand curves, as well as the chapter on the role of expectations in monetary policy. *The Economics of Money, Banking, and Financial Markets*, Business School Edition, will more closely fit the needs of those professors whose courses put less emphasis on monetary theory.

For professors who desire a comprehensive discussion of monetary theory and monetary policy, *The Economics of Money, Banking, and Financial Markets*, Eleventh Edition, contains all of the chapters on monetary theory. Professors who *do* want this coverage are often hard-pressed to cover all of the finance and institutions chapters. To that end, the Eleventh Edition omits the chapters on nonbank finance, financial derivatives, and conflicts of interest. The Companion Website at http://www.pearsonhighered .com/mishkin provides the omitted chapters, making them readily available for those who wish to utilize them in their courses.

Reorganization of Part 3, Financial Institutions

The global financial crisis of 2007–2009 has become a central topic in the teaching of money and banking. When I teach this material, I find that students understand the dynamics of the crisis more deeply if they are taught about bank management, financial regulation, and the shadow banking system before they delve into the details of the global financial crisis. For this reason, I have moved the chapter titled "Financial Crises" so that it follows the three chapters titled "Banking and the Management of Financial Institutions," "Economic Analysis and Financial Regulation," and "Banking Industry: Structure and Competition."

In addition, I have added the following new material to Part 3 of the text:

- A new FYI box on the tyranny of collateral (Chapter 8)
- A new section that provides more detail on securitization and the shadow banking system (Chapter 11)

- A new section on the response of financial regulation to the global financial crisis (Chapter 12)
- A new section exploring what can be done about the too-big-to-fail problem (Chapter 12)

Nonconventional Monetary Policy and the Zero Lower Bound

Monetary policy entered a brave new world when policymakers had to resort to nonconventional measures when the policy interest rate—the federal funds rate in the United States—hit a floor of zero, or the so-called "zero lower bound." Because the policy rate cannot be driven lower than zero, under this condition conventional monetary policy becomes infeasible. Nonconventional monetary policy at the zero lower bound, such as quantitative easing, has become a very controversial topic that stimulates a lot of student interest. The Eleventh Edition contains extensive discussion of this topic, including the following new material:

- A new application on quantitative easing and the money supply from 2007 to 2014 (Chapter 14)
- An updated section on forward guidance and the commitment to future policy actions (Chapter 15)
- A new section on monetary policy at the zero lower bound that uses the aggregate demand and aggregate supply models to explain how the zero lower bound affects the conduct of monetary policy (Chapter 23)
- A new application on nonconventional monetary policy and quantitative easing (Chapter 23)
- A new application on Abenomics and the shift in Japanese monetary policy in 2013 (Chapter 23)

The Euro Crisis

The Euro crisis has been a continuing drama since 2010, and so this edition includes the following new material:

- A new global box on the European sovereign debt crisis (Chapter 12)
- A new section on monetary unions (Chapter 18)
- A new global box on whether the Euro will survive (Chapter 18)

Additional New Material

New developments in the money and banking field have prompted me to add the following new material that I feel is necessary to keep the text current:

- A new application on whether Bitcoin will become the money of the future (Chapter 3)
- A new application on the effects of the Obama tax increase on bond interest rates (Chapter 6)
- An updated section on the evolution of the Fed's communication strategy (Chapter 13)
- A new section on movements along versus shifts in the *MP* curve, with a new application that discusses the movement along the *MP* curve that occurred when the Fed raised the federal funds target during the years 2004 to 2006 (Chapter 21)
- A new FYI box that describes the meaning of the word *autonomous* (Chapter 22)
- A new section on nominal GDP targeting (Chapter 23)

Chapters and Appendices on the Web

The Companion Website for the book, http://www.pearsonhighered.com/mishkin, is an essential resource for additional content.

The web chapters for the Eleventh Edition of *The Economics of Money, Banking, and Financial Markets* include the unique chapters from the Business School Edition along with web chapters on financial crises in emerging market economies and the *ISLM* model. These chapters are numbered as follows:

Web Chapter 1:   Financial Crises in Emerging Market Economies
Web Chapter 2:   The *ISLM* Model
Web Chapter 3:   Nonbank Finance
Web Chapter 4:   Financial Derivatives
Web Chapter 5:   Conflicts of Interest in the Financial Industry

The web appendices include:

Appendix to Chapter 4:   Measuring Interest-Rate Risk: Duration
Appendix 1 to Chapter 5:   Models of Asset Pricing
Appendix 2 to Chapter 5:   Applying the Asset Market Approach to a Commodity Market: The Case of Gold
Appendix 3 to Chapter 5:   Loanable Funds Framework
Appendix to Chapter 7:   Evidence on the Efficient Market Hypothesis
Appendix 1 to Chapter 9:   Duration Gap Analysis
Appendix 2 to Chapter 9:   Measuring Bank Performance
Appendix 1 to Chapter 10:   The 1980s Banking and Savings and Loan Crisis
Appendix 2 to Chapter 10:   Banking Crises Throughout the World
Appendix 1 to Chapter 14:   The Fed's Balance Sheet and the Monetary Base
Appendix 2 to Chapter 14:   The M2 Money Multiplier
Appendix 3 to Chapter 14:   Explaining the Behavior of the Currency Ratio
Appendix 4 to Chapter 14:   The Great Depression Bank Panics, 1930–1933, and the Money Supply
Appendix 1 to Chapter 16:   Monetary Targeting
Appendix 2 to Chapter 16:   A Brief History of Federal Reserve Policymaking
Appendix 1 to Chapter 19:   The Baumol-Tobin and Tobin Mean-Variance Models of the Demand for Money
Appendix 2 to Chapter 19:   Empirical Evidence on the Demand for Money
Appendix 1 to Chapter 22:   The Effects of Macroeconomic Shocks on Asset Prices
Appendix 2 to Chapter 22:   Aggregate Demand and Supply: A Numerical Example
Appendix 3 to Chapter 22:   The Algebra of the Aggregate Demand and Supply Model
Appendix 4 to Chapter 22:   The Taylor Principle and Inflation Stability
Appendix to Chapter 25:   Evaluating Empirical Evidence: The Debate Over the Importance of Money in Economic Fluctuations

Instructors can either use these web chapters and appendices in class to supplement the material in the textbook, or recommend them to students who want to expand their knowledge of the money and banking field.

FLEXIBILITY AND MODULARITY

In using previous editions, adopters, reviewers, and survey respondents have continually praised this text's flexibility and modularity—that is, the option to pick and choose which chapters to cover and in what order to cover them. Flexibility and modularity are especially important in the money and banking course because there are as many ways to teach this course as there are instructors. To satisfy the diverse needs of instructors, the text achieves flexibility as follows:

- Core chapters provide the basic analysis used throughout the book, and other chapters or sections of chapters can be used or omitted according to instructor preferences. For example, Chapter 2 introduces the financial system and basic concepts such as transaction costs, adverse selection, and moral hazard. After covering Chapter 2, the instructor may decide to give more detailed coverage of financial structure by assigning Chapter 8 or may choose to skip Chapter 8 and take any of a number of different paths through the book.
- The text allows instructors to cover the most important issues in monetary theory even if they do not wish to present a detailed development of the *IS, MP,* and *AD* curves (provided in Chapters 20 and 21). Instructors who want to teach a more complete treatment of monetary theory can make use of these chapters.
- Part 6 on monetary theory can easily be taught before Part 4 of the text if the instructor wishes to give students a deeper understanding of the rationale behind monetary policy.
- Chapter 25 on the transmission mechanisms of monetary policy can be taught at many different points in the course—either with Part 4, when monetary policy is discussed, or with Chapter 20 or Chapter 22, when the concept of aggregate demand is developed. Transmission mechanisms of monetary policy can also be taught as a special topic at the end of the course.
- The international approach of the text, accomplished through marked international sections within chapters as well as separate chapters on the foreign exchange market and the international monetary system, is comprehensive yet flexible. Although many instructors will teach all the international material, others will not. Instructors who wish to put less emphasis on international topics can easily skip Chapter 17 on the foreign exchange market and Chapter 18 on the international financial system and monetary policy. The international sections within chapters are self-contained and can be omitted with little loss of continuity.

To illustrate how this book can be used for courses with varying emphases, several course outlines are suggested for a one-semester teaching schedule. More detailed information about how the text can be used flexibly in your course is available in the Instructor's Manual.

- *General Money and Banking Course:* Chapters 1–5, 9–13, 15, 16, 22–23, with a choice of 5 of the remaining 11 chapters
- *General Money and Banking Course with an International Emphasis:* Chapters 1–5, 9–13, 15–18, 22–23, with a choice of 3 of the remaining 9 chapters
- *Financial Markets and Institutions Course:* Chapters 1–12, with a choice of 7 of the remaining 13 chapters
- *Monetary Theory and Policy Course:* Chapters 1–5, 13–16, 19–24, with a choice of 4 of the remaining 10 chapters

PEDAGOGICAL AIDS

Whether teaching theory or its applications, a textbook must be a solid motivational tool. To this end, I have incorporated a wide variety of pedagogical features that will make the material easy to learn:

1. **Previews** at the beginning of each chapter tell students where the chapter is heading, why specific topics are important, and how these topics relate to other topics discussed in the book.
2. **Applications**, numbering over 50, demonstrate how the analysis presented in the book can be used to explain many important real-world situations.
3. **Following the Financial News boxes** introduce students to relevant news articles and data that are reported daily in the press, and teach students how to interpret these data.
4. **Inside the Fed boxes** give students a feel for the operation and structure of the Federal Reserve System.
5. **Global boxes** present interesting material with an international focus.
6. **FYI boxes** highlight dramatic historical episodes, interesting ideas, and intriguing facts related to the subject matter.
7. **Summary tables** provide a useful study aid for reviewing material.
8. **Key statements** are important points set in boldface italic type so that students can easily find them for later reference.
9. **Graphs** with captions, numbering more than 120, help students clearly understand the interrelationships among the plotted variables and the principles of analysis.
10. A **Summary** at the end of each chapter lists the main points covered in the chapter.
11. **Key terms** are important words or phrases introduced in the chapter. They are set in boldface when they are defined for the first time, and they are listed by page number at the end of each chapter.
12. **End-of-chapter questions and applied problems**, numbering more than 600, help students learn the subject matter by applying economic concepts.
13. **Real-Time Data Analysis Problems** ask students to apply up-to-the-minute data, taken from the St. Louis Federal Reserve Bank's FRED database, so that they can understand what is happening in the economy in real time.
14. **Web Exercises** encourage students to collect information from online sources or use online resources to enhance their learning experience.
15. **Web sources** report the URL sources of the data used to create the many tables and charts.
16. **Web References** point the student to websites that provide information or data that supplement the text material.
17. A **Glossary** at the back of the book provides definitions of all of the key terms.

AN EASIER WAY TO TEACH: SUPPLEMENTS TO ACCOMPANY THE ELEVENTH EDITION

The Economics of Money, Banking, and Financial Markets, Eleventh Edition, includes the most comprehensive program of supplements of any money, banking, and financial markets textbook.

MyEconLab

MyEconLab has been designed and refined with a single purpose in mind: to create those moments of understanding that transform the difficult into the clear and obvious. With comprehensive homework, quiz, test, and tutorial options, instructors can manage all of their assessment needs within one program.

MyEconLab for *The Economics of Money, Banking, and Financial Markets* offers the following resources for students and instructors:

- **All end-of-chapter questions and applied problems** from the text are available in MyEconLab.
- **Applications** from the text are provided, along with assignable questions.
- **Mini-Lecture Videos** provide a step-by-step analysis of all the data and analytic figures included in the text. The videos can be used in class or viewed by students on their own time.
- A **Personal Study Plan** is created for each individual student based on his or her performance on assigned and sample exercises.
- **Instant tutorial feedback** is provided for problems and graphing responses to questions.
- **Interactive learning aids**, such as *Help Me Solve This* (a step-by-step tutorial), are designed to help the student exactly when he or she needs support.
- **News articles** are available for classroom and assignment use. Up-to-date news articles and complimentary discussion questions are posted weekly to bring today's news into the classroom and course.
- **Real-Time Data Analysis Problems** allow instructors to assign problems that use up-to-the-minute data. Each RTDA exercise loads the appropriate and most current data from FRED, a comprehensive and up-to-date data set maintained by the Federal Reserve Bank of St. Louis. Exercises are graded based on the particular data used, and feedback is provided.
- An **Enhanced Pearson eText** is available within the online course materials and off-line via iPad and Android apps. The enhanced Pearson eText enables instructors and students to highlight, bookmark, and take notes.
- **Auto-graded problems and graphs** are available for assignments.
- A powerful **Gradebook,** flexible and rich with information, provides data on student and class assignment performance and time on task.
- **Advanced communication tools** enable students and instructors to communicate through email, discussion board, chat, and ClassLive.
- **Customization options** provide new and enhanced ways to share documents, add content, and rename menu items.
- **Temporary access.** A fourteen-day grace period of temporary access is provided for students who are awaiting financial aid.
- **One place for students to access all of their MyLab courses**. Students and instructors can register, create, and access all of their MyLab courses, regardless of discipline, from one convenient online location: http://www.pearsonmylab.com.

For more information, please visit http://www.myeconlab.com.

Additional Instructor Resources

1. **Instructor's Resource Manual**. This online supplement, prepared by me, offers conventional elements such as sample course outlines, chapter outlines, and answers to questions and problems in the text.

2. **PowerPoint® Presentation**. This online supplement provides all of the tables and graphs presented in the text, along with very detailed lecture notes for all the course material. The lecture notes are, in fact, based on the notes I use in class, and they should help other instructors prepare their lectures as they have helped me prepare mine. In this edition, Paul Kubik of DePaul University has enhanced the presentation by adding additional lecture notes. Instructors who prefer to teach with a blackboard can use these PowerPoint slides as their own class notes; for those who prefer to teach with visual aids, the PowerPoint slides afford them the flexibility to do so. The analytic figures within the PowerPoint slides are completely manipulable by the user so that instructors can custom-design their PowerPoint lectures with step-by-step animations of all key text figures.

3. **Test Bank**. This online supplement, updated and revised by James Hueng of Western Michigan University and Kathy Kelly of the University of Texas at Arlington, is comprised of more than 2,500 multiple-choice and essay test items, many with graphs. The authors of the test bank have connected questions to the general knowledge and skill guidelines found in The Association to Advance Collegiate Schools of Business (AACSB) assurance of learning standards. AACSB is a not-for-profit corporation of educational institutions, corporations, and other organizations devoted to the promotion and improvement of higher education in business administration and accounting. One of the criteria for AACSB accreditation is quality of the curriculum. Although no specific courses are required, the AACSB expects a curriculum to include learning experiences in the following areas: Written and oral communication, ethical understanding and reasoning, analytical thinking, information technology, interpersonal relations and teamwork, diverse and multicultural work environments, reflective thinking, and application of knowledge. Questions that test skills relevant to these guidelines are appropriately tagged for easy identification and assessment of student mastery.

4. **TestGen**. This online supplement enables the instructor to produce exams efficiently. This product consists of the multiple-choice and essay questions provided in the online Test Bank, and offers editing capabilities. It is available in Windows and Macintosh versions.

5. **Mishkin Companion Website.** This online supplement, located at http://www .pearsonhighered.com/mishkin, features appendices on a wide variety of topics (see "Appendices on the Web"), omitted chapters, and links to the URLs that are listed at the ends of the chapters.

ACKNOWLEDGMENTS

As always in so large a project, there are many people to thank. My gratitude goes especially to Donna Battista, Vice President of Business Publishing at Pearson; and Christina Masturzo, my Acquisitions Editor. I would like to thank Alison Kalil, Carolyn Philips, and Kathy Smith for their contributions as well. I also have been assisted by comments from my colleagues at Columbia and from my students.

In addition, I have been guided by the thoughtful commentary of outside reviewers and correspondents, especially Jim Eaton and Aaron Jackson. Their feedback has made this a better book. In particular, I thank the following professors who reviewed the text in preparation for this edition:

Thomas Bernardin, Smith College
Diego Escobari, The University of Texas–Pan American
Layton W. Franko, Queens College
Hyeongwoo Kim, Auburn University
Mary H. Lesser, Lenoir–Rhyne University
Robin McCutcheon, Marshall University
Andrew Nahlik, Illinois College
Hiranya K. Nath, Sam Houston State University
William R. Parke, University of North Carolina, Chapel Hill
Prosper Raynold, Miami University
Burak Sungu, Miami University
Demetri Tsanacas, Ferrum College and Hollins University
Rubina Vohra, New Jersey City University
Liping Zheng, Drake University

My special thanks go to the following individuals who analyzed the manuscript in previous editions:

Burt Abrams, University of Delaware
Francis W. Ahking, University of Connecticut
Mohammed Akacem, Metropolitan State College of Denver
Stefania Albanesi, Columbia University
Nancy Anderson, Mississippi College
Muhammad Anwar, University of Massachusetts
Harjit K. Arora, Le Moyne College
Bob Barnes, Northern Illinois University
Stacie Beck, University of Delaware
Larry Belcher, Stetson University
Gerry Bialka, University of North Florida
Daniel K. Biederman, University of North Dakota
John Bishop, East Carolina University
Daniel Blake, California State University, Northridge
Robert Boatler, Texas Christian University
Henning Bohn, University of California, Santa Barbara
Michael W. Brandl, University of Texas at Austin
Oscar T. Brookins, Northeastern University
William Walter Brown, California State University, Northridge
James L. Butkiewicz, University of Delaware

Colleen M. Callahan, Lehigh University
Ray Canterbery, Florida State University
Mike Carew, Baruch University
Tina Carter, University of Florida
Sergio Castello, University of Mobile
Matthew S. Chambers, Towson University
Jen-Chi Cheng, Wichita State University
Chi-Young Choi, University of Texas, Arlington
Patrick Crowley, Middlebury College
Sarah E. Culver, University of Alabama, Birmingham
Julie Dahlquist, University of Texas, San Antonio
Maria Davis, San Antonio College
Ranjit S. Dighe, State University of New York, Oswego
Richard Douglas, Bowling Green University
Donald H. Dutkowsky, Syracuse University
Richard Eichhorn, Colorado State University
Paul Emberton, Southwest Texas State University
Erick Eschker, Humboldt State University
Robert Eyler, Sonoma State University
L. S. Fan, Colorado State University
Imran Farooqi, University of Iowa
Sasan Fayazmanesh, California State University, Fresno
Dennis Fixler, George Washington University
Gary Fleming, Roanoke College
Grant D. Forsyth, Eastern Washington University
Timothy Fuerst, Bowling Green State University
Marc Fusaro, Arkansas Tech University
James Gale, Michigan Technological University
Shirley Gedeon, University of Vermont
Edgar Ghossoub, University of Texas, San Antonio
Mark Gibson, Washington State University
Lance Girton, University of Utah
Stuart M. Glosser, University of Wisconsin, Whitewater
Fred C. Graham, American University
Jo Anna Gray, University of Oregon
David Gulley, Bentley University
Ralph Gunderson, University of Wisconsin
Daniel Haak, Stanford University
Larbi Hammami, McGill University
Bassan Harik, Western Michigan University
J. C. Hartline, Rutgers University
Scott Hein, Texas Tech
Robert Stanley Herren, North Dakota State University
Jane Himarios, University of Texas, Arlington
Chad Hogan, University of Michigan
Linda Hooks, Washington and Lee University
James Hueng, Western Michigan University
Dar-Yeh Hwang, National Taiwan University
Jayvanth Ishwaran, Stephen F. Austin State University
Aaron Jackson, Bentley University

Jonatan Jelen, Queens College and City College of CUNY
U Jin Jhun, State University of New York, Oswego
Frederick L. Joutz, George Washington University
Ahmed Kalifa, Colorado State University
Bryce Kanago, University of Northern Iowa
Magda Kandil, International Monetary Fund
Theodore Kariotis, Towson University
George G. Kaufman, Loyola University Chicago
Richard H. Keehn, University of Wisconsin, Parkside
Elizabeth Sawyer Kelly, University of Wisconsin, Madison
Kathy Kelly, University of Texas, Arlington
Michael Kelsay, University of Missouri, Kansas City
Paul Kubik, DePaul University
Sungkyu Kwak, Washburn University
Fritz Laux, Northeastern State University
Jim Lee, Fort Hays State University
Robert Leeson, University of Western Ontario
Tony Lima, California State University, Hayward
Fiona Maclachlan, Manhattan College
Elham Mafi-Kreft, Indiana University
Bernard Malamud, University of Nevada, Las Vegas
James Maloy, University of Pittsburgh
James Marchand, Mercer University
Marvin Margolis, Millersville University
Elaine McBeth, College of William and Mary
Stephen McCafferty, Ohio State University
James McCown, Ohio State University
Cheryl McGaughey, Angelo State University
W. Douglas McMillin, Louisiana State University
William Merrill, Iowa State University
Carrie Meyer, George Mason University
Stephen M. Miller, University of Connecticut
Masoud Moghaddam, Saint Cloud State University
Thomas S. Mondschean, DePaul University
George Monokroussos, University of Albany
Clair Morris, U.S. Naval Academy
Jon Nadenichek, California State University, Northridge
John Nader, Grand Valley State University
Leonce Ndikumana, University of Massachusetts, Amherst
Ray Nelson, Brigham Young University
Inder P. Nijhawan, Fayetteville State University
Nick Noble, Miami University of Ohio
Dennis O'Toole, Virginia Commonwealth University
Mark J. Perry, University of Michigan, Flint
Chung Pham, University of New Mexico
Marvin M. Phaup, George Washington University
Andy Prevost, Ohio University
Ganga P. Ramdas, Lincoln University
Ronald A. Ratti, University of Missouri, Columbia
Hans Rau, Ball State University

Prosper Raynold, Miami University
Javier Reyes, Texas A&M University
Jack Russ, San Diego State University
Steve Russell, IUPUI
Robert S. Rycroft, Mary Washington College
Joe Santos, South Dakota State University
Lynn Schneider, Auburn University, Montgomery
Walter Schwarm, Colorado State University
John Shea, University of Maryland
Harinder Singh, Grand Valley State University
Rajesh Singh, Iowa State University
Richard Stahl, Louisiana State University
Larry Taylor, Lehigh University
Leigh Tesfatsion, Iowa State University
Aditi Thapar, New York University
Frederick D. Thum, University of Texas, Austin
Robert Tokle, Idaho State University
C. Van Marrewijk, Erasmus University
Rubina Vohra, New Jersey City University
Christopher J. Waller, Indiana University
Yongsheng Wang, Washington and Jefferson College
Chao Wei, George Washington University
Maurice Weinrobe, Clark University
James R. Wible, University of New Hampshire
Philip R. Wiest, George Mason University
William Wilkes, Athens State University
Thomas Williams, William Paterson University
Elliot Willman, New Mexico State University
Donald Wills, University of Washington, Tacoma
Laura Wolff, Southern Illinois University, Edwardsville
JaeJoon Woo, DePaul University
Robert Wright, University of Virginia
Ben T. Yu, California State University, Northridge
Ky H. Yuhn, Florida Atlantic University
Ed Zajicek, Winston-Salem State University
David Zalewski, Providence College
Jeffrey Zimmerman, Methodist College

Finally, I want to thank my wife, Sally; my son, Matthew; and my daughter, Laura, who provide me with a warm and happy environment that enables me to do my work; and also my father, Sidney, now deceased, who a long time ago put me on the path that led to this book.

FREDERIC S. MISHKIN

About the Author

Frederic S. Mishkin is the Alfred Lerner Professor of Banking and Financial Institutions at the Graduate School of Business, Columbia University. He is also a Research Associate at the National Bureau of Economic Research, co-director of the U.S. Monetary Policy Forum, a member of the Squam Lake Working Group on Financial Reform, and past president of the Eastern Economics Association. Since receiving his Ph.D. from the Massachusetts Institute of Technology in 1976, he has taught at the University of Chicago, Northwestern University, Princeton University, and Columbia. He has also received an honorary professorship from the People's (Renmin) University of China. From 1994 to 1997, he was Executive Vice President and Director of Research at the Federal Reserve Bank of New York and an associate economist of the Federal Open Market Committee of the Federal Reserve System. From September 2006 to August 2008, he was a member (governor) of the Board of Governors of the Federal Reserve System.

Professor Mishkin's research focuses on monetary policy and its impact on financial markets and the aggregate economy. He is the author of more than twenty books, including *Macroeconomics: Policy and Practice,* Second Edition (Pearson, 2015); *Financial Markets and Institutions,* Eighth Edition (Pearson, 2015); *Monetary Policy Strategy* (MIT Press, 2007); *The Next Great Globalization: How Disadvantaged Nations Can Harness Their Financial Systems to Get Rich* (Princeton University Press, 2006); *Inflation Targeting: Lessons from the International Experience* (Princeton University Press, 1999); *Money, Interest Rates, and Inflation* (Edward Elgar, 1993); and *A Rational Expectations Approach to Macroeconometrics: Testing Policy Ineffectiveness and Efficient Markets Models* (University of Chicago Press, 1983). In addition, he has published more than 200 articles in such journals as *American Economic Review, Journal of Political Economy, Econometrica, Quarterly Journal of Economics, Journal of Finance*, and *Journal of Monetary Economics*.

Professor Mishkin has served on the editorial board of *American Economic Review* and has been an associate editor at *Journal of Business and Economic Statistics,* the *Journal of Applied Econometrics, Journal of Economic Perspectives, Journal of International Money and Finance,* and *Journal of Money, Credit and Banking*; he also served as the editor of the Federal Reserve Bank of New York's *Economic Policy Review*. He is currently an associate editor (member of the editorial board) at five academic journals, including *International Finance; Finance India; Review of Development Finance; Borsa Economic Review;* and *Emerging Markets, Finance and Trade*. He has been a consultant to the Board of Governors of the Federal Reserve System, the World Bank, and the International Monetary Fund, as well as to many central banks throughout the world. He was also a member of the International Advisory Board to the Financial Supervisory Service of South Korea and an advisor to the Institute for Monetary and Economic Research at the Bank of Korea. Professor Mishkin was a Senior Fellow at the Federal Deposit Insurance Corporation's Center for Banking Research and was an academic consultant to and serves on the Economic Advisory Panel of the Federal Reserve Bank of New York.

Introduction

Crisis and Response: Global Financial Crisis and Its Aftermath

In August 2007, financial markets began to seize up, and over the next two years the world economy experienced a global financial crisis that was the most severe since the Great Depression years of the 1930s. Housing prices plummeted, the stock market crashed, unemployment skyrocketed, and both businesses and households found they couldn't get credit. Not only did the central bank of the United States, the Federal Reserve, respond by sharply lowering interest rates and intervening in credit markets to provide them with massive amounts of liquidity, but the federal government also entered into the act with a $700 billion bailout of weakened financial institutions and huge fiscal stimulus packages totaling over $1 trillion. However, even with these aggressive actions aimed at stabilizing the financial system and boosting the economy, seven years after the crisis the U.S. economy was still experiencing an unemployment rate above 6%, with many homeowners losing their homes. The financial systems of many governments throughout the world were also in tatters.

The global financial crisis and its aftermath demonstrate the importance of banks and financial systems to economic well-being, as well as the major role of money in the economy. Part I of this book provides an introduction to the study of money, banking, and financial markets. Chapter 1 outlines a road map of the book and discusses why it is so worthwhile to study money, banking, and financial markets. Chapter 2 provides a general overview of the financial system. Chapter 3 then explains what money is and how it is measured.

1 Why Study Money, Banking, and Financial Markets?

Learning Objectives

- Recognize the importance of financial markets in the economy.
- Describe how financial intermediation and financial innovation affect banking and the economy.
- Identify the basic links among monetary policy, the business cycle, and economic variables.
- Explain the importance of exchange rates in a global economy.

Preview

You have just heard on the evening news that the Federal Reserve is raising the federal funds rate by $\frac{1}{2}$ of a percentage point. What effect might this have on the interest rate of an automobile loan when you finance your purchase of a sleek new sports car? Does it mean that a house will be more or less affordable in the future? Will it make it easier or harder for you to get a job next year?

This book provides answers to these and other questions by examining how financial markets (such as those for bonds, stocks, and foreign exchange) and financial institutions (banks, insurance companies, mutual funds, and other institutions) work and by exploring the role of money in the economy. Financial markets and institutions affect not only your everyday life but also the flow of trillions of dollars of funds throughout our economy, which in turn affects business profits, the production of goods and services, and even the economic well-being of countries other than the United States. What happens to financial markets, financial institutions, and money is of great concern to politicians and can have a major impact on elections. The study of money, banking, and financial markets will reward you with an understanding of many exciting issues. In this chapter, we provide a road map of this book by outlining these issues and exploring why they are worth studying.

WHY STUDY FINANCIAL MARKETS?

Part 2 of this book focuses on **financial markets**—markets in which funds are transferred from people who have an excess of available funds to people who have a shortage. Financial markets, such as bond and stock markets, are crucial to promoting greater economic efficiency by channeling funds from people who do not have a productive use for them to those who do. Indeed, well-functioning financial markets are a key factor in producing high economic growth, and poorly-performing financial markets are one reason that many countries in the world remain desperately poor. Activities in financial markets also have a direct effect on personal wealth, the behavior of businesses and consumers, and the cyclical performance of the economy.

2

The Bond Market and Interest Rates

A **security** (also called a *financial instrument*) is a claim on the issuer's future income or **assets** (any financial claim or piece of property that is subject to ownership). A **bond** is a debt security that promises to make periodic payments for a specified period of time.[1] The bond market is especially important to economic activity because it enables corporations and governments to borrow money to finance their activities, and because it is where interest rates are determined. An **interest rate** is the cost of borrowing or the price paid for the rental of funds (usually expressed as a percentage of the rental of $100 per year). Many types of interest rates are found in the economy—mortgage interest rates, car loan rates, and interest rates on many different types of bonds.

Interest rates are important on a number of levels. On a personal level, high interest rates might deter you from buying a house or a car because the cost of financing would be high. Conversely, high interest rates might encourage you to save because you can earn more interest income by putting aside some of your earnings as savings. On a more general level, interest rates have an impact on the overall health of the economy because they affect not only consumers' willingness to spend or save, but also businesses' investment decisions. High interest rates, for example, might cause a corporation to postpone building a new plant that would provide more jobs.

Because changes in interest rates affect individuals, financial institutions, businesses, and the overall economy, it is important to explain substantial fluctuations in interest rates over the past 35 years. For example, the interest rate on three-month Treasury bills peaked at over 16% in 1981. This interest rate fell to 3% in late 1992 and 1993, rose to above 5% in the mid-to-late 1990s, fell to below 1% in 2004, rose to 5% by 2007, and fell to close to zero from 2008 to 2014.

Because different interest rates have a tendency to move in unison, economists frequently lump interest rates together and refer to "the" interest rate. As Figure 1 shows, however, interest rates on several types of bonds can differ substantially. The interest rate on three-month Treasury bills, for example, fluctuates more than the other interest rates, and is lower on average. The interest rate on Baa (medium-quality) corporate bonds is higher, on average, than the other interest rates, and the spread between it and the other rates became larger in the 1970s, narrowed in the 1990s, rose briefly in the early 2000s, narrowed again, and then rose sharply starting in the summer of 2007. It then began to decline toward the end of 2009, returning to low levels by 2014.

In Chapter 2 we study the role of bond markets in the economy, and in Chapters 4 through 6 we examine what an interest rate is, how the common movements in interest rates come about, and why the interest rates on different bonds vary.

The Stock Market

A **common stock** (typically called simply a **stock**) represents a share of ownership in a corporation. It is a security that is a claim on the earnings and assets of the corporation. Issuing stock and selling it to the public is a way for corporations to raise funds to finance their activities. The stock market, in which claims on the earnings of corporations (shares of stock) are traded, is the most widely followed financial

---

[1]The definition of *bond* used throughout this book is the broad one commonly used in academic settings, which covers both short- and long-term debt instruments. However, some practitioners in financial markets use the word *bond* to describe only specific long-term debt instruments such as corporate bonds or U.S. Treasury bonds.

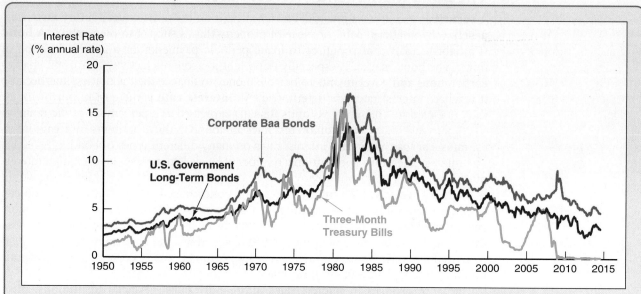

FIGURE 1   **Interest Rates on Selected Bonds, 1950–2014**

Although different interest rates have a tendency to move in unison, they often differ substantially, and the spreads between them fluctuate.

Source: **Federal Reserve Bank of St. Louis, FRED database:** http://research.stlouisfed.org/fred2/

market in almost every country that has one; that's why it's often called simply "the market." A big swing in the prices of shares in the stock market is always a major story on the evening news. People often speculate on where the market is heading and get very excited when they can brag about their latest "big killing," but they become depressed when they suffer a big loss. The attention the market receives can probably be best explained by one simple fact: It is a place where people can get rich—or poor—very quickly.

As Figure 2 indicates, stock prices are extremely volatile. After rising steadily during the 1980s, the market experienced the worst one-day drop in its entire history on October 19, 1987—"Black Monday"—with the Dow Jones Industrial Average (DJIA) falling by 22%. From then until 2000, the stock market experienced one of the greatest rises (often referred to as a "bull market") in its history, with the Dow climbing to a peak of over 11,000. With the collapse of the high-tech bubble in 2000, the stock market fell sharply, dropping by over 30% by late 2002. It then rose to an all-time high above the 14,000 level in 2007, only to fall by over 50% of its value to a low below 7,000 in 2009. Another bull market then began, with the Dow reaching new highs of 17,000 by 2014. These considerable fluctuations in stock prices affect the size of people's wealth and, as a result, their willingness to spend.

The stock market is also an important factor in business investment decisions, because the price of shares affects the amount of funds that can be raised by selling newly issued stock to finance investment spending. A higher price for a firm's shares means that the firm can raise a larger amount of funds, which it can then use to buy production facilities and equipment.

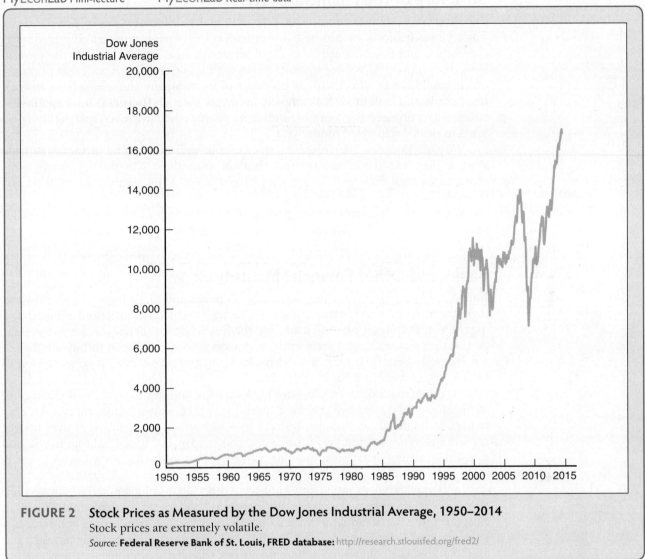

FIGURE 2   Stock Prices as Measured by the Dow Jones Industrial Average, 1950–2014
Stock prices are extremely volatile.
Source: **Federal Reserve Bank of St. Louis, FRED database:** http://research.stlouisfed.org/fred2/

In Chapter 2 we examine the role that the stock market plays in the financial system, and in Chapter 7 we return to the issue of how stock prices behave and respond to information in the marketplace.

WHY STUDY FINANCIAL INSTITUTIONS AND BANKING?

Part 3 of this book focuses on financial institutions and the business of banking. Banks and other financial institutions are what make financial markets work. Without them, financial markets would not be able to move funds from people who save to people who have productive investment opportunities. Thus financial institutions play a crucial role in the economy.

Structure of the Financial System

The financial system is complex, comprising many different types of private sector financial institutions, including banks, insurance companies, mutual funds, finance companies, and investment banks, all of which are heavily regulated by the government. If an individual wanted to make a loan to IBM or General Motors, for example, he or she would not go directly to the president of the company and offer a loan. Instead, he or she would lend to such a company indirectly through **financial intermediaries**, which are institutions that borrow funds from people who have saved and in turn make loans to people who need funds.

Why are financial intermediaries so crucial to well-functioning financial markets? Why do they extend credit to one party but not to another? Why do they usually write complicated legal documents when they extend loans? Why are they the most heavily regulated businesses in the economy?

We answer these questions in Chapter 8 by developing a coherent framework for analyzing financial structure in the United States and in the rest of the world.

Banks and Other Financial Institutions

Banks are financial institutions that accept deposits and make loans. The term *banks* includes firms such as commercial banks, savings and loan associations, mutual savings banks, and credit unions. Banks are the financial intermediaries that the average person interacts with most frequently. A person who needs a loan to buy a house or a car usually obtains it from a local bank. Most Americans keep a large portion of their financial wealth in banks in the form of checking accounts, savings accounts, or other types of bank deposits. Because banks are the largest financial intermediaries in our economy, they deserve the most careful study. However, banks are not the only important financial institutions. Indeed, in recent years, other financial institutions, such as insurance companies, finance companies, pension funds, mutual funds, and investment banks, have been growing at the expense of banks, so we need to study them as well.

In Chapter 9, we examine how banks and other financial institutions manage their assets and liabilities to make profits. In Chapter 10, we extend the economic analysis in Chapter 8 to understand why financial regulation takes the form it does and what can go wrong in the regulatory process. In Chapter 11, we look at the banking industry and examine how the competitive environment has changed this industry. We also learn why some financial institutions have been growing at the expense of others.

Financial Innovation

In Chapter 11, we study **financial innovation**, the development of new financial products and services. We will see why and how financial innovation takes place, with particular emphasis on how the dramatic improvements in information technology have led to new financial products and the ability to deliver financial services electronically through what has become known as **e-finance**. We also study financial innovation because it shows us how creative thinking on the part of financial institutions can lead to higher profits but can also sometimes result in financial disasters. By studying how financial institutions have been creative in the past, we obtain a better grasp of how they may be creative in the future. This knowledge provides us with useful clues about how the financial system may change over time.

Financial Crises

At times, the financial system seizes up and produces **financial crises**, which are major disruptions in financial markets that are characterized by sharp declines in asset prices and the failures of many financial and nonfinancial firms. Financial crises have been a feature of capitalist economies for hundreds of years, and are typically followed by severe business cycle downturns. Starting in August 2007, the U.S. economy was hit by the worst financial crisis since the Great Depression. Defaults in subprime residential mortgages led to major losses in financial institutions, producing not only numerous bank failures but also the demise of Bear Stearns and Lehman Brothers, two of the largest investment banks in the United States. The crisis produced the worst economic downturn since the Great Depression, and as a result, it is now referred to as the "Great Recession."

We discuss why these crises occur and why they do so much damage to the economy in Chapter 12.

WHY STUDY MONEY AND MONETARY POLICY?

Money, also referred to as the **money supply**, is defined as anything that is generally accepted as payment for goods or services or in the repayment of debts. Money is linked to changes in economic variables that affect all of us and are important to the health of the economy. The final two parts of this book examine the role of money in the economy.

Money and Business Cycles

During 1981–1982, the total production of goods and services (called **aggregate output**) in the U.S. economy fell and the **unemployment rate** (the percentage of the available labor force unemployed) rose to over 10%. After 1982, the economy began to expand rapidly, and by 1989, the unemployment rate had declined to 5%. In 1990, the eight-year expansion came to an end, with the unemployment rate rising to above 7%. The economy bottomed out in 1991, and the subsequent recovery was the longest in U.S. history, with the unemployment rate falling to around 4%. A mild economic downturn began in March 2001, with unemployment rising to 6%; the economy began to recover in November 2001, with unemployment eventually declining to a low of 4.4%. Starting in December 2007, the economy went into a steep economic downturn and unemployment rose to over 10% before the economy slowly began to recover in June 2009.

Why did the economy undergo such pronounced fluctuations? Evidence suggests that money plays an important role in generating **business cycles**, the upward and downward movement of aggregate output produced in the economy. Business cycles affect all of us in immediate and important ways. When output is rising, for example, it is easier to find a good job; when output is falling, finding a good job might be difficult. Figure 3 shows the movements of the rate of growth of the money supply over the 1950–2014 period, with the shaded areas representing **recessions**, or periods of declining aggregate output. We see that the rate of money growth declined before most recessions, indicating that changes in money growth might be a driving force behind business cycle fluctuations. However, declines in the rate of money growth are often not followed by a recession.

We explore how money and monetary policy might affect aggregate output in Chapters 19 through 25 (Part 6) of this book, where we study **monetary theory**, the theory that relates the quantity of money and monetary policy to changes in aggregate economic activity and inflation.

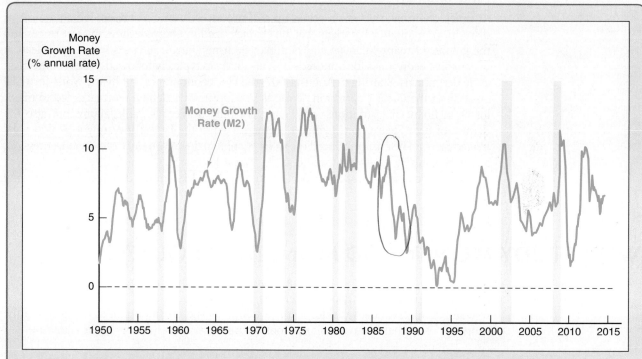

FIGURE 3   **Money Growth (M2 Annual Rate) and the Business Cycle in the United States, 1950–2014**
Although money growth has declined before almost every recession, not every decline in the rate
of money growth is followed by a recession. Shaded areas represent recessions.
Source: **Federal Reserve Bank of St. Louis, FRED database:** http://research.stlouisfed.org/fred2/

Money and Inflation

The movie you paid $10 to see last week would have set you back only a dollar or two
thirty years ago. In fact, for $10, you probably could have had dinner, seen the movie, and
bought yourself a big bucket of hot buttered popcorn. As shown in Figure 4, which illustrates the movement of average prices in the U.S. economy from 1950 to 2014, the prices
of most items are quite a bit higher now than they were then. The average price of goods
and services in an economy is called the **aggregate price level** or, more simply, the *price
level* (a more precise definition is found in the appendix to this chapter). From 1950 to
2014, the price level has increased more than sevenfold. **Inflation**, a continual increase in
the price level, affects individuals, businesses, and the government. It is generally regarded
as an important problem to be solved and is often at the top of political and policymaking
agendas. To solve the inflation problem, we need to know something about its causes.

What explains inflation? One clue to answering this question is found in Figure 4,
which plots the money supply versus the price level. As we can see, the price level and
the money supply generally rise together. These data seem to indicate that a continuing
increase in the money supply might be an important factor in causing the continuing
increase in the price level that we call inflation.

Further evidence that inflation may be tied to continuing increases in the money
supply is found in Figure 5, which plots the average **inflation rate** (the rate of change
of the price level, usually measured as a percentage change per year) for a number of
countries over the ten-year period 2003–2013 against the average rate of money growth

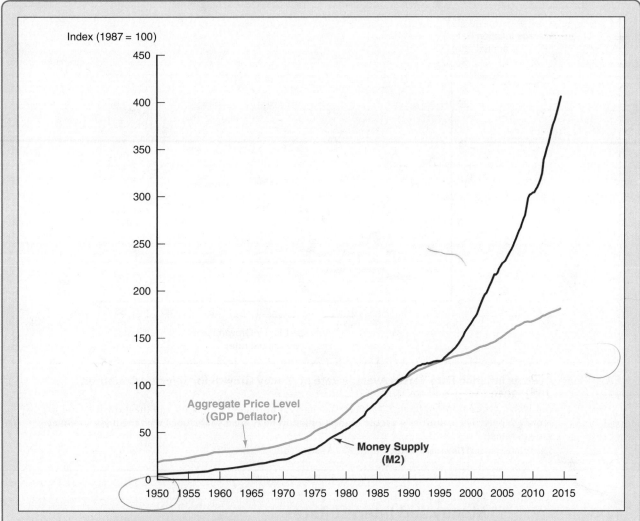

FIGURE 4   **Aggregate Price Level and the Money Supply in the United States, 1950–2014**
From 1950 to 2014, the price level has increased more than tenfold.
Source: **Federal Reserve Bank of St. Louis, FRED database:** http://research.stlouisfed.org/fred2/

over the same period. As you can see, a positive association exists between inflation and the growth rate of the money supply: The countries with the highest inflation rates are also the ones with the highest money growth rates. Turkey, Ukraine, and Zambia, for example, experienced high inflation during this period, and their rates of money growth were high. By contrast, Sweden and the United States experienced low inflation rates over the same period, and their rates of money growth were low. Such evidence led Milton Friedman, a Nobel laureate in economics, to make the famous statement, "Inflation is always and everywhere a monetary phenomenon."[2] We look at the quantity of money and monetary policy's role in creating inflation in Chapters 19 and 23.

[2]Milton Friedman, *Dollars and Deficits* (Upper Saddle River, NJ: Prentice Hall, 1968), p. 39.

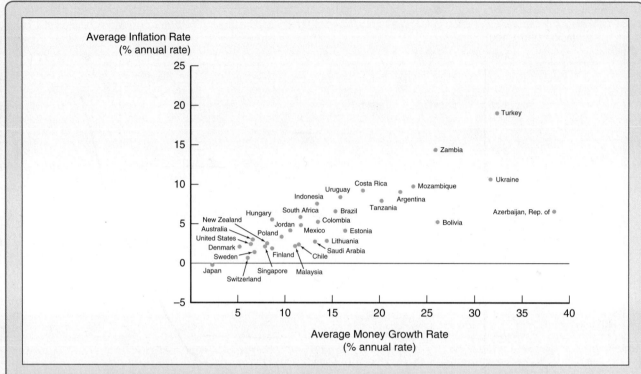

FIGURE 5 **Average Inflation Rate Versus Average Rate of Money Growth for Selected Countries, 2003–2013**
A positive association can be seen between the ten-year averages of inflation and the growth rate of the money supply: The countries with the highest inflation rates are also the ones with the highest money growth rates.
Source: **International Financial Statistics.** http://www.imf.org/external/data.htm

Money and Interest Rates

In addition to other factors, money plays an important role in interest-rate fluctuations, which are of great concern to businesses and consumers. Figure 6 shows changes in the interest rate on long-term Treasury bonds and the rate of money growth from 1950 to 2014. As the money growth rate rose in the 1960s and 1970s, the long-term bond rate rose with it. However, the relationship between money growth and interest rates has been less clear-cut since 1980. We analyze the relationship between money growth and interest rates when we examine the behavior of interest rates in Chapter 5.

Conduct of Monetary Policy

Because money affects many economic variables that are important to the well-being of our economy, politicians and policymakers throughout the world care about the conduct of **monetary policy**, the management of money and interest rates. The organization responsible for the conduct of a nation's monetary policy is the **central bank**. The United States' central bank is the **Federal Reserve System** (also called simply "**the Fed**"). In Chapters 13 through 16 (Part 4), we study how central banks such as

MyEconLab Mini-lecture   MyEconLab Real-time data

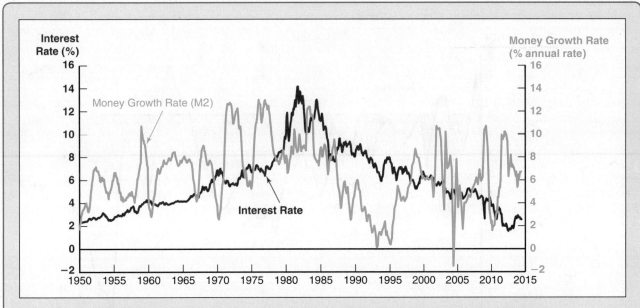

FIGURE 6   **Money Growth (M2 Annual Rate) and Interest Rates (Long-Term U.S. Treasury Bonds), 1950–2014**

As the money growth rate rose in the 1960s and 1970s, the long-term bond rate rose with it. However, the relationship between money growth and interest rates has been less clear-cut since 1980.

Source: **Federal Reserve Bank of St. Louis, FRED database:** http://research.stlouisfed.org/fred2/

the Federal Reserve System can affect the quantity of money and interest rates in the economy, and then we look at how monetary policy is actually conducted in the United States and elsewhere.

Fiscal Policy and Monetary Policy

Fiscal policy involves decisions about government spending and taxation. A **budget deficit** is an excess of government expenditures with respect to tax revenues for a particular time period, typically a year, while a **budget surplus** arises when tax revenues exceed government expenditures. The government must finance any budget deficit by borrowing, whereas a budget surplus leads to a lower government debt burden. As Figure 7 shows, the budget deficit, relative to the size of the U.S. economy, peaked in 1983 at 6% of national output (as calculated by the **gross domestic product**, or **GDP**, a measure of aggregate output described in the appendix to this chapter). Since then, the budget deficit at first declined to less than 3% of GDP, rose again to 5% of GDP by the early 1990s, and fell subsequently, leading to budget surpluses from 1999 to 2001. In the aftermath of the terrorist attacks of September 11, 2001, the war in Iraq that began in March 2003, and the 2007–2009 financial crisis, the budget swung back into deficit, with deficits at one point exceeding 10% of GDP and then falling substantially thereafter. What to do about budget deficits has been the subject of legislation and the source of bitter battles between the president and Congress in recent years.

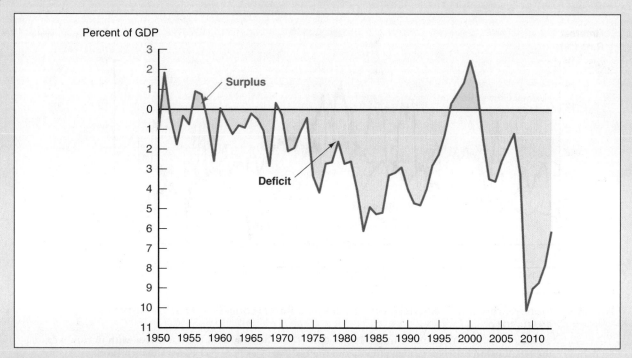

FIGURE 7 **Government Budget Surplus or Deficit as a Percentage of Gross Domestic Product, 1950–2013**

The budget deficit, relative to the size of the U.S. economy, has fluctuated substantially over the years. It rose to 6% of GDP in 1983 and then fell, eventually leading to budget surpluses from 1999 to 2001. Subsequently, budget deficits climbed, peaking at over 10% of GDP in 2009 and falling substantially thereafter.

Source: **Economic Report of the President, Table B79 at** http://www.gpoaccess.gov/eop/tables09.html

You may have read statements in newspapers or heard on TV that budget surpluses are a good thing, while deficits are undesirable. In Chapter 19, we examine why deficits might result in a higher rate of money growth, a higher rate of inflation, and higher interest rates.

WHY STUDY INTERNATIONAL FINANCE?

The globalization of financial markets has accelerated at a rapid pace in recent years. Financial markets have become increasingly integrated throughout the world. American companies often borrow in foreign financial markets, and foreign companies borrow in U.S. financial markets. Banks and other financial institutions, such as JP Morgan Chase, Citigroup, UBS, and Deutschebank, have become increasingly international, with operations in many countries throughout the world. Part 5 of this book explores the foreign exchange market and the international financial system.

The Foreign Exchange Market

For funds to be transferred from one country to another, they have to be converted from the currency of the country of origin (say, dollars) into the currency of the country

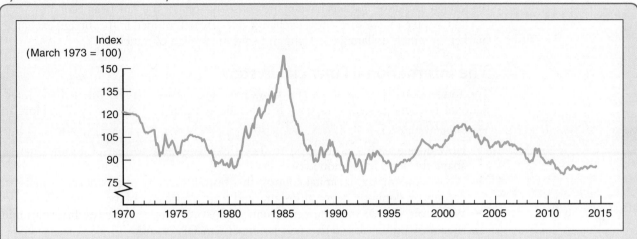

FIGURE 8   **Exchange Rate of the U.S. Dollar, 1970–2014**
The value of the U.S. dollar relative to other currencies has fluctuated substantially over the years.
Source: **Federal Reserve Bank of St. Louis, FRED database:** http://research.stlouisfed.org/fred2/

they are going to (say, euros). The **foreign exchange market** is where this conversion takes place, so it is instrumental in moving funds between countries. It is also important because it is where the **foreign exchange rate**, or the price of one country's currency in terms of another's, is determined.

Figure 8 shows the exchange rate for the U.S. dollar from 1970 to 2014 (measured as the value of the U.S. dollar in terms of a basket of major foreign currencies). The fluctuations in prices in this market have been substantial: The dollar's value weakened considerably from 1971 to 1973, rose slightly until 1976, and then reached a low point in the 1978–1980 period. From 1980 to early 1985, the dollar's value appreciated dramatically, and then declined again, reaching another low in 1995. From 2000 to 2014, the dollar depreciated substantially, with only a temporary upturn in 2008 and 2009.

What have these fluctuations in the exchange rate meant to the American public and businesses? A change in the exchange rate has a direct effect on American consumers because it affects the cost of imports. In 2001, when the euro was worth around 85 cents, 100 euros of European goods (say, French wine) cost $85. When the dollar subsequently weakened, raising the cost of one euro to a peak of nearly $1.50, the same 100 euros of wine now cost $150. Thus a weaker dollar leads to more expensive foreign goods, makes vacationing abroad more expensive, and raises the cost of indulging your desire for imported delicacies. When the value of the dollar drops, Americans decrease their purchases of foreign goods and increase their consumption of domestic goods (such as travel within the United States or American-made wine).

Conversely, a strong dollar means that U.S. goods exported abroad will cost more in foreign countries, and hence foreigners will buy fewer of them. Exports of steel, for example, declined sharply when the dollar strengthened during the 1980–1985 and 1995–2001 periods. A strong dollar benefited American consumers by making foreign goods cheaper, but hurt American businesses and eliminated some jobs by cutting both domestic and foreign sales of the businesses' products. The decline in the value of the dollar from 1985 to 1995 and from 2001 to 2014 had the opposite effect: It made foreign goods more expensive but made American businesses more competitive. Fluctuations in the foreign exchange markets have major consequences for the American economy.

In Chapter 17, we study how exchange rates are determined in the foreign exchange market, in which dollars are bought and sold for foreign currencies.

The International Financial System

The tremendous increase in capital flows among countries has heightened the international financial system's impact on domestic economies. Issues we will explore in Chapter 18 include:

- How does a country's decision to fix its exchange rate to that of another nation shape the conduct of monetary policy?
- What is the impact of capital controls that restrict mobility of capital across national borders on domestic financial systems and the performance of the economy?
- What role should international financial institutions, such as the International Monetary Fund, play in the international financial system?

HOW WE WILL STUDY MONEY, BANKING, AND FINANCIAL MARKETS

This textbook stresses the "economic way of thinking" by developing a unifying framework in which you will study money, banking, and financial markets. This analytic framework uses a few basic economic concepts to organize your thinking about the determination of asset prices, the structure of financial markets, bank management, and the role of money in the economy. It encompasses the following basic concepts:

- A simplified approach to the demand for assets
- The concept of equilibrium
- Basic supply and demand analysis to explain behavior of financial markets
- The search for profits
- An approach to financial structure based on transaction costs and asymmetric information
- Aggregate supply and demand analysis

The unifying framework used in this book will keep your knowledge from becoming obsolete and make the material more interesting. It will enable you to learn what *really* matters without having to memorize a mass of dull facts that you will forget soon after the final exam. This framework will also provide you with the tools you need to understand trends in the financial marketplace and in variables such as interest rates, exchange rates, inflation, and aggregate output.

To help you understand and apply the unifying analytic framework, simple models are constructed in which the variables held constant are carefully delineated. Each step in the derivation of the model is clearly and carefully laid out, and the models are then used to explain various phenomena by focusing on changes in one variable at a time, holding all other variables constant.

To reinforce the models' usefulness, this text uses case studies, applications, and special-interest boxes to present evidence that supports or casts doubts on the theories being discussed. This exposure to real-life events and empirical data should dissuade you from thinking that all economists make abstract assumptions and develop theories that have little to do with actual behavior.

To function better financially in the real world outside the classroom, you must have the tools with which to follow the financial news that is reported in leading financial publications and on the Web. To help and encourage you to read the financial news, this book contains special boxed inserts titled "Following the Financial News" that provide detailed information and definitions to help you evaluate data that are discussed frequently in the media. This book also contains over 700 end-of-chapter questions and applied problems that ask you to apply the analytic concepts you have learned to real-world issues.

Exploring the Web

The World Wide Web has become an extremely valuable and convenient resource for financial research. This book emphasizes the importance of this tool in several ways. First, you can view the most current data for a high percentage of the in-text data figures by using eText to access the Federal Reserve Bank of St. Louis's FRED database. Figures for which you can do this are labeled *MyEconLab Real-Time Data*. Second, at the end of almost every chapter there are several real-time data analysis problems, which ask you to download the most recent data from the Federal Reserve Bank of St. Louis's FRED database and then use these data to answer interesting questions. Third, there are additional Web exercises at the end of many chapters that prompt you to visit sites related to the chapter and use them to learn more about macroeconomic issues. Web references are also supplied at the end of each chapter; these list the URLs of sites related to the material being discussed. You can visit these sites to further explore a topic you find of particular interest. *Note:* Website URLs are subject to frequent change. We have tried to select stable sites, but we realize that even government URLs change. The publisher's website (http://www.myeconlab.com) will maintain an updated list of current URLs for your reference.

CONCLUDING REMARKS

The study of money, banking, and financial markets is an exciting field that directly affects your life. Interest rates influence the earnings you make on your savings and the payments on loans you may seek for a car or a house, and monetary policy may affect your job prospects and the prices you will pay for goods in the future. Your study of money, banking, and financial markets will introduce you to many of the controversies related to economic policy that are hotly debated in the political arena, and will help you gain a clearer understanding of the economic phenomena you hear about in the news media. The knowledge you gain will stay with you and benefit you long after this course is over.

SUMMARY

1. Activities in financial markets directly affect individuals' wealth, the behavior of businesses, and the efficiency of our economy. Three financial markets deserve particular attention: the bond market (where interest rates are determined), the stock market (which has a major effect on people's wealth and on firms' investment decisions), and the foreign exchange market (because fluctuations in the foreign exchange rate have major consequences for the U.S. economy).

2. Banks and other financial institutions channel funds from people who might not put them to productive use to people who can do so, and thus play a crucial role in improving the efficiency of the economy. When the financial system seizes up and produces a financial crisis, financial firms fail, which causes severe damage to the economy.

3. Money and monetary policy appear to have a major influence on inflation, business cycles, and interest rates. Because these economic variables are so

important to the health of the economy, we need to understand how monetary policy is and should be conducted. We also need to study government fiscal policy because it can be an influential factor in the conduct of monetary policy.

4. This textbook stresses the "economic way of thinking" by developing a unifying analytic framework in which to study money, banking, and financial markets, using a few basic economic principles. This textbook also emphasizes the interaction of theoretical analysis and empirical data.

KEY TERMS

aggregate income, p. 19
aggregate output, p. 7
aggregate price level, p. 8
asset, p. 3
banks, p. 6
bond, p. 3
budget deficit, p. 11
budget surplus, p. 11
business cycles, p. 7
central bank, p. 10

common stock, p. 3
e-finance, p. 6
Federal Reserve System (the Fed), p. 10
financial crises, p. 7
financial innovation, p. 6
financial intermediaries, p. 6
financial markets, p. 2
fiscal policy, p. 11
foreign exchange market, p. 13
foreign exchange rate, p. 13

gross domestic product (GDP), p. 11
inflation, p. 8
inflation rate, p. 8
interest rate, p. 3
monetary policy, p. 10
monetary theory, p. 7
money (money supply), p. 7
recession, p. 7
security, p. 3
stock, p. 3
unemployment rate, p. 7

QUESTIONS

All questions are available in MyEconLab at http://www.myeconlab.com.

1. What is the typical relationship among interest rates on three-month Treasury bills, long-term Treasury bonds, and Baa corporate bonds?

2. What effect might a fall in stock prices have on business investment?

3. What effect might a rise in stock prices have on consumers' decisions to spend?

4. Why are financial markets important to the health of the economy?

5. What was the main cause of the recession that began in 2007?

6. What is the basic activity of banks?

7. What are the other important financial intermediaries in the economy, besides banks?

8. Can you think of any financial innovation in the past ten years that has affected you personally? Has it made you better off or worse off? Why?

9. Has the inflation rate in the United States increased or decreased in the past few years? What about interest rates?

10. If history repeats itself and we see a decline in the rate of money growth, what might you expect to happen to

 a. real output?

 b. the inflation rate?

 c. interest rates?

11. When interest rates decrease, how might businesses and consumers change their economic behavior?

12. Is everybody worse off when interest rates rise?

13. Why do managers of financial institutions care so much about the activities of the Federal Reserve System?

14. How does the current size of the U.S. budget deficit compare to the historical budget deficit or surplus for the time period since 1950?

15. How would a fall in the value of the pound sterling affect British consumers?

16. How would an increase in the value of the pound sterling affect American businesses?

17. How can changes in foreign exchange rates affect the profitability of financial institutions?

18. According to Figure 8, in which years would you have chosen to visit the Grand Canyon in Arizona rather than the Tower of London?

19. When the dollar is worth more in relation to currencies of other countries, are you more likely to buy American-made or foreign-made jeans? Are U.S. companies that

manufacture jeans happier when the dollar is strong or when it is weak? What about an American company that is in the business of importing jeans into the United States?

20. Much of the U.S. government debt is held by foreign investors as treasury bonds and bills. How do fluctuations in the dollar exchange rate affect the value of that debt held by foreigners?

APPLIED PROBLEMS

All applied problems are available in MyEconLab *at* http://www.myeconlab.com.

21. The following table lists foreign exchange rates between U.S. dollars and British pounds (GBP) during April.

Which day would have been the best for converting $200 into British pounds? Which day would have been the worst? What would be the difference in pounds?

Date	U.S. Dollars per GBP
4/1	1.9564
4/4	1.9293
4/5	1.914
4/6	1.9374
4/7	1.961
4/8	1.8925
4/11	1.8822
4/12	1.8558
4/13	1.796
4/14	1.7902
4/15	1.7785
4/18	1.7504
4/19	1.7255
4/20	1.6914
4/21	1.672
4/22	1.6684
4/25	1.6674
4/26	1.6857
4/27	1.6925
4/28	1.7201
4/29	1.7512

DATA ANALYSIS PROBLEMS

The Problems update with real-time data in MyEconLab *and are available for practice or instructor assignment.*

 1. Go to the St. Louis Federal Reserve FRED database and find data on the three-month treasury bill rate (TB3MS), the three-month AA nonfinancial commercial paper rate (CPN3M), the 30-year treasury bond rate (GS30), the 30-year conventional mortgage rate (MORTG), and the NBER recession indicators (USREC).

a. In general, how do these interest rates behave during recessions and during expansionary periods?

b. In general, how do the three-month rates compare to the 30-year rates? How do the treasury rates compare to the respective commercial paper and mortgage rates?

c. For the most recent available month of data, take the average of each of the three-month rates and compare it to the average of the three-month rates from January 2000. How do the averages compare?

d. For the most recent available month of data, take the average of each of the 30-year rates and compare it to the average of the 30-year rates from January 2000. How do the averages compare?

2. Go to the St. Louis Federal Reserve FRED database and find data on the M1 money supply (M1SL) and the 10-year treasury bond rate (GS10). Add the two series into a single graph by using the "Add Data Series" feature. Transform the M1 money supply variable into the M1 growth rate by adjusting the *units* for the M1 money supply to "Percent Change from Year Ago."

a. In general, how have the growth rate of the M1 money supply and the 10-year treasury bond rate behaved during recessions and during expansionary periods since the year 2000?

b. In general, is there an obvious, stable relationship between money growth and the 10-year interest rate since the year 2000?

c. Compare the money growth rate and the 10-year interest rate for the most recent month available to the rates for January 2000. How do the rates compare?

WEB EXERCISES

1. In this exercise, we will practice collecting data from the Web and graphing it using Excel. Go to http://www.forecasts.org/data/index.htm, click on Stock Index Data at the top of the page, and choose the U.S. Stock Indices—Monthly option. Finally, choose the Dow Jones Industrial Average option.

a. Move the data into an Excel spreadsheet.
b. Using the data from part (a), prepare a graph. Use the Excel Chart Wizard to properly label your axes.

2. In Web Exercise 1, you collected data on and then graphed the Dow Jones Industrial Average (DJIA). This same site reports forecast values of the DJIA. Go to http://www.forecasts.org/data/index.htm, and click on FFC Home at the top of the page. Click on the Dow Jones Industrial link under Forecasts in the far-left column.

a. What is the Dow forecast to be in six months?
b. What percentage increase is forecast for the next six months?

WEB REFERENCES

http://www.federalreserve.gov/releases/

Daily, weekly, monthly, quarterly, and annual releases and historical data for selected interest rates, foreign exchange rates, and so on.

http://stockcharts.com/charts/historical/

Historical charts of various stock indexes over differing time periods.

http://www.federalreserve.gov

General information, monetary policy, banking system, research, and economic data of the Federal Reserve.

http://www.bls.gov/data/inflation_calculator.htm

This calculator lets you compute how the dollar's buying power has changed since 1913.

http://www.kowaldesign.com/budget/

This site reports the current federal budget deficit or surplus and how it has changed since the 1950s. It also reports how the federal budget is spent.

http://www.brillig.com/debt_clock/

National debt clock. This site reports the exact national debt at each point in time.

Defining Aggregate Output, Income, the Price Level, and the Inflation Rate

Because these terms are used so frequently throughout the text, we need to have a clear understanding of the definitions of *aggregate output*, *income*, the *price level*, and the *inflation rate*.

AGGREGATE OUTPUT AND INCOME

The most commonly reported measure of aggregate output, the **gross domestic product (GDP)**, is the market value of all final goods and services produced in a country during the course of a year. This measure excludes two sets of items that at first glance you might think it would include. Purchases of goods that have been produced in the past, whether a Rembrandt painting or a house built twenty years ago, are not counted as part of GDP; nor are purchases of stocks or bonds. Neither of these categories enters into the GDP because these categories do not include goods and services produced during the course of the year. Intermediate goods, which are used up in producing final goods and services, such as the sugar in a candy bar or the energy used to produce steel, are also not counted separately as part of the GDP. Because the value of the final goods already includes the value of the intermediate goods, to count them separately would be to count them twice.

Aggregate income, the total income of *factors of production* (land, labor, and capital) from producing goods and services in the economy during the course of the year, is best thought of as being equal to aggregate output. Because the payments for final goods and services must eventually flow back to the owners of the factors of production as income, income payments must equal payments for final goods and services. For example, if the economy has an aggregate output of $10 trillion, total income payments in the economy (aggregate income) are also $10 trillion.

REAL VERSUS NOMINAL MAGNITUDES

When the total value of final goods and services is calculated using current prices, the resulting GDP measure is referred to as *nominal GDP*. The word *nominal* indicates that values are measured using current prices. If all prices doubled but actual production of goods and services remained the same, nominal GDP would double, even though people would not enjoy the benefits of twice as many goods and services. As a result, nominal variables can be misleading measures of economic well-being.

nominal = current

A more reliable measure of economic production expresses values in terms of prices for an arbitrary base year, currently 2005. GDP measured with constant prices is referred to as *real GDP*, the word *real* indicating that values are measured in terms of fixed prices. Real variables thus measure the quantities of goods and services and do not change because prices have changed, but rather only if actual quantities have changed.

A brief example will make the distinction clearer. Suppose that you have a nominal income of $30,000 in 2016 and that your nominal income was $15,000 in 2005. If all prices doubled between 2005 and 2016, are you better off? The answer is no: Although your income has doubled, your $30,000 buys you only the same amount of goods because prices have also doubled. A *real* income measure indicates that your income in terms of the goods it can buy is the same. Measured in 2005 prices, the $30,000 of nominal income in 2016 turns out to be only $15,000 of real income. Because your real income is actually the same for the two years, you are no better or worse off in 2016 than you were in 2005.

Because real variables measure quantities in terms of real goods and services, they are typically of more interest than nominal variables. In this text, discussion of aggregate output or aggregate income always refers to real measures (such as real GDP).

AGGREGATE PRICE LEVEL

In this chapter, we defined the aggregate price level as a measure of average prices in the economy. Three measures of the aggregate price level are commonly encountered in economic data. The first is the *GDP deflator*, which is defined as nominal GDP divided by real GDP. Thus, if 2016 nominal GDP is $10 trillion but 2016 real GDP in 2005 prices is $9 trillion,

$$\text{GDP deflator} = \frac{\$10 \text{ trillion}}{\$9 \text{ trillion}} = 1.11$$

The GDP deflator equation indicates that, on average, prices have risen 11% since 2005. Typically, measures of the price level are presented in the form of a price index, which expresses the price level for the base year (in our example, 2005) as 100. Thus the GDP deflator for 2016 would be 111.

Another popular measure of the aggregate price level (which officials in the Fed frequently focus on) is the *PCE deflator*, which is similar to the GDP deflator and is defined as nominal personal consumption expenditures (PCE) divided by real PCE.

The measure of the aggregate price level that is most frequently reported in the press is the *consumer price index (CPI)*. The CPI is measured by pricing a "basket" of goods and services bought by a typical urban household. If, over the course of the year, the cost of this basket of goods and services rises from $500 to $600, the CPI has risen by 20%. The CPI is also expressed as a price index with the base year equal to 100.

The CPI, the PCE deflator, and the GDP deflator measures of the price level can be used to convert or deflate a nominal magnitude into a real magnitude. This is accomplished by dividing the nominal magnitude by the price index. In our example, in which the GDP deflator for 2016 is 1.11 (expressed as an index value of 111), real GDP for 2016 equals

$$\frac{\$10 \text{ trillion}}{1.11} = \$9 \text{ trillion in 2005 prices}$$

which corresponds to the real GDP figure for 2016 assumed earlier.

GROWTH RATES AND THE INFLATION RATE

The media often talk about the economy's growth rate, and particularly the growth rate of real GDP. A growth rate is defined as the percentage change in a variable, i.e.,

$$\text{growth rate of } x = \frac{x_t - x_{t-1}}{x_{t-1}} \times 100$$

where t indicates today and $t - 1$ indicates a year earlier.

For example, if real GDP grew from $9 trillion in 2016 to $9.5 trillion in 2017, then the GDP growth rate for 2017 would be 5.6%:

$$\text{GDP growth rate} = \frac{\$9.5 \text{ trillion} - \$9 \text{ trillion}}{\$9 \text{ trillion}} \times 100 = 5.6\%$$

The inflation rate is defined as the growth rate of the aggregate price level. Thus, if the GDP deflator rose from 111 in 2016 to 113 in 2017, the inflation rate using the GDP deflator would be 1.8%:

$$\text{inflation rate} = \frac{113 - 111}{111} \times 100 = 1.8\%$$

If the growth rate is for a period of less than one year, it is usually reported on an annualized basis; that is, it is converted to the growth rate over a year's time, assuming that the growth rate remains constant. For GDP, which is reported quarterly, the annualized growth rate would be approximately four times the percentage change in GDP from the previous quarter. For example, if GDP rose $\frac{1}{2}$% from the first quarter of 2016 to the second quarter of 2016, then the annualized GDP growth rate for the second quarter of 2016 would be reported as 2% ($= 4 \times \frac{1}{2}$%). (A more accurate calculation would be 2.02%, because a precise quarterly growth rate should be compounded on a quarterly basis.)

2 An Overview of the Financial System

Learning Objectives

- Compare and contrast direct and indirect finance.
- Identify the structure and components of financial markets.
- List and describe the different types of financial market instruments.
- Recognize the international dimensions of financial markets.
- Summarize the roles of transaction costs, risk sharing, and information costs as they relate to financial intermediaries.
- List and describe the different types of financial intermediaries.
- Identify the reasons for and list the types of financial market regulations.

Preview

Inez the Inventor has designed a low-cost robot that cleans the house (even does the windows!), washes the car, and mows the lawn, but she has no funds to put her wonderful invention into production. Walter the Widower has plenty of savings, which he and his wife accumulated over the years. If Inez and Walter could get together so that Walter could provide funds to Inez, Inez's robot would see the light of day, and the economy would be better off: We would have cleaner houses, shinier cars, and more beautiful lawns.

Financial markets (bond and stock markets) and financial intermediaries (such as banks, insurance companies, and pension funds) serve the basic function of getting people like Inez and Walter together so that funds can move from those who have a surplus of funds (Walter) to those who have a shortage of funds (Inez). More realistically, when Apple invents a better iPod, it may need funds to bring its new product to market. Similarly, when a local government needs to build a road or a school, it may require more funds than local property taxes provide. Well-functioning financial markets and financial intermediaries are crucial to economic health.

To study the effects of financial markets and financial intermediaries on the economy, we need to acquire an understanding of their general structure and operation. In this chapter, we learn about the major financial intermediaries and the instruments that are traded in financial markets, as well as how these markets are regulated.

This chapter presents an overview of the fascinating study of financial markets and institutions. We return to a more detailed treatment of the regulation, structure, and evolution of the financial system in Chapters 8 through 12.

FUNCTION OF FINANCIAL MARKETS

Financial markets perform the essential economic function of channeling funds from households, firms, and governments that have saved surplus funds by spending less than their income to those that have a shortage of funds because they wish to spend more than their income. This function is shown schematically in Figure 1. Those who have saved and are lending funds, the lender-savers, are at the left, and those who must borrow funds to finance their spending, the borrower-spenders, are at the right. The

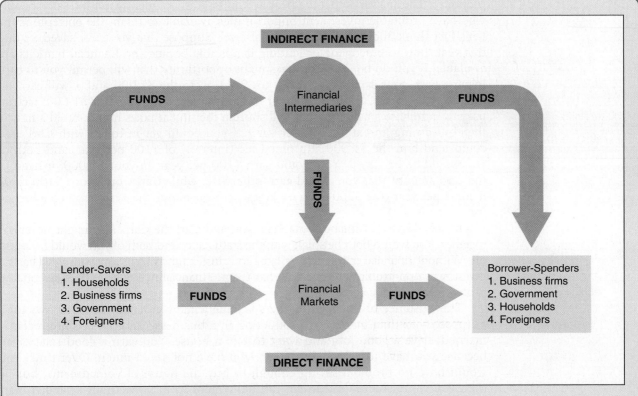

FIGURE 1   Flows of Funds Through the Financial System

The arrows show that funds flow from lender-savers to borrower-spenders via two routes: *direct finance,* in which borrowers borrow funds directly from financial markets by selling securities, and *indirect finance,* in which a financial intermediary borrows funds from lender-savers and then uses these funds to make loans to borrower-spenders.

principal lender-savers are households, but business enterprises and the government (particularly state and local government), as well as foreigners and their governments, sometimes also find themselves with excess funds and so lend them out. The most important borrower-spenders are businesses and the government (particularly the federal government), but households and foreigners also borrow to finance their purchases of cars, furniture, and houses. The arrows show that funds flow from lender-savers to borrower-spenders via two routes.

In *direct finance* (the route at the bottom of Figure 1), borrowers borrow funds directly from lenders in financial markets by selling the lenders *securities* (also called *financial instruments*), which are claims on the borrower's future income or assets. Securities are assets for the person who buys them but **liabilities** (IOUs or debts) for the individual or firm that sells (issues) them. For example, if Ford needs to borrow funds to pay for a new factory to manufacture electric cars, it might borrow the funds from savers by selling them a *bond,* a debt security that promises to make periodic payments for a specified period of time, or a *stock,* a security that entitles the owner to a share of the company's profits and assets.

Why is this channeling of funds from savers to spenders so important to the economy? The answer is that the people who save are frequently not the same people who have profitable investment opportunities available to them, the entrepreneurs. Let's first think about this on a personal level. Suppose that you have saved $1,000 this year, but no borrowing or lending is possible because no financial markets are available. If you do not have an investment opportunity that will permit you to earn income with your savings, you will just hold on to the $1,000 and it will earn no interest. However, Carl the Carpenter has a productive use for your $1,000: He can use it to purchase a new tool that will shorten the time it takes him to build a house, thereby earning an extra $200 per year. If you could get in touch with Carl, you could lend him the $1,000 at a rental fee (interest) of $100 per year, and both of you would be better off. You would earn $100 per year on your $1,000, instead of the zero amount that you would earn otherwise, while Carl would earn $100 more income per year (the $200 extra earnings per year minus the $100 rental fee for the use of the funds).

In the absence of financial markets, you and Carl the Carpenter might never get together. You would both be stuck with the status quo, and both of you would be worse off. Without financial markets, it is hard to transfer funds from a person who has no investment opportunities to one who has them. Financial markets are thus essential to promoting economic efficiency.

The existence of financial markets is beneficial even if someone borrows for a purpose other than increasing production in a business. Say that you are recently married, have a good job, and want to buy a house. You earn a good salary, but because you have just started to work, you have not saved much. Over time, you would have no problem saving enough to buy the house of your dreams, but by then you would be too old to get full enjoyment from it. Without financial markets, you are stuck; you cannot buy the house and must continue to live in your tiny apartment.

If a financial market were set up so that people who had built up savings could lend you the funds to buy the house, you would be more than happy to pay them some interest so that you could own a home while you are still young enough to enjoy it. Then, over time, you would pay back your loan. If this loan could occur, you would be better off, as would the persons who made you the loan. They would now earn some interest, whereas they would not if the financial market did not exist.

Now we can see why financial markets have such an important function in the economy. They allow funds to move from people who lack productive investment opportunities to people who have such opportunities. Financial markets are critical for producing an efficient allocation of **capital** (wealth, either financial or physical, that is employed to produce more wealth), which contributes to higher production and efficiency for the overall economy. Indeed, as we will explore in Chapter 12, when financial markets break down during financial crises, as they did during the recent global financial crisis, severe economic hardship results, which can sometimes lead to dangerous political instability.

Well-functioning financial markets also directly improve the well-being of consumers by allowing them to time their purchases better. They provide funds to young people to buy what they need (and will eventually be able to afford) without forcing them to wait until they have saved up the entire purchase price. Financial markets that are operating efficiently improve the economic welfare of everyone in the society.

STRUCTURE OF FINANCIAL MARKETS

Now that we understand the basic function of financial markets, let's look at their structure. The following descriptions of several categories of financial markets illustrate essential features of these markets.

Debt and Equity Markets

A firm or an individual can obtain funds in a financial market in two ways. The most common method is through the issuance of a debt instrument, such as a bond or a mortgage, which is a contractual agreement by the borrower to pay the holder of the instrument fixed dollar amounts at regular intervals (interest and principal payments) until a specified date (the maturity date), when a final payment is made. The **maturity** of a debt instrument is the number of years (term) until that instrument's expiration date. A debt instrument is **short-term** if its maturity term is less than a year and **long-term** if its maturity term is ten years or longer. Debt instruments with a maturity term between one and ten years are said to be **intermediate-term**.

The second method of raising funds is through the issuance of **equities**, such as common stock, which are claims to share in the *net income* (income after expenses and taxes) and the assets of a business. If you own one share of common stock in a company that has issued one million shares, you are entitled to 1 one-millionth of the firm's net income and 1 one-millionth of the firm's assets. Equities often make periodic payments (**dividends**) to their holders and are considered long-term securities because they have no maturity date. In addition, owning stock means that you own a portion of the firm and thus have the right to vote on issues important to the firm and to elect its directors.

The main disadvantage of owning a corporation's equities rather than its debt is that an equity holder is a *residual claimant*; that is, the corporation must pay all its debt holders before it pays its equity holders. The advantage of holding equities is that equity holders benefit directly from any increases in the corporation's profitability or asset value because equities confer ownership rights on the equity holders. Debt holders do not share in this benefit, because their dollar payments are fixed. We examine the pros and cons of debt versus equity instruments in more detail in Chapter 8, which provides an economic analysis of financial structure.

The total value of equities in the United States has fluctuated between $4 and $25 trillion since the early 1990s, depending on the prices of shares. Although the average person is more aware of the stock market than of any other financial market, the size of the debt market is often substantially larger than the size of the equities market: At the end of 2013, the value of debt instruments was $42 trillion, while the value of equities was $21.3 trillion.

Primary and Secondary Markets

A **primary market** is a financial market in which new issues of a security, such as a bond or a stock, are sold to initial buyers by the corporation or government agency borrowing the funds. A **secondary market** is a financial market in which securities that have been previously issued can be resold.

The primary markets for securities are not well known to the public because the selling of securities to initial buyers often takes place behind closed doors. An important financial institution that assists in the initial sale of securities in the primary market is the **investment bank**. The investment bank does this by **underwriting** securities: It guarantees a price for a corporation's securities and then sells them to the public.

The New York Stock Exchange and NASDAQ (National Association of Securities Dealers Automated Quotation System), in which previously issued stocks are traded, are the best-known examples of secondary markets, although the bond markets, in which previously-issued bonds of major corporations and the U.S. government are bought and sold, actually have a larger trading volume. Other examples of secondary markets are foreign exchange markets, futures markets, and options markets. Securities brokers and dealers are crucial to a well-functioning secondary market. **Brokers** are agents of investors who match buyers with sellers of securities; **dealers** link buyers and sellers by buying and selling securities at stated prices.

When an individual buys a security in the secondary market, the person who has sold the security receives money in exchange for the security, but the corporation that issued the security acquires no new funds. A corporation acquires new funds only when its securities are first sold in the primary market. Nonetheless, secondary markets serve two important functions. First, they make it easier and quicker to sell these financial instruments to raise cash; that is, they make the financial instruments more **liquid**. The increased liquidity of these instruments then makes them more desirable and thus easier for the issuing firm to sell in the primary market. Second, secondary markets determine the price of the security that the issuing firm sells in the primary market. The investors who buy securities in the primary market will pay the issuing corporation no more than the price they think the secondary market will set for this security. The higher the security's price in the secondary market, the higher the price the issuing firm will receive for a new security in the primary market, and hence the greater the amount of financial capital it can raise. Conditions in the secondary market are therefore the most relevant to corporations issuing securities. For this reason, books like this one, which deal with financial markets, focus on the behavior of secondary markets rather than that of primary markets.

Exchanges and Over-the-Counter Markets

Secondary markets can be organized in two ways. One method is through **exchanges**, where buyers and sellers of securities (or their agents or brokers) meet in one central location to conduct trades. The New York Stock Exchange for stocks and the Chicago Board of Trade for commodities (wheat, corn, silver, and other raw materials) are examples of organized exchanges.

The other forum for a secondary market is an **over-the-counter (OTC) market**, in which dealers at different locations who have an inventory of securities stand ready to buy and sell securities "over the counter" to anyone who comes to them and is willing to accept their prices. Because over-the-counter dealers are in contact via computers and know the prices set by one another, the OTC market is very competitive and not very different from a market with an organized exchange.

Many common stocks are traded over-the-counter, although a majority of the largest corporations have their shares traded at organized stock exchanges. The U.S. government bond market, with a larger trading volume than the New York Stock Exchange, by contrast, is set up as an over-the-counter market. Forty or so dealers establish a "market" in these securities by standing ready to buy and sell U.S. government bonds. Other over-the-counter markets include those that trade other types of financial instruments, such as negotiable certificates of deposit, federal funds, and foreign exchange instruments.

Money and Capital Markets

Another way of distinguishing between markets is on the basis of the maturity of the securities traded in each market. The **money market** is a financial market in which only short-term debt instruments (generally those with original maturity terms of less than one year) are traded; the **capital market** is the market in which longer-term debt instruments (generally those with original maturity terms of one year or greater) and equity instruments are traded. Money market securities are usually more widely traded than longer-term securities and so tend to be more liquid. In addition, as we will see in Chapter 4, short-term securities have smaller fluctuations in prices than long-term securities, making them safer investments. As a result, corporations and banks actively use the money market to earn interest on surplus funds that they expect to have only temporarily. Capital market securities, such as stocks and long-term bonds, are often held by financial intermediaries such as insurance companies and pension funds, which have little uncertainty about the amount of funds they will have available in the future.

FINANCIAL MARKET INSTRUMENTS

To complete our understanding of how financial markets perform the important role of channeling funds from lender-savers to borrower-spenders, we need to examine the securities (instruments) traded in financial markets. We first focus on the instruments traded in the money market and then turn to those traded in the capital market.

Money Market Instruments

Because of their short terms to maturity, the debt instruments traded in the money market undergo the least price fluctuations and so are the least risky investments. The money market has undergone great changes in the past three decades, with the amounts of some financial instruments growing at a far more rapid rate than others.

The principal money market instruments are listed in Table 1, along with the amount at the end of 1980, 1990, 2000, and 2013. The Following the Financial News box discusses the money market interest rates most frequently reported in the media.

TABLE 1	Principal Money Market Instruments			
	Amount ($ billions, end of year)			
Type of Instrument	**1980**	**1990**	**2000**	**2013**
U.S. Treasury bills	216	527	647	1,591
Negotiable bank certificates of deposit (large denominations)	317	543	1,053	1,762
Commercial paper	122	557	1,619	951
Federal funds and security repurchase agreements	64	388	768	1,919

Source: Federal Reserve Flow of Funds Accounts; http://www.federalreserve.gov

The four money market interest rates discussed most frequently in the media are:

Prime rate: The base interest rate on corporate bank loans, an indicator of the cost of businesses borrowing from banks

Federal funds rate: The interest rate charged on overnight loans in the federal funds market, a sensitive indicator of the cost to banks of borrowing funds from other banks and the stance of monetary policy

Treasury bill rate: The interest rate on U.S. Treasury bills, an indicator of general interest-rate movements

Libor rate: The British Banker's Association average of interbank rates for dollar deposits in the London market

The data for these interest rates are reported daily in newspapers and on Internet sites such as http://www.bankrate.com.

U.S. Treasury Bills   These short-term debt instruments of the U.S. government are issued in one-, three-, and six-month maturities to finance the federal government. They pay a set amount at maturity and have no interest payments, but they effectively pay interest by initially selling at a discount—that is, at a price lower than the set amount paid at maturity. For instance, in May 2016, you might buy a six-month Treasury bill for $9,000 that can be redeemed in November 2016 for $10,000.

U.S. Treasury bills are the most liquid of all money market instruments because they are the most actively traded. They are also the safest money market instrument because there is a low probability of **default**, a situation in which the party issuing the debt instrument (the federal government, in this case) is unable to make interest payments or pay off the amount owed when the instrument matures. The federal government can always meet its debt obligations because it can raise taxes or issue **currency** (paper money or coins) to pay off its debts. Treasury bills are held mainly by banks, although small amounts are held by households, corporations, and other financial intermediaries.

Negotiable Bank Certificates of Deposit   A *certificate of deposit (CD)* is a debt instrument sold by a bank to depositors that pays annual interest of a given amount and at maturity pays back the original purchase price. Negotiable CDs are those sold in secondary markets, with the amount outstanding currently around $1.8 trillion. Negotiable CDs are an extremely important source of funds for commercial banks from corporations, money market mutual funds, charitable institutions, and government agencies.

Commercial Paper   *Commercial paper* is a short-term debt instrument issued by large banks and well-known corporations, such as Microsoft and General Motors. Growth of the commercial paper market has been substantial: The amount of commercial paper outstanding has increased by over 700% (from $122 billion to $951 billion) in the period 1980–2013. We will discuss why the commercial paper market has had such tremendous growth in Chapter 11.

Repurchase Agreements   *Repurchase agreements (repos)* are effectively short-term loans (usually with a maturity term of less than two weeks) for which Treasury bills serve as *collateral,* an asset that the lender receives if the borrower does not pay back the loan. Repos are made as follows: A large corporation, such as Microsoft, may have some idle funds in its bank account, say $1 million, which it would like to lend for a week. Microsoft uses this excess $1 million to buy Treasury bills from a bank, which agrees to repurchase them the next week at a price slightly above Microsoft's purchase price. The net effect of this agreement is that Microsoft makes a loan of $1 million to the bank and holds $1 million of the bank's Treasury bills until the bank repurchases the bills to pay off the loan. Repurchase agreements are now an important source of bank funds (over $493 billion). The most important lenders in this market are large corporations.

Federal (Fed) Funds These instruments are typically overnight loans between banks of their deposits at the Federal Reserve. The *federal funds* designation is somewhat confusing because these loans are not made by the federal government or by the Federal Reserve but rather by banks to other banks. One reason why a bank might borrow in the federal funds market is that it might find it does not have enough funds in its deposit accounts at the Fed to meet the amount required by regulators. It can then borrow these funds from another bank, which transfers them to the borrowing bank using the Fed's wire transfer system. This market is very sensitive to the credit needs of the banks, so the interest rate on these loans, called the **federal funds rate**, is a closely watched barometer of the tightness of credit market conditions in the banking system and the stance of monetary policy. When high, the federal funds rate indicates that banks are strapped for funds; when low, it indicates that banks' credit needs are low.

Capital Market Instruments

Capital market instruments are debt and equity instruments with maturities of greater than one year. They have far wider price fluctuations than money market instruments and are considered to be fairly risky investments. The principal capital market instruments are listed in Table 2, which shows the amount at the end of 1980, 1990, 2000,

TABLE 2	Principal Capital Market Instruments			
	Amount			
	($ billions, end of year)			
Type of Instrument	**1980**	**1990**	**2000**	**2013**
Corporate stocks (market value)	1,601	4,146	17,627	21,363
Residential mortgages	1,106	2,886	5,463	9,863
Corporate bonds	366	1,008	2,230	6,436
U.S. government securities (marketable long-term)	407	1,653	2,184	4,359
U.S. government agency securities	193	435	1,616	6,199
State and local government bonds	310	870	1,192	2,925
Bank commercial loans	459	818	1,091	1,175
Consumer loans	355	813	536	679
Commercial and farm mortgages	352	829	1,214	2,463

Source: Federal Reserve Flow of Funds Accounts; http://www.federalreserve.gov.

Following the Financial News   Capital Market Interest Rates

The five interest rates on capital market instruments discussed most frequently in the media are:

30-year mortgage rate: The interest rate on a 30-year, fixed-rate residential mortgage that is less than $417,000 ($625,500 in high-cost areas) in amount and is guaranteed by the **Federal Housing Administration (FHA)**.

Jumbo mortgage rate: The interest rate on a 30-year, fixed-rate residential mortgage for prime customers that is in excess of $417,000 ($625,500 in high-cost areas) in amount.

Five-year adjustable rate mortgage (ARM) rate: The interest rate for the first five years on a residential mortgage that adjusts after five years for prime customers.

New-car loan rate: The interest rate on a four-year, fixed-rate new-car loan.

10-year Treasury rate: The interest rate on U.S. Treasury bonds maturing in ten years.

The data for these interest rates are reported daily in newspapers and on Internet sites such as http://www.bankrate.com and http://www.finance.yahoo.com.

---

and 2013. The Following the Financial News box discusses the capital market interest rates most frequently reported in the media.

Stocks   *Stocks* are equity claims on the net income and assets of a corporation. Their value of $21 trillion at the end of 2013 exceeds that of any other type of security in the capital market. However, the amount of new stock issues in any given year is typically quite small, less than 1% of the total value of shares outstanding. Individuals hold around half of the value of stocks; the rest is held by pension funds, mutual funds, and insurance companies.

Mortgages and Mortgage-Backed Securities   **Mortgages** are loans to households or firms to purchase land, housing, or other real structures, in which the structure or land itself serves as collateral for the loans. The mortgage market is the largest debt market in the United States, with the amount of residential mortgages (used to purchase residential housing) outstanding more than quadruple the amount of commercial and farm mortgages. Mortgages are provided by financial institutions such as savings and loan associations, mutual savings banks, commercial banks, and insurance companies. However, in recent years a growing amount of the funds for mortgages have been provided by **mortgage-backed securities**, bond-like debt instruments backed by a bundle of individual mortgages, whose interest and principal payments are collectively paid to the holders of the security. As we will see in Chapter 12, mortgage-backed securities and more complicated variants (CDOs) have become notorious because they played a key role in promoting the recent global financial crisis. The federal government plays an active role in the mortgage market via the three government agencies—the Federal National Mortgage Association (FNMA, "Fannie Mae"), the Government National Mortgage Association (GNMA, "Ginnie Mae"), and the Federal Home Loan Mortgage Corporation (FHLMC, "Freddie Mac")—that provide funds to the mortgage market by selling bonds and using the proceeds to buy mortgages.

Corporate Bonds   These long-term bonds are issued by corporations with very strong credit ratings. The typical *corporate bond* sends the holder an interest payment twice a year and pays off the face value when the bond matures. Some corporate bonds, called *convertible bonds,* have the additional feature of allowing the holder to convert them into a specified number of shares of stock at any time up to the maturity date. This feature makes these convertible bonds more desirable to prospective purchasers than bonds without it, and it allows the corporation to reduce its interest payments because the bonds can increase in value if the price of the stock appreciates sufficiently. Because the outstanding amount of both convertible and nonconvertible bonds for any given corporation is small, corporate bonds are not nearly as liquid as other securities such as U.S. government bonds.

Although the size of the corporate bond market is substantially smaller than that of the stock market, with the amount of corporate bonds outstanding less than one-third that of stocks, the volume of new corporate bonds issued each year is substantially greater than the volume of new stock issues. Thus the behavior of the corporate bond market is probably far more important to a firm's financing decisions than is the behavior of the stock market. The principal buyers of corporate bonds are life insurance companies; pension funds and households are other large holders.

U.S. Government Securities   These long-term debt instruments are issued by the U.S. Treasury to finance the deficits of the federal government. Because they are the most widely traded bonds in the United States (the volume of transactions on average exceeds $500 billion daily), they are the most liquid security traded in the capital market. They are held by the Federal Reserve, banks, households, and foreigners.

U.S. Government Agency Securities   These long-term bonds are issued by various government agencies such as Ginnie Mae, the Federal Farm Credit Bank, and the Tennessee Valley Authority to finance such items as mortgages, farm loans, or power-generating equipment. Many of these securities are guaranteed by the federal government. They function much like U.S. government bonds and are held by similar parties.

State and Local Government Bonds   State and local bonds, also called *municipal bonds,* are long-term debt instruments issued by state and local governments to finance expenditures on schools, roads, and other large programs. An important feature of these bonds is that their interest payments are exempt from federal income tax and generally from state taxes in the issuing state. Commercial banks, with their high income tax rates, are the biggest buyers of these securities, owning over half the total amount outstanding. The next biggest group of holders consists of wealthy individuals in high income-tax brackets, followed by insurance companies.

Consumer and Bank Commercial Loans   These loans to consumers and businesses are made principally by banks but, in the case of consumer loans, also by finance companies.

INTERNATIONALIZATION OF FINANCIAL MARKETS

The growing internationalization of financial markets has become an important trend. Before the 1980s, U.S. financial markets were much larger than those outside the United States, but in recent years the dominance of U.S. markets has been weakening. (See the Global box "Are U.S. Capital Markets Losing Their Edge?") The extraordinary growth of

Global Are U.S. Capital Markets Losing Their Edge?

Over the past few decades, the United States lost its international dominance in a number of manufacturing industries, including automobiles and consumer electronics, as other countries became more competitive in global markets. Recent evidence suggests that financial markets now are undergoing a similar trend: Just as Ford and General Motors have lost global market share to Toyota and Honda, U.S. stock and bond markets recently have seen their share of sales of newly-issued corporate securities slip. The London and Hong Kong stock exchanges now handle a larger share of initial public offerings (IPOs) of stock than does the New York Stock Exchange, which had been by far the dominant exchange in terms of IPO value before 2000. Furthermore, the number of stocks listed on U.S. exchanges has been falling, while stock listings abroad have been growing rapidly: Listings outside the United States are now about ten times greater than those in the United States. Likewise, the portion of new corporate bonds issued worldwide that are initially sold in U.S. capital markets has fallen below the share sold in European debt markets.

Why do corporations that issue new securities to raise capital now conduct more of this business in financial markets in Europe and Asia? Among the factors contributing to this trend are quicker adoption of technological innovation by foreign financial markets, tighter immigration controls in the United States following the terrorist attacks of 2001, and perceptions that listing on American exchanges will expose foreign securities issuers to greater risks of lawsuits. Many people see burdensome financial regulation as the main cause, however, and point specifically to the Sarbanes-Oxley Act of 2002. Congress passed this act after a number of accounting scandals involving U.S. corporations and the accounting firms that audited them came to light. Sarbanes-Oxley aims to strengthen the integrity of the auditing process and the quality of information provided in corporate financial statements. The costs to corporations of complying with the new rules and procedures are high, especially for smaller firms, but largely avoidable if firms choose to issue their securities in financial markets outside the United States. For this reason, there is much support for revising Sarbanes-Oxley to lessen its allegedly harmful effects and induce more securities issuers back to U.S. financial markets. However, evidence is not conclusive to support the view that Sarbanes-Oxley is the main cause of the relative decline of U.S. financial markets and therefore in need of reform.

Discussion of the relative decline of U.S. financial markets and debate about the factors that are contributing to it likely will continue. Chapter 8 provides more detail on the Sarbanes-Oxley Act and its effects on the U.S. financial system.

foreign financial markets has been the result of both large increases in the pool of savings in foreign countries such as Japan and the deregulation of foreign financial markets, which has enabled foreign markets to expand their activities. American corporations and banks are now more likely to tap international capital markets to raise needed funds, and American investors often seek investment opportunities abroad. Similarly, foreign corporations and banks raise funds from Americans, and foreigners have become important investors in the United States. A look at international bond markets and world stock markets will give us a picture of how this globalization of financial markets is taking place.

International Bond Market, Eurobonds, and Eurocurrencies

The traditional instruments in the international bond market are known as **foreign bonds**. Foreign bonds are sold in a foreign country and are denominated in that country's currency. For example, if the German automaker Porsche sells a bond in the

United States denominated in U.S. dollars, it is classified as a foreign bond. Foreign bonds have been an important instrument in the international capital market for centuries. In fact, a large percentage of U.S. railroads built in the nineteenth century were financed by sales of foreign bonds in Britain.

A more recent innovation in the international bond market is the **Eurobond**, a bond denominated in a currency other than that of the country in which it is sold—for example, a bond denominated in U.S. dollars sold in London. Currently, over 80% of the new issues in the international bond market are Eurobonds, and the market for these securities has grown very rapidly. As a result, the Eurobond market is now larger than the U.S. corporate bond market.

A variant of the Eurobond is **Eurocurrencies**, which are foreign currencies deposited in banks outside the home country. The most important of the Eurocurrencies are **Eurodollars**, which are U.S. dollars deposited in foreign banks outside the United States or in foreign branches of U.S. banks. Because these short-term deposits earn interest, they are similar to short-term Eurobonds. American banks borrow Eurodollar deposits from other banks or from their own foreign branches, and Eurodollars are now an important source of funds for American banks.

Note that the currency, the euro, can create some confusion about the terms Eurobond, Eurocurrencies, and Eurodollars. A bond denominated in euros is called a Eurobond *only if it is sold outside the countries that have adopted the euro*. In fact, most Eurobonds are not denominated in euros but are instead denominated in U.S. dollars. Similarly, Eurodollars have nothing to do with euros, but are instead U.S. dollars deposited in banks outside the United States.

World Stock Markets

Until recently, the U.S. stock market was by far the largest in the world, but foreign stock markets have been growing in importance, with the United States not always number one. The increased interest in foreign stocks has prompted the development in the United States of mutual funds that specialize in trading in foreign stock markets. As the Following the Financial News box indicates, American investors now pay attention not only to the Dow Jones Industrial Average but also to stock price indexes for foreign stock markets, such as the Nikkei 300 Average (Tokyo) and the Financial Times Stock Exchange (FTSE) 100-Share Index (London).

The internationalization of financial markets is having profound effects on the United States. Foreigners, particularly Japanese investors, are not only providing funds to corporations in the United States but are also helping finance the federal government. Without these foreign funds, the U.S. economy would have grown far less rapidly in the past twenty years. The internationalization of financial markets is also leading the way to a more integrated world economy in which flows of goods and technology between countries are more commonplace. In later chapters, we will encounter many examples of the important roles that international factors play in our economy.

FUNCTION OF FINANCIAL INTERMEDIARIES: INDIRECT FINANCE

As shown in Figure 1 (p. 23), funds can move from lenders to borrowers by a second route, called *indirect finance* because it involves a financial intermediary that stands between the lender-savers and the borrower-spenders and helps transfer funds from

Following the Financial News   Foreign Stock Market Indexes

Foreign stock market indexes are published daily in newspapers and on Internet sites such as finance .yahoo.com.

The most important of these stock market indexes are:

Dow Jones Industrial Average (DJIA): An index of the 30 largest publicly-traded corporations in the United States, maintained by the Dow Jones Corporation

S&P 500: An index of 500 of the largest companies traded in the United States, maintained by Standard & Poor's

NASDAQ Composite: An index for all the stocks that trade on the NASDAQ stock market, where most of the technology stocks in the United States are traded

FTSE 100: An index of the 100 most highly capitalized UK companies listed on the London Stock Exchange

DAX: An index of the 30 largest German companies trading on the Frankfurt Stock Exchange

CAC 40: An index of the 40 largest French companies trading on Euronext Paris

Hang Seng: An index of the largest companies trading on the Hong Kong stock markets

Strait Times: An index of the 30 largest companies trading on the Singapore Exchange

These indexes are reported daily in newspapers and on Internet sites such as http://www.finance .yahoo.com.

---

one to the other. A financial intermediary does this by borrowing funds from lender-savers and then using these funds to make loans to borrower-spenders. For example, a bank might acquire funds by issuing a liability to the public in the form of savings deposits (an asset for the public). It might then use the funds to acquire an asset by making a loan to General Motors or by buying a U.S. Treasury bond in the financial market. The ultimate result is that funds have been transferred from the public (the lender-savers) to General Motors or the U.S. Treasury (the borrower-spender) with the help of the financial intermediary (the bank).

The process of indirect financing using financial intermediaries, called **financial intermediation**, is the primary route for moving funds from lenders to borrowers. Indeed, although the media focus much of their attention on securities markets, particularly the stock market, financial intermediaries are a far more important source of financing for corporations than securities markets are. This is true not only for the United States but for other industrialized countries as well (see the Global box). Why are financial intermediaries and indirect finance so important in financial markets? To answer this question, we need to understand the roles of transaction costs, risk sharing, and information costs in financial markets.

Transaction Costs

Transaction costs, the time and money spent in carrying out financial transactions, are a major problem for people who have excess funds to lend. As we have seen, Carl the Carpenter needs $1,000 for his new tool, and you know that it is an excellent investment opportunity. You have the cash and would like to lend him the money, but to protect your investment, you have to hire a lawyer to write up the loan contract that specifies how much interest Carl will pay you, when he will make these interest payments, and when he will repay you the $1,000. Obtaining the contract will cost

Global The Importance of Financial Intermediaries Relative to Securities Markets: An International Comparison

Patterns of financing corporations differ across countries, but one key fact emerges: Studies of the major developed countries, including the United States, Canada, the United Kingdom, Japan, Italy, Germany, and France, show that when businesses go looking for funds to finance their activities, they usually obtain them indirectly through financial intermediaries and not directly from securities markets.* Even in the United States and Canada, which have the most developed securities markets in the world, loans from financial intermediaries are far more important for corporate finance than securities markets are. The countries that have made the least use of securities markets are Germany and Japan; in these two countries, financing from financial intermediaries has been almost ten times greater than that from securities markets. However, after the deregulation of Japanese securities markets in recent years, the share of corporate financing by financial intermediaries has been declining relative to the use of securities markets.

Although the dominance of financial intermediaries over securities markets is clear in all countries, the relative importance of bond versus stock markets differs widely across countries. In the United States, the bond market is far more important as a source of corporate finance: On average, the amount of new financing raised using bonds is ten times the amount raised using stocks. By contrast, countries such as France and Italy make more use of equities markets than of the bond market to raise capital.

*See, for example, Colin Mayer, "Financial Systems, Corporate Finance, and Economic Development," in *Asymmetric Information, Corporate Finance, and Investment*, ed. R. Glenn Hubbard (Chicago: University of Chicago Press, 1990), pp. 307–332.

you $500. When you figure in this transaction cost for making the loan, you realize that you can't earn enough from the deal (you spend $500 to make perhaps $100) and reluctantly tell Carl that he will have to look elsewhere.

This example illustrates that small savers like you or potential borrowers like Carl might be frozen out of financial markets and thus be unable to benefit from them. Can anyone come to the rescue? Financial intermediaries can.

Financial intermediaries can substantially reduce transaction costs because they have developed expertise in lowering them and because their large size allows them to take advantage of **economies of scale**, the reduction in transaction costs per dollar of transactions as the size (scale) of transactions increases. For example, a bank knows how to find a good lawyer to produce an airtight loan contract, and this contract can be used over and over again in its loan transactions, thus lowering the legal cost per transaction. Instead of a loan contract (which may not be all that well written) costing $500, a bank can hire a top-flight lawyer for $5,000 to draw up an airtight loan contract that can be used for 2,000 loans at a cost of $2.50 per loan. At a cost of $2.50 per loan, it now becomes profitable for the financial intermediary to lend Carl the $1,000.

Because financial intermediaries are able to reduce transaction costs substantially, they make it possible for you to provide funds indirectly to people like Carl with productive investment opportunities. In addition, a financial intermediary's low transaction costs mean that it can provide its customers with **liquidity services**, services that make it easier for customers to conduct transactions. For example, banks provide depositors with checking accounts that enable them to pay their bills easily. In addition, depositors can earn interest on checking and savings accounts and yet still convert them into goods and services whenever necessary.

Risk Sharing

Another benefit made possible by the low transaction costs of financial institutions is that these institutions can help reduce the exposure of investors to **risk**—that is, uncertainty about the returns investors will earn on assets. Financial intermediaries do this through the process known as **risk sharing**: They create and sell assets with risk characteristics that people are comfortable with, and the intermediaries then use the funds they acquire by selling these assets to purchase other assets that may have far more risk. Low transaction costs allow financial intermediaries to share risk at low cost, enabling them to earn a profit on the spread between the returns they earn on risky assets and the payments they make on the assets they have sold. This process of risk sharing is also sometimes referred to as **asset transformation**, because in a sense, risky assets are turned into safer assets for investors.

Financial intermediaries also promote risk sharing by helping individuals to diversify and thereby lower the amount of risk to which they are exposed. **Diversification** entails investing in a collection (**portfolio**) of assets whose returns do not always move together, with the result that overall risk is lower than for individual assets. (Diversification is just another name for the old adage "You shouldn't put all your eggs in one basket.") Low transaction costs allow financial intermediaries to pool a collection of assets into a new asset and then sell it to individuals.

Asymmetric Information: Adverse Selection and Moral Hazard

The presence of transaction costs in financial markets explains, in part, why financial intermediaries and indirect finance play such an important role in financial markets. An additional reason is that in financial markets, one party often does not know enough about the other party to make accurate decisions. This inequality is called **asymmetric information**. For example, a borrower who takes out a loan usually has better information about the potential returns and risks associated with the investment projects for which the funds are earmarked than the lender does. Lack of information creates problems in the financial system on two fronts: before the transaction is entered into, and afterward.[1]

Adverse selection is the problem created by asymmetric information *before* the transaction occurs. Adverse selection in financial markets occurs when the potential borrowers who are the most likely to produce an undesirable (*adverse*) outcome—the bad credit risks—are the ones who most actively seek out a loan and are thus most likely to be selected. Because adverse selection makes it more likely that loans might be made to bad credit risks, lenders may decide not to make any loans, even though good credit risks exist in the marketplace.

To understand why adverse selection occurs, suppose you have two aunts to whom you might make a loan—Aunt Louise and Aunt Sheila. Aunt Louise is a conservative type who borrows only when she has an investment she is quite sure will pay off. Aunt Sheila, by contrast, is an inveterate gambler who has just come across a get-rich-quick scheme that will make her a millionaire if she can just borrow $1,000 to invest in it. Unfortunately, as with most get-rich-quick schemes, the probability is high that the investment won't pay off and that Aunt Sheila will lose the $1,000.

---

[1]Asymmetric information and the adverse selection and moral hazard concepts are also crucial problems for the insurance industry.

Which of your aunts is more likely to call you to ask for a loan? Aunt Sheila, of course, because she has so much to gain if the investment pays off. You, however, would not want to make a loan to her because the probability is high that her investment will turn sour and she will be unable to pay you back.

If you know both your aunts very well—that is, if your information is not asymmetric—you won't have a problem, because you will know that Aunt Sheila is a bad risk and so you will not lend to her. Suppose, though, that you don't know your aunts well. You will be more likely to lend to Aunt Sheila than to Aunt Louise because Aunt Sheila will be hounding you for the loan. Because of the possibility of adverse selection, you might decide not to lend to either of your aunts, even though there are times when Aunt Louise, who is an excellent credit risk, might need a loan for a worthwhile investment.

Moral hazard is the problem created by asymmetric information *after* the transaction occurs. Moral hazard in financial markets is the risk (*hazard*) that the borrower might engage in activities that are undesirable (*immoral*) from the lender's point of view, because they make it less likely that the loan will be paid back. Because moral hazard lowers the probability that the loan will be repaid, lenders may decide that they would rather not make a loan.

As an example of moral hazard, suppose that you made a $1,000 loan to another relative, Uncle Melvin, who needs the money to purchase a computer so that he can set up a business typing students' term papers. Once you have made the loan, however, Uncle Melvin is more likely to slip off to the track and play the horses than to purchase the computer. If he bets on a 20-to-1 long shot and wins with your money, he is able to pay back your $1,000 and live high-off-the-hog with the remaining $19,000. But if he loses, as is likely, you won't get paid back, and all he has lost is his reputation as a reliable, upstanding uncle. Uncle Melvin therefore has an incentive to go to the track because his gains ($19,000) if he bets correctly are much greater than the cost to him (his reputation) if he bets incorrectly. If you knew what Uncle Melvin was up to, you would prevent him from going to the track, and he would not be able to increase the moral hazard. However, because it is hard for you to keep informed about his whereabouts—that is, because information is asymmetric—there is a good chance that Uncle Melvin will go to the track and you will not get paid back. The risk of moral hazard might therefore discourage you from making the $1,000 loan to Uncle Melvin, even if you are sure that you will be paid back if he uses it to set up his business.

The problems created by adverse selection and moral hazard are a major impediment to well-functioning financial markets. Again, financial intermediaries can alleviate these problems.

With financial intermediaries in the economy, small savers can provide their funds to the financial markets by lending these funds to a trustworthy intermediary—say, the Honest John Bank—which in turn lends the funds out either by making loans or by buying securities such as stocks or bonds. Successful financial intermediaries have higher earnings on their investments than do small savers, because they are better equipped than individuals to screen out bad credit risks from good ones, thereby reducing losses due to adverse selection. In addition, financial intermediaries have high earnings because they develop expertise in monitoring the parties they lend to, thus reducing losses due to moral hazard. The result is that financial intermediaries can afford to pay lender-savers interest or provide substantial services and still earn a profit.

As we have seen, financial intermediaries play an important role in the economy because they provide liquidity services, promote risk sharing, and solve information problems, thereby allowing small savers and borrowers to benefit from the existence of financial markets. The success of financial intermediaries in performing this role is evidenced by the fact that most Americans invest their savings with them and obtain loans from them. Financial intermediaries play a key role in improving economic efficiency because they help financial markets channel funds from lender-savers to people with productive investment opportunities. Without a well-functioning set of financial intermediaries, it is very hard for an economy to reach its full potential. We will explore further the role of financial intermediaries in the economy in Part 3.

Economies of Scope and Conflicts of Interest

Another reason why financial intermediaries play such an important part in the economy is that by providing multiple financial services to their customers, such as offering them bank loans or selling their bonds for them, they can also achieve **economies of scope**; that is, they can lower the cost of information production for each service by applying one information resource to many different services. A bank, for example, when making a loan to a corporation, can evaluate how good a credit risk the firm is, which then helps the bank decide whether it would be easy to sell the bonds of this corporation to the public.

Although economies of scope may substantially benefit financial institutions, they also create potential costs in terms of **conflicts of interest**. Conflicts of interest, a type of moral hazard problem, arise when a person or institution has multiple objectives (interests), some of which conflict with each other. Conflicts of interest are especially likely to occur when a financial institution provides multiple services. The potentially competing interests of those services may lead an individual or firm to conceal information or disseminate misleading information. We care about conflicts of interest because a substantial reduction in the quality of information in financial markets increases asymmetric information problems and prevents financial markets from channeling funds into the most productive investment opportunities. Consequently, the financial markets and the economy become less efficient.

TYPES OF FINANCIAL INTERMEDIARIES

We have seen why financial intermediaries have such an important function in the economy. Now we take a look at the principal financial intermediaries and how they perform the intermediation function. Financial intermediaries fall into three categories: depository institutions (banks), contractual savings institutions, and investment intermediaries. Table 3 describes the primary liabilities (sources of funds) and assets (uses of funds) of the financial intermediaries in each category. The relative sizes of these intermediaries in the United States are indicated in Table 4, which lists the amounts of their assets at the end of 1980, 1990, 2000, and 2013.

Depository Institutions

Depository institutions (for simplicity, we refer to these as *banks* throughout this text) are financial intermediaries that accept deposits from individuals and institutions and make loans. The study of money and banking focuses special attention on this group of financial institutions because they are involved in the creation of deposits, an important component of the money supply. These institutions include commercial banks and the so-called **thrift institutions (thrifts)**: savings and loan associations, mutual savings banks, and credit unions.

TABLE 3	Primary Assets and Liabilities of Financial Intermediaries	
Type of Intermediary	**Primary Liabilities (Sources of Funds)**	**Primary Assets (Uses of Funds)**
Depository institutions (banks)		
Commercial banks	Deposits ·	Business and consumer loans, mortgages, U.S. government securities, and municipal bonds
Savings and loan associations	Deposits	Mortgages
Mutual savings banks	Deposits	Mortgages
Credit unions	Deposits	Consumer loans
Contractual savings institutions		
Life insurance companies	Premiums from policies	Corporate bonds and mortgages
Fire and casualty insurance companies	Premiums from policies	Municipal bonds, corporate bonds and stock, and U.S. government securities
Pension funds, government retirement funds	Employer and employee contributions	Corporate bonds and stock
Investment intermediaries		
Finance companies	Commercial paper, stocks, bonds	Consumer and business loans
Mutual funds	Shares	Stocks, bonds
Money market mutual funds	Shares	Money market instruments
Hedge funds	Partnership participation	Stocks, bonds, loans, foreign currencies, and many other assets

Commercial Banks   These financial intermediaries raise funds primarily by issuing checkable deposits (deposits on which checks can be written), savings deposits (deposits that are payable on demand but do not allow their owners to write checks), and time deposits (deposits with fixed terms to maturity). They then use these funds to make commercial, consumer, and mortgage loans and to buy U.S. government securities and municipal bonds. Slightly fewer than 5,700 commercial banks are found in the United States and, as a group, they are the largest financial intermediary and have the most diversified portfolios (collections) of assets.

Savings and Loan Associations (S&Ls) and Mutual Savings Banks   These depository institutions, of which there are approximately 900 in the United States, obtain funds primarily through savings deposits (often called *shares*) and time and checkable deposits. In the past, these institutions were constrained in their activities and mostly made mortgage loans for residential housing. Over time, these restrictions have been loosened, so the distinction between these depository institutions and commercial banks has blurred. These intermediaries have become more alike and are now more competitive with each other.

TABLE 4 Primary Financial Intermediaries and Value of Their Assets

Type of Intermediary	Value of Assets ($ billions, end of year)			
	1980	1990	2000	2013
Depository institutions (banks)				
Commercial banks	1,481	3,334	6,469	12,670
Savings and loan associations and mutual savings banks	792	1,365	1,218	2,157
Credit unions	67	215	441	1,005
Contractual savings institutions				
Life insurance companies	464	1,367	3,136	6,035
Fire and casualty insurance companies	182	533	862	1,527
Pension funds (private)	504	1,629	4,355	7,966
State and local government retirement funds	197	737	2,293	4,846
Investment intermediaries				
Finance companies	205	610	1,140	1,474
Mutual funds	70	654	4,435	11,527
Money market mutual funds	76	498	1,812	2,678

Source: Federal Reserve Flow of Funds Accounts; http://www.federalreserve.gov/releases/Z1/.

Credit Unions   These financial institutions, numbering about 7,000 in the United States, are typically very small cooperative lending institutions organized around a particular group: union members, employees of a particular firm, and so forth. They acquire funds from deposits called *shares* and primarily make consumer loans.

Contractual Savings Institutions

Contractual savings institutions, such as insurance companies and pension funds, are financial intermediaries that acquire funds at periodic intervals on a contractual basis. Because they can predict with reasonable accuracy how much they will have to pay out in benefits in the coming years, they do not have to worry as much as depository institutions about losing funds quickly. As a result, the liquidity of assets is not as important a consideration for them as it is for depository institutions, and they tend to invest their funds primarily in long-term securities such as corporate bonds, stocks, and mortgages.

Life Insurance Companies   Life insurance companies insure people against financial hazards following a death and sell annuities (annual income payments upon retirement). They acquire funds from the premiums that people pay to keep their policies in force and use them mainly to buy corporate bonds and mortgages. They also purchase stocks, but are restricted in the amount that they can hold. Currently, with $6 trillion in assets, they are among the largest of the contractual savings institutions.

Fire and Casualty Insurance Companies These companies insure their policyholders against loss from theft, fire, and accidents. They are very much like life insurance companies, receiving funds through premiums for their policies, but they have a greater possibility of loss of funds if major disasters occur. For this reason, they use their funds to buy more liquid assets than life insurance companies do. Their largest holding of assets consists of municipal bonds; they also hold corporate bonds and stocks and U.S. government securities.

Pension Funds and Government Retirement Funds Private pension funds and state and local retirement funds provide retirement income in the form of annuities to employees who are covered by a pension plan. Funds are acquired by contributions from employers and from employees, who either have a contribution automatically deducted from their paychecks or contribute voluntarily. The largest asset holdings of pension funds are corporate bonds and stocks. The establishment of pension funds has been actively encouraged by the federal government, both through legislation requiring pension plans and through tax incentives to encourage contributions.

Investment Intermediaries

This category of financial intermediary includes finance companies, mutual funds, money market mutual funds, and hedge funds.

Finance Companies Finance companies raise funds by selling commercial paper (a short-term debt instrument) and by issuing stocks and bonds. They lend these funds to consumers, who use them to purchase such items as furniture, automobiles, and home improvements, and to small businesses. Some finance companies are organized by a parent corporation to help sell its product. For example, Ford Motor Credit Company makes loans to consumers who purchase Ford automobiles.

Mutual Funds These financial intermediaries acquire funds by selling shares to many individuals and then using the proceeds to purchase diversified portfolios of stocks and bonds. Mutual funds allow shareholders to pool their resources so that they can take advantage of lower transaction costs when buying large blocks of stocks or bonds. In addition, mutual funds allow shareholders to hold more diversified portfolios than they otherwise would. Shareholders can sell (redeem) shares at any time, but the value of these shares will be determined by the value of the mutual fund's holdings of securities. Because these fluctuate greatly, the value of mutual fund shares will, too; therefore, investments in mutual funds can be risky.

Money Market Mutual Funds These financial institutions are similar to mutual funds but also function to some extent as depository institutions because they offer deposit-type accounts. Like most mutual funds, they sell shares to acquire funds that are then used to buy money market instruments that are both safe and very liquid. The interest on these assets is paid out to the shareholders.

A key feature of these funds is that shareholders can write checks against the value of their shareholdings. In effect, shares in a money market mutual fund function like checking account deposits that pay interest. Money market mutual funds have experienced extraordinary growth since 1971, when they first appeared. In 2013, their assets had climbed to $2.7 trillion.

Hedge Funds Hedge funds are a type of mutual fund with special characteristics. Hedge funds are organized as limited partnerships with minimum investments ranging from $100,000 to, more typically, $1 million or more. These limitations mean that hedge funds are subject to much weaker regulation than other mutual funds. Hedge funds invest in many types of assets, with some specializing in stocks, others in bonds, others in foreign currencies, and still others in far more exotic assets.

Investment Banks Despite its name, an investment bank is not a bank or a financial intermediary in the ordinary sense; that is, it does not take in funds and then lend them out. Instead, an investment bank is a different type of intermediary that helps a corporation issue securities. First it advises the corporation on which type of securities to issue (stocks or bonds); then it helps sell (**underwrite**) the securities by purchasing them from the corporation at a predetermined price and reselling them in the market. Investment banks also act as deal makers and earn enormous fees by helping corporations acquire other companies through mergers or acquisitions.

REGULATION OF THE FINANCIAL SYSTEM

The financial system is among the most heavily regulated sectors of the American economy. The government regulates financial markets for two main reasons: to increase the information available to investors and to ensure the soundness of the financial system. We will examine how these two goals have led to the present regulatory environment. As a study aid, the principal regulatory agencies of the U.S. financial system are listed in Table 5.

Increasing Information Available to Investors

Asymmetric information in financial markets means that investors may be subject to adverse selection and moral hazard problems that may hinder the efficient operation of financial markets. Risky firms or outright crooks may be the most eager to sell securities to unwary investors, and the resulting adverse selection problem may keep investors out of financial markets. Furthermore, once an investor has bought a security, thereby lending money to a firm, the borrower may have incentives to engage in risky activities or to commit outright fraud. The presence of this moral hazard problem may also keep investors away from financial markets. Government regulation can reduce adverse selection and moral hazard problems in financial markets and enhance the efficiency of the markets by increasing the amount of information available to investors.

As a result of the stock market crash of 1929 and revelations of widespread fraud in the aftermath, political demands for regulation culminated in the Securities Act of 1933 and the establishment of the Securities and Exchange Commission (SEC) in 1934. The SEC requires corporations issuing securities to disclose certain information about their sales, assets, and earnings to the public, and restricts trading by the largest stockholders (known as *insiders*) in the corporation. By requiring disclosure and by discouraging insider trading, which could be used to manipulate security prices, the SEC hopes that investors will be better informed and protected from the types of abuses that occurred in financial markets before 1933. Indeed, in recent years, the SEC has been particularly active in prosecuting people involved in insider trading.

TABLE 5	Principal Regulatory Agencies of the U.S. Financial System	
Regulatory Agency	**Subject of Regulation**	**Nature of Regulations**
Securities and Exchange Commission (SEC)	Organized exchanges and financial markets	Requires disclosure of information; restricts insider trading
Commodities Futures Trading Commission (CFTC)	Futures market exchanges	Regulates procedures for trading in futures markets
Office of the Comptroller of the Currency	Federally-chartered commercial banks and thrift institutions	Charters and examines the books of federally-chartered commercial banks and thrift institutions; imposes restrictions on assets they can hold
National Credit Union Administration (NCUA)	Federally-chartered credit unions	Charters and examines the books of federally-chartered credit unions and imposes restrictions on assets they can hold
State banking and insurance commissions	State-chartered depository institutions and insurance companies	Charter and examine the books of state-chartered banks and insurance companies, impose restrictions on assets they can hold, and impose restrictions on branching
Federal Deposit Insurance Corporation (FDIC)	Commercial banks, mutual savings banks, savings and loan associations	Provides insurance of up to $250,000 for each depositor at a bank, examines the books of insured banks, and imposes restrictions on assets they can hold
Federal Reserve System	All depository institutions	Examines the books of commercial banks and systemically important financial institutions; sets reserve requirements for all banks

Ensuring the Soundness of Financial Intermediaries

Asymmetric information can lead to the widespread collapse of financial intermediaries, referred to as a **financial panic**. Because providers of funds to financial intermediaries may not be able to assess whether the institutions holding their funds are sound, if they have doubts about the overall health of financial intermediaries, they may want to pull their funds out of both sound and unsound institutions. The possible outcome is a financial panic that produces large losses for the public and causes serious damage to the economy. To protect the public and the economy from financial panics, the government has implemented six types of regulations.

Restrictions on Entry State banking and insurance commissions, as well as the Office of the Comptroller of the Currency (an agency of the federal government), have created tight regulations governing who is allowed to set up a financial intermediary. Individuals or groups that want to establish a financial intermediary, such as a bank or an insurance company, must obtain a charter from the state or the federal government.

Only upstanding citizens with impeccable credentials and a large amount of initial funds will be given a charter.

Disclosure   Reporting requirements for financial intermediaries are stringent. Their bookkeeping must follow certain strict principles, their books are subject to periodic inspection, and they must make certain information available to the public.

Restrictions on Assets and Activities   Financial intermediaries are restricted in what they are allowed to do and what assets they can hold. Before you put funds into a bank or similar institution, you will want to know that your funds are safe and that the bank or other financial intermediary will be able to meet its obligations to you. One way of ensuring the trustworthiness of financial intermediaries is to restrict them from engaging in certain risky activities. Legislation passed in 1933 (and repealed in 1999) separated commercial banking from the securities industry so that banks could not engage in risky ventures associated with this industry. Another way to limit a financial intermediary's behavior is to restrict it from holding certain risky assets, or at least from holding a greater quantity of these risky assets than is prudent. For example, commercial banks and other depository institutions are not allowed to hold common stock because stock prices experience substantial fluctuations. Insurance companies are allowed to hold common stock, but their holdings cannot exceed a certain fraction of their total assets.

Deposit Insurance   The government can insure people's deposits so that they do not suffer great financial loss if the financial intermediary that holds these deposits should fail. The most important government agency that provides this type of insurance is the Federal Deposit Insurance Corporation (FDIC), which insures each depositor at a commercial bank or mutual savings bank up to a loss of $250,000 per account. Premiums paid by these financial institutions go into the FDIC's Deposit Insurance Fund, which is used to pay off depositors if an institution fails. The FDIC was created in 1934 after the massive bank failures of 1930–1933, in which the savings of many depositors at commercial banks were wiped out. The National Credit Union Share Insurance Fund (NCUSIF) does the same for credit unions.

Limits on Competition   Politicians have often declared that unbridled competition among financial intermediaries promotes failures that harm the public. Although the evidence that competition does indeed have this effect is extremely weak, state and federal governments at times have imposed restrictions on the opening of additional locations (branches). In the past, banks were not allowed to open branches in other states, and in some states banks were restricted from opening branches in additional locations.

Restrictions on Interest Rates   Competition has also been inhibited by regulations that impose restrictions on interest rates that can be paid on deposits. For decades after 1933, banks were prohibited from paying interest on checking accounts. In addition, until 1986, the Federal Reserve System had the power under *Regulation Q* to set maximum interest rates that banks could pay on savings deposits. These regulations were instituted because of the widespread belief that unrestricted interest-rate competition helped encourage bank failures during the Great Depression. Later evidence does not seem to support this view, and Regulation Q has been abolished (although there are still restrictions on paying interest on checking accounts held by businesses).

In later chapters, we will look more closely at government regulation of financial markets and explore whether it has improved their functioning.

Financial Regulation Abroad

Not surprisingly, given the similarity of the economic systems here and in Japan, Canada, and the nations of Western Europe, financial regulation in these countries is similar to that in the United States. Provision of information is improved by requiring corporations issuing securities to report details about assets and liabilities, earnings, and sales of stock, and by prohibiting insider trading. The soundness of intermediaries is ensured by licensing, periodic inspection of financial intermediaries' books, and provision of deposit insurance (although its coverage is smaller than that in the United States and its existence is often intentionally not advertised).

The major differences between financial regulation in the United States and abroad relate to bank regulation. In the past, the United States was the only industrialized country that subjected banks to restrictions on branching, which limited their size and confined them to certain geographic regions. (These restrictions were abolished by legislation in 1994.) U.S. banks are also the most restricted in the range of assets they may hold. Banks abroad frequently hold shares in commercial firms; in Japan and Germany, those stakes can be sizable.

SUMMARY

1. The basic function of financial markets is to channel funds from savers who have an excess of funds to spenders who have a shortage of funds. Financial markets can do this either through direct finance, in which borrowers borrow funds directly from lenders by selling them securities, or through indirect finance, which involves a financial intermediary that stands between the lender-savers and the borrower-spenders and helps transfer funds from one to the other. This channeling of funds improves the economic welfare of everyone in society. Because they allow funds to move from people who have no productive investment opportunities to those who have such opportunities, financial markets contribute to economic efficiency. In addition, channeling of funds directly benefits consumers by allowing them to make purchases when they need them most.

2. Financial markets can be classified as debt and equity markets, primary and secondary markets, exchanges and over-the-counter markets, and money and capital markets.

3. The principal money market instruments (debt instruments with maturities of less than one year) are U.S. Treasury bills, negotiable bank certificates of deposit, commercial paper, repurchase agreements, and federal funds. The principal capital market instruments (debt and equity instruments with maturities greater than one year) are stocks, mortgages, corporate bonds, U.S. government securities, U.S. government agency securities, state and local government bonds, and consumer and bank commercial loans.

4. An important trend in recent years is the growing internationalization of financial markets. Eurobonds, which are denominated in a currency other than that of the country in which they are sold, are now the dominant security in the international bond market and have surpassed U.S. corporate bonds as a source of new funds. Eurodollars, which are U.S. dollars deposited in foreign banks, are an important source of funds for American banks.

5. Financial intermediaries are financial institutions that acquire funds by issuing liabilities and, in turn, use those funds to acquire assets by purchasing securities or making loans. Financial intermediaries play an important role in the financial system because they reduce transaction costs, allow risk sharing, and solve problems created by adverse selection and moral hazard. As a result, financial intermediaries allow small savers and borrowers to benefit from the existence of financial markets, thereby increasing the efficiency of the economy. However, the economies of scope that help make financial intermediaries successful can lead

to conflicts of interest that make the financial system less efficient.

6. The principal financial intermediaries fall into three categories: (a) banks—commercial banks, savings and loan associations, mutual savings banks, and credit unions; (b) contractual savings institutions—life insurance companies, fire and casualty insurance companies, and pension funds; and (c) investment intermediaries—finance companies, mutual funds, money market mutual funds and hedge funds.

7. The government regulates financial markets and financial intermediaries for two main reasons: to increase the information available to investors and to ensure the soundness of the financial system. Regulations include requiring disclosure of information to the public, restrictions on who can set up a financial intermediary, restrictions on what assets financial intermediaries can hold, the provision of deposit insurance, limits on competition, and restrictions on interest rates.

KEY TERMS

adverse selection, p. 36
asset transformation, p. 36
asymmetric information, p. 36
brokers, p. 26
capital, p. 24
capital market, p. 27
conflicts of interest, p. 38
currency, p. 28
dealers, p. 26
default, p. 28
diversification, p. 36
dividends, p. 25
economies of scale, p. 35
economies of scope, p. 38
equities, p. 25

Eurobond, p. 33
Eurocurrencies, p. 33
Eurodollars, p. 33
exchanges, p. 26
federal funds rate, p. 29
financial intermediation, p. 34
financial panic, p. 43
foreign bonds, p. 32
intermediate-term, p. 25
investment bank, p. 26
liabilities, p. 23
liquid, p. 26
liquidity services, p. 35
long-term, p. 25
maturity, p. 25

money market, p. 27
moral hazard, p. 37
mortgages, p. 30
mortgage-backed securities, p. 30
over-the-counter (OTC) market, p. 26
portfolio, p. 36
primary market, p. 25
risk, p. 36
risk sharing, p. 36
secondary market, p. 25
short-term, p. 25
thrift institutions (thrifts), p. 38
transaction costs, p. 34
underwrite, p. 42
underwriting, p. 26

QUESTIONS

All questions are available in MyEconLab *at* http://www.myeconlab.com.

1. If I can buy a car today for $5,000 and it is worth $10,000 in extra income to me next year because it enables me to get a job as a traveling salesman, should I take out a loan from Larry the Loan Shark at a 90% interest rate if no one else will give me a loan? Will I be better or worse off as a result of taking out this loan? Can you make a case for legalizing loan sharking?

2. Some economists suspect that one of the reasons economies in developing countries grow so slowly is that they do not have well-developed financial markets. Does this argument make sense?

3. Why is a share of Microsoft common stock an asset for its owner and a liability for Microsoft?

4. If you suspect that a company will go bankrupt next year, which would you rather hold, bonds issued by the company or equities issued by the company? Why?

5. "Because corporations do not actually raise any funds in secondary markets, secondary markets are less important to the economy than primary markets are." Is this statement true, false, or uncertain?

6. Describe who issues each of the following money market instruments:

   a. Treasury bills

   b. Certificates of deposit

   c. Commercial paper

   d. Repurchase agreement

   e. Fed funds

7. What is the difference between a *mortgage* and a *mortgage-backed security*?

8. The U.S. economy borrowed heavily from the British in the nineteenth century to build a railroad system. Why did this make both countries better off?

9. A significant number of European banks held large amounts of assets as mortgage-backed securities derived from the U.S. housing market, which crashed after 2006. How does this demonstrate both a benefit and a cost to the internationalization of financial markets?

10. How does risk sharing benefit both financial intermediaries and private investors?

11. How can the adverse selection problem explain why you are more likely to make a loan to a family member than to a stranger?

12. One of the factors contributing to the financial crisis of 2007–2009 was the widespread issuance of subprime mortgages. How does this demonstrate adverse selection?

13. Why do loan sharks worry less about moral hazard in connection with their borrowers than some other lenders do?

14. If you are an employer, what kinds of moral hazard problems might you worry about with regard to your employees?

15. If there were no asymmetry in the information that a borrower and a lender had, could a moral hazard problem still exist?

16. "In a world without information costs and transaction costs, financial intermediaries would not exist." Is this statement true, false, or uncertain? Explain your answer.

17. Why might you be willing to make a loan to your neighbor by putting funds in a savings account earning a 5% interest rate at the bank and having the bank lend her the funds at a 10% interest rate, rather than lend her the funds yourself?

18. How do conflicts of interest make the asymmetric information problem worse?

19. How can the provision of several types of financial services by one firm be both beneficial and problematic?

20. If you were going to get a loan to purchase a new car, which financial intermediary would you use: a credit union, a pension fund, or an investment bank?

21. Why would a life insurance company be concerned about the financial stability of major corporations or the health of the housing market?

22. In 2008, as a financial crisis began to unfold in the United States, the FDIC raised the limit on insured losses to bank depositors from $100,000 per account to $250,000 per account. How would this help stabilize the financial system?

APPLIED PROBLEMS

All applied problems are available in MyEconLab *at* http://www.myeconlab.com.

23. Suppose you have just inherited $10,000 and are considering the following options for investing the money to maximize your return:

    Option 1: Put the money in an interest-bearing checking account that earns 2%. The FDIC insures the account against bank failure.

    Option 2: Invest the money in a corporate bond with a stated return of 5%, although there is a 10% chance the company could go bankrupt.

    Option 3: Loan the money to one of your friend's roommates, Mike, at an agreed-upon interest rate of 8%, even though you believe there is a 7% chance that Mike will leave town without repaying you.

    Option 4: Hold the money in cash and earn zero return.

    a. If you are risk-neutral (that is, neither seek out nor shy away from risk), which of the four options should you choose to maximize your expected return? (*Hint:* To calculate the *expected return* of an outcome, multiply the probability that an event will occur by the outcome of that event.)

    b. Suppose Option 3 is your only possibility. If you could pay your friend $100 to find out extra information about Mike that would indicate with certainty whether he will leave town without paying, would you pay the $100? What does this say about the value of better information regarding risk?

DATA ANALYSIS PROBLEMS

The Problems update with real-time data in MyEconLab and are available for practice or instructor assignment.

 1. Go to the St. Louis Federal Reserve FRED database, and find data on federal debt held by the Federal Reserve (FDHBFRBN), by private investors (FDHBPIN), and by international and foreign investors (FDHBFIN). Using these series, calculate the total amount held and the percentage held in each of the three categories for the most recent quarter available. Repeat for the first quarter of 2000, and compare the results.

 2. Go to the St. Louis Federal Reserve FRED database, and find data on the total assets of all commercial banks (TLAACBM027SBOG) and the total assets of money market mutual funds (MMMFFAQ027S). Transform the commercial bank assets series to quarterly by adjusting the *Frequency* setting to "Quarterly." Calculate the percent increase in growth of assets for each series, from January 2000 to the most recent quarter available. Which of the two financial intermediaries has experienced the most growth?

WEB EXERCISES

1. One of the single best sources of information about financial institutions is the U.S. Flow of Funds report, produced by the Federal Reserve. This document contains data on most financial intermediaries. Go to http://www.federalreserve.gov/releases/Z1/ and find the most current release. You may have to get Acrobat Reader if your computer does not already have it; the site has a link for a free download. Go to the Level Tables and answer the following questions.

   a. What percentage of assets do commercial banks hold in loans? What percentage of assets is held in mortgage loans?

   b. What percentage of assets do savings and loans hold in mortgage loans?

   c. What percentage of assets do credit unions hold in mortgage loans and in consumer loans?

2. The most famous financial market in the world is the New York Stock Exchange. Go to http://www.nyse.com.

   a. What is the mission of the NYSE?

   b. Firms must pay a fee to list their shares for sale on the NYSE. What would be the fee for a firm with five million common shares outstanding?

WEB REFERENCES

http://stockcharts.com/charts/historical

Contains historical stock index charts for the Dow Jones Industrial Average, S&P 500, NASDAQ, 30-year Treasury Bond, and gold prices.

http://www.nyse.com

New York Stock Exchange. Find listed companies, quotes, company historical data, real-time market indexes, and more.

http://www.nasdaq.com

Detailed market and security information for the NASDAQ OTC stock exchange.

http://finance.yahoo.com

Major world stock indexes, with charts, news, and components.

http://www.sec.gov

The United States Securities and Exchange Commission home page. Contains vast SEC resources, laws and regulations, investor information, and litigation.

3

What Is Money?

Learning Objectives

- Describe what money is.
- List and summarize the functions of money.
- Identify different types of payment systems.
- Compare and contrast the M1 and M2 money supplies.

Preview

If you had lived in America before the Revolutionary War, your money might have consisted primarily of Spanish doubloons (silver coins that were also called *pieces of eight*). Before the Civil War, the principal forms of money in the United States were gold and silver coins and paper notes, called *banknotes*, issued by private banks. Today, you use as money not only coins and paper bills issued by the government, but also debit cards and checks written on accounts held at banks. Money has taken different forms at different times, but it has *always* been important to people and to the economy.

To understand the effects of money on the economy, we must understand exactly what money is. In this chapter, we develop precise definitions by exploring the functions of money, looking at why and how it promotes economic efficiency, tracing how its forms have evolved over time, and examining how money is currently measured.

MEANING OF MONEY

As used in everyday conversation, the word *money* can mean many things, but to economists it has a very specific meaning. To avoid confusion, we must clarify how economists' use of the word *money* differs from conventional usage.

Economists define *money* (also referred to as the *money supply*) as anything that is generally accepted as payment for goods or services or in the repayment of debts. Currency, consisting of paper bills and coins, clearly fits this definition and is one type of money. When most people talk about money, they're talking about **currency** (paper money and coins). If, for example, someone comes up to you and says, "Your money or your life," you should quickly hand over all of your currency rather than ask, "What exactly do you mean by 'money'?"

To define money merely as currency is much too narrow a definition for economists. Because checks are also accepted as payment for purchases, checking account deposits are considered money as well. An even broader definition of money is needed because other items, such as savings deposits, can, in effect, function as money if they can be quickly and easily converted into currency or checking account deposits. As you can see, no single, precise definition of money or the money supply is possible, even for economists.

To complicate matters further, the word *money* is frequently used synonymously with *wealth*. When people say, "Joe is rich—he has an awful lot of money," they probably mean that Joe not only has a lot of currency and a high balance in his checking account but also has stocks, bonds, four cars, three houses, and a yacht. Thus, while "currency" is too narrow a definition of money, this other popular usage is much too broad. Economists make a distinction between money in the form of currency, demand deposits, and other items that are used to make purchases, and **wealth**, the total collection of pieces of property that serve to store value. Wealth includes not only money but also other assets such as bonds, common stock, art, land, furniture, cars, and houses.

People also use the word *money* to describe what economists call *income*, as in the sentence "Sheila would be a wonderful catch; she has a good job and earns a lot of money." **Income** is a *flow* of earnings per unit of time. Money, by contrast, is a *stock*: It is a certain amount at a given point in time. If someone tells you that he has an income of $1,000, you cannot tell whether he earns a lot or a little without knowing whether this $1,000 is earned per year, per month, or even per day. But if someone tells you that she has $1,000 in her pocket, you know exactly how much this is.

Keep in mind that the money discussed in this book refers to anything that is generally accepted as payment for goods and services or in the repayment of debts, and is distinct from income and wealth.

FUNCTIONS OF MONEY

Whether money is shells or rocks or gold or paper, it has three primary functions in any economy: as a medium of exchange, as a unit of account, and as a store of value. Of the three functions, its function as a medium of exchange is what distinguishes money from other assets such as stocks, bonds, and houses.

Medium of Exchange

In almost all market transactions in our economy, money in the form of currency or checks is a **medium of exchange**; it is used to pay for goods and services. The use of money as a medium of exchange promotes economic efficiency by minimizing the time spent in exchanging goods and services. To see why, let's look at a *barter economy*, one without money, in which goods and services are exchanged directly for other goods and services.

Take the case of Ellen the Economics Professor, who can do just one thing well: give brilliant economics lectures. In a barter economy, if Ellen wants to eat, she must find a farmer who not only produces the food she likes but also wants to learn economics. As you might expect, this search will be difficult and time-consuming, and Ellen might spend more time looking for such an economics-hungry farmer than she will teaching. It is even possible that she will have to quit lecturing and go into farming herself. Even so, she may still starve to death.

The time spent trying to exchange goods or services is called a *transaction cost*. In a barter economy, transaction costs are high because people have to satisfy a "double coincidence of wants"—they have to find someone who has a good or service they want and who also wants the good or service they have to offer.

Let's see what happens if we introduce money into Ellen the Economics Professor's world. Ellen can teach anyone who is willing to pay money to hear her lecture. She can then go to any farmer (or his representative at the supermarket) and buy the food she needs with the money she has been paid. The problem of the double coincidence of wants is avoided, and Ellen saves a lot of time, which she may spend doing what she does best: teaching.

As this example shows, money promotes economic efficiency by eliminating much of the time spent exchanging goods and services. It also promotes efficiency by allowing people to specialize in what they do best. Money is therefore essential in an economy: It is a lubricant that allows the economy to run more smoothly by lowering transaction costs, thereby encouraging specialization and division of labor.

The need for money is so strong that almost every society beyond the most primitive invents it. For a commodity to function effectively as money, it has to meet several criteria: (1) It must be easily standardized, making it simple to ascertain its value; (2) it must be widely accepted; (3) it must be divisible, so that it is easy to "make change"; (4) it must be easy to carry; and (5) it must not deteriorate quickly. Objects that have satisfied these criteria have taken many unusual forms throughout human history, ranging from wampum (strings of beads) used by Native Americans; to tobacco and whiskey, used by the early American colonists; to cigarettes, used in prisoner-of-war camps during World War II.[1] The diverse forms of money that have been developed over the years are as much a testament to the inventiveness of the human race as are the developments of tools and language.

Unit of Account

The second role of money is to provide a **unit of account**; that is, money is used to measure value in an economy. We measure the value of goods and services in terms of money, just as we measure weight in terms of pounds or distance in terms of miles. To see why this function is important, let's look again at a barter economy, in which money does not perform this function. If the economy has only three goods—say, peaches, economics lectures, and movies—then we need to know only three prices to tell us how to exchange one for another: the price of peaches in terms of economics lectures (that is, how many economics lectures you have to pay for a peach), the price of peaches in terms of movies, and the price of economics lectures in terms of movies. If there were 10 goods, we would need to know 45 prices in order to exchange one good for another; with 100 goods, we would need 4,950 prices; and with 1,000 goods, we would need 499,500 prices.[2]

Imagine how hard it would be in a barter economy to shop at a supermarket with 1,000 different items on its shelves and be faced with deciding whether chicken or fish is a better buy if the price of a pound of chicken were quoted as 4 pounds of butter and the price of a pound of fish as 8 pounds of tomatoes. To make it possible to compare prices, the tag on each item would have to list up to 999 different prices, and the time spent reading them would result in very high transaction costs.

---

[1]An extremely entertaining article on the development of money in a prisoner-of-war camp during World War II is R. A. Radford, "The Economic Organization of a P.O.W. Camp," *Economica* 12 (November 1945): 189–201.

[2]The formula for telling us the number of prices we need when we have N goods is the same formula that tells us the number of pairs when there are N items. It is

$$\frac{N(N-1)}{2}$$

In the case of ten goods, for example, we would need

$$\frac{10(10-1)}{2} = \frac{90}{2} = 45 \text{ prices.}$$

The solution to the problem is to introduce money into the economy and have all prices quoted in terms of units of that money, enabling us to quote the price of economics lectures, peaches, and movies in terms of, say, dollars. If there were only three goods in the economy, this would not be a great advantage over the barter system, because we would still need three prices to conduct transactions. But for 10 goods we would need only 10 prices; for 100 goods, 100 prices; and so on. At the 1,000-goods supermarket, now only 1,000 prices need to beconsidered, not 499,500!

We can see that using money as a unit of account lowers transaction costs in an economy by reducing the number of prices that need to be considered. The benefits of this function of money grow as the economy becomes more complex.

Store of Value

Money also functions as a **store of value**; it is a repository of purchasing power available over time. A store of value is used to save purchasing power from the time income is received until the time it is spent. This function of money is useful because most of us do not want to spend our income immediately upon receiving it, but rather prefer to wait until we have the time or the desire to shop.

Money is not unique as a store of value; any asset—whether money, stocks, bonds, land, houses, art, or jewelry—can be used to store wealth. Many such assets have advantages over money as a store of value: They often pay the owner a higher interest rate than money, experience price appreciation, and deliver services such as providing a roof over one's head. If these assets are a more desirable store of value than money, why do people hold money at all?

The answer to this question relates to the important economic concept of **liquidity**, the relative ease and speed with which an asset can be converted into a medium of exchange. Liquidity is highly desirable. Money is the most liquid asset of all because it is the medium of exchange; it does not have to be converted into anything else to make purchases. Other assets involve transaction costs when they are converted into money. When you sell your house, for example, you have to pay a brokerage commission (usually 4–6% of the sales price), and if you need cash immediately to pay some pressing bills, you might have to settle for a lower price if you want to sell the house quickly. Because money is the most liquid asset, people are willing to hold it even if it is not the most attractive store of value.

How good a store of value money is depends on the price level. A doubling of all prices, for example, means that the value of money has dropped by half; conversely, a halving of all prices means that the value of money has doubled. During times of inflation, when the price level is increasing rapidly, money loses value rapidly, and people become more reluctant to hold their wealth in this form. This is especially true during periods of extreme inflation, known as **hyperinflation**, in which the inflation rate exceeds 50% per month.

Hyperinflation occurred in Germany after World War I, with inflation rates sometimes exceeding 1,000% per month. By the end of the hyperinflation of 1923, the price level had risen to more than 30 billion times what it had been just two years before. The quantity of money needed to purchase even the most basic items became excessive. There are stories, for example, that near the end of the hyperinflation, a wheelbarrow of cash would be required to pay for a loaf of bread. Money was losing its value so rapidly that workers were paid and then given time off on several occasions during the day to spend their wages before the money became worthless. No one wanted to hold on to money, so the use of money to carry out transactions declined, and barter became more and more dominant. Transaction costs skyrocketed and, as we would expect, output in the economy fell sharply.

EVOLUTION OF THE PAYMENTS SYSTEM

We can obtain a better picture of the functions of money and the forms it has taken over time by looking at the evolution of the **payments system**, the method of conducting transactions in the economy. The payments system has been evolving over centuries, and with it the form of money. At one point, precious metals such as gold were used as the principal means of payment and were the main form of money. Later, paper assets such as checks and currency began to be used in the payments system and viewed as money. Where the payments system is heading has an important bearing on how money will be defined in the future.

Commodity Money

To obtain perspective on where the payments system is heading, it's worth exploring how it has evolved. For any object to function as money, it must be universally acceptable; everyone must be willing to take it in payment for goods and services. An object that clearly has value to everyone is a likely candidate to serve as money, and a natural choice is a precious metal such as gold or silver. Money made up of precious metals or another valuable commodity is called **commodity money**, and from ancient times until several hundred years ago, commodity money functioned as the medium of exchange in all but the most primitive societies. The problem with a payments system based exclusively on precious metals is that such a form of money is very heavy and is hard to transport from one place to another. Imagine the holes you'd wear in your pockets if you had to buy things only with coins! Indeed, for a large purchase such as a house, you'd have to rent a truck to transport the money payment.

Fiat Money

The next development in the payments system was *paper currency* (pieces of paper that function as a medium of exchange). Initially, paper currency carried a guarantee that it was convertible into coins or into a fixed quantity of precious metal. However, currency has evolved into **fiat money**, paper currency decreed by governments as legal tender (meaning that it must be accepted as legal payment for debts) but not convertible into coins or precious metal. Paper currency has the advantage of being much lighter than coins or precious metal, but it can be accepted as a medium of exchange only if there is some trust in the authorities who issue it and if printing has reached a sufficiently advanced stage that counterfeiting is extremely difficult. Because paper currency has evolved into a legal arrangement, countries can change the currency they use at will. Indeed, this is what many European countries did when they abandoned their currencies for the euro in 2002.

Major drawbacks of paper currency and coins are that they are easily stolen and can be expensive to transport in large amounts because of their bulk. To combat this problem, another step in the evolution of the payments system occurred with the development of modern banking: the invention of *checks*.

Checks

A check is an instruction from you to your bank to transfer money from your account to someone else's account when she deposits the check. Checks allow transactions to take place without the need to carry around large amounts of currency. The introduction of checks was a major innovation that improved the efficiency of the payments system. Frequently, payments made back and forth cancel each other; without checks, this would involve the movement of a lot of currency. With checks, payments that cancel each other can be settled by canceling the checks, and no currency need be moved. The use of checks thus reduces the transportation costs associated with the payments system and improves economic efficiency. Another advantage of checks is that they can be written for any amount up to the balance in the account, making transactions for large amounts much easier. Checks are also advantageous in that loss from theft is greatly reduced and because they provide convenient receipts for purchases.

Two problems arise, however, with a payments system based on checks. First, it takes time to get checks from one place to another, a particularly serious problem if you are paying someone in a different location who needs to be paid quickly. In addition, if you have a checking account, you know that it often takes several business days before a bank will allow you to make use of the funds from a check you have deposited. If your need for cash is urgent, this feature of paying by check can be frustrating. Second, the paper shuffling required to process checks is costly; currently, the cost of processing all checks written in the United States is estimated at over $10 billion per year.

Electronic Payment

The development of inexpensive computers and the spread of the Internet now make it cheap to pay bills electronically. In the past, you had to pay a bill by mailing a check, but now banks provide websites at which you just log on, make a few clicks, and thereby transmit your payment electronically. Not only do you save the cost of the stamp, but paying bills becomes (almost) a pleasure, requiring little effort. Electronic payment systems provided by banks now even spare you the step of logging on to pay the bill. Instead, recurring bills can be automatically deducted from your bank account. Estimated cost savings when a bill is paid electronically rather than by a check exceed one dollar per transaction. Electronic payment is thus becoming more and more common in the United States.

E-Money

Electronic payments technology can substitute not only for checks but also for cash, in the form of **electronic money** (or **e-money**)—money that exists only in electronic form. The first form of e-money was the *debit card*. Debit cards, which look like credit cards, enable consumers to purchase goods and services by electronically transferring funds directly from their bank accounts to a merchant's account. Debit cards are used in many of the same places that accept credit cards and are now often faster to use than cash. At most supermarkets, for example, you can swipe your debit card through the card reader at the checkout station, press a button, and the amount of your purchase is deducted from your bank account. Most banks, as well as companies such as Visa and MasterCard, issue debit cards, and your ATM card typically can function as a debit card.

A more advanced form of e-money is the *stored-value card*. The simplest form of stored-value card is purchased for a preset dollar amount that the consumer pays up front, like a prepaid phone card. The more sophisticated stored-value card is known as a **smart card**. It contains a computer chip that allows it to be loaded with digital cash from the owner's bank account whenever needed. In Asian countries, such as Japan and Korea, cell phones now have a smart card feature that raises the expression "pay by phone" to a new level. Smart cards can be loaded from ATM machines, personal computers with a smart card reader, or specially equipped telephones.

A third form of electronic money, often referred to as **e-cash**, is used on the Internet to purchase goods or services. A consumer gets e-cash by setting up an account with

FYI   Are We Headed for a Cashless Society?

Predictions of a cashless society have been around for decades, but they have not come to fruition. For example, *Business Week* predicted in 1975 that electronic means of payment "would soon revolutionize the very concept of money itself," only to reverse its view several years later. In recent years, pilot projects aimed at converting consumers to the use of e-money in the form of smart cards have not been a success. Mondex, which was launched in Great Britain in 1995 and was one of the first widely-touted stored-value cards, is now used only on a few British university campuses. In Germany and Belgium, millions of people carry bank cards with computer chips embedded in them that enable them to make use of e-money, but very few people actually use them. Why has the movement to a cashless society been so slow in coming?

Although e-money might be more convenient and efficient than a payments system based on paper, several factors work against the disappearance of the paper system. First, it is very expensive to set up the computer, card reader, and telecommunications networks necessary to make electronic money the dominant form of payment. Second, electronic means of payment raise security and privacy concerns. We often hear media reports of an unauthorized hacker who has been able to access a computer database and alter the information stored there. Because this is not an uncommon occurrence, unscrupulous persons might be able to access bank accounts in electronic payments systems and steal funds by moving them from someone else's accounts into their own. The prevention of this type of fraud is no easy task, and a whole new field of computer science has developed to cope with such security issues. A further concern is that the use of electronic means of payment leaves an electronic trail that contains a large amount of personal data on buying habits. There are worries that government agencies, employers, and marketers might be able to access these data, thereby enabling them to encroach on our privacy if they choose to do so.

In conclusion, although the use of e-money will surely increase in the future, to paraphrase Mark Twain, "the reports of cash's death are greatly exaggerated."

a bank that has links to the Internet and then transferring the e-cash to her PC. When she wants to buy something with e-cash, she surfs to a store on the Web and clicks the "buy" option for a particular item, whereupon the e-cash is automatically transferred from her computer to the merchant's computer. The merchant can then have the funds transferred from the consumer's bank account to his own before the goods are shipped.

Given the convenience of e-money, you might think that we would move quickly to a cashless society in which all payments are made electronically. However, this hasn't happened, as discussed in the FYI box, "Are We Headed for a Cashless Society?"

APPLICATION   Will Bitcoin Become the Money of the Future?

Bitcoin is a new type of electronic money created by software developer Satoshi Nakamoto in 2009. Bitcoin is not controlled by a single entity like a central bank, but rather is created in a decentralized fashion by users who generate new bitcoins when they use their computing power to verify and process Bitcoin transactions, a process referred to as "mining." Some tech enthusiasts have characterized Bitcoin as the money of the future. But does Bitcoin satisfy the three key functions of money that we discussed earlier? That is, does it function as a medium of exchange, a unit of account, and a store of value?

Bitcoin certainly functions well as a medium of exchange. It has two features that make it attractive for conducting transactions. First, the fees for conducting transactions with bitcoins are substantially lower than those associated with credit cards and debit cards. Second, transactions made with bitcoins can be made anonymously, which is very attractive to those who want to preserve their privacy.

Bitcoin, however, does not do well with regard to the other two functions of money—as a unit of account and a store of value. The price of Bitcoin has been extremely volatile, with its volatility estimated to be over seven times that of the price of gold and over eight times that of stock market indexes such as the S&P 500. For example, in 2011, the price of a bitcoin fluctuated between 30 cents and $32. It then rose to a peak of $255 on April 10, 2013, only to fall back down to $55 on April 17. On November 30, 2013, the price of a bitcoin peaked at $1125, but it then fell to below the $500 level by May of 2014.

The high volatility of the value of the bitcoin means that it does not function well as a store of value; it is just too risky. Because of this volatility, the Bitcoin has not become a unit of account: Almost no one quotes the prices of their products in terms of bitcoins.

Despite the hype, Bitcoin does not satisfy two of the three key functions of money and thus its use as money is likely to be quite limited. Furthermore, governments are concerned about the use of Bitcoin to conduct drug transactions and money laundering. The Department of Homeland Security seized Bitcoin assets from the Mt. Gox exchange when the FBI shut down the Silk Road drug website in May of 2013. Countries such as China have outlawed the use of Bitcoin as a currency. There also have been high-profile thefts of Bitcoin, with Mt. Gox, one of the largest Bitcoin exchanges, experiencing a theft of almost $500 million worth of Bitcoin in February of 2014, leading Mt. Gox to file for bankruptcy.

Our understanding of the functions of money strongly suggests that Bitcoin will not be the money of the future. However, some of its technology, which enables users to conduct electronic transactions cheaply, may become a feature of future electronic payments systems. ◆

MEASURING MONEY

The definition of money as anything that is generally accepted as payment for goods and services tells us that money is defined by people's behavior. An asset is considered money only if people believe it will be accepted by others when making payment. As we have seen, many different assets have performed this role over the centuries, ranging from gold to paper currency to checking accounts. For this reason, a behavioral definition does not tell us which assets in our economy should be considered money. To measure money, we need a precise definition that tells us exactly which assets should be included.

The Federal Reserve's Monetary Aggregates

The Federal Reserve System (the Fed), the central banking authority responsible for monetary policy in the United States, has conducted many studies on how to measure money. The problem of measuring money has recently become especially crucial because extensive financial innovation has produced new types of assets that might properly belong in a measure of money. Since 1980, the Fed has modified its measures of money several times and has settled on the following measures of the money supply, which are also referred to as **monetary aggregates** (see Table 1 and the Following the Financial News box).

The narrowest measure of money reported by the Fed is **M1**, which includes the most liquid assets: currency, checking account deposits, and traveler's checks. The

TABLE 1	Measures of the Monetary Aggregates	
		Value as of August 18, 2014, ($ billions)
M1 = Currency		1,206.1
+ Traveler's checks		3.3
+ Demand deposits		1,089.9
+ Other checkable deposits		477.4
Total M1		2,776.7
M2 = M1		
+ Small-denomination time deposits		533.0
+ Savings deposits and money market deposit accounts		7,338.2
+ Money market mutual fund shares (retail)		642.5
Total M2		11,290.4

Source: http://www.federalreserve.gov/releases/h6/hist.

components of M1 are shown in Table 1. The *currency* component of M1 includes only paper money and coins in the hands of the nonbank public and does not include cash held in ATMs or bank vaults. Surprisingly, more than $4,000 cash is in circulation for each person in the United States (see the FYI box). The *traveler's checks* component of M1 includes only traveler's checks not issued by banks. The *demand deposits* component includes business checking accounts that do not pay interest, as well as traveler's checks issued by banks. The *other checkable deposits* item includes all other checkable deposits, particularly interest-bearing checking accounts held by households. These assets are clearly money because they can be used directly as a medium of exchange.

Until the mid-1970s, only commercial banks were permitted to establish checking accounts, and they were not allowed to pay interest on them. With the advent of financial innovation (discussed more extensively in Chapter 11), regulations have changed so that other types of banks, such as savings and loan associations, mutual savings banks, and credit unions, can also offer checking accounts. In addition, banking institutions can offer other checkable deposits, such as NOW (negotiated order of withdrawal) accounts and ATS (automatic transfer from savings) accounts, that do pay interest on their balances.

Following the Financial News   The Monetary Aggregates

Every week on Thursday, the Federal Reserve publishes the data for M1 and M2 in its H.6 release. These numbers are often reported on in the media. The H.6 release can be found at http://www.federalreserve.gov/releases/h6/current/h6.htm.

FYI   Where Are All the U.S. Dollars?

The almost $4,000 of U.S. currency held per person in the United States is a surprisingly large number. U.S. currency is bulky, can be easily stolen, and pays no interest, so it doesn't make sense for most of us to keep a lot of it. Do you know anyone who carries $4,000 in his or her pockets? We have a puzzle: Where are all these dollars, and who is holding them?

Criminals are one group that holds a lot of dollars. If you were engaged in illegal activity, you would not conduct your transactions with checks because they are traceable and therefore a potentially powerful piece of evidence against you. That explains why gangsters like Tony Soprano have so much cash buried in their backyards. Some businesses like to retain a lot of cash because, if they operate as a cash business, it makes their transactions less traceable; thus they can avoid declaring income on which they would otherwise have to pay taxes.

Foreigners are the other group that routinely holds U.S. dollars. In many countries, people do not trust their own currency because their country often experiences high inflation, which erodes the value of that currency; these people hold U.S. dollars as a hedge against this inflation risk. Lack of trust in the ruble, for example, has led Russians to hoard enormous amounts of U.S. dollars. More than half of U.S. dollars are held abroad.

The **M2** monetary aggregate adds to M1 other assets that are not quite as liquid as those included in M1: assets that have check-writing features (money market deposit accounts and money market mutual fund shares) and other assets (savings deposits and small-denomination time deposits) that can be turned into cash quickly and at very little cost. *Small-denomination time deposits* are certificates of deposit with a denomination of less than $100,000 that can be redeemed without a penalty only at a fixed maturity date. *Savings deposits* are nontransaction deposits that can be added to or taken out at any time. *Money market deposit accounts* are similar to money market mutual funds but are issued by banks. The *money market mutual fund shares* are retail accounts on which households can write checks.

Because economists and policymakers cannot be sure which of the monetary aggregates is the best measure of money, it is logical to wonder if the movements of M1 and M2 closely parallel one another. If they do, then using one monetary aggregate to predict future economic performance and to conduct policy will be the same as using the other, and it does not much matter that we are not sure of the appropriate definition of money for a given policy decision. However, if the monetary aggregates do *not* move together, then what one monetary aggregate tells us is happening to the money supply might be quite different from what the other monetary aggregate would tell us. Conflicting information would present a confusing picture, making it hard for policymakers to decide on the right course of action.

Figure 1 plots the growth rates of M1 and M2 from 1960 to 2014. The growth rates of these two monetary aggregates do tend to move together; the timing of their rise and fall is roughly similar until the 1990s, and they both show a higher growth rate, on average, in the 1970s than in the 1960s.

Yet some glaring discrepancies exist between the movements of these aggregates. Contrast M1's high rates of growth from 1992 to 1994 with the much lower growth rates of M2. Also notice that from 2004 to 2007, M2's growth rate increased slightly, while M1's growth rate decelerated sharply and became negative. In 2009 and 2011, M1 growth surged to over 15% from near zero the year before, while M2 growth rose

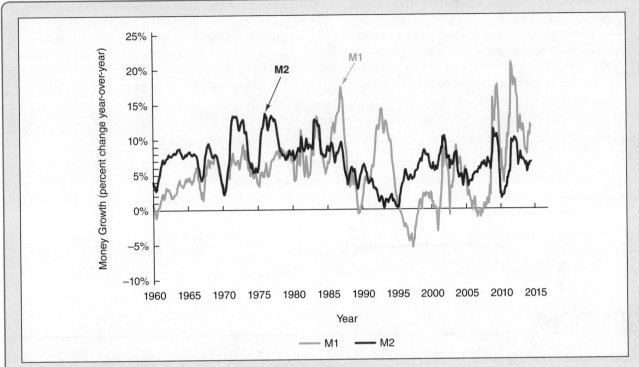

FIGURE 1   **Growth Rates of the M1 and M2 Aggregates, 1960–2014**
The timing of the rise and fall of growth rates is roughly similar for both M1 and M2. There were periods, however, such as 1992–1994 and 2004–2007, during which M1 and M2 moved in opposite directions, leading to conflicting recommendations about the best course of monetary policy.
Source: **Federal Reserve Bank of St. Louis, FRED database:** http://research.stlouisfed.org/fred2/

less dramatically. Thus, the different measures of money tell a very different story about the results of monetary policy in recent years.

From the data in Figure 1, you can see that obtaining a single, precise, and correct measure of money does seem to matter, and that it does make a difference which monetary aggregate policymakers and economists choose as the best measure of money.

SUMMARY

1. To economists, the word *money* has a different meaning than *income* or *wealth*. Money is anything that is generally accepted as payment for goods or services or in the repayment of debts.

2. Money serves three primary functions: as a medium of exchange, as a unit of account, and as a store of value. Money as a medium of exchange helps an economy avoid the problem of double coincidence of wants that arises in a barter economy, and thus lowers transaction costs and

encourages specialization and the division of labor. Money as a unit of account reduces the number of prices needed in an economy, which also reduces transaction costs. Money also functions as a store of value, but performs this role poorly if it is rapidly losing value due to inflation.

3. The payments system has evolved over time. Until several hundred years ago, the payments systems in all but the most primitive societies were based primarily on precious metals. The introduction of paper currency lowered the cost of transporting money. The next major advance was the introduction of checks, which lowered transaction costs still further. We are currently moving toward an electronic payments system in which paper is eliminated and all transactions are handled by computers. Despite the potential efficiency of such a system, obstacles are slowing the movement to a checkless society and the development of new forms of electronic money.

4. The Federal Reserve System has defined two different measures of the money supply—M1 and M2. These measures are not equivalent and do not always move together, so they cannot be used interchangeably by policymakers. Obtaining the precise, correct measure of money does seem to matter and has implications for the conduct of monetary policy.

KEY TERMS

commodity money, p. 53
currency, p. 49
e-cash, p. 54
electronic money (e-money), p. 54
fiat money, p. 53
hyperinflation, p. 52

income, p. 50
liquidity, p. 52
M1, p. 56
M2, p. 58
medium of exchange, p. 50
monetary aggregates, p. 56

payments system, p. 53
smart card, p. 54
store of value, p. 52
unit of account, p. 51
wealth, p. 50

QUESTIONS

All questions are available in MyEconLab *at* http://www.myeconlab.com.

1. Why is simply counting currency an inadequate measure of money?

2. In prison, cigarettes are sometimes used among inmates as a form of payment. How is it possible for cigarettes to solve the "double coincidence of wants" problem, even if a prisoner does not smoke?

3. Three goods are produced in an economy by three individuals:

Good	Producer
Apples	Orchard owner
Bananas	Banana grower
Chocolate	Chocolatier

   If the orchard owner likes only bananas, the banana grower likes only chocolate, and the chocolatier likes only apples, will any trade between these three persons take place in a barter economy? How will introducing money into the economy benefit these three producers?

4. Why did cavemen not need money?

5. Most of the time it is quite difficult to separate the three functions of money. Money performs its three functions at all times, but sometimes we can stress one

in particular. For each of the following situations, identify which function of money is emphasized.

   a. Brooke accepts money in exchange for performing her daily tasks at her office, since she knows she can use that money to buy goods and services.

   b. Tim wants to calculate the relative value of oranges and apples, and therefore checks the price per pound of each of these goods as quoted in currency units.

   c. Maria is currently pregnant. She expects her expenditures to increase in the future and decides to increase the balance in her savings account.

6. In Brazil, a country that underwent a rapid inflation before 1994, many transactions were conducted in dollars rather than in reals, the domestic currency. Why?

7. Was money a better store of value in the United States in the 1950s than in the 1970s? Why or why not? In which period would you have been more willing to hold money?

8. Why have some economists described money during a hyperinflation as a "hot potato" that is quickly passed from one person to another?

9. Why were people in the United States in the nineteenth century sometimes willing to be paid by check rather than with gold, even though they knew there was a possibility that the check might bounce?

10. In ancient Greece, why was gold a more likely candidate for use as money than wine?

11. If you use an online payment system such as PayPal to purchase goods or services on the Internet, does this affect the M1 money supply, the M2 money supply, both, or neither? Explain.

12. Rank the following assets from most liquid to least liquid:

    a. Checking account deposits

    b. Houses

    c. Currency

    d. Automobiles

    e. Savings deposits

    f. Common stock

13. Which of the Federal Reserve's measures of the monetary aggregates—M1 or M2—is composed of the most liquid assets? Which is the larger measure?

14. It is not unusual to find a business that displays a sign saying "no personal checks, please." On the basis of this observation, comment on the relative degree of liquidity of a checking account versus currency.

15. For each of the following assets, indicate which of the monetary aggregates (M1 and M2) includes them:

    a. Currency

    b. Money market mutual funds

    c. Small-denomination time deposits

    d. Checkable deposits

16. Assume that you are interested in earning some return on the idle balances you usually keep in your checking account and decide to buy some money market mutual funds shares by writing a check. Comment on the effect of your action (with everything else the same) on M1 and M2.

17. In April 2009, the growth rate of M1 fell to 6.1%, while the growth rate of M2 rose to 10.3%. In September 2013, the year-over-year growth rate of the M1 money supply was 6.5%, while the growth rate of the M2 money supply was about 8.3%. How should Federal Reserve policymakers interpret these changes in the growth rates of M1 and M2?

18. Suppose a researcher discovers that a measure of the total amount of debt in the U.S. economy over the past twenty years was a better predictor of inflation and the business cycle than M1 or M2. Does this discovery mean that we should define money as equal to the total amount of debt in the economy?

APPLIED PROBLEMS

All applied problems are available in MyEconLab *at* http://www.myeconlab.com.

19. The table below shows hypothetical values, in billions of dollars, of different forms of money.

    a. Use the table to calculate the M1 and M2 money supplies for each year, as well as the growth rates of the M1 and M2 money supplies from the previous year.

    b. Why are the growth rates of M1 and M2 so different? Explain.

		2015	**2016**	**2017**	**2018**
A.	Currency	900	920	925	931
B.	Money market mutual fund shares	680	681	679	688
C.	Saving account deposits	5,500	5,780	5,968	6,105
D.	Money market deposit accounts	1,214	1,245	1,274	1,329
E.	Demand and checkable deposits	1,000	972	980	993
F.	Small denomination time deposits	830	861	1,123	1,566
G.	Traveler's checks	4	4	3	2
H.	3-month treasury bills	1,986	2,374	2,436	2,502

DATA ANALYSIS PROBLEMS

The Problems update with real-time data in MyEconLab and are available for practice or instructor assignment.

 1. Go to the St. Louis Federal Reserve FRED database, and find data on currency (CURRSL), traveler's checks (TVCKSSL), demand deposits (DEMDEPSL), and other checkable deposits (OCDSL). Calculate the M1 money supply, and calculate the percentage change in M1 and in each of the four components of M1 from the most recent month of data available to the same time one year prior. Which component has the highest growth rate? The lowest growth rate? Repeat the calculations using the data from January 2000 to the most recent month of data available, and compare your results.

 2. Go to the St. Louis Federal Reserve FRED database, and find data on small-denomination time deposits (STDSL), savings deposits and money market deposit accounts (SAVINGSL), and retail money market funds (RMFSL). Calculate the percentage change of each of these three components of M2 (not included in M1) from the most recent month of data available to the same time one year prior. Which component has the highest growth rate? The lowest growth rate? Repeat the calculations using the data from January 2000 to the most recent month of data available, and compare your results. Use your answers from question 1 to determine which grew faster: the non-M1 components of M2, or the M1 money supply.

WEB EXERCISES

1. Go to http://www.federalreserve.gov/releases/h6/Current/.

   a. What have been the growth rates of M1 and M2 over the past twelve months?

   b. From what you know about the state of the economy, do these growth rates seem expansionary or restrictive?

WEB REFERENCES

http://www.federalreserve.gov/paymentsystems/default.htm

This site reports on the Federal Reserve's policies regarding payments systems.

http://www.federalreserve.gov/releases/h6/Current/

The Federal Reserve reports the current levels of M1 and M2 on this website.

Financial Markets

Crisis and Response: Credit Market Turmoil and the Stock Market Crash of October 2008

The financial crisis that started during the summer of 2007 began to snowball as the value of mortgage-backed securities on financial institutions' balance sheets plummeted. When the House of Representatives, fearing the wrath of constituents who were angry about proposals to bail out Wall Street, voted down a $700 billion bailout package proposed by the Bush administration on Monday, September 29, 2008, the financial crisis took an even more virulent turn, despite the bailout package that was passed four days later.

A "flight to quality" drove three-month Treasury bill rates down to almost zero, rates not seen since the Great Depression of the 1930s. Credit spreads—an indicator of risk—shot through the roof, with the gap between Eurodollar and Treasury bill rates (the TED spread) going from around 40 basis points (0.40 percentage point) before the financial crisis began to over 450 basis points in mid-October, the highest value in its history. After earlier sharp declines, the stock market crashed further, with the week beginning on October 6, 2008, showing the worst weekly decline in U.S. history.

The recent financial crisis illustrates how volatile financial markets can be. This volatility hit financial consumers directly, leading to difficulty in getting loans, falling home values, and declining retirement account values, and putting jobs in jeopardy. How can policy respond to disruptions in financial markets? We begin addressing this question by examining the inner workings of financial markets, particularly interest rate dynamics. Chapter 4 explains what an interest rate is, as well as the relationships among interest rates, bond prices, and returns. Chapter 5 examines how the overall level of interest rates is determined. In Chapter 6, we extend the analysis of the bond market to explain changes in credit spreads and the relationship of long-term to short-term interest rates. Chapter 7 looks at the role of expectations in the stock market and explores what drives stock prices.

4 The Meaning of Interest Rates

Learning Objectives

- Calculate the present value of future cash flows and the yield to maturity on the four types of credit market instruments.
- Recognize the distinctions among yield to maturity, current yield, rate of return, and rate of capital gain.
- Interpret the distinction between real and nominal interest rates.

Preview

Interest rates are among the most closely watched variables in the economy. Their movements are reported almost daily by the news media because they directly affect our everyday lives and have important consequences for the health of the economy. They influence personal decisions such as whether to consume or save, whether to buy a house, and whether to purchase bonds or put funds into a savings account. Interest rates also affect the economic decisions of businesses and households, such as whether to use their funds to invest in new equipment for factories or to save rather than spend their money.

Before we can go on with the study of money, banking, and financial markets, we must understand exactly what the phrase *interest rates* means. In this chapter, we see that a concept known as the *yield to maturity* is the most accurate measure of interest rates; the yield to maturity is what economists mean when they use the term *interest rate*. We'll discuss how the yield to maturity is measured. We'll also see that a bond's interest rate does not necessarily indicate how good an investment the bond is, because what the bond earns (its rate of return) does not necessarily equal its interest rate. Finally, we'll explore the distinction between real interest rates, which are adjusted for inflation, and nominal interest rates, which are not.

Although learning definitions is not always the most exciting of pursuits, it is important to read carefully and understand the concepts presented in this chapter. Not only are they used continually throughout the remainder of this text, but a firm grasp of these terms will give you a clearer understanding of the role that interest rates play in your life as well as in the general economy.

MEASURING INTEREST RATES

Different debt instruments have very different streams of cash payments (known as **cash flows**) to the holder, with very different timing. Thus we first need to understand how we can compare the value of one kind of debt instrument with the value of another before we see how interest rates are measured. To do this, we make use of the concept of *present value*.

Present Value

The concept of **present value** (or **present discounted value**) is based on the commonsense notion that a dollar paid to you one year from now is less valuable than a dollar paid to you today. This notion is true because you can deposit a dollar today in a savings account that earns interest and have more than a dollar in one year. Economists use a more formal definition, as explained in this section.

Let's look at the simplest kind of debt instrument, which we will call a **simple loan**. In this loan, the lender provides the borrower with an amount of funds (called the *principal*) that must be repaid to the lender at the *maturity date*, along with an additional payment for the interest. For example, if you made your friend, Jane, a simple loan of $100 for one year, you would require her to repay the principal of $100 in one year's time, along with an additional payment for interest—say, $10. In the case of a simple loan like this one, the interest payment divided by the amount of the loan is a natural and sensible way to measure the interest rate. This measure of the so-called *simple interest rate*, i, is

$$i = \frac{\$10}{\$100} = 0.10 = 10\%$$

If you make this $100 loan, at the end of the year you will have $110, which can be rewritten as

$$\$100 \times (1 + 0.10) = \$110$$

If you then lent out the $110 at the same interest rate, at the end of the second year you would have

$$\$110 \times (1 + 0.10) = \$121$$

or, equivalently,

$$\$100 \times (1 + 0.10) \times (1 + 0.10) = \$100 \times (1 + 0.10)^2 = \$121$$

Continuing with the loan again, at the end of the third year you would have

$$\$121 \times (1 + 0.10) = \$100 \times (1 + 0.10)^3 = \$133$$

Generalizing, we can see that at the end of n years, your $100 would turn into

$$\$100 \times (1 + i)^n$$

The amounts you would have at the end of each year by making the $100 loan today can be seen in the following timeline:

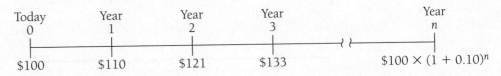

Today 0	Year 1	Year 2	Year 3	Year n
$100	$110	$121	$133	$100 × (1 + 0.10)^n

This timeline clearly indicates that you are just as happy having $100 today as you will be having $110 a year from now (of course, as long as you are sure that Jane will pay you back). You are also just as happy having $100 today as you will be having $121 two years from now, or $133 three years from now, or $100 × (1 + 0.10)^n$ dollars n years from now. The timeline indicates that we can also work backward from future amounts to the present. For example, $133 = \$100 \times (1 + 0.10)^3$ three years from now is worth $100 today, so

$$\$100 = \frac{\$133}{(1 + 0.10)^3}$$

The process of calculating today's value of dollars received in the future, as we have done above, is called ⌐discounting the future.⌐ We can generalize this process by writing today's (present) value of $100 as PV and the future cash flow (payment) of $133 as CF, and then replacing 0.10 (the 10% interest rate) by i. This leads to the following formula:

$$PV = \frac{CF}{(1 + i)^n} \qquad (1)$$

Intuitively, Equation 1 tells us that if you are promised $1 of cash flow, for certain, ten years from now, this dollar would not be as valuable to you as $1 is today because, if you had the $1 today, you could invest it and end up with more than $1 in ten years.

The concept of present value is extremely useful, because it allows us to figure out today's value (price) of a credit (debt) market instrument at a given simple interest rate i by just adding up the individual present values of all the future payments received. This information enables us to compare the values of two or more instruments that have very different timing of their payments.

APPLICATION   Simple Present Value

What is the present value of $250 to be paid in two years if the interest rate is 15%?

Solution

The present value would be $189.04. We find this value by using Equation 1,

$$PV = \frac{CF}{(1 + i)^n}$$

where

$$\begin{aligned}
CF &= \text{cash flow in two years} = 250 \\
i &= \text{annual interest rate} \quad = 0.15 \\
n &= \text{number of years} \quad = 2
\end{aligned}$$

Thus

$$PV = \frac{\$250}{(1 + 0.15)^2} = \frac{\$250}{1.3225} = \$189.04$$

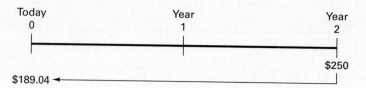

APPLICATION   How Much Is That Jackpot Worth?

Assume that you just hit the $20 million jackpot in the New York State Lottery, which promises you a payment of $1 million every year for the next twenty years. You are clearly excited, but have you really won $20 million?

Solution

No, not in the present value sense. In today's dollars, that $20 million is worth a lot less. If we assume an interest rate of 10% as in the earlier examples, the first payment of $1 million is clearly worth $1 million today, but the second payment next year is worth only $1 million/$(1 + 0.10)$ = $909,090, a lot less than $1 million. The following year, the payment is worth $1 million/$(1 + 0.10)^2$ = $826,446 in today's dollars, and so on. When you add up all these amounts, they total $9.4 million. You are still pretty excited (who wouldn't be?), but because you understand the concept of present value, you recognize that you are the victim of false advertising. In present-value terms, you didn't really win $20 million, but instead won less than half that amount. ◆

Four Types of Credit Market Instruments

In terms of the timing of their cash flow payments, there are four basic types of credit market instruments.

1. A simple loan, which we have already discussed, in which the lender provides the borrower with an amount of funds that must be repaid to the lender at the maturity date, along with an additional payment for the interest. Many money market instruments are of this type—for example, commercial loans to businesses.

2. A **fixed-payment loan** (also called a **fully amortized loan**) in which the lender provides the borrower with an amount of funds that the borrower must repay by making the same payment, consisting of part of the principal and interest, every period (such as a month) for a set number of years. For example, if you borrow $1,000, a fixed-payment loan might require you to pay $126 every year for 25 years. Installment loans (such as auto loans) and mortgages are frequently of the fixed-payment type.

3. A **coupon bond** pays the owner of the bond a fixed interest payment (coupon payment) every year until the maturity date, when a specified final amount (**face value** or **par value**) is repaid. (The coupon payment is so named because in the past, the bondholder obtained payment by clipping a coupon off the bond and sending it to the bond issuer, who then sent the payment to the holder. Today, it is no longer necessary to send in coupons to receive payments.) A coupon bond with $1,000 face value, for example, might pay you a coupon payment of $100 per year for ten years, and then repay you the face value amount of $1,000 at the maturity date. (The face value of a bond is usually in $1,000 increments.)

   A coupon bond is identified by four pieces of information: First is the bond's face value; second is the corporation or government agency that issues the bond; third is the maturity date of the bond; and fourth is the bond's **coupon rate**, which is the dollar amount of the yearly coupon payment expressed as a percentage of the face value of the bond. In our example, the coupon bond has a yearly coupon payment of $100 and a face value of $1,000. The coupon rate is then $100/$1,000 = 0.10, or 10%. Capital market instruments such as U.S. Treasury bonds and notes and corporate bonds are examples of coupon bonds.

4. A **discount bond** (also called a **zero-coupon bond**) is bought at a price below its face value (at a discount), and the face value is repaid at the maturity date. Unlike a

coupon bond, a discount bond does not make any interest payments; it just pays off the face value. For example, a one-year discount bond with a face value of $1,000 might be bought for $900; in a year's time, the owner would be repaid the face value of $1,000. U.S. Treasury bills, U.S. savings bonds, and long-term zero-coupon bonds are examples of discount bonds.

These four types of instruments make payments at different times: Simple loans and discount bonds make payments only at their maturity dates, whereas fixed-payment loans and coupon bonds make payments periodically until maturity. How can you decide which of these instruments will provide you with the most income? They all seem so different because they make payments at different times. To solve this problem, we use the concept of present value, explained earlier, to provide us with a procedure for measuring interest rates on these different types of instruments.

Yield to Maturity

Of the several common ways of calculating interest rates, the most important is the **yield to maturity**, which is the interest rate that equates the present value of cash flow payments received from a debt instrument with its value today.[1] Because the concept behind the calculation of the yield to maturity makes good economic sense, economists consider it the most accurate measure of interest rates.

To better understand the yield to maturity, we now look at how it is calculated for the four types of credit market instruments. In all of these examples, the key to understanding the calculation of the yield to maturity is realizing that we are equating today's value of the debt instrument with the present value of all of its future cash flow payments.

Simple Loan   Using the concept of present value, the yield to maturity on a simple loan is easy to calculate. For the one-year loan we discussed, today's value is $100, and the payments in one year's time would be $110 (the repayment of $100 plus the interest payment of $10). We can use this information to solve for the yield to maturity i by recognizing that the present value of the future payments must equal today's value of the loan.

Yield to Maturity on a Simple Loan

If Pete borrows $100 from his sister and next year she wants $110 back from him, what is the yield to maturity on this loan?

Solution

The yield to maturity on the loan is 10%.

$$PV = \frac{CF}{(1 + i)^n}$$

where
$$
\begin{aligned}
PV &= \text{amount borrowed} &&= \$100 \\
CF &= \text{cash flow in one year} &&= \$110 \\
n &= \text{number of years} &&= 1
\end{aligned}
$$

[1]In other contexts, the yield to maturity is also called the *internal rate of return*.

Thus

$$\$100 = \frac{\$110}{(1 + i)}$$

$$(1 + i)\$100 = \$110$$

$$(1 + i) = \frac{\$110}{\$100}$$

$$i = 1.10 - 1 = 0.10 = 10\%$$

```
          Today                    Year
            0                       1
            ├───────────────────────┤
          $100                     $110
                ───────► i = 10% ◄───────
```

This calculation of the yield to maturity should look familiar because it equals the interest payment of $10 divided by the loan amount of $100; that is, it equals the simple interest rate on the loan. An important point to recognize is that *for simple loans, the simple interest rate equals the yield to maturity*. Hence the same term i is used to denote both the yield to maturity and the simple interest rate.

Fixed-Payment Loan   Recall that this type of loan has the same cash flow payment every period throughout the life of the loan. On a fixed-rate mortgage, for example, the borrower makes the same payment to the bank every month until the maturity date, at which time the loan will be completely paid off. To calculate the yield to maturity for a fixed-payment loan, we follow the same strategy that we used for the simple loan—we equate today's value of the loan with its present value. Because the fixed-payment loan involves more than one cash flow payment, the present value of the fixed-payment loan is calculated (using Equation 1) as the sum of the present values of all cash flow payments.

In the case of our earlier example, the loan is $1,000 and the yearly payment is $126 for the next 25 years. The present value (*PV*) is calculated as follows: At the end of one year, there is a $126 payment with a *PV* of $126/(1 + i)$; at the end of two years, there is another $126 payment with a *PV* of $126/(1 + i)^2$; and so on until, at the end of the twenty-fifth year, the last payment of $126 with a *PV* of $126/(1 + i)^{25}$ is made. Setting today's value of the loan ($1,000) equal to the sum of the present values of all the yearly payments gives us

$$\$1,000 = \frac{\$126}{1 + i} + \frac{\$126}{(1 + i)^2} + \frac{\$126}{(1 + i)^3} + \cdots + \frac{\$126}{(1 + i)^{25}}$$

More generally, for any fixed-payment loan,

$$LV = \frac{FP}{(1 + i)} + \frac{FP}{(1 + i)^2} + \frac{FP}{(1 + i)^3} + \cdots + \frac{FP}{(1 + i)^n} \tag{2}$$

where
$$LV = \text{loan value}$$
$$FP = \text{fixed yearly payment}$$
$$n = \text{number of years until maturity}$$

For a fixed-payment loan, the loan value, the fixed yearly payment, and the number of years until maturity are known quantities, and only the yield to maturity is not. So we can solve this equation for the yield to maturity i. Because this calculation is not easy, many financial calculators have programs that enable you to find i given the loan's numbers for LV, FP, and n. For example, in the case of a 25-year $1,000 loan with yearly payments of $85.81, the yield to maturity that results from solving Equation 2 is 7%. Real estate brokers always have a financial calculator that can solve such equations handy, so that they can immediately tell the prospective house buyer exactly what the yearly (or monthly) payments will be if the house purchase is financed by a mortgage.

APPLICATION # Yield to Maturity and the Yearly Payment on a Fixed-Payment Loan

You decide to purchase a new home and need a $100,000 mortgage. You take out a loan from the bank that has an interest rate of 7%. What is the yearly payment to the bank if you wish to pay off the loan in twenty years?

Solution

The yearly payment to the bank is $9,439.29.

$$LV = \frac{FP}{(1 + i)} + \frac{FP}{(1 + i)^2} + \frac{FP}{(1 + i)^3} + \cdots + \frac{FP}{(1 + i)^n}$$

where
$$LV = \text{loan value amount} = 100{,}000$$
$$i = \text{annual interest rate} = 0.07$$
$$n = \text{number of years} = 20$$

Thus

$$\$100{,}000 = \frac{FP}{(1 + 0.07)} + \frac{FP}{(1 + 0.07)^2} + \frac{FP}{(1 + 0.07)^3} + \cdots + \frac{FP}{(1 + 0.07)^{20}}$$

To find the monthly payment for the loan using a financial calculator:

$$n = \text{number of years} = 20$$
$$PV = \text{amount of the loan } (LV) = 100{,}000$$
$$FV = \text{amount of the loan after 20 years} = 0$$
$$i = \text{annual interest rate} = 0.07$$

Then push the *PMT* button to get the fixed yearly payment $(FP) = \$9{,}439.29.$ ◆

Coupon Bond To calculate the yield to maturity for a coupon bond, follow the same strategy used for the fixed-payment loan: Equate today's value of the bond with its present value. Because coupon bonds also have more than one cash flow payment, the present value of the bond is calculated as the sum of the present values of all the coupon payments plus the present value of the final payment of the face value of the bond.

The present value of a $1,000-face-value bond with ten years to maturity and yearly coupon payments of $100 (a 10% coupon rate) can be calculated as follows: At the end of one year, there is a $100 coupon payment with a *PV* of $100/(1 + i)$; at the end of the second year, there is another $100 coupon payment with a *PV* of $100/(1 + i)^2$; and so on until, at maturity, there is a $100 coupon payment with a *PV* of $100/(1 + i)^{10}$ plus the repayment of the $1,000 face value with a *PV* of $1,000/(1 + i)^{10}$. Setting today's value of the bond (its current price, denoted by *P*) equal to the sum of the present values of all the cash flow payments for the bond gives

$$P = \frac{\$100}{1 + i} + \frac{\$100}{(1 + i)^2} + \frac{\$100}{(1 + i)^3} + \cdots + \frac{\$100}{(1 + i)^{10}} + \frac{\$1,000}{(1 + i)^{10}}$$

More generally, for any coupon bond,[2]

$$P = \frac{C}{1 + i} + \frac{C}{(1 + i)^2} + \frac{C}{(1 + i)^3} + \cdots + \frac{C}{(1 + i)^n} + \frac{F}{(1 + i)^n} \qquad (3)$$

where
$$P = \text{price of the coupon bond}$$
$$C = \text{yearly coupon payment}$$
$$F = \text{face value of the bond}$$
$$n = \text{years to maturity date}$$

In Equation 3, the coupon payment, the face value, the years to maturity, and the price of the bond are known quantities, and only the yield to maturity is not. Hence we can solve this equation for the yield to maturity *i*. As in the case of the fixed-payment loan, this calculation is not easy, so business-oriented software and financial calculators have built-in programs that solve the equation for you.

APPLICATION

Yield to Maturity and Bond Price for a Coupon Bond

Find the price of a 10% coupon bond with a face value of $1000, a 12.25% yield to maturity, and eight years to maturity.

Solution
The price of the bond is $889.20. To solve using a financial calculator:

$$n = \text{years to maturity} \qquad\qquad = 8$$
$$FV = \text{face value of the bond } (F) \quad = 1,000$$
$$i = \text{annual interest rate} \qquad\quad = 12.25\%$$
$$PMT = \text{yearly coupon payments}(C) = 100$$

Then push the *PV* button to get the price of the bond = $889.20.

---

[2]Most coupon bonds actually make coupon payments on a semiannual basis rather than once a year as we assumed here. The effect on the calculations is very slight and will be ignored here.

Alternatively, you could solve for the yield to maturity given the bond price by entering $889.20 for *PV* and pushing the *i* button to get a yield to maturity of 12.25%. ◆

Table 1 shows the yields to maturity calculated for several bond prices. Three interesting facts emerge:

1. When the coupon bond is priced at its face value, the yield to maturity equals the coupon rate.
2. The price of a coupon bond and the yield to maturity are negatively related; that is, as the yield to maturity rises, the price of the bond falls. As the yield to maturity falls, the price of the bond rises.
3. The yield to maturity is greater than the coupon rate when the bond price is below its face value and is less than the coupon rate when the bond price is above its face value.

These three facts are true for any coupon bond and are really not surprising if you think about the reasoning behind the calculation of the yield to maturity. When you put $1,000 in a bank account with an interest rate of 10%, you can take out $100 every year and you will be left with the $1,000 at the end of ten years. This process is similar to buying the $1,000 bond with a 10% coupon rate analyzed in Table 1, which pays a $100 coupon payment every year and then repays $1,000 at the end of ten years. If the bond is purchased at the par value of $1,000, its yield to maturity must equal 10%, which is also equal to the coupon rate of 10%. The same reasoning applied to any coupon bond demonstrates that if the coupon bond is purchased at its par value, the yield to maturity and the coupon rate must be equal.

It is a straightforward process to show that the bond price and the yield to maturity are negatively correlated. As *i*, the yield to maturity, increases, all denominators in the bond price formula (Equation 3) must necessarily increase, because the rise in *i* lowers the present value of all future cash flow payments for this bond. Hence a rise in the interest rate, as measured by the yield to maturity, means that the price of the bond must fall. Another way to explain why the bond price falls when the interest rate rises is to consider that a higher interest rate implies that the future coupon payments and final payment are worth less when discounted back to the present; hence the price of the bond must be lower.

The third fact, that the yield to maturity is greater than the coupon rate when the bond price is below its par value, follows directly from facts 1 and 2. When the yield to maturity equals the coupon rate, then the bond price is at the face value; when the

TABLE 1	Yields to Maturity on a 10%-Coupon-Rate Bond Maturing in Ten Years (Face Value = $1,000)
Price of Bond ($)	**Yield to Maturity (%)**
1,200	7.13
1,100	8.48
1,000	10.00
900	11.75
800	13.81

yield to maturity rises above the coupon rate, the bond price necessarily falls and so must be below the face value of the bond.

One special case of a coupon bond is worth discussing here because its yield to maturity is particularly easy to calculate. This bond is called a **consol** or a **perpetuity**; it is a perpetual bond with no maturity date and no repayment of principal that makes fixed coupon payments of C forever. Consols were first sold by the British Treasury during the Napoleonic Wars and are still traded today; they are quite rare, however, in American capital markets. The formula in Equation 3 for the price of the consol Pc simplifies to the following:[3]

$$P_c = \frac{C}{i_c} \tag{4}$$

where

P_c = price of the perpetuity (consol)
C = yearly payment
i_c = yield to maturity of the perpetuity (consol)

One nice feature of perpetuities is that you can immediately see that as i_c increases, the price of the bond falls. For example, if a perpetuity pays $100 per year forever and the interest rate is 10%, its price will be $1,000 = $100/0.10. If the interest rate rises to 20%, its price will fall to $500 = $100/0.20. We can rewrite this formula as

$$i_c = \frac{C}{P_c} \tag{5}$$

APPLICATION Yield to Maturity on a Perpetuity

What is the yield to maturity on a bond that has a price of $2,000 and pays $100 of interest annually forever?

Solution
The yield to maturity is 5%.

$$i_c = \frac{C}{P_c} \qquad \frac{100}{\$2,000}$$

---

[3]The bond price formula for a consol is

$$P = \frac{C}{1 + i} + \frac{C}{(1 + i)^2} + \frac{C}{(1 + i)^3} + \dots$$

which can be written as

$$P = C(x + x^2 + x^3 + \dots)$$

in which $x = 1/(1 + i)$. The formula for an infinite sum is

$$1 + x + x^2 + x^3 + \dots = \frac{1}{1 - x} \text{ for } x < 1$$

and so

$$P = C\left(\frac{1}{1 - x} - 1\right) = C\left[\frac{1}{1 - 1/(1 + i)} - 1\right]$$

which by suitable algebraic manipulation becomes

$$P = C\left(\frac{1 + i}{i} - \frac{i}{i}\right) = \frac{C}{i}$$

where

C = yearly payment   = \$100
P_c = price of perpetuity (consol) = \$2,000

Thus

$$i_c = \frac{\$100}{\$2,000}$$

$$i_c = 0.05 = 5\%$$
                                                                    ◆

The formula given in Equation 5, which describes the calculation of the yield to maturity for a perpetuity, also provides a useful approximation for the yield to maturity on coupon bonds. When a coupon bond has a long term to maturity (say, twenty years or more), it is very much like a perpetuity, which pays coupon payments forever. This is because the cash flows more than twenty years in the future have such small present discounted values that the value of a long-term coupon bond is very close to the value of a perpetuity with the same coupon rate. Thus i_c in Equation 5 will be very close to the yield to maturity for any long-term bond. For this reason, i_c, the yearly coupon payment divided by the price of the security, has been given the name **current yield** and is frequently used as an approximation to describe interest rates on long-term bonds.

Discount Bond   The yield-to-maturity calculation for a discount bond is similar to that for a simple loan. Let's consider a discount bond such as a one-year U.S. Treasury bill that pays a face value of \$1,000 in one year's time but today has a price of \$900.

APPLICATION   Yield to Maturity on a Discount Bond

What is the yield to maturity on a one-year, \$1,000 Treasury bill with a current price of \$900?

Solution
The yield to maturity is 11.1%.
   Using the present value formula,

$$PV = \frac{CF}{(1 + i)^n}$$

and recognizing that the present value (*PV*) is the current price of \$900, the cash flow in one year is \$1,000, and the number of years is 1, we can write:

$$\$900 = \frac{\$1,000}{1 + i}$$

Solving for *i*, we get

$$(1 + i) \times \$900 = \$1,000$$
$$\$900 + \$900i = \$1,000$$
$$\$900i = \$1,000 - \$900$$

$$i = \frac{\$1,000 - \$900}{\$900} = 0.111 = 11.1\%   ◆$$

As we just saw in the preceding application, the yield to maturity for a one-year discount bond equals the increase in price over the year, $1,000 – $900, divided by the initial price, $900. Hence, more generally, for any one-year discount bond, the yield to maturity can be written as

$$i = \frac{F - P}{P}$$

(6)

where
F = face value of the discount bond
P = current price of the discount bond

An important feature of this equation is that it indicates that, for a discount bond, the yield to maturity is negatively related to the current bond price. This is the same conclusion that we reached for a coupon bond. Equation 6 shows that a rise in the bond price—say, from $900 to $950—means that the bond will have a smaller increase in its price at maturity and so the yield to maturity will fall, from 11.1% to 5.3% in our example. Similarly, a fall in the yield to maturity means that the current price of the discount bond has risen.

Summary   The concept of present value tells you that a dollar in the future is not as valuable to you as a dollar today because you can earn interest on a dollar you have today. Specifically, a dollar received n years from now is worth only $\$1/(1 + i)^n$ today. The present value of a set of future cash flow payments on a debt instrument equals the sum of the present values of each of the future payments. The yield to maturity for an instrument is the interest rate that equates the present value of the future payments on that instrument to its value today. Because the procedure for calculating the yield to maturity is based on sound economic principles, the yield to maturity is the measure that economists think most accurately describes the interest rate.

Our calculations of the yield to maturity for a variety of bonds reveal the important fact that *current bond prices and interest rates are negatively related: When the interest rate rises, the price of the bond falls, and vice versa*.

THE DISTINCTION BETWEEN INTEREST RATES AND RETURNS

Many people think that the interest rate on a bond tells them all they need to know about how well off they are as a result of owning it. If Irving the Investor thinks he is well off when he owns a long-term bond yielding a 10% interest rate, and the interest rate then rises to 20%, he will have a rude awakening: As we will shortly see, if he has to sell the bond, Irving will lose his shirt! How well a person does financially by holding a bond or any other security over a particular time period is accurately measured by the security's **return**, or, in more precise terminology, the **rate of return**. We will use the concept of *return* continually throughout this book: Understanding this concept will make the material presented later in the book easier to follow.

For any security, the rate of return is defined as the amount of each payment to the owner plus the change in the security's value, expressed as a fraction of its purchase price. To make this definition clearer, let us see what the return would look like for a $1,000-face-value coupon bond with a coupon rate of 10% that is bought for \$1,000, held for one year, and then sold for \$1,200. The payments to the owner are the yearly coupon payments of \$100, and the change in the bond's value is \$1,200 − \$1,000 = \$200. Adding these values together and expressing them as a fraction of the purchase price of \$1,000 gives us the one-year holding-period return for this bond:

$$\frac{\$100 + \$200}{\$1,000} = \frac{\$300}{\$1,000} = 0.30 = 30\%$$

You may have noticed something quite surprising about the return that we just calculated: It equals 30%, yet as Table 1 indicates, initially the yield to maturity was only 10%. This discrepancy demonstrates that *the return on a bond will not necessarily equal the yield to maturity on that bond*. We now see that the distinction between interest rate and return can be important, although for many securities the two may be closely related.

More generally, the return on a bond held from time t to time $t + 1$ can be written as

$$R = \frac{C + P_{t+1} - P_t}{P_t} \tag{7}$$

where
$$\begin{aligned} R &= \text{return from holding the bond from time } t \text{ to time } t + 1 \\ P_t &= \text{price of the bond at time } t \\ P_{t+1} &= \text{price of the bond at time } t + 1 \\ C &= \text{coupon payment} \end{aligned}$$

A convenient way to rewrite the return formula in Equation 7 is to recognize that it can be split into two separate terms:

$$R = \frac{C}{P_t} + \frac{P_{t+1} - P_t}{P_t}$$

The first term is the current yield i_c (the coupon payment over the purchase price):

$$\frac{C}{P_t} = i_c$$

The second term is the **rate of capital gain**, or the change in the bond's price relative to the initial purchase price:

$$\frac{P_{t+1} - P_t}{P_t} = g$$

where g is the rate of capital gain. Equation 7 can then be rewritten as

$$R = i_c + g \tag{8}$$

which shows that the return on a bond is the current yield i_c plus the rate of capital gain g. This rewritten formula illustrates the point we just discovered: Even for a bond for which the current yield i_c is an accurate measure of the yield to maturity, the return can differ substantially from the interest rate. Returns will differ substantially from the interest rate if the price of the bond experiences sizable fluctuations that produce substantial capital gains or losses.

TABLE 2	One-Year Returns on Different-Maturity 10%-Coupon-Rate Bonds When Interest Rates Rise from 10% to 20%				
(1) Years to Maturity When Bond Is Purchased	(2) Initial Current Yield (%)	(3) Initial Price ($)	(4) Price Next Year* ($)	(5) Rate of Capital Gain (%)	(6) Rate of Return [col (2) + col (5)] (%)
30	10	1,000	503	−49.7	−39.7
20	10	1,000	516	−48.4	−38.4
10	10	1,000	597	−40.3	−30.3
5	10	1,000	741	−25.9	−15.9
2	10	1,000	917	−8.3	+1.7
1	10	1,000	1,000	0.0	+10.0

*Calculated with a financial calculator, using Equation 3.

To explore this point even further, let's look at what happens to the returns on bonds of different maturities when interest rates rise. Table 2 calculates the one-year returns, using Equation 8 above, on several 10%-coupon-rate bonds, all purchased at par, when interest rates on all these bonds rise from 10% to 20%. Several key findings from this table are generally true of all bonds:

- The only bonds whose returns will equal their initial yields to maturity are those whose times to maturity are the same as their holding periods (see, for example, the last bond in Table 2).
- A rise in interest rates is associated with a fall in bond prices, resulting in capital losses on bonds whose terms to maturity are longer than their holding periods.
- The more distant a bond's maturity date, the greater the size of the percentage price change associated with an interest rate change.
- The more distant a bond's maturity date, the lower the rate of return that occurs as a result of an increase in the interest rate.
- Even though a bond may have a substantial initial interest rate, its return can turn out to be negative if interest rates rise.

At first, students are frequently puzzled (as was poor Irving the Investor) that a rise in interest rates can mean that a bond has been a poor investment. The trick to understanding this fact is to recognize Irving has already purchased the bond, so that a rise in the interest rate means that the price of the bond Irving is holding falls and he experiences a capital loss. If this loss is large enough, the bond can be a poor investment indeed. For example, we see in Table 2 that the bond that has 30 years to maturity when purchased has a capital loss of 49.7% when the interest rate rises from 10% to 20%. This loss is so large that it exceeds the current yield of 10%, resulting in a negative return (loss) of −39.7%. If Irving does not sell the bond, his capital loss is often referred to as a "paper loss." This is a loss nonetheless because if Irving had not bought this bond and had instead put his money in the bank, he would now be able to buy more bonds at their lower price than he presently owns.

Maturity and the Volatility of Bond Returns: Interest-Rate Risk

The finding that the prices of longer-maturity bonds respond more dramatically to changes in interest rates helps explain an important fact about the behavior of bond markets: *Prices and returns for long-term bonds are more volatile than those for shorter-term bonds*. Price changes of +20% and −20% within a year, with corresponding variations in returns, are common for bonds that are more than twenty years away from maturity.

We now see that changes in interest rates make investments in long-term bonds quite risky. Indeed, the risk level associated with an asset's return that results from interest-rate changes is so important that it has been given a special name, **interest-rate risk**.[4] Dealing with interest-rate risk is a major concern of managers of financial institutions and investors, as we will see in later chapters.

Although long-term debt instruments have substantial interest-rate risk, short-term debt instruments do not. Indeed, bonds with a maturity term that is as short as the holding period have no interest-rate risk.[5] We see this for the coupon bond at the bottom of Table 2, which has no uncertainty about the rate of return because it equals the yield to maturity, which is known at the time the bond is purchased. The key to understanding why there is no interest-rate risk for *any* bond whose time to maturity matches the holding period is to recognize that (in this case) the price at the end of the holding period is already fixed at the face value. A change in interest rates can then have no effect on the price at the end of the holding period for these bonds, and the return will therefore be equal to the yield to maturity, which is known at the time the bond is purchased.[6]

---

[4] Interest-rate risk can be quantitatively measured using the concept of *duration*. This concept and its calculation are discussed in an appendix to this chapter, which can be found on the Companion Website at http://www.pearsonhighered.com/mishkin.

[5] The statement that there is no interest-rate risk for any bond whose time to maturity matches the holding period is literally true only for discount (zero-coupon) bonds that make no intermediate cash payments before the holding period is over. A coupon bond that makes an intermediate cash payment before the holding period is over requires that this payment be reinvested. Because the interest rate at which this payment can be reinvested is uncertain, some uncertainty exists about the return on this coupon bond even when the time to maturity equals the holding period. However, the riskiness of the return on a coupon bond from reinvesting the coupon payments is typically quite small, so a coupon bond with a time to maturity equal to its holding period still has very little risk.

[6] In this text we assume that holding periods on all short-term bonds are equal to the term to maturity, and thus the bonds are not subject to interest-rate risk. However, if the term to maturity of the bond is shorter than an investor's holding period, the investor is exposed to a type of interest-rate risk called *reinvestment risk*. Reinvestment risk occurs because the proceeds from the short-term bond need to be reinvested at a future interest rate that is uncertain.

To understand reinvestment risk, suppose that Irving the Investor has a holding period of two years and decides to purchase a $1,000, one-year bond at face value and then another one at the end of the first year. If the initial interest rate is 10%, Irving will have $1,100 at the end of the first year. If the interest rate rises to 20%, as in Table 2, Irving will find that buying $1,100 worth of another one-year bond will leave him at the end of the second year with $1,100 × (1 + 0.20) = $1,320. Thus Irving's two-year return will be ($1,320 − $,1000)/1,000 = 0.32 = 32%, which equals 14.9% at an annual rate. In this case, Irving has earned more by buying the one-year bonds than he would have if he had initially purchased a two-year bond with an interest rate of 10%. Thus, when Irving has a holding period that is longer than the term to maturity of the bonds he purchases, he benefits from a rise in interest rates. Conversely, if interest rates fall to 5%, Irving will have only $1,155 at the end of two years: $1,100 × (1 + 0.05). His two-year return will be ($1,555 − $1,000)/1,000 = 0.155 = 15.5%, which is 7.2% at an annual rate. With a holding period greater than the term to maturity of the bond, Irving now loses from a decline in interest rates.

We have seen that when the holding period is longer than the term to maturity of a bond, the return is uncertain because the future interest rate when reinvestment occurs is also uncertain—in short, there is reinvestment risk. We also see that if the holding period is longer than the term to maturity of the bond, the investor benefits from a rise in interest rates and is hurt by a fall in interest rates.

Summary

The return on a bond, which tells you how good an investment it has been over the holding period, is equal to the yield to maturity in only one special case—when the holding period and the term to maturity of the bond are identical. Bonds whose terms to maturity are longer than their holding periods are subject to interest-rate risk: Changes in interest rates lead to capital gains and losses that produce substantial differences between the return and the yield to maturity known at the time the bond is purchased. Interest-rate risk is especially important for long-term bonds, on which capital gains and losses can be substantial. This is why long-term bonds are not considered safe assets with a sure return over short holding periods.

THE DISTINCTION BETWEEN REAL AND NOMINAL INTEREST RATES

So far in our discussion of interest rates, we have ignored the effects of inflation on the cost of borrowing. What we up to this point have been calling the interest rate makes no allowance for inflation, and it is more precisely referred to as the **nominal interest rate**. We must distinguish the nominal interest rate from the **real interest rate**, which is the interest rate that is adjusted by subtracting expected changes in the price level (inflation) so that it more accurately reflects the true cost of borrowing. This interest rate is more precisely referred to as the *ex ante real interest rate* because it is adjusted for *expected* changes in the price level. The ex ante real interest rate is veryimportant to economic decisions, and typically it is what economists mean when they make reference to the "real" interest rate. The interest rate that is adjusted for *actual* changes in the price level is called the *ex post real interest rate*. It describes how well a lender has done in real terms *after the fact*.

The real interest rate is more accurately defined from the *Fisher equation*, named for Irving Fisher, one of the great monetary economists of the twentieth century. The Fisher equation states that the nominal interest rate i equals the real interest rate r plus the expected rate of inflation π^e:[7]

$$i = r + \pi^e \tag{9}$$

Rearranging terms, we find that the real interest rate equals the nominal interest rate minus the expected inflation rate:

$$r = i - \pi^e \tag{10}$$

To see why this definition makes sense, let's first consider a situation in which you have made a simple one-year loan with a 5% interest rate ($i = 5\%$), and you expect the price level to rise by 3% over the course of the year ($\pi^e = 3\%$). As a result of making

[7]A more precise formulation of the Fisher equation is

$$i = r + \pi^e + (r \times \pi^e)$$

because

$$1 + i = (1 + r)(1 + \pi^e) = 1 + r + \pi^e + (r \times \pi^e)$$

and subtracting 1 from both sides gives us the first equation. For small values of r and π^e, the term $r \times \pi^e$ is so small that we ignore it, as in the text.

the loan, at the end of the year you expect to have 2% more in **real terms**—that is, in terms of real goods and services you can buy. In this case, the interest rate you expect to earn in terms of real goods and services is 2%:

$$r = 5\% - 3\% = 2\%$$

as indicated by Equation 10.[8]

APPLICATION   Calculating Real Interest Rates

What is the real interest rate if the nominal interest rate is 8% and the expected inflation rate is 10% over the course of a year?

Solution

The real interest rate is −2%. Although you will be receiving 8% more dollars at the end of the year, you will be paying 10% more for goods. The result is that you will be able to buy 2% fewer goods at the end of the year, and you will be 2% worse off in real terms. Mathematically,

$$r = i - \pi^e$$

where
$$i = \text{nominal interest rate} = 0.08$$
$$\pi^e = \text{expected inflation rate} = 0.10$$

Thus

$$r = 0.08 - 0.10 = -0.02 = -2\%$$ ◆

As a lender, you are clearly less eager to make a loan in this case, because in terms of real goods and services you have actually earned a negative interest rate of 2%. By contrast, as a borrower, you fare quite well because at the end of the year, the amounts you will have to pay back will be worth 2% less in terms of goods and services—you

---

[8]Because most interest income in the United States is subject to federal income taxes, the true earnings in real terms from holding a debt instrument are not reflected by the real interest rate defined by the Fisher equation but rather by the *after-tax real interest rate,* which equals the nominal interest rate *after income tax payments have been subtracted,* minus the expected inflation rate. For a person facing a 30% tax rate, the after-tax interest rate earned on a bond yielding 10% is only 7% because 30% of the interest income must be paid to the Internal Revenue Service. Thus the after-tax real interest rate on this bond when expected inflation is 5% equals 2% (=7% − 5%). More generally, the after-tax real interest rate can be expressed as

$$i(1 - \tau) - \pi^e$$

where τ = the income tax rate.

This formula for the after-tax real interest rate also provides a better measure of the effective cost of borrowing for many corporations and homeowners in the United States because, in calculating income taxes, they can deduct interest payments on loans from their income. Thus, if you face a 30% tax rate and take out a mortgage loan with a 10% interest rate, you are able to deduct the 10% interest payment and lower your taxes by 30% of this amount. Your after-tax nominal cost of borrowing is then 7% (10% minus 30% of the 10% interest payment), and when the expected inflation rate is 5%, the effective cost of borrowing in real terms is again 2% (=7% − 5%).

As the example (and the formula) indicates, after-tax real interest rates are always below the real interest rate defined by the Fisher equation. For a further discussion of measures of after-tax real interest rates, see Frederic S. Mishkin, "The Real Interest Rate: An Empirical Investigation," *Carnegie-Rochester Conference Series on Public Policy* 15 (1981): 151–200.

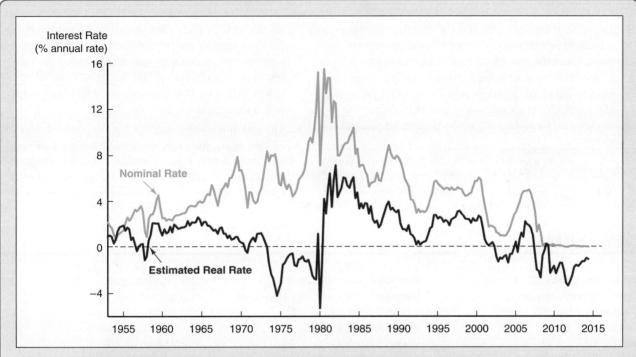

FIGURE 1   Real and Nominal Interest Rates (Three-Month Treasury Bill), 1953–2014

Nominal and real interest rates often do not move together. When U.S. nominal rates were high in the 1970s, real rates were actually extremely low—often negative.

Sources: Nominal rates from Federal Reserve Bank of St. Louis FRED database: http://research.stlouisfed.org/fred2/. The real rate is constructed using the procedure outlined in Frederic S. Mishkin, "The Real Interest Rate: An Empirical Investigation," *Carnegie-Rochester Conference Series on Public Policy* 15 (1981): 151–200. This procedure involves estimating expected inflation as a function of past interest rates, inflation, and time trends, and then subtracting the expected inflation measure from the nominal interest rate.

as the borrower will be ahead by 2% in real terms. **When the real interest rate is low, there are greater incentives to borrow and fewer incentives to lend.**

A similar distinction can be made between nominal returns and real returns. Nominal returns, which do not allow for inflation, are what we have been referring to as simply "returns." When inflation is subtracted from a nominal return, we have the real return, which indicates the amount of extra goods and services that we can purchase as a result of holding the security.

The distinction between real and nominal interest rates is important because the real interest rate, which reflects the real cost of borrowing, is likely to be a better indicator of the incentives to borrow and lend. It appears to be a better guide to how people will respond to what is happening in credit markets. Figure 1, which presents estimates from 1953 to 2014 of the real and nominal interest rates on three-month U.S. Treasury bills, shows us that nominal and real rates usually move together but do not always do so. (This is also true for nominal and real interest rates in the rest of the world.) In particular, when nominal rates in the United States were high in the 1970s, real rates were actually extremely low—often negative. By the standard of nominal interest rates, you would have thought that credit market conditions were tight during this period because it was expensive to borrow. However, the estimates of the real rates indicate that you would have been mistaken. In real terms, the cost of borrowing was actually quite low.

SUMMARY

1. The yield to maturity, which is the measure that most accurately reflects the interest rate, is the interest rate that equates the present value of future payments of a debt instrument with the instrument's value today. Application of this principle reveals that bond prices and interest rates are negatively correlated: When the interest rate rises, the price of the bond must fall, and vice versa.

2. The return on a security, which tells you how well you have done by holding the security over a stated period of time, can differ substantially from the interest rate as measured by the yield to maturity. Long-term bond prices experience substantial fluctuations when interest rates change and thus bear interest-rate risk. The resulting capital gains and losses can be large, which is why long-term bonds are not considered safe assets with a sure return.

3. The real interest rate is defined as the nominal interest rate minus the expected rate of inflation. It is both a better measure of the incentives to borrow and lend and a more accurate indicator of the tightness of credit market conditions than is the nominal interest rate.

KEY TERMS

cash flows, p. 64
consol or perpetuity, p. 73
coupon bond, p. 67
coupon rate, p. 67
current yield, p. 74
discount bond (zero-coupon bond), p. 67

face value (par value), p. 67
fixed-payment loan (fully amortized loan), p. 67
interest-rate risk, p. 78
nominal interest rate, p. 79
present value (present discounted value), p. 64

rate of capital gain, p. 76
real interest rate, p. 79
real terms, p. 80
return (rate of return), p. 75
simple loan, p. 65
yield to maturity, p. 68

QUESTIONS

All questions are available in MyEconLab *at* http://www.myeconlab.com.

1. Would a dollar tomorrow be worth more to you today when the interest rate is 20% or when it is 10%?

2. Write down the formula that is used to calculate the yield to maturity on a twenty-year 10% coupon bond with a $1,000 face value that sells for $2,000.

3. To help pay for college, you have just taken out a $1,000 government loan that makes you pay $126 per year for 25 years. However, you don't have to start making these payments until you graduate from college two years from now. Why is the yield to maturity necessarily less than 12%? (This is the yield to maturity on a normal $1,000 fixed-payment loan on which you pay $126 per year for 25 years.)

4. Do bondholders fare better when the yield to maturity increases or when it decreases? Why?

5. A financial adviser has just given you the following advice: "Long-term bonds are a great investment because their interest rate is over 20%." Is the financial adviser necessarily right?

6. If mortgage rates rise from 5% to 10% but the expected rate of increase in housing prices rises from 2% to 9%, are people more or less likely to buy houses?

7. When is the current yield a good approximation of the yield to maturity?

8. Why would a government choose to issue a perpetuity, which requires payments forever, instead of a terminal loan, such as a fixed-payment loan, discount bond, or coupon bond?

9. Under what conditions will a discount bond have a negative nominal interest rate? Is it possible for a coupon bond or a perpetuity to have a negative nominal interest rate?

10. True or False: With a discount bond, the return on the bond is equal to the rate of capital gain.

11. If interest rates decline, which would you rather be holding, long-term bonds or short-term bonds? Why? Which type of bond has the greater interest-rate risk?

12. Interest rates were lower in the mid-1980s than in the late 1970s, yet many economists have commented that real interest rates were actually much higher in the mid-1980s than in the late 1970s. Does this make sense? Do you think that these economists are right?

13. Retired persons often have much of their wealth placed in savings accounts and other interest-bearing investments, and complain whenever interest rates are low. Do they have a valid complaint?

APPLIED PROBLEMS

All applied problems are available in MyEconLab at http://www.myeconlab.com.

14. If the interest rate is 10%, what is the present value of a security that pays you $1,100 next year, $1,210 the year after, and $1,331 the year after that?

15. Calculate the present value of a $1,000 discount bond with five years to maturity if the yield to maturity is 6%.

16. A lottery claims its grand prize is $10 million, payable over 5 years at $2,000,000 per year. If the first payment is made immediately, what is this grand prize really worth? Use an interest rate of 6%.

17. What is the yield to maturity on a $1,000-face-value discount bond maturing in one year that sells for $800?

18. What is the yield to maturity on a simple loan for $1 million that requires a repayment of $2 million in five years' time?

19. Which $1,000 bond has the higher yield to maturity, a twenty-year bond selling for $800 with a current yield of 15% or a one-year bond selling for $800 with a current yield of 5%?

20. Consider a bond with a 4% annual coupon and a face value of $1,000. Complete the following table. What relationships do you observe between years to maturity, yield to maturity, and the current price?

Years to Maturity	Yield to Maturity	Current Price
2	2%	
2	4%	
3	4%	
5	2%	
5	6%	

21. Consider a coupon bond that has a $1,000 par value and a coupon rate of 10%. The bond is currently selling for $1,044.89 and has two years to maturity. What is the bond's yield to maturity?

22. What is the price of a perpetuity that has a coupon of $50 per year and a yield to maturity of 2.5%? If the yield to maturity doubles, what will happen to the perpetuity's price?

23. Property taxes in a particular district are 4% of the purchase price of a home every year. If you just purchased a $250,000 home, what is the present value of all the future property tax payments? Assume that the house remains worth $250,000 forever, property tax rates never change, and a 6% interest rate is used for discounting.

24. A $1000-face-value bond has a 10% coupon rate, its current price is $960, and its price is expected to increase to $980 next year. Calculate the current yield, the expected rate of capital gain, and the expected rate of return.

25. Assume you just deposited $1,000 into a bank account. The current real interest rate is 2%, and inflation is expected to be 6% over the next year. What nominal rate would you require from the bank over the next year? How much money will you have at the end of one year? If you are saving to buy a fancy bicycle that currently sells for $1,050, will you have enough money to buy it?

DATA ANALYSIS PROBLEMS

The Problems update with real-time data in MyEconLab and are available for practice or instructor assignment.

1. Go to the St. Louis Federal Reserve FRED database, and find data on the interest rate on a four-year auto loan (TERMCBAUTO48NS). Assume that you borrow $20,000 to purchase a new automobile and that you finance it with a four-year loan at the most recent interest rate given in the database. If you make one payment per year for four years, what will the yearly payment be? What is the total amount that will be paid out on the $20,000 loan?

2. The U.S. Treasury issues some bonds as *Treasury Inflation Indexed Securities, or TIIS*, which are bonds adjusted for inflation; hence the yields can be roughly interpreted as real interest rates. Go to the St. Louis Federal Reserve FRED database, and find data on the following TIIS bonds and their nominal counterparts. Then answer the questions below.

- 5 year U.S. treasury (DGS5) and 5 year TIIS (DFII5)

- 7 year U.S. treasury (DGS7) and 7 year TIIS (DFII7)

- 10 year U.S. treasury (DGS10) and 10 year TIIS (DFII10)

- 20 year U.S. treasury (DGS20) and 20 year TIIS (DFII20)

- 30 year U.S. treasury (DGS30) and 30 year TIIS (DFII30)

  a. Following the Great Recession of 2008–2009, the 5, 7, 10, and even the 20 year TIIS yields became negative for a period of time. How is this possible?

  b. Using the most recent data available, calculate the difference between the yields for each of the pairs of bonds (DGS5 – DFII5, etc.) listed above. What does this difference represent?

  c. Based on your answer to part (b), are there significant variations among the differences in the bond-pair yields? Interpret the magnitude of the variation in differences among the pairs.

WEB EXERCISES

1. In this chapter, we discussed long-term bonds as if there were only one type, coupon bonds. In fact, investors can also purchase long-term discount bonds. A discount bond is sold at a low price, and the whole return comes in the form of a price appreciation. You can easily compute the current price of a discount bond by using the financial calculator at http://www.treasurydirect.gov/indiv/tools/tools_savingsbondcalc.htm.

To compute the values for savings bonds, read the instructions on the page and click on Get Started. Fill in the information (you do not need to fill in the Bond Serial Number field) and click on Calculate.

WEB REFERENCES

http://www.bloomberg.com/markets/

Under Rates & Bonds, you can access information on key interest rates, U.S. Treasuries, government bonds, and municipal bonds.

http://www.teachmefinance.com

A review of the key financial concepts: time value of money, annuities, perpetuities, and so on.

WEB APPENDICES

Please visit the Companion Website at http://www.pearsonhighered.com/mishkin to read the Web appendix to Chapter 4.

Appendix 1: **Measuring Interest-Rate Risk: Duration**

5

The Behavior of Interest Rates

Learning Objectives

- Identify the factors that affect the demand for assets.
- Draw the demand and supply curves for the bond market, and identify the equilibrium interest rate.
- List and describe the factors that affect the equilibrium interest rate in the bond market.
- Describe the connection between the bond market and the money market through the liquidity preference framework.
- List and describe the factors that affect the money market and the equilibrium interest rate.
- Identify and illustrate the effects on the interest rate of changes in money growth over time.

Preview

In the early 1950s, nominal interest rates on three-month Treasury bills were about 1% at an annual rate; by 1981, they had reached over 15%. They fell below 1% in 2003, rose to 5% in 2007, and then fell to close to zero in 2008 and for many years afterward. What explains these substantial fluctuations in interest rates? One reason why we study money, banking, and financial markets is to provide some answers to this question.

In this chapter, we examine how the overall level of nominal interest rates (which we refer to simply as "interest rates") is determined and which factors influence their behavior. We learned in Chapter 4 that interest rates are negatively related to the price of bonds, so if we can explain why bond prices change, we can also explain why interest rates fluctuate. We make use of supply and demand analysis for bond markets and markets for money to examine how interest rates change.

To derive a demand curve for assets such as money or bonds, the first step in our analysis, we must first understand what determines the demand for these assets. We do this by examining *portfolio theory*, an economic theory that outlines criteria that are important when deciding how much of an asset to buy. Armed with this theory, we can then go on to derive the demand curve for bonds or money. After deriving supply curves for these assets, we develop the concept of *market equilibrium*, which is defined as the point at which the quantity supplied equals the quantity demanded. Then we use this model to explain changes in equilibrium interest rates.

Because interest rates on different securities tend to move together, in this chapter we will proceed as if there were only one type of security and one interest rate in the entire economy. In the following chapter, we expand our analysis to look at why interest rates on different types of securities differ.

DETERMINANTS OF ASSET DEMAND

Before going on to our supply and demand analysis of the bond market and the market for money, we must first understand what determines the quantity demanded of an asset. Recall that an asset is a piece of property that is a store of value. Items such as money, bonds, stocks, art, land, houses, farm equipment, and manufacturing machinery are all assets. Faced with the question of whether to buy and hold an asset or whether to buy one asset rather than another, an individual must consider the following factors:

1. **Wealth**, the total resources owned by the individual, including all assets
2. **Expected return** (the return expected over the next period) on one asset relative to alternative assets
3. **Risk** (the degree of uncertainty associated with the return) on one asset relative to alternative assets
4. **Liquidity** (the ease and speed with which an asset can be turned into cash) relative to alternative assets

Wealth

When we find that our wealth has increased, we have more resources available with which to purchase assets, and so, not surprisingly, the quantity of assets we demand increases. Therefore, the effect of changes in wealth on the quantity demanded of an asset can be summarized as follows: *Holding everything else constant, an increase in wealth raises the quantity demanded of an asset.*

Expected Returns

In Chapter 4, we saw that the return on an asset (such as a bond) measures how much we gain from holding that asset. When we make a decision to buy an asset, we are influenced by what we expect the return on that asset to be. If an ExxonMobil bond, for example, has a return of 15% half the time and 5% the other half, its expected return (which you can think of as the average return) is 10% ($=0.5 \times 15\% + 0.5 \times 5\%$).[1] If the expected return on the ExxonMobil bond rises relative to expected returns on alternative assets, then, holding everything else constant, it becomes more desirable to purchase the ExxonMobil bond, and the quantity demanded increases. This can occur in either of two ways: (1) when the expected return on the ExxonMobil bond rises while the return on an alternative asset—say, stock in Google—remains unchanged or (2) when the return on the alternative asset, the Google stock, falls while the return on the ExxonMobil bond remains unchanged. To summarize, *an increase in an asset's expected return relative to that of an alternative asset, holding everything else unchanged, raises the quantity demanded of the asset.*

Risk

The degree of risk or uncertainty of an asset's returns also affects demand for the asset. Consider two assets, stock in Fly-by-Night Airlines and stock in Feet-on-the-Ground Bus Company. Suppose that Fly-by-Night stock has a return of 15% half the time and 5% the other half, making its expected return 10%, while Feet-on-the-Ground stock has a fixed return of 10%. Fly-by-Night stock has uncertainty associated with its returns and so has greater risk than Feet-on-the-Ground stock, whose return is a sure thing.

---

[1] If you are interested in finding out more information on how to calculate expected returns, as well as standard deviations of returns that measure risk, the Companion Website at http://www.pearsonhighered.com/mishkin contains an appendix to this chapter describing models of asset pricing. This appendix also describes how diversification lowers the overall risk of a portfolio and includes a discussion of systematic risk and basic asset pricing models, such as the capital asset pricing model and the arbitrage pricing theory.

A *risk-averse* person prefers stock in Feet-on-the-Ground (the sure thing) to Fly-by-Night stock (the riskier asset), even though the stocks have the same expected return, 10%. By contrast, a person who prefers risk is a *risk preferrer* or *risk lover*. Most people are risk-averse, especially in their financial decisions: Everything else being equal, they prefer to hold the less risky asset. Hence, **holding everything else constant, if an asset's risk rises relative to that of alternative assets, its quantity demanded will fall.**

Liquidity

Another factor that affects the demand for an asset is how quickly it can be converted into cash at low costs—its liquidity. An asset is liquid if the market in which it is traded has depth and breadth, that is, if the market has many buyers and sellers. A house is not a very liquid asset because it may be hard to find a buyer quickly; if a house must be sold to pay off bills, it might have to be sold for a much lower price. And the transaction costs associated with selling a house (broker's commissions, lawyer's fees, and so on) are substantial. A U.S. Treasury bill, by contrast, is a highly liquid asset. It can be sold in a well-organized market with many buyers, and so it can be sold quickly at low cost. **The more liquid an asset is relative to alternative assets, holding everything else unchanged, the more desirable it is and the greater the quantity demanded will be.**

Theory of Portfolio Choice

All the determining factors we have just discussed can be assembled into the **theory of portfolio choice**, which tells us how much of an asset people will want to hold in their portfolios. It states that, holding all other factors constant:

1. The quantity demanded of an asset is positively related to wealth.
2. The quantity demanded of an asset is positively related to its expected return relative to alternative assets.
3. The quantity demanded of an asset is negatively related to the risk of its returns relative to alternative assets.
4. The quantity demanded of an asset is positively related to its liquidity relative to alternative assets.

These results are summarized in Table 1.

SUMMARY TABLE 1

Response of the Quantity of an Asset Demanded to Changes in Wealth, Expected Returns, Risk, and Liquidity

Variable	Change in Variable	Change in Quantity Demanded
Wealth	↑	↑
Expected return relative to other assets	↑	↑
Risk relative to other assets	↑	↓
Liquidity relative to other assets	↑	↑

Note: Only increases in the variables are shown. The effects of decreases in the variables on the quantity demanded would be the opposite of those indicated in the rightmost column.

SUPPLY AND DEMAND IN THE BOND MARKET

Our first approach to the analysis of interest-rate determination looks at supply and demand in the bond market so that we can better understand how the prices of bonds are determined. Thanks to our knowledge from Chapter 4 of how interest rates are measured, we know that each bond price is associated with a particular level of the interest rate. Specifically, the negative relationship between bond prices and interest rates means that when a bond's price rises, its interest rate falls, and vice versa.

The first step in our analysis is to obtain a bond **demand curve**, which shows the relationship between the quantity demanded and the price when all other economic variables are held constant (that is, values of other variables are taken as given). You may recall from previous economics courses that the assumption that all other economic variables are held constant is called *ceteris paribus*, which means "other things being equal" in Latin.

Demand Curve

To clarify and simplify our analysis, let's consider the demand for one-year discount bonds, which make no coupon payments but pay the owner the $1,000 face value in a year. If the holding period is one year, then, as we saw in Chapter 4, the return on the bonds is known absolutely and is equal to the interest rate as measured by the yield to maturity. This means that the expected return on this bond is equal to the interest rate i, which, using Equation 6 in Chapter 4, is

$$i = R^e = \frac{F - P}{P}$$

where

$$
\begin{aligned}
i &= \text{interest rate} = \text{yield to maturity} \\
R^e &= \text{expected return} \\
F &= \text{face value of the discount bond} \\
P &= \text{initial purchase price of the discount bond}
\end{aligned}
$$

This formula shows that a particular value of the interest rate corresponds to each bond price. If the bond sells for $950, the interest rate and expected return are

$$\frac{\$1{,}000 - \$950}{\$950} = 0.053 = 5.3\%$$

At this 5.3% interest rate and expected return corresponding to a bond price of $950, let us assume that the quantity of bonds demanded is $100 billion, which is plotted as point A in Figure 1.

At a price of $900, the interest rate and expected return are

$$\frac{\$1{,}000 - \$900}{\$900} = 0.111 = 11.1\%$$

Because the expected return is higher, with all other economic variables (such as income, expected returns on other assets, risk, and liquidity) held constant, the quantity demanded of these bonds will be higher, as predicted by portfolio theory. Point B in Figure 1 shows that the quantity of bonds demanded at the price of $900 has risen to $200 billion. Continuing with this reasoning, we see that if the bond price is $850 (interest rate and expected return = 17.6%), the quantity of bonds demanded (point C)

MyEconLab Mini-lecture

FIGURE 1
Supply and Demand for Bonds

Equilibrium in the bond market occurs at point C, the intersection of the demand curve B^d and the bond supply curve B^s. The equilibrium price is $P^* = \$850$, and the equilibrium interest rate is $i^* = 17.6\%$.

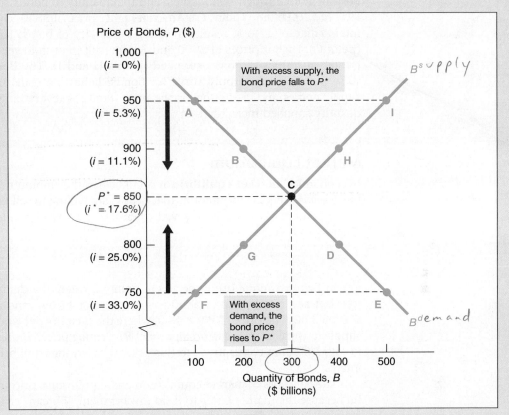

will be greater than at point B. Similarly, at the even lower prices of $800 (interest rate = 25%) and $750 (interest rate = 33.3%), the quantity of bonds demanded will be even higher (points D and E). The curve B^d, which connects these points, is the demand curve for bonds. It has the usual downward slope, indicating that at lower prices of the bond (everything else being equal), the quantity demanded is higher.[2]

Supply Curve

An important assumption behind the demand curve for bonds in Figure 1 is that all other economic variables besides the bond's price and interest rate are held constant. We use the same assumption in deriving a **supply curve**, which shows the relation-ship between the quantity supplied and the price when all other economic variables are held constant.

In Figure 1, when the price of the bonds is $750 (interest rate = 33.3%), point F shows that the quantity of bonds supplied is $100 billion for the example we are con-sidering. If the price is $800, the interest rate is the lower rate of 25%. Because at this

---

[2]Although our analysis indicates that the demand curve is downward-sloping, it does not imply that the curve is a straight line. For ease of exposition, however, we will draw demand curves and supply curves as straight lines.

interest rate it is now less costly to borrow by issuing bonds, firms will be willing to borrow more through bond issues, and the quantity of bonds supplied is at the higher level of $200 billion (point G). An even higher price of $850, corresponding to a lower interest rate of 17.6%, results in a larger quantity of bonds supplied of $300 billion (point C). Higher prices of $900 and $950 result in even lower interest rates and even greater quantities of bonds supplied (points H and I). The B^s curve, which connects these points, is the supply curve for bonds. It has the usual upward slope found in supply curves, indicating that as the price increases (everything else being equal), the quantity supplied increases.

Market Equilibrium

In economics, **market equilibrium** occurs when the amount that people are willing to buy (*demand*) equals the amount that people are willing to sell (*supply*) at a given price. In the bond market, this is achieved when the quantity of bonds demanded equals the quantity of bonds supplied:

$$B^d = B^s \tag{1}$$

In Figure 1, equilibrium occurs at point C, where the demand and supply curves intersect at a bond price of $850 (interest rate of 17.6%) and a quantity of bonds of $300 billion. The price of $P^* = 850$, where the quantity demanded equals the quantity supplied, is called the *equilibrium* or *market-clearing* price. Similarly, the interest rate of $i^* = 17.6\%$ that corresponds to this price is called the equilibrium or market-clearing interest rate.

The concepts of market equilibrium and equilibrium price or interest rate are useful because the market tends to head toward them. We can see this in Figure 1 by first looking at what happens when we have a bond price that is above the equilibrium price. When the price of bonds is set too high, at, say, $950, the quantity of bonds supplied at point I is greater than the quantity of bonds demanded at point A. A situation like this, in which the quantity of bonds supplied exceeds the quantity of bonds demanded, is called a condition of **excess supply**. Because people want to sell more bonds than others want to buy, the price of the bonds will fall, as shown by the downward arrow in the figure at the bond price of $950. As long as the bond price remains above the equilibrium price, an excess supply of bonds will continue to be available, and the price of bonds will continue to fall. This decline will stop only when the price has reached the equilibrium price of $850, the price at which the excess supply of bonds has been eliminated.

Now let's look at what happens when the price of bonds is below the equilibrium price. If the price of the bonds is set too low, at, say, $750, the quantity demanded at point E is greater than the quantity supplied at point F. This is called a condition of **excess demand**. People now want to buy more bonds than others are willing to sell, so the price of bonds will be driven up, as illustrated by the upward arrow in the figure at the bond price of $750. Only when the excess demand for bonds is eliminated by the bond price rising to the equilibrium level of $850 is there no further tendency for the price to rise.

We can see that the concept of equilibrium price is a useful one because it indicates where the market will settle. Because each price on the vertical axis of Figure 1 corresponds to a particular value of the interest rate, the same diagram also shows that the interest rate will head toward the equilibrium interest rate of 17.6%. When the interest rate is below the equilibrium interest rate, as it is when it is at 5.3%, the price of the bond is above the equilibrium price, and an excess supply of bonds results. The price of the bond then falls, leading to a rise in the interest rate toward the equilibrium level. Similarly, when the interest rate is above the equilibrium level, as it is when it is at 33.3%, an excess demand for bonds occurs, and the bond price rises, driving the interest rate back down to the equilibrium level of 17.6%.

Supply and Demand Analysis

Our Figure 1 is a conventional supply and demand diagram with price on the vertical axis and quantity on the horizontal axis. Because the interest rate that corresponds to each bond price is also marked on the vertical axis, this diagram allows us to read the equilibrium interest rate, giving us a model that describes the determination of interest rates. It is important to recognize that a supply and demand diagram like Figure 1 can be drawn for *any* type of bond because the interest rate and price of a bond are *always* negatively related for all kinds of bonds, whether a discount bond or a coupon bond.

An important feature of the analysis here is that supply and demand are always described in terms of *stocks* (amounts at a given point in time) of assets, not in terms of *flows*. The **asset market approach** for understanding behavior in financial markets—which emphasizes stocks of assets, rather than flows, in determining asset prices—is the dominant methodology used by economists, because correctly conducting analyses in terms of flows is very tricky, especially when we encounter inflation.[3]

CHANGES IN EQUILIBRIUM INTEREST RATES

We will now use the supply and demand framework for bonds to analyze why interest rates change. To avoid confusion, it is important to make the distinction between *movements along* a demand (or supply) curve and *shifts in* a demand (or supply) curve. When quantity demanded (or supplied) changes as a result of a change in the price of the bond (or, equivalently, a change in the interest rate), we have a *movement along* the demand (or supply) curve. The change in the quantity demanded when we move from point A to B to C in Figure 1, for example, is a movement along a demand curve. A *shift in* the demand (or supply) curve, by contrast, occurs when the quantity demanded (or supplied) changes *at each given price (or interest rate)* of the bond in response to a change in some other factor besides the bond's price or interest rate. When one of these factors changes, causing a shift in the demand or supply curve, there will be a new equilibrium value for the interest rate.

In the following pages, we will look at how the supply and demand curves shift in response to changes in variables, such as expected inflation and wealth, and what effects these changes have on the equilibrium value of interest rates.

---

[3]The asset market approach developed in the text is useful in understanding not only how interest rates behave but also how any asset price is determined. A second appendix to this chapter, which is on the Companion Website at http://www.pearsonhighered.com/mishkin, shows how the asset market approach can be applied to understanding the behavior of commodity markets—in particular, the gold market. The analysis of the bond market that we have developed here has another interpretation that uses a different terminology and framework involving the supply and demand for loanable funds. This loanable funds framework is discussed in a third appendix to this chapter, which is also available on the book's website.

Shifts in the Demand for Bonds

The theory of portfolio choice, which we developed at the beginning of the chapter, provides a framework for deciding which factors will cause the demand curve for bonds to shift. These factors include changes in the following four parameters:

1. Wealth
2. Expected returns on bonds relative to alternative assets
3. Risk of bonds relative to alternative assets
4. Liquidity of bonds relative to alternative assets

To see how a change in each of these factors (holding all other factors constant) can shift the demand curve, let's look at some examples. (As a study aid, Table 2 summarizes the effects of changes in these factors on the bond demand curve.)

Wealth When the economy is growing rapidly in a business cycle expansion and wealth is increasing, the quantity of bonds demanded at each bond price (or interest rate) increases, as shown in Figure 2. To see how this works, consider point B on the initial demand curve for bonds, B_1^d. With higher wealth, the quantity of bonds demanded at the same price must rise, to point B'. Similarly, for point D, the higher wealth causes the quantity demanded at the same bond price to rise to point D'. Continuing with this reasoning for every point on the initial demand curve B_1^d, we can see that the demand curve shifts to the right from B_1^d to B_2^d, as indicated by the arrows.

We can conclude that *in a business cycle expansion with growing wealth, the demand for bonds rises and the demand curve for bonds shifts to the right.* Applying the same reasoning, *in a recession, when income and wealth are falling, the demand for bonds falls, and the demand curve shifts to the left.*

MyEconLab Mini-lecture

FIGURE 2
Shift in the Demand Curve for Bonds

When the demand for bonds increases, the demand curve shifts to the right as shown.

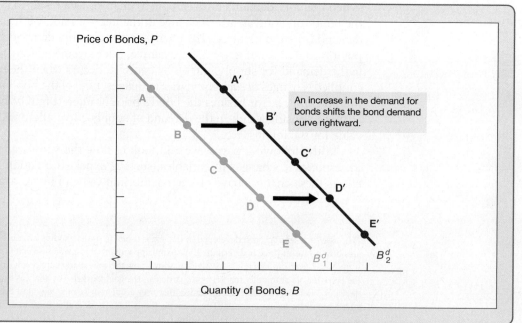

An increase in the demand for bonds shifts the bond demand curve rightward.

SUMMARY TABLE 2

Factors That Shift the Demand Curve for Bonds

Variable	Change in Variable	Change in Quantity Demanded at Each Bond Price	Shift in Demand Curve
Wealth	↑	↑	
Expected interest rate	↑	↓	
Expected inflation	↑	↓	
Riskiness of bonds relative to other assets	↑	↓	
Liquidity of bonds relative to other assets	↑	↑	

Note: Only increases in the variables are shown. The effects of decreases in the variables on demand would be the opposite of those indicated in the remaining columns.

Another factor that affects wealth is the public's propensity to save. If households save more, wealth increases and, as we have seen, the demand for bonds rises and the demand curve for bonds shifts to the right. Conversely, if people save less, wealth and the demand for bonds fall, and the demand curve shifts to the left.

Expected Returns   For a one-year discount bond and a one-year holding period, the expected return and the interest rate are identical, so nothing other than today's interest rate affects the expected return.

For bonds with maturities of greater than one year, the expected return may differ from the interest rate. For example, we saw in Chapter 4, Table 2, that a rise in the interest rate on a long-term bond from 10% to 20% would lead to a sharp decline in price and a very large negative return. Hence, if people began to think that interest rates would be higher next year than they had originally anticipated, the expected return today on long-term bonds would fall, and the quantity demanded would fall at each interest rate. *Higher expected future interest rates lower the expected return for long-term bonds, decrease the demand, and shift the demand curve to the left.*

By contrast, an expectation of lower future interest rates would mean that long-term bond prices would be expected to rise more than originally anticipated, and the resulting higher expected return today would raise the quantity demanded at each bond price and interest rate. *Lower expected future interest rates increase the demand for long-term bonds and shift the demand curve to the right* (as in Figure 2).

Changes in expected returns on other assets can also shift the demand curve for bonds. If people suddenly become more optimistic about the stock market and begin to expect higher stock prices in the future, both expected capital gains and expected returns on stocks will rise. With the expected return on bonds held constant, the expected return on bonds today relative to stocks will fall, lowering the demand for bonds and shifting the demand curve to the left. *An increase in expected return on alternative assets lowers the demand for bonds and shifts the demand curve to the left.*

A change in expected inflation is likely to alter expected returns on physical assets (also called *real assets*), such as automobiles and houses, which affect the demand for bonds. An increase in expected inflation from, say, 5% to 10% will lead to higher prices on cars and houses in the future and hence higher nominal capital gains. The resulting rise in the expected returns today on these real assets will lead to a fall in the expected return on bonds relative to the expected return on real assets today and thus cause the demand for bonds to fall. Alternatively, we can think of the rise in expected inflation as lowering the real interest rate on bonds, and thus the resulting decline in the relative expected return on bonds will cause the demand for bonds to fall. *An increase in the expected rate of inflation lowers the expected return on bonds, causing their demand to decline and the demand curve to shift to the left.*

Risk   If prices in the bond market become more volatile, the risk associated with bonds increases, and bonds become a less attractive asset. *An increase in the riskiness of bonds causes the demand for bonds to fall and the demand curve to shift to the left.*

Conversely, an increase in the volatility of prices in another asset market, such as the stock market, would make bonds more attractive. *An increase in the riskiness of alternative assets causes the demand for bonds to rise and the demand curve to shift to the right* (as in Figure 2).

Liquidity   If more people started trading in the bond market, and as a result it became easier to sell bonds quickly, the increase in their liquidity would cause the quantity of bonds demanded at each interest rate to rise. *Increased liquidity of bonds results in an increased demand for bonds, and the demand curve shifts to the right* (see Figure 2).

Similarly, increased liquidity of alternative assets lowers the demand for bonds and shifts the demand curve to the left. The reduction of brokerage commissions for trading common stocks that occurred when the fixed-rate commission structure was abolished in 1975, for example, increased the liquidity of stocks relative to bonds, and the resulting lower demand for bonds shifted the demand curve to the left.

Shifts in the Supply of Bonds

Certain factors can cause the supply curve for bonds to shift. Among these factors are:

1. Expected profitability of investment opportunities
2. Expected inflation
3. Government budget deficits

We will look at how the supply curve shifts when each of these factors changes (all others remaining constant). (As a study aid, Table 3 summarizes the effects of changes in these factors on the bond supply curve.)

SUMMARY TABLE 3

Factors That Shift the Supply of Bonds

Variable	Change in Variable	Change in Quantity Supplied at Each Bond Price	Shift in Supply Curve
Profitability of investments	↑	↑	
Expected inflation	↑	↑	
Government deficit	↑	↑	

Note: Only increases in the variables are shown. The effects of decreases in the variables on the supply would be the opposite of those indicated in the remaining columns.

MyEconLab Mini-lecture

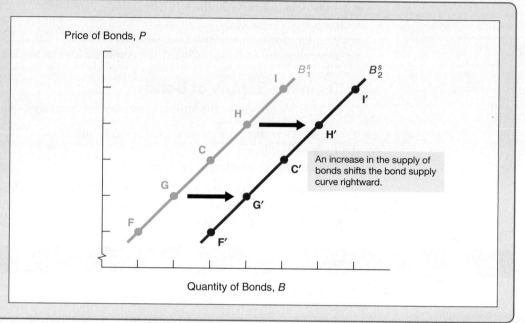

FIGURE 3
Shift in the Supply Curve for Bonds
When the supply of bonds increases, the supply curve shifts to the right.

Expected Profitability of Investment Opportunities
When opportunities for profitable plant and equipment investments are plentiful, firms are more willing to borrow to finance these investments. When the economy is growing rapidly, as in a business cycle expansion, investment opportunities that are expected to be profitable abound, and the quantity of bonds supplied at any given bond price increases (see Figure 3). *Therefore, in a business cycle expansion, the supply of bonds increases and the supply curve shifts to the right. Likewise, in a recession, when far fewer profitable investment opportunities are expected, the supply of bonds falls and the supply curve shifts to the left.*

Expected Inflation
As we saw in Chapter 4, the real cost of borrowing is most accurately measured by the real interest rate, which equals the (nominal) interest rate minus the expected inflation rate. For a given interest rate (and bond price), when expected inflation increases, the real cost of borrowing falls; hence, the quantity of bonds supplied increases at any given bond price. *An increase in expected inflation causes the supply of bonds to increase and the supply curve to shift to the right* (see Figure 3) *and a decrease in expected inflation causes the supply of bonds to decrease and the supply curve to shift to the left.*

Government Budget Deficits
The activities of the government can influence the supply of bonds in several ways. The U.S. Treasury issues bonds to finance government deficits, caused by gaps between the government's expenditures and its revenues. When these deficits are large, the Treasury sells more bonds, and the quantity of bonds supplied at each bond price increases. *Higher government deficits increase the supply of bonds and shift the supply curve to the right* (see Figure 3). *On the other hand, government surpluses, as occurred in the late 1990s, decrease the supply of bonds and shift the supply curve to the left.*

State and local governments and other government agencies also issue bonds to finance their expenditures, and this can affect the supply of bonds as well. We will see in later chapters that the conduct of monetary policy involves the purchase and sale of bonds, which in turn influences the supply of bonds.

We now can use our knowledge of how supply and demand curves shift to analyze how the equilibrium interest rate can change. The best way to do this is to pursue several applications that are particularly relevant to our understanding of how monetary policy affects interest rates. In studying these applications, keep two things in mind:

1. When we examine the effect of a variable change, remember we are assuming that all other variables are unchanged; that is, we are making use of the *ceteris paribus* assumption.

2. Remember that the interest rate is negatively related to the bond price, so when the equilibrium bond price rises, the equilibrium interest rate falls. Conversely, if the equilibrium bond price moves downward, the equilibrium interest rate rises.

APPLICATION

Changes in the Interest Rate Due to Expected Inflation: The Fisher Effect

We have already done most of the work necessary to evaluate how a change in expected inflation affects the nominal interest rate, in that we have already analyzed how a change in expected inflation shifts the supply and demand curves. Figure 4 shows the effect on the equilibrium interest rate of an increase in expected inflation.

MyEconLab Mini-lecture

FIGURE 4
Response to a Change in Expected Inflation

When expected inflation rises, the supply curve shifts from B_1^s to B_2^s, and the demand curve shifts from B_1^d to B_2^d. The equilibrium moves from point 1 to point 2, causing the equilibrium bond price to fall from P_1 to P_2 and the equilibrium interest rate to rise.

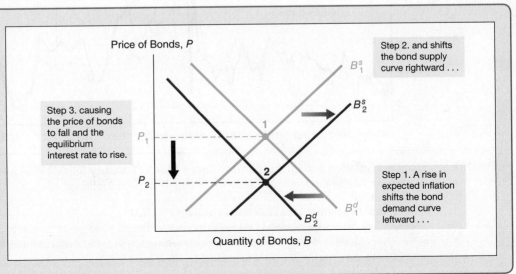

Step 2. and shifts the bond supply curve rightward . . .

Step 3. causing the price of bonds to fall and the equilibrium interest rate to rise.

Step 1. A rise in expected inflation shifts the bond demand curve leftward . . .

Suppose that expected inflation is initially 5% and the initial supply and demand curves B_1^s and B_1^d intersect at point 1, where the equilibrium bond price is P_1. If expected inflation rises to 10%, the expected return on bonds relative to real assets falls for any given bond price and interest rate. As a result, the demand for bonds falls, and the demand curve shifts to the left from B_1^d to B_2^d. The rise in expected inflation also shifts the supply curve. At any given bond price and interest rate, the real cost of borrowing declines, causing the quantity of bonds supplied to increase and the supply curve to shift to the right, from B_1^s to B_2^s.

When the demand and supply curves shift in response to the change in expected inflation, the equilibrium moves from point 1 to point 2, at the intersection of B_2^d and B_2^s. The equilibrium bond price falls from P_1 to P_2 and, because the bond price is negatively related to the interest rate, this means that the interest rate rises. Note that Figure 4 has been drawn so that the equilibrium quantity of bonds remains the same at both point 1 and point 2. However, depending on the size of the shifts in the supply and demand curves, the equilibrium quantity of bonds can either rise or fall when expected inflation rises.

Our supply and demand analysis has led us to an important observation: *When expected inflation rises, interest rates will rise.* This result has been named the **Fisher effect**, after Irving Fisher, the economist who first pointed out the relationship of expected inflation to interest rates. The accuracy of this prediction is shown in Figure 5. The interest rate on three-month Treasury bills has usually moved along with the expected inflation rate. Consequently, many economists recommend that inflation must be kept low if we want to keep nominal interest rates low.

MyEconLab Mini-lecture   MyEconLab Real-time data

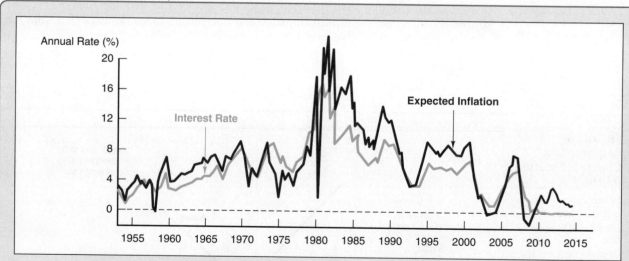

FIGURE 5   Expected Inflation and Interest Rates (Three-Month Treasury Bills), 1953–2014
The interest rate on three-month Treasury bills and the expected inflation rate generally move together, as the Fisher effect predicts.

Sources: **Federal Reserve Bank of St. Louis FRED database:** http://research.stlouisfed.org/fred2/. Expected inflation calculated using procedures outlined in Frederic S. Mishkin, "The Real Interest Rate: An Empirical Investigation," Carnegie-Rochester Conference Series on Public Policy 15 (1981): 151–200. These procedures involve estimating expected inflation as a function of past interest rates, inflation, and time trends.

APPLICATION   Changes in the Interest Rate Due to a Business Cycle Expansion

Figure 6 analyzes the effects of a business cycle expansion on interest rates. In a business cycle expansion, the amounts of goods and services being produced in the economy increase, so national income rises. When this occurs, businesses are more willing to borrow because they are likely to have many profitable investment opportunities for which they need financing. Hence, at a given bond price, the quantity of bonds that firms want to sell (that is, the supply of bonds) will increase. This means that during a business cycle expansion, the supply curve for bonds shifts to the right (see Figure 6) from B_1^s to B_2^s.

Expansion in the economy also affects the demand for bonds. As the economy expands, wealth is likely to increase, and the theory of portfolio choice tells us that the demand for bonds will rise as well. We see this in Figure 6, where the demand curve has shifted to the right, from B_1^d to B_2^d.

Given that both the supply and demand curves have shifted to the right, we know that the new equilibrium reached at the intersection of B_2^d and B_2^s must also move to the right. However, depending on whether the supply curve shifts more than the demand curve or vice versa, the new equilibrium interest rate can either rise or fall.

MyEconLab Mini-lecture

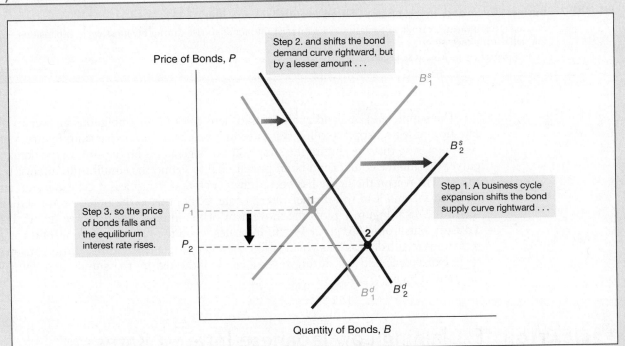

FIGURE 6   **Response to a Business Cycle Expansion**

In a business cycle expansion, when income and wealth are rising, the demand curve shifts rightward from B_1^d to B_2^d. If the supply curve shifts to the right more than the demand curve, as in this figure, the equilibrium bond price moves down from P_1 to P_2 and the equilibrium interest rate rises.

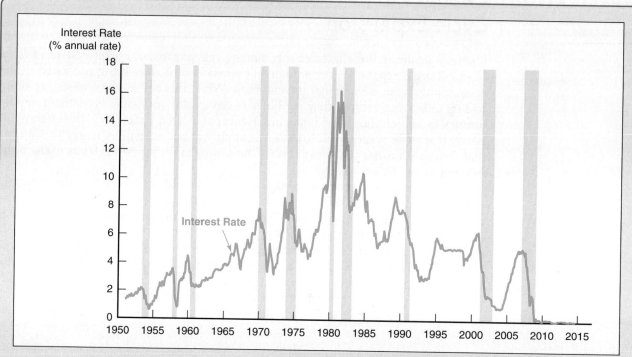

FIGURE 7   Business Cycle and Interest Rates (Three-Month Treasury Bills), 1951–2014

Shaded areas indicate periods of recession. The interest rate tends to rise during business cycle expansions and fall during recessions.

Source: **Federal Reserve Bank of St. Louis FRED database:** http://research.stlouisfed.org/fred2/

The supply and demand analysis used here gives us an ambiguous answer to the question of what happens to interest rates in a business cycle expansion. Figure 6 has been drawn so that the shift in the supply curve is greater than the shift in the demand curve, causing the equilibrium bond price to fall to P_2 and the equilibrium interest rate to rise. The reason the figure has been drawn such that a business cycle expansion and a rise in income lead to a higher interest rate is that this is the outcome we actually see in the data. Figure 7 plots the movement of the interest rate on three-month U.S. Treasury bills from 1951 to 2014 and indicates when the business cycle went through recessions (shaded areas). As you can see, the interest rate tends to rise during business cycle expansions and fall during recessions, as indicated by the supply and demand diagram in Figure 6.

APPLICATION   Explaining Low Japanese Interest Rates

In the 1990s and early 2000s, Japanese interest rates became the lowest in the world. Indeed, in November 1998, an extraordinary event occurred: Interest rates on Japanese six-month Treasury bills even turned slightly negative! Why did Japanese interest rates drop to such low levels?

In the late 1990s and early 2000s, Japan experienced a prolonged recession, which was accompanied by deflation (a negative inflation rate). We can use these facts, along with an analysis similar to that used in the preceding applications, to explain the low Japanese interest rates.

Negative inflation caused the demand for bonds to rise because the expected return on real assets fell, thereby raising the relative expected return on bonds and in turn causing the demand curve to shift to the right. Negative inflation also raised the real interest rate and therefore the real cost of borrowing for any given nominal rate, thereby causing the supply of bonds to contract and the supply curve to shift to the left. The outcome was then exactly the opposite of that graphed in Figure 4: The rightward shift of the demand curve and leftward shift of the supply curve led to a rise in the bond price and a fall in interest rates.

The business cycle contraction and the resulting lack of profitable investment opportunities in Japan also led to lower interest rates by decreasing the supply of bonds and shifting the supply curve to the left. Although the demand curve also shifted to the left because wealth decreased during the business cycle contraction, the demand curve shifted less than the supply curve, just as we saw in the preceding application. Thus, the bond price rose and interest rates fell (the opposite outcome of that in Figure 6).

Usually we think that low interest rates are a good thing because they make it cheap to borrow. But the Japanese example shows that just as a fallacy is present in the adage "You can never be too rich or too thin" (maybe you can't be too rich, but you can certainly be too thin and thereby damage your health), a fallacy is present in always thinking that lower interest rates are better. In Japan, the low and even negative interest rates were a sign that the country was in real trouble, with falling prices and a contracting economy. Only when the Japanese economy returns to health will interest rates rise back to more normal levels. ◆

SUPPLY AND DEMAND IN THE MARKET FOR MONEY: THE LIQUIDITY PREFERENCE FRAMEWORK

An alternative model for determining the equilibrium interest rate, developed by John Maynard Keynes, is known as the **liquidity preference framework**. This framework determines the equilibrium interest rate in terms of the supply of and demand for money rather than the supply of and demand for bonds. Although the two frameworks look different, the liquidity preference analysis of the market for money is closely related to the supply and demand framework of the bond market.[4]

The starting point of Keynes's analysis is his assumption that people use two main categories of assets to store their wealth: money and bonds. Therefore, total wealth in the economy must equal the total quantity of bonds plus money in the economy, which equals the quantity of bonds supplied (B^s) plus the quantity of money supplied (M^s).

[4]Note that the term *market for money* refers to the market for the medium of exchange, money. This market differs from the *money market* referred to by finance practitioners, which, as discussed in Chapter 2, is the financial market in which short-term debt instruments are traded.

The quantity of bonds demanded (B^d) plus the quantity of money demanded (M^d) must also equal the total amount of wealth, because people cannot purchase more assets than their available resources allow. Thus the quantity of bonds and money supplied must equal the quantity of bonds and money demanded:

$$B^s + M^s = B^d + M^d \tag{2}$$

Collecting the bond terms on one side of the equation and the money terms on the other, this equation can be rewritten as

$$B^s - B^d = M^d - M^s \tag{3}$$

Equation 3 tells us that if the market for money is in equilibrium ($M^s = M^d$), then the right-hand side of the equation equals zero, implying that $B^s = B^d$, which in turn means the bond market is also in equilibrium.

Thus we arrive at the same result whether we determine the equilibrium interest rate by equating the supply and demand for bonds or by equating the supply and demand for money. In this sense, the liquidity preference framework, which analyzes the market for money, is equivalent to a framework analyzing supply and demand in the bond market. In practice, the approaches differ because, by assuming there are only two kinds of assets, money and bonds, the liquidity preference approach implicitly ignores any effects on interest rates that arise from changes in the expected returns on real assets such as automobiles and houses. In most instances, however, both frameworks yield the same predictions.

The reason we approach the determination of interest rates using both frameworks is that the bond supply and demand framework is easier to use when analyzing the effects caused by changes in expected inflation, whereas the liquidity preference framework is easier to use when analyzing the effects caused by changes in income, the price level, and the supply of money.

Because the definition of money used by Keynes includes currency (which earns no interest) and checking account deposits (which in his time typically earned little or no interest), he assumed that money has a zero rate of return. Bonds, the only alternative asset to money in Keynes's framework, have an expected return equal to the interest rate i.[5] As this interest rate rises (holding everything else unchanged), the expected return on money falls relative to the expected return on bonds, causing a fall in the quantity of money demanded, as predicted by the theory of portfolio choice.

We can also see that the quantity of money demanded and the interest rate should be negatively related by using the concept of **opportunity cost**, which is the amount of interest (expected return) sacrificed by not holding the alternative asset—in this case, a bond. As the interest rate on bonds, i, rises, the opportunity cost of holding money rises; thus money is less desirable and the quantity of money demanded falls.

Figure 8 shows the quantity of money demanded at a number of interest rates, with all other economic variables, such as income and the price level, held constant. At an interest rate of 25%, point A shows that the quantity of money demanded is

---

[5]Keynes did not actually assume that the expected returns on bonds equaled the interest rate but rather argued that they were closely related. This distinction makes no appreciable difference in our analysis.

MyEconLab Mini-lecture

FIGURE 8
Equilibrium in the Market for Money

Equilibrium in the market for money occurs at point C, the intersection of the money demand curve M^d and the money supply curve M^s. The equilibrium interest rate is $i^* = 15\%$.

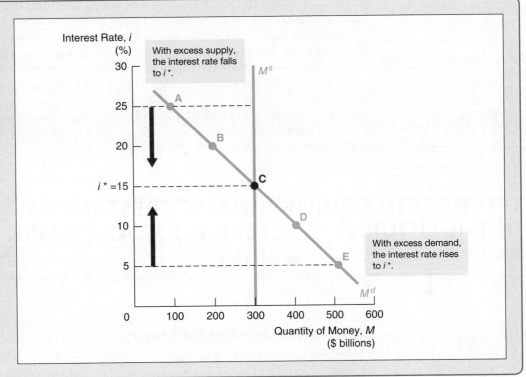

$100 billion. If the interest rate is at the lower rate of 20%, the opportunity cost of holding money is lower, and the quantity of money demanded rises to $200 billion, as indicated by the move from point A to point B. If the interest rate is even lower, the quantity of money demanded is even higher, as is indicated by points C, D, and E. The curve M^d connecting these points is the demand curve for money, and it slopes downward.

At this point in our analysis, we will assume that a central bank controls the amount of money supplied at a fixed quantity of $300 billion, so that the supply curve for money M^s in the figure is a vertical line at $300 billion. The equilibrium at which the quantity of money demanded equals the quantity of money supplied occurs at the intersection of the supply and demand curves at point C, where

$$M^d = M^s \tag{4}$$

The resulting equilibrium interest rate is $i^* = 15\%$.

We can again see that there is a tendency to approach this equilibrium rate by first looking at the relationship of money demand and supply when the interest rate is above the equilibrium interest rate. When the interest rate is 25%, the quantity of money demanded at point A is $100 billion, yet the quantity of money supplied is $300 billion. The excess supply of money means that people are holding more money than they desire, so they will try to get rid of their excess money balances by trying to buy bonds.

Accordingly, they will bid up the price of bonds. As the bond price rises, the interest rate will fall toward the equilibrium interest rate of 15%. This tendency is shown by the downward arrow drawn at the interest rate of 25%.

Likewise, if the interest rate is 5%, the quantity of money demanded at point E is $500 billion, but the quantity of money supplied is only $300 billion. An excess demand for money now exists because people want to hold more money than they currently have. To try to obtain more money, they will sell their only other asset—bonds—and the price will fall. As the price of bonds falls, the interest rate will rise toward the equilibrium rate of 15%. Only when the interest rate is at its equilibrium value will there be no tendency for it to move further, and so the interest rate will settle at this value.

CHANGES IN EQUILIBRIUM INTEREST RATES IN THE LIQUIDITY PREFERENCE FRAMEWORK

In order to use the liquidity preference framework to analyze how the equilibrium interest rate changes, we must understand what causes the demand and supply curves for money to shift.

Shifts in the Demand for Money

In Keynes's liquidity preference analysis, two factors cause the demand curve for money to shift: income and the price level.

Income Effect   In Keynes's view, there were two reasons why income would affect the demand for money. First, as an economy expands and income rises, wealth increases and people want to hold more money as a store of value. Second, as the economy expands and income rises, people want to carry out more transactions using money as a medium of exchange, and so they also want to hold more money. The conclusion is that *a higher level of income causes the demand for money at each interest rate to increase and the demand curve to shift to the right.*

Price-Level Effect   Keynes took the view that people care about the amount of money they hold in real terms—that is, in terms of the goods and services it can buy. When the price level rises, the same nominal quantity of money is no longer as valuable; it cannot be used to purchase as many real goods or services. To restore their holdings of money in real terms to the former level, people will want to hold a greater nominal quantity of money, so *a rise in the price level causes the demand for money at each interest rate to increase and the demand curve to shift to the right.*

Shifts in the Supply of Money

We will assume that the supply of money is completely controlled by the central bank, which in the United States is the Federal Reserve. (Actually, the process that determines the money supply is substantially more complicated, involving banks, depositors, and borrowers from banks. We will study it in more detail later in the book.) For now, all we need to know is that *an increase in the money supply engineered by the Federal Reserve will shift the supply curve for money to the right.*

APPLICATION Changes in the Equilibrium Interest Rate Due to Changes in Income, the Price Level, or the Money Supply

To see how we can use the liquidity preference framework to analyze the movement of interest rates, we will again look at several applications that will help us evaluate the effect of monetary policy on interest rates. In going through these applications, remember to use the *ceteris paribus* assumption: When examining the effect of a change in one variable, hold all other variables constant. (As a study aid, Table 4 summarizes the shifts in the demand and supply curves for money.)

SUMMARY TABLE 4				
Factors That Shift the Demand for and Supply of Money				
Variable	**Change in Variable**	**Change in Money Demand (M^d) or Supply (M^s) at Each Interest Rate**	**Change in Interest Rate**	
Income	↑	M^d↑	↑	
Price level	↑	M^d↑	↑	
Money supply	↑	M^s↑	↓	

Note: Only increases in the variables are shown. The effects of decreases in the variables on demand and supply would be the opposite of those indicated in the remaining columns.

MyEconLab Mini-lecture

FIGURE 9
Response to a Change in Income or the Price Level

In a business cycle expansion, when income is rising, or when the price level rises, the demand curve shifts from M_1^d to M_2^d. The supply curve is fixed at $M^s = \overline{M}$. The equilibrium interest rate rises from i_1 to i_2.

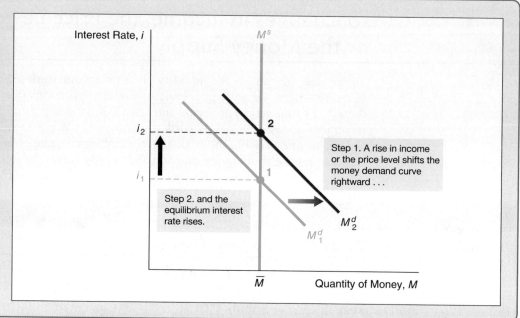

Step 1. A rise in income or the price level shifts the money demand curve rightward . . .

Step 2. and the equilibrium interest rate rises.

Changes in Income

We have seen that when income is rising during a business cycle expansion, the demand for money will rise, shown in Figure 9 by the rightward shift in the demand curve from M_1^d to M_2^d. The new equilibrium is reached at point 2, at the intersection of the M_2^d curve with the money supply curve M^s. As you can see, the equilibrium interest rate rises from i_1 to i_2. The liquidity preference framework thus generates the conclusion that **when income is rising during a business cycle expansion (holding other economic variables constant), interest rates will rise.** This conclusion is unambiguous, unlike the conclusion we reached using the bond demand and supply framework.

Changes in the Price Level

When the price level rises, the value of money in terms of its purchasing power is lower. To restore their money's purchasing power in real terms to its former level, people will want to hold a greater nominal quantity of money. A higher price level shifts the demand curve for money to the right from M_1^d to M_2^d (see Figure 9). The equilibrium moves from point 1 to point 2, where the equilibrium interest rate has risen from i_1 to i_2, illustrating that **when the price level increases, with the supply of money and other economic variables held constant, interest rates will rise.**

Changes in the Money Supply

An increase in the money supply due to expansionary monetary policy by the Federal Reserve implies that the supply curve for money will shift to the right. As shown in Figure 10 by the movement of the supply curve from M_1^s to M_2^s, the equilibrium moves

MyEconLab Mini-lecture

FIGURE 10
**Response to a
Change in the
Money Supply**
When the money
supply increases, the
supply curve shifts
from M_1^s to M_2^s and
the equilibrium
interest rate falls
from i_1 to i_2.

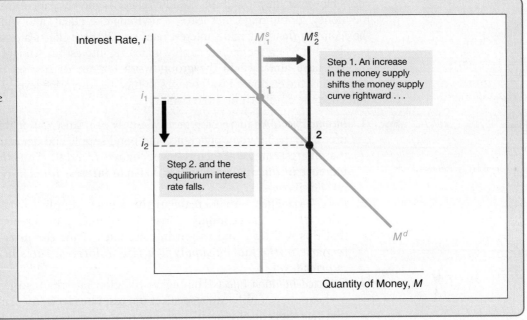

from point 1 down to point 2, where the M_2^s supply curve intersects with the demand curve M^d and the equilibrium interest rate has fallen from i_1 to i_2. **When the money supply increases (everything else remaining equal), interest rates will decline.**[6]

MONEY AND INTEREST RATES

The liquidity preference analysis in Figure 10 seems to suggest that an increase in the money supply will lower interest rates. This conclusion has important policy implications because it has frequently caused politicians to call for a more rapid growth of the money supply in an effort to drive down interest rates.

But is it correct to conclude that money and interest rates should be negatively related? Might other important factors have been left out of the liquidity preference analysis in Figure 10, factors that would reverse this conclusion? We will provide answers to these questions by applying the supply and demand analysis we used in this chapter to obtain a deeper understanding of the relationship between money and interest rates.

An important criticism of the idea that an increase in the money supply lowers interest rates was raised by Milton Friedman, a Nobel laureate in economics. He acknowledged that the liquidity preference analysis was correct and called the result—that an increase

[6]This same result can be generated using the bond supply and demand framework. As we will see in Chapter 14, a central bank increases the money supply primarily by buying bonds and thereby decreasing the supply of bonds available to the public. The resulting shift to the left of the supply curve for bonds leads to an increase in the equilibrium price of bonds and a decline in the equilibrium interest rate.

in the money supply (*everything else remaining equal*) lowers interest rates—the *liquidity effect*. However, he viewed the liquidity effect as merely part of the story: An increase in the money supply might not leave "everything else equal" and will have other effects on the economy that may make interest rates rise. If these effects are substantial, it is entirely possible that when the money supply increases, interest rates might also increase.

We have already laid the groundwork for our discussion of these other effects, because we have shown how changes in income, the price level, and expected inflation influence the equilibrium interest rate.

1. *Income Effect*. An increasing money supply can cause national income and wealth to rise. Both the liquidity preference and bond supply and demand frameworks indicate that interest rates will then rise (see Figures 6 and 9). Thus **the income effect of an increase in the money supply is a rise in interest rates in response to the higher level of income.**

2. *Price-Level Effect*. An increase in the money supply can also cause the overall price level in the economy to rise. The liquidity preference framework predicts that this will lead to a rise in interest rates. Thus **the price-level effect from an increase in the money supply is a rise in interest rates in response to the rise in price level.**

3. *Expected-Inflation Effect*. The higher inflation rate that can result from an increase in the money supply can also affect interest rates by influencing the expected inflation rate. Specifically, an increase in the money supply may lead people to expect a higher price level in the future—and hence the expected inflation rate will be higher. The bond supply and demand framework has shown us that this increase in expected inflation will lead to a higher level of interest rates. Therefore, **the expected-inflation effect of an increase in the money supply is a rise in interest rates in response to the rise in the expected inflation rate.**

At first glance it might appear that the price-level effect and the expected-inflation effect are the same thing. They both indicate that increases in the price level induced by an increase in the money supply will raise interest rates. However, there is a subtle difference between the two, and this is why they are discussed as two separate effects.

Suppose that a one-time increase in the money supply today leads to a rise in prices to a permanently higher level by next year. As the price level rises over the course of this year, the interest rate will rise via the price-level effect. Only at the end of the year, when the price level has risen to its peak, will the price-level effect be at a maximum.

The rising price level will also raise interest rates via the expected-inflation effect, because people will expect that inflation will be higher over the course of the year. However, when the price level stops rising next year, inflation and the expected inflation rate will return to zero. Any rise in interest rates as a result of the earlier rise in expected inflation will then be reversed. We thus see that in contrast to the price-level effect, which reaches its greatest impact next year, the expected-inflation effect will have its smallest impact (zero impact) next year. The basic difference between the two effects, then, is that the price-level effect remains even after prices have stopped rising, whereas the expected-inflation effect disappears.

An important point is that the expected-inflation effect will persist only as long as the price level continues to rise. As we will see in our discussion of monetary theory in subsequent chapters, a one-time increase in the money supply will not produce a continually rising price level; only a higher rate of money supply growth will. Thus a higher rate of money supply growth is needed if the expected-inflation effect is to persist.

APPLICATION Does a Higher Rate of Growth of the Money Supply Lower Interest Rates?

We can now put together all the effects we have discussed to help us decide whether our analysis supports the politicians who advocate a greater rate of growth of the money supply when they feel that interest rates are too high. Of all the effects, only the liquidity effect indicates that a higher rate of money growth will cause a decline in interest rates. In contrast, the income, price-level, and expected-inflation effects indicate that interest rates will rise when money growth is higher. Which of these effects is largest, and how quickly does each take effect? The answers are critical in determining whether interest rates will rise or fall when money supply growth is increased.

Generally, the liquidity effect from greater money growth takes effect immediately, because the rising money supply leads to an immediate decline in the equilibrium interest rate. The income and price-level effects take longer to work because time is needed for the increasing money supply to raise the price level and income, which in turn raise interest rates. The expected-inflation effect, which also raises interest rates, can be slow or fast, depending on whether people adjust their expectations of inflation slowly or quickly when the money growth rate is increased.

Three possibilities are outlined in Figure 11; each shows how interest rates respond over time to an increased rate of money supply growth, starting at time T. Panel (a) shows a case in which the liquidity effect dominates the other effects so that the interest rate falls from i_1 at time T to a final level of i_2. The liquidity effect operates quickly to lower the interest rate, but as time goes by, the other effects start to reverse some of the decline. Because the liquidity effect is larger than the others, however, the interest rate never rises back to its initial level.

In panel (b), the liquidity effect is smaller than the other effects, with the expected-inflation effect operating slowly because expectations of inflation are slow to adjust upward. Initially, the liquidity effect drives down the interest rate. Then the income, price-level, and expected-inflation effects begin to raise it. Because these effects are dominant, the interest rate eventually rises above its initial level to i_2. In the short run, lower interest rates result from increased money growth, but eventually they end up climbing above the initial level.

In panel (c), the expected-inflation effect dominates and operates rapidly because people quickly raise their expectations of inflation when the rate of money growth increases. The expected-inflation effect begins immediately to overpower the liquidity effect, and the interest rate immediately starts to climb. Over time, as the income and price-level effects start to take hold, the interest rate rises even higher, and the eventual outcome is an interest rate that is substantially higher than the initial interest rate. The result shows clearly that increasing money supply growth is not the answer to reducing interest rates; rather, money growth should be *reduced* to lower interest rates!

An important issue for economic policymakers is deciding which of these three scenarios is closest to reality. If a decline in interest rates is desired, then an increase in money supply growth is called for when the liquidity effect dominates the other effects, as in panel (a). A decrease in money growth is appropriate when the other effects dominate the liquidity effect and expectations of inflation adjust rapidly, as in panel (c). If the other effects dominate the liquidity effect but expectations of inflation adjust only slowly, as in panel (b), then the decision to increase or decrease money growth depends on whether policymakers care more about what happens in the short run or in the long run.

MyEconLab Mini-lecture

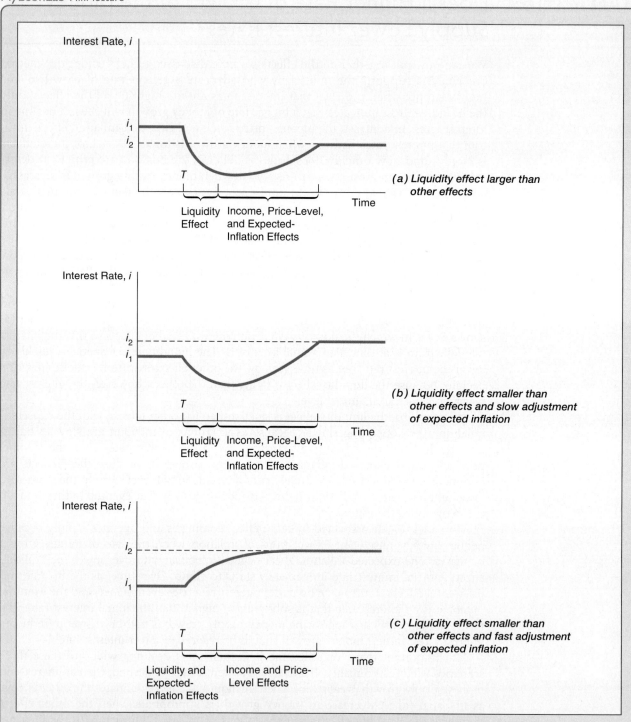

FIGURE 11   Response over Time to an Increase in Money Supply Growth
Each panel shows how interest rates respond over time to an increased rate of money supply growth, starting at time *T*.

MyEconLab Mini-lecture   MyEconLab Real-time data

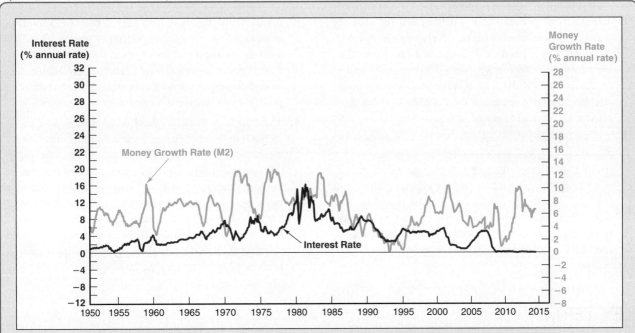

FIGURE 12   **Money Growth (M2, Annual Rate) and Interest Rates (Three-Month Treasury Bills), 1950–2014**

When the rate of money supply growth began to climb in the mid-1960s, interest rates rose, indicating that the liquidity effect was dominated by the price-level, income, and expected-inflation effects. By the 1970s, both interest rates and money growth reached levels unprecedented in the post–World War II period.

Source: **Federal Reserve Bank of St. Louis FRED database:** http://research.stlouisfed.org/fred2/

Which scenario is supported by the evidence? The relationship between interest rates and money growth from 1950 to 2014 is plotted in Figure 12. When the rate of money supply growth began to climb in the mid-1960s, interest rates rose, indicating that the liquidity effect was dominated by the price-level, income, and expected-inflation effects. By the 1970s, interest rates reached levels unprecedented in the post–World War II period, as did the rate of money supply growth.

The scenario depicted in panel (a) of Figure 11 seems doubtful, and the case for lowering interest rates by raising the rate of money growth is much weakened. Looking back at Figure 5, which shows the relationship between interest rates and expected inflation, you should not find this too surprising. The rise in the rate of money supply growth in the 1960s and 1970s is matched by a large rise in expected inflation, which would lead us to predict that the expected-inflation effect would be dominant. It is the most plausible explanation for why interest rates rose in the face of higher money growth. However, Figure 12 does not really tell us which one of the two scenarios depicted in panels (b) and (c) of Figure 11 is more accurate. It depends critically on how fast people's expectations about inflation adjust. Research done using more sophisticated methods than just looking at a graph like Figure 12 indicates that increased money growth temporarily lowers short-term interest rates and thus conforms to the scenario in panel (b). ◆

SUMMARY

1. The theory of portfolio choice tells us that the quantity demanded of an asset is (a) positively related to wealth, (b) positively related to the expected return on the asset relative to alternative assets, (c) negatively related to the riskiness of the asset relative to alternative assets, and (d) positively related to the liquidity of the asset relative to alternative assets.

2. The supply and demand analysis for bonds provides one theory of how interest rates are determined. It predicts that interest rates will change when there is a change in demand caused by changes in income (or wealth), expected returns, risk, or liquidity, or when there is a change in supply caused by changes in the attractiveness of investment opportunities, the real cost of borrowing, or the government budget.

3. An alternative theory of how interest rates are determined is provided by the liquidity preference framework, which analyzes the supply of and demand for money. It shows that interest rates will change when the demand for money changes because of alterations in income or the price level, or when the supply of money changes.

4. There are four possible effects on interest rates of an increase in the money supply: the liquidity effect, the income effect, the price-level effect, and the expected-inflation effect. The liquidity effect indicates that a rise in money supply growth will lead to a decline in interest rates; the other effects work in the opposite direction. The evidence seems to indicate that the income, price-level, and expected-inflation effects dominate the liquidity effect such that an increase in money supply growth leads to higher—rather than lower—interest rates.

KEY TERMS

asset market approach, p. 91
demand curve, p. 88
excess demand, p. 90
excess supply, p. 90
expected return, p. 86

Fisher effect, p. 98
liquidity, p. 86
liquidity preference framework, p. 101
market equilibrium, p. 90

opportunity cost, p. 102
risk, p. 86
supply curve, p. 89
theory of portfolio choice, p. 87
wealth, p. 86

QUESTIONS

All questions are available in MyEconLab *at* http://www.myeconlab.com.

1. Explain why you would be more or less willing to buy a share of Microsoft stock in the following situations:

   a. Your wealth falls.

   b. You expect the stock to appreciate in value.

   c. The bond market becomes more liquid.

   d. You expect gold to appreciate in value.

   e. Prices in the bond market become more volatile.

2. Explain why you would be more or less willing to buy a house under the following circumstances:

   a. You just inherited $100,000.

   b. Real estate commissions fall from 6% of the sales price to 5% of the sales price.

   c. You expect Microsoft stock to double in value next year.

   d. Prices in the stock market become more volatile.

   e. You expect housing prices to fall.

3. Explain why you would be more or less willing to buy gold under the following circumstances:

   a. Gold again becomes acceptable as a medium of exchange.

   b. Prices in the gold market become more volatile.

   c. You expect inflation to rise, and gold prices tend to move with the aggregate price level.

   d. You expect interest rates to rise.

4. Explain why you would be more or less willing to buy long-term AT&T bonds under the following circumstances:

   a. Trading in these bonds increases, making them easier to sell.

   b. You expect a bear market in stocks (stock prices are expected to decline).

c. Brokerage commissions on stocks fall.

d. You expect interest rates to rise.

e. Brokerage commissions on bonds fall.

5. What will happen to the demand for Rembrandt paintings if the stock market undergoes a boom? Why?

6. "The more risk-averse people are, the more likely they are to diversify." Is this statement true, false, or uncertain? Explain your answer.

7. "No one who is risk-averse will ever buy a security that has a lower expected return, more risk, and less liquidity than another security." Is this statement true, false, or uncertain? Explain your answer.

8. What effect will a sudden increase in the volatility of gold prices have on interest rates?

9. How might a sudden increase in people's expectations of future real estate prices affect interest rates?

10. Explain what effect a large federal deficit should have on interest rates.

11. In the aftermath of the global economic crisis that started to take hold in 2008, U.S. government budget deficits increased dramatically, yet interest rates on U.S. Treasury debt fell sharply and stayed low for quite some time. Does this make sense? Why or why not?

12. Will there be an effect on interest rates if brokerage commissions on stocks fall? Explain your answer.

13. The president of the United States announces in a press conference that he will fight the higher inflation rate with a new anti-inflation program. Predict what will happen to interest rates if the public believes him.

14. Predict what will happen to interest rates if the public suddenly expects a large increase in stock prices.

15. Predict what will happen to interest rates if prices in the bond market become more volatile.

16. Would fiscal policymakers ever have reason to worry about potentially inflationary conditions? Why or why not?

17. Why should a rise in the price level (but not in expected inflation) cause interest rates to rise when the nominal money supply is fixed?

18. If the next chair of the Federal Reserve Board has a reputation for advocating an even slower rate of money growth than the current chair, what will happen to interest rates? Discuss the possible resulting situations.

19. M1 money growth in the U.S. was about 15% in 2011 and 2012, and 10% in 2013. Over the same time period, the yield on 3-month Treasury bills was close to 0%. Given these high rates of money growth, why did interest rates stay so low, rather than increase? What does this say about the income, price-level, and expected-inflation effects?

APPLIED PROBLEMS

All applied problems are available in MyEconLab *at* http://www.myeconlab.com.

20. Suppose you visit with a financial adviser, and you are considering investing some of your wealth in one of three investment portfolios: stocks, bonds, or commodities. Your financial adviser provides you with the following table, which gives the probabilities of possible returns from each investment:

a. Which investment should you choose to maximize your expected return: stocks, bonds, or commodities?

b. If you are risk-averse and have to choose between the stock and the bond investments, which should you choose? Why?

Stocks		Bonds		Commodities	
Probability	Return	Probability	Return	Probability	Return
0.25	12%	0.6	10%	0.2	20%
0.25	10%	0.4	7.50%	0.25	12%
0.25	8%			0.25	6%
0.25	6%			0.25	4%
				0.05	0%

21. An important way in which the Federal Reserve decreases the money supply is by selling bonds to the public. Using a supply and demand analysis for bonds, show what effect this action has on interest rates. Is your answer consistent with what you would expect to find with the liquidity preference framework?

22. Using both the liquidity preference framework and the supply and demand for bonds framework, show why interest rates are procyclical (rising when the economy is expanding and falling during recessions).

23. Using both the supply and demand for bonds and liquidity preference frameworks, show how interest rates are affected when the riskiness of bonds rises. Are the results the same in the two frameworks?

24. The demand curve and supply curve for one-year discount bonds with a face value of $1,000 are represented by the following equations:

    B^d: Price $= -0.6 \times$ Quantity $+ 1140$

    B^s: Price $=$ Quantity $+ 700$

    a. What is the expected equilibrium price and quantity of bonds in this market?

    b. Given your answer to part (a), what is the expected interest rate in this market?

25. The demand curve and supply curve for one-year discount bonds with a face value of $1,000 are represented by the following equations:

    B^d: Price $= -0.6 \times$ Quantity $+ 1140$

    B^s: Price $=$ Quantity $+ 700$

    Suppose that, as a result of monetary policy actions, the Federal Reserve sells 80 bonds that it holds. Assume that bond demand and money demand are held constant.

    a. How does the Federal Reserve policy affect the bond supply equation?

    b. Calculate the effect of the Federal Reserve's action on the equilibrium interest rate in this market.

DATA ANALYSIS PROBLEMS

The Problems update with real-time data in MyEconLab *and are available for practice or instructor assignment.*

 1. Go to the St. Louis Federal Reserve FRED database, and find data on net worth of households and non-profits (HNONWRQ027S) and the 10-year U.S. treasury bond (GS10). For the net worth indicator, adjust the *units* setting to "Percent Change from Year Ago," and for the 10-year bond, adjust the *frequency* setting to "Quarterly."

   a. What is the percent change in net worth over the most recent year of data available? All else being equal, what do you expect should happen to the price and yield on the 10-year treasury bond? Why?

   b. What is the change in yield on the 10-year treasury bond over the last year of data available? Is this result consistent with your answer to part (a)? Briefly explain.

2. Go to the St. Louis Federal Reserve FRED database, and find data on the M1 money supply (M1SL) and the 10-year U.S. treasury bond rate. For the M1 money supply indicator, adjust the *units* setting to "Percent Change from Year Ago," and for the 10-year treasury bond, adjust the *frequency* setting to "Quarterly." Download the data into a spreadsheet.

   a. Create a scatter plot, with money growth on the horizontal axis and the 10-year treasury rate on the vertical axis, from 2000:Q1 to the most recent quarter of data available. On the scatter plot, graph a fitted (regression) line of the data (there are several ways to do this; however, one particular chart layout has this option built in). Based on the fitted line, are the data consistent with the liquidity effect? Briefly explain.

   b. Repeat part (a), but this time compare the contemporaneous money growth rate with the interest rate four quarters later. For example, create a scatter plot comparing money growth from 2000:Q1 with the interest rate from 2001:Q1, and so on, up to the most recent pairwise data available. Compare your results to those obtained in part (a), and interpret the liquidity effect as it relates to the income, price-level, and expected-inflation effects.

   c. Repeat part (a) again, except this time compare the contemporaneous money growth rate with the interest rate eight quarters later. For example, create a scatter plot comparing money growth from 2000:Q1 with the interest rate from 2002:Q1, and so on, up to the most recent pairwise data available. Assuming the liquidity and other effects are fully incorporated into the bond market after two years, what do your results imply about the overall effect of money growth on interest rates?

d. Based on your answers to parts (a) through (c), how do the actual data on money growth and interest rates compare to the three scenarios presented in Figure 11 of this chapter?

WEB EXERCISES

1. Increasing prices erode the purchasing power of the dollar. It is interesting to compute what goods would have cost at some point in the past after adjusting for inflation. Go to http://minneapolisfed.org/index.cfm. What would a car that costs $22,000 today have cost the year you were born?

2. One of the points made in this chapter is that inflation erodes investment returns. Go to http://www

.moneychimp.com/articles/econ/inflation_calculator .htm and review how changes in inflation alter your real return. What happens to the difference between the adjusted value of an investment and its inflation-adjusted value as

a. inflation increases?

b. the investment horizon lengthens?

c. expected returns increase?

WEB REFERENCES

http://www.federalreserve.gov/releases/H6/Current

The Federal Reserve reports money supply data at 4:30 p.m. every Thursday.

WEB APPENDICES

Please visit the Companion Website at http://www .pearsonhighered.com/mishkin to read the Web appendices to Chapter 5.

Appendix 1: **Models of Asset Pricing**

Appendix 2: **Applying the Asset Market Approach to a Commodity Market: The Case of Gold**

Appendix 3: **Loanable Funds Framework**

The Risk and Term Structure of Interest Rates

Preview

In our supply and demand analysis of interest-rate behavior in Chapter 5, we examined the determination of just one interest rate. Yet we saw earlier that there are enormous numbers of bonds on which the interest rates can and do differ. In this chapter, we complete the interest-rate picture by examining the relationships of the various interest rates to one another. Understanding why interest rates differ from bond to bond can help businesses, banks, insurance companies, and private investors decide which bonds to purchase as investments and which ones to sell.

We first look at why bonds with the same term to maturity have different interest rates. The relationship among these interest rates is called the **risk structure of interest rates**, although risk, liquidity, and income tax rules all play a role in determining the risk structure. A bond's term to maturity also affects its interest rate, and the relationship among interest rates on bonds with different terms to maturity is called the **term structure of interest rates**. In this chapter, we examine the sources and causes of fluctuations in interest rates relative to one another, and look at a number of theories that explain these fluctuations.

RISK STRUCTURE OF INTEREST RATES

Figure 1 shows the yields to maturity for several categories of long-term bonds from 1919 to 2014. It shows us two important features of interest-rate behavior for bonds of the same maturity: Interest rates on different categories of bonds, although they generally move together, differ from one another in any given year, and the spread (or difference) between the interest rates varies over time. The interest rates on municipal bonds, for example, were higher than those on U.S. government (Treasury) bonds in the late 1930s but lower thereafter. In addition, the spread between the interest rates on Baa corporate bonds (riskier than Aaa corporate bonds) and U.S. government bonds was very large during the Great Depression years from 1930–1933, was smaller during the 1940s–1960s, and then widened again afterward. Which factors are responsible for these phenomena?

Default Risk

One attribute of a bond that influences its interest rate is its risk of **default**. Default occurs when the issuer of the bond is unable or unwilling to make interest payments when promised or pay off the face value when the bond matures. Corporations suffering

MyEconLab Mini-lecture   MyEconLab Real-time data

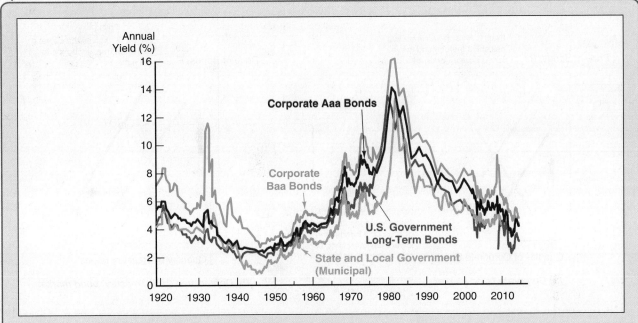

FIGURE 1   Long-Term Bond Yields, 1919–2014

Interest rates on different categories of bonds differ from one another in any given year, and the spread (or difference) between the interest rates varies over time.

Sources: **Board of Governors of the Federal Reserve System,** *Banking and Monetary Statistics, 1941–1970;* **Federal Reserve Bank of St. Louis FRED database:** http://research.stlouisfed.org/fred2.

big losses, such as the major airline companies like United, Delta, US Airways, and Northwest in the mid-2000s, and then American Airlines in 2011, might be more likely to suspend interest payments on their bonds. The default risk on their bonds would therefore be quite high. By contrast, U.S. Treasury bonds have usually been considered to have no default risk because the federal government can always increase taxes or print money to pay off its obligations. Bonds like these with no default risk are called **default-free bonds**. (However, during the budget negotiations in Congress in 2013, which led to a government shutdown, the Republicans threatened to let Treasury bonds default, and this threat had an adverse impact on the bond market.) The spread between interest rates on bonds with default risk and interest rates on default-free bonds, both of the same maturity, is called the **risk premium**. The risk premium indicates how much additional interest people must earn to be willing to hold the risky bond. Our supply and demand analysis of the bond market in Chapter 5 can be used to explain why a bond with default risk always has a positive risk premium, and why a higher default risk means a larger risk premium.

To examine the effect of default risk on interest rates, let's look at the supply and demand diagrams for the default-free (U.S. Treasury) and corporate long-term bond markets in Figure 2. To make the diagrams somewhat easier to read, let's assume that initially corporate bonds have the same default risk as U.S. Treasury bonds. In this case, these two bonds have the same attributes (identical risk and maturity); their equilibrium

MyEconLab Mini-lecture

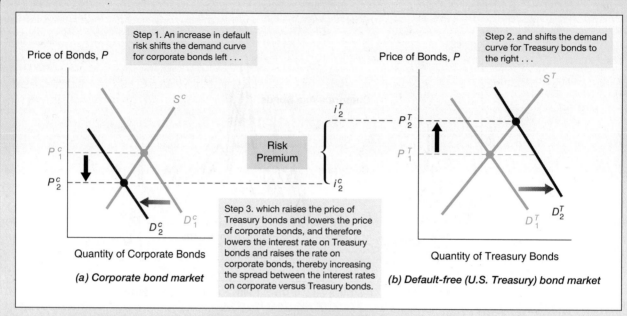

FIGURE 2 **Response to an Increase in Default Risk on Corporate Bonds**
Initially, $P_1^c = P_1^T$, $i_1^c = i_1^T$, and the risk premium is zero. An increase in default risk on corporate bonds shifts the demand curve from D_1^c to D_2^c; simultaneously, it shifts the demand curve for Treasury bonds from D_1^T to D_2^T. The equilibrium price for corporate bonds falls from P_1^c to P_2^c, and the equilibrium interest rate on corporate bonds rises to i_2^c. In the Treasury market, the equilibrium bond price rises from P_1^T to P_2^T, and the equilibrium interest rate falls to i_2^T. The brace indicates the difference between i_2^c and i_2^T, the risk premium on corporate bonds. (Note that because P_2^c is lower than P_2^T, i_2^c is greater than i_2^T.)

prices and interest rates will initially be equal ($P_1^c = P_1^T$ and $i_1^c = i_1^T$), and the risk premium on corporate bonds ($i_1^c - i_1^T$) will be zero.

If the possibility of a default increases because a corporation begins to suffer large losses, the default risk on corporate bonds will increase, and the expected return on these bonds will decrease. In addition, the corporate bond's return will be more uncertain. The theory of portfolio choice predicts that because the expected return on the corporate bond falls relative to the expected return on the default-free Treasury bond while its relative riskiness rises, the corporate bond is less desirable (holding everything else equal), and demand for it will fall. Another way of thinking about this is that if you were an investor, you would want to hold (demand) a smaller amount of corporate bonds. The demand curve for corporate bonds in panel (a) of Figure 2 then shifts to the left, from D_1^c to D_2^c.

At the same time, the expected return on default-free Treasury bonds increases relative to the expected return on corporate bonds, while their relative riskiness declines. The Treasury bonds thus become more desirable, and demand rises, as shown in panel (b) by the rightward shift in the demand curve for these bonds from D_1^T to D_2^T.

As we can see in Figure 2, the equilibrium price for corporate bonds falls from P_1^c to P_2^c, and since the bond price is negatively correlated to the interest rate, the equilibrium interest rate on corporate bonds rises to i_2^c. At the same time, however, the equilibrium price for the Treasury bonds rises from P_1^T to P_2^T and the equilibrium interest rate falls to i_2^T. The spread between the interest rates on corporate and default-free bonds—that is, the risk premium on corporate bonds—has risen from zero to $i_2^c - i_2^T$. We can now conclude that *a bond with default risk will always have a positive risk premium, and an increase in its default risk will raise the risk premium.*

Because default risk is so important to the size of the risk premium, purchasers of bonds need to know whether a corporation is likely to default on its bonds. This information is provided by **credit-rating agencies**, investment advisory firms that rate the quality of corporate and municipal bonds in terms of their probability of default. Credit-rating agencies have become very controversial in recent years because of the role they played in the global financial crisis of 2007–2009 (see the FYI box, "Conflicts of Interest at Credit-Rating Agencies and the Global Financial Crisis"). Table 1 provides

TABLE 1	Bond Ratings by Moody's, Standard and Poor's, and Fitch		
Rating Agency			
Moody's	**S&P**	**Fitch**	**Definitions**
Aaa	AAA	AAA	Prime Maximum Safety
Aa1	AA+	AA+	High Grade High Quality
Aa2	AA	AA	
Aa3	AA−	AA−	
A1	A+	A+	Upper Medium Grade
A2	A	A	
A3	A−	A−	
Baa1	BBB+	BBB+	Lower Medium Grade
Baa2	BBB	BBB	
Baa3	BBB−	BBB−	
Ba1	BB+	BB+	Noninvestment Grade
Ba2	BB	BB	Speculative
Ba3	BB−	BB−	
B1	B−	B−	Highly Speculative
B2	B	B	
B3	B−	B−	
Caa1	CCC+	CCC	Substantial Risk
Caa2	CCC	—	In Poor Standing
Caa3	CCC−	—	
Ca	—	—	Extremely Speculative
C	—	—	May Be in Default
—	—	DDD	Default
—	—	D	
—	D	D	

FYI   Conflicts of Interest at Credit-Rating Agencies and the Global Financial Crisis

Debt ratings play a major role in the pricing of debt securities and in the regulatory process. Conflicts of interest arose for credit-rating agencies in the years leading up to the global financial crisis when these agencies advised clients on how to structure complex financial instruments that paid out cash flows from subprime mortgages. At the same time, the agencies were rating these identical products, leading to potential for severe conflicts of interest. Specifically, the large fees they earned from advising clients on how to structure products that the agencies themselves were rating meant they did not have sufficient incentives to make sure their ratings were accurate.

When housing prices began to fall and subprime mortgages began to default, it became crystal clear that the ratings agencies had done a terrible job of assessing the risk in the subprime products they had helped to structure. Many AAA-rated products had to be downgraded over and over again until they reached junk status. The resulting massive losses on these assets were one reason why so many financial institutions that were holding them got into trouble. Indeed, some commentators have cited credit-rating agencies as among the chief villains that should be blamed for the global financial crisis.

the bond ratings and their descriptions as defined by the three largest credit-rating agencies, Moody's Investor Service, Standard and Poor's Corporation, and Fitch Ratings. Bonds with relatively low risk of default are called *investment-grade* securities and have a rating of Baa (or BBB) and above. Bonds with ratings below Baa (or BBB) have higher default risk and have been aptly dubbed speculative-grade or **junk bonds**. Because these bonds always have higher interest rates than investment-grade securities, they are also referred to as high-yield bonds.

Next let's look at Figure 1 at the beginning of the chapter and see if we can explain the relationship between interest rates on corporate and those on U.S. Treasury bonds. Corporate bonds always have higher interest rates than U.S. Treasury bonds because they always have some risk of default, whereas U.S. Treasury bonds do not. Because Baa-rated corporate bonds have a greater default risk than the higher-rated Aaa bonds, their risk premium is greater, and the Baa rate therefore always exceeds the Aaa rate. We can use the same analysis to explain the huge jump in the risk premium on Baa corporate bond rates during the Great Depression years of 1930–1933, as well as the rise in the risk premium after 1970 (see Figure 1). The Depression period saw a very high rate of business failures and defaults. As we would expect, these factors led to a substantial increase in the default risk for bonds issued by vulnerable corporations, and the risk premium for Baa bonds reached unprecedentedly high levels. Since 1970, we have again seen higher levels of business failures and defaults, although they have been well below Great Depression levels. Again, as expected, both default risks and risk premiums for corporate bonds rose, widening the spread between interest rates on corporate bonds and those on Treasury bonds.

APPLICATION ## The Global Financial Crisis and the Baa-Treasury Spread

Starting in August 2007, the collapse of the subprime mortgage market led to large losses among financial institutions (which we will discuss more extensively in Chapter 12). As a consequence of the subprime collapse and the subsequent global financial crisis, many investors began to doubt the financial health of corporations with low credit ratings such as Baa and even the reliability of the ratings themselves. The perceived increase in default risk for Baa bonds made them less desirable at any given interest rate, decreased the quantity demanded, and shifted the demand curve for Baa bonds to the left. As shown in panel (a) of Figure 2, the interest rate on Baa bonds should have risen, which is indeed what happened. Interest rates on Baa bonds rose by 280 basis points (2.80 percentage points) from 6.63% at the end of July 2007 to 9.43% at the most virulent stage of the global financial crisis in mid-October 2008. But the increase in perceived default risk for Baa bonds in October 2008 made default-free U.S. Treasury bonds relatively more attractive and shifted the demand curve for these securities to the right—an outcome described by some analysts as a "flight to quality." Just as our analysis in Figure 2 predicts, interest rates on Treasury bonds fell by 80 basis points, from 4.78% at the end of July 2007 to 3.98% in mid-October 2008. The spread between interest rates on Baa and Treasury bonds rose by 360 basis points, from 1.85% before the crisis to 5.45% afterward. ◆

Liquidity

Another attribute of a bond that influences its interest rate is its liquidity. As we learned in Chapter 4, a liquid asset is one that can be quickly and cheaply converted into cash if the need arises. The more liquid an asset is, the more desirable it is (holding everything else constant). U.S. Treasury bonds are the most liquid of all long-term bonds; because they are so widely traded, they are the easiest to sell quickly, and the cost of selling them is low. Corporate bonds are not as liquid because fewer bonds for any one corporation are traded; thus it can be costly to sell these bonds in an emergency because it might be hard to find buyers quickly.

How does the reduced liquidity of the corporate bonds affect their interest rates relative to the interest rate on Treasury bonds? We can use supply and demand analysis with the same figure that was used to analyze the effect of default risk, Figure 2, to show that the lower liquidity of corporate bonds relative to Treasury bonds increases the spread between the interest rates on these two bonds. Let's start the analysis by assuming that, initially, corporate and Treasury bonds are equally liquid and all their other attributes are the same. As shown in Figure 2, their equilibrium prices and interest rates will initially be equal: $P_1^c = P_1^T$ and $i_1^c = i_1^T$. If the corporate bond becomes less liquid than the Treasury bond because it is less widely traded, then (as the theory of portfolio choice indicates) demand for it will fall, shifting its demand curve leftward from D_1^c to D_2^c, as in panel (a). The Treasury bond now becomes relatively more liquid in comparison with the corporate bond, so its demand curve shifts rightward from D_1^T to D_2^T, as in panel (b). The shifts in the curves in Figure 2 show that the price of the less liquid corporate bond falls and its interest rate rises, while the price of the more liquid Treasury bond rises and its interest rate falls.

The result is that the spread between the interest rates on the two bond types rises. Therefore, the differences between interest rates on corporate bonds and Treasury bonds (that is, the risk premiums) reflect not only the corporate bond's default risk but also its lesser liquidity. This is why a risk premium should more accurately be called a "risk and liquidity premium," but convention dictates the label *risk premium*.

Income Tax Considerations

Returning to Figure 1, we are still left with one puzzle—the behavior of municipal bond rates. Municipal bonds are certainly not default-free: State and local governments have defaulted on municipal bonds in the past, particularly during the Great Depression, and even more recently in the cases of Detroit, Michigan; San Bernadino, Mammoth Lakes, and Stockton, all in California; Jefferson County, Alabama; Harrisburg, Pennsylvania; Central Falls, Rhode Island; and Boise County, Idaho. Also, municipal bonds are not as liquid as U.S. Treasury bonds.

Why is it, then, that these bonds have had lower interest rates than U.S. Treasury bonds for most of the past 70 years, as indicated in Figure 1? The explanation lies in the fact that interest payments on municipal bonds are exempt from federal income taxes, a factor that has the same effect on the demand for municipal bonds as an increase in their expected return.

Let's imagine that your income is high enough to put you in the 40% income tax bracket, where for every extra dollar of income you earn you have to pay 40 cents to the government. If you own a $1,000-face-value U.S. Treasury bond that sells for $1,000 and has a coupon payment of $100, you get to keep only $60 of the payment after taxes. Although the bond has a 10% interest rate, you actually earn only 6.0% after taxes.

Suppose, however, that you put your savings into a $1,000-face-value municipal bond that sells for $1,000 and pays only $80 in coupon payments. Its interest rate is only 8%, but because it is a tax-exempt security, you pay no taxes on the $80 coupon payment, so you earn 8% after taxes. Clearly, you earn more on the municipal bond after taxes, so you are willing to hold the riskier and less liquid municipal bond even though it has a lower interest rate than the U.S. Treasury bond. (This was not true before World War II, when the tax-exempt status of municipal bonds did not convey much of an advantage because income tax rates were extremely low.)

Another way of understanding why municipal bonds have lower interest rates than Treasury bonds is to use the supply and demand analysis depicted in Figure 3. We initially assume that municipal and Treasury bonds have identical attributes and so have the same bond prices as drawn in the figure, $P_1^m = P_1^T$, and the same interest rates. Once the municipal bonds are given a tax advantage that raises their after-tax expected return relative to Treasury bonds and makes them more desirable, demand for them rises, and their demand curve shifts to the right, from D_1^m to D_2^m. Their equilibrium bond price then rises from P_1^m to P_2^m, and their equilibrium interest rate falls. By contrast, Treasury bonds have now become less desirable relative to municipal bonds; demand for Treasury bonds decreases, and D_1^T shifts to the left to D_2^T. The Treasury bond price falls from P_1^T to P_2^T, and the interest rate rises. The resulting lower interest rates for municipal bonds and higher interest rates for Treasury bonds explain why municipal bonds can have interest rates below those of Treasury bonds.[1]

[1]In contrast to corporate bonds, Treasury bonds are exempt from state and local income taxes. Using the analysis in the text, you should be able to show that this feature of Treasury bonds provides an additional reason why interest rates on corporate bonds are higher than those on Treasury bonds.

MyEconLab Mini-lecture

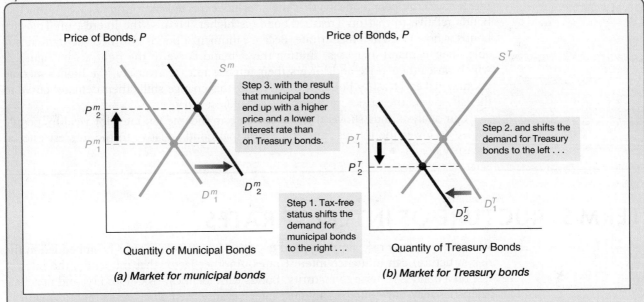

Step 3. with the result that municipal bonds end up with a higher price and a lower interest rate than on Treasury bonds.

Step 1. Tax-free status shifts the demand for municipal bonds to the right . . .

Step 2. and shifts the demand for Treasury bonds to the left . . .

(a) Market for municipal bonds

(b) Market for Treasury bonds

FIGURE 3   Interest Rates on Municipal and Treasury Bonds

When a municipal bond is given tax-free status, demand for the municipal bond shifts rightward from D_1^m to D_2^m, and demand for the Treasury bond shifts leftward from D_1^T to D_2^T. The equilibrium price of the municipal bond rises from P_1^m to P_2^m, so its interest rate falls, while the equilibrium price of the Treasury bond falls from P_1^T to P_2^T and its interest rate rises. The result is that municipal bonds end up with lower interest rates than Treasury bonds.

Summary

The risk structure of interest rates (the relationships among interest rates on bonds with the same maturity) is explained by three factors: default risk, liquidity, and the income tax treatment of a bond's interest payments. As a bond's default risk increases, the risk premium on that bond (the spread between its interest rate and the interest rate on a default-free Treasury bond) rises. The greater liquidity of Treasury bonds also explains why their interest rates are lower than those on less liquid bonds. If a bond has a favorable tax treatment, as do municipal bonds, whose interest payments are exempt from federal income taxes, its interest rate will be lower.

APPLICATION   # Effects of the Obama Tax Increase on Bond Interest Rates

In 2013, Congress approved legislation proposed by the Obama administration to increase the income tax rate on high-income taxpayers fom 35% to 39% when it repealed tax cuts implemented under the Bush administration. What was the effect of this income tax increase on interest rates in the municipal bond market relative to those in the Treasury bond market?

Our supply and demand analysis provides the answer. An increased income tax rate for wealthy people means that the after-tax expected return on tax-free municipal bonds relative to that on Treasury bonds is higher, because the interest on Treasury bonds is now taxed at a higher rate. Because municipal bonds now become more desirable, their demand increases, shifting the demand curve to the right, as in Figure 3, which raises their price and lowers their interest rate. Conversely, the higher income tax rate makes Treasury bonds less desirable; this change shifts their demand curve to the left, lowers their price, and raises their interest rates.

Our analysis thus shows that the increase in income tax rates for wealthy people helped to lower the interest rates on municipal bonds relative to the interest rate on Treasury bonds. ◆

TERM STRUCTURE OF INTEREST RATES

We have seen how risk, liquidity, and tax considerations (collectively embedded in the risk structure) can influence interest rates. Another factor that influences the interest rate on a bond is its term to maturity: Bonds with identical risk, liquidity, and tax characteristics may have different interest rates because their times remaining to maturity are different. A plot of the yields on bonds with differing terms to maturity but the same risk, liquidity, and tax considerations is called a **yield curve**, and it describes the term structure of interest rates for particular types of bonds, such as government bonds. The Following the Financial News box shows a yield curve for Treasury securities. Yield

Following the Financial News   Yield Curves

Many newspapers and Internet sites such as http:// www.finance.yahoo.com publish a daily plot of the yield curves for Treasury securities. An example for July 7, 2014 is presented here. The numbers on the vertical axis indicate the interest rate for the Treasury security, with the maturity term given on the horizontal axis, with "m" denoting "month" and "y" denoting "year."

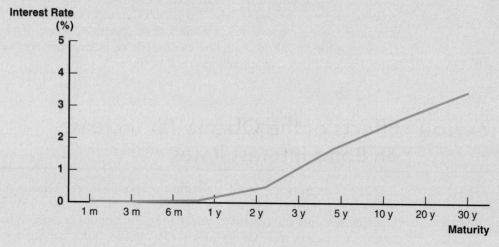

MyEconLab Mini-lecture   MyEconLab Real-time data

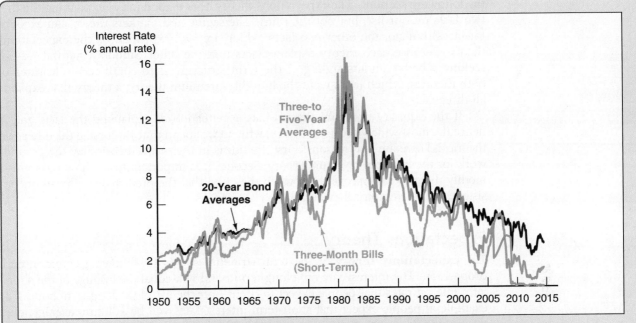

FIGURE 4   **Movements over Time of Interest Rates on U.S. Government Bonds with Different Maturities**

Interest rates on bonds of different maturities move together over time.

Source: **Federal Reserve Bank of St. Louis FRED database:** http://research.stlouisfed.org/fred2/

curves can be classified as upward-sloping, flat, or downward-sloping (the last sort is often referred to as an **inverted yield curve**). When yield curves slope upward, which is the most common case, long-term interest rates are above short-term interest rates; when yield curves are flat, short- and long-term interest rates are the same; and when yield curves are inverted, long-term interest rates are below short-term interest rates. Yield curves can also have more complicated shapes in which they first slope up and then down, or vice versa. Why does the yield curve usually slope upward, but sometimes take on other shapes?

In addition to explaining why yield curves take on different shapes at different times, a good theory of the term structure of interest rates must explain the following three important empirical facts:

1. As we see in Figure 4, interest rates on bonds of different maturities move together over time.
2. When short-term interest rates are low, yield curves are more likely to have an upward slope; when short-term interest rates are high, yield curves are more likely to slope downward and be inverted.
3. Yield curves almost always slope upward, as appears in the Following the Financial News box.

Three theories have been put forward to explain the term structure of interest rates—that is, the relationships among interest rates on bonds of different maturities reflected in yield curve patterns: (1) the expectations theory, (2) the segmented markets theory, and (3) the liquidity premium theory. Each of these theories is described in the following sections. The expectations theory does a good job of explaining the first two facts on our list, but not the third. The segmented markets theory can account for fact 3 but not the other two facts, which are well explained by the expectations theory. Because each theory explains facts that the other cannot, a natural way of seeking a better understanding of the term structure is to combine the features of both theories, which leads us to the liquidity premium theory, a theory that explains all three facts.

If the liquidity premium theory does a better job of explaining the facts and is hence the most widely accepted theory, why do we spend time discussing the other two theories? There are two reasons. First, the ideas in these two theories lay the groundwork for the liquidity premium theory. Second, it is important to see how economists modify theories to improve them when they find that the predicted results are inconsistent with the empirical evidence.

Expectations Theory

The **expectations theory** of the term structure states the following commonsense proposition: The interest rate on a long-term bond will equal the average of the short-term interest rates that people expect to occur over the life of the long-term bond. For example, if people expect that short-term interest rates will be 10%, on average, over the coming five years, the expectations theory predicts that the interest rate on bonds with five years to maturity will be 10%, too. If short-term interest rates are expected to rise even higher after this five-year period, so that the average short-term interest rate over the coming 20 years is 11%, then the interest rate on 20-year bonds will equal 11% and will be higher than the interest rate on five-year bonds. Thus the expectations theory predicts that interest rates on bonds of different maturities differ because short-term interest rates are expected to have different values at future dates.

The key assumption behind this theory is that buyers of bonds do not prefer bonds of one maturity over another, so they will not hold any quantity of a bond if its expected return is less than that of another bond with a different maturity. Bonds that have this characteristic are said to be *perfect substitutes*. In practice, this means that if bonds with different maturities are perfect substitutes, then the expected returns on those bonds must be equal.

To see how the assumption that bonds with different maturities are perfect substitutes leads to the expectations theory, let us consider the following two investment strategies:

1. Purchase a one-year bond, and when it matures in one year, purchase another one-year bond.
2. Purchase a two-year bond and hold it until maturity.

Because both strategies must have the same expected return, the interest rate on the two-year bond must equal the average of the two one-year interest rates. For example, let's say that the current interest rate on the one-year bond is 9%, and you expect the interest rate on the one-year bond next year to be 11%. If you pursue the first strategy of buying the two one-year bonds, the expected return over the two years will average out to be $(9\% + 11\%)/2 = 10\%$ per year. You will be willing to hold both the one- and two-year bonds only if the expected return per year on the two-year bond equals this return. Therefore, the interest rate on the two-year bond must equal 10%, the average interest rate on the two one-year bonds.

We can make this argument more general. For an investment of $1, consider the choice of holding, for two periods, a two-period bond or two one-period bonds. Using the definitions

i_t = today's (time t) interest rate on a one-period bond
i_{t+1}^e = interest rate on a one-period bond expected for next period (time $t + 1$)
i_{2t} = today's (time t) interest rate on the two-period bond

the expected return from investing $1 in the two-period bond and holding it for the two periods can be calculated as

$$(1 + i_{2t}^e)(1 + i_{2t}^e) - 1 = 1 + 2i_{2t} + (i_{2t})^2 - 1 = 2i_{2t} + (i_{2t})^2$$

After the second period, the $1 investment is worth $(1 + i_{2t})(1 + i_{2t})$. Subtracting the $1 initial investment from this amount and dividing by the initial $1 investment gives the rate of return calculated in the previous equation. Because $(i_{2t})^2$ is extremely small—if $i_{2t} = 10\% = 0.10$, then $(i_{2t})^2 = 0.01$—we can simplify the expected return for holding the two-period bond for the two periods to

$$2i_{2t}$$

With the other strategy, in which one-period bonds are bought, the expected return on the $1 investment over the two periods is

$$(1 + i_t)(1 + i_{t+1}^e) - 1 = 1 + i_t + i_{t+1}^e + i_t(i_{t+1}^e) - 1 = i_t + i_{t+1}^e + i_t(i_{t+1}^e)$$

This calculation is derived by recognizing that, after the first period, the $1 investment becomes $1 + i_t$, and this is reinvested in the one-period bond for the next period, yielding an amount $(1 + i_t)(1 + i_{t+1}^e)$. Then, subtracting the $1 initial investment from this amount and dividing by the initial investment of $1 gives the expected return for the strategy of holding one-period bonds for the two periods. Because $i_t(i_{t+1}^e)$ is also extremely small—if $i_t = i_{t+1}^e = 0.10$, then $i_t(i_{t+1}^e) = 0.01$—we can simplify this to

$$i_t + i_{t+1}^e$$

Both bonds will be held only if these expected returns are equal—that is, when

$$2i_{2t} = i_t + i_{t+1}^e$$

Solving for i_{2t} in terms of the one-period rates, we have

$$i_{2t} = \frac{i_t + i_{t+1}^e}{2} \tag{1}$$

which tells us that the two-period rate must equal the average of the two one-period rates. Graphically, this can be shown as

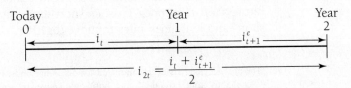

We can conduct the same steps for bonds with longer maturities so that we can examine the whole term structure of interest rates. By doing so, we find that the interest rate i_{nt} on an n-period bond must be

$$i_{nt} = \frac{i_t + i_{t+1}^e + i_{t+2}^e + \ldots + i_{t+(n-1)}^e}{n} \tag{2}$$

Equation 2 states that the n-period interest rate equals the average of the one-period interest rates expected to occur over the n-period life of the bond. This is a restatement of the expectations theory, in more precise terms.[2]

A simple numerical example might help clarify the expectations theory presented in Equation 2. If the one-year interest rates over the next five years are expected to be 5%, 6%, 7%, 8%, and 9%, Equation 2 indicates that the interest rate on the two-year bond will be

$$\frac{5\% + 6\%}{2} = 5.5\%$$

On the five-year bond, it will be

$$\frac{5\% + 6\% + 7\% + 8\% + 9\%}{5} = 7\%$$

By doing similar calculations for the one-, three-, and four-year interest rates, you should be able to verify that the one- to five-year interest rates are 5.0%, 5.5%, 6.0%, 6.5%, and 7.0%, respectively. Thus we see that the rising trend in expected short-term interest rates produces an upward-sloping yield curve along which interest rates rise as maturity lengthens.

The expectations theory is an elegant theory that explains why the term structure of interest rates (as represented by yield curves) changes at different times. When the yield curve is upward-sloping, the expectations theory suggests that short-term interest rates are expected to rise in the future, as we have seen in our numerical example. In this situation, in which the long-term rate is currently higher than the short-term rate, the average of future short-term rates is expected to be higher than the current short-term rate, which can occur only if short-term interest rates are expected to rise. This result is depicted in our numerical example. When the yield curve is inverted (slopes downward), the average of future short-term interest rates is expected to be lower than the current short-term rate, implying that short-term interest rates are expected to fall, on average, in the future. Only when the yield curve is flat does the expectations theory suggest that short-term interest rates are not expected to change, on average, in the future.

The expectations theory also explains fact 1, which states that interest rates on bonds with different maturities move together over time. Historically, short-term interest rates have shown the following trend: If they increase today, they will tend to be higher in the future. Hence a rise in short-term rates will raise people's expectations of future higher short-term rates. Because long-term rates are the average of expected future short-term rates, a rise in short-term rates will also raise long-term rates, causing short- and long-term rates to move together.

[2]The analysis here has been conducted for discount bonds. Formulas for interest rates on coupon bonds would differ slightly from those used here, but would convey the same principle.

The expectations theory also explains fact 2, which states that yield curves tend to have an upward slope when short-term interest rates are low and be inverted when short-term rates are high. When short-term rates are low, people generally expect them to rise to some normal level in the future, and the average of future expected short-term rates is high relative to the current short-term rate. Therefore, long-term interest rates will be substantially higher than current short-term rates, and the yield curve will have an upward slope. Conversely, if short-term rates are high, people usually expect them to come back down. Long-term rates will then drop below short-term rates because the average of expected future short-term rates will be lower than current short-term rates, and the yield curve will slope downward and become inverted.[3]

The expectations theory is an attractive theory because it provides a simple explanation of the behavior of the term structure, but unfortunately it has a major shortcoming: It cannot explain fact 3, which states that yield curves usually slope upward. The typical upward slope of yield curves implies that short-term interest rates are usually expected to rise in the future. In practice, short-term interest rates are just as likely to fall as they are to rise, and so the expectations theory suggests that the typical yield curve should be flat rather than upward-sloping.

Segmented Markets Theory

As the name suggests, the **segmented markets theory** of the term structure sees markets for different-maturity bonds as completely separate and segmented. The interest rate on a bond of a particular maturity is then determined by the supply of and demand for that bond, and is not affected by expected returns on other bonds with other maturities.

The key assumption of the segmented markets theory is that bonds of different maturities are not substitutes at all, and so the expected return from holding a bond of one maturity has no effect on the demand for a bond of another maturity. This theory of the term structure is the opposite extreme of the expectations theory, which assumes that bonds of different maturities are perfect substitutes.

The argument for why bonds of different maturities are not substitutes is that investors have very strong preferences for bonds of one maturity as opposed to another, so they are concerned only with the expected returns on bonds of the maturity they prefer. This might be because they have a particular holding period in mind, and if they match the maturity of the bond to the desired holding period, they can obtain a certain return with no risk at all.[4] (We saw in Chapter 4 that if the term to maturity equals the holding period, then the return is known for certain because it equals the yield exactly, and

---

[3]The expectations theory explains another important fact about the relationship between short-term and long-term interest rates. As you can see in Figure 4, short-term interest rates are more volatile than long-term rates. If interest rates are *mean-reverting*—that is, if they tend to head back down after they reach unusually high levels or go back up after they fall to unusually low levels—then an average of these short-term rates must necessarily have less volatility than the short-term rates themselves. Because the expectations theory suggests that the long-term rate will be equal to an average of future short-term rates, it implies that the long-term rate will have less volatility than short-term rates.

[4]The statement that there is no uncertainty about the return if the term to maturity equals the holding period is literally true only for a discount bond. For a coupon bond with a long holding period, some risk exists because coupon payments must be reinvested before the bond matures. Our analysis here is thus being conducted for discount bonds. However, the gist of the analysis remains the same for coupon bonds because the amount of risk from reinvestment is small when coupon bonds have the same term to maturity as the holding period.

no interest-rate risk exists.) For example, people who are limited by a short holding period will prefer to hold short-term bonds. Conversely, if you are putting away funds for your young child to go to college in the future, your desired holding period will be much longer, and you will want to hold longer-term bonds.

In the segmented markets theory, differing yield curve patterns are accounted for by supply and demand differences associated with bonds of different maturities. If, as seems sensible, risk-averse investors have short desired holding periods and generally prefer bonds with shorter maturities that have less interest-rate risk, the segmented markets theory can explain fact 3, which states that yield curves typically slope upward. Because the demand for long-term bonds is typically relatively lower than that for short-term bonds, long-term bonds will have lower prices and higher interest rates, and hence the yield curve will typically slope upward.

Although the segmented markets theory can explain why yield curves usually tend to slope upward, it has a major flaw in that it cannot explain facts 1 and 2. First, because it views the market for bonds of different maturities as completely segmented, there is no reason that a rise in the interest rate on a bond of one maturity would affect the interest rate on a bond of another maturity. Therefore, the segmented markets theory cannot explain why interest rates on bonds of different maturities tend to move together (fact 1). Second, because it is not clear how the demand for and supply of short- versus long-term bonds change with the level of short-term interest rates, the theory does not explain why yield curves tend to slope upward when short-term interest rates are low and to be inverted when short-term interest rates are high (fact 2).

Because each of our two theories explains empirical facts that the other cannot, a logical step is to combine the theories, which leads us to the liquidity premium theory.

Liquidity Premium and Preferred Habitat Theories

The **liquidity premium theory** of the term structure states that the interest rate on a long-term bond will equal an average of short-term interest rates expected to occur over the life of the long-term bond plus a liquidity premium (also referred to as a term premium) that responds to supply and demand conditions for that bond.

The liquidity premium theory's key assumption is that bonds of different maturities are substitutes, which means that the expected return on one bond *does* influence the expected return on a bond of a different maturity. However, the theory allows investors to prefer one bond maturity over another. In other words, bonds of different maturities are assumed to be substitutes, but not *perfect* substitutes. Investors tend to prefer shorter-term bonds because these bonds bear less interest-rate risk. For this reason, investors must be offered a positive liquidity premium to induce them to hold longer-term bonds. Thus the expectations theory is modified by adding a positive liquidity premium to the equation that describes the relationship between long- and short-term interest rates. The liquidity premium theory is written as

$$i_{nt} = \frac{i_t + i_{t+1}^e + i_{t+2}^e + \; \ldots \; + i_{t+(n-1)}^e}{n} + l_{nt} \tag{3}$$

where l_{nt} is the liquidity (term) premium for the n-period bond at time t, which is always positive and rises with the term to maturity of the bond, n.

Closely related to the liquidity premium theory is the **preferred habitat theory**, which takes a somewhat less direct approach to modifying the expectations hypothesis but comes to a similar conclusion. It assumes that investors have a preference for bonds

MyEconLab Mini-lecture

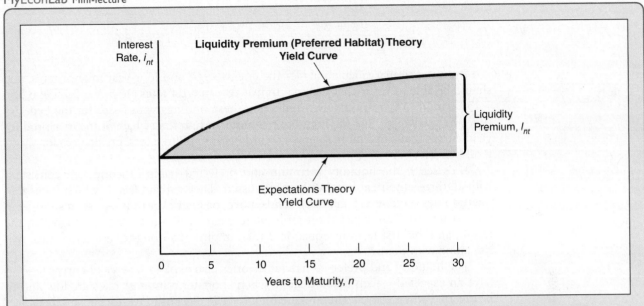

FIGURE 5   The Relationship Between the Liquidity Premium (Preferred Habitat) and Expectations Theory
Because the liquidity premium is always positive and grows as the term to maturity increases, the yield curve implied by the liquidity premium and preferred habitat theories is always above the yield curve implied by the expectations theory and has a steeper slope. For simplicity, the yield curve implied by the expectations theory shown here assumes unchanging future one-year interest rates.

of one maturity over bonds of another—a particular bond maturity ("preferred habitat") in which they prefer to invest. Because they prefer bonds of one maturity over bonds of another, they are willing to buy bonds that do not have the preferred maturity (habitat) only if those bonds earn a somewhat higher expected return. Because risk-averse investors are likely to prefer the habitat of short-term bonds over that of longer-term bonds, they are willing to hold long-term bonds only if they have higher expected returns. This reasoning leads to the same Equation 3 implied by the liquidity premium theory, with a term premium that typically rises with maturity.

The relationship between the expectations theory and the liquidity premium and preferred habitat theories is shown in Figure 5. There we see that because the liquidity premium is always positive and typically grows as the term to maturity increases, the yield curve implied by the liquidity premium theory is always above the yield curve implied by the expectations theory and generally has a steeper slope. (For simplicity, we are assuming that the expectations theory yield curve is flat.)

A simple numerical example, similar to the one we used for the expectations hypothesis, further clarifies the liquidity premium and preferred habitat theories given in Equation 3. Again suppose that the one-year interest rates over the next five years are expected to be 5%, 6%, 7%, 8%, and 9%, while investors' preferences for holding short-term bonds means that the liquidity premiums for one- to five-year bonds are 0%, 0.25%, 0.5%, 0.75%, and 1.0%, respectively. Equation 3 then indicates that the interest rate on the two-year bond would be

$$\frac{5\% + 6\%}{2} + 0.25\% = 5.75\%$$

For the five-year bond, it would be

$$\frac{5\% + 6\% + 7\% + 8\% + 9\%}{5} + 1\% = 8\%$$

By doing similar calculations for the one-, three-, and four-year interest rates, you should be able to verify that the one- to five-year interest rates are 5.0%, 5.75%, 6.5%, 7.25%, and 8.0%, respectively. Comparing these findings with those for the expectations theory, we see that the liquidity premium and preferred habitat theories produce yield curves that slope more steeply upward because of investors' preferences for short-term bonds.

Let's see if the liquidity premium and preferred habitat theories are consistent with all three empirical facts we have discussed. They explain fact 1, which states that interest rates on different-maturity bonds move together over time: A rise in short-term interest rates indicates that short-term interest rates will, on average, be higher in the future, and the first term in Equation 3 then implies that long-term interest rates will rise along with them.

The liquidity and preferred habitat theories also explain why yield curves tend to have an especially steep upward slope when short-term interest rates are low and to be inverted when short-term rates are high (fact 2). Because investors generally expect short-term interest rates to rise to some normal level when they are low, the average of future expected short-term rates will be high relative to the current short-term rate. With the additional boost of a positive liquidity premium, long-term interest rates will be substantially higher than current short-term rates, and the yield curve will have a steep upward slope. Conversely, if short-term rates are high, people usually expect them to come back down. Long-term rates will then drop below short-term rates because the average of expected future short-term rates will be far below current short-term rates, despite positive liquidity premiums, and so the yield curve will slope downward.

The liquidity premium and preferred habitat theories explain fact 3, which states that yield curves typically slope upward, by recognizing that the liquidity premium rises with a bond's maturity because of investors' preferences for short-term bonds. Even if short-term interest rates are expected to stay the same, on average, in the future, long-term interest rates will be above short-term interest rates, and yield curves will typically slope upward.

How can the liquidity premium and preferred habitat theories explain the occasional appearance of inverted yield curves if the liquidity premium is positive? It must be that, at times, short-term interest rates are expected to fall so much in the future that the average of the expected short-term rates is well below the current short-term rate. Even when the positive liquidity premium is added to this average, the resulting long-term rate is still lower than the current short-term interest rate.

As our discussion indicates, a particularly attractive feature of the liquidity premium and preferred habitat theories is that you can see what the market is predicting about future short-term interest rates just from the slope of the yield curve. A steeply rising yield curve, as in panel (a) of Figure 6, indicates that short-term interest rates are expected to rise in the future. A moderately steep yield curve, as in panel (b), indicates that short-term interest rates are not expected to rise or fall much in the future. A flat yield curve, as in panel (c), indicates that short-term rates are expected to fall moderately in the future. Finally, an inverted yield curve, as in panel (d), indicates that short-term interest rates are expected to fall sharply in the future.

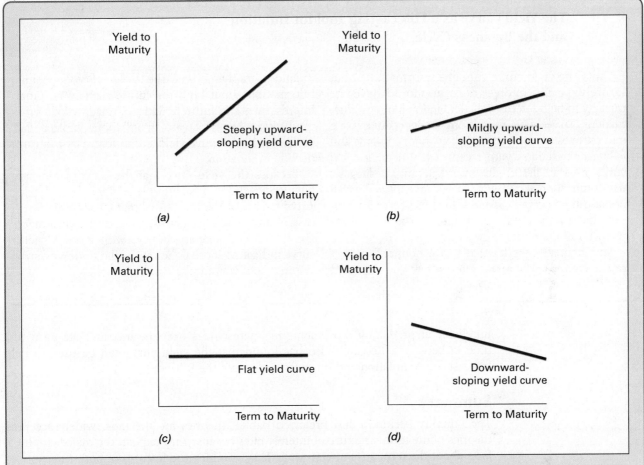

FIGURE 6   Yield Curves and the Market's Expectations of Future Short-Term Interest Rates According to the Liquidity Premium (Preferred Habitat) Theory

A steeply rising yield curve, as in panel (a), indicates that short-term interest rates are expected to rise in the future. A moderately steep yield curve, as in panel (b), indicates that short-term interest rates are not expected to rise or fall much in the future. A flat yield curve, as in panel (c), indicates that short-term rates are expected to fall moderately in the future. Finally, an inverted yield curve, as in panel (d), indicates that short-term interest rates are expected to fall sharply in the future.

Evidence on the Term Structure

In the 1980s, researchers examining the term structure of interest rates questioned whether the slope of the yield curve provides information about movements of future short-term interest rates. They found that the spread between long- and short-term interest rates does not always help predict future short-term interest rates, a finding that may stem from substantial fluctuations in the liquidity (term) premium for long-term bonds. More recent research using more discriminating tests now favors a different view. It shows that the term structure contains quite a bit of information for the very short run (over the next several months) and the long run (over several years) but is

FYI **The Yield Curve as a Forecasting Tool for Inflation and the Business Cycle**

Because the yield curve contains information about future expected interest rates, it should have the capacity to help forecast inflation and real output fluctuations. To see why, recall from Chapter 5 that rising interest rates are associated with economic booms and falling interest rates with recessions. When the yield curve is either flat or downward-sloping, it suggests that future short-term interest rates are expected to fall because the economy is more likely to enter a recession. Indeed, the yield curve is found to be an accurate predictor of the business cycle.

In Chapter 4, we learned that a nominal interest rate is composed of a real interest rate and expected inflation, implying that the yield curve contains information about both the future path of nominal interest rates and future inflation. A steep yield curve predicts a future increase in inflation, while a flat or downward-sloping yield curve forecasts a future decline in inflation.

Because the yield curve can be used to forecast business cycles and inflation, the slope of the yield curve is part of the tool kit of many economic forecasters and is often viewed as a useful indicator of the stance of monetary policy, with a steep yield curve indicating loose policy and a flat or downward-sloping yield curve indicating tight policy.

unreliable at predicting movements in interest rates over the intermediate term (the time in between). Research also has found that the yield curve can be used to help forecast future inflation and business cycles (see the FYI box).

Summary

The liquidity premium and preferred habitat theories are the most widely accepted theories of the term structure of interest rates because they explain the major empirical facts about the term structure so well. They combine the features of both the expectations theory and the segmented markets theory by asserting that a long-term interest rate will be the sum of a liquidity (term) premium and the average of the short-term interest rates that are expected to occur over the life of the bond.

The liquidity premium and preferred habitat theories explain the following facts: (1) Interest rates on bonds of different maturities tend to move together over time; (2) when short-term interest rates are low, yield curves are more likely to have a steep upward slope; (3) yield curves usually slope upward, but when short-term interest rates are high, yield curves are more likely to be inverted.

The theories also help us predict the movement of short-term interest rates in the future. A steep upward slope of the yield curve means that short-term rates are expected to rise, a mild upward slope means that short-term rates are expected to remain the same, a flat slope means that short-term rates are expected to fall moderately, and an inverted yield curve means that short-term rates are expected to fall sharply.

APPLICATION Interpreting Yield Curves, 1980–2014

Figure 7 illustrates several yield curves for U.S. government bonds, for selected dates from 1981 to 2014. What do these yield curves tell us about the public's expectations of future movements of short-term interest rates?

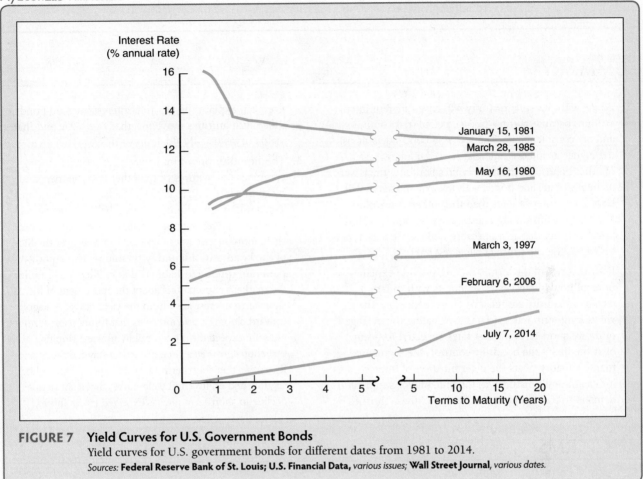

FIGURE 7   Yield Curves for U.S. Government Bonds
Yield curves for U.S. government bonds for different dates from 1981 to 2014.
Sources: **Federal Reserve Bank of St. Louis; U.S. Financial Data,** *various issues;* **Wall Street Journal,** *various dates.*

The steep inverted yield curve that occurred on January 15, 1981, indicated that short-term interest rates were expected to decline sharply in the future. In order for longer-term interest rates, along with their positive liquidity premiums, to be well below short-term interest rates, short-term interest rates must be expected to decline so sharply that their average would be far below the current short-term rate. Indeed, the public's expectations of sharply lower short-term interest rates evident in the yield curve were realized soon after January 15; by March, three-month Treasury bill rates had declined from the 16% level to 13%.

The steep, upward-sloping yield curves that occurred on March 28, 1985, and July 7, 2014, indicated that short-term interest rates were expected to climb in the future. Long-term interest rates are higher than short-term interest rates when short-term interest rates are expected to rise because their average plus the liquidity premium will be higher than the current short-term rate. The moderately upward-sloping yield curves on May 16, 1980, and March 3, 1997, indicated that short-term interest rates were expected neither to rise nor to fall in the near future. In this case, their average remains the same as the current short-term rate, and the positive liquidity premium for longer-term bonds explains the moderate upward slope of the yield curve. The flat yield curve of February 6, 2006, indicated that short-term interest rates were expected to fall slightly. ◆

SUMMARY

1. Bonds with the same maturity will have different interest rates because of three factors: default risk, liquidity, and tax considerations. The greater a bond's default risk, the higher its interest rate relative to the interest rates of other bonds; the greater a bond's liquidity, the lower its interest rate; and bonds with tax-exempt status will have lower interest rates than they otherwise would. The relationship among interest rates on bonds with the same maturity that arises because of these three factors is known as the *risk structure of interest rates*.

2. Four theories of the term structure provide explanations of how interest rates on bonds with different terms to maturity are related. The expectations theory views long-term interest rates as equaling the average of future short-term interest rates expected to occur over the life of the bond. By contrast, the segmented markets theory treats the determination of interest rates for each bond's maturity as the outcome of supply and demand in that market only. Neither of these theories by

itself can explain the fact that interest rates on bonds of different maturities move together over time and that yield curves usually slope upward.

3. The liquidity premium (preferred habitat) theory combines the features of the other two theories, and by so doing is able to explain the facts just mentioned. The liquidity premium (preferred habitat) theory views long-term interest rates as equaling the average of future short-term interest rates expected to occur over the life of the bond plus a liquidity premium. The liquidity premium (preferred habitat) theory allows us to infer the market's expectations about the movement of future short-term interest rates from the yield curve. A steeply upward-sloping curve indicates that future short-term rates are expected to rise; a mildly upward-sloping curve, that short-term rates are expected to stay the same; a flat curve, that short-term rates are expected to decline slightly; and an inverted yield curve, that a substantial decline in short-term rates is expected in the future.

KEY TERMS

credit-rating agencies, p. 119
default, p. 116
default-free bonds, p. 117
expectations theory, p. 126
inverted yield curve, p. 125

junk bonds, p. 120
liquidity premium theory, p. 130
preferred habitat theory, p. 130
risk premium, p. 117
risk structure of interest rates, p. 116

segmented markets theory, p. 129
term structure of interest rates, p. 116
yield curve, p. 124

QUESTIONS

All questions are available in MyEconLab *at* http://www.myeconlab.com.

1. If junk bonds are "junk," then why do investors buy them?

2. Which should have the higher risk premium on its interest rates, a corporate bond with a Moody's Baa rating or a corporate bond with a C rating? Why?

3. Why do U.S. Treasury bills have lower interest rates than large-denomination negotiable bank CDs?

4. In the fall of 2008, AIG, the largest insurance company in the world at the time, was at risk of defaulting due to the severity of the global financial crisis. As a result, the U.S. government stepped in to support AIG with large capital injections and an ownership stake. How would this affect, if at all, the yield and risk premium on AIG corporate debt?

5. Risk premiums on corporate bonds are usually *anticyclical*; that is, they decrease during business cycle expansions and increase during recessions. Why is this so?

6. "If bonds of different maturities are close substitutes, their interest rates are more likely to move together." Is this statement true, false, or uncertain? Explain your answer.

7. The U.S. Treasury offers some of its debt as Treasury Inflation Protected Securities, or TIPS, in which the price of bonds is adjusted for inflation over the life of the debt instrument. TIPS bonds are traded on a much smaller scale than nominal U.S. Treasury bonds of equivalent maturity. What can you conclude about the liquidity premiums of TIPS versus nominal U.S. bonds?

8. Predict what will happen to interest rates on a corporation's bonds if the federal government guarantees today that it will pay creditors if the corporation goes bankrupt in the future. What will happen to the interest rates on Treasury securities?

9. Predict what will happen to the risk premiums on corporate bonds if brokerage commissions are lowered in the corporate bond market.

10. During 2008, the difference in yield (the *yield spread*) between three-month AA-rated financial commercial paper and three-month AA-rated nonfinancial commercial paper steadily increased from its usual level of close to zero, spiking to over a full percentage point at its peak in October 2008. What explains this sudden increase?

11. If the income tax exemption on municipal bonds were abolished, what would happen to the interest rates on these bonds? What effect would the change have on interest rates on U.S. Treasury securities?

12. Prior to 2008, mortgage lenders required a house inspection to assess a home's value, and often used the same one or two inspection companies in the same geographical market. Following the collapse of the housing market in 2008, mortgage lenders required a house inspection, but this inspection was arranged through a third party. How does the pre-2008 scenario illustrate a conflict of interest similar to the role that credit-rating agencies played in the global financial crisis?

13. "According to the expectations theory of the term structure, it is better to invest in one-year bonds, reinvested over two years, than to invest in a two-year bond if interest rates on one-year bonds are expected to be the same in both years." Is this statement true, false, or uncertain?

14. If bond investors decide that 30-year bonds are no longer as desirable an investment as they were previously,

predict what will happen to the yield curve, assuming (a) the expectations theory of the term structure holds; and (b) the segmented markets theory of the term structure holds.

15. Suppose the interest rates on one-, five-, and ten-year U.S. Treasury bonds are currently 3%, 6%, and 6%, respectively. Investor A chooses to hold only one-year bonds, and Investor B is indifferent with regard to holding five- and ten-year bonds. How can you explain the behavior of Investors A and B?

16. If a yield curve looks like the one shown in the figure below, what is the market predicting about the movement of future short-term interest rates? What might the yield curve indicate about the market's predictions for the inflation rate in the future?

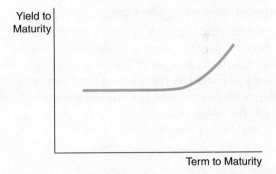

17. If a yield curve looks like the one shown in the figure below, what is the market predicting about the movement of future short-term interest rates? What might the yield curve indicate about the market's predictions for the inflation rate in the future?

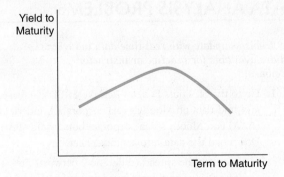

18. If yield curves, on average, were flat, what would this say about the liquidity (term) premiums in the term structure? Would you be more or less willing to accept the expectations theory?

19. If the yield curve suddenly became steeper, how would you revise your predictions of interest rates in the future?

20. If expectations of future short-term interest rates suddenly fell, what would happen to the slope of the yield curve?

21. Following a policy meeting on March 19, 2009, the Federal Reserve made an announcement that it would purchase up to $300 billion of longer-term Treasury securities over the following six months. What effect might this policy have on the yield curve?

APPLIED PROBLEMS

All applied problems are available in MyEconLab at http://www.myeconlab.com.

22. In 2010 and 2011, the government of Greece risked defaulting on its debt due to a severe budget crisis. Using bond market graphs, compare the effects on the risk premium between U.S. Treasury debt and comparable-maturity Greek debt.

23. Assuming the expectations theory is the correct theory of the term structure, calculate the interest rates in the term structure for maturities of one to five years, and plot the resulting yield curves for the following paths of one-year interest rates over the next five years:

a. 5%, 7%, 7%, 7%, 7%

b. 5%, 4%, 4%, 4%, 4%

How would your yield curves change if people preferred shorter-term bonds to longer-term bonds?

24. Assuming the expectations theory is the correct theory of the term structure, calculate the interest rates in the term structure for maturities of one to five years, and plot the resulting yield curves for the following paths of one-year interest rates over the next five years:

a. 5%, 6%, 7%, 6%, 5%

b. 5%, 4%, 3%, 4%, 5%

How would your yield curves change if people preferred shorter-term bonds over longer-term bonds?

25. The table below shows current and expected future one-year interest rates, as well as current interest rates on multiyear bonds. Use the table to calculate the liquidity premium for each multiyear bond.

Year	One-Year Bond Rate	Multiyear Bond Rate
1	2%	2%
2	3%	3%
3	4%	5%
4	6%	6%
5	7%	8%

DATA ANALYSIS PROBLEMS

The Problems update with real-time data in MyEconLab and are available for practice or instructor assignment.

 1. Go to the St. Louis Federal Reserve FRED database, and find data on Moody's Aaa corporate bond yield (AAA) and Moody's Baa corporate bond yield (BAA). Download the data into a spreadsheet.

a. Calculate the spread (difference) between the Baa and Aaa corporate bond yields for the most recent month of data available. What does this difference represent?

b. Calculate the spread again, for the same month but one year prior, and compare the result to your answer to part (a). What do your answers

say about how the risk premium has changed over the past year?

c. Identify the month of highest and lowest spreads since the beginning of the year 2000. How do these spreads compare to the most current spread data available? Interpret the results.

2. Go to the St. Louis Federal Reserve FRED database, and find daily yield data on the following U.S. treasuries securities: one-month (DGS1MO), three-month (DGS3MO), six-month (DGS6MO), one-year (DGS1), two-year (DGS2), three-year (DGS3), five-year (DGS5), seven-year (DGS7), 10-year (DGS10), 20-year (DGS20), and 30-year (DGS30). Download the last full year of data available into a spreadsheet.

a. Construct a yield curve by creating a line graph for the most recent day of data available, and for the same day (or as close to the same day as possible) one year prior, across all the maturities. How do the yield curves compare? What does the changing slope say about potential changes in economic conditions?

b. Determine the date of the most recent Federal Open Market Committee policy statement. Construct yield curves for both the day before the policy statement was released and the day on which the policy statement was released. Was there any significant change in the yield curve as a result of the policy statement? How might this be explained?

WEB EXERCISES

1. The amount of additional interest investors receive due to various risk premiums changes over time. Sometimes risk premiums are much larger than at other times. For example, the default risk premium was very small in the late 1990s when the economy was so healthy that business failures were rare. This risk premium increases during recessions.

    Go to http://www.federalreserve.gov/releases/h15 (historical data), and find the following three interest rate listings for AAA- and Baa-rated bonds: the most current listing; the listing for June 1, 2013; and the listing for June 1, 2008. Prepare a graph that shows the interest rate information for these bonds over these three time periods (see Figure 1 for an example). Are the risk premiums stable, or do they change over time?

2. Figure 7 shows a number of yield curves at various points in time. Go to http://www.bloomberg.com/markets/rates/index.html and find the Treasury yield curve. Does the current yield curve fall above or below the most recent one listed in Figure 7? Is the current yield curve flatter or steeper than the most recent one reported in Figure 7?

WEB REFERENCES

http://www.federalreserve.gov/Releases/h15/update/

The Federal Reserve reports the yields on different-quality bonds. Look at the bottom of the listing of interest rates for AAA- and BBB-rated bonds.

http://stockcharts.com/charts/YieldCurve.html

This site lets you look at the dynamic yield curve at any point in time since 1995.

7 The Stock Market, the Theory of Rational Expectations, and the Efficient Market Hypothesis

Learning Objectives
- Calculate the price of common stock.
- Recognize the impact of new information on stock prices.
- Compare and contrast adaptive expectations and rational expectations.
- Explain why arbitrage opportunities imply that the efficient market hypothesis holds.
- Identify and explain the implications of the efficient market hypothesis for financial markets.
- Summarize the reasons why behavioral finance suggests that the efficient market hypothesis may not hold.

Preview

Rarely does a day go by that the stock market isn't a major news item. We have witnessed huge swings in the stock market in recent years. The 1990s were an extraordinary decade for stocks: The Dow Jones and S&P 500 indexes increased by more than 400%, while the tech-laden NASDAQ index rose by more than 1,000%. By early 2000, all three indexes had reached record highs. Unfortunately, the good times did not last. Starting in early 2000, the stock market began to decline and many investors lost their shirts. The NASDAQ crashed, falling by more than 50%, while the Dow Jones and S&P 500 indexes fell by 30% through January 2003. After subsequently rising by over 30%, the stock market crashed again during the global financial crisis, falling by over 50% from its peak in the fall of 2007. Starting in 2009, the stock market recovered quickly, more than doubling and reaching new highs by 2014.

Because so many people invest in the stock market and the prices of stocks affect the ability of people to retire comfortably, the market for stocks is undoubtedly the financial market that receives the most attention and scrutiny. In this chapter, we look first at how this important market works.

We begin by discussing the fundamental theories that underlie the valuation of stocks. These theories are critical to understanding the forces that cause the value of stocks to rise and fall minute by minute and day by day. Once we have learned the methods for stock valuation, we need to explore how expectations about the market affect its behavior. We do so by examining the *theory of rational expectations*. When this theory is applied to financial markets, the outcome is the *efficient market hypothesis*, which has some general implications for how markets in other securities besides stocks operate. The theory of rational expectations is also central to debates about the conduct of monetary policy, to be discussed in Chapter 24.

COMPUTING THE PRICE OF COMMON STOCK

Common stock is the principal medium through which corporations raise equity capital. **Stockholders**—those who hold stock in a corporation—own an interest in the corporation equal to the percentage of outstanding shares they own. This ownership interest gives them a bundle of rights. The most important are the right to vote and to be a **residual claimant** of all funds flowing into the firm (known as **cash flows**), meaning that the stockholder receives whatever remains after all other claims against the firm's

140

assets have been satisfied. Stockholders may receive dividends from the net earnings of the corporation. **Dividends** are payments made periodically, usually every quarter, to stockholders. The board of directors of the firm sets the level of the dividend, usually based on the recommendation of management. In addition, the stockholder has the right to sell the stock.

One basic principle of finance is that the value of any investment is calculated by computing the present value of all cash flows the investment will generate over its life. For example, a commercial building will sell for a price that reflects the net cash flows (rents minus expenses) it is projected to have over its useful life. Similarly, we value common stock as the value in today's dollars of all future cash flows. The cash flows that a stockholder might earn from stock are dividends, the sales price, or both.

To develop the theory of stock valuation, we begin with the simplest possible scenario: You buy the stock, hold it for one period to get a dividend, then sell the stock. We call this the *one-period valuation model*.

The One-Period Valuation Model

Suppose that you have some extra money to invest for one year. After a year, you will need to sell your investment to pay tuition. After watching CNBC or *Nightly Business Report* on TV, you decide that you want to buy Intel Corp. stock. You call your broker and find that Intel is currently selling for $50 per share and pays $0.16 per year in dividends. The analyst on CNBC predicts that the stock will be selling for $60 in one year. Should you buy this stock?

To answer this question, you need to determine whether the current price accurately reflects the analyst's forecast. To value the stock today, you need to find the present discounted value of the expected cash flows (future payments) using the formula in Equation 1 of Chapter 4. In this equation, the discount factor used to discount the cash flows is the required return on investments in equity rather than the interest rate. The cash flows consist of one dividend payment plus a final sales price. When these cash flows are discounted back to the present, the following equation computes the current price of the stock:

$$P_0 = \frac{D_1}{(1 + k_e)} + \frac{P_1}{(1 + k_e)} \tag{1}$$

where

P_0 = the current price of the stock. The zero subscript refers to time period zero, or the present.

D_1 = the dividend paid at the end of year 1

k_e = the required return on investments in equity

P_1 = the price at the end of the first period; the predicted sales price of the stock

To see how Equation 1 works, let's compute the price of the Intel stock if, after careful consideration, you decide that you would be satisfied to earn a 12% return on the investment. If you have decided that $k_e = 0.12$, are told that Intel pays $0.16 per year in dividends ($D_1 = 0.16$), and forecast the share price of $60 for next year ($P_1 = \$60$), you get the following result from Equation 1:

$$P_0 = \frac{0.16}{1 + 0.12} + \frac{\$60}{1 + 0.12} = \$0.14 + \$53.57 = \$53.71$$

On the basis of your analysis, you find that the present value of all cash flows from the stock is $53.71. Because the stock is currently priced at $50 per share, you would choose to buy it. However, you should be aware that the stock may be selling for less than $53.71, because other investors have placed a greater risk on the cash flows or estimated the cash flows to be less than you did.

The Generalized Dividend Valuation Model

Using the present value concept, we can extend the one-period dividend valuation model to any number of periods: The value of a stock today is the present value of all future cash flows. The only cash flows that an investor will receive are dividends and a final sales price when the stock is ultimately sold in period n. The generalized multiperiod formula for stock valuation can be written as

$$P_0 = \frac{D_1}{(1 + k_e)^1} + \frac{D_2}{(1 + k_e)^2} + \cdots + \frac{D_n}{(1 + k_e)^n} + \frac{P_n}{(1 + k_e)^n} \tag{2}$$

where

P_n = the price of the stock in period n
D_i = the dividend paid at the end of year i

If you tried to use Equation 2 to find the value of a share of stock, you would soon realize that you must first estimate the value the stock will have at some point in the future before you can estimate its value today. In other words, you must find P_n before you can find P_0. However, if P_n is far in the future, it will not affect P_0. For example, the present value of a share of stock that sells for $50 seventy-five years from now, using a 12% discount rate, is just one cent [$50/(1.12^{75}) = \$0.01$]. This reasoning implies that the current value of a share of stock can be calculated as simply the present value of the future dividend stream. The **generalized dividend model** is given in Equation 3. Note that it is the same formula as Equation 2, but without the final sales price:

$$P_0 = \sum_{t=1}^{\infty} \frac{D_t}{(1 + k_e)^t} \tag{3}$$

Consider the implications of Equation 3 for a moment. The generalized dividend model states that the price of a stock is determined only by the present value of the dividends and that nothing else matters. Many stocks do not pay dividends, so how is it that these stocks have value? *Buyers of the stock expect that the firm will pay dividends someday.* Most of the time a firm institutes dividends as soon as it has completed the rapid growth phase of its life cycle.

The generalized dividend valuation model requires that we compute the present value of an infinite stream of dividends, a process that could be difficult, to say the least. Therefore, simplified models have been developed to make the calculations easier. One such model is the **Gordon growth model**, which assumes constant dividend growth.

The Gordon Growth Model

Many firms strive to increase their dividends at a constant rate each year. Equation 4 is derived from Equation 3 to reflect this constant growth in dividends:

$$P_0 = \frac{D_0 \times (1 + g)^1}{(1 + k_e)^1} + \frac{D_0 \times (1 + g)^2}{(1 + k_e)^2} + \cdots + \frac{D_0 \times (1 + g)^{\infty}}{(1 + k_e)^{\infty}} \tag{4}$$

where
$$D_0 = \text{the most recent dividend paid}$$
$$g = \text{the expected constant growth rate in dividends}$$
$$k_e = \text{the required return on an investment in equity}$$

Equation 4 can be simplified to obtain Equation 5:[1]

$$P_0 = \frac{D_0 \times (1 + g)}{(k_e - g)} = \frac{D_1}{(k_e - g)} \tag{5}$$

This model is useful for finding the value of a stock, given a few assumptions:

1. *Dividends are assumed to continue growing at a constant rate forever.* Actually, as long as the dividends are expected to grow at a constant rate for an extended period of time, the model should yield reasonable results. This is because errors about distant cash flows become small when discounted to the present.
2. *The growth rate is assumed to be less than the required return on equity,* k_e. Myron Gordon, in his development of the model, demonstrated that this is a reasonable assumption. In theory, if the growth rate were faster than the rate demanded by holders of the firm's equity, then in the long run the firm would grow impossibly large.

HOW THE MARKET SETS STOCK PRICES

Suppose you go to an auto auction. The cars are available for inspection before the auction begins, and you find a little Mazda Miata that you like. You test-drive it in the parking lot and notice that it makes a few strange noises, but you decide that you still like the car. You decide that $5,000 is a fair price that will allow you to pay some repair bills should the noises turn out to be serious. You see that the auction is ready to begin, so you go in and wait for the Miata to be auctioned.

Suppose another buyer also spots the Miata. He test-drives the car and recognizes that the noises are simply the result of worn brake pads that he can fix himself at a nominal cost. He decides that the car is worth $7,000. He also goes in and waits for the Miata to come up for auction.

---

[1]To generate Equation 5 from Equation 4, first multiply both sides of Equation 4 by $(1 + k_e)/(1 + g)$, and then subtract Equation 4 from the result. This yields

$$\frac{P_0 \times (1 + k_e)}{(1 + g)} - P_0 = D_0 - \frac{D_0 \times (1 + g)^\infty}{(1 + k_e)^\infty}$$

Assuming that k_e is greater than g, the term on the far right will approach zero and so can be dropped. Thus, after factoring P_0 out of the left-hand side,

$$P_0 \times \left[\frac{1 + k_e}{1 + g} - 1 \right] = D_0$$

Next, simplify by combining terms:

$$P_0 \times \frac{(1 + k_e) - (1 + g)}{1 + g} = D_0$$

$$P_0 = \frac{D_0 \times (1 + g)}{k_e - g} = \frac{D_1}{k_e - g}$$

Who will buy the car, and for how much? Suppose only the two of you are interested in the Miata. You begin the bidding at $4,000. Your competitor ups your bid to $4,500. You bid your top price of $5,000. He counters with $5,100. The price is now higher than you are willing to pay, so you stop bidding. The car is sold to the more informed buyer for $5,100.

This simple example raises a number of important points. First, the price is set by the buyer who is willing to pay the highest price. This price is not necessarily the highest price the asset could fetch, but it is incrementally greater than what any other buyer is willing to pay.

Second, the market price will be set by the buyer who can take best advantage of the asset. The buyer who purchased the car knew that he could fix the noise easily and cheaply. As a consequence, he was willing to pay more for the car than you were. The same concept holds for other assets. For example, a piece of property or a building will sell to the buyer who can put the asset to the most productive use.

Finally, the example shows the role played by information in asset pricing. Superior information about an asset can increase its value by reducing its risk. When you consider buying a stock, the future cash flows are subject to many unknowns. The buyer who has the best information about these cash flows will discount them at a lower interest rate than will a buyer who is very uncertain.

Now let's apply these ideas to stock valuation. Suppose you are considering the purchase of stock expected to pay a $2 dividend next year. Market analysts expect the firm to grow at 3% indefinitely. You are *uncertain* about both the constancy of the dividend stream and the accuracy of the estimated growth rate. To compensate yourself for this uncertainty (risk), you require a return of 15%.

Now suppose Jennifer, another investor, has spoken with industry insiders and feels more confident about the projected cash flows. Jennifer requires only a 12% return because her perceived risk is lower than yours. Bud, on the other hand, is dating the CEO of the company. He knows with more certainty what the future of the firm actually looks like, and thus requires only a 10% return.

What value will each investor give to the stock? Applying the Gordon growth model yields the following stock prices:

Investor	Discount Rate	Stock Price
You	15%	$16.67
Jennifer	12%	$22.22
Bud	10%	$28.57

You are willing to pay $16.67 for the stock. Jennifer will pay up to $22.22, and Bud will pay $28.57. The investor with the lowest perceived risk is willing to pay the most for the stock. If there were no other traders but these three, the market price would be between $22.22 and $28.57. If you already held the stock, you would sell it to Bud.

We thus see that the players in the market, bidding against one another, establish the market price. When new information is released about a firm, expectations change, and with them, prices change. New information can cause changes in expectations about the level of future dividends or the risk of those dividends. Because market participants are constantly receiving new information and revising their expectations, it is reasonable that stock prices are constantly changing as well.

APPLICATION   Monetary Policy and Stock Prices

Stock market analysts tend to hang on every word uttered by the chair of the Federal Reserve because they know that an important determinant of stock prices is monetary policy. But how does monetary policy affect stock prices?

The Gordon growth model in Equation 5 explains this relationship. Monetary policy can affect stock prices in two ways. First, when the Fed lowers interest rates, the return on bonds (an alternative asset to stocks) declines, and investors are likely to accept a lower required rate of return on an investment in equity (k_e). The resulting decline in k_e lowers the denominator in the Gordon growth model (Equation 5), leads to a higher value of P_0, and raises stock prices. Furthermore, a lowering of interest rates is likely to stimulate the economy, so the growth rate in dividends, g, is likely to be somewhat higher. This rise in g also causes the denominator in Equation 5 to decrease, which also leads to a higher P_0 and a rise in stock prices.

As we will see in Chapter 25, the impact of monetary policy on stock prices is one of the key ways in which monetary policy affects the economy.

APPLICATION   The Global Financial Crisis and the Stock Market

The global financial crisis that started in August 2007 led to one of the worst stock market declines in the past 50 years. Our analysis of stock price valuation, again using the Gordon growth model, can help us understand how this event affected stock prices.

The global financial crisis had a major negative impact on the economy, leading to a downward revision of the growth prospects for U.S. companies, thus lowering the dividend growth rate (g) in the Gordon model. In terms of Equation 5, the resulting increase in the denominator would lead to a decline in P_0 and hence a decline in stock prices.

Increased uncertainty about the U.S. economy and the widening credit spreads caused by the subprime crisis also raised the required return on investment in equity. In terms of Equation 5, a higher k_e leads to an increase in the denominator, a decline in P_0, and a general fall in stock prices.

In the early stages of the global financial crisis, the declines in growth prospects and credit spreads were moderate, and so, as the Gordon model predicts, the stock market decline was also moderate. However, when the crisis entered a particularly virulent stage in October 2008, credit spreads shot through the roof, the economy tanked, and as the Gordon model predicts, the stock market crashed. From its peak in October 2007 (high of 14,066 for the DJIA) to its lowest point in March 2009 (DJIA low of 6,547), the market lost 53% of its value. ◆

THE THEORY OF RATIONAL EXPECTATIONS

The analysis of stock price evaluation we outlined in the previous section depends on people's expectations—especially expectations of cash flows. Indeed, it is difficult to think of any sector of the economy in which expectations are not crucial; this is why it is important to examine how expectations are formed. We do so by outlining the *theory of rational expectations*, currently the most widely used theory to describe the formation of business and consumer expectations.

In the 1950s and 1960s, economists regularly viewed expectations as formed from past experience only. Expectations of inflation, for example, were typically viewed as being an average of past inflation rates. This view of expectation formation, called **adaptive expectations**, suggests that changes in expectations will occur slowly over time, as data for a variable evolve.[2] So, if inflation had formerly been steady at a 5% rate, expectations of future inflation would be 5%, too. If inflation rose to a steady rate of 10%, expectations of future inflation would rise toward 10%, but slowly: In the first year, expected inflation might rise only to 6%; in the second year, to 7%; and so on.

The adaptive expectations hypothesis has been faulted on the grounds that people use more information than just past data on a single variable to form their expectations of that variable. Their expectations of inflation will almost surely be affected by their predictions of future monetary policy, as well as by current and past monetary policy. In addition, people often change their expectations quickly in the light of new information. To address these objections to the validity of adaptive expectations, John Muth developed an alternative theory of expectations, called **rational expectations**, which can be stated as follows: ***Expectations will be identical to optimal forecasts (the best guess of the future) using all available information.***[3]

What exactly does this mean? To explain it more clearly, let's use the theory of rational expectations to examine how expectations are formed in a situation that most of us will encounter at some point in our lifetime: our drive to work. Suppose that if Joe Commuter travels when it is not rush hour, his trip takes an average of 30 minutes. Sometimes his trip takes 35 minutes; other times, 25 minutes; but the average, non-rush-hour driving time is 30 minutes. If, however, Joe leaves for work during the rush hour, it takes him, on average, an additional 10 minutes to get to work. Given that he leaves for work during the rush hour, the best guess of his driving time—the **optimal forecast**—is 40 minutes.

If the only information available to Joe before he leaves for work related to his driving time is that he is leaving during the rush hour, what does rational expectations theory allow you to predict about Joe's expectations of his driving time? Since the best guess of his driving time, using all available information, is 40 minutes, Joe's expectation should be the same. Clearly, an expectation of 35 minutes would not be rational, because it is not equal to the optimal forecast, or the best guess of the driving time.

Suppose that the next day, given the same conditions and expectations, it takes Joe 45 minutes to drive to work because he hits an abnormally large number of red lights. The day after that, Joe hits all the lights right and it takes him only 35 minutes to drive to work. Do these variations mean that Joe's 40-minute expectation is irrational? No; an expectation of 40 minutes' driving time is still a rational expectation. In both cases, the

---

[2]More specifically, adaptive expectations—say, of inflation—are written as a weighted average of past inflation rates:

$$\pi_t^e = (1 - \lambda) \sum_{j=0}^{\infty} \lambda^j \pi_{t-j}$$

where
π_t^e = adaptive expectation of inflation at time t
π_{t-j} = inflation at time $t - j$
λ = a constant between the values of 0 and 1

[3]John Muth, "Rational Expectations and the Theory of Price Movements," *Econometrica* 29 (1961): 315–335.

forecast is off by five minutes, so the expectation has not been perfectly accurate each time. However, the forecast does not have to be perfectly accurate to be rational—it need only be the *best possible* forecast given the available information; that is, it has to be correct *on average,* and the 40-minute expectation meets this requirement. As there is bound to be some randomness in Joe's driving time regardless of driving conditions, an optimal forecast will never be completely accurate.

The example makes the following important point about rational expectations: ***Even though a rational expectation equals the optimal forecast using all available information, a prediction based on it may not always be perfectly accurate.***

What if an item of information relevant to predicting driving time is unavailable or ignored? Suppose that on Joe's usual route to work, an accident occurs and causes a two-hour traffic jam. If Joe has no way of ascertaining this information, his rush-hour expectation of 40 minutes' driving time is still rational, because the accident information is not available to him for incorporation into his optimal forecast. However, if there was a radio or TV traffic report about the accident that Joe did not bother to listen to, or heard but ignored, his 40-minute expectation is no longer rational. In light of the availability of this information, Joe's optimal forecast should have been two hours and 40 minutes.

Accordingly, an expectation may fail to be rational for two reasons:

1. People might be aware of all available information but find it takes too much effort to make their expectation the best guess possible.
2. People might be unaware of some available relevant information, so their best guess of the future will not be accurate.

Nonetheless, it is important to recognize that if an additional factor is important but information about it is not available, an expectation that does not take that factor into account can still be rational.

Formal Statement of the Theory

We can state the theory of rational expectations somewhat more formally. If X stands for the variable that is being forecast (in our example, Joe Commuter's driving time), X^e for the expectation of this variable (Joe's expectation of his driving time), and X^{of} for the optimal forecast of X using all available information (the best guess possible of Joe's driving time), the theory of rational expectations then simply states

$$X^e = X^{of} \tag{6}$$

That is, the expectation of X equals the optimal forecast using all available information.

Rationale Behind the Theory

Why do people try to make their expectations match their best possible guess of future results, using all available information? The simplest explanation is that it is costly for people not to do so. Joe Commuter has a strong incentive to make his expectation of the time it takes him to drive to work as accurate as possible. If he underpredicts his driving time, he will often be late to work and risk being fired. If he overpredicts, he will, on average, get to work too early and will have given up sleep or leisure time unnecessarily. Accurate expectations are desirable, and therefore people have a strong incentive to try to make expectations equal to optimal forecasts by using all available information.

The same principle applies to businesses. Suppose an appliance manufacturer—say, General Electric—knows that interest-rate movements are important to the sales of appliances. If GE makes poor forecasts of interest rates, it will earn less profit, because it will produce either too many or too few appliances. The incentives are strong for GE to acquire all available information to help it forecast interest rates and make the best possible guess of future interest-rate movements.

Implications of the Theory

Rational expectations theory leads to two commonsense implications regarding the formation of expectations. These implications are important in the analysis of both the stock market and the aggregate economy:

1. *If there is a change in the way a variable moves, the way in which expectations of this variable are formed will change as well.* This tenet of rational expectations theory can be most easily understood through a concrete example. Suppose interest rates move in such a way that they tend to return to a "normal" level over time. If today's interest rate is high relative to the normal level, an optimal forecast of the interest rate in the future is that it will decline to the normal level. Rational expectations theory would imply that when today's interest rate is high, the expectation is that it will fall in the future.

Suppose now that the way in which the interest rate moves changes so that when the interest rate is high, it stays high. In this case, when today's interest rate is high, the optimal forecast of the future interest rate, and hence the rational expectation, is that it will stay high. Expectations of the future interest rate will no longer indicate that the interest rate will fall. The change in the way the interest-rate variable moves has therefore led to a change in the way that expectations of future interest rates are formed. The rational expectations analysis here is generalizable to expectations of any variable. Hence, when a change occurs in the way any variable moves, the way in which expectations of this variable are formed will change, too.

2. *The forecast errors of expectations will, on average, be zero and cannot be predicted ahead of time.* The forecast error of an expectation is $X - X^e$, the difference between the realization of a variable X and the expectation of the variable. That is, if Joe Commuter's driving time on a particular day is 45 minutes and his expectation of the driving time is 40 minutes, the forecast error is five minutes.

Suppose that in violation of the rational expectations tenet, Joe's forecast error is not, on average, equal to zero; instead, it equals five minutes. The forecast error is now predictable ahead of time because Joe will soon notice that he is, on average, five minutes late for work and can improve his forecast by increasing it by five minutes. Rational expectations theory implies that this is exactly what Joe will do because he will want his forecast to be the best guess possible. When Joe has revised his forecast upward by five minutes, on average, the forecast error will equal zero, so it cannot be predicted ahead of time. Rational expectations theory implies that forecast errors of expectations cannot be predicted.

The incentives for equating expectations with optimal forecasts are especially strong in financial markets. In these markets, people with better forecasts of the future get rich. The application of the theory of rational expectations to financial markets (where it is called the **efficient market hypothesis** or the **theory of efficient capital markets**) is thus particularly useful.

THE EFFICIENT MARKET HYPOTHESIS: RATIONAL EXPECTATIONS IN FINANCIAL MARKETS

While monetary economists were developing the theory of rational expectations, financial economists were developing a parallel theory of expectations formation for financial markets. It led them to the same conclusion as that of the rational expectations theorists: Expectations in financial markets are equal to optimal forecasts using all available information.[4] Although financial economists, such as Eugene Fama, winner of the Nobel Prize in economics, gave their theory another name, calling it the *efficient market hypothesis*, in fact their theory is just an application of rational expectations to the pricing of stocks and other securities.

The efficient market hypothesis is based on the assumption that prices of securities in financial markets fully reflect all available information. You may recall from Chapter 4 that the rate of return from holding a security equals the sum of the capital gain on the security (the change in the price), plus any cash payments, divided by the initial purchase price of the security:

$$R = \frac{P_{t+1} - P_t + C}{P_t} \tag{7}$$

where

R = rate of return on the security held from time t to time $t + 1$ (say, the end of 2015 to the end of 2016)

P_{t+1} = price of the security at time $t + 1$, the end of the holding period

P_t = price of the security at time t, the beginning of the holding period

C = cash payment (coupon or dividend payments) made in the period t to $t + 1$

Let's look at the expectation of this return at time t, the beginning of the holding period. Because the current price P_t and the cash payment C are known at the outset, the only variable in the definition of the return that is uncertain is the price next period, P_{t+1}.[5] Denoting expectation of the security's price at the end of the holding period as P^e_{t+1}, the expected return R^e is

$$R^e = \frac{P^e_{t+1} - P_t + C}{P_t}$$

The efficient market hypothesis views expectations of future prices as equal to optimal forecasts using all currently available information. In other words, the market's expectations of future securities prices are rational, so that

$$P^e_{t+1} = P^{of}_{t+1}$$

which in turn implies that the expected return on the security will equal the optimal forecast of the return:

$$R^e = R^{of} \tag{8}$$

---

[4]The development of the efficient market hypothesis was not wholly independent of the development of rational expectations theory in that financial economists were aware of Muth's work.

[5]There are cases in which C might not be known at the beginning of the period, but that does not make a substantial difference to the analysis. We would in that case assume that not only price expectations but also the expectations of C are optimal forecasts using all available information.

Unfortunately, we cannot observe either R^e or P^e_{t+1}, so the rational expectations equations by themselves do not tell us much about how the financial market behaves. However, if we can devise some way to measure the value of R^e, these equations will have important implications for how prices of securities change in financial markets.

The supply and demand analysis of the bond market that we developed in Chapter 5 showed us that the expected return on a security (the interest rate, in the case of the one-year discount bond we examined) will have a tendency to move toward the equilibrium return that equates the quantity demanded to the quantity supplied. Supply and demand analysis enables us to determine the expected return on a security with the following equilibrium condition:

The expected return on a security R^e equals the equilibrium return R^*, which equates the quantity of the security demanded to the quantity supplied; that is,

$$R^e = R^* \tag{9}$$

The academic field of finance explores the factors (risk and liquidity, for example) that influence the equilibrium returns on securities. For our purposes, it is sufficient to know that we can determine the equilibrium return and thus determine the expected return with the equilibrium condition.

We can derive an equation to describe pricing behavior in an efficient market by using the equilibrium condition to replace R^e with R^* in the rational expectations equation (Equation 8). In this way, we obtain

$$R^{of} = R^* \tag{10}$$

This equation tells us that *current prices in a financial market will be set so that the optimal forecast of a security's return using all available information equals the security's equilibrium return*. Financial economists state it more simply: In an efficient market, a security's price fully reflects all available information.

Rationale Behind the Hypothesis

To see why the efficient market hypothesis makes sense, we make use of the concept of **arbitrage**, in which market participants (*arbitrageurs*) eliminate **unexploited profit opportunities**, that is, returns on a security that are larger than what is justified by the characteristics of that security. Arbitrage is of two types: *pure arbitrage*, in which the elimination of unexploited profit opportunities involves no risk, and the type of arbitrage we discuss here, in which the arbitrageur takes on some risk when eliminating the unexploited profit opportunities. To see how arbitrage leads to the efficient market hypothesis given a security's risk characteristics, let's look at an example. Suppose the normal return on ExxonMobil common stock is 10% at an annual rate, and its current price P_t is lower than the optimal forecast of tomorrow's price P^{of}_{t+1}, so that the optimal forecast of the return at an annual rate is 50%, which is greater than the equilibrium return of 10%. We are now able to predict that, on average, ExxonMobil's return will be abnormally high, so there is an unexploited profit opportunity. Knowing that, on average, you can earn an abnormally high rate of return on ExxonMobil stock (because $R^{of} > R^*$), you will buy more, which will in turn drive up the stock's current price P_t relative to its expected future price P^{of}_{t+1}, thereby lowering R^{of}. When the current price has risen sufficiently so that R^{of} equals R^* and the efficient market condition (Equation 10) is satisfied, the buying of ExxonMobil stock will stop, and the unexploited profit opportunity will disappear.

Similarly, a security for which the optimal forecast of the return is -5% and the equilibrium return is 10% ($R^{of} < R^*$) would be a poor investment because, on average, the security earns less than the equilibrium return. In such a case, you would sell the security and drive down its current price relative to the expected future price until R^{of} rose to the level of R^* and the efficient market condition was again satisfied. Our discussion can be summarized as follows:

$$R^{of} > R^* \rightarrow P_t\uparrow \rightarrow R^{of}\downarrow$$

$$R^{of} < R^* \rightarrow P_t\downarrow \rightarrow R^{of}\uparrow$$

until

$$R^{of} = R^*$$

Another way to state the efficient market condition is this: *In an efficient market, all unexploited profit opportunities will be eliminated.*

An extremely important factor in this reasoning is that *not everyone in a financial market must be well informed about a security or have rational expectations for its price to be driven to the point at which the efficient market condition holds*. Financial markets are structured so that many participants can play. As long as a few people (often referred to as the "smart money") keep their eyes open for unexploited profit opportunities, they will eliminate the profit opportunities that appear, because in doing so they make a profit. The efficient market hypothesis makes sense because it does not require that everyone in a market be cognizant of what is happening to every security.

Random-Walk Behavior of Stock Prices

The term **random walk** describes the movements of a variable whose future values cannot be predicted (are random) because, given today's value, the value of the variable is just as likely to fall as it is to rise. An important implication of the efficient market hypothesis is that stock prices should approximately follow a random walk; that is, *future changes in stock prices should, for all practical purposes, be unpredictable*. The random-walk implication of the efficient market hypothesis is the one most commonly mentioned in the press because it is the most readily comprehensible to the public. In fact, when people mention the "random-walk theory of stock prices," they are in reality referring to the efficient market hypothesis.

The case for random-walk stock prices can be demonstrated. Suppose people could predict that the price of Happy Feet Corporation (HFC) stock would rise 1% in the coming week. The predicted rate of capital gains and rate of return on HFC stock would then exceed 50% at an annual rate. Since this is very likely to be far higher than the equilibrium rate of return on HFC stock ($R^{of} > R^*$), the efficient market hypothesis indicates that people would immediately buy this stock and bid up its current price. The action would stop only when the predictable change in the price dropped to near zero, so that $R^{of} = R^*$.

Similarly, if people could predict that the price of HFC stock would fall by 1%, the predicted rate of return would be negative ($R^{of} > R^*$), and people would immediately sell the stock. The current price would fall until the predictable change in the price rose back to near zero, where the efficient market condition again would hold. The efficient market hypothesis suggests that the predictable change in stock prices will be near zero, leading to the conclusion that stock prices will generally follow a

Global — Should Foreign Exchange Rates Follow a Random Walk?

Although the efficient market hypothesis is usually applied to the stock market, it can also be used to show that foreign exchange rates, like stock prices, should generally follow a random walk. To see why this is the case, consider what would happen if investors could predict that a currency would rise in value by 1% in the coming week. By buying this currency, they could earn a greater than 50% return at an annual rate, which is likely to be far above the equilibrium return for holding a currency. As a result, investors would immediately buy the currency and bid up its current price, thereby reducing the expected return. The process would only stop when

the predictable change in the exchange rate dropped to near zero so that the optimal forecast of the return no longer differed from the equilibrium return. Likewise, if investors could predict that the currency would fall in value by 1% in the coming week, they would sell it until the predictable change in the exchange rate was again near zero. The efficient market hypothesis therefore implies that future changes in exchange rates should, for all practical purposes, be unpredictable; in other words, exchange rates should follow random walks. Indeed, the random-walk behavior of exchange rates is exactly what is found in the data.

random walk.[6] As the Global Box "Should Foreign Exchange Rates Follow a Random Walk?" indicates, the efficient market hypothesis suggests that foreign exchange rates should also follow a random walk.

APPLICATION — Practical Guide to Investing in the Stock Market

The efficient market hypothesis has numerous applications to the real world.[7] It is especially valuable because it can be applied directly to an issue that concerns many of us: how to get rich (or at least not get poor) by investing in the stock market. A practical guide to investing in the stock market, which we develop here, provides a better understanding of the use and implications of the efficient market hypothesis.

How Valuable Are Reports Published by Investment Advisers?

Suppose you have just read in the "Heard on the Street" column of the *Wall Street Journal* that investment advisers are predicting a boom in oil stocks because an oil shortage is developing. Should you proceed to withdraw all of your hard-earned savings from the bank and invest them in oil stocks?

---

[6]Note that the random-walk behavior of stock prices is only an *approximation* derived from the efficient market hypothesis. Random-walk behavior would hold *exactly* only for a stock for which an unchanged price leads to its having the equilibrium return. Then, when the predictable change in the stock price is exactly zero, $R^{of} = R^*$.

[7]The empirical evidence on the efficient market hypothesis is discussed in an appendix to this chapter, which can be found on the Companion Website at http://www.pearsonhighered.com/mishkin.

The efficient market hypothesis tells us that when purchasing a security, we cannot expect to earn an abnormally high return, or a return greater than the equilibrium return.

Information in newspapers and in the published reports of investment advisers is readily available to many market participants and is already reflected in market prices. So acting on this information will not yield abnormally high returns, on average. The empirical evidence for the most part confirms that recommendations from investment advisers cannot help us outperform the general market. Indeed, as the FYI box suggests, human investment advisers in San Francisco do not, on average, even outperform an orangutan!

Probably no other conclusion is met with more skepticism by students than this one when they first hear it. We all know, or have heard of, someone who has been successful in the stock market for a period of many years. We wonder, "How could someone be so consistently successful if he or she did not really know how to predict when returns would be abnormally high?" The following story, reported in the press, illustrates why such anecdotal evidence is not reliable.

A get-rich-quick artist invented a clever scam. Every week, he wrote two letters. In letter A, he would pick team A to win a particular football game; in letter B, he would pick the opponent, team B. He would then separate a mailing list into two groups, and he would send letter A to the people in one group and letter B to the people in the other. The following week he would do the same thing, but this time he would send these letters only to the group who had received the first letters containing the correct prediction. After doing this for ten games, he had a small cluster of people who had received letters predicting the correct winning team for every game. He then mailed a final letter to this group, declaring that since he was obviously an expert predictor of the outcome of football games (he had picked the winning teams ten weeks in a row), and since his predictions were profitable for the recipients who bet on the games, he would continue to send his predictions only if he were paid a substantial amount of money. When one of his clients figured out what he was up to, the con man was prosecuted and thrown in jail!

What is the lesson of the story? Even if no forecaster is an accurate predictor of the market, there will always be a group of consistent winners. A person who has done well regularly in the past cannot guarantee that he or she will do well in the future. Note that there will also be a group of persistent losers, but you rarely hear about them because no one brags about a poor forecasting record.

Should You Be Skeptical of Hot Tips?

Suppose your broker phones you with a hot tip to buy stock in the Happy Feet Corporation (HFC) because it has just developed a product that is completely effective in curing athlete's foot. The stock price is sure to go up. Should you follow this advice and buy HFC stock?

The efficient market hypothesis indicates that you should be skeptical of such news. If the stock market is efficient, it has already priced HFC stock so that its expected return will equal the equilibrium return. The hot tip is not particularly valuable and will not enable you to earn an abnormally high return.

You might wonder, though, if the hot tip is based on new information and would give you an edge on the rest of the market. If other market participants have gotten this information before you, the answer again is no. As soon as the information hits the street, the unexploited profit opportunity it creates will be quickly eliminated. The stock's price will already reflect the information, and you should expect to realize only the equilibrium return. But if you are one of the first to gain the new information, it *can* do you some good. Only then can you be one of the lucky ones who, on average, will earn an abnormally high return by helping eliminate the profit opportunity by buying HFC stock.

Do Stock Prices Always Rise When There Is Good News?

If you follow the stock market, you might have noticed a puzzling phenomenon: When good news about a corporation, such as a particularly favorable earnings report, is announced, the price of the corporation's stock frequently does not rise. The efficient market hypothesis explains this phenomenon.

Because changes in stock prices are unpredictable, when information is announced that has already been expected by the market, stock prices will remain unchanged. The announcement does not contain any new information that would lead to a change in stock prices. If this were not the case, and the announcement led to a change in stock prices, it would mean that the change was predictable. Because such a scenario is ruled out in an efficient market, **stock prices will respond to announcements only when the information being announced is new and unexpected**. If the news is expected, no stock price response will occur. This is exactly what the evidence shows: Stock prices do reflect publicly available information.

Sometimes an individual stock price declines when good news is announced. Although this seems somewhat peculiar, it is completely consistent with the workings of an efficient market. Suppose that although the announced news is good, it is not as good as expected. HFC's earnings may have risen by 15%, but if the market expected earnings to rise by 20%, the new information is actually unfavorable, and the stock price declines.

Efficient Market Prescription for the Investor

What does the efficient market hypothesis recommend for investing in the stock market? It tells us that hot tips and investment advisers' published recommendations—all of which make use of publicly available information—cannot help an investor outperform the market. Indeed, it indicates that anyone without better information than other market participants cannot expect to beat the market. So what is an investor to do?

The efficient market hypothesis leads to the conclusion that such an investor (and almost all of us fit into this category) should not try to outguess the market by constantly buying and selling securities. This process does nothing but boost the income of brokers, who earn commissions on each trade.[8] Instead, the investor should pursue a "buy and hold" strategy—purchase stocks and hold them for long periods of time. This will lead to the same returns, on average, but the investor's net profits will be higher because fewer brokerage commissions will have to be paid.

A sensible strategy for a small investor, whose costs of managing a portfolio may be high relative to its size, is to buy into a mutual fund rather than to buy individual stocks. Because the efficient market hypothesis indicates that no mutual fund can consistently outperform the market, an investor should not buy into a fund that has high management fees or pays sales commissions to brokers, but rather should purchase a no-load (commission-free) mutual fund that has low management fees.

The evidence indicates that it will not be easy to beat the prescription suggested here, although some anomalies (discussed in an appendix found on this book's website) to the efficient market hypothesis suggest that an extremely clever investor (that rules out most of us) may be able to outperform a buy-and-hold strategy. ◆

WHY THE EFFICIENT MARKET HYPOTHESIS DOES NOT IMPLY THAT FINANCIAL MARKETS ARE EFFICIENT

Many financial economists take the efficient market hypothesis one step further in their analysis of financial markets. Not only do they believe that expectations in financial markets are rational—that is, equal to optimal forecasts using all available information—but they also add the condition that prices in financial markets reflect the true fundamental (intrinsic) value of the securities. In other words, all prices are always correct and reflect **market fundamentals** (items that have a direct impact on future income streams of the securities), and so financial markets are efficient.

This stronger view of market efficiency has several important implications in the academic field of finance. First, it implies that in an efficient capital market, one investment is as good as any other because the securities' prices are correct. Second, it implies that a security's price reflects all available information about the intrinsic value of the security. Third, it implies that security prices can be used by managers of both financial and nonfinancial firms to assess their costs of capital (costs of financing their investments) accurately and hence that security prices can be used to help these managers make correct decisions about whether a specific investment is worth making. This stronger version of market efficiency is a basic tenet of much analysis in the finance field.

The efficient market hypothesis may be misnamed, however. It does not imply the stronger view of market efficiency, but rather just that prices in markets like the stock market are unpredictable. Indeed, as the following application suggests, the existence of market crashes and **bubbles**, in which the prices of assets rise well above their fundamental values, casts serious doubt on the stronger view that financial markets are efficient. However, market crashes and bubbles do not necessarily provide strong evidence against the basic tenets of the efficient market hypothesis.

---

[8]The investor may also have to pay Uncle Sam capital gains taxes on any profits that are realized when a security is sold—an additional reason why continual buying and selling does not make sense.

APPLICATION   # What Do Stock Market Crashes Tell Us About the Efficient Market Hypothesis and the Efficiency of Financial Markets?

On October 19, 1987, dubbed "Black Monday," the Dow Jones Industrial Average declined by more than 20%, the largest one-day decline in U.S. history. The collapse of the high-tech companies' share prices from their peaks in March 2000 caused the heavily-tech-laden NASDAQ index to fall from about 5,000 in March 2000 to about 1,500 in 2001 and 2002, a decline of well over 60%. These stock market crashes caused many economists to question the validity of the efficient market hypothesis. These economists do not believe that a rational marketplace could have produced such a massive swing in share prices. To what degree should these stock market crashes make us doubt the validity of the efficient market hypothesis?

Nothing in efficient markets theory rules out large changes in stock prices. A large change in stock prices can result from new information that produces a dramatic decline in optimal forecasts of the future valuation of firms. However, economists are hard pressed to find fundamental changes in the economy that would have caused the Black Monday and tech crashes. One lesson from these crashes is that factors other than market fundamentals probably have an effect on asset prices. Indeed, as we will explore in Chapters 8 and 12, there are good reasons to believe that impediments to the proper functioning of financial markets do exist. Hence these crashes have convinced many economists that the stronger version of market efficiency, which states that asset prices reflect the true fundamental (intrinsic) value of securities, is incorrect. These economists attribute a large role in determination of stock and other asset prices to market psychology and to the institutional structure of the marketplace. However, nothing in this view contradicts the basic reasoning behind rational expectations or the efficient market hypothesis—that market participants eliminate unexploited profit opportunities. Even though stock market prices may not always solely reflect market fundamentals, as long as market crashes are unpredictable, the basic premises of efficient markets theory hold.

However, other economists believe that market crashes and bubbles suggest that unexploited profit opportunities may exist and that the efficient market hypothesis might be fundamentally flawed. The controversy over the efficient market hypothesis continues. ◆

BEHAVIORAL FINANCE

Doubts about the efficiency of financial markets, triggered by the stock market crash of 1987, led economists such as Nobel Prize winner Robert Shiller to develop a new field of study called **behavioral finance**. It applies concepts from other social sciences, such as anthropology, sociology, and particularly psychology, to explain the behavior of securities prices.[9]

[9]Surveys of this field can be found in Hersh Shefrin, *Beyond Greed and Fear: Understanding of Behavioral Finance and the Psychology of Investing* (Boston: Harvard Business School Press, 2000); Andrei Shleifer, *Inefficient Markets* (Oxford, UK: Oxford University Press, 2000); and Robert J. Shiller, "From Efficient Market Theory to Behavioral Finance," Cowles Foundation Discussion Paper No. 1385 (October 2002).

As we have seen, the efficient market hypothesis assumes that unexploited profit opportunities are eliminated by "smart money" market participants. But can smart money dominate ordinary investors so that financial markets are efficient? Specifically, the efficient market hypothesis suggests that smart money participants will sell when a stock price goes up irrationally, with the result that the stock price falls back down to a level that is justified by fundamentals. For this to occur, smart money investors must be able to engage in **short sales**; that is, they must borrow stock from brokers and then sell it in the market, with the aim of earning a profit by buying the stock back again ("covering the short") after it has fallen in price. Work by psychologists, however, suggests that people are subject to loss aversion: They are more unhappy when they suffer losses than they are happy when they achieve gains. Short sales can result in losses far in excess of an investor's initial investment if the stock price climbs sharply higher than the price at which the short sale is made (and losses might be unlimited if the stock price climbs to astronomical heights).

Loss aversion can thus explain an important phenomenon: Very little short selling actually takes place. Short selling may also be constrained by rules restricting it, because it seems unsavory for someone to make money from another person's misfortune. The existence of so little short selling can explain why stock prices are sometimes overvalued. That is, the lack of enough short selling means that smart money does not drive stock prices back down to their fundamental value.

Psychologists have also found that people tend to be overconfident in their own judgments. As a result, investors tend to believe that they are smarter than other investors. Because investors are willing to assume that the market typically doesn't get it right, they trade on their beliefs rather than on pure facts. This theory may explain why securities markets have such a large trading volume—something that the efficient market hypothesis does not predict.

Overconfidence and social contagion (fads) provide an explanation for stock market bubbles. When stock prices go up, investors attribute their profits to their intelligence and talk up the stock market. This word-of-mouth enthusiasm and glowing media reports then can produce an environment in which even more investors think stock prices will rise in the future. The result is a positive feedback loop in which prices continue to rise, producing a speculative bubble, which finally crashes when prices get too far out of line with fundamentals.[10]

The field of behavioral finance is a young one, but it holds out hope that we might be able to explain some features of securities markets' behavior that are not well explained by the efficient market hypothesis.

---

[10]See Robert J. Shiller, *Irrational Exuberance* (New York: Broadway Books, 2001).

SUMMARY

1. Stocks are valued as the present value of future dividends. Unfortunately, we do not know very precisely what these dividends will be. This uncertainty introduces a great deal of error into the valuation process. The Gordon growth model is a simplified method of computing stock value that depends on the assumption that the dividends are growing at a constant rate forever. Given our uncertainty regarding future dividends, this assumption is often the best we can do.

2. The interaction among traders in the market is what actually sets prices on a day-to-day basis. The trader who values the security the most (either because of less uncertainty about cash flows or because of greater estimated cash flows) will be willing to pay the most.

As new information is released, investors will revise their estimates of the true value of the security and will either buy or sell it, depending on how the market price compares with their estimated valuation. Because small changes in estimated growth rates or required returns result in large changes in price, it is not surprising that the markets are often volatile.

3. The efficient market hypothesis states that current security prices will fully reflect all available information, because in an efficient market, all unexploited profit opportunities are eliminated. The elimination of unexploited profit opportunities necessary for a financial market to be efficient does not require that all market participants be well informed. The efficient markets hypothesis implies that stock prices generally follow a random walk.

4. The efficient market hypothesis indicates that hot tips and investment advisers' published recommendations cannot help an investor outperform the market. The best prescription for investors is to pursue a buy-and-hold strategy—purchase stocks and hold them for long periods of time. Empirical evidence generally supports these implications of the efficient market hypothesis in the stock market.

5. The existence of market crashes and bubbles has convinced many economists that the stronger version of market efficiency, which states that asset prices reflect the true fundamental (intrinsic) value of securities, is not correct. There is, however, less evidence that these crashes prove that the efficient market hypothesis is wrong. Even if the stock market were driven by factors other than fundamentals, these crashes do not clearly demonstrate that many basic tenets of the efficient market hypothesis are no longer valid, as long as the crashes could not have been predicted.

6. The new field of behavioral finance applies concepts from other social sciences, such as anthropology, sociology, and psychology, to our understanding of the behavior of securities prices. Loss aversion, overconfidence, and social contagion can explain why trading volume is so high, why stock prices become overvalued, and why speculative bubbles occur.

KEY TERMS

adaptive expectations, p. 146
arbitrage, p. 150
behavioral finance, p. 156
bubbles, p. 155
cash flows, p. 140
dividends, p. 141
efficient market hypothesis, p. 148

generalized dividend model, p. 142
Gordon growth model, p. 142
market fundamentals, p. 155
optimal forecast, p. 146
random walk, p. 151
rational expectations, p. 146
residual claimant, p. 140

short sales, p. 157
stockholders, p. 140
theory of efficient capital markets, p. 148
unexploited profit opportunity, p. 150

QUESTIONS

All questions are available in MyEconLab at http://www.myeconlab.com.

1. What basic principle of finance can be applied to the valuation of any investment asset?

2. What are the two main sources of cash flows for a stockholder? How reliably can these cash flows be estimated? Compare the problem of estimating stock cash flows to the problem of estimating bond cash flows. Which security would you predict to be more volatile?

3. Some economists think that central banks should try to prick bubbles in the stock market before they get out of hand and cause later damage when they burst. How can monetary policy be used to prick a market bubble? Explain using the Gordon growth model.

4. If monetary policy becomes more transparent about the future course of interest rates, how will stock prices be affected, if at all?

5. "Forecasters' predictions of inflation are notoriously inaccurate, so their expectations of inflation cannot be rational." Is this statement true, false, or uncertain? Explain your answer.

6. "Anytime it is snowing when Joe Commuter gets up in the morning, he misjudges how long it will take him to drive to work. When it is not snowing, his expectations

of the driving time are perfectly accurate. Considering that it snows only once every ten years where Joe lives, Joe's expectations are almost always perfectly accurate." Are Joe's expectations rational? Why or why not?

7. If a forecaster spends hours every day studying data to forecast interest rates, but his expectations are not as accurate as predicting that tomorrow's interest rate will be identical to today's interest rate, are his expectations rational?

8. "If stock prices did not follow a random walk, there would be unexploited profit opportunities in the market." Is this statement true, false, or uncertain? Explain your answer.

9. Suppose that increases in the money supply lead to a rise in stock prices. Does this mean that when you see that the money supply has sharply increased in the past week, you should go out and buy stocks? Why or why not?

10. If the public expects a corporation to lose $5 per share this quarter and it actually loses $4, which is still the largest loss in the history of the company, what does the efficient market hypothesis predict will happen to the price of the stock when the $4 loss is announced?

11. If you read in the *Wall Street Journal* that the "smart money" on Wall Street expects stock prices to fall, should you follow that lead and sell all your stocks?

12. If your broker has been right in her five previous buy and sell recommendations, should you continue listening to her advice?

13. Can a person with rational expectations expect the price of a share of Google to rise by 10% in the next month?

14. "If most participants in the stock market do not follow what is happening to the monetary aggregates, prices of common stocks will not fully reflect information about them." Is this statement true, false, or uncertain? Explain your answer.

15. "An efficient market is one in which no one ever profits from having better information than the rest of the market participants." Is this statement true, false, or uncertain? Explain your answer.

16. If higher money growth is associated with higher future inflation, and if announced money growth turns out to be extremely high but is still less than the market expected, what do you think will happen to long-term bond prices?

17. "Foreign exchange rates, like stock prices, should follow a random walk." Is this statement true, false, or uncertain? Explain your answer.

18. Can we expect the value of the dollar to rise by 2% next week if our expectations are rational?

19. "Human fear is the source of stock market crashes, so these crashes indicate that expectations in the stock market cannot be rational." Is this statement true, false, or uncertain? Explain your answer.

20. In the late 1990s, as information technology advanced rapidly and the Internet was widely developed, U.S. stock markets soared, peaking in early 2001. Later that year, these markets began to unwind and then crashed, with many commentators identifying the previous few years as a "stock market bubble." How might it be possible for this episode to be a bubble but still adhere to the efficient market hypothesis?

21. Why might the efficient market hypothesis be less likely to hold when fundamentals suggest stocks should be at a lower level?

APPLIED PROBLEMS

All applied problems are available in MyEconLab *at* http://www.myeconlab.com.

22. Compute the price of a share of stock that pays a $1 per year dividend and that you expect to be able to sell in one year for $20, assuming you require a 15% return.

23. After careful analysis, you have determined that a firm's dividends should grow at 7%, on average, in the foreseeable future. The firm's last dividend was $3. Compute the current price of this stock, assuming the required return is 18%.

24. The current price of a stock is $65.88. If dividends are expected to be $1 per share for the next five years, and the required return is 10%, then what should the price of the stock be in 5 years when you plan to sell it? If the dividend and required return remain the same, and the stock price is expected to increase by $1 five years from now, does the current stock price also increase by $1? Why or why not?

25. A company has just announced a 3-for-1 stock split, effective immediately. Prior to the split, the company had a market value of $5 billion with 100 million shares outstanding. Assuming the split conveys no

new information about the company, what are the value of the company, the number of shares outstanding, and the price per share after the split? If the actual market price immediately following the split is $17.00 per share, what does this tell us about market efficiency?

DATA ANALYSIS PROBLEMS

The Problems update with real-time data in MyEconLab and are available for practice or instructor assignment.

 1. Go to the St. Louis Federal Reserve FRED database, and find data on the Dow Jones Industrial Average (DJIA). Assume the DJIA is a stock that pays no dividends. Apply the one-period valuation model, using the data from one year prior up to the most current date available, to determine the required return on equity investment. In other words, assume the most recent stock price of DJIA is known one year prior. What rate of return would be required in order to "buy" a share of DJIA? Suppose that a $100 dividend is paid out instead. How does this change the required rate of return?

2. Go to the St. Louis Federal Reserve FRED database, and find data on net corporate dividend payments

(B056RC1A027NBEA). Adjust the *units* setting to "Percent Change from Year Ago," and download the data into a spreadsheet.

a. Calculate the average annual growth rate of dividends from 1960 to the most recent year of data available.

b. Find data on the Dow Jones Industrial Average (DJIA) for the most recent day of data available. Suppose that a $100 dividend is paid out at the end of next year. Use the Gordon growth model and your answer to part (a) to calculate the rate of return that would be required for equity investment over the next year, assuming you could buy a share of DJIA.

WEB EXERCISES

1. Visit http://www.forecasts.org/data/index.htm. Click on Stock Index at the very top of the page. Now choose U.S. Stock Indices—monthly. Review the indexes for the DJIA, the S&P 500, and the NASDAQ composite. Which index appears most volatile? In which index would you rather have invested in 1985 if the investment had been allowed to compound until now?

2. The Internet is a great source of information on stock prices and stock price movements. Yahoo Finance is a great source for stock market data. Go to http://finance .yahoo.com and click on the DOW ticker in the Market

Summary section to view current data on the Dow Jones Industrial Average. Click on the chart to manipulate the different variables. Change the time range and observe the stock trend over various intervals. Have stock prices been going up or down over the past day, week, three months, and year?

3. Eugene Fama and Robert Shiller recently won the Nobel Prize in economics. Go to http://nobelprize.org/ nobel_prizes/economics/ and locate the press release on Eugene Fama and Robert Shiller. What was the Nobel Prize to them awarded for? When was it awarded?

WEB REFERENCES

http://stocks.tradingcharts.com

Access detailed stock quotes, charts, and historical stock data.

http://www.investorhome.com/emh.htm

Learn more about the efficient market hypothesis.

WEB APPENDIX

Please visit the Companion Website at http://www .pearsonhighered.com/mishkin to read the Web appendix to Chapter 7.

Appendix: **Evidence on the Efficient Market Hypothesis**

PART

3

Financial Institutions

Crisis and Response: The $700 Billion Bailout Package

After a heated national debate, the U.S. House of Representatives passed the Emergency Economic Stabilization Act on October 3, 2008. This stunning $700 billion bailout package sought to promote economic recovery from the global financial crisis by authorizing the Treasury to purchase troubled mortgage assets from struggling financial institutions or to inject capital into banking institutions. To calm fears further, the Act raised the federal deposit insurance limit from $100,000 to $250,000.

The initial bill was voted down on September 29, when constituents flooded their representatives with complaints about bailing out the greedy Wall Street executives behind the crisis. The national debate pitted Wall Street against Main Street: Many people who sided with struggling homeowners saw the proposed federal bailout of financial institutions as government hypocrisy. How could injecting capital into the financial system help those fearful of losing their jobs or, worse yet, those who found themselves suddenly without work?

The central role of financial institutions in the workings of the economy—the focus of Part 3—was being overlooked. Banks and other financial institutions make financial markets work by moving funds from people who save to people who have productive investment opportunities. That bank branch on Main Street was not going to be able to lend freely to a small business owner or recent college graduate looking to fund a new car purchase until capital once again flowed.

The global financial crisis highlights how financial systems change over time, be it from financial innovations or through hard lessons learned from such crises. Chapter 8 analyzes financial structure in the United States and in the rest of the world. In Chapter 9, we look at the business and process of banking. In Chapter 10, we extend the economic analysis developed in Chapter 8 to understand the motivations for bank regulation, and we examine the pitfalls of the regulatory process. Chapter 11 examines the development of the American banking system over time and the growing internationalization of banking. In Chapter 12, we develop a framework for understanding the dynamics of financial crises, and focus in particular on the red-hot global crisis of 2007–2009.

An Economic Analysis of Financial Structure

Preview

A healthy and vibrant economy requires a financial system that moves funds from people who save to people who have productive investment opportunities. But how does the financial system make sure that your hard-earned savings get channeled to Paula the Productive Investor rather than to Benny the Bum?

This chapter answers that question by providing an economic analysis of how our financial structure is designed to promote economic efficiency. The analysis focuses on a few simple but powerful economic concepts that enable us to explain features of our financial system, such as why financial contracts are written as they are and why financial intermediaries are more important than securities markets for getting funds to borrowers. The analysis also demonstrates the important link between the financial system and the performance of the aggregate economy, which is the subject of Part 6 of this book.

BASIC FACTS ABOUT FINANCIAL STRUCTURE THROUGHOUT THE WORLD

The financial system is complex in structure and function throughout the world. It includes many different types of institutions: banks, insurance companies, mutual funds, stock and bond markets, and so on—all of which are regulated by government. The financial system channels trillions of dollars per year from savers to people with productive investment opportunities. If we take a close look at financial structure all over the world, we find eight basic facts, some of which are quite surprising, that we must explain if we are to understand how the financial system works.

The bar chart in Figure 1 shows how American businesses financed their activities using external funds (those obtained from outside the business itself) in the period 1970–2000 and compares U.S. data with data for Germany, Japan, and Canada. The conclusions drawn from this period still hold true today. The *Bank Loans* category is made up primarily of loans from depository institutions; *Nonbank Loans* are primarily loans by other financial intermediaries; the *Bonds* category includes marketable debt securities, such as corporate bonds and commercial paper; and *Stock* consists of new issues of equity (stock market shares).

Now let's explore the eight facts.

1. **Stocks are not the most important source of external financing for businesses.** Because so much attention in the media is focused on the stock market, many people

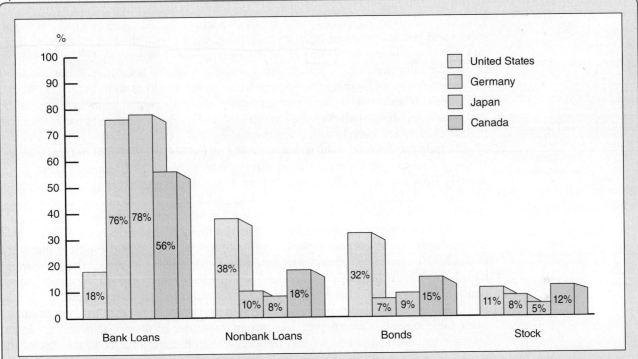

FIGURE 1   Sources of External Funds for Nonfinancial Businesses: A Comparison of the United States with Germany, Japan, and Canada

The *Bank Loans* category is made up primarily of loans from depository institutions; the *Nonbank Loans* are primarily loans by other financial intermediaries; the *Bonds* category includes marketable debt securities, such as corporate bonds and commercial paper; and *Stock* consists of new issues of new equity (stock market shares).

Source: Andreas Hackethal and Reinhard H. Schmidt, "Financing Patterns: Measurement Concepts and Empirical Results," Johann Wolfgang Goethe-Universitat Working Paper No. 125, January 2004. The data are for 1970–2000 and are gross flows as percentages of the total, not including trade and other credit data, which are not available.

have the impression that stocks are the most important source of financing for American corporations. However, as we can see from the bar chart in Figure 1, the stock market accounted for only a small fraction of the external financing of American businesses in the 1970–2000 period: 11%.[1] Similarly low figures apply for the other countries presented in Figure 1. Why is the stock market less important than other sources of financing in the United States and other countries?

---

[1]The 11% figure for the percentage of external financing provided by stocks is based on the flows of external funds to corporations. However, this flow figure is somewhat misleading because when a share of stock is issued, it raises funds permanently, whereas when a bond is issued, it raises funds only temporarily until it is paid back at maturity. To see this, suppose a firm raises $1,000 by selling a share of stock and another $1,000 by selling a $1,000 one-year bond. In the case of the stock issue, the firm can hold on to the $1,000 it raised by selling the stock. However, in order to hold on to the $1,000 it raised through debt, the firm has to issue a new $1,000 bond every year. If we look at the flow of funds to corporations over a 30-year period, as shown in Figure 1, the firm will have raised $1,000 through a stock issue only once in the 30-year period, while it will have raised $1,000 through debt 30 times, once in each of the 30 years. Thus it looks as though debt is 30 times more important than stocks in raising funds, even though our example indicates that the two methods are actually equally important for the firm.

2. Issuing marketable debt and equity securities is not the primary way in which businesses finance their operations. Figure 1 shows that bonds are a far more important source of financing in the United States than stocks are (32% versus 11%). However, stocks and bonds combined (43%), which make up the total share of marketable securities, still supply less than one-half of the external funds needed by U.S. corporations to finance their activities. The fact that issuing marketable securities is not the most important source of financing is true elsewhere in the world as well. Indeed, as we see in Figure 1, other countries have a much smaller share of external financing supplied by marketable securities than does the United States. Why don't businesses use marketable securities more extensively to finance their activities?

3. Indirect finance, which involves the activities of financial intermediaries, is many times more important than direct finance, in which businesses raise funds directly from lenders in financial markets. Direct finance involves the sale to households of marketable securities, such as stocks and bonds. The 43% share of stocks and bonds used as a source of external financing for American businesses actually greatly overstates the importance of direct finance in our financial system. Since 1970, less than 5% of newly-issued corporate bonds and commercial paper, and less than one-third of stocks, have been sold directly to American households. The rest of these securities have been bought primarily by financial intermediaries such as insurance companies, pension funds, and mutual funds. These figures indicate that direct finance is used in less than 10% of the external funding of American business. Because in most countries marketable securities are an even less important source of finance than in the United States, direct finance is also far less important than indirect finance in the rest of the world. Why are financial intermediaries and indirect finance so important in financial markets? In recent years, however, indirect finance has been declining in importance. Why is this happening?

4. Financial intermediaries, particularly banks, are the most important source of external funds used to finance businesses. As we can see in Figure 1, the primary source of external funds for businesses throughout the world is loans made by banks and other nonbank financial intermediaries, such as insurance companies, pension funds, and finance companies (56% in the United States, but more than 70% in Germany, Japan, and Canada). In other industrialized countries, bank loans are the largest category of sources of external finance (more than 70% in Germany and Japan, and more than 50% in Canada). Thus the data suggest that banks in these countries have the most important role in financing business activities. In developing countries, banks play an even more important role in the financial system than they do in industrialized countries. What makes banks so important to the workings of the financial system? Although banks remain important, their contributions to external funds for businesses have been declining in recent years. What is driving this decline?

5. The financial system is among the most heavily regulated sectors of the economy. The financial system is heavily regulated in the United States and in all other developed countries. Governments regulate financial markets primarily to promote the provision of information and to ensure the soundness (stability) of the financial system. Why are financial markets so extensively regulated throughout the world?

6. Only large, well-established corporations have easy access to securities markets to finance their activities. Individuals and smaller businesses that are not well established are less likely to raise funds by issuing marketable securities. Instead, they most often obtain their financing from banks. Why do only large, well-known corporations find it easier to raise funds in securities markets?

7. *Collateral is a prevalent feature of debt contracts for both households and businesses.* **Collateral** is property that is pledged to a lender to guarantee payment in the event that the borrower is unable to make debt payments. Collateralized debt (also known as **secured debt** to contrast it with **unsecured debt**, such as credit card debt, which is not collateralized) is the predominant form of household debt and is widely used in business borrowing as well. The majority of household debt in the United States consists of collateralized loans: Your automobile is collateral for your auto loan, and your house is collateral for your mortgage. Commercial and farm mortgages, for which property is pledged as collateral, make up one-quarter of borrowing by nonfinancial businesses; corporate bonds and other bank loans also often involve pledges of collateral. Why is collateral such an important feature of debt contracts?

8. *Debt contracts typically are extremely complicated legal documents that place substantial restrictions on the behavior of the borrower.* Many students think of a debt contract as a simple IOU that can be written on a single piece of paper. The reality of debt contracts is far different, however. In all countries, bond or loan contracts typically are long legal documents with provisions (called **restrictive covenants**) that restrict and specify certain activities that the borrower can engage in. Restrictive covenants are not just a feature of debt contracts for businesses; for example, personal automobile loan and home mortgage contracts include covenants that require the borrower to maintain sufficient insurance on the automobile or house purchased with the loan. Why are debt contracts so complex and restrictive?

As you may recall from Chapter 2, an important feature of financial markets is their substantial transaction and information costs. An economic analysis of how these costs affect financial markets will help us understand the eight facts, which will in turn give us a much deeper understanding of how our financial system works. In the next section, we examine the impact of transaction costs on the structure of our financial system. Then we turn to the effects of information costs on financial structure.

TRANSACTION COSTS

Transaction costs are a major problem in financial markets. An example will make this clear.

How Transaction Costs Influence Financial Structure

Say you have $5,000 that you would like to invest, and you are thinking about investing in the stock market. Because you have only $5,000, you can buy only a small number of shares. Even if you use online trading, your purchase is so small that the brokerage commission for buying the stock you pick will be a large percentage of the purchase price of the shares. If, instead, you decide to buy a bond, the problem becomes even worse; the smallest denomination offered on some bonds that you might want to buy is as large as $10,000, and you do not have that much money to invest. You are disappointed and realize that you will not be able to use financial markets to earn a return on your hard-earned savings. You can take some consolation, however, in the fact that you are not alone in being stymied by high transaction costs. This is a fact of life for many of us: Only about one-half of American households own any securities.

You also face another problem related to transaction costs. Because you have only a small amount of funds available, you can make only a restricted number of investments, because a large number of small transactions would result in very high transaction costs. That is, you have to put all your eggs in one basket, and your inability to diversify will subject you to a lot of risk.

How Financial Intermediaries Reduce Transaction Costs

This example of the problems posed by transaction costs, along with the example outlined in Chapter 2, in which legal costs kept you from making a loan to Carl the Carpenter, illustrate that small savers like you are frozen out of financial markets and are unable to benefit from them. Fortunately, financial intermediaries, an important part of the financial structure, have evolved to reduce transaction costs and allow small savers and borrowers to benefit from the existence of financial markets.

Economies of Scale   One solution to the problem of high transaction costs is to bundle the funds of many investors together so that they can take advantage of *economies of scale*, the reduction in transaction costs per dollar of investment as the size (scale) of transactions increases. Bundling investors' funds together reduces transaction costs for each individual investor. Economies of scale exist because the total cost of carrying out a transaction in financial markets increases only a little as the size of the transaction grows. For example, the cost of arranging a purchase of 10,000 shares of stock is not much greater than the cost of arranging a purchase of 50 shares of stock.

The presence of economies of scale in financial markets helps explain the development of financial intermediaries and why financial intermediaries have become such an important part of our financial structure. The clearest example of a financial intermediary that arose because of economies of scale is a mutual fund. A *mutual fund* is a financial intermediary that sells shares to individuals and then invests the proceeds in bonds or stocks. Because it buys large blocks of stocks or bonds, a mutual fund can take advantage of lower transaction costs. These cost savings are then passed on to individual investors after the mutual fund has taken its cut in the form of management fees for administering their accounts. An additional benefit for individual investors is that a mutual fund is large enough to purchase a widely diversified portfolio of securities. The increased diversification for individual investors reduces their risk, making them better off.

Economies of scale are also important in lowering the costs of resources that financial institutions need to accomplish their tasks, such as computer technology. Once a large mutual fund has invested a lot of money in setting up a telecommunications system, for example, the system can be used for a huge number of transactions at a low cost per transaction.

Expertise   Financial intermediaries are also better able to develop expertise that can be used to lower transaction costs. Their expertise in computer technology, for example, enables them to offer their customers convenient services such as check-writing privileges on their accounts and toll-free numbers that customers can call for information on how well their investments are doing.

Low transaction costs enable financial intermediaries to provide their customers with *liquidity services,* which are services that make it easier for customers to conduct transactions. Money market mutual funds, for example, not only pay shareholders relatively high interest rates but also allow them to write checks for convenient bill paying.

ASYMMETRIC INFORMATION: ADVERSE SELECTION AND MORAL HAZARD

The presence of transaction costs in financial markets partly explains why financial intermediaries and indirect finance play such an important role in financial markets (fact 3). To understand financial structure more fully, however, we turn to the role of information in financial markets.

Asymmetric information—a situation that arises when one party's insufficient knowledge about the other party involved in a transaction makes it impossible for the first party to make accurate decisions when conducting the transaction—is an important aspect of financial markets. For example, managers of a corporation know whether they are honest and usually have better information about how well their business is doing than stockholders do. The presence of asymmetric information leads to adverse selection and moral hazard problems, which were introduced in Chapter 2.

Adverse selection is an asymmetric information problem that occurs *before* a transaction occurs: Potential bad credit risks are the ones who most actively seek out loans. Thus the parties who are most likely to produce an undesirable outcome are also the ones most likely to want to engage in the transaction. For example, big risk takers or outright crooks are often the most eager to take out a loan because they know they are unlikely to pay it back. Because adverse selection increases the chances that a loan might be made to a bad credit risk, lenders might decide not to make any loans, even though good credit risks can be found in the marketplace.

Moral hazard arises *after* the transaction occurs: The lender runs the risk that the borrower will engage in activities that are undesirable from the lender's point of view, because such activites make it less likely that the loan will be paid back. For example, once borrowers have obtained a loan, they may take on big risks (which have possible high returns but also run a greater risk of default) because they are playing with someone else's money. Because moral hazard lowers the probability that the loan will be repaid, lenders may decide that they would rather not make a loan.

The analysis of how asymmetric information problems affect economic behavior is called **agency theory**. We will apply this theory here to explain why financial structure takes the form it does, thereby explaining the facts outlined at the beginning of the chapter.

THE LEMONS PROBLEM: HOW ADVERSE SELECTION INFLUENCES FINANCIAL STRUCTURE

A particular aspect of the way the adverse selection problem interferes with the efficient functioning of a market was outlined in a famous article by Nobel Prize winner George Akerlof. It is called the "lemons problem" because it resembles the problem created by "lemons," that is, bad cars, in the used-car market.[2] Potential buyers of used cars are

---

[2]George Akerlof, "The Market for 'Lemons': Quality, Uncertainty and the Market Mechanism," *Quarterly Journal of Economics* 84 (1970): 488–500. Two important papers that have applied the lemons problem analysis to financial markets are Stewart Myers and N. S. Majluf, "Corporate Financing and Investment Decisions: When Firms Have Information That Investors Do Not Have," *Journal of Financial Economics* 13 (1984): 187–221; and Bruce Greenwald, Joseph E. Stiglitz, and Andrew Weiss, "Information Imperfections in the Capital Market and Macroeconomic Fluctuations," *American Economic Review* 74 (1984): 194–199.

frequently unable to assess the quality of a car; that is, they can't tell whether a particular used car is one that will run well or a lemon that will continually give them grief. The price that a buyer pays must therefore reflect the *average* quality of the cars in the market, somewhere between the low value of a lemon and the high value of a good car.

The owner of a used car, by contrast, is more likely to know whether the car is a peach or a lemon. If the car is a lemon, the owner is more than happy to sell it at the price the buyer is willing to pay, which, being somewhere between the value of a lemon and that of a good car, is greater than the lemon's value. However, if the car is a peach, that is, a good car, the owner knows that the car is undervalued at the price the buyer is willing to pay, and so the owner may not want to sell it. As a result of this adverse selection problem, fewer good used cars will come to the market. Because the average quality of a used car available in the market will be low, and because very few people want to buy a lemon, there will be few sales. The used-car market will function poorly, if at all.

Lemons in the Stock and Bond Markets

A similar lemons problem arises in securities markets—that is, the debt (bond) and equity (stock) markets. Suppose that our friend Irving the Investor, a potential buyer of securities such as common stock, can't distinguish between good firms with high expected profits and low risk and bad firms with low expected profits and high risk. In this situation, Irving will be willing to pay only a price that reflects the *average* quality of firms issuing securities—a price that lies between the value of securities from bad firms and the value of those from good firms. If the owners or managers of a good firm have better information than Irving and *know* that they have a good firm, then they know that their securities are undervalued and will not want to sell them to Irving at the price he is willing to pay. The only firms willing to sell Irving securities will be bad firms (because his price is higher than the securities are worth). Our friend Irving is not stupid; he does not want to hold securities in bad firms, and hence he will decide not to purchase securities in the market. In an outcome similar to that in the used-car market, this securities market will not work very well because few firms will sell securities in it to raise capital.

The analysis is similar if Irving considers purchasing a corporate debt instrument in the bond market rather than an equity share. Irving will buy a bond only if its interest rate is high enough to compensate him for the average default risk of the good and bad firms trying to sell the debt. The knowledgeable owners of a good firm realize that they will be paying a higher interest rate than they should, so they are unlikely to want to borrow in this market. Only the bad firms will be willing to borrow, and because investors like Irving are not eager to buy bonds issued by bad firms, they will probably not buy any bonds at all. Few bonds are likely to sell in this market, so it will not be a good source of financing.

The analysis we have just conducted explains fact 2—why marketable securities are not the primary source of financing for businesses in any country in the world. It also partly explains fact 1—why stocks are not the most important source of financing for American businesses. The presence of the lemons problem keeps securities markets such as the stock and bond markets from being effective in channeling funds from savers to borrowers.

Tools to Help Solve Adverse Selection Problems

In the absence of asymmetric information, the lemons problem goes away. If buyers know as much about the quality of used cars as sellers, so that all involved can tell a good car from a bad one, buyers will be willing to pay full value for good used cars.

Because the owners of good used cars can now get a fair price, they will be willing to sell them in the market. The market will have many transactions and will perform its intended job of channeling good cars to people who want them.

Similarly, if purchasers of securities can distinguish good firms from bad, they will pay the full value of securities issued by good firms, and good firms will sell their securities in the market. The securities market will then be able to move funds to the good firms that have the most productive investment opportunities.

Private Production and Sale of Information   The solution to the adverse selection problem in financial markets is to reduce asymmetric information by furnishing the people supplying funds with more details about the individuals or firms seeking to finance their investment activities. One way for saver-lenders to get this information is through private companies that collect and produce information distinguishing good firms from bad firms, and then sell it to the saver-lenders. In the United States, companies such as Standard and Poor's, Moody's, and Value Line gather information on firms' balance sheet positions and investment activities, publish these data, and sell them to subscribers (individuals, libraries, and financial intermediaries involved in purchasing securities).

The system of private production and sale of information does not completely solve the adverse selection problem in securities markets, however, because of the **free-rider problem**. The free-rider problem occurs when people who do not pay for information take advantage of the information that other people have paid for. The free-rider problem suggests that the private sale of information is only a partial solution to the lemons problem. To see why, suppose you have just purchased information that tells you which firms are good and which are bad. You believe that this purchase is worthwhile because you can make up the cost of acquiring this information, and then some, by purchasing the securities of good firms that are undervalued. However, when our savvy (free-riding) investor Irving sees you buying certain securities, he buys right along with you, even though he has not paid for any information. If many other investors act as Irving does, the increased demand for the undervalued good securities causes their low price to be bid up immediately to reflect the securities' true value. Because of all these free riders, you can no longer buy the securities for less than their true value. Now, because you will not gain any profit from purchasing the information, you realize that you never should have paid for the information in the first place. If other investors come to the same realization, private firms and individuals may not be able to sell enough of this information to make it worth their while to gather and produce it. The weakened ability of private firms to profit from selling information will mean that less information is produced in the marketplace, so adverse selection (the lemons problem) will still interfere with the efficient functioning of securities markets.

Government Regulation to Increase Information   The free-rider problem prevents the private market from producing enough information to eliminate all the asymmetric information that leads to adverse selection. Could financial markets benefit from government intervention? The government could, for instance, produce information to help investors distinguish good from bad firms and provide it to the public free of charge. This solution, however, would involve the government releasing negative information about firms, a practice that might be politically difficult. A second possibility (and one followed by the United States and most governments throughout the world) is for the government to regulate securities markets in a way that encourages firms to reveal honest information about themselves so that investors can determine how good or bad the firms are. In the United States, the Securities and Exchange Commission

FYI   The Enron Implosion

Until 2001, Enron Corporation, a firm that specialized in trading in the energy market, appeared to be spectacularly successful. It controlled a quarter of the energy-trading market and was valued as high as $77 billion in August 2000 (just a little over a year before its collapse), making it the seventh-largest corporation in the United States at that time. However, toward the end of 2001, Enron came crashing down. In October 2001, Enron announced a third-quarter loss of $618 million and disclosed accounting "mistakes." The SEC then engaged in a formal investigation of Enron's financial dealings with partnerships led by its former finance chief. It became clear that Enron was engaged in a complex set of transactions by which it was keeping substantial amounts of debt and financial contracts off its balance sheet. These transactions enabled Enron to hide its financial difficulties. Despite securing as much as $1.5 billion of new financing from J. P. Morgan Chase and Citigroup, the company was forced to declare bankruptcy in December 2001, up to that point the largest bankruptcy declaration in U.S. history.

The Enron collapse illustrates that government regulation can lessen asymmetric information problems but cannot eliminate them. Managers have tremendous incentives to hide their companies' problems, making it hard for investors to know the true value of firms.

The Enron bankruptcy not only increased concerns in financial markets about the quality of accounting information supplied by corporations, but also led to hardship for many of the firm's former employees, who found that their pensions had become worthless. Outrage against the duplicity of executives at Enron was high, and several of them were convicted and sent to jail.

(SEC) is the government agency that requires firms selling their securities to undergo independent audits, in which accounting firms certify that the firm is adhering to standard accounting principles and disclosing accurate information about sales, assets, and earnings. Similar regulations are found in other countries. However, disclosure requirements do not always work well, as the collapse of Enron and accounting scandals at other corporations, such as WorldCom and Parmalat (an Italian company), suggest (see the FYI box, "The Enron Implosion").

The asymmetric information problem of adverse selection in financial markets helps explain why financial markets are among the most heavily regulated sectors of the economy (fact 5). Government regulation aimed at increasing the information available to investors is necessary to reduce the adverse selection problem, which interferes with the efficient functioning of securities (stock and bond) markets.

Although government regulation lessens the adverse selection problem, it does not eliminate it entirely. Even when firms provide information to the public about their sales, assets, or earnings, they still have more information than investors: A lot more is involved in knowing the quality of a firm than statistics alone can provide. Furthermore, bad firms have an incentive to make themselves look like good firms because this enables them to fetch a higher price for their securities. Bad firms will slant the information they are required to transmit to the public, thus making it harder for investors to sort out the good firms from the bad.

Financial Intermediation   So far we have seen that private production of information and government regulation to encourage provision of information lessen, but do not eliminate, the adverse selection problem in financial markets. How, then, can the financial structure help promote the flow of funds to people with productive investment opportunities when asymmetric information exists? A clue is provided by the structure of the used-car market.

An important feature of the used-car market is that most used cars are not sold directly by one individual to another. An individual who considers buying a used car might pay for privately produced information by subscribing to a magazine like *Consumer Reports* to find out if a particular make of car has a good repair record. Nevertheless, reading *Consumer Reports* does not solve the adverse selection problem, because even if a particular make of car has a good reputation, the specific car someone is trying to sell could be a lemon. The prospective buyer might also bring the used car to a mechanic for a once-over. But what if the prospective buyer doesn't know a mechanic who can be trusted or the mechanic charges a high fee to evaluate the car?

Because these roadblocks make it hard for individuals to acquire enough information about used cars, most used cars are not sold directly by one individual to another. Instead, they are sold by an intermediary, a used-car dealer who purchases used cars from individuals and resells them to other individuals. Used-car dealers produce information in the market by becoming experts in determining whether a car is a peach or a lemon. Once a dealer knows that a car is good, the dealer can sell it with some form of a guarantee: either an explicit guarantee such as a warranty or an implicit guarantee in which the dealer stands by its reputation for honesty. People are more likely to purchase a used car because of a dealer's guarantee, and the dealer is able to sell the used car at a higher price than the dealer paid for it. Thus the dealer profits from the production of information about automobile quality. If dealers purchase and then resell cars on which they have produced information, they avoid the problem of other people free-riding on the information they produced.

Just as used-car dealers help solve adverse selection problems in the automobile market, financial intermediaries play a similar role in financial markets. A financial intermediary, such as a bank, becomes an expert in producing information about firms so that it can sort out good credit risks from bad ones. It then can acquire funds from depositors and lend them to the good firms. Because the bank is able to lend mostly to good firms, it is able to earn a higher return on its loans than the interest it has to pay to its depositors. The resulting profit that the bank earns gives it the incentive to engage in this information production activity.

An important element of the bank's ability to profit from the information it produces is that it avoids the free-rider problem by primarily making private loans, rather than by purchasing securities that are traded in the open market. Because a private loan is not traded, other investors cannot watch what the bank is doing and bid down the loan's interest rate to the point that the bank receives no compensation for the information it has produced. The bank's role as an intermediary that holds mostly nontraded loans is the key to its success in reducing asymmetric information in financial markets.

Our analysis of adverse selection indicates that financial intermediaries in general—and banks in particular, because they hold a large fraction of nontraded loans—should play a greater role in moving funds to corporations than securities markets do. Our analysis thus explains facts 3 and 4: why indirect finance is so much more important than direct finance and why banks are the most important source of external funds for financing businesses.

Our analysis also explains the greater importance of banks, as opposed to securities markets, in the financial systems of developing countries. As we have seen, better information about the quality of firms lessens asymmetric information problems, making it easier for firms to issue securities. Information about private firms is harder to collect in developing countries than in industrialized countries; therefore, the smaller role played by securities markets leads to a greater role for financial intermediaries such as banks. As a corollary to our analysis, as information about firms becomes easier to acquire, the role of banks should decline. A major development in the past 30 years in the United States has been huge improvements in information technology. Thus our analysis suggests that the lending role of financial institutions such as banks in the United States should have declined, and this is exactly what has occurred (see Chapter 11).

Our analysis of adverse selection also explains fact 6, which questions why large firms are more likely to obtain funds from securities markets, a direct route, rather than from banks and financial intermediaries, an indirect route. The better known a corporation is, the more information about its activities is available in the marketplace. Thus it is easier for investors to evaluate the quality of the corporation and determine whether it is a good firm or a bad one. Because investors have fewer worries about adverse selection when dealing with well-known corporations, they are more willing to invest directly in their securities. Thus, in accordance with adverse selection, a pecking order for firms that can issue securities should exist. Hence we have an explanation for fact 6: The larger and more established a corporation is, the more likely it will be to issue securities to raise funds.

Collateral and Net Worth   Adverse selection interferes with the functioning of financial markets only if a lender suffers a loss when a borrower is unable to make loan payments and thereby defaults on the loan. *Collateral*, property promised to the lender if the borrower defaults, reduces the consequences of adverse selection because it reduces the lender's losses in the event of a default. If a borrower defaults on a loan, the lender can sell the collateral and use the proceeds to make up for the losses on the loan. For example, if you fail to make your mortgage payments, the lender can take the title to your house, auction it off, and use the receipts to pay off the loan. Lenders are thus more willing to make loans secured by collateral, and borrowers are willing to supply collateral because the reduced risk for the lender makes it more likely that the loan will be made, perhaps even at a better loan rate. The presence of adverse selection in credit markets thus explains why collateral is an important feature of debt contracts (fact 7).

Net worth (also called **equity capital**), the difference between a firm's assets (what it owns or is owed) and its liabilities (what it owes), can perform a similar role to that of collateral. If a firm has a high net worth, then even if it engages in investments that lead to negative profits and so defaults on its debt payments, the lender can take title to the firm's net worth, sell it off, and use the proceeds to recoup some of the losses from the loan. In addition, the more net worth a firm has in the first place, the less likely it is to default, because the firm has a cushion of assets that it can use to pay off its loans. Hence, when firms seeking credit have high net worth, the consequences of adverse selection are less important and lenders are more willing to make loans. This concept lies behind the often-heard lament, "Only the people who don't need money can borrow it!"

Summary   So far we have used the concept of adverse selection to explain seven of the eight facts about financial structure introduced earlier: The first four facts emphasize the importance of financial intermediaries and the relative unimportance of securities markets with regard to the financing of corporations; the fifth, that financial markets are among the most heavily regulated sectors of the economy; the sixth, that only large, well-established corporations have access to securities markets; and the seventh, that collateral is an important feature of debt contracts. In the next section, we will see that the other asymmetric information concept, moral hazard, provides additional reasons for the importance of financial intermediaries and the relative unimportance of securities markets as related to the financing of corporations, the prevalence of government regulation, and the importance of collateral in debt contracts. In addition, the concept of moral hazard can be used to explain our final fact (fact 8): why debt contracts are complicated legal documents that place substantial restrictions on the behavior of the borrower.

HOW MORAL HAZARD AFFECTS THE CHOICE BETWEEN DEBT AND EQUITY CONTRACTS

Moral hazard is the asymmetric information problem that occurs after a financial transaction takes place, when the seller of a security may have incentives to hide information and engage in activities that are undesirable for the purchaser of the security. Moral hazard has important consequences for whether a firm finds it easier to raise funds with debt than with equity contracts.

Moral Hazard in Equity Contracts: The Principal–Agent Problem

Equity contracts, such as common stock, are claims to a share in the profits and assets of a business. Equity contracts are subject to a particular type of moral hazard called the **principal–agent problem**. When managers own only a small fraction of the firm they work for, the stockholders who own most of the firm's equity (called the *principals*) are not the same people as the managers of the firm. Thus the managers are the *agents* of the owners. This separation of ownership and control involves moral hazard, in that the managers in control (the agents) may act in their own interest rather than in the interest of the stockholder-owners (the principals) because the managers have less incentive to maximize profits than the stockholder-owners do.

To understand the principal–agent problem more fully, suppose that your friend Steve asks you to become a silent partner in his ice-cream store. The store set-up requires an initial investment of $10,000, and Steve has only $1,000. So you purchase an equity stake (stock shares) for $9,000, which entitles you to 90% of the ownership of the firm, while Steve owns only 10%. If Steve works hard to make tasty ice cream, keeps the store clean, smiles at all the customers, and hustles to wait on tables quickly, after all expenses (including Steve's salary) have been paid, the store will make $50,000 in profits per year, of which Steve will receive 10% ($5,000) and you will receive 90% ($45,000).

But if Steve doesn't provide quick and friendly service to his customers, uses the $50,000 in income to buy artwork for his office, and even sneaks off to the beach while he should be at the store, the store will not earn any profit. Steve can earn the additional $5,000 (his 10% share of the profits) over his salary only if he works hard and forgoes unproductive investments (such as art for his office). Steve might decide that the extra $5,000 just isn't enough to make him expend the effort to be a good manager. If Steve feels this way, he does not have enough incentive to be a good manager and will end up with a beautiful office, a good tan, and a store that doesn't show any profits. Because the store won't show any profits, Steve's decision not to act in your interest will cost you $45,000 (your 90% of the profits had he chosen to be a good manager instead).

The moral hazard arising from the principal–agent problem might be even worse if Steve is not totally honest. Because his ice-cream store is a cash business, Steve has the incentive to pocket $50,000 in cash and tell you that the profits were zero. He now gets a return of $50,000, and you get nothing.

Further proof that the principal–agent problem created by equity contracts can be severe is provided by past scandals involving corporations such as Enron and Tyco International, in which managers were found to have diverted corporate funds for their own personal use. In addition to pursuing personal benefits, managers might also pursue corporate strategies (such as the acquisition of other firms) that enhance their personal power but do not increase the corporation's profitability.

The principal–agent problem would not arise if the owners of a firm had complete information about what the managers were up to and could prevent wasteful expenditures or fraud. The principal–agent problem, which is an example of moral hazard, arises only because a manager, such as Steve, has more information about his activities than the stockholder does—that is, information is asymmetric. The principal–agent problem also would not occur if Steve alone owned the store, and ownership and control were not separate. If this were the case, Steve's hard work and avoidance of unproductive investments would yield him a profit (and extra income) of $50,000, an amount that would make it worth his while to be a good manager.

Tools to Help Solve the Principal–Agent Problem

Production of Information: Monitoring   You have seen that the principal–agent problem arises because managers have more information about their activities and actual profits than stockholders do. One way for stockholders to reduce this moral hazard problem is for them to engage in a particular type of information production: monitoring the firm's activities by auditing the firm frequently and checking on what the management is doing. The problem is that the monitoring process can be expensive in terms of time and money, as reflected in the name economists give it: **costly state verification**. Costly state verification makes the equity contract less desirable and explains in part why equity is not a more important element in our financial structure.

As with adverse selection, the free-rider problem decreases the amount of private information production that would reduce the moral hazard (principal–agent) problem. In this example, the free-rider problem decreases monitoring. If you know that other stockholders are paying to monitor the activities of the company you hold shares in, you can take a free ride on their activities. Then you can use the money you save by not engaging in monitoring to vacation on a Caribbean island. If you can do this, though, so can other stockholders. Perhaps all the stockholders will go to the islands, and no one will spend any resources on monitoring the firm. The moral hazard problem for shares of common stock will then be severe, making it hard for firms to issue them to raise capital (providing an additional explanation for fact 1).

Government Regulation to Increase Information . As with adverse selection, the government has an incentive to try to reduce the moral hazard problem created by asymmetric information, which provides another reason why the financial system is so heavily regulated (fact 5). Governments everywhere have laws to force firms to adhere to standard accounting principles that make profit verification easier. They also pass laws to impose stiff criminal penalties on people who commit the fraud of hiding and stealing profits. However, these measures can be only partly effective. Catching this kind of fraud is not easy; fraudulent managers have the incentive to make it very hard for government agencies to find or prove fraud.

Financial Intermediation   Financial intermediaries have the ability to avoid the free-rider problem in the face of moral hazard, and this is another reason why indirect finance is so important (fact 3). One financial intermediary that helps reduce the moral hazard arising from the principal–agent problem is the **venture capital firm**. Venture capital firms pool the resources of their partners and use the funds to help budding entrepreneurs start new businesses. In exchange for supplying the venture capital, the firm receives an equity share in the new business. Because verification of earnings and profits is so important in eliminating moral hazard, venture capital firms usually insist on having several of their own people participate as members of the managing body—the board of directors—of the new business so that they can keep a close watch on the new firm's activities. When a venture capital firm supplies start-up funds, the equity in the new firm is private—that is, not marketable to anyone *except* the venture capital firm.[3] Thus other investors are unable to take a free ride on the venture capital firm's verification activities. As a result of this arrangement, the venture capital firm is able to garner the full benefits of its verification activities and is given the appropriate incentives to reduce the moral hazard problem. Venture capital firms have been important in the development of the high-tech sector in the United States, which has resulted in job creation, economic growth, and increased international competitiveness.

Debt Contracts   Moral hazard arises with an equity contract, which is a claim on profits in all situations, whether the firm is making or losing money. If a contract could be structured so that moral hazard would exist only in certain situations, the need to monitor managers would be reduced, and the contract would be more attractive than the equity contract. The debt contract has exactly these attributes because it is a contractual agreement by the borrower to pay the lender *fixed* dollar amounts at periodic intervals. When a firm has high profits, the lender receives the contractual payments and does not need to know the exact profits of the firm. If the managers are hiding profits or pursuing activities that are personally beneficial but don't increase the firm's profitability, the lender doesn't care, as long as these activities do not interfere with the ability of the firm to make its debt payments on time. Only when the firm cannot meet its debt payments, thereby putting itself in a state of default, does the lender need to verify the state of the firm's profits. Only in this situation do lenders involved in debt contracts need to act more like equity holders; to get their fair share, they now must know how much income the firm has.

The less frequent need to monitor the firm, and thus the lower cost of state verification, helps explain why debt contracts are used more frequently than equity contracts to raise capital. The concept of moral hazard therefore helps explain fact 1, which states that stocks are not the most important source of financing for businesses.[4]

---

[3]Private equity firms, which also engage in private equity investment, solve the free-rider problem in a way that is similar to the method used by venture capital firms. Venture capital firms invest in new businesses and then, when the new company matures, sell shares to the public. In contrast to venture capital firms, which take new companies public, private equity firms take older, public companies and make them private—that is, they purchase all the publicly-traded shares and retire them. They then exercise control over the company using methods similar to those used by venture capital firms.

[4]Another factor that encourages the use of debt contracts rather than equity contracts in the United States is our tax code. Debt interest payments are a deductible expense for American firms, whereas dividend payments to equity shareholders are not.

HOW MORAL HAZARD INFLUENCES FINANCIAL STRUCTURE IN DEBT MARKETS

Even with the advantages just described, debt contracts are still subject to moral hazard. Because a debt contract requires the borrowers to pay out a fixed amount and lets them keep any profits above this amount, the borrowers have an incentive to take on investment projects that are riskier than the lenders would like.

For example, suppose you are concerned about the problem of verifying the profits of Steve's ice-cream store, and so you decide not to become an equity partner. Instead, you lend Steve the $9,000 he needs to set up his business, and you and he sign a debt contract that pays you an interest rate of 10%. As far as you are concerned, this is a surefire investment, because the demand for ice cream is strong and steady in your neighborhood. However, once you give Steve the funds, he might use them for purposes other than what he proposed to you. Instead of opening up the ice-cream store, Steve might use your $9,000 loan to invest in chemical research equipment because he thinks he has a 1-in-10 chance of inventing a diet ice cream that tastes every bit as good as the premium brands but has no fat or calories.

Obviously, this is a very risky investment, but if Steve is successful, he will become a multimillionaire. He has a strong incentive to undertake the riskier investment with your money because the gains to him would be so large if he succeeded. You would clearly be very unhappy if Steve used your loan for the riskier investment, because if he were unsuccessful, which is highly likely, you would lose most, if not all, of the money you gave him. And if he were successful, you wouldn't share in his success—you would still get only a 10% return on the loan because the principal and interest payments are fixed. Because of the potential moral hazard (that Steve might use your money to finance a very risky venture), you would probably not make the loan to Steve, even though an ice-cream store in the neighborhood is a good investment that would provide benefits to everyone.

Tools to Help Solve Moral Hazard in Debt Contracts

Net Worth and Collateral   When borrowers have more at stake because their net worth (the difference between their assets and their liabilities) is high or the collateral they have pledged to the lender is valuable, the risk of moral hazard—the temptation to act in a manner that lenders find objectionable—is greatly reduced because the borrowers themselves have a lot to lose. In other words, if borrowers have more "skin in the game" because they have higher net worth or pledge collateral, they are likely to take less risk at the lender's expense. Let's return to Steve and his ice-cream business. Suppose that the cost of setting up either the ice-cream store or the research equipment is $100,000 instead of $10,000. Now Steve needs to invest $91,000 (instead of $1,000) of his own money in the business, in addition to the $9,000 supplied by your loan. If Steve is unsuccessful in inventing the no-calorie, nonfat ice cream, he has a lot to lose—the $91,000 of net worth (the $100,000 in assets minus the $9,000 loan from you). He will think twice about undertaking the riskier investment and is more likely to invest in the ice-cream store, which is more of a sure thing. Thus, when Steve has more of his own money (net worth) invested in the business, and hence more skin in the game, you are more likely to make him the loan. Similarly, if you have pledged your house as collateral, you are less likely to go to Las Vegas and gamble away your earnings that month, because you might not be able to make your mortgage payments and therefore might lose your house.

One way of describing the solution that high net worth and collateral provide to the moral hazard problem is to say that it makes the debt contract **incentive-compatible**; that is, it aligns the incentives of the borrower with those of the lender. The greater the borrower's net worth and collateral pledged, then the greater the borrower's incentive to behave in the way that the lender expects and desires, the smaller the moral hazard problem in the debt contract, and the easier it is for the firm or household to borrow. Conversely, when the borrower's net worth and collateral are lower, the moral hazard problem is greater, making it harder to borrow.

Monitoring and Enforcement of Restrictive Covenants

As the example of Steve and his ice-cream store shows, if you could make sure that Steve doesn't invest in anything riskier than the ice-cream store, it would be worth your while to make him the loan. You can ensure that Steve uses your money for the purpose *you* expect by writing provisions (restrictive covenants) into the debt contract that restrict his firm's activities. By monitoring Steve's activities to check whether he is complying with the restrictive covenants and by enforcing the covenants if he is not, you can make sure that he will not take on risks at your expense. Restrictive covenants are directed at reducing moral hazard either by ruling out undesirable behavior or by encouraging desirable behavior. There are four types of restrictive covenants that achieve this objective:

1. *Covenants to discourage undesirable behavior.* Covenants can be designed to lower moral hazard by keeping the borrower from engaging in the undesirable behavior of undertaking risky investment projects. Some covenants mandate that a loan be used only to finance specific activities, such as the purchase of particular equipment or inventories. Others restrict the borrowing firm from engaging in certain risky business activities, such as purchasing other businesses.

2. *Covenants to encourage desirable behavior.* Restrictive covenants can encourage the borrower to engage in desirable activities that make it more likely that the loan will be paid off. One such restrictive covenant requires the breadwinner in a household to carry life insurance that will pay off the mortgage upon that person's death. For businesses, restrictive covenants of this type focus on encouraging the borrowing firm to keep its net worth high because higher borrower net worth reduces moral hazard and makes it less likely that the lender will suffer losses. These restrictive covenants typically specify that the borrowing firm must maintain minimum holdings of certain assets relative to the firm's size.

3. *Covenants to keep collateral valuable.* Because collateral is an important protection for the lender, restrictive covenants can encourage the borrower to keep the collateral in good condition and make sure that it stays in the possession of the borrower. This is the type of covenant ordinary people encounter most often. Automobile loan contracts, for example, require the car owner to maintain a minimum amount of collision and theft insurance and prevent the sale of the car unless the loan is paid off. Similarly, the recipient of a home mortgage must have adequate insurance on the home and must pay off the mortgage when the property is sold.

4. *Covenants to provide information.* Restrictive covenants also require a borrowing firm to provide information about its activities periodically, in the form of quarterly accounting and income reports, thereby making it easier for the lender to monitor the firm and reduce moral hazard. This type of covenant may also stipulate that the lender has the right to audit and inspect the firm's books at any time.

We now see why debt contracts are often complicated legal documents with numerous restrictions on the borrower's behavior (fact 8): Debt contracts require complicated restrictive covenants to lower moral hazard.

Financial Intermediation   Although restrictive covenants help reduce the moral hazard problem, they do not eliminate it completely. It is almost impossible to write covenants that rule out *every* risky activity. Furthermore, borrowers may be clever enough to find loopholes in restrictive covenants that make them ineffective.

Another problem with restrictive covenants is that they must be monitored and enforced. A restrictive covenant is meaningless if the borrower can violate it knowing that the lender won't check up or is unwilling to pay for legal recourse. Because monitoring and enforcement of restrictive covenants are costly, the free-rider problem arises in the debt securities (bond) market just as it does in the stock market. If you know that other bondholders are monitoring and enforcing the restrictive covenants, you can free-ride on their monitoring and enforcement. But other bondholders can do the same thing, so the likely outcome is that not enough resources will be devoted to monitoring and enforcing the restrictive covenants. Moral hazard therefore continues to be a severe problem for marketable debt.

As we have seen before, financial intermediaries—particularly banks—can avoid the free-rider problem by primarily making *private* loans. Private loans are not traded, so no one else can free-ride on the intermediary's monitoring and enforcement of the restrictive covenants. The intermediary making private loans thus receives the full benefits of monitoring and enforcement, and will work to shrink the moral hazard problem inherent in debt contracts. The concept of moral hazard has provided us with additional reasons why financial intermediaries play a more important role in channeling funds from savers to borrowers than marketable securities do, as described in facts 3 and 4.

Summary

Asymmetric information in financial markets leads to adverse selection and moral hazard problems that interfere with the efficient functioning of those markets. Tools to help solve these problems involve the private production and sale of information, government regulation to increase information in financial markets, the importance of collateral and net worth to debt contracts, and the use of monitoring and restrictive covenants. Our analysis suggests that the existence of the free-rider problem for traded securities such as stocks and bonds indicates that financial intermediaries—particularly banks—should play a greater role than securities markets in financing the activities of businesses. Economic analysis of the consequences of adverse selection and moral hazard has helped explain the basic features of our financial system, including the eight facts about our financial structure outlined at the beginning of this chapter.

As a study aid, Table 1 summarizes the asymmetric information problems and tools that help solve them. In addition, it notes how these tools and asymmetric information problems explain the eight facts of financial structure described at the beginning of the chapter.

SUMMARY TABLE 1

Asymmetric Information Problems and Tools to Solve Them

Asymmetric Information Problem	Tools to Solve It	Explains Fact Number
Adverse selection	Private production and sale of information	1, 2
	Government regulation to increase information	5
	Financial intermediation	3, 4, 6
	Collateral and net worth	7
Moral hazard in equity contracts (principal–agent problem)	Production of information: monitoring	1
	Government regulation to increase information	5
	Financial intermediation	3
	Debt contracts	1
Moral hazard in debt contracts	Collateral and net worth	6, 7
	Monitoring and enforcement of restrictive covenants	8
	Financial intermediation	3, 4

Note: List of facts:
1. Stocks are not the most important source of external financing.
2. Marketable securities are not the primary source of financing.
3. Indirect finance is more important than direct finance.
4. Banks are the most important source of external funds.
5. The financial system is heavily regulated.
6. Only large, well-established firms have access to securities markets.
7. Collateral is prevalent in debt contracts.
8. Debt contracts have numerous restrictive covenants.

APPLICATION   Financial Development and Economic Growth

Recent research has found that an important reason why many developing countries and ex-communist countries like Russia (which are referred to as *transition countries*) experience very low rates of economic growth is that their financial systems are underdeveloped (a situation referred to as *financial repression*).[5] The economic analysis of financial structure helps explain how an underdeveloped financial system leads to a low state of economic development and economic growth.

The financial systems of developing and transition countries face several difficulties that keep them from operating efficiently. As we have seen, two important tools used

[5]See World Bank, *Finance for Growth: Policy Choices in a Volatile World* (World Bank and Oxford University Press, 2001), and Frederic S. Mishkin, *The Next Great Globalization: How Disadvantaged Nations Can Harness Their Financial Systems to Get Rich* (Princeton University Press, 2006) for a survey of the literature linking economic growth with financial development and a list of additional references.

to help solve adverse selection and moral hazard problems in credit markets are collateral and restrictive covenants. In many developing countries, the system of property rights (the rule of law, constraints on government expropriation, and the absence of corruption) functions poorly, making it hard for these two tools to function effectively.

As discussed in the FYI box, "The Tyranny of Collateral," the weak systems of property rights common in developing and transition countries impede the use of collateral, making adverse selection problems worse because the lender will need even more information about the quality of the borrower in order to screen out a good loan from a bad one. As a result, it is harder for lenders to channel funds to the borrowers with the most productive investment opportunities, ultimately leading to less productive investment and hence a slower-growing economy.

FYI   The Tyranny of Collateral

To use property, such as land or capital, as collateral, a person must legally own it. Unfortunately, as Hernando De Soto documents in his book *The Mystery of Capital*, it is extremely expensive and time-consuming for the poor in developing countries to make their ownership of property legal. Obtaining legal title to a dwelling on urban land in the Philippines, for example, involved 168 bureaucratic steps and 53 public and private agencies, and the process took anywhere from thirteen to twenty-five years. Obtaining legal title to desert land in Egypt took 77 steps, 31 public and private agencies, and anywhere from five to fourteen years. To legally buy government land in Haiti, an ordinary citizen had to go through 176 steps over nineteen years. These legal barriers do not mean that the poor do not invest: they still build houses and buy equipment, even if they don't have legal title to these assets. By De Soto's calculations, the "total value of the real estate held but not legally owned by the poor of the Third World and former communist nations is at least $9.3 trillion."*

Without legal title, however, none of this property can be used as collateral to borrow funds, a requirement for most lenders. Even when people have legal title to their property, the legal system in most developing countries is so inefficient that collateral does not mean much. Typically, creditors must first sue the defaulting debtor for payment, which takes several years, and then, upon obtaining a favorable judgment, the creditor has to sue again to obtain title to the collateral. This process

often takes in excess of five years. By the time the lender acquires the collateral, it is likely to have been neglected or stolen and thus has little value. In addition, governments often block lenders from foreclosing on borrowers in politically powerful sectors of a society, such as agriculture.

When the financial system is unable to use collateral effectively, the adverse selection problem worsens because the lender needs even more information about the quality of the borrower in order to distinguish a good loan from a bad one. Little lending will take place, especially in transactions that involve collateral, such as mortgages. In Peru, for example, the value of mortgage loans relative to the size of the economy is less than 1/20 that in the United States.

The poor in developing countries have an even harder time obtaining loans because it is too costly for them to get title to their property, and therefore they have no collateral to offer, resulting in what Raghuram Rajan, the governor of India's central bank, and Luigi Zingales of the University of Chicago refer to as the "tyranny of collateral."** Even when poor people have a good idea for a business and are willing to work hard, they cannot get the funds to finance the business, making it difficult for them to escape poverty.

*Hernando De Soto, *The Mystery of Capital: Why Capitalism Triumphs in the West and Fails Everywhere Else* (New York: Basic Books, 2000), 35.

**Raghuram Rajan and Luigi Zingales, *Saving Capitalism from the Capitalists: Unleashing the Power of Financial Markets to Create Wealth and Spread Opportunity* (New York: Crown Business, 2003).

Similarly, a poorly developed or corrupt legal system makes it extremely difficult for lenders to enforce restrictive covenants. Thus their ability to reduce moral hazard on the part of borrowers is severely limited, and so they are less willing to lend. Again, the outcome is less productive investment and a lower growth rate for the economy. The importance of an effective legal system in promoting economic growth suggests that lawyers play a more positive role in the economy than we give them credit for.

Governments in developing and transition countries often use their financial systems to direct credit to themselves or to favored sectors of the economy by setting interest rates at artificially low levels for certain types of loans, by creating development finance institutions to make specific types of loans, or by directing existing institutions to lend to certain entities. As we have seen, private institutions have an incentive to solve adverse selection and moral hazard problems and to lend to borrowers with the most productive investment opportunities. Governments have less incentive to do so because they are not driven by the profit motive and thus their directed credit programs may not channel funds to sectors that will produce high growth for the economy. The likely outcome is, again, less efficient investment and slower economic growth.

In addition, banks in many developing and transition countries are owned by their governments. Again, because of the absence of the profit motive, these **state-owned banks** have little incentive to allocate their capital to the most productive uses. Not surprisingly, the primary loan customer of these state-owned banks is often the government itself, which does not always use the funds wisely.

We have seen that government regulation can increase the amount of information available in financial markets and thus help them work more efficiently. Many developing and transition countries have an underdeveloped regulatory apparatus that retards the provision of adequate information to the marketplace. For example, these countries often have weak accounting standards, making it very hard to ascertain the quality of a borrower's balance sheet. As a result, asymmetric information problems are more severe, and the financial system is severely hampered in channeling funds to the most productive uses.

The institutional environment of a poor legal system, weak accounting standards, inadequate government regulation, and government intervention through directed credit programs and state ownership of banks all help explain why many countries stay poor while others grow rich.

APPLICATION   Is China a Counterexample to the Importance of Financial Development?

Although China appears to be on its way to becoming an economic powerhouse, its financial development remains in the early stages. The country's legal system is weak, so that financial contracts are difficult to enforce, and accounting standards are lax, making high-quality information about creditors hard to obtain. Regulation of the banking system is still in its formative stages, and the banking sector is dominated by large, state-owned banks. Yet the Chinese economy has enjoyed one of the highest growth rates in the world over the past twenty years. How has China been able to grow so rapidly, given its low level of financial development?

As noted above, China is in an early state of financial development, with a per capita income that is still less than $10,000, one-fifth the per capita income in the United States. With an extremely high savings rate, averaging around 40% over the past two decades, the country has been able to rapidly build up its capital stock and shift a massive pool of underutilized labor from the subsistence-agriculture sector into higher-productivity activities that use capital. Even though available savings have not always been allocated to their most productive uses, the huge increase in capital, combined with the gains in productivity achieved by moving labor out of low-productivity, subsistence agriculture, have been enough to produce high growth.

As China gets richer, however, this strategy is unlikely to continue to work. The Soviet Union provides a graphic example. In the 1950s and 1960s, the Soviet Union shared many characteristics with modern-day China: high growth fueled by a high savings rate, a massive buildup of capital, and shifts of a large pool of underutilized labor from subsistence agriculture to manufacturing. During this high-growth phase, however, the Soviet Union was unable to develop the institutions needed to allocate capital efficiently. As a result, once the pool of subsistence laborers was used up, the Soviet Union's growth slowed dramatically and it was unable to keep up with the Western economies. Today, no one considers the Soviet Union an economic success story, and its inability to develop the institutions necessary to sustain financial development and growth is an important reason for the demise of this superpower.

To move into the next stage of development, China will need to allocate its capital more efficiently, which requires that it improve its financial system. The Chinese leadership is well aware of this challenge; the government has announced that state-owned banks are being put on the path to privatization. In addition, the government is engaged in legal reform aimed at making financial contracts more enforceable. New bankruptcy law is being developed so that lenders will have the ability to take over the assets of firms that default on their loan contracts. Whether the Chinese government will succeed in developing a first-rate financial system, thereby enabling China to join the ranks of developed countries, is a big question mark. ◆

SUMMARY

1. There are eight basic facts that summarize the U.S. financial structure. The first four emphasize the importance of financial intermediaries and the relative unimportance of securities markets with regard to the financing of corporations; the fifth recognizes that financial markets are among the most heavily regulated sectors of the economy; the sixth states that only large, well-established corporations have access to securities markets; the seventh indicates that collateral is an important feature of debt contracts; and the eighth presents debt contracts as complicated legal documents that place substantial restrictions on the behavior of the borrower.

2. Transaction costs freeze many small savers and borrowers out of direct involvement with financial markets. Financial intermediaries can take advantage of economies of scale and are better able to develop expertise, leading to lower transaction costs and thus enabling

their savers and borrowers to benefit from the existence of financial markets.

3. Asymmetric information results in two problems: adverse selection, which occurs before the transaction takes place, and moral hazard, which occurs after the transaction has taken place. Adverse selection refers to the fact that bad credit risks are the ones most likely to seek loans, and moral hazard refers to the risk of the borrower engaging in activities that are undesirable from the lender's point of view.

4. Adverse selection interferes with the efficient functioning of financial markets. Tools that help reduce the adverse selection problem include private production and sale of information, government regulation to increase information, financial intermediation, and collateral and net worth. The free-rider problem occurs when people who do not pay for information take advantage of information that other people have paid for. This problem

explains why financial intermediaries, particularly banks, play a more important role in financing the activities of businesses than do securities markets.

5. Moral hazard in equity contracts, known as the principal–agent problem, occurs because managers (the agents) have less incentive to maximize profits than stockholders (the principals). The principal–agent problem explains why debt contracts are so much more

prevalent in financial markets than equity contracts. Tools that help reduce the principal–agent problem include monitoring, government regulation to increase information, and financial intermediation.

6. Tools that are used to reduce the moral hazard problem in debt contracts include net worth, monitoring and enforcement of restrictive covenants, and financial intermediaries.

KEY TERMS

agency theory, p. 167
collateral, p. 165
costly state verification, p. 174
free-rider problem, p. 169

incentive-compatible, p. 177
net worth (equity capital), p. 172
principal–agent problem, p. 173
restrictive covenants, p. 165

secured debt, p. 165
state-owned banks, p. 181
unsecured debt, p. 165
venture capital firm, p. 175

QUESTIONS

All questions are available in MyEconLab at http://www.myeconlab.com.

1. For each of the following countries, identify the single most important (largest) and least important (smallest) source of external funding: United States; Germany; Japan; Canada. Comment on the similarities and differences among the countries' funding sources.

2. How can economies of scale help explain the existence of financial intermediaries?

3. Describe two ways in which financial intermediaries help lower transaction costs in an economy.

4. Why are financial intermediaries willing to engage in information collection activities when investors in financial instruments may be unwilling to do so?

5. Suppose you go to your local bank, intending to buy a certificate of deposit with your savings. Explain why you would not offer a loan, at an interest rate that is higher than the rate the bank pays on certificates of deposit (but lower than the rate the bank charges for car loans), to the next individual who enters the bank and applies for a car loan.

6. Wealthy people often worry that others will seek to marry them only for their money. Is this a problem of adverse selection?

7. Do you think the lemons problem would be more severe for stocks traded on the New York Stock Exchange or for those traded over-the-counter? Explain.

8. Would you be more willing to lend to a friend if she had put all of her life savings into her business than you would be if she had not done so? Why?

9. What specific procedures do financial intermediaries use to reduce asymmetric information problems in lending?

10. What steps can the government take to reduce asymmetric information problems and help the financial system function more smoothly and efficiently?

11. How can asymmetric information problems lead to a bank panic?

12. In December 2001, Argentina announced it would not honor its sovereign (government-issued) debt. Many investors were left holding Argentinean bonds priced at a fraction of their previous value. A few years later, Argentina announced it would pay back 25% of the face value of its debt. Comment on the effects of information asymmetries on government bond markets. Do you think investors are currently willing to buy bonds issued by the government of Argentina?

13. How does the free-rider problem aggravate adverse selection and moral hazard problems in financial markets?

14. Would moral hazard and adverse selection still arise in financial markets if information were not asymmetric? Explain.

15. How do standardized accounting principles help financial markets work more efficiently?

16. Which firms are most likely to use bank financing rather than issue bonds or stocks to finance their activities? Why?

17. How can the existence of asymmetric information provide a rationale for government regulation of financial markets?

18. "The more collateral there is backing a loan, the less the lender has to worry about adverse selection." Is this statement true, false, or uncertain? Explain your answer.

19. Explain how the separation of ownership and control in American corporations might lead to poor management.

20. Many policymakers in developing countries have proposed the implementation of a system of deposit insurance similar to the system that exists in the United States. Explain why this might create more problems than solutions in the financial system of a developing country.

21. Gustavo is a young doctor who lives in a country with a relatively inefficient legal and financial system. When Gustavo applied for a mortgage, he found that banks usually required collateral for up to 300% of the amount of the loan. Explain why banks might require that much collateral in such a financial system. Comment on the consequences of such a system for economic growth.

APPLIED PROBLEMS

All applied problems are available in MyEconLab *at* http://www.myeconlab.com.

For Problems 22–25, use the fact that the expected value of an event is a probability weighted average, the sum of each possible outcome multiplied by the probability of the event occurring.

22. You are in the market for a used car and decide to visit a used car dealership. You know that the Blue Book value of the car you are looking at is between $20,000 and $24,000. If you believe the dealer knows *as much* about the car as you do, how much are you willing to pay? Why? Assume that you care only about the expected value of the car you will buy and that the car values are symmetrically distributed.

23. Refer to Problem 22. Now you believe the dealer knows *more* about the car than you do. How much are you willing to pay? Why? How can this asymmetric information problem be resolved in a competitive market?

24. You wish to hire Ron to manage your Dallas operations. The profits from the operations depend partially on how hard Ron works, as follows.

Profit Probabilities		
	Profit = $10,000	Profit = $50,000
Lazy	60%	40%
Hard worker	20%	80%

If Ron is lazy, he will surf the Internet all day, and he views this as a zero cost opportunity. However, Ron views working hard as a "personal cost" valued at $1,000. What fixed percentage of the profits should you offer Ron? Assume Ron cares only about his expected payment less any "personal cost."

25. You own a house worth $400,000 that is located on a river. If the river floods moderately, the house will be completely destroyed. Moderate flooding happens about once every 50 years. If you build a seawall, the river would have to flood heavily to destroy your house, and such heavy flooding happens only about once every 200 years. What would be the annual premium for a flood insurance policy that offers full insurance? For a policy that pays only 75% of the home value, what are your expected costs with and without a seawall? Do the different policies provide an incentive to be safer (i.e., to build the seawall)?

DATA ANALYSIS PROBLEMS

The Problems update with real-time data in MyEconLab and are available for practice or instructor assignment.

 1. Go to the St. Louis Federal Reserve FRED database, and find data on the percent of value of loans secured by collateral for all commercial and industrial loans (ESANQ) and the net percentage of domestic banks tightening standards for commercial and industrial loans to large and middle-market firms (DRTSCILM). Download the data into a spreadsheet.

   a. Calculate the average, over the most recent four quarters and the four quarters prior to that, for the bank standards indicator and the "percent of loans secured by collateral" indicator. Do these averages behave as you would expect?

   b. Use the Data Analysis tool in Excel to calculate the correlation coefficient for the two data series from 1997:Q3 to the most recent quarter of data available. What can you conclude about the relationship between collateral and bank C&I lending standards? Is this result consistent with efforts to reduce asymmetric information?

 2. Go to the St. Louis Federal Reserve FRED database, and find data on net worth of households (TNWBSHNO) and the net percentage of domestic banks tightening standards for prime mortgage loans (DRTSPM). Adjust the *units* setting for the net worth indicator to "Percent Change from Year Ago," and download the data into a spreadsheet.

   a. Calculate the average, over the most recent four quarters and the four quarters prior to that, for the bank standards indicator and the "percent change in net worth" indicator. Do these averages behave as you would expect?

   b. Use the Data Analysis tool in Excel to calculate the correlation coefficient for the two data series from 2007:Q3 to the most recent quarter of data available. What can you conclude about the relationship between the net worth of households and bank mortgage lending standards? Is this result consistent with efforts to reduce asymmetric information?

WEB EXERCISES

1. In this chapter, we discuss the lemons problem and its effect on the efficient functioning of a market. This theory was initially developed by George Akerlof. Go to http://www.nobel.se/economics/laureates/2001/public .html. This site reports that Akerlof, Spence, and Stiglitz were awarded the Nobel Prize in economics in 2001 for their work. Read this report down through the section on George Akerlof. Summarize his research ideas in one page.

WEB REFERENCES

http://nobelprize.org/nobel_prize/economics/laureates/2001/public.html

A complete discussion of the lemons problem on a site dedicated to Nobel Prize winners.

9 Banking and the Management of Financial Institutions

Learning Objectives

- Summarize the features of a bank balance sheet.
- Apply changes to a bank's assets and liabilities on a T-account.
- Identify the ways in which banks can manage their assets and liabilities to maximize profit.
- List the ways in which banks deal with credit risk.
- Apply gap analysis and duration analysis, and identify interest-rate risk.
- Summarize the types of off-balance-sheet activities.

Preview

Because banking plays such a major role in channeling funds to borrowers with productive investment opportunities, this financial activity is important in ensuring that the financial system and the economy run smoothly and efficiently. In the United States, banks (depository institutions) supply on the order of $10 trillion in credit annually. They provide loans to businesses, help us finance our college educations and our purchases of new cars and homes, and provide us with services such as checking and savings accounts, debit cards, and ATMs.

In this chapter, we examine how banking is conducted to earn the highest profits possible: how and why banks make loans, how they acquire funds and manage their assets and liabilities (debts), and how they earn income. Although we focus on commercial banks, because commercial banks are the most important financial intermediary, many of the same principles are applicable to other types of financial intermediaries.

THE BANK BALANCE SHEET

To understand how banking works, we start by looking at the bank **balance sheet**, a list of the bank's assets and liabilities. As the name implies, this list balances; that is, it has the characteristic that

$$\text{total assets} = \text{total liabilities} + \text{capital}$$

A bank's balance sheet is also a list of its *sources* of bank funds (liabilities and capital) and *uses* to which the funds are put (assets). Banks obtain funds by borrowing and by issuing other liabilities, such as deposits. They then use these funds to acquire assets such as securities and loans. Banks make profits by earning interest on their asset holdings of securities and loans that is higher than the interest and other expenses on their liabilities. The balance sheet used by all commercial banks as of June 2014 is shown in Table 1.

Liabilities

A bank acquires funds by issuing (selling) liabilities, which are the *sources of funds* the bank uses. The funds obtained from issuing liabilities are used to purchase income-earning assets.

TABLE 1	Balance Sheet of All Commercial Banks (items as a percentage of the total, June 2014)			
Assets (Uses of Funds)*			**Liabilities (Sources of Funds)**	
Reserves and cash items	19%		Checkable deposits	11%
Securities			Nontransaction deposits	
U.S. government and agency	13		Small-denomination time deposits (<$100,000) + savings deposits	47
State and local government and other securities	6		Large-denomination time deposits	11
Loans			Borrowings	20
Commercial and industrial	12		Bank capital	11
Real estate	25			
Consumer	8			
Interbank	1			
Other	7			
Other assets (for example, physical capital)	9			
Total	100		Total	100

*In order of decreasing liquidity.

Source: http://www.federalreserve.gov/releases/h8/current/.

Checkable Deposits   Checkable deposits are bank accounts that allow the owner of the account to write checks to third parties. Checkable deposits include all accounts on which checks can be drawn. Table 1 shows that the category of checkable deposits accounts for 11% of bank liabilities. Checkable deposits were once the most important source of bank funds (more than 60% of bank liabilities in 1960), but with the advent of new, more attractive financial instruments, such as money market deposit accounts, the share of checkable deposits in total bank liabilities has shrunk over time.

Checkable deposits are payable on demand; that is, if a depositor shows up at the bank and requests payment by making a withdrawal, the bank must pay the depositor immediately. Similarly, if a person who receives a check written on an account from a bank presents that check at the bank, the bank must pay the funds out immediately (or credit them to that person's account).

A checkable deposit is an asset for the depositor because it is part of his or her wealth. Because the depositor can withdraw funds and the bank is obligated to pay, checkable deposits are a liability for the bank. They are usually the lowest-cost source of bank funds, because depositors are willing to forgo some interest in exchange for access to a liquid asset that they can use to make purchases immediately. The bank's costs of maintaining checkable deposits include interest payments and the costs incurred in servicing these accounts—processing, preparing, and sending out monthly statements; providing efficient tellers (human or otherwise); maintaining an impressive building and conveniently located branches; and advertising and marketing aimed at enticing customers to deposit their funds in the bank. In recent years, interest paid on deposits (checkable and nontransaction) has accounted for around 10% of total bank operating expenses, whereas the costs involved in servicing accounts (employee salaries, building rent, and so on) have been approximately 85% of operating expenses.

Nontransaction Deposits Nontransaction deposits are the primary source of bank funds (58% of bank liabilities in Table 1). Owners cannot write checks on nontransaction deposits, but the interest rates paid on these deposits are usually higher than those on checkable deposits. There are two basic types of nontransaction deposits: savings accounts and time deposits (also called certificates of deposit, or CDs).

Savings accounts were once the most common type of nontransaction deposit. Funds can be added to or withdrawn from savings accounts at any time. For these accounts, transactions and interest payments are recorded in a monthly statement or in a passbook held by the owner of the account.

Time deposits have a fixed maturity length, ranging from several months to over five years, and assess substantial penalties (the forfeiture of several months' interest) for early withdrawal of funds. Small-denomination time deposits (deposits of less than $100,000) are less liquid for the depositor than passbook savings, earn higher interest rates, and are a more costly source of funds for the banks.

Large-denomination time deposits (CDs) are available in denominations of $100,000 or more and are typically bought by corporations or other banks. Large-denomination CDs are negotiable; like bonds, they can be resold in a secondary market before they mature. For this reason, negotiable CDs are held by corporations, money market mutual funds, and other financial institutions as alternative assets to Treasury bills and other short-term bonds. Since 1961, when they first appeared, negotiable CDs have become an important source of bank funds (11% in Table 1).

Borrowings Banks also obtain funds by borrowing from the Federal Reserve System, the Federal Home Loan banks, other banks, and corporations. Borrowings from the Fed are called **discount loans** (also known as *advances*). Banks also borrow reserves overnight in the federal (fed) funds market from other U.S. banks and financial institutions. Banks borrow funds overnight in order to have enough deposits at the Federal Reserve to meet the amount required by the Fed. (The *federal funds* designation is somewhat confusing, because these loans are not made by the federal government or by the Federal Reserve, but rather by banks to other banks.) Other sources of borrowed funds are loans made to banks by their parent companies (bank holding companies), loan arrangements with corporations (such as repurchase agreements), and borrowings of Eurodollars (deposits denominated in U.S. dollars residing in foreign banks or foreign branches of U.S. banks). Borrowings have become a more important source of bank funds over time: In 1960, they made up only 2% of bank liabilities; currently, they account for 20% of bank liabilities.

Bank Capital The final category on the right-hand side of the balance sheet is bank capital, or the bank's net worth, which equals the difference between total assets and liabilities (11% of total bank assets in Table 1). Bank capital is raised by selling new equity (stock) or from retained earnings. A bank's capital is its cushion against a drop in the value of its assets, which could force the bank into insolvency, which occurs when a bank has liabilities in excess of assets, meaning that the bank can be forced into liquidation.

Assets

A bank uses the funds that it has acquired by issuing liabilities to purchase income-earning assets. Bank assets are thus naturally referred to as *uses of funds*, and the interest payments earned on them are what enable banks to make profits.

Reserves   All banks hold some of the funds they acquire as deposits in an account at the Fed. **Reserves** consist of these deposits plus currency that is physically held by banks (called **vault cash** because it is stored in bank vaults overnight). Although reserves earn a low interest rate, banks hold them for two reasons. First, some reserves, called **required reserves**, are held because of **reserve requirements**, the regulation that for every dollar of checkable deposits at a bank, a certain fraction (10 cents, for example) must be kept as reserves. This fraction (10% in our example) is called the **required reserve ratio**. Banks hold additional reserves, called **excess reserves**, because they are the most liquid of all bank assets and a bank can use them to meet its obligations when funds are withdrawn, either directly by a depositor or indirectly when a check is written on an account.

Cash Items in Process of Collection   Suppose that a check written on an account at another bank is deposited in your bank, and the funds for this check have not yet been received (collected) from the other bank. The check is classified as a "cash item in process of collection," and it is an asset for your bank because it is a claim on another bank for funds that will be paid within a few days.

Deposits at Other Banks   Many small banks hold deposits in larger banks in exchange for a variety of services, including check collection, foreign exchange transactions, and help with securities purchases. This is one aspect of a system called *correspondent banking*.

Collectively, cash items in process of collection and deposits at other banks are referred to as *cash items*. As can be seen in Table 1, in June 2014, reserves and cash items made up 19% of total assets.

Securities   A bank's holdings of securities are an important income-earning asset: Securities (made up entirely of debt instruments for commercial banks, because banks are not allowed to hold stock) account for 19% of bank assets in Table 1, and they provide commercial banks with about 10% of their revenue. These securities can be classified into three categories: U.S. government and agency securities, state and local government securities, and other securities. The U.S. government and agency securities are the most liquid because they can be easily traded and converted into cash with low transaction costs. Because of their high liquidity, short-term U.S. government securities are called **secondary reserves**.

Banks hold state and local government securities because state and local governments are more likely to do business with banks that hold their securities. State and local government and other securities are both less marketable (less liquid) and riskier than U.S. government securities, primarily because of default risk: Some possibility exists that the issuer of the securities may not be able to make its interest payments or pay back the face value of the securities when they mature.

Loans   Banks make their profits primarily by issuing loans. In Table 1, some 53% of bank assets are in the form of loans, and in recent years loans have generally produced more than half of bank revenues. A loan is a liability for the individual or corporation receiving it, but an asset for a bank, because it provides income to the bank. Loans are typically less liquid than other assets because they cannot be turned into cash until the loan matures. If a bank makes a one-year loan, for example, it cannot get its funds back until the loan comes due in one year. Loans also have a higher probability of default than other assets. Because of their lack of liquidity and their higher default risk, the bank earns its highest return on loans.

As indicated in Table 1, the largest categories of loans for commercial banks are commercial and industrial loans made to businesses and real estate loans. Commercial banks also make consumer loans and lend to each other. The bulk of these interbank loans are overnight loans lent in the federal funds market. The major difference in the balance sheets of the various categories of depository institutions is primarily in the type of loan in which they specialize. Savings and loans and mutual savings banks, for example, specialize in residential mortgages, while credit unions tend to make consumer loans.

Other Assets The physical capital (bank buildings, computers, and other equipment) owned by banks is included in the other assets category.

BASIC BANKING

Before proceeding to a more detailed study of how a bank manages its assets and liabilities to make the highest profit, you should understand the basic operation of a bank.

In general terms, banks make profits by selling liabilities with one set of characteristics (a particular combination of liquidity, risk, size, and return) and using the proceeds to buy assets with a different set of characteristics. This process is often referred to as **asset transformation**. For example, a savings deposit held by one person can provide the funds that enable the bank to make a mortgage loan to another person. The bank has, in effect, transformed the savings deposit (an asset held by the depositor) into a mortgage loan (an asset held by the bank). Another way of describing this process of asset transformation is to say that the bank "borrows short and lends long" because it makes long-term loans and funds them by issuing short-term deposits.

The process of transforming assets and providing a set of services (check clearing, record keeping, credit analysis, and so forth) is like any other production process in a firm. If the bank produces desirable services at low cost and earns substantial income on its assets, it earns profits; if not, the bank suffers losses.

To make our analysis of the operation of a bank more concrete, we use a tool called a **T-account**. A T-account is a simplified balance sheet, with lines in the form of a T, that lists only the changes that occur in balance sheet items starting from some initial balance sheet position. Let's say that Jane Brown has heard that the First National Bank provides excellent service, so she opens a checking account with a $100 bill. She now has a $100 checkable deposit at the bank, which shows up as a $100 liability on the bank's balance sheet. The bank now puts her $100 bill into its vault so that the bank's assets rise by the $100 increase in vault cash. The T-account for the bank looks like this:

First National Bank			
Assets		**Liabilities**	
Vault cash	+$100	Checkable deposits	+$100

Because vault cash is also part of the bank's reserves, we can rewrite the T-account as follows:

Assets		Liabilities	
Reserves	+$100	Checkable deposits	+$100

Note that Jane Brown's opening of a checking account leads to **an increase in the bank's reserves equal to the increase in checkable deposits**.

If Jane had opened her account with a $100 check written on an account at another bank, say, the Second National Bank, we would get the same result. The initial effect on the T-account of the First National Bank would be as follows:

Assets		Liabilities	
Cash items in process of collection	+$100	Checkable deposits	+$100

Checkable deposits increase by $100 as before, but now the First National Bank is owed $100 by the Second National Bank. This asset for the First National Bank is entered in the T-account as $100 of cash items in process of collection because the First National Bank will now try to collect the funds that it is owed. It could go directly to the Second National Bank and ask for payment of the funds, but if the two banks are in separate states, that would be a time-consuming and costly process. Instead, the First National Bank deposits the check in its account at the Fed, and the Fed collects the funds from the Second National Bank. The net result is that the Fed transfers $100 of reserves from the Second National Bank to the First National Bank, and the final balance sheet positions of the two banks are as follows:

First National Bank				Second National Bank			
Assets		Liabilities		Assets		Liabilities	
Reserves	+$100	Checkable deposits	+$100	Reserves	−$100	Checkable deposits	−$100

The process initiated by Jane Brown can be summarized as follows: When a check written on an account at one bank is deposited in another, the bank receiving the deposit gains reserves equal to the amount of the check, while the bank on which the check is written sees its reserves fall by the same amount. Therefore, **when a bank receives additional deposits, it gains an equal amount of reserves; when it loses deposits, it loses an equal amount of reserves.**

Now that you understand how banks gain and lose reserves, we can examine how a bank rearranges its balance sheet to make a profit when it experiences a change in its deposits. Let's return to the situation in which the First National Bank has just received the extra $100 of checkable deposits. As you know, the bank is obliged to keep a certain fraction of its checkable deposits as required reserves. If the fraction (the required reserve ratio) is 10%, the First National Bank's required reserves have increased by $10, and we can rewrite its T-account as follows:

First National Bank			
Assets		**Liabilities**	
Required reserves	+$10	Checkable deposits	+$100
Excess reserves	+$90		

Let's see how well the bank is doing as a result of the additional checkable deposits. Servicing the extra $100 of checkable deposits is costly, because the bank must keep records, pay tellers, pay for check clearing, and so forth. Because reserves earn little interest, the bank is taking a loss! The situation is even worse if the bank makes interest payments on the deposits, as with NOW accounts. To make a profit, the bank must put to productive use all or part of the $90 of excess reserves it has available. One way to do this is to invest in securities. The other is to make loans; as we have seen, loans account for approximately 50% of the total value of bank assets (uses of funds). Because lenders are subject to the asymmetric information problems of adverse selection and moral hazard (discussed in Chapter 8), banks take steps to reduce the incidence and severity of these problems. Bank loan officers evaluate potential borrowers using what are called the "five C's"—character, capacity (ability to repay), collateral, conditions (in the local and national economies), and capital (net worth)—before they agree to lend. (A more detailed discussion of the methods banks use to reduce the risk involved in lending is given later in this chapter.)

Let's assume that the First National Bank chooses not to hold any excess reserves but to make loans instead. The T-account then looks like this:

Assets		**Liabilities**	
Required reserves	+$10	Checkable deposits	+$100
Loans	+$90		

The bank is now making a profit because it holds short-term liabilities, such as checkable deposits, and uses the proceeds to fund longer-term assets, such as loans with higher interest rates. As mentioned earlier, this process of asset transformation is frequently described by saying that banks are in the business of "borrowing short and lending long." For example, if the loans have an interest rate of 10% per year, the bank earns $9 in income from its loans over the year. If the $100 of checkable deposits is in a NOW account with a 5% interest rate and it costs another $3 per year to service the account, the cost per year of these deposits is $8. The bank's profit on the new deposits is then $1 per year, plus any interest that it earns on required reserves.

GENERAL PRINCIPLES OF BANK MANAGEMENT

Now that you have some idea of how a bank operates, let's look at how a bank manages its assets and liabilities to earn the highest possible profit. The bank manager has four primary concerns. The first is to make sure that the bank has enough ready cash to pay its depositors when there are **deposit outflows**—that is, when deposits are lost because depositors make withdrawals and demand payment. To keep enough cash on hand, the bank must engage in **liquidity management**, the acquisition of assets that are liquid enough to meet the bank's obligations to depositors. Second, the bank manager must pursue an acceptably low level of risk by acquiring assets that have a low rate of default and by diversifying asset holdings (**asset management**). The manager's third concern is acquiring funds at low cost (**liability management**). Finally, the manager must decide the amount of capital the bank should maintain and then acquire the needed capital (**capital adequacy management**).

To understand bank (and other financial institution) management fully, we must go beyond the general principles of bank asset and liability management described next and look in more detail at how a financial institution manages its assets. The two sections following this one provide an in-depth discussion of how a financial institution manages **credit risk**, the risk arising because borrowers may default, and how it manages **interest-rate risk**, the riskiness of earnings and returns on bank assets caused by interest-rate changes.

Liquidity Management and the Role of Reserves

Let's see how a typical bank, the First National Bank, can deal with deposit outflows that occur when its depositors withdraw cash from checking or savings accounts or write checks that are deposited in other banks. In the example that follows, we assume that the bank has ample excess reserves and that all deposits have the same required reserve ratio of 10% (the bank is required to keep 10% of deposits as reserves). Suppose that the First National Bank's initial balance sheet is as follows:

Assets		Liabilities	
Reserves	$20 million	Deposits	$100 million
Loans	$80 million	Bank capital	$ 10 million
Securities	$10 million		

The bank's required reserves are 10% of $100 million, or $10 million. Given that it holds $20 million of reserves, the First National Bank has excess reserves of $10 million.

If a deposit outflow of $10 million occurs, the bank's balance sheet becomes

Assets		Liabilities	
Reserves	$10 million	Deposits	$90 million
Loans	$80 million	Bank capital	$10 million
Securities	$10 million		

The bank loses $10 million of deposits *and* $10 million of reserves, but because its required reserves are now 10% of only $90 million (that is, $9 million), its reserves still exceed this amount by $1 million. In short, *if a bank has ample excess reserves, a deposit outflow does not necessitate changes in other parts of its balance sheet.*

The situation is quite different when a bank holds insufficient excess reserves. Let's assume that instead of initially holding $10 million in excess reserves, the First National Bank makes additional loans of $10 million, so that it holds no excess reserves. Its initial balance sheet would then be

Assets		Liabilities	
Reserves	$10 million	Deposits	$100 million
Loans	$90 million	Bank capital	$ 10 million
Securities	$10 million		

When it suffers the $10 million deposit outflow, its balance sheet becomes

Assets		Liabilities	
Reserves	$ 0	Deposits	$90 million
Loans	$90 million	Bank capital	$10 million
Securities	$10 million		

After $10 million has been withdrawn from deposits and hence reserves, the bank has a problem: It has a reserve requirement of 10% of $90 million, or $9 million, but it has no reserves! To eliminate this shortfall, the bank has four basic options. One option is to acquire the reserves needed to meet a deposit outflow by borrowing them from other banks in the federal funds market, or by borrowing from corporations.[1] If the First National Bank acquires the $9 million shortfall in reserves by borrowing it from other banks or corporations, its balance sheet becomes

Assets		Liabilities	
Reserves	$ 9 million	Deposits	$90 million
Loans	$90 million	Borrowings from other banks or corporations	$ 9 million
Securities	$10 million		
		Bank capital	$10 million

---

[1]One way in which the First National Bank can borrow from other banks and corporations is by selling negotiable certificates of deposit. This method for obtaining funds is discussed in the section on liability management.

The cost of this activity is the interest rate on these borrowings, such as the federal funds rate.

A second alternative is for the bank to sell some of its securities to help cover the deposit outflow. For example, it might sell $9 million of its securities and deposit the proceeds with the Fed, resulting in the following balance sheet:

Assets		Liabilities	
Reserves	$ 9 million	Deposits	$90 million
Loans	$90 million	Bank capital	$10 million
Securities	$ 1 million		

The bank incurs some brokerage and other transaction costs when it sells these securities. The U.S. government securities that are classified as secondary reserves are very liquid, so the transaction costs of selling them are quite modest. However, the other securities the bank holds are less liquid, and the transaction costs can be appreciably higher.

The bank has a third option for meeting a deposit outflow: It can acquire reserves by borrowing from the Fed. In our example, the First National Bank could leave its security and loan holdings the same, and borrow $9 million in discount loans from the Fed. Its balance sheet would then be

Assets		Liabilities	
Reserves	$ 9 million	Deposits	$90 million
Loans	$90 million	Borrowings from the Fed	$ 9 million
Securities	$10 million	Bank capital	$10 million

The cost associated with discount loans is the interest rate that must be paid to the Fed (called the **discount rate**).

As a last option, a bank can acquire the $9 million of reserves to meet the deposit outflow by reducing its loans by this amount and depositing the $9 million it then receives with the Fed, thereby increasing its reserves by $9 million. This transaction changes the balance sheet as follows:

Assets		Liabilities	
Reserves	$ 9 million	Deposits	$90 million
Loans	$81 million	Bank capital	$10 million
Securities	$10 million		

The First National Bank is once again in good shape because its $9 million of reserves satisfies the reserve requirement.

However, this process of reducing its loans is the bank's costliest way of acquiring reserves when a deposit outflow exists. If the First National Bank has numerous short-term loans renewed at fairly short intervals, it can reduce its total amount of loans outstanding fairly quickly by *calling in* loans—that is, by not renewing some loans when they come due. Unfortunately for the bank, this is likely to antagonize the customers whose loans are not being renewed because they have not done anything to deserve such treatment. Indeed, they are likely to take their business elsewhere in the future, a very costly consequence for the bank.

A second method of reducing its loans is for the bank to sell them off to other banks. Again, this is very costly because other banks do not know how risky these loans are and so may not be willing to buy the loans at their full value. (This is an example of the lemons adverse selection problem described in Chapter 8.)

The foregoing discussion explains why banks hold excess reserves even though loans or securities earn a higher return. When a deposit outflow occurs, excess reserves enable the bank to escape the costs of (1) borrowing from other banks or corporations, (2) selling securities, (3) borrowing from the Fed, or (4) calling in or selling off loans. ***Excess reserves are insurance against the costs associated with deposit outflows. The higher the costs associated with deposit outflows, the more excess reserves a bank will want to hold.***

Just as you and I would be willing to pay an insurance company to insure us against a casualty loss such as the theft of a car, a bank is willing to pay the cost of holding excess reserves (the opportunity cost—that is, the earnings forgone by not holding income-earning assets such as loans or securities) to insure against losses due to deposit outflows. Because excess reserves, like insurance, have a cost, banks also take other steps to protect themselves; for example, they might shift their holdings of assets to more liquid securities (secondary reserves).

Asset Management

Now that you understand a bank's need for liquidity, we can examine the basic strategy a bank pursues in managing its assets. To maximize its profits, a bank must simultaneously seek the highest returns possible on loans and securities, reduce risk, and make adequate provisions for liquidity by holding liquid assets. Banks try to accomplish these three goals in four basic ways.

First, banks try to find borrowers who will pay high interest rates and are unlikely to default on their loans. They seek out loan business by advertising their borrowing rates and by approaching corporations directly to solicit loans. It is up to the bank's loan officer to decide if potential borrowers are good credit risks who will make interest and principal payments on time (i.e., banks engage in screening to reduce the adverse selection problem). Typically, banks are conservative in their loan policies; the default rate is usually less than 1%. It is important, however, that banks not be so conservative that they miss out on attractive lending opportunities that earn high interest rates.

Second, banks try to purchase securities with high returns and low risk.

Third, in managing their assets, banks must attempt to lower risk by diversifying. They accomplish this by purchasing many different types of assets (short- and long-term, U.S. Treasury, and municipal bonds) and approving many types of loans to a variety of customers. Banks that have not sufficiently sought the benefits of diversification often come to regret it later. For example, banks that had overspecialized in making loans to energy companies, real estate developers, or farmers suffered huge losses in the 1980s with the slump in energy, property, and farm prices. Indeed, many of these banks went broke because they had "put too many eggs in one basket."

Finally, the bank must manage the liquidity of its assets so that it can meet deposit outflows and still satisfy its reserve requirements without bearing huge costs. This means that it will hold liquid securities even if they earn a somewhat lower return than other assets. The bank must decide, for example, how much it should hold in excess reserves to avoid the costs associated with a deposit outflow. In addition, it will want to hold U.S. government securities as secondary reserves so that even if a deposit outflow forces some costs on the bank, these will not be terribly high. Again, it is not wise for a bank to be too conservative. If it avoids all costs associated with deposit outflows by holding only excess reserves, the bank suffers losses, because reserves earn low interest, while the bank's liabilities are costly to maintain. The bank must balance its desire for liquidity against the benefits of the increased earnings that can be obtained from less liquid assets, such as loans.

Liability Management

Before the 1960s, liability management was a staid affair: For the most part, banks took their liabilities as fixed and spent their time trying to achieve an optimal mix of assets. There were two main reasons for the emphasis on asset management. First, more than 60% of bank funds were obtained through checkable (demand) deposits that by law could not pay any interest. Thus banks could not actively compete with one another for these deposits by paying interest on them, and so their amount was effectively a given for an individual bank. Second, because the markets for making overnight loans between banks were not well developed, banks rarely borrowed from other banks to meet their reserve needs.

Starting in the 1960s, however, large banks (called **money center banks**) in key financial centers, such as New York, Chicago, and San Francisco, began to explore ways in which the liabilities on their balance sheets could provide them with reserves and liquidity. This move led to an expansion of overnight loan markets, such as the federal funds market, and the development of new financial instruments, such as negotiable CDs (first developed in 1961), which enabled money center banks to acquire funds quickly.[2]

This new flexibility in liability management meant that banks could take a different approach to bank management. They no longer needed to depend on checkable deposits as the primary source of bank funds and as a result no longer treated their sources of funds (liabilities) as given. Instead, they aggressively set target goals for their asset growth and tried to acquire funds (by issuing liabilities) as they were needed.

For example, today, when a money center bank finds an attractive loan opportunity, it can acquire funds by selling a negotiable CD. Or, if it has a reserve shortfall, it can borrow funds from another bank in the federal funds market without incurring high transaction costs. The federal funds market can also be used to finance loans. Because of the increased importance of liability management, most banks now manage both sides of the balance sheet together in an *asset–liability management (ALM) committee*.

The greater emphasis on liability management explains some of the important changes over the past three decades in the composition of banks' balance sheets. While

---

[2]Because small banks are not as well known as money center banks and so might be a higher credit risk, they find it harder to raise funds in the negotiable CD market. Hence they do not engage nearly as actively in liability management.

negotiable CDs and bank borrowings have greatly increased in importance as a source of bank funds in recent years (rising from 2% of bank liabilities in 1960 to 31% by mid-2014), checkable deposits have decreased in importance (from 61% of bank liabilities in 1960 to 11% by mid-2014). Newfound flexibility in liability management and the search for higher profits have also stimulated banks to increase the proportion of their assets held in loans, which earn higher income (from 46% of bank assets in 1960 to 53% by mid-2014) than other assets.

Capital Adequacy Management

Banks have to make decisions about the amount of capital they need to hold for three reasons. First, bank capital helps prevent *bank failure*, a situation in which the bank cannot satisfy its obligations to pay its depositors and other creditors, and so goes out of business. Second, the amount of capital held affects returns for the owners (equity holders) of the bank. Third, a minimum amount of bank capital (bank capital requirements) is required by regulatory authorities.

How Bank Capital Helps Prevent Bank Failure   Let's consider two banks with identical balance sheets, except that High Capital Bank has a ratio of capital to assets of 10%, while Low Capital Bank has a ratio of 4%.

High Capital Bank				Low Capital Bank			
Assets		**Liabilities**		**Assets**		**Liabilities**	
Reserves	$10 million	Deposits	$90 million	Reserves	$10 million	Deposits	$96 million
Loans	$90 million	Bank capital	$10 million	Loans	$90 million	Bank capital	$ 4 million

Suppose both banks get caught up in the euphoria of the housing market, only to find later that $5 million of their housing loans have become worthless. When these bad loans are written off (valued at zero), the total value of assets declines by $5 million. As a consequence, bank capital, which equals total assets minus liabilities, also declines by $5 million. The balance sheets of the two banks now look like this:

High Capital Bank				Low Capital Bank			
Assets		**Liabilities**		**Assets**		**Liabilities**	
Reserves	$10 million	Deposits	$90 million	Reserves	$10 million	Deposits	$96 million
Loans	$85 million	Bank capital	$ 5 million	Loans	$85 million	Bank capital	−$ 1 million

High Capital Bank takes the $5 million loss in stride because its initial cushion of $10 million in capital means that it still has a positive net worth (bank capital) of $5 million after the loss. Low Capital Bank, however, is in big trouble. The value of its assets has fallen below that of its liabilities, and its net worth is now –$1 million. Because the bank has a negative net worth, it is insolvent: It does not have sufficient assets to pay off all holders of its liabilities. When a bank becomes insolvent, government regulators close the bank, its assets are sold off, and its managers are fired. Because the owners of Low Capital Bank will find their investment wiped out, they clearly would have preferred the bank to have had a large enough cushion of bank capital to absorb the losses, as was the case for High Capital Bank. We therefore see an important rationale for a bank to maintain a sufficient level of capital: *A bank maintains bank capital to lessen the chance that it will become insolvent.*

How the Amount of Bank Capital Affects Returns to Equity Holders   Because owners of a bank must know whether their bank is being managed well, they need good measures of bank profitability. A basic measure of bank profitability is the **return on assets (ROA)**, the net profit after taxes per dollar of assets:

$$ROA = \frac{\text{net profit after taxes}}{\text{assets}}$$

The return on assets provides information on how efficiently a bank is being run because it indicates how much profit is generated, on average, by each dollar of assets.

However, what the bank's owners (equity holders) care about most is how much the bank is earning on their equity investment. This information is provided by the other basic measure of bank profitability, the **return on equity (ROE)**, which is defined as the net profit after taxes per dollar of equity (bank) capital:

$$ROE = \frac{\text{net profit after taxes}}{\text{equity capital}}$$

There is a direct relationship between the return on assets (which measures how efficiently the bank is run) and the return on equity (which measures how well the owners are doing on their investment). This relationship is determined by the **equity multiplier (EM)**, or the amount of assets per dollar of equity capital:

$$EM = \frac{\text{assets}}{\text{equity capital}}$$

To see this, we note that

$$\frac{\text{net profit after taxes}}{\text{equity capital}} = \frac{\text{net profit after taxes}}{\text{assets}} \times \frac{\text{assets}}{\text{equity capital}}$$

which, using our definitions, yields

$$ROE = ROA \times EM \tag{1}$$

The formula in Equation 1 tells us what happens to the return on equity when a bank holds a smaller amount of capital (equity) for a given amount of assets. As we have seen, High Capital Bank initially has $100 million of assets and $10 million of equity, which gives it an equity multiplier of 10 (= $100 million/$10 million). Low Capital Bank, by contrast, has only $4 million of equity, so its equity multiplier is higher, equaling 25 (= $100 million/$4 million). Suppose these banks have been equally well run, so that they both have the same return on assets, 1%. The return on equity for High

Capital Bank equals $1\% \times 10 = 10\%$, whereas the return on equity for Low Capital Bank equals $1\% \times 25 = 25\%$. The equity holders in Low Capital Bank are clearly a lot happier than the equity holders in High Capital Bank because they are earning more than twice as high a return. We now see why the owners of a bank may not want it to hold too much capital. *Given the return on assets, the lower the bank capital, the higher the return for the owners of the bank.*

Trade-off Between Safety and Returns to Equity Holders   We now see that bank capital has both benefits and costs. Bank capital benefits the owners of a bank in that it makes their investment safer by reducing the likelihood of bankruptcy. But bank capital is costly because the higher it is, the lower will be the return on equity for a given return on assets. In determining the optimal amount of bank capital, managers must compare the benefit of maintaining higher capital (increased safety) with the cost of higher capital (the lower return on equity for bank owners).

In more uncertain times, when the possibility of large losses on loans increases, bank managers might want to hold more capital in order to protect the equity holders. Conversely, if the managers have confidence that loan losses won't occur, they might want to reduce the amount of bank capital, have a high equity multiplier, and thereby increase the return on equity.

Bank Capital Requirements   Banks also hold capital because they are required to do so by regulatory authorities. Because of the high costs of holding capital (for the reasons just described), bank managers often want to hold less bank capital relative to assets than is required by the regulatory authorities. In this case, the amount of bank capital is determined by the bank capital requirements. We discuss the details of bank capital requirements and their important role in bank regulation in Chapter 10.

APPLICATION   ## Strategies for Managing Bank Capital

Suppose that, as the manager of the First National Bank, you have to make decisions about the appropriate amount of bank capital to hold in your bank. Looking at the balance sheet of the bank, which, like that of High Capital Bank, has a ratio of bank capital to assets of 10% ($10 million of capital and $100 million of assets), you are concerned that the large amount of bank capital is causing the return on equity to be too low. You conclude that the bank has a capital surplus and should increase the equity multiplier to raise the return on equity. What should you do next?

To lower the amount of capital relative to assets and raise the equity multiplier, you can do any of three things: (1) You can reduce the amount of bank capital by buying back some of the bank's stock; (2) you can reduce the bank's capital by paying out higher dividends to its stockholders, thereby reducing the bank's retained earnings; or (3) you can keep bank capital constant but increase the bank's assets by acquiring new funds—say, by issuing CDs—and then seeking out loan business or purchasing more securities with these new funds. Because you think it will enhance your position with the stockholders, you decide to pursue the second alternative and raise the dividend on the First National Bank stock.

Now suppose that the First National Bank is in a situation similar to that of Low Capital Bank and has a ratio of bank capital to assets of 4%. You now worry that the bank is short on capital relative to assets because it does not have a sufficient cushion to prevent bank failure. To raise the amount of capital relative to assets, you now have the following three choices: (1) You can raise capital for the bank by having it issue equity (common stock); (2) you can raise capital by reducing the bank's dividends to shareholders, thereby increasing retained earnings that it can put into its capital account; or (3) you can keep capital at the same level but reduce the bank's assets by making fewer loans or by selling off securities and then using the proceeds to reduce the bank's liabilities. Suppose that raising bank capital is not easy to do at the current time because bank stock is selling at low prices or because shareholders will protest if their dividends are cut. Then you might have to choose the third alternative and shrink the size of the bank.

Our discussion of the strategies for managing bank capital at the First National Bank leads to the following conclusion, which deserves particular emphasis: ***A shortfall of bank capital is likely to lead a bank to reduce its assets and therefore is likely to cause a contraction in lending***. In past years, many banks experienced capital shortfalls and had to restrict asset and lending growth. The important consequences of this decision for the credit markets are illustrated by the application that follows.

APPLICATION | How a Capital Crunch Caused a Credit Crunch During the Global Financial Crisis

The dramatic slowdown in the growth of credit in the wake of the financial crisis that began in 2007 triggered a "credit crunch" during which credit was hard to get. As a result, the performance of the economy in 2008 and 2009 was very poor. What caused the credit crunch?

Our analysis of how a bank manages its capital indicates that the 2008–2009 credit crunch was caused, at least in part, by the capital crunch, in which shortfalls of bank capital led to slower credit growth.

A major boom and bust in the housing market led to huge losses for banks from their holdings of securities backed by residential mortgages. These losses reduced bank capital, which led to capital shortfalls: Banks had to either raise new capital or restrict asset growth by cutting back on lending. Banks did raise some capital, but with the growing weakness of the economy, raising new capital was extremely difficult, so banks also chose to tighten their lending standards and reduce lending. Both of these reactions to capital shortfalls helped produce a weak economy in 2008 and 2009. ◆

MANAGING CREDIT RISK

As noted in our earlier discussion of the general principles of asset management, banks and other financial institutions must make successful loans that are paid back in full (and so subject the institution to little credit risk) if they are to earn high profits. The economic concepts of adverse selection and moral hazard (discussed in Chapters 2 and 8) provide a framework for understanding the principles that financial institutions must follow if they are to reduce credit risk and make successful loans.[3]

---

[3]Other financial intermediaries, such as insurance companies, pension funds, and finance companies, also make private loans, and the credit risk management principles we outline here apply to them as well.

Adverse selection in loan markets occurs because bad credit risks (those most likely to default on their loans) are the ones who usually line up for loans; in other words, those who are most likely to produce an *adverse* outcome are also the most likely to be *selected*. Borrowers with very risky investment projects have much to gain if their projects are successful, so they are the most eager to obtain loans. Clearly, however, they are the least desirable borrowers because of the greater possibility that they will be unable to pay back their loans.

Moral hazard exists in loan markets because borrowers may have incentives to engage in activities that are undesirable from the lender's point of view. In such situations, it is more likely that the lender will be subjected to the *hazard* of default. Once borrowers have obtained a loan, they are more likely to invest in high-risk investment projects—projects that pay high returns to the borrower if successful. The high risk associated with these investments, however, makes it less likely that these borrowers will be able to pay back their loans.

To be profitable, financial institutions must overcome the adverse selection and moral hazard problems that make loan defaults more likely. Financial institutions attempt to solve these problems by using a number of principles for managing credit risk: screening and monitoring, establishment of long-term customer relationships, loan commitments, collateral and compensating balance requirements, and credit rationing.

Screening and Monitoring

Asymmetric information is present in loan markets because lenders have less information about the investment opportunities and activities of borrowers than borrowers do. This situation leads banks and other financial institutions to perform two information-producing activities:screening and monitoring. Indeed, Walter Wriston, a former head of Citicorp, one of the largest bank corporations in the United States, was often quoted as stating that the business of banking is the production of information.

Screening   Adverse selection in loan markets requires that lenders screen out the bad credit risks from the good ones, so that loans are profitable to them. To accomplish effective screening, lenders must collect reliable information from prospective borrowers. Effective screening and information collection together form an important principle of credit risk management.

When you apply for a consumer loan (such as a car loan or a mortgage to purchase a house), the first thing you are asked to do is fill out forms that elicit a great deal of information about your personal finances. You are asked about your salary, your bank accounts and other assets (such as cars, insurance policies, and furnishings), and your outstanding loans; your record of loan, credit card, and charge account repayments; and the number of years you've worked and the names of your employers. You also are asked personal questions such as your age, marital status, and number of children. The lender uses this information to evaluate how good a credit risk you are by calculating your credit score, a statistical measure derived from your answers that is used to predict whether you are likely to have trouble making your loan payments. Deciding how good a risk you are cannot be entirely scientific, so the lender must also use judgment. The loan officer, whose job it is to decide whether you should be given the loan, might call your employer or talk to some of the personal references you have supplied. The officer might even make a judgment based on your demeanor or your appearance. (This is why most people dress neatly and conservatively when they go to a bank to apply for a loan.)

The process of screening and collecting information is similar when a financial institution makes a business loan. It collects information about the company's profits and losses (income) along with information about its assets and liabilities. The lender also has to evaluate the likely future success of the business. So, in addition to obtaining information such as sales figures, a loan officer might ask questions about the company's future plans, the purpose of the loan, and competition within the industry. The officer may even visit the company to obtain a firsthand look at its operations. The bottom line is that, whether they are considering making personal loans or business loans, bankers and other financial institutions need to be nosy.

Specialization in Lending One puzzling feature of bank lending is that a bank often specializes in lending to local firms or to firms in particular industries, such as energy. In one sense, this behavior seems surprising because it means that the bank is not diversifying its portfolio of loans and thus is exposing itself to more risk. But from another perspective, such specialization makes perfect sense. The adverse selection problem requires that the bank screen out bad credit risks. It is easier for the bank to collect information about local firms and determine their creditworthiness than to collect comparable information on firms that are farther away. Similarly, by concentrating its lending on firms in specific industries, the bank becomes more knowledgeable about these industries and is therefore better able to predict which firms will be able to make timely payments on their debt.

Monitoring and Enforcement of Restrictive Covenants Once a loan has been made, the borrower has an incentive to engage in risky activities that make it less likely that the loan will be paid off. To reduce this moral hazard, financial institutions must write provisions (restrictive covenants) into loan contracts that restrict borrowers from engaging in risky activities. By monitoring borrowers' activities to see whether they are complying with the restrictive covenants and by enforcing the covenants if they are not, lenders can make sure that borrowers are not taking on risks at their expense. The need for banks and other financial institutions to engage in screening and monitoring explains why they spend so much money on auditing and information-collecting activities.

Long-Term Customer Relationships

An additional way for banks and other financial institutions to obtain information about their borrowers is through long-term customer relationships, another important principle of credit risk management.

If a prospective borrower has had a checking account, a savings account, or a loan with a bank over a long period of time, a loan officer can look at past activity on the accounts and learn quite a bit about the borrower. The balances in the checking and savings accounts tell the banker how liquid the potential borrower is and at what time of year the borrower has a strong need for cash. A review of the checks the borrower has written reveals the borrower's suppliers. If the borrower has borrowed previously from the bank, the bank has a record of the loan payments. Thus long-term customer relationships reduce the costs of information collection and make it easier to screen out bad credit risks.

The need for monitoring by lenders adds to the importance of long-term customer relationships. If the borrower has borrowed from the bank before, the bank has already established procedures for monitoring that customer. Therefore, the costs of monitoring long-term customers are lower than the costs of monitoring new customers.

Long-term relationships benefit customers as well as banks. A firm that has had a previous relationship with a bank will find it easier to obtain a loan from the bank at a low interest rate because the bank has an easier time determining if the prospective borrower is a good credit risk and therefore incurs fewer costs in monitoring the borrower.

A long-term customer relationship has another advantage for the bank. No bank can think of every contingency when it writes a restrictive covenant into a loan contract; there will always be risky borrower activities that are not ruled out. However, what if a borrower wants to preserve a long-term relationship with a bank because it will be easier to get future loans from the bank, at low interest rates? The borrower then has the incentive to avoid risky activities that would upset the bank, even if restrictions on these risky activities are not specified in the loan contract. Indeed, if a bank doesn't like what a borrower is doing even when the borrower isn't violating any restrictive covenants, it has some power to discourage the borrower from such activity: The bank can threaten not to give the borrower new loans in the future. Long-term customer relationships therefore enable banks to deal with even unanticipated moral hazard contingencies.

Loan Commitments

Banks also create long-term relationships and gather information by issuing **loan commitments** to commercial customers. A loan commitment is a bank's commitment (for a specified future period of time) to provide a firm with loans up to a given amount at an interest rate that is tied to some market interest rate. The majority of commercial and industrial loans are made under the loan commitment arrangement. The advantage for the firm is that it has a source of credit when it needs it. The advantage for the bank is that the loan commitment promotes a long-term relationship, which in turn facilitates information collection. In addition, provisions in the loan commitment agreement require that the firm continually supply the bank with information about the firm's income, asset and liability position, business activities, and so on. A loan commitment arrangement is a powerful method for reducing the bank's costs of screening and information collection.

Collateral and Compensating Balances

Collateral requirements for loans are important credit risk management tools. Collateral, which is property promised to the lender as compensation if the borrower defaults, lessens the consequences of adverse selection because it reduces the lender's losses in the case of a loan default. It also reduces moral hazard because the borrower has more to lose from a default. If a borrower defaults on a loan, the lender can sell the collateral and use the proceeds to make up for its losses on the loan. One particular form of collateral required when a bank makes commercial loans is called **compensating balances**: A firm receiving a loan must keep a required minimum amount of funds in a checking account at the bank. For example, a business getting a $10 million loan may be required to keep compensating balances of at least $1 million in its checking account at the bank. This $1 million in compensating balances can then be taken by the bank to make up some of the losses on the loan if the borrower defaults.

In addition to serving as collateral, compensating balances increase the likelihood that a loan will be paid off. They do this by helping the bank monitor the borrower and consequently reduce moral hazard. Specifically, by requiring the borrower to use a checking account at the bank, the bank can observe the firm's check payment practices, which may yield a great deal of information about the borrower's financial condition. For example, a sustained drop in the borrower's checking account balance may signal that the borrower is having financial trouble, or account activity may suggest that the borrower is engaging in risky activities; perhaps a change in suppliers means the borrower is pursuing a new line of business. Any significant change in the borrower's payment procedures is a signal to the bank that it should make inquiries. Compensating balances therefore make it easier for banks to monitor borrowers more effectively and are an important credit risk management tool.

Credit Rationing

Another way in which financial institutions deal with adverse selection and moral hazard is through **credit rationing**: refusing to make loans even though borrowers are willing to pay the stated interest rate, or even a higher rate. Credit rationing takes two forms. The first occurs when a lender refuses to make a loan *of any amount* to a borrower, even if the borrower is willing to pay a higher interest rate. The second occurs when a lender is willing to make a loan but restricts the size of the loan to less than the borrower would like.

Initially, you might be puzzled by the first type of credit rationing. After all, even if the potential borrower is a credit risk, why doesn't the lender just extend the loan, but at a higher interest rate? The answer is that adverse selection prevents this from being a wise course of action. Individuals and firms with the riskiest investment projects are exactly those that are willing to pay the highest interest rates. If a borrower took on a high-risk investment and succeeded, the borrower would become extremely rich. But a lender wouldn't want to make such a loan precisely because the credit risk is high; the likely outcome is that the borrower will *not* succeed and the lender will not be paid back. Charging a higher interest rate just makes adverse selection worse for the lender; that is, it increases the likelihood that the lender is lending to a bad credit risk. The lender would therefore rather not make any loans at a higher interest rate; instead, it would engage in the first type of credit rationing and would turn down loans.

Financial institutions engage in the second type of credit rationing to guard against moral hazard: They grant loans to borrowers, but loans that are not as large as the borrowers want. Such credit rationing is necessary because the larger the loan, the greater the benefits from moral hazard. If a bank gives you a $1,000 loan, for example, you are likely to take actions that enable you to pay it back because you don't want to hurt your credit rating for the future. However, if the bank lends you $10 million, you are more likely to fly down to Rio to celebrate. The larger your loan, the greater your incentives to engage in activities that make it less likely that you will repay the loan. Because more borrowers repay their loans if the loan amounts are small, financial institutions ration credit by providing borrowers with smaller loans than they seek.

MANAGING INTEREST-RATE RISK

With the increased volatility of interest rates that occurred in the 1980s, banks and other financial institutions became more concerned about their exposure to interest-rate risk, the riskiness of earnings and returns that is associated with changes in interest rates. To see what interest-rate risk is all about, let's again take a look at the First National Bank, which has the following balance sheet:

First National Bank			
Assets		**Liabilities**	
Rate-sensitive assets	$20 million	Rate-sensitive liabilities	$50 million
Variable-rate and		Variable-rate CDs	
short-term loans		Money market deposit	
Short-term securities		accounts	
Fixed-rate assets	$80 million	Fixed-rate liabilities	$50 million
Reserves		Checkable deposits	
Long-term loans		Savings deposits	
Long-term securities		Long-term CDs	
		Equity capital	

A total of $20 million of First National Bank's assets are rate-sensitive, with interest rates that change frequently (at least once a year), and $80 million of its assets are fixed-rate, with interest rates that remain unchanged for a long period (over a year). On the liabilities side, the First National Bank has $50 million of rate-sensitive liabilities and $50 million of fixed-rate liabilities. Suppose that interest rates rise by 5 percentage points on average, from 10% to 15%. The income on the assets increases by $1 million (= 5% × $20 million of rate-sensitive assets), while the payments on the liabilities increase by $2.5 million (= 5% × $50 million of rate-sensitive liabilities). The First National Bank's profits now decline by $1.5 million (= $1 million − $2.5 million). Conversely, if interest rates fall by 5 percentage points, similar reasoning tells us that the First National Bank's profits increase by $1.5 million. This example illustrates the following point: *If a bank has more rate-sensitive liabilities than assets, a rise in interest rates will reduce bank profits, and a decline in interest rates will raise bank profits.*

Gap and Duration Analysis

The sensitivity of bank profits to changes in interest rates can be measured more directly using **gap analysis**, in which the amount of rate-sensitive liabilities is subtracted from the amount of rate-sensitive assets. In our example, this calculation (called the "gap") is −$30 million (= $20 million − $50 million). By multiplying the gap times the change in the interest rate, we can immediately obtain the effect on bank profits. For example, when interest rates rise by 5 percentage points, the change in profits is 5% × −$30 million, which equals −$1.5 million, as we saw.

The analysis we just conducted is known as *basic gap analysis*, and it can be refined in two ways. Clearly, not all assets and liabilities in the fixed-rate category have the same maturity. One refinement, the *maturity bucket approach*, is to measure the gap for several maturity subintervals, called *maturity buckets*, so that effects of interest-rate changes over a multiyear period can be calculated. The second refinement, called *standardized gap analysis*, accounts for the differing degrees of rate sensitivity among rate-sensitive assets and liabilities.

An alternative method for measuring interest-rate risk, called **duration analysis**, examines the sensitivity of the market value of the bank's total assets and liabilities to changes in interest rates. Duration analysis is based on what is known as Macaulay's concept of *duration*, which measures the average lifetime of a security's stream of payments.[4] Duration is a useful concept because it provides a good approximation of the sensitivity of a security's market value to a change in its interest rate:

percent change in market value of security $\approx$

$-$percentage-point change in interest rate $\times$ duration in years

where $\approx$ denotes "approximately equals."

Duration analysis involves using the average (weighted) duration of a financial institution's assets and of its liabilities to see how its net worth responds to a change in interest rates. Going back to our example of the First National Bank, suppose the average duration of the bank's assets is three years (that is, the average lifetime of the stream of payments is three years), whereas the average duration of its liabilities is two years. In addition, the First National Bank has $100 million of assets and, say, $90 million of liabilities, so its bank capital is 10% of assets. With a 5-percentage-point increase in interest rates, the market value of the bank's assets falls by 15% ($= -5\% \times 3$ years), a decline of $15 million on the $100 million of assets. However, the market value of the liabilities falls by 10% ($= -5\% \times 2$ years), a decline of $9 million on the $90 million of liabilities. The net result is that the net worth (the market value of the assets minus the liabilities) has declined by $6 million, or 6% of the total original asset value. Similarly, a 5-percentage-point decline in interest rates increases the net worth of the First National Bank by 6% of the total asset value.

As our example makes clear, both duration analysis and gap analysis indicate that the First National Bank will suffer if interest rates rise but will gain if they fall. Duration analysis and gap analysis are thus useful tools for a manager of a financial institution who is concerned about its degree of exposure to interest-rate risk.

APPLICATION Strategies for Managing Interest-Rate Risk

Suppose that as manager of the First National Bank, you have done a duration and gap analysis for the bank. Now you need to decide which alternative strategies you should pursue to manage the interest-rate risk.

---

[4]Algebraically, Macaulay's duration, D, is defined as

$$D = \sum_{\tau=1}^{N} \tau \frac{CP_\tau}{(1 + i^\tau)} \Big/ \sum_{\tau=1}^{N} \frac{CP_\tau}{(1 + i^\tau)}$$

where $\tau =$ time until cash payment is made
$CP_\tau =$ cash payment (interest plus principal) at time τ
$i =$ interest rate
$N =$ time to maturity of the security

For a more detailed discussion of duration gap analysis using the concept of Macaulay's duration, see the appendix to this chapter on the Companion Website at http://www.pearsonhighered.com/mishkin.

If you firmly believe that interest rates will fall in the future, you may be willing to forego action because you know that the bank has more rate-sensitive liabilities than rate-sensitive assets and so will benefit from the expected interest-rate decline. However, you also realize that the First National Bank is subject to substantial interest-rate risk because there is always a possibility that interest rates will rise rather than fall. What should you do to eliminate this interest-rate risk? One thing you could do is to shorten the duration of the bank's assets to increase their rate sensitivity. Alternatively, you could lengthen the duration of the liabilities. By this adjustment of the bank's assets or liabilities, the bank's income will be less affected by interest-rate swings.

One problem with eliminating the First National Bank's interest-rate risk by altering the balance sheet is that doing so might be very costly in the short run. The bank may be locked into assets and liabilities of particular durations because of where its expertise lies. Fortunately, recently developed financial instruments known as financial derivatives—financial forwards and futures, options, and swaps—can help the bank reduce its interest-rate risk exposure but do not require that the bank rearrange its balance sheet. ◆

OFF-BALANCE-SHEET ACTIVITIES

Although asset and liability management has traditionally been the primary concern of banks, in the more competitive environment of recent years banks have been aggressively seeking out profits by engaging in off-balance-sheet activities.[5] **Off-balance-sheet activities** involve trading financial instruments and generating income from fees and loan sales, activities that affect bank profits but do not appear on bank balance sheets. Indeed, off-balance-sheet activities have been growing in importance for banks: The income from these activities as a percentage of assets has nearly doubled since 1980.

Loan Sales

One type of off-balance-sheet activity that has grown in importance in recent years involves income generated by loan sales. A **loan sale**, also called a *secondary loan participation*, involves a contract that sells all or part of the cash stream from a specific loan and thereby removes the loan so that it is no longer an asset on the bank's balance sheet. Banks earn profits by selling loans for amounts that are slightly greater than the amounts of the original loans. Because the high interest rate on these loans makes them attractive, institutions are willing to buy them, even though the higher price means that they earn a slightly lower interest rate than the original interest rate on the loan, usually on the order of 0.15 percentage point.

Generation of Fee Income

Another type of off-balance-sheet activity involves the generation of income from fees that banks receive for providing specialized services to their customers, such as making foreign exchange trades on a customer's behalf, servicing a mortgage-backed security by

---

[5]Managers of financial institutions also need to know how well their banks are doing at any point in time. A second appendix to this chapter discusses how bank performance is measured; it can be found on the Companion Website at http://www.pearsonhighered.com/mishkin.

collecting interest and principal payments and then paying them out, guaranteeing debt securities such as banker's acceptances (by which the bank promises to make interest and principal payments if the party issuing the security cannot), and providing backup lines of credit. There are several types of backup lines of credit. We have already mentioned the most important, the loan commitment, under which, for a fee, the bank agrees to provide a loan at the customer's request, up to a given dollar amount, over a specified period of time. Credit lines with "overdraft privileges" are also now available to bank depositors—these bank customers can write checks in excess of their deposit balances and, in effect, write themselves a loan. Other lines of credit for which banks get fees include standby letters of credit to back up issues of commercial paper and other securities, and credit lines (called *note issuance facilities*, NIFs, and *revolving underwriting facilities*, RUFs) for underwriting Euronotes, which are medium-term Eurobonds.

Off-balance-sheet activities involving guarantees of securities and backup credit lines increase the risk a bank faces. Even though a guaranteed security does not appear on a bank's balance sheet, it still exposes the bank to default risk: If the issuer of the security defaults, the bank is left holding the bag and must pay off the security's owner. Backup credit lines also expose the bank to risk because the bank may be forced to provide loans when it does not have sufficient liquidity or when the borrower is a very poor credit risk.

Trading Activities and Risk Management Techniques

We have already mentioned that banks' attempts to manage interest-rate risk have led them to trading in financial futures, options for debt instruments, and interest-rate swaps. Banks engaged in international banking also conduct transactions in the foreign exchange market. All transactions in these markets are off-balance-sheet activities because they do not have a direct effect on the bank's balance sheet. Although bank trading in these markets is often directed toward reducing risk or facilitating other bank business, banks also try to outguess the markets and engage in speculation. This speculation can be a very risky business and has led to bank insolvencies, the most dramatic being the failure of Barings, a British bank, in 1995.

Trading activities, although often highly profitable, are also highly risky because they make it easy for financial institutions and their employees to make huge bets quickly. The principal–agent problem, discussed in Chapter 8, is an especially severe problem for management of trading activities. Because a trader (the agent) has the opportunity to place large bets, whether she trades in bond markets, foreign exchange markets, or financial derivatives, she has an incentive to take on excessive risks: If her trading strategy leads to large profits, she is likely to receive a high salary and bonuses, but if she takes large losses, the financial institution (the principal) will have to cover them. As the Barings Bank failure of 1995 so forcefully demonstrated, a trader subject to the principal–agent problem can take an institution that is quite healthy and drive it into insolvency very rapidly (see the Global box).

To reduce the principal–agent problem, managers of financial institutions must set up internal controls to prevent debacles like the one at Barings. Such controls include the complete separation of the people in charge of trading activities from those in charge of the bookkeeping for trades. In addition, managers must set limits on the total amount of traders' transactions and on the institution's risk exposure. Managers must also scrutinize risk assessment procedures using the latest computer technology. One such method involves the value-at-risk approach. In this approach, the institution

Global Barings, Daiwa, Sumitomo, Société Générale, and JP Morgan Chase: Rogue Traders and the Principal–Agent Problem

The demise of Barings, a venerable British bank more than a century old, is a sad morality tale of how the principal–agent problem operating through a rogue trader can take a financial institution that has a healthy balance sheet one month and turn it into an insolvent tragedy the next.

In July 1992, Nick Leeson, Barings's new head clerk at its Singapore branch, began to speculate on the Nikkei, the Japanese version of the Dow Jones stock index. By late 1992, Leeson had suffered losses of $3 million, which he hid from his superiors by stashing the losses in a secret account. He even fooled his superiors into thinking he was generating large profits, thanks to a failure of internal controls at his firm, which allowed him to execute trades on the Singapore exchange *and* oversee the bookkeeping of those trades. (As anyone who runs a cash business, such as a bar, knows, there is always a lower likelihood of fraud if more than one person handles the cash. Similarly, in trading operations, you never mix management of the back room with management of the front room; this principle was grossly violated by Barings management.)

Things didn't get better for Leeson, who by late 1994 had suffered losses exceeding $250 million. In January and February of 1995, Leeson bet the bank. On January 17, 1995, the day of the earthquake in Kobe, Japan, he lost $75 million, and by the end of the week he had lost more than $150 million. When the stock market declined on February 23, leaving him with a further loss of $250 million, he called it quits and fled Singapore. Three days later, he turned himself in at the Frankfurt airport. By the end of his wild ride, Leeson's losses, $1.3 billion in all, ate up Barings's capital and caused the bank to fail. Leeson was subsequently convicted and sent to jail in Singapore for his activities. He was released in 1999 and apologized for his actions.

Our asymmetric information analysis of the principal–agent problem explains Leeson's behavior and highlights the danger of a management lapse like Barings's. Letting Leeson control both his own trades and the back room increased asymmetric information, because it reduced the principal's (Barings's) knowledge about Leeson's trading activities. This lapse

increased the moral hazard incentive for him to take risks at the bank's expense, as he was now less likely to be caught. Furthermore, once he had experienced large losses, he had even greater incentives to take on even higher risk because, if his bets worked out, he could reverse his losses and keep in good standing with the company; whereas if his bets soured, he had little to lose because he was out of a job anyway. Indeed, the bigger his losses, the more he had to gain by bigger bets, which explains the escalation of the amount of his trades as his losses mounted. If Barings's managers had understood the principal–agent problem, they would have been more vigilant at finding out what Leeson was up to, and the bank might still be here today.

Unfortunately, Nick Leeson is no longer a rarity in the rogue traders' billionaires club, made up of those who have lost more than $1 billion. Over eleven years, Toshihide Iguchi, an officer in the New York branch of Daiwa Bank, also had control of both the bond trading operation and the back room bookkeeping activities, and he racked up $1.1 billion in losses over the period. In July 1995, Iguchi disclosed his losses to his superiors, but the management of the bank did not disclose them to its regulators. The result was that Daiwa was slapped with a $340 million fine and the bank was thrown out of the country by U.S. bank regulators.

Yasuo Hamanaka is another member of the billionaires club. In July 1996, he topped Leeson's and Iguchi's record, losing $2.6 billion for his employer, the Sumitomo Corporation, one of Japan's top trading companies. In January 2008, Jerome Kerviel's loss for his bank, Société Générale, set the all-time record for a rogue trader: His unauthorized trades cost the French bank $7.2 billion. In 2012, even the highly successful JP Morgan Chase bank experienced a trading loss of over $2 billion, caused by rogue trader Bruno Iksill, who was colorfully nicknamed "the London Whale."

The moral of these stories is that management of firms engaged in trading activities must reduce the principal–agent problem by closely monitoring their traders' activities, or the rogues' gallery will continue to grow.

develops a statistical model with which it can calculate the maximum loss that its portfolio is likely to sustain over a given time interval, dubbed the value at risk, or VaR. For example, a bank might estimate that the maximum loss it would be likely to sustain over one day with a probability of 1 in 100 is $1 million; the $1 million figure is the bank's calculated value at risk. Another approach is called "stress testing." In this approach, a manager uses a computer model to project what would happen if a doomsday scenario occurred; that is, she looks at the losses the institution would sustain in the event of an unusual combination of bad events. With the value-at-risk approach and stress testing, a financial institution can assess its risk exposure and take steps to reduce it.

U.S. bank regulators have become concerned about the increased risk that banks are facing from their off-balance-sheet activities and, as we will see in Chapter 10, are encouraging banks to pay increased attention to risk management. In addition, the Bank for International Settlements is developing additional bank capital requirements based on value-at-risk calculations for a bank's trading activities.

SUMMARY

1. The balance sheet of a commercial bank can be thought of as a list of the sources and uses of bank funds. A bank's liabilities are its sources of funds, which include checkable deposits, time deposits, discount loans from the Fed, borrowings from other banks and corporations, and bank capital. A bank's assets are its uses of funds, which include reserves, cash items in process of collection, deposits at other banks, securities, loans, and other assets (mostly physical capital).

2. Banks make profits through the process of asset transformation: They borrow short (accept short-term deposits) and lend long (make long-term loans). When a bank takes in additional deposits, it gains an equal amount of reserves; when it pays out deposits, it loses an equal amount of reserves.

3. Although more-liquid assets tend to earn lower returns, banks still desire to hold them. Specifically, banks hold excess and secondary reserves because they provide insurance against the costs of a deposit outflow. Banks manage their assets to maximize profits by seeking the highest returns possible on loans and securities while at the same time trying to lower risk and make adequate provisions for liquidity. Although liability management was once a staid affair, large (money center) banks now actively seek out sources of funds by issuing liabilities such as negotiable CDs or by actively borrowing from other banks and corporations. Banks manage the amount of capital they hold with

the goals of preventing bank failure and meeting bank capital requirements set by the regulatory authorities. However, banks do not want to hold too much capital because by so doing they will lower the returns to equity holders.

4. The concepts of adverse selection and moral hazard explain many credit risk management principles involving loan activities: screening and monitoring, establishment of long-term customer relationships and loan commitments, collateral and compensating balances, and credit rationing.

5. With the increased volatility of interest rates that occurred in the 1980s, financial institutions became more concerned about their exposure to interest-rate risk. Gap and duration analyses tell a financial institution if it has more rate-sensitive liabilities than assets (in which case a rise in interest rates will reduce profits, and a fall in interest rates will raise profits). Financial institutions manage their interest-rate risk by modifying their balance sheets, but can also use strategies involving financial derivatives.

6. Off-balance-sheet activities consist of trading financial instruments and generating income from fees and loan sales, all of which affect bank profits but are not visible on bank balance sheets. Because these off-balance-sheet activities expose banks to increased risk, bank management must pay particular attention to risk assessment procedures and internal controls to restrict employees from taking on too much risk.

KEY TERMS

QUESTIONS

All questions are available in MyEconLab at
http://www.myeconlab.com.

1. Why might a bank be willing to borrow funds from other banks at a higher rate than the rate at which it can borrow from the Fed?

2. Rank the following bank assets from most to least liquid:

   a. Commercial loans

   b. Securities

   c. Reserves

   d. Physical capital

3. The bank you own has the following balance sheet:

Assets		Liabilities	
Reserves	$ 75 million	Deposits	$500 million
Loans	$525 million	Bank capital	$100 million

   If the bank suffers a deposit outflow of $50 million with a required reserve ratio on deposits of 10%, what actions should you take?

4. If a deposit outflow of $50 million occurs, which balance sheet would a bank rather have initially, the balance sheet in Question 3 or the following balance sheet? Why?

Assets		Liabilities	
Reserves	$100 million	Deposits	$500 million
Loans	$500 million	Bank capital	$100 million

5. Why has the development of overnight loan markets made it more likely that banks will hold fewer excess reserves?

6. If the bank you own has no excess reserves and a sound customer comes in asking for a loan, should you automatically turn the customer down, explaining that you don't have any excess reserves to lend out? Why or why not? What options are available that will enable you to provide the funds your customer needs?

7. If a bank finds that its ROE is too low because it has too much bank capital, what can it do to raise its ROE?

8. If a bank is falling short of meeting its capital requirements by $1 million, what three things can it do to rectify the situation?

9. Why do equity holders care more about ROE than about ROA?

10. If a bank doubles the amount of its capital and ROA stays constant, what will happen to ROE?

11. What are the benefits and costs for a bank when it decides to increase the amount of its bank capital?

12. Why is being nosy a desirable trait for a banker?

13. A bank almost always insists that the firms it lends to keep compensating balances at the bank. Why?

14. If the president of a bank told you that the bank was so well run that it has never had to call in loans, sell securities, or borrow as a result of a deposit outflow, would you be willing to buy stock in that bank? Why or why not?

15. "Because diversification is a desirable strategy for avoiding risk, it never makes sense for a bank to specialize in

making specific types of loans." Is this statement true, false, or uncertain? Explain your answer.

16. If you are a banker and expect interest rates to rise in the future, would you prefer to make short-term loans or long-term loans?

17. "Bank managers should always seek the highest return possible on their assets." Is this statement true, false, or uncertain? Explain your answer.

18. Why has noninterest income been growing as a source of bank operating income?

APPLIED PROBLEMS

All applied problems are available in MyEconLab at http://www.myeconlab.com.

19. Using the T-accounts of the First National Bank and the Second National Bank given in this chapter, describe what happens when Jane Brown writes a $50 check on her account at the First National Bank to pay her friend Joe Green, who in turn deposits the check in his account at the Second National Bank.

20. What happens to reserves at the First National Bank if one person withdraws $1,000 of cash and another person deposits $500 of cash? Use T-accounts to explain your answer.

Questions 21 and 22 relate to the first month's operations of NewBank.

21. NewBank started its first day of operations with $6 million in capital. A total of $100 million in checkable deposits is received. The bank makes a $25 million commercial loan and lends another $25 million in mortgage loans. If required reserves are 8%, what does the bank balance sheet look like?

22. NewBank decides to invest $45 million in 30-day T-bills. The T-bills are currently trading at $4,986.70 (including commissions) for a $5,000 face value instrument. How many T-bills does NewBank purchase? What does the balance sheet look like?

23. X-Bank reported an ROE of 15% and an ROA of 1%. How well capitalized is this bank?

24. Suppose you are the manager of a bank whose $100 billion of assets have an average duration of four years and whose $90 billion of liabilities have an average duration of six years. Conduct a duration analysis for the bank, and show what will happen to the net worth of the bank if interest rates rise by 2 percentage points. What actions could you take to reduce the bank's interest-rate risk?

25. Suppose you are the manager of a bank that has $15 million of fixed-rate assets, $30 million of rate-sensitive assets, $25 million of fixed-rate liabilities, and $20 million of rate-sensitive liabilities. Conduct a gap analysis for the bank, and show what will happen to bank profits if interest rates rise by 5 percentage points. What actions could you take to reduce the bank's interest-rate risk?

DATA ANALYSIS PROBLEMS

The Problems update with real-time data in MyEconLab and are available for practice or instructor assignment.

 1. Go to the St. Louis Federal Reserve FRED database, and find data for all commercial banks on total liabilities (TLBACBM027SBOG), total deposits (DPSACBM027SBOG), and residual of assets less liabilities (RALACBM027SBOG).

   a. What is the balance sheet interpretation of the residual of assets less liabilities?

   b. For the most recent month of data available, use the three indicators listed above to calculate the total amount of borrowings by banks.

2. Go to the St. Louis Federal Reserve FRED database, and find data for all commercial banks on total assets (TLAACBM027SBOG), U.S. government and agency securities held (USGSEC), other securities held (OTHSEC), commercial and industrial loans (BUSLOANS), real estate loans (REALLN), consumer loans (CONSUMER), interbank loans (IBLACBM027S-BOG), other loans (OLLACBM027SBOG), and other assets (OATACBM027SBOG). Use the most recent month of data available across all indicators.

   a. What is the total amount of loans held by banks? What is this number as a percentage of total bank assets?

b. What is the total amount of securities held by banks? What is this number as a percentage of total bank assets?

c. What is the total amount of reserves and cash items? What is this number as a percentage of total bank assets?

WEB EXERCISES

1. Table 1 reports the balance sheet of all commercial banks based on aggregate data found in the Federal Reserve *Bulletin*. Compare this table to the most recent balance sheet reported by Bank of America. Go to http://www.bankofamerica.com/investor.index .cfm?section=700 and click on Annual Reports to view the balance sheet. Does Bank of America have more or less of its portfolio in loans than the average bank? Which type of loan is most common?

2. It is relatively easy to find up-to-date information on banks because of their extensive reporting requirements. Go to http://www2.fdic.gov/qbp/, where you

will find summary data on financial institutions. This site is sponsored by the Federal Deposit Insurance Corporation. Go to the most recent Quarterly Banking Profile. Scroll to the bottom and open Table 1-A.

a. Have banks' returns on assets been increasing or decreasing over the past few years?

b. Has the core capital been increasing, and how does it compare to the capital ratio reported in Table 1 of the text?

c. How many institutions are currently reporting to the FDIC?

WEB REFERENCES

http://www.bankofamerica.com/investor/index .cfm?section=700

Click on Annual Reports to view the balance sheet.

http://www.federalreserve.gov/boarddocs/SupManual/ default.htm#trading

The Federal Reserve Bank Trading and Capital Market Activities Manual offers an in-depth discussion of a wide range of risk management issues encountered in trading operations.

WEB APPENDIX

Please visit the Companion Website at http://www .pearsonhighered.com/mishkin to read the Web appendices to Chapter 9.

Appendix 1: **Duration Gap Analysis**

Appendix 2: **Measuring Bank Performance**

10 Economic Analysis of Financial Regulation

Learning Objectives

- Identify the reasons for and forms of a government safety net in financial markets.
- List and summarize the types of financial regulation and how each reduces asymmetric information problems.

Preview

As we have seen in previous chapters, the financial system is among the most heavily regulated sectors of the economy, and banks are among the most heavily regulated of financial institutions. In this chapter, we develop an economic analysis of why regulation of the financial system takes the form it does.

Unfortunately, the regulatory process may not always work very well, as evidenced by the recent global financial crisis. Here we also use our economic analysis of financial regulation to explain the worldwide crises in banking and to consider how the regulatory system can be reformed to prevent future such disasters.

ASYMMETRIC INFORMATION AS A RATIONALE FOR FINANCIAL REGULATION

In earlier chapters, we saw how asymmetric information—the fact that different parties in a financial contract do not have the same information—leads to adverse selection and moral hazard problems, which have an important impact on our financial system. The concepts of asymmetric information, adverse selection, and moral hazard are especially useful in understanding why governments pursue financial regulation.

Government Safety Net

As we saw in Chapter 8, financial intermediaries, like banks, are particularly well suited to solving adverse selection and moral hazard problems because they make private loans that help avoid the free-rider problem. However, this solution to the free-rider problem creates another asymmetric information problem, because depositors lack information about the quality of these private loans. This asymmetric information problem leads to other problems that interfere with the proper functioning of the financial system.

Bank Panics and the Need for Deposit Insurance   Before the FDIC (Federal Deposit Insurance Corporation) started operations in 1934, a **bank failure** (in which a bank is unable to meet its obligations to pay its depositors and other creditors, and so must go out of business) meant that depositors would have to wait until the bank was liquidated (until its assets had been turned into cash) to get their deposit funds; at that time, they would be paid only a fraction of the value of their deposits. Because they couldn't know if bank managers were taking on too much risk or were outright crooks, depositors would be reluctant to put money in banks, thus making banking institutions less viable. Second, depositors' lack of information about the quality of bank assets can lead to a **bank panic**, in which many banks fail simultaneously. Because the simultaneous failure of many banks leads to a sharp decline in bank lending, bank panics have serious, harmful consequences for the economy.

To understand why bank panics occur, consider the following situation. Deposit insurance does not exist, and an adverse shock hits the economy. As a result of the shock, 5% of banks have such large losses on loans that they become insolvent (have a negative net worth and so are bankrupt). Because of asymmetric information, depositors are unable to tell whether their bank is a "good" bank or one of the 5% that are insolvent. Depositors at bad *and* good banks recognize that they may not get back 100 cents on the dollar for their deposits, and therefore are inclined to withdraw them. Indeed, because banks operate on a "sequential service constraint" (a first-come, first-served basis), depositors have a very strong incentive to be the first to show up at the bank, because if they are last in line, the bank may have paid out all its funds and they will get nothing. The incentive to "run" to the bank to be first is why withdrawals when there is fear about the health of a bank is described as a "bank run." Uncertainty about the health of the banking system in general can lead to runs on both good and bad banks, and the failure of one bank can hasten the failure of others (referred to as the *contagion effect*). If nothing is done to restore the public's confidence, a bank panic can ensue.

Indeed, bank panics were a fact of American life in the nineteenth and early twentieth centuries, with major panics occurring every 20 years or so, in 1819, 1837, 1857, 1873, 1884, 1893, 1907, and 1930–1933. Bank failures were a serious problem even during the boom years of the 1920s, when the number of bank failures averaged around 600 per year.

A government safety net for depositors can short-circuit runs on banks and bank panics, and by providing protection for the depositor, it can overcome depositors' reluctance to put funds into the banking system. One form of safety net is deposit insurance, such as that provided by the Federal Deposit Insurance Corporation (FDIC) of the United States. The FDIC guarantees that current depositors will be paid off in full on the first $250,000 they have deposited in a bank if the bank fails. (In 1934, deposits were insured up to $2,500.) With fully insured deposits, depositors don't need to run to the bank to make withdrawals—even if they are worried about the bank's health—because their deposits will be worth 100 cents on the dollar no matter what. From 1930 to 1933, the years immediately preceding the creation of the FDIC, the number of bank failures averaged more than 2,000 per year. After the establishment of the FDIC in 1934, bank failures averaged fewer than 15 per year until 1981.

The FDIC uses two primary methods to handle a failed bank. In the first, called the *payoff method*, the FDIC allows the bank to fail and pays off depositors up to the $250,000 insurance limit (with funds acquired from the insurance premiums paid by the banks who have bought FDIC insurance). After the bank has been liquidated, the FDIC lines up with other creditors of the bank and is paid its share of the proceeds from the liquidated assets. Typically, when the payoff method is used, account holders with deposits in excess of the $250,000 limit get back more than 90 cents on the dollar, although the process can take several years to complete.

In the second method, called the *purchase and assumption method*, the FDIC reorganizes the bank, typically by finding a willing merger partner who assumes (takes over) all of the failed bank's liabilities so that no depositor or other creditor loses a penny. The FDIC often sweetens the pot for the merger partner by providing it with subsidized loans or by buying some of the failed bank's weaker loans. The net effect of the purchase and assumption method is that the FDIC has guaranteed *all* liabilities and deposits, not just deposits under the $250,000 limit. The purchase and assumption method is typically more costly for the FDIC than the payoff method, but nevertheless was the FDIC's more common procedure for dealing with a failed bank before new banking legislation was introduced in 1991.

In recent years, government deposit insurance has been growing in popularity and has spread to many countries throughout the world. Whether this trend is desirable is discussed in the Global box, "The Spread of Government Deposit Insurance Throughout the World: Is This a Good Thing?"

Other Forms of the Government Safety Net   Deposit insurance is not the only form of government safety net. In other countries, governments have often stood ready to provide support to domestic banks facing runs even in the absence of explicit deposit insurance. Furthermore, banks are not the only financial intermediaries that can pose a systemic threat to the financial system. When financial institutions are very large or highly interconnected with other financial institutions or markets, their failure has the potential to bring down the entire financial system. This is exactly what happened with Bear Stearns and Lehman Brothers, two investment banks, and AIG, an insurance company, during the global financial crisis in 2008.

Global   The Spread of Government Deposit Insurance Throughout the World: Is This a Good Thing?

For the first 30 years after federal deposit insurance was established in the United States, only six countries emulated the United States and adopted deposit insurance. However, this began to change in the late 1960s, with the trend accelerating in the 1990s, when the number of countries adopting deposit insurance topped 70. Government deposit insurance has taken off throughout the world because of growing concern about the health of banking systems, particularly after the increasing number of banking crises in recent years (documented at the end of this chapter). Has this spread of deposit insurance been a good thing? Has it helped improve the performance of the financial system and prevent banking crises?

The answer seems to be "no" under many circumstances. Research at the World Bank has found that, on average, the adoption of explicit government deposit insurance is associated with less banking sector stability and a higher incidence of banking crises.* Furthermore, on average, deposit insurance seems to retard financial development. However, these negative effects of deposit insurance occur only in countries with weak institutional environments: an absence of rule of law, ineffective regulation and supervision of the financial sector, and high corruption. This situation is exactly what might be expected because, as we will see later in this chapter, a strong institutional environment is needed to limit the moral hazard incentives for banks to engage in the excessively risky behavior encouraged by deposit insurance. The problem is that development of a strong institutional environment may be very difficult to achieve in many emerging market countries. We are left with the following conclusion: Adoption of deposit insurance may be exactly the wrong medicine for promoting stability and efficiency of banking systems in emerging market countries.

*See World Bank, *Finance for Growth: Policy Choices in a Volatile World* (Oxford: World Bank and Oxford University Press, 2001).

One way in which governments provide support is through lending from the central bank to troubled institutions, as the Federal Reserve did during the global financial crisis (more on this in Chapter 15). This form of support is often referred to as the "lender of last resort" role of the central bank. In other cases, funds are provided directly to troubled institutions, as was done by the U.S. Treasury and by other governments in 2008 during a particularly virulent phase of the global financial crisis (see Chapter 12). Governments can also take over (nationalize) troubled institutions and guarantee that all creditors' loans will be paid in full.

Drawbacks of the Government Safety Net

Although a government safety net can help protect depositors and other creditors and prevent, or ameliorate, financial crises, it is a mixed blessing.

Moral Hazard and the Government Safety Net   The most serious drawback of the government safety net stems from moral hazard, the incentives of one party in a transaction to engage in activities detrimental to the other party. Moral hazard is an important concern in insurance arrangements in general because the existence of insurance provides increased incentives for taking risks that might result in an insurance payoff. For example, some drivers with automobile collision insurance that has a low deductible might be more likely to drive recklessly, because if they get into an accident, the insurance company pays most of the costs for damage and repairs.

Moral hazard is a prominent concern associated with government safety nets. With a safety net, depositors and creditors know they will not suffer losses if a financial institution fails, so they do not impose the discipline of the marketplace on these institutions by withdrawing funds when they suspect that the financial institution is taking on too much risk. Consequently, financial institutions with a government safety net have an incentive to take on greater risks than they otherwise would, because taxpayers will foot the bill if the bank subsequently goes belly up. Financial institutions can place the following bet: "Heads, I win; tails, the taxpayer loses."

Adverse Selection and the Government Safety Net   A further problem with a government safety net like deposit insurance is adverse selection, the fact that the people who are most likely to produce the adverse outcome the bank is insured against (bank failure) are the same people who most want to take advantage of the insurance. For example, bad drivers are more likely than good drivers to take out automobile collision insurance with a low deductible. Because depositors and creditors protected by a government safety net have little reason to impose discipline on financial institutions, risk-loving entrepreneurs might find the financial industry a particularly attractive one—they know they will be able to engage in highly risky activities. Even worse, because protected depositors and creditors have so little reason to monitor the financial institution's activities, without government intervention outright crooks might also find finance an attractive industry for their activities because it is easy for them to get away with fraud and embezzlement.

"Too Big to Fail"   The moral hazard created by a government safety net and the desire to prevent financial institution failures have presented financial regulators with a particular quandary, the **too-big-to-fail problem**, in which regulators are reluctant to close down large financial institutions and impose losses on their depositors and creditors because doing so might precipitate a financial crisis. The too-big-to-fail problem first arose when Continental Illinois, one of the ten largest banks in the United States, became insolvent in May 1984. Not only did the FDIC guarantee depositors up to the

$100,000 insurance limit (the maximum at that time), but it also guaranteed accounts exceeding $100,000 and even prevented losses for Continental Illinois bondholders. Shortly thereafter, the Comptroller of the Currency (the regulator of national banks) testified to Congress that eleven of the largest banks would receive treatment similar to that received by Continental Illinois. Although the comptroller did not use the term "too big to fail" (it was actually used by Congressman Stewart McKinney in those Congressional hearings), this term is now applied to a policy in which the government provides guarantees of repayment of large, uninsured creditors of the largest banks, so that no depositor or creditor suffers a loss, even when these depositors and creditors are not automatically entitled to this guarantee. The FDIC does this by using the purchase and assumption method, giving the insolvent bank a large infusion of capital and then finding a willing merger partner to take over the bank and its deposits. The too-big-to-fail policy was extended to big banks that were not even among the eleven largest. (Note that "too big to fail" is a somewhat misleading term, because when a financial institution is closed or merged into another financial institution, the managers are usually fired and the stockholders in the financial institution lose their investment.)

One problem with the too-big-to-fail policy is that it increases the moral hazard incentives for big banks. If the FDIC were willing to close a bank using the payoff method, paying depositors only up to the current $250,000 limit, large depositors with more than $250,000 would suffer losses if the bank failed. Thus they would have an incentive to monitor the bank by examining the bank's activities closely and pulling their money out if the bank was taking on too much risk. To prevent such a loss of deposits, the bank would be more likely to engage in less risky activities. However, once large depositors know that a bank is too big to fail, they have no incentive to monitor the bank and pull out their deposits when it takes on too much risk: No matter what the bank does, large depositors will not suffer any losses. The result of the too-big-to-fail policy is that big financial institutions might take on even greater risks, thereby making bank failures more likely.

Similarly, the too-big-to-fail policy increases the moral hazard incentives for non-bank financial institutions that are extended a government safety net. Knowing that the financial institution will be bailed out, creditors have little incentive to monitor the institution and pull their money out when the institution is taking on excessive risk. As a result, large or interconnected financial institutions are more likely to engage in highly risky activities, making a financial crisis more likely.

Indeed, financial institutions that were considered too big to fail—including Bear Stearns, Lehman Brothers, and AIG—did take on excessive risk in the period leading to the global financial crisis, and their subsequent collapse helped trigger the worst financial crisis (discussed in Chapter 12) since the Great Depression.

Financial Consolidation and the Government Safety Net   With financial innovation and the passage of the Riegle-Neal Interstate Banking and Branching Efficiency Act of 1994 and the Gramm-Leach-Bliley Financial Services Modernization Act in 1999, financial consolidation has been proceeding at a rapid pace, leading to both larger and more complex financial organizations. Financial consolidation poses two challenges to financial regulation because of the existence of the government safety net. First, the increased size of financial institutions resulting from financial consolidation increases the too-big-to-fail problem, because there are now more large institutions whose failure would expose the financial system to systemic (system-wide) risk. Thus more financial institutions are likely to be treated as too big to fail, and the increased moral hazard incentives for these large institutions to take on greater risk increases the fragility of the financial system. Second, financial consolidation of banks with other financial services firms means that the government safety net may be extended to new activities, such as securities underwriting, insurance, or real estate activities, as occurred during the global financial crisis. This situation increases incentives for greater risk-taking in these activities, which can also weaken the fabric of the financial system. Limiting the moral hazard incentives for the larger, more complex financial organizations that have arisen as a result of recent changes in legislation is one of the key issues facing banking regulators in the aftermath of the global financial crisis.

TYPES OF FINANCIAL REGULATION

There are eight basic types of financial regulation aimed at lessening asymmetric information problems and excessive risk taking in the financial system: (1) restrictions on asset holdings, (2) capital requirements, (3) prompt corrective action, (4) chartering and examination, (5) assessment of risk management, (6) disclosure requirements, (7) consumer protection, and (8) restrictions on competition.

Restrictions on Asset Holdings

As we have seen, the moral hazard associated with a government safety net encourages too much risk taking on the part of financial institutions. Bank regulations that restrict asset holdings are directed at minimizing this moral hazard, which can cost taxpayers dearly.

Even in the absence of a government safety net, financial institutions still have the incentive to take on too much risk. Risky assets may provide the financial institution with higher earnings when they pay off, but if they do not pay off and the institution fails, depositors and creditors are left holding the bag. If depositors and creditors were able to monitor the bank easily by acquiring information on its risk-taking activities, they would be able to withdraw their funds immediately if the institution was taking on too much risk. To prevent such a loss of funds, the institution would be more likely to reduce its risk-taking activities. Unfortunately, acquiring information on an institution's activities to learn how much risk it is taking on can be a difficult task. Hence most depositors and many creditors are incapable of imposing the discipline that might prevent financial institutions from engaging in risky activities. A strong rationale for government regulation aimed at reducing risk taking on the part of financial institutions therefore existed even before the establishment of government safety nets like federal deposit insurance.

Because banks are the financial institutions most prone to panics, they are subjected to strict regulations that restrict their holdings of risky assets, such as common stocks. Bank regulations also promote diversification, which reduces risk by limiting the dollar amounts of loans in particular categories or to individual borrowers. With the extension of the government safety net during the global financial crisis, and the calls for regulatory reform in its aftermath, it is likely that nonbank financial institutions may face greater restrictions on their holdings of risky assets in the future. The danger exists, however, that these restrictions may become so onerous that the efficiency of the financial system will be impaired.

Capital Requirements

Government-imposed capital requirements are another way of minimizing moral hazard at financial institutions. When a financial institution is forced to hold a large amount of equity capital, the institution has more to lose if it fails and is thus more likely to pursue less risky activities. In addition, as was illustrated in Chapter 9, capital functions as a cushion when bad shocks occur, making it less likely that a financial institution will fail, thereby directly adding to the safety and soundness of financial institutions.

Capital requirements for banks take two forms. The first type is based on the **leverage ratio**, the amount of capital divided by the bank's total assets. To be classified as well capitalized, a bank's leverage ratio must exceed 5%; a lower leverage ratio, especially one below 3%, triggers increased regulatory restrictions on the bank. Through most of the 1980s, minimum bank capital in the United States was set solely by specifying a minimum leverage ratio.

In the wake of the Continental Illinois and savings and loans bailouts of the 1980s, regulators in the United States and the rest of the world have become increasingly worried about banks' holdings of risky assets and about the increase in banks' **off-balance-sheet activities**. Off-balance-sheet activities, which do not appear on bank balance sheets but nevertheless expose banks to risk, involve trading financial instruments and generating income from fees. To help combat the problems of risky assets and off-balance-sheet activities, banking officials from industrialized nations agreed to set up the **Basel Committee on Banking Supervision** (so named because it meets under the auspices of the Bank for International Settlements in Basel, Switzerland), which implemented the **Basel Accord**, which deals with a second type of capital requirements, risk-based capital requirements. The Basel Accord, which requires that banks hold as capital at least 8% of their risk-weighted assets, has been adopted by more than 100 countries, including the United States. Assets are allocated into four categories, each with a different weight to reflect the degree of credit risk. The first category carries a zero weight and includes items that have little default risk, such as reserves and government securities issued by the Organization for Economic Cooperation and Development (OECD—industrialized) countries. The second category has a 20% weight and includes claims on banks in OECD countries. The third category has a weight of 50% and includes municipal bonds and residential mortgages. The fourth category has the maximum weight of 100% and includes loans to consumers and corporations. Off-balance-sheet activities are treated in a similar manner. They are assigned a credit-equivalent percentage that converts them to on-balance-sheet items to which the appropriate risk weight applies, and there are minimum capital requirements for risks in banks' trading accounts.

Over time, the limitations of the Basel Accord have become apparent, because the regulatory measure of bank risk, as stipulated by the risk weights, can differ substantially from the actual risk the bank faces. This discrepancy has resulted in **regulatory arbitrage**, a practice in which banks keep on their books assets that have the same risk-based capital requirement but are relatively risky, such as a loan to a company with a very low credit rating, while taking off their books low-risk assets, such as a loan to a company with a very high credit rating. The Basel Accord thus might lead to increased risk taking, the opposite of its intent. To address these limitations, the Basel Committee on Bank Supervision came up with a new capital accord, often referred to as Basel 2. However, in the aftermath of the global financial crisis, the committee developed an even newer accord, which the media has dubbed "Basel 3." These accords are described in the Global box, "Where Is the Basel Accord Heading After the Global Financial Crisis?"

Prompt Corrective Action

If the amount of a financial institution's capital falls to low levels, two serious problems result. First, the bank is more likely to fail because it has a smaller capital cushion if it suffers loan losses or other asset write-downs. Second, with less capital, a financial institution has less "skin in the game" and is therefore more likely to take on excessive risks. In other words, the moral hazard problem becomes more severe, making it more likely that the institution will fail and the taxpayer will be left holding the bag. To prevent this, the Federal Deposit Insurance Corporation Improvement Act of 1991

Global Where Is the Basel Accord Heading After the Global Financial Crisis?

Starting in June 1999, the Basel Committee on Banking Supervision released several proposals to reform the original 1988 Basel Accord. These efforts have culminated in what bank supervisors refer to as Basel 2, which is based on three pillars.

1. Pillar 1 links capital requirements for large, internationally active banks more closely to actual risk of three types: market risk, credit risk, and operational risk. It does so by specifying many more categories of assets, with different risk weights, in its standardized approach. Alternatively, it allows sophisticated banks to pursue an internal ratings-based approach that permits these banks to use their own models of credit risk.

2. Pillar 2 focuses on strengthening the supervisory process, particularly in assessing the quality of risk management in banking institutions and evaluating whether these institutions have adequate procedures in place for determining how much capital they need.

3. Pillar 3 focuses on improving market discipline through increased disclosure of details about a bank's credit exposures, its amount of reserves and capital, the officials who control the bank, and the effectiveness of its internal rating system.

Although Basel 2 made great strides toward limiting excessive risk taking by internationally active banking institutions, it greatly increased the complexity of the accord. The document describing the original Basel Accord was 26 pages long, whereas the final draft of Basel 2 exceeded 500 pages. The original timetable called for the completion of the final round of consultation by the end of 2001, with the new rules taking effect by 2004. However, criticism from banks, trade associations, and national regulators led to several postponements. The final draft of Basel 2 was not published until June 2004, and European banks began to implement the new accord at the start of 2008. U.S. banks submitted plans for compliance with Basel 2 in 2008, but full implementation did not occur until 2009. Only the dozen or so largest U.S. banks are subject to Basel 2; all others are allowed to use a simplified version of the standards it imposes.

The global financial crisis, however, revealed many limitations of the new accord. First, Basel 2 did not require banks to have sufficient capital to weather the financial disruption that occurred during this period. Second, risk weights in the standardized approach are heavily reliant on credit ratings, which proved to be extremely unreliable in the run-up to the financial crisis. Third, Basel 2 is very procyclical—that is, it demands that banks hold less capital when times are good but more when times are bad, thereby exacerbating credit cycles. Because the probability of default and expected losses on different classes of assets rises during bad times, Basel 2 may require more capital at exactly the time when capital is most short. This has been a particularly serious concern in the aftermath of the global financial crisis. As a result of this crisis, banks' capital balances eroded, leading to a cutback on lending that was a big drag on the economy. Basel 2 made this cutback in lending even worse, doing yet more harm to the economy. Fourth, Basel 2 did not focus sufficiently on the dangers of a possible drying up of liquidity, a problem that brought down financial institutions during the financial crisis.

As a result of these limitations, in 2010 the Basel Committee developed a new accord, Basel 3. It beefs up capital standards not only by raising them substantially but also by improving the quality of the capital, makes capital standards less procyclical by raising capital requirements in good times and lowering them in bad, makes new rules on the use of credit ratings, and requires financial institutions to have more stable funding so that they are better able to withstand liquidity shocks. Measures to achieve these objectives are highly controversial because of concerns that tightening up capital standards might cause banks to restrict their lending, which would make it harder for economies throughout the world to recover from the recent deep recession. Basel 3 is being implemented slowly over time, with the target for full implementation extending out to the end of 2019. Whether Basel 3 will be fully in place by that date, and whether it will be successful in restraining risk taking, is highly uncertain.

adopted prompt corrective action provisions that require the FDIC to intervene earlier and more vigorously when a bank gets into trouble.

Banks are now classified into five groups based on bank capital. Group 1, classified as "well capitalized," comprises banks that significantly exceed minimum capital requirements and are allowed privileges such as the ability to do some securities underwriting. Banks in group 2, classified as "adequately capitalized," meet minimum capital requirements and are not subject to corrective actions but are not allowed the privileges of the well-capitalized banks. Banks in group 3, "undercapitalized," fail to meet capital requirements. Banks in groups 4 and 5 are "significantly undercapitalized" and "critically undercapitalized," respectively, and are not allowed to pay interest on their deposits at rates that are higher than average. In addition, for group 4 and 5 banks, the FDIC is required to take prompt corrective actions, such as requiring these banks to submit capital restoration plans, restrict their asset growth, and seek regulatory approval to open new branches or develop new lines of business. Banks that are so undercapitalized as to have equity capital that amounts to less than 2% of assets fall into group 5, and the FDIC must take steps to close them down.

Financial Supervision: Chartering and Examination

Overseeing who operates financial institutions and how they are operated, referred to as **financial supervision** or **prudential supervision**, is an important method for reducing adverse selection and moral hazard in the financial industry. Because financial institutions can be used by crooks or overambitious entrepreneurs to engage in highly speculative activities, such undesirable people are often eager to run a financial institution. Chartering financial institutions is one method of preventing this adverse selection problem; through chartering, proposals for new institutions are screened to prevent undesirable people from controlling them.

A commercial bank obtains a charter either from the Comptroller of the Currency (in the case of a national bank) or from a state banking authority (in the case of a state bank). To obtain a charter, the people planning to organize the bank must submit an application that shows how they plan to operate the bank. In evaluating the application, the regulatory authority looks at whether the bank is likely to be sound by examining the quality of the bank's intended management, the likely earnings of the bank, and the amount of the bank's initial capital. Before 1980, the chartering agency typically explored the issue of whether the community needed a new bank. Often a new bank charter would not be granted if existing banks in a community would be hurt by its presence. Today this anticompetitive stance (justified by the desire to prevent failures of existing banks) is no longer as strong in the chartering agencies.

Once a bank has been chartered, it is required to file periodic (usually quarterly) *call reports* that reveal the bank's assets and liabilities, income and dividends, ownership, foreign exchange operations, and other details. The bank is also subject to examination by the bank regulatory agencies to ascertain its financial condition at least once a year. To avoid duplication of effort, the three federal agencies work together and usually accept each other's examinations. This means that, typically, national banks are examined by the Office of the Comptroller of the Currency, state banks that are members of the Federal Reserve System are examined by the Fed, and insured nonmember state banks are examined by the FDIC.

Regular on-site examinations, which allow regulators to monitor whether the institution is complying with capital requirements and restrictions on asset holdings, function to limit moral hazard. Bank examiners give banks a *CAMELS rating*. The acronym is based on the six areas assessed: capital adequacy, asset quality, management, earnings, liquidity, and sensitivity to market risk. With this information about a bank's activities, regulators can enforce regulations by taking formal actions such as issuing *cease and desist orders* to alter the bank's behavior, or even closing a bank if its CAMELS rating is sufficiently low. Actions taken to reduce moral hazard by restricting banks from taking on too much risk also help reduce the adverse selection problem further, because with less opportunity for risk taking, risk-loving entrepreneurs are less likely to be attracted to the banking industry.

Note that the methods used by regulators to cope with adverse selection and moral hazard have their counterparts in private financial markets (see Chapters 8 and 9). Chartering is similar to the screening of potential borrowers; regulations that restrict risky asset holdings are similar to restrictive covenants that prevent borrowing firms from engaging in risky investment activities; capital requirements act like restrictive covenants that require minimum amounts of net worth for borrowing firms; and regular examinations are similar to the monitoring of borrowers by lending institutions.

Bank examinations are conducted by bank examiners, who sometimes make unannounced visits to the bank (so that nothing can be "swept under the rug" in anticipation of their examination). The examiners study a bank's books to see whether it is complying with the rules and regulations that apply to its holdings of assets. If a bank is holding securities or loans that are too risky, the bank examiner can force the bank to get rid of them. If a bank examiner decides that a loan is unlikely to be repaid, the examiner can force the bank to declare the loan worthless (to write off the loan, which reduces the bank's capital). If, after examining the bank, the examiner feels that it does not have sufficient capital or has engaged in dishonest practices, the bank can be declared a "problem bank" and will be subject to more frequent examinations.

Assessment of Risk Management

Traditionally, on-site examinations have focused primarily on assessment of the quality of a financial institution's balance sheet at a point in time and whether it complies with capital requirements and restrictions on asset holdings. Although the traditional focus is still important in reducing excessive risk taking by financial institutions, it is no longer thought to be adequate in today's world, in which financial innovation has produced new markets and instruments that make it easy for financial institutions and their employees to make huge bets easily and quickly. In this new financial environment, a financial institution that is healthy at a particular point in time can be driven into insolvency extremely rapidly by trading losses, as forcefully demonstrated by the failure of Barings in 1995 (discussed in Chapter 9). Thus an examination that focuses only on a financial institution's position at a point in time may not be effective in indicating whether it will, in fact, be taking on excessive risk in the near future.

This change in the financial environment resulted in a major shift in thinking about the prudential supervisory process throughout the world. Bank examiners, for example, now place far greater emphasis on evaluating the soundness of a bank's management processes with regard to controlling risk. This shift in thinking was reflected in a new focus on risk management by the Federal Reserve System, starting with 1993 guidelines for examiners regarding trading and derivatives activities. The focus was expanded and formalized in the Trading Activities Manual issued early in 1994, which provided bank examiners with tools to evaluate risk management systems. In late 1995, the Federal Reserve and the Comptroller of the Currency announced that they would be assessing risk management processes at the banks they supervised. Now, bank examiners give a separate risk management rating, from 1 to 5, that feeds into the overall management rating as part of the CAMELS system. Four elements of sound risk management are assessed to arrive at the risk management rating: (1) the quality of oversight provided by the board of directors and senior management; (2) the adequacy of policies and limits for all activities that present significant risks; (3) the quality of the risk measurement and monitoring systems; and (4) the adequacy of internal controls to prevent fraud or unauthorized activities on the part of employees.

This shift toward focusing on management processes is also reflected in recent guidelines adopted by the U.S. bank regulatory authorities to deal with interest-rate risk. These guidelines require the bank's board of directors to establish interest-rate risk limits, appoint officials of the bank to manage this risk, and monitor the bank's risk exposure. The guidelines also require that senior management of a bank develop formal risk management policies and procedures to ensure that the board of directors' risk limits are not violated and to implement internal controls to monitor interest-rate risk and compliance with the board's directives. Particularly important is the implementation of **stress tests**, which calculate potential losses and the need for more capital under fictional dire scenarios, and **value-at-risk (VaR)** calculations, which measure the size of the loss on a trading portfolio—say, over a two-week period—that might happen 1% of the time. In addition to these guidelines, bank examiners will continue to consider interest-rate risk in deciding the bank's capital requirements.

Disclosure Requirements

The free-rider problem described in Chapter 8 indicates that individual depositors and creditors do not have enough incentive to produce private information about the quality of a financial institution's assets. To ensure that better information is available in the marketplace, regulators can require that financial institutions adhere to certain standard accounting principles and disclose a wide range of information that helps the market assess the quality of an institution's portfolio and the amount of its exposure to risk. More public information about the risks incurred by financial institutions and the quality of their portfolios can better enable stockholders, creditors, and depositors to evaluate and monitor financial institutions and so act as a deterrent to excessive risk taking.

Disclosure requirements are a key element of financial regulation. Basel 2 puts a particular emphasis on disclosure requirements, with one of its three pillars focusing on increasing market discipline by mandating increased disclosure by banking institutions of their credit exposure, amount of reserves, and capital. The Securities Act of 1933 and the Securities and Exchange Commission (SEC), which was established in 1934, also impose disclosure requirements on any corporation, including financial institutions, that issues publicly-traded securities. In addition, the SEC has required financial institutions to provide additional disclosure regarding their off-balance-sheet positions and more information about how they value their portfolios.

Regulation to increase disclosure is needed to limit incentives to take on excessive risk and to upgrade the quality of information in the marketplace so that investors can make informed decisions, thereby improving the ability of financial markets to allocate capital to its most productive uses. The efficiency of markets is assisted by the SEC's disclosure requirements mentioned above, as well as its regulation of brokerage firms, mutual funds, exchanges, and credit-rating agencies to ensure that they produce reliable information and protect investors. The Sarbanes-Oxley Act of 2002 took disclosure of information even further by increasing the incentives to produce accurate audits of corporate income statements and balance sheets, establishing the Public Company Accounting Oversight Board (PCAOB) to oversee the audit industry, and putting in place regulations to limit conflicts of interest in the financial services industry.

Particularly controversial in the wake of the global financial crisis is the move to so-called **mark-to-market accounting**, also called **fair-value accounting**, in which

FYI Mark-to-Market Accounting and the Global Financial Crisis

The controversy over mark-to-market accounting has made accounting a hot topic. Mark-to-market accounting was made standard practice in the U.S. accounting industry in 1993. The rationale behind mark-to-market accounting is that market prices provide the best basis for estimating the true value of assets, and hence capital, in a firm. Before mark-to-market accounting, firms relied on traditional historical-cost (book value) accounting, in which the value of an asset is set at its initial purchase price. The problem with historical-cost accounting is that fluctuations in the values of assets and liabilities caused by changes in interest rates or default risk are not reflected in the calculation of the firm's equity capital. Yet changes in the market values of assets and liabilities—and hence changes in the market value of equity capital—are what indicate whether a firm is in good shape or, alternatively, is getting into trouble and may therefore be more susceptible to moral hazard.

Mark-to-market accounting, however, is subject to a major flaw: At times, markets stop working, as occurred during the global financial crisis. The price of an asset sold at a time of financial distress does not reflect its fundamental value. That is, the fire-sale liquidation value of an asset can at times be well below the present value of its expected future cash flows. Many people, particularly bankers, have criticized mark-to-market accounting, claiming that it was an important factor driving the recent global financial crisis. They claim that the seizing up of financial markets led to market prices that were well below their fundamental values. Mark-to-market accounting requires that financial firms' assets be marked down in value. This markdown creates a shortfall in capital that leads to a cutback in lending, which causes a further deterioration in asset prices, which in turn causes a further cutback in lending. The resulting adverse feedback loop can then make the financial crisis even worse. Although the criticisms of mark-to-market accounting have some validity, some of the criticism by bankers is self-serving. The criticism was made only when asset values were falling and mark-to-market accounting was painting a bleaker picture of banks' balance sheets, as opposed to when asset prices were booming and mark-to-market accounting made banks' balance sheets look very good.

The criticisms of mark-to-market accounting led to a Congressional focus on mark-to-market accounting that resulted in a provision in the Emergency Economic Stabilization Act of 2008, that required the SEC, in consultation with the Federal Reserve and the U.S. Treasury, to submit a study of mark-to-market accounting applicable to financial institutions. The resulting report concluded that the rules requiring mark-to-market accounting were not a major cause of the global financial crisis and should be retained. However, the report did suggest some improvements. Who knew that accounting could get even politicians worked up!

assets are valued in the balance sheet at what they could sell for in the market (see the FYI box, "Mark-to-Market Accounting and the Global Financial Crisis").

Consumer Protection

The existence of asymmetric information suggests that consumers may not have enough information to protect themselves fully in financial dealings. Consumer protection regulation has taken several forms. The Consumer Protection Act of 1969 (more commonly referred to as the Truth in Lending Act) requires all lenders, not just banks, to provide information to consumers about the cost of borrowing, including the disclosure of a standardized interest rate (called the *annual percentage rate*, or *APR*) and the total finance charges on the loan. The Fair Credit Billing Act of 1974 requires creditors, especially credit card issuers, to provide information on the method of assessing finance charges, and requires that billing complaints be handled quickly.

Congress also passed legislation to reduce discrimination in credit markets. The Equal Credit Opportunity Act of 1974 and its extension in 1976 forbid discrimination by lenders based on race, gender, marital status, age, or national origin. The act is administered by the Federal Reserve under Regulation B. The Community Reinvestment Act (CRA) of 1977 was enacted to prevent "redlining," a lender's refusal to lend in a particular area (marked off by a hypothetical red line on a map). The Community Reinvestment Act requires that banks show that they lend in all areas in which they take deposits, and if banks are found to be in noncompliance with the act, regulators can reject their applications for mergers, branching, or other new activities.

The global financial crisis has illustrated the need for greater consumer protection, because so many borrowers took out loans with terms they did not understand and that were well beyond their means to repay. (Most infamous were so-called NINJA loans, which were issued to borrowers with No Income, No Job, and No Assets.) The result was millions of foreclosures, with many households losing their homes. As we will see in Chapter 12, Congress responded by creating a new consumer protection agency to prevent this type of lending from happening again.

Restrictions on Competition

Increased competition can also increase moral hazard incentives for financial institutions to take on more risk. Declining profitability resulting from increased competition could tip the incentives of financial institutions toward assuming greater risk in an effort to maintain former profit levels. Thus governments in many countries have instituted regulations to protect financial institutions from competition. These regulations took two forms in the United States in the past. First were restrictions on branching, described in Chapter 11, which reduced competition between banks. These restrictions were eliminated, however, in 1994. The second form involved preventing nonbank institutions from competing with banks by preventing them from engaging in banking business, as embodied in the Glass-Steagall Act, which was repealed in 1999.

Although restrictions on competition propped up the health of banks, they had some serious disadvantages: They led to higher charges to consumers and decreased the efficiency of banking institutions, which now did not have to compete as vigorously. Thus, although the existence of asymmetric information provided a rationale for anticompetitive regulations, it did not mean they would be beneficial. Indeed, in recent years, the impulse of governments in industrialized countries to restrict competition has been waning.

Summary

Asymmetric information analysis explains the types of financial regulations that are needed to reduce moral hazard and adverse selection problems in the financial system. However, understanding the theory behind regulation does not mean that regulation and supervision of the financial system are easy in practice. Getting regulators and supervisors to do their job properly is difficult for several reasons. First, as we will see in our discussion of financial innovation in Chapter 11, financial institutions, in their search for profits, have strong incentives to avoid existing regulations by loophole mining. Thus regulation applies to a moving target. Regulators are continually playing cat-and-mouse with financial institutions—financial institutions think up clever ways to avoid regulations, which then leads regulators to modify their regulation activities. Regulators continually face new challenges in a dynamically changing financial system, and unless they can respond rapidly, they may not be able to keep financial institutions from taking on excessive risk. This problem can be exacerbated if regulators and supervisors do not have the resources or expertise necessary to keep up with clever people seeking to circumvent the existing regulations.

Global International Financial Regulation

Because asymmetric information problems in the banking industry are a fact of life throughout the world, financial regulation in other countries is similar to that in the United States. Financial institutions are chartered and supervised by government regulators, just as they are in the United States. Disclosure requirements for financial institutions and corporations issuing securities are similar in other developed countries. Deposit insurance is also a feature of the regulatory systems of most other countries, although its coverage is often smaller than that in the United States, and it is intentionally not advertised. We have also seen that capital requirements are in the process of being standardized across countries in compliance with agreements like the Basel Accord.

Particular problems in financial regulation occur when financial institutions operate in many countries and thus can shift their business readily from one country to another. Financial regulators closely examine the domestic operations of financial institutions in their own country, but they often do not have the knowledge or ability to keep a close watch on operations in other countries, operations run either by domestic institutions' foreign affiliates or by foreign institutions with domestic branches. In addition, when a financial institution operates in many countries, it is not always clear which national regulatory authority should have primary responsibility for keeping the institution from engaging in overly risky activities.

The difficulties inherent in international financial regulation were highlighted by the collapse of the Bank of Credit and Commerce International (BCCI). BCCI, although it operated in more than 70 countries, including the United States and the United Kingdom, was supervised by Luxembourg, a tiny country unlikely to be up to the task. When massive fraud was discovered, the Bank of England closed BCCI down, but not before depositors and stockholders were exposed to huge losses. Cooperation among regulators in different countries and standardization of regulatory requirements provide potential solutions to the problems of international financial regulation. The world has moved in this direction through agreements like the Basel Accord and oversight procedures announced by the Basel Committee in July 1992, which require a bank's worldwide operations to be under the scrutiny of a single home-country regulator with enhanced powers to acquire information on the bank's activities. The Basel Committee also ruled that regulators in other countries can restrict the operations of a foreign bank if they believe it lacks effective oversight. Whether agreements of this type will solve the problem of international financial regulation in the future is an open question.

Financial regulation and supervision are difficult for two other reasons. In the regulation and supervision game, the devil is in the details. Subtle differences in the details may have unintended consequences; unless regulators get the regulation and supervision just right, they may be unable to prevent excessive risk taking. In addition, regulated firms may lobby politicians to lean on regulators and supervisors to go easy on them.

For all of these reasons, there is no guarantee that regulators and supervisors will be successful in promoting a healthy financial system. These same problems bedevil financial regulators in other countries as well, as the Global box, "International Financial Regulation," indicates. Indeed, financial regulation and supervision have not always worked well, leading to banking crises in the United States and throughout the world.[1]

[1] The United States suffered a major banking crisis in the 1980s, a crisis that hit the savings and loan industry particularly hard. The story of this banking crisis is a fascinating one, involving juicy scandals and even Senator John McCain, who was a presidential candidate in 2008. This crisis is discussed in the first Web appendix to this chapter, "The 1980s Banking and Saving and Loan Crisis," which can be found on the book's Companion Website at http://www.pearsonhighered.com/mishkin. A second Web appendix to this chapter, "Banking Crises Throughout the World," discusses banking crises in other countries. The second Web appendix can also be found on the Companion Website.

Because so many laws regulating the financial system have been passed in the United States, it is hard to keep track of them all. As a study aid, Table 1 lists the major financial legislation passed since the beginning of the twentieth century and outlines the key provisions of each act.

TABLE 1	Major Financial Legislation in the United States

Federal Reserve Act (1913)

Created the Federal Reserve System

McFadden Act of 1927

Effectively prohibited banks from branching across state lines

Put national and state banks on equal footing regarding branching

Banking Acts of 1933 (Glass-Steagall) and 1935

Created the FDIC

Separated commercial banking from the securities industry

Prohibited interest on checkable deposits and restricted such deposits to commercial banks

Put interest-rate ceilings on other deposits

Securities Act of 1933 and Securities Exchange Act of 1934

Required that investors receive financial information on securities offered for public sale

Prohibited misrepresentations and fraud in the sale of securities

Created the Securities and Exchange Commission (SEC)

Investment Company Act of 1940 and Investment Advisers Act of 1940

Regulated investment companies, including mutual funds

Regulated investment advisers

Bank Holding Company Act and Douglas Amendment (1956)

Clarified the status of bank holding companies (BHCs)

Gave the Federal Reserve regulatory responsibility for BHCs

Depository Institutions Deregulation and Monetary Control Act (DIDMCA) of 1980

Gave thrift institutions wider latitude in activities

Approved NOW and sweep accounts nationwide

Phased out interest-rate ceilings on deposits

Imposed uniform reserve requirements on depository institutions

Eliminated usury ceilings on loans

Increased deposit insurance to $100,000 per account

Depository Institutions Act of 1982 (Garn–St. Germain)

Gave the FDIC and the Federal Savings and Loan Insurance Corporation (FSLIC) emergency powers to merge banks and thrifts across state lines

Allowed depository institutions to offer money market deposit accounts (MMDAs)

Granted thrifts wider latitude in commercial and consumer lending

TABLE 1 (continued)

Competitive Equality in Banking Act (CEBA) of 1987

Provided $10.8 billion to shore up the FSLIC

Made provisions for regulatory forbearance in depressed areas

Financial Institutions Reform, Recovery, and Enforcement Act (FIRREA) of 1989

Provided funds to resolve savings and loan (S&L) failures

Eliminated FSLIC and the Federal Home Loan Bank Board

Created the Office of Thrift Supervision to regulate thrifts

Created the Resolution Trust Corporation to resolve insolvent thrifts

Raised deposit insurance premiums

Reimposed restrictions on S&L activities

Federal Deposit Insurance Corporation Improvement Act (FDICIA) of 1991

Recapitalized the FDIC

Limited brokered deposits and the too-big-to-fail policy

Set provisions for prompt corrective action

Instructed the FDIC to establish risk-based premiums

Increased examinations, capital requirements, and reporting requirements

Included the Foreign Bank Supervision Enhancement Act (FBSEA), which strengthened the Fed's authority to supervise foreign banks

Riegle-Neal Interstate Banking and Branching Efficiency Act of 1994

Overturned prohibition of interstate banking

Allowed branching across state lines

Gramm-Leach-Bliley Financial Services Modernization Act of 1999

Repealed Glass-Steagall and removed the separation of banking and securities industries

Sarbanes-Oxley Act of 2002

Created Public Company Accounting Oversight Board (PCAOB)

Prohibited certain conflicts of interest

Required certification by CEO and CFO of financial statements and independence of audit committee

Federal Deposit Insurance Reform Act of 2005

Merged the Bank Insurance Fund and the Savings Association Insurance Fund

Increased deposit insurance on individual retirement accounts to $250,000 per account

Dodd-Frank Wall Street Reform and Consumer Protection Act of 2010

Created Consumer Financial Protection Bureau to regulate mortgages and other financial products

Required routine derivatives to be cleared through central clearinghouses and exchanges

Authorized government takeovers of financial holding companies

Created Financial Stability Oversight Council to regulate systemically important financial institutions

Banned banks from proprietary trading and from owning large percentages of hedge funds

SUMMARY

1. The concepts of asymmetric information, adverse selection, and moral hazard help explain why governments pursue financial regulation.

2. There are eight basic types of financial regulation aimed at lessening asymmetric information problems and excessive risk taking in the financial system: (1) restrictions on asset holdings; (2) capital requirements; (3) prompt corrective action; (4) chartering and examination; (5) assessment of risk management: (6) disclosure requirements; (7) consumer protection; and (8) restrictions on competition.

KEY TERMS

bank failure, p. 215
bank panic, p. 216
Basel Accord, p. 221
Basel Committee on Banking
   Supervision, p. 221

fair-value accounting, p. 225
financial supervision (prudential
   supervision), p. 223
leverage ratio, p. 221
mark-to-market accounting, p. 225

off-balance-sheet activities, p. 221
regulatory arbitrage, p. 221
stress tests, p. 225
too-big-to-fail problem, p. 218
value-at-risk (VaR), p. 225

QUESTIONS

All questions are available in MyEconLab at
http://www.myeconlab.com.

1. Why are deposit insurance and other types of government safety nets important to the health of the economy?

2. If casualty insurance companies provided fire insurance without any restrictions, what kind of adverse selection and moral hazard problems might result?

3. Do you think that eliminating or limiting the amount of deposit insurance would be a good idea? Explain your answer.

4. How could higher deposit insurance premiums for banks with riskier assets benefit the economy?

5. What are the costs and benefits of a too-big-to-fail policy?

6. What types of bank regulations are designed to reduce moral hazard problems? Will they completely eliminate moral hazard problems?

7. Why does imposing bank capital requirements on banks help limit risk taking?

8. At the height of the global financial crisis in October 2008, the U.S. Treasury forced nine of the largest U.S. banks to accept capital injections in exchange for nonvoting ownership stock, even though some of the banks did not need the capital and did not want to participate. What could be the Treasury's rationale for doing this?

9. What special problem do off-balance-sheet activities present to bank regulators, and what have they done about it?

10. What are some of the limitations to the Basel and Basel 2 Accords? How does the Basel 3 Accord attempt to address these limitations?

11. How does bank chartering reduce adverse selection problems? Does it always work?

12. Why has the trend in bank supervision moved away from a focus on capital requirements to a focus on risk management?

13. How do disclosure requirements help limit excessive risk taking by banks?

14. Suppose Universal Bank holds $100 million in assets, which are composed of the following:

Required reserves:	$10 million
Excess reserves:	$ 5 million
Mortgage loans:	$20 million
Corporate bonds:	$15 million
Stocks:	$25 million
Commodities:	$25 million

a. Do you think it is a good idea for Universal Bank to hold stocks, corporate bonds, and commodities as assets? Why or why not?

b. If the housing market suddenly crashed, would Universal Bank be better off using a mark-to-market accounting system or the historical-cost system?

c. If the price of commodities suddenly increased sharply, would Universal Bank be better off using a mark-to-market accounting system or the historical-cost system?

d. What do your answers to parts (b) and (c) tell you about the tradeoffs between the two accounting systems?

15. Why might more competition in financial markets be a bad idea? Would restrictions on competition be a better idea? Why or why not?

APPLIED PROBLEMS

All applied problems are available in MyEconLab at http://www.myeconlab.com.

16. Consider a failing bank. How much is a deposit of $350,000 worth if the FDIC uses the *payoff method*? The *purchase and assumption method*? Which method is more costly to taxpayers?

17. Consider a bank with the following balance sheet:

Assets		Liabilities	
Required reserves	$ 8 million	Checkable deposits	$100 million
Excess reserves	$ 3 million	Bank capital	$ 6 million
T-bills	$45 million		
Commercial loans	$50 million		

The bank makes a loan commitment for $10 million to a commercial customer. Calculate the bank's capital ratio before and after the agreement. Calculate the bank's risk-weighted assets before and after the agreement.

Problems 18–20 relate to a sequence of transactions at Oldhat Financial.

18. Oldhat Financial starts its first day of operations with $9 million in capital. A total of $130 million in checkable deposits is received. The bank makes a $25 million commercial loan and another $50 million in mortgages with the following terms: 200 standard, 30-year, fixed-rate mortgages with a nominal annual rate of 5.25%, each for $250,000.

Assume that required reserves are 8%.

a. What does the bank balance sheet look like?

b. How well capitalized is the bank?

c. Calculate the risk-weighted assets and risk-weighted capital ratio after Oldhat's first day.

19. Early the next day, the bank invests $50 million of its excess reserves in commercial loans. Later that day, terrible news hits the mortgage markets, and mortgage rates jump to 13%, implying a present value of Oldhat's current mortgage holdings of $124,798 per mortgage. Bank regulators force Oldhat to sell its mortgages to recognize the fair market value. What does Oldhat's balance sheet look like? How do these events affect its capital position?

20. To avoid insolvency, regulators decide to provide the bank with $25 million in bank capital. However, the bad news about the mortgages is featured in the local newspaper, causing a bank run. As a result, $30 million in deposits is withdrawn. Show the effects of the capital injection and the bank run on the balance sheet. Was the capital injection enough to stabilize the bank? If the bank regulators decide that the bank needs a capital ratio of 10% to prevent further runs on the bank, how much of an additional capital injection is required to reach a 10% capital ratio?

DATA ANALYSIS PROBLEMS

The Problems update with real-time data in MyEconLab and are available for practice or instructor assignment.

1. Go to the St. Louis Federal Reserve FRED database, and find data on the number of commercial banks in the U.S. in each of the following categories: average assets less than $100 million (US100NUM), average assets between $100 million and $300 million (US13NUM), average assets between $300 million

and $1 billion (US31NUM), average assets between $1 billion and $15 billion (US115NUM), and average assets greater than $15 billion (USG15NUM). Download the data into a spreadsheet. Calculate the percentage of banks in the smallest (less than $100 million) and largest (greater than $15 billion) categories, as a percentage of the total number of banks, for the most recent quarter of data available and for 1990:Q1. What has happened to the proportion of very large banks? What has happened to the proportion of very small banks? What does this say about the "too-big-to-fail" problem and moral hazard?

 2. Go to the St. Louis Federal Reserve FRED database, and find data on the residual of assets less liabilities, or bank capital (RALACBM027SBOG), and total assets of commercial banks (TLAACBM027SBOG). Download the data from January 1990 through the most recent month available into a spreadsheet. For each monthly observation, calculate the bank leverage ratio as the ratio of bank capital to total assets. Create a line graph of the leverage ratio over time. All else being equal, what can you conclude about leverage and moral hazard in commercial banks over time?

WEB EXERCISES

1. The Office of the Comptroller of the Currency is responsible for many of the regulations affecting bank operations. Go to http://www.occ.treas.gov/. Click on "OCC Regulations" under "Law and Regulations." Now click on "12 CFR Parts 1 to 199." What does Part 1 cover? How many parts are there in 12 CFR? Open Part 18. What topic does it cover? Summarize its purpose.

WEB REFERENCES

http://www.ny.frb.org/banking/supervisionregulate.html

View bank regulation information.

http://www.federalreserve.gov/Regulations/default.htm

Access regulatory publications of the Federal Reserve Board.

http://www.fdic.gov/regulations/laws/important/index.html

Describes the most important laws that have affected the banking industry in the United States.

http://www.fdic.gov/bank/historical/bank/index.html

Search for data on bank failures in any year.

WEB APPENDICES

Please visit the Companion Website at http://www.pearsonhighered.com/mishkin to read the Web appendices to Chapter 10.

Appendix 1: **The 1980s Banking and Savings and Loan Crisis**

Appendix 2: **Banking Crises Throughout the World**

11 Banking Industry: Structure and Competition

Learning Objectives

- Recognize the key features of the banking system and the historical context of the implementation of these features.
- Explain how financial innovation led to the growth of the shadow banking system.
- Identify the key structural changes in the commercial banking industry.
- Summarize the factors that led to consolidation in the commercial banking industry.
- Assess the reasons for separating banking from other financial services through legislation.
- Summarize the distinctions between thrift institutions and commercial banks.
- Identify the reasons for U.S. banks to operate in foreign countries and for foreign banks to operate in the United States.

Preview

The operations of individual banks (how they acquire, use, and manage funds to make a profit) are roughly similar throughout the world. In all countries, banks are financial intermediaries in the business of earning profits. When you consider the structure and operation of the banking industry as a whole, however, the United States is in a class by itself. In most countries, four or five large banks typically dominate the banking industry, but in the United States there are on the order of 5,700 commercial banks, 800 savings and loan associations, 350 mutual savings banks, and 7,000 credit unions.

Is more necessarily better? Does this diversity mean that the American banking system is more competitive and therefore more economically efficient and sound than banking systems in other countries? What in the American economic and political system explains this large number of banking institutions? In this chapter, we try to answer these questions by examining the historical trends in the banking industry and its overall structure.

We start by examining the historical development of the banking system and how financial innovation has increased the competitive environment for the banking industry and is causing fundamental changes in it. We go on to look at the commercial banking industry in detail and then discuss the thrift industry, which includes savings and loan associations, mutual savings banks, and credit unions. We spend more time on commercial banks because they are by far the largest depository institutions, accounting for more than two-thirds of the deposits in the banking system. In addition to looking at our domestic banking system, we examine the forces behind the growth of international banking to see how it has affected us in the United States.

HISTORICAL DEVELOPMENT OF THE BANKING SYSTEM

The modern commercial banking industry in the United States began when the Bank of North America was chartered in Philadelphia in 1782. With the success of this bank, other banks opened for business, and the American banking industry was off and running. (As a study aid, Figure 1 provides a time line of the most important dates in the history of American banking before World War II.)

A major controversy involving the industry in its early years was whether the federal government or the states should charter banks. The Federalists, particularly

MyEconLab Mini-lecture

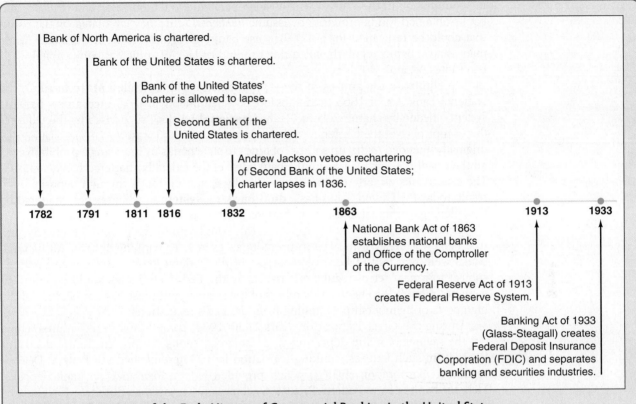

FIGURE 1   Time Line of the Early History of Commercial Banking in the United States
The most important dates in the history of American banking before World War II.

Alexander Hamilton, advocated greater centralized control of banking and federal chartering of banks. Their efforts led to the creation in 1791 of the Bank of the United States, which had elements of both a private bank and a **central bank**, a government institution that has responsibility for the amount of money and credit supplied in the economy as a whole. Agricultural and other interests, however, were quite suspicious of centralized power and hence advocated chartering by the states. Furthermore, their distrust of moneyed interests in the big cities led them to exert political pressure in an effort to eliminate the Bank of the United States, and in 1811 their efforts met with success when its charter was not renewed. Because of abuses by state banks and the clear need for a central bank to help the federal government raise funds during the War of 1812, Congress was stimulated to create the Second Bank of the United States in 1816. Tensions between advocates and opponents of centralized banking power were a recurrent theme during the operation of this second attempt at central banking in the United States, and with the election of Andrew Jackson, a strong advocate of states' rights, the fate of the Second Bank was sealed. After the election in 1832, Jackson vetoed the rechartering of the Second Bank of the United States as a national bank, and its charter lapsed in 1836.

Until 1863, all commercial banks in the United States were chartered by the banking commission of the state in which each operated. No national currency existed, and banks obtained funds primarily by issuing *banknotes* (currency circulated by the banks that could be redeemed for gold). Because banking regulations were extremely lax in many states, banks regularly failed due to fraud or lack of sufficient bank capital; their banknotes became worthless.

To eliminate the abuses of the state-chartered banks (called **state banks**), the National Bank Act of 1863 (and subsequent amendments to it) created a new banking system of federally chartered banks (called **national banks**), supervised by the Office of the Comptroller of the Currency, a department of the U.S. Treasury. This legislation was originally intended to dry up sources of funds to state banks by imposing a prohibitive tax on their banknotes while leaving the banknotes of the federally chartered banks untaxed. The state banks cleverly escaped extinction by acquiring funds through deposits. As a result, today the United States has a **dual banking system** in which banks chartered by the federal government and banks chartered by the states operate side by side.

Central banking did not reappear in this country until the Federal Reserve System (the Fed) was created in 1913 to promote an even safer banking system. All national banks were required to become members of the Federal Reserve System and became subject to a new set of regulations issued by the Fed. State banks could choose (but were not required) to become members of the system, and most did not because of the high costs of membership stemming from the Fed's regulations.

During the Great Depression years 1930–1933, some 9,000 bank failures wiped out the savings of many depositors at commercial banks. To prevent future depositor losses from such failures, banking legislation in 1933 established the Federal Deposit Insurance Corporation (FDIC), which provided federal insurance on bank deposits. Member banks of the Federal Reserve System were required to purchase FDIC insurance for their depositors, and non–Federal Reserve commercial banks could choose to buy this insurance (almost all of them did). The purchase of FDIC insurance made banks subject to another set of regulations imposed by the FDIC.

Because the investment banking activities of the commercial banks were blamed for many bank failures, provisions in the banking legislation in 1933 (also known as the Glass-Steagall Act) prohibited commercial banks from underwriting or dealing in corporate securities (though allowing them to sell new issues of government securities) and limited banks to the purchase of debt securities approved by the bank regulatory agencies. Likewise, this legislation prohibited investment banks from engaging in commercial banking activities. In effect, the Glass-Steagall Act separated the activities of commercial banks from those of the securities industry.

Under the conditions of the Glass-Steagall Act, which was repealed in 1999, commercial banks had to sell off their investment banking operations. The First National Bank of Boston, for example, spun off its investment banking operations into the First Boston Corporation, now part of one of the most important investment banking firms in America, Credit Suisse First Boston. Investment banking firms typically discontinued their deposit business, although J.P. Morgan discontinued its investment banking business and reorganized as a commercial bank; however, some senior officers of J.P. Morgan went on to organize Morgan Stanley, another one of the largest investment banking firms today.

Multiple Regulatory Agencies

Commercial bank regulation in the United States has developed into a crazy quilt of multiple regulatory agencies with overlapping jurisdictions. The Office of the Comptroller of the Currency has the primary supervisory responsibility for national banks that own more than half of the assets in the commercial banking system. The Federal Reserve and the state banking authorities have joint primary responsibility for state banks that are members of the Federal Reserve System. The Fed also has regulatory responsibility over companies that own one or more banks (called **bank holding companies**) and secondary responsibility for the national banks. The FDIC and the state banking authorities jointly supervise state banks that have FDIC insurance but are not members of the Federal Reserve System. The state banking authorities have sole jurisdiction over state banks without FDIC insurance. (Such banks hold less than 0.2% of the deposits in the commercial banking system.)

If you find the U.S. bank regulatory system confusing, imagine how confusing it is for the banks, which have to deal with multiple regulatory agencies. Several proposals have been raised by the U.S. Treasury to rectify this situation by centralizing the regulation of all depository institutions under one independent agency. However, none of these proposals has been successful in Congress, and whether there will be regulatory consolidation in the future is highly uncertain.

FINANCIAL INNOVATION AND THE GROWTH OF THE "SHADOW BANKING SYSTEM"

Although banking institutions are still the most important financial institutions in the U.S. economy, in recent years the traditional banking business of making loans that are funded by deposits has been in decline. Some of this business has been replaced by the **shadow banking system**, in which bank lending has been replaced by lending via the securities markets, with the involvement of a number of different financial institutions.

To understand how the banking industry has evolved over time, we must first understand the process of financial innovation, which has transformed the entire financial system. Like other industries, the financial industry is in business to earn profits by selling its products. If a soap company perceives that a need exists in the marketplace for a laundry detergent with fabric softener, it develops a product to fit that need. Similarly, to maximize their profits, financial institutions develop new products to satisfy their own needs as well as those of their customers; in other words, innovation—which can be extremely beneficial to the economy—is driven by the desire to get (or stay) rich. This view of the innovation process leads to the following simple analysis: *A change in the financial environment will stimulate a search by financial institutions for innovations that are likely to be profitable.*

Starting in the 1960s, individuals and financial institutions operating in financial markets were confronted with drastic changes in the economic environment: Inflation and interest rates climbed sharply and became harder to predict, a situation that changed demand conditions in financial markets. The rapid advances in computer technology changed supply conditions. In addition, financial regulations became more burdensome. Financial institutions found that many of the old ways of doing business were no longer profitable; the financial services and products they had been offering to the public were not selling. Many financial intermediaries found that they were no longer able to acquire funds with their traditional financial instruments, and without these funds they would soon be out of business. To survive in the new economic environment, financial institutions had to research and develop new products and services that would meet customer needs and prove profitable, a process referred to as **financial engineering**. In their case, necessity was the mother of innovation.

Our discussion of the factors that drive financial innovation suggests that there are three basic types of financial innovation: responses to changes in demand conditions, responses to changes in supply conditions, and avoidance of existing regulations. These three motivations often interact to produce particular financial innovations. Now that we have a framework for understanding why financial institutions produce innovations, let's look at examples of how financial institutions, in their search for profits, have produced financial innovations of the three basic types.

Responses to Changes in Demand Conditions: Interest-Rate Volatility

The most significant change in the economic environment that altered the demand for financial products in recent years has been the dramatic increase in the volatility of interest rates. In the 1950s, the interest rate on three-month Treasury bills fluctuated between 1.0% and 3.5%; in the 1970s, it fluctuated between 4.0% and 11.5%; in the 1980s, it ranged from 5% to more than 15%. Large fluctuations in interest rates lead to substantial capital gains or losses and greater uncertainty about returns on investments. Recall that the risk that is related to the uncertainty about interest-rate movements and returns is called *interest-rate risk*, and high volatility of interest rates, such as we saw in the 1970s and 1980s, leads to a higher level of interest-rate risk.

We would expect the increase in interest-rate risk to increase the demand for financial products and services that could reduce that risk. This change in the economic environment would thus stimulate a search by financial institutions for profitable innovations that meet this new demand and would spur the creation of new financial instruments that help lower interest-rate risk. Two financial innovations that were developed in the 1970s confirm this prediction: adjustable-rate mortgages and financial derivatives.

Adjustable-Rate Mortgages   Like other investors, financial institutions find that lending is more attractive if interest-rate risk is lower. They would not want to make a mortgage loan at a 10% interest rate and two months later find that they could obtain 12% in interest on the same mortgage. To reduce interest-rate risk, in 1975 savings and loans in California began to issue adjustable-rate mortgages, that is, mortgage loans on which the interest rate changes when a market interest rate (usually the Treasury bill rate) changes. Initially, an adjustable-rate mortgage might have a 5% interest rate. In six months, this interest rate might increase or decrease by the amount of the increase or decrease in, say, the six-month Treasury bill rate, and the mortgage payment would then change. Because adjustable-rate mortgages allow mortgage-issuing institutions to earn higher interest rates on existing mortgages when market rates rise, profits remain high during these periods.

This attractive feature of adjustable-rate mortgages has encouraged mortgage-issuing institutions to issue adjustable-rate mortgages with lower initial interest rates than those on conventional fixed-rate mortgages, making them popular with many households. However, because the mortgage payment on a variable-rate mortgage can increase, many households continue to prefer fixed-rate mortgages. Hence both types of mortgages are widespread.

Financial Derivatives   Given the greater demand for the reduction of interest-rate risk, commodity exchanges such as the Chicago Board of Trade recognized that if they could develop a product that would help investors and financial institutions protect themselves from, or **hedge**, interest-rate risk, then they could make profits by selling this new instrument. **Futures contracts**, in which the seller agrees to provide a certain standardized commodity to the buyer on a specific future date at an agreed-on price, had been around for a long time. Officials at the Chicago Board of Trade realized that if they created futures contracts in financial instruments, which are called **financial derivatives** because their payoffs are linked to (i.e., derived from) previously issued securities, they could be used to hedge risk. Thus, in 1975, financial derivatives were born.

Responses to Changes in Supply Conditions: Information Technology

The most important source of the changes in supply conditions that stimulated financial innovation has been the improvement in computer and telecommunications technology. This technology, called *information technology,* has had two effects. First, it has lowered the cost of processing financial transactions, making it profitable for financial institutions to create new financial products and services for the public. Second, it has made it easier for investors to acquire information, thereby making it easier for firms to issue securities. The rapid developments in information technology have resulted in many new financial products and services, which we examine here.

Bank Credit and Debit Cards Credit cards have been around since well before World War II. Many individual stores (Sears, Macy's) institutionalized charge accounts by providing customers with credit cards that allowed them to make purchases at these stores without cash. Nationwide credit cards were not established until after World War II, when Diners Club developed a card to be used in restaurants all over the country (and abroad). Similar credit card programs were started by American Express and Carte Blanche, but because of the high cost of operating these programs, cards were issued only to select persons and businesses that could afford expensive purchases.

A firm issuing credit cards earns income from loans it makes to credit card holders and from payments made by stores on credit card purchases (a percentage of the purchase price, say, 5%). A credit card program's costs arise from loan defaults, stolen cards, and the expense involved in processing credit card transactions.

Seeing the success of Diners Club, American Express, and Carte Blanche, bankers wanted to share in the profitable credit card business. Several commercial banks attempted to expand the credit card business to a wider market in the 1950s, but the cost per transaction of running these programs was so high that their early attempts failed.

In the late 1960s, improved computer technology, which lowered the transaction costs for providing credit card services, made it more likely that bank credit card programs would be profitable. The banks tried to enter this business again, and this time their efforts led to the creation of two successful bank credit card programs: BankAmericard (originally started by Bank of America but now an independent organization called Visa) and MasterCharge (now MasterCard, run by the Interbank Card Association). These programs have become phenomenally successful; around 500 million of their cards are in use in the United States and over a billion more in the rest of the world. Indeed, bank credit cards have been so profitable that nonfinancial institutions such as Sears (which launched the Discover card), General Motors, and AT&T have also entered the credit card business. Consumers have benefited because credit cards are more widely accepted than checks as a method of paying for purchases (particularly abroad), and they allow consumers to take out loans more easily.

The success of bank credit cards led these institutions to come up with another financial innovation, *debit cards*. Debit cards often look just like credit cards and can be used to make purchases in an identical fashion. However, in contrast to credit cards, which extend the purchaser a loan that does not have to be paid off immediately, a debit card purchase is immediately deducted from the card holder's bank account. Debit cards depend even more on low costs of processing transactions, because their profits are generated entirely from the fees paid by merchants on debit card purchases at their stores. Debit cards have grown extremely popular in recent years.

Electronic Banking   The wonders of modern computer technology have also enabled banks to lower the cost of bank transactions by having the customer interact with an electronic banking (e-banking) facility rather than with a human being. One important form of an e-banking facility is the **automated teller machine (ATM)**, an electronic machine that allows customers to get cash, make deposits, transfer funds from one account to another, and check balances. ATM machines do not have to be paid overtime and never sleep, and thus are available for use 24 hours a day. Not only does this result in cheaper transactions for the bank, but it also provides more convenience for the customer. Because of their low cost, ATMs can be put at locations other than a bank or its branches, further increasing customer convenience. The low cost of ATMs has encouraged banks to install them everywhere, and ATMs now number more than 400,000 in the United States alone. Furthermore, it is now just as easy to get foreign currency from an ATM when you are traveling in Europe as it is to get cash from your local bank.

With the drop in the cost of telecommunications, banks have developed another financial innovation, *home banking*. It is now cost-effective for banks to set up an electronic banking facility in which the bank's customer is linked up with the bank's computer and allowed to carry out transactions by using a smart phone, tablet, or personal computer. Now a bank's customers can conduct many of their bank transactions without ever leaving the comfort of home. The advantage for the customer is the convenience of home banking, while banks find that the cost of transactions is substantially less than the cost associated with brick-and-mortar banking. The success of ATMs and home banking has led to another innovation, the **automated banking machine (ABM)**, which combines in one location an ATM, an Internet connection to the bank's website, and a telephone link to customer service.

With the decline in the price of personal computers and their increasing presence in the home, we have seen a further innovation in the home banking area, the creation of a new type of banking institution, the **virtual bank**, a bank that has no physical location but rather exists only in cyberspace. In 1995, Security First Network Bank, based in Atlanta but now owned by Royal Bank of Canada, became the first virtual bank, offering an array of banking services on the Internet—accepting checking account and savings deposits, selling certificates of deposits, issuing ATM cards, providing bill-paying facilities, and so on. The virtual bank thus takes home banking one step further, enabling the customer to have a full set of banking services at home, 24 hours a day. In 1996, Bank of America and Wells Fargo entered the virtual banking market, to be followed by many others, with Bank of America now being the largest Internet bank in the United States. Will virtual banking be the predominant form of banking in the future? (See the FYI box, "Will 'Clicks' Dominate 'Bricks' in the Banking Industry?")

Junk Bonds   Before the advent of computers and advanced telecommunications, it was difficult to acquire information about the financial situations of firms that might want to sell securities. Because of the difficulty in screening out bad from good credit risks, the only firms that were able to sell bonds were very well-established corporations

---

FYI   **Will "Clicks" Dominate "Bricks" in the Banking Industry?**

With the advent of virtual banks ("clicks") and the convenience they provide, a key question is whether they will become the primary form in which banks do their business, eliminating the need for physical bank branches ("bricks") as the main delivery mechanism for banking services. Indeed, will stand-alone Internet banks be the wave of the future?

The answer seems to be no. Internet-only banks such as Wingspan (owned by Bank One), First-e (Dublin-based), and Egg (a British Internet-only bank owned by Prudential) have had disappointing revenue growth and profits. The result is that pure online banking has not been the success that proponents had hoped for. Why has Internet banking been a disappointment?

Internet banking has several strikes against it. First, bank depositors want to know that their savings are secure, and so are reluctant to put their money into new institutions without a long track record. Second, customers worry about the security of their online transactions and whether their transactions will truly be kept

private. Traditional banks are viewed as being more secure and trustworthy in terms of protecting private information. Third, many customers prefer that certain services be provided by physical branches. For example, banking customers seem to prefer purchasing long-term savings products face-to-face. Fourth, Internet banking has run into technical problems—server crashes, slow connections over phone lines, mistakes in conducting transactions—that will probably diminish over time as technology improves.

The wave of the future thus does not appear to be pure Internet banks. Instead, it looks as though "clicks and bricks" will be the predominant form of banking, in which online banking is used to complement the services provided by traditional banks. Nonetheless, the delivery of banking services is undergoing massive changes, with more and more banking services delivered over the Internet and the number of physical bank branches likely to decline in the future.

---

that had high credit ratings.[1] Before the 1980s, then, only corporations that could issue bonds with ratings of Baa or above could raise funds by selling newly issued bonds. Some firms that had fallen on bad times, known as *fallen angels*, had previously issued long-term corporate bonds with ratings that had now fallen below Baa, bonds that were pejoratively dubbed "junk bonds."

With the improvement in information technology in the 1970s, it became easier for investors to acquire financial information about corporations, making it easier to screen out bad from good credit risks. With easier screening, investors were more willing to buy long-term debt securities from less-well-known corporations with lower credit ratings. With this change in supply conditions, we would expect that some smart individual would pioneer the concept of selling new public issues of junk bonds, not for fallen angels but for companies that had not yet achieved investment-grade status. This is exactly what Michael Milken of Drexel Burnham Lambert, an investment banking firm, started to do in 1977. Junk bonds became an important factor in the corporate bond market, with the amount outstanding exceeding $200 billion by the late 1980s. Although there was a sharp slowdown in activity in the junk bond market after Milken was indicted for securities law violations in 1989, the junk bond market heated up again in the 1990s and 2000s.

---

[1]The discussion of adverse selection problems in Chapter 8 provides a more detailed analysis of why only well-established firms with high credit ratings were able to sell securities.

Commercial Paper Market   *Commercial paper* is a short-term debt security issued by large banks and corporations. The commercial paper market has undergone tremendous growth since 1970, when $33 billion was outstanding, to around $1 trillion outstanding at the end of 2013. Indeed, commercial paper has been one of the fastest-growing money market instruments.

Improvements in information technology also help explain the rapid rise of the commercial paper market. We have seen that improvements in information technology made it easier for investors to screen out bad from good credit risks, thus making it easier for corporations to issue debt securities. Not only did this make it simpler for corporations to issue long-term debt securities, as in the junk bond market, but it also meant they could raise funds by issuing short-term debt securities, such as commercial paper, with greater ease. Many corporations that used to do their short-term borrowing from banks now frequently raise short-term funds in the commercial paper market instead.

The development of money market mutual funds has been another factor in the rapid growth of the commercial paper market. Because money market mutual funds need to hold liquid, high-quality, short-term assets such as commercial paper, the growth of assets in these funds to around $2.7 trillion has created a ready market in commercial paper. The growth of pension and other large funds that invest in commercial paper has also stimulated the growth of this market.

Securitization and the Shadow Banking System

One of the most important financial innovations of the past two decades, arising from improvements in information technology, is securitization. **Securitization** is the process of bundling small and otherwise illiquid financial assets (such as residential mortgages, auto loans, and credit card receivables), which have typically been the bread and butter of banking institutions, into marketable capital market securities. Securitization is the fundamental building block of the shadow banking system.

How the Shadow Banking System Works   In traditional banking, one entity engages in the process of asset transformation—that is, it issues liabilities with one set of desirable characteristics (say, deposits with high liquidity and low risk) to fund the purchase of assets with a different set of characteristics (say, loans with low liquidity and high returns). Securitization, on the other hand, is a process of asset transformation that involves a number of different financial institutions working together. These institutions comprise the shadow banking system. In other words, asset transformation accomplished through securitization and the shadow banking system is not done "under one roof," as is traditional banking.

For example, a mortgage broker (more generally referred to as a *loan originator*) will arrange for a residential mortgage loan to be made by a financial institution that will then service the loan (that is, collect the interest and principal payments). This *servicer* then sells the mortgage to another financial institution, which bundles the mortgage with a large number of other residential mortgages. The *bundler* takes the interest and principal payments on the portfolio of mortgages and "passes them through" (pays them out) to third parties. The bundler goes to a *distributor* (typically an investment bank), which designs a security that divides the portfolio of loans into standardized amounts. The distributor then sells the claims to these interest and principal payments as securities, mostly to other financial intermediaries that are also part of the shadow banking system—for example, a money market mutual fund or a pension fund. Schematically, the securitization process is described by the following sequence:

$$\text{Loan origination} \Rightarrow \text{servicing} \Rightarrow \text{bundling} \Rightarrow \text{distribution}$$

Because the securitization process involves the origination of loans and then finally the distribution of securities, securitization is also characterized as an **originate-to-distribute** business model.

At each step of the securitization process, the loan originator, servicer, bundler and distributor earn a fee. Each of these four institutions has specialized in a particular element of the financial intermediation process. The shadow banking system, which comprises all of the financial institutions involved in the securitization process, can thus be very profitable if transaction costs and the costs of collecting information are low. Advances in information technology have therefore been critical to the growth of securitization and the shadow banking system. Lower costs of acquiring information make it far easier to sell capital market securities, while lower transaction costs make it cheaper for financial institutions to collect interest and principal payments on bundled loans and then pay them out to the securities holders.

Subprime Mortgage Market   A particularly important financial innovation that developed in the 2000s as a result of securitization and the shadow banking system was the **subprime mortgage**, a new class of residential mortgages offered to borrowers with less-than-stellar credit records. Before 2000, only the most credit-worthy (prime) borrowers could obtain residential mortgages. Advances in computer technology and new statistical techniques, known as data mining, led to enhanced, quantitative evaluation of the credit risk for residential mortgages. Households with credit records could now be assigned a numerical credit score, known as a FICO score (named after the Fair Isaac Corporation that developed it), that predicted how likely the household would be to default on its loan payments. Because it now became easier to assess the risk associated with a pool of subprime mortgages, it became possible to bundle them into a mortgage-backed-security, providing a new source of funding for these mortgages. The result was an explosion of subprime mortgage lending which, as we will see in Chapter 12, was a key factor that led to the global financial crisis of 2007–2009.

Avoidance of Existing Regulations

The process of financial innovation, as we have discussed it so far, is much like innovation in other areas of the economy: It occurs in response to changes in demand and supply conditions. However, because the financial industry is more heavily regulated than other industries, government regulation is a much greater spur to innovation in this industry. Government regulation leads to financial innovation by creating incentives for firms to skirt regulations that restrict their ability to earn profits. Edward Kane, an economist at Boston College, describes this process of avoiding regulations as "loophole mining." The economic analysis of innovation suggests that when the economic environment changes such that regulatory constraints are so burdensome that large profits can be made by avoiding them, loophole mining and innovation are more likely to occur.

Because banking is one of the most heavily regulated industries in America, loophole mining is especially likely to occur. The rise in inflation and interest rates from the late 1960s to 1980 made the regulatory constraints imposed on this industry even more burdensome, leading to financial innovation.

Two sets of regulations have seriously restricted the ability of banks to make profits: reserve requirements that force banks to keep a certain fraction of their deposits as reserves (vault cash and deposits in the Federal Reserve System) and restrictions on the interest rates that can be paid on deposits. For the following reasons, these regulations have been major forces behind financial innovation.

1. *Reserve requirements.* The key to understanding why reserve requirements led to financial innovation is to recognize that they act, in effect, as a tax on deposits. Because up until 2008 the Fed did not pay interest on reserves, the opportunity cost of holding them was the interest that a bank could otherwise earn by lending the reserves out. For each dollar of deposits, reserve requirements therefore imposed a cost on the bank equal to the interest rate, i, that could be earned if the reserves could be lent out times the fraction of deposits required as reserves, r. The cost of $i \times r$ imposed on the bank was just like a tax on bank deposits of $i \times r$ per dollar of deposits. This "tax" on deposits rises as interest rates rise.

It is a great tradition to avoid taxes if possible, and banks also play this game. Just as taxpayers look for loopholes to lower their tax bills, banks seek to increase their profits by mining loopholes and by producing financial innovations that enable them to escape the tax on deposits imposed by reserve requirements.

2. *Restrictions on interest paid on deposits.* Until 1980, legislation prohibited banks in most states from paying interest on checking account deposits, and through Regulation Q, the Fed set maximum limits on the interest rate that could be paid on time deposits. To this day, banks are not allowed to pay interest on corporate checking accounts. The desire of banks to avoid these **deposit rate ceilings** also led to financial innovations.

If market interest rates rose above the maximum rates that banks paid on time deposits under Regulation Q, depositors withdrew funds from banks to put them into higher-yielding securities. This loss of deposits from the banking system restricted the amount of funds that banks could lend (called **disintermediation**) and thus limited bank profits. Banks had an incentive to get around deposit rate ceilings, because by so doing, they could acquire more funds to make loans and earn higher profits.

We can now look at how the desire to avoid restrictions on interest payments and the tax effect of reserve requirements led to two important financial innovations.

Money Market Mutual Funds Money market mutual funds issue shares that are redeemable at a fixed price (usually $1) by writing checks. For example, if you buy 5,000 shares for $5,000, the money market fund uses these funds to invest in short-term money market securities (Treasury bills, negotiable certificates of deposit, commercial paper) that provide you with interest payments. In addition, you are able to write checks up to the $5,000 held as shares in the money market fund. Although money market fund shares effectively function as checking account deposits that earn interest, they are not legally deposits and so are not subject to reserve requirements or prohibitions on interest payments. For this reason, they can pay higher interest rates than deposits at banks.

The first money market mutual fund was created by two Wall Street mavericks, Bruce Bent and Henry Brown, in 1970. However, the low market interest rates from 1970 to 1977 (which were just slightly above Regulation Q ceilings of 5.25–5.5%) kept money market mutual funds from being particularly advantageous relative to bank deposits. In early 1978, the situation changed rapidly as inflation rose and market interest rates began to climb over 10%, well above the 5.5% maximum interest rates

---

Bruce Bent, one of the originators of money market mutual funds, almost brought down the industry during the global financial crisis in the fall of 2008. Mr. Bent told his shareholders in a letter written in July 2008 that the fund was managed on a basis of "unwavering discipline focused on protecting your principal." He also wrote to the Securities and Exchange Commission in September 2007, stating "When I first created the money market fund back in 1970, it was designed with the tenets of safety and liquidity." He added that these principles had "fallen by the wayside as portfolio managers chased the highest yield and compromised the integrity of the money fund." Alas, Bent did not follow his own advice, and his fund, the Reserve Primary Fund, bought risky assets that made its yield higher than the industry average.

When Lehman Brothers went into bankruptcy on September 15, 2008, the Reserve Primary Fund, with assets over $60 billion, was caught holding the bag on $785 million of Lehman's debt, which then had to be marked down to zero. The resulting losses meant that on September 16, Bent's fund could no longer afford to redeem its shares at the par value of $1, a situation known as "breaking the buck." Bent's shareholders began to pull their money out of the fund, causing it to lose 90% of its assets.

The fear that this could happen to other money market mutual funds led to a classic panic in which shareholders began to withdraw their funds at an alarming rate. The whole money market mutual fund industry looked as though it would come crashing down. To prevent this, the Federal Reserve and the U.S. Treasury rode to the rescue on September 19. The Fed set up a facility, discussed in Chapter 15, to make loans to be used to purchase commercial paper from money market mutual funds so that they could meet the demands for redemptions from their investors. The Treasury then put in a temporary guarantee for all money market mutual fund redemptions, and the panic subsided.

Not surprisingly, given the extension of a government safety net to the money market mutual fund industry, there are calls to regulate this industry more heavily. The money market mutual fund industry will never be the same.

---

payable on savings accounts and time deposits under Regulation Q. In 1977, money market mutual funds had assets of less than $4 billion; in 1978, their assets climbed to close to $10 billion; in 1979, to more than $40 billion; and in 1982, to $230 billion. Currently, their assets are around $2.7 trillion. To say the least, money market mutual funds have been a successful financial innovation, which is exactly what we would have predicted given the financial climate of the late 1970s and early 1980s, in which interest rates soared beyond Regulation Q ceilings.

In a supreme irony, risky investments by a money market mutual fund founded by Bruce Brent almost brought down the money market mutual fund industry during the global financial crisis in 2008 (see the FYI box, "Bruce Bent and the Money Market Mutual Fund Panic of 2008").

Sweep Accounts   Another innovation that enables banks to avoid the "tax" from reserve requirements is the **sweep account**. In this arrangement, any balances above a certain amount in a corporation's checking account at the end of a business day are "swept out" of the account and invested in overnight securities that pay interest. Because the "swept out" funds are no longer classified as checkable deposits, they are not subject to reserve requirements and thus are not "taxed." They also have the advantage that they allow banks, in effect, to pay interest on these checking accounts, which otherwise is not allowed under existing regulations. Because sweep accounts have become so popular, they have lowered the amount of required reserves to the degree that most banking institutions do not find reserve requirements binding: In other words, they voluntarily hold more reserves than they are required to.

The financial innovations of sweep accounts and money market mutual funds are particularly interesting because they were stimulated not only by the desire to avoid a costly regulation, but also by a change in supply conditions—in this case, information technology. Without low-cost computers to process inexpensively the additional transactions required by these innovations, they would not have been profitable and therefore would not have been developed. Technological factors often combine with other incentives, such as the desire to get around a regulation, to produce innovation.

Financial Innovation and the Decline of Traditional Banking

The traditional financial intermediation role of banking has been to make long-term loans and to fund them by issuing short-term deposits, a process of asset transformation commonly referred to as "borrowing short and lending long." Here we examine how financial innovations have created a more competitive environment for the banking industry, causing the industry to change dramatically, with its traditional banking business going into decline.

In the United States, the importance of commercial banks as a source of funds for nonfinancial borrowers has shrunk dramatically. As we can see in Figure 2, in 1974,

 MyEconLab Mini-lecture

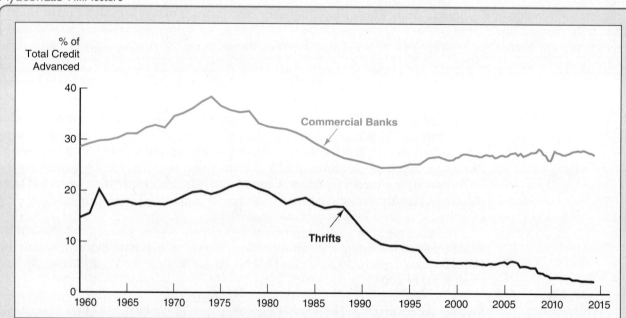

FIGURE 2 Bank Share of Total Nonfinancial Borrowing, 1960–2014

In 1974, commercial banks provided close to 40% of these funds; by 2014, their market share was down to 27%. The decline in market share for thrift institutions has been even more precipitous, from more than 20% in the late 1970s to 2.5% today.

Source: Federal Reserve Bank of St. Louis, FRED data base: http://research.stlouisfed.org/fred2/; https://www2.fdic.gov/hsob/index.asp.

commercial banks provided close to 40% of these funds; by 2014, their market share was down to 27%. The decline in market share for thrift institutions has been even more precipitous, from more than 20% in the late 1970s to 2.5% today. To understand why the traditional banking business has declined in size, we need to look at how the financial innovations described earlier have caused banks to suffer declines in their cost advantages in acquiring funds—that is, on the liabilities side of their balance sheet—while at the same time losing income advantages on the assets side of their balance sheet. The simultaneous decline of cost and income advantages has resulted in reduced profitability of traditional banking and an effort by banks to leave this business and engage in new and more profitable activities.

Decline in Cost Advantages in Acquiring Funds (Liabilities)

Until 1980, banks were subject to deposit rate ceilings that restricted them from paying any interest on checkable deposits and (under Regulation Q) limited them to paying a maximum interest rate of a little more than 5% on time deposits. Until the 1960s, these restrictions worked to the banks' advantage because their major source of funds (in excess of 60%) was checkable deposits, and the zero interest cost on these deposits meant that the banks had a very low cost of funds. Unfortunately, this cost advantage for banks did not last. The rise in inflation beginning in the late 1960s led to higher interest rates, which made investors more sensitive to yield differentials on different assets. The result was the *disintermediation* process, in which people began to take their money out of banks, with their low interest rates on both checkable and time deposits, and began to seek out higher-yielding investments. At the same time, as we have seen, attempts to get around deposit rate ceilings and reserve requirements led to the financial innovation of money market mutual funds, which put the banks at an even further disadvantage because depositors could now obtain checking account–like services while earning high interest on their money market mutual fund accounts. One manifestation of these changes in the financial system was that the low-cost source of funds, checkable deposits, declined dramatically in importance for banks, falling from more than 60% of bank liabilities to 11% today.

The growing difficulty for banks in raising funds led them to support legislation in the 1980s that eliminated Regulation Q ceilings on time and savings deposit interest rates and allowed checkable deposit accounts that paid interest. Although these changes in regulation helped make banks more competitive in their quest for funds, it also meant that their cost of acquiring funds had risen substantially, thereby reducing their earlier cost advantage over other financial institutions.

Decline in Income Advantages on Uses of Funds (Assets)

The loss of cost advantages on the liabilities side of the balance sheet for American banks is one reason they have become less competitive, but they have also been hit by a decline in income advantages on the assets side from the financial innovations we discussed earlier—junk bonds, securitization, and the rise of the commercial paper market. The resulting loss of income advantages for banks relative to these innovations has resulted in a loss of market share and has led to the growth of the shadow banking system, which has made use of these innovations to enable borrowers to bypass the traditional banking system.

We have seen that improvements in information technology have made it easier for firms to issue securities directly to the public. This change means that instead of going to banks to finance short-term credit needs, many of the banks' best business customers now find it cheaper to go instead to the commercial paper market for funds. In addition, the commercial paper market has allowed finance companies, which depend primarily on commercial paper to acquire funds, to expand their operations at the expense of banks. Finance companies, which lend to many of the same businesses that borrow from banks, have maintained their market share relative to banks: Before 1980, finance company loans to business equaled about 30% of commercial and industrial bank loans; currently, they account for 32%.

The emergence of the junk bond market has also eaten into banks' loan business. Improvements in information technology have made it easier for corporations to sell their bonds to the public directly, thereby bypassing banks. Although *Fortune* 500 companies started taking this route in the 1970s, now lower-quality corporate borrowers are using banks less often because they have access to the junk bond market.

We have also seen that improvements in computer technology have led to the growth of the shadow banking system and securitization, whereby illiquid financial assets such as bank loans and mortgages are transformed into marketable securities. Computers enable other financial institutions to originate loans because these institutions can now accurately evaluate credit risk with statistical methods. Computers also have lowered transaction costs, making it possible to bundle these loans and sell them as securities. When default risk can be easily evaluated using computers, banks no longer have an advantage in making loans. Without their former advantages, banks have lost loan business to other financial institutions even though the banks themselves are involved in the process of securitization. Securitization has been a particular problem for mortgage-issuing institutions such as S&Ls, because most residential mortgages are now securitized.

Banks' Responses   In any industry, a decline in profitability usually results in an exit from the industry (often due to widespread bankruptcies) and a shrinkage of market share. This occurred in the U.S. banking industry during the 1980s via consolidations and bank failures (discussed in Chapter 10).

In an attempt to survive and maintain adequate profit levels, many U.S. banks faced two alternatives. First, they could attempt to maintain their traditional lending activity by expanding into new and riskier areas of lending. For example, U.S. banks increased their risk taking by placing a greater percentage of their total funds in commercial real estate loans, traditionally a riskier type of loan. In addition, they increased lending for corporate takeovers and leveraged buyouts, which are highly leveraged transactions. The decline in the profitability of banks' traditional business may thus have helped lead to the global financial crisis of 2007 to 2009.

The second way in which banks have sought to maintain their former profit levels is by pursuing new off-balance-sheet activities that are more profitable and in effect embrace the shadow banking system. U.S. commercial banks did this during the early 1980s, more than doubling the share of their income coming from off-balance-sheet, non–interest-income activities. Nontraditional bank activities can be riskier and, therefore, result in excessive risk taking by banks. Indeed, they led to a substantial weakening of bank balance sheets during the global financial crisis.

The decline of banks' traditional business has driven the banking industry to seek out new lines of business. This search for business opportunities may be beneficial because it may ultimately keep banks vibrant and healthy. Indeed, bank profitability was high up until 2007, and nontraditional, off-balance-sheet activities played an important role in the high bank profits. However, the new directions in banking led to increased risk taking, and thus the decline in traditional banking has required regulators to be more vigilant. Nontraditional bank activities pose new challenges for bank regulators, who, as we saw in Chapter 10, must now be far more concerned about banks' off-balance-sheet activities.

Decline of Traditional Banking in Other Industrialized Countries Forces similar to those in the United States have led to the decline of traditional banking in other industrialized countries. The loss of banks' monopoly power over depositors has occurred outside the United States as well. Financial innovation and deregulation are occurring worldwide and have created attractive alternatives for both depositors and borrowers. In Japan, for example, deregulation opened a wide array of new financial instruments to the public, causing a disintermediation process similar to that in the United States. In European countries, innovations have steadily eroded the barriers that have traditionally protected banks from competition.

In other countries, banks also faced increased competition from the expansion of securities markets and the growth of the shadow banking system. Both financial deregulation and advances in information technology in other countries have improved the availability of information in securities markets, making it easier and less costly for firms to finance their activities by issuing securities rather than going to banks. Further, even in countries where securities markets have not grown, banks have still lost loan business because their best corporate customers have had increasing access to foreign and offshore capital markets, such as the Eurobond market. In smaller economies, like that of Australia, which still do not have as well-developed corporate bond or commercial paper markets, banks have lost loan business to international securities markets. In addition, the same forces that drove the securitization process in the United States have been at work in other countries and have undercut the profitability of traditional banking in these countries as well. The United States has not been unique in seeing its banks face a more difficult competitive environment. Thus, although the decline of traditional banking occurred earlier in the United States than in other countries, the same forces have caused a decline in traditional banking abroad.

STRUCTURE OF THE U.S. COMMERCIAL BANKING INDUSTRY

There are approximately 5,700 commercial banks in the United States, far more than in any other country in the world. As Table 1 indicates, we have an extraordinary number of small banks. Thirty percent of the banks have less than $100 million

TABLE 1	Size Distribution of Insured Commercial Banks, June 30, 2014		
Assets	Number of Banks	Share of Banks (%)	Share of Assets Held (%)
Less than $100 million	1,744	30.3	0.7
$100 million–$1 billion	3,469	60.3	7.4
$1 billion–$10 billion	451	7.8	8.5
More than $10 billion	93	1.6	83.4
Total	5,757	100.00	100.00

Source: https://www2.fdic.gov/qbp/2014jun/cb4.html.

TABLE 2	Ten Largest U.S. Banks, June 30, 2014	
Bank	**Assets ($ millions)**	**Share of All Commercial Bank Assets (%)**
1. J.P. Morgan Chase	1,945,467	14.23
2. Bank of America Corp.	1,433,716	10.49
3. Wells Fargo	1,373,600	10.05
4. Citibank	1,346,747	9.85
5. U.S. Bank	360,478	2.64
6. PNC	310,000	2.27
7. Bank of NY Mellon	296,626	2.17
8. State Street	239,051	1.75
9. Capital One	238,483	1.74
10. TD Bank	217,626	1.59
Total	7,761,794	56.78

Source: http://www.federalreserve.gov/Releases/Lbr/

in assets. Far more typical is the size distribution in Canada or the United Kingdom, where five or fewer banks dominate the industry. In contrast, the ten largest commercial banks in the United States (listed in Table 2) together hold just 57% of the assets in their industry.

Most industries in the United States have far fewer firms than the commercial banking industry; typically, large firms tend to dominate these industries to a greater extent than in the commercial banking industry. (Consider the computer software industry, which is dominated by Microsoft, or the automobile industry, which is dominated by General Motors, Ford, Daimler-Chrysler, Toyota, and Honda.) Does the large number of banks in the commercial banking industry and the absence of a few dominant firms suggest that commercial banking is more competitive than other industries?

Restrictions on Branching

The presence of so many commercial banks in the United States actually reflects past regulations that restricted the ability of these financial institutions to open **branches** (additional offices for the conduct of banking operations). Each state had its own regulations on the type and number of branches that a bank could open. Regulations on both coasts, for example, tended to allow banks to open branches throughout a state; in the middle part of the country, regulations on branching were more restrictive, in some cases allowing no branches at all. The McFadden Act of 1927, which was designed to put national banks and state banks on equal footing (and the Douglas Amendment of 1956, which closed a loophole in the McFadden Act), effectively prohibited banks from branching across state lines and forced all national banks to conform to the branching regulations of the state in which their headquarters were located.

The McFadden Act and state branching regulations constituted strong anticompetitive forces in the commercial banking industry, allowing many small banks to stay in existence because larger banks were prevented from opening branches nearby. If competition is beneficial to society, why did regulations restricting branching arise in America? The simplest explanation is that the American public has historically been hostile to large banks. States with the most restrictive branching regulations were typically ones in which populist antibank sentiment was strongest in the nineteenth century. (These states usually had large farming populations whose relations with banks periodically became tempestuous when banks would foreclose on farmers who couldn't pay their debts.) The legacy of nineteenth-century politics was a banking system with restrictive branching regulations and hence an inordinate number of small banks. However, as we will see later in this chapter, branching restrictions have been eliminated, and we have moved toward nationwide banking.

Response to Branching Restrictions

An important feature of the U.S. banking industry is that competition can be repressed by regulation but not completely quashed. As we saw earlier in this chapter, the existence of restrictive regulation stimulates financial innovations that get around these regulations, in the banks' search for profits. Regulations restricting branching have stimulated similar economic forces and have promoted the development of two financial innovations: bank holding companies and automated teller machines.

Bank Holding Companies   A holding company is a corporation that owns several different companies. This form of corporate ownership has important advantages for banks. It has allowed them to circumvent restrictive branching regulations, because the holding company can own a controlling interest in several banks even if branching is not permitted. Furthermore, a bank holding company can engage in other activities related to banking, such as the provision of investment advice, data processing and transmission services, leasing, credit card services, and servicing of loans in other states.

The growth of bank holding companies has been dramatic over the past three decades. Today bank holding companies own almost all large banks, and more than 90% of all commercial bank deposits are held in banks owned by holding companies.

Automated Teller Machines   Another financial innovation that resulted from the desire to avoid restrictions on branching is the automated teller machine (ATM). Banks quickly realized that if they did not own or rent an ATM, but instead let it be owned by someone else and paid a fee for each transaction, the ATM would probably not be considered a branch of the bank and thus would not be subject to branching regulations. This is exactly what the regulatory agencies and courts in most states concluded. Because they enable banks to widen their markets, a number of these shared facilities (such as Cirrus and NYCE) have been established nationwide. Furthermore, even when an ATM is owned by a bank, states typically have special provisions that allow wider establishment of ATMs than is permissible for traditional "brick and mortar" branches.

As we saw earlier in this chapter, avoiding regulation was not the only reason for the development of the ATM. The advent of cheaper computer and telecommunications technology enabled banks to provide ATMs at low cost, making them a profitable innovation. This example further illustrates that technological factors often combine with incentives, such as the desire to avoid restrictive regulations, to produce financial innovation.

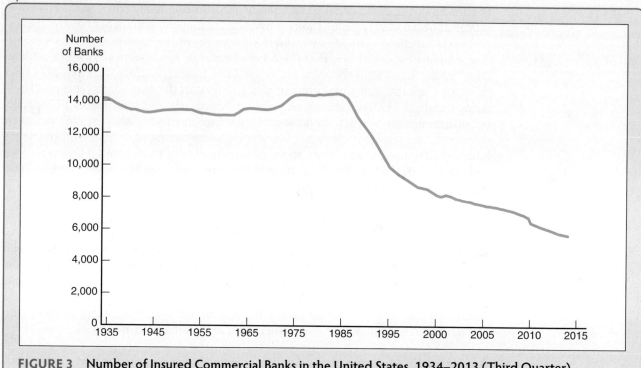

FIGURE 3   **Number of Insured Commercial Banks in the United States, 1934–2013 (Third Quarter)**

After a period of stability from 1934 to the mid-1980s, the number of commercial banks began to fall dramatically.

Source: Federal Reserve Bank of St. Louis, FRED database: http://research.stlouisfed.org/fred2/.

BANK CONSOLIDATION AND NATIONWIDE BANKING

As we can see in Figure 3, after a remarkable period of stability from 1934 to the mid-1980s, the number of commercial banks in the United States began to fall dramatically. Why did this sudden decline take place?

The banking industry hit some hard times in the 1980s and early 1990s, with bank failures running at a rate of over 100 per year from 1985 to 1992 (more on this later in the chapter; also see Chapter 10). But bank failures are only part of the story. In the years 1985–1992, the number of banks declined by 3,000—more than double the number of failures. And in the period 1992–2007, when the banking industry returned to health, the number of commercial banks decreased by a little over 3,800, less than 5% of which were bank failures, and most of these were of small banks. Thus we see that bank failures played an important, though not predominant, role in reducing the number of banks in the 1985–1992 period, and an almost negligible role through 2007. The global financial crisis, however, led to additional declines in the number of banks because of bank failures.

So what explains the rest of the story? The answer is bank consolidation. Banks have been merging to create larger entities or have been buying up other banks. This gives rise to a new question: Why has bank consolidation been taking place in recent years?

As we have seen, loophole mining by banks reduced the effectiveness of branching restrictions, with the result that many states recognized it would be in their best interest if they allowed ownership of banks across state lines. The result was the formation of reciprocal regional compacts in which banks in one state were allowed to own banks in other states in the region. In 1975, Maine enacted the first interstate banking legislation that allowed out-of-state bank holding companies to purchase banks in that state. In 1982, Massachusetts enacted a regional compact with other New England states to allow interstate banking, and many other regional compacts were adopted thereafter until, by the early 1990s, almost all states allowed some form of interstate banking.

With the barriers to interstate banking breaking down in the early 1980s, banks recognized that they could gain the benefits of diversification because they would now be able to make loans in many states rather than just one. This gave them an advantage: If one state's economy was weak, another state in which they operated might have a strong economy, thus decreasing the likelihood that loans in different states would default at the same time. In addition, allowing banks to own banks in other states meant that they could increase their size through out-of-state acquisition of banks or by merging with banks in other states. Mergers and acquisitions explain the first phase of banking consolidation, which has played such an important role in the decline in the number of banks since 1985. Another result of the loosening of restrictions on interstate branching is the development of a new class of banks, called **superregional banks**, which are bank holding companies that have begun to rival the money center banks in size but whose headquarters are not in one of the money center cities (New York, Chicago, and San Francisco). Examples of these superregional banks are Bank of America of Charlotte, North Carolina, and Banc One of Columbus, Ohio.

Not surprisingly, the advent of the Web and improved computer technology is another factor driving bank consolidation. Economies of scale have increased because large, upfront investments are required to set up information technology platforms for financial institutions. To take advantage of these economies of scale, banks have needed to get bigger, and this development has led to additional consolidation. Information technology has also been increasing **economies of scope**, the ability to use one resource to provide many different products and services. For example, details about the quality and creditworthiness of firms not only inform decisions about whether to make loans to them but also can be useful in determining at what price their shares should trade. Similarly, once you have marketed one financial product to an investor, you probably know how to market another. Business people describe economies of scope by saying there are "synergies" between different lines of business, and information technology is making these synergies more likely. The result is that consolidation is taking place not only to make financial institutions bigger, but also to increase the combination of products and services they can provide. This consolidation has had two consequences. First, different types of financial intermediaries are encroaching on each other's territory, making them more alike. Second, consolidation has led to the development of large, complex banking organizations. This development has been facilitated by the repeal of the Glass-Steagall restrictions on combinations of banking and other financial service industries, as discussed in the next section.

The Riegle-Neal Interstate Banking and Branching Efficiency Act of 1994

Banking consolidation was given further stimulus by the passage in 1994 of the Riegle-Neal Interstate Banking and Branching Efficiency Act. This legislation expanded the regional compacts to the entire nation and overturned the McFadden Act and Douglas

Amendment's prohibition of interstate banking. Not only did this act allow bank holding companies to acquire banks in any other state, notwithstanding any state laws to the contrary, but bank holding companies could also merge the banks they owned into one bank with branches in different states. States were, however, given the option of opting out of interstate branching, but only Texas did so, although it later reversed its position and now allows it.

The Riegle-Neal Act finally established the basis for a true nationwide banking system. Although interstate banking was accomplished previously by out-of-state purchase of banks by bank holding companies, until 1994 it was virtually nonexistent because very few states had enacted interstate branching legislation. Allowing banks to conduct interstate banking through branching is especially important because many bankers feel that economies of scale cannot be fully exploited through the bank holding company structure, but only through branching networks in which all of the bank's operations are fully coordinated.

Nationwide banks have now emerged. Starting with the merger in 1998 of Bank of America and NationsBank, which created the first bank with branches on both coasts, consolidation in the banking industry has created some banking organizations with operations in all 50 states.

What Will the Structure of the U.S. Banking Industry Look Like in the Future?

Now that true nationwide banking in the United States is a reality, the benefits of bank consolidation for the banking industry have increased substantially, driving the next phase of mergers and acquisitions and accelerating the decline in the number of commercial banks. With great changes occurring in the structure of this industry, the question naturally arises: What will the industry look like in ten years?

One view is that the industry will become more like that in many other countries (see the Global box, "Comparison of Banking Structure in the United States and Abroad"), and we will end up with only a couple of hundred banks. A more extreme view is that the industry will look like that of Canada or the United Kingdom, with a few large banks dominating the industry. Most experts come up with a different answer: The structure of the U.S. banking industry will still be unique, but not to the degree it once was. The consolidation surge is likely to settle down as the U.S. banking industry approaches several thousand, rather than several hundred, banks.

Banking consolidation will result not only in a smaller number of banks but also, as the mergers between Chase Manhattan Bank and Chemical Bank and between Bank of America and NationsBank suggest, in a shift in assets from smaller banks to larger banks. Within ten years, the share of bank assets in banks with less than $100 million in assets is expected to halve, while the amount at the megabanks, those with more than $100 billion in assets, is expected to more than double. Indeed, the United States now has several trillion-dollar banks (e.g., Citibank, J.P. Morgan Chase, and Bank of America).

Are Bank Consolidation and Nationwide Banking Good Things?

Advocates of nationwide banking believe that it will produce more efficient banks and a healthier banking system that is less prone to bank failures. However, critics of bank consolidation fear that it will eliminate small banks, referred to as **community banks**,

Global   Comparison of Banking Structure in the United States and Abroad

The structure of the commercial banking industry in the United States is radically different from that in other industrialized nations. The United States came late to developing a true national banking system in which banks have branches throughout the country. One result is that many more banks are found in the United States than in other industrialized countries. In contrast to the United States, which has on the order of 5,700 commercial banks, every other industrialized country has far fewer than 1,000. Japan, for example, has fewer than 100 commercial banks—a mere fraction of the number in the United States, even though its economy and population are half the size of those of the United States. Another result of past restrictions on branching in the United States is that our banks tend to be much smaller than those in other countries.

and that this will result in less lending to small businesses. In addition, they worry that a few banks will come to dominate the industry, making the banking business less competitive.

Most economists are skeptical of these criticisms of bank consolidation. As we have seen, research indicates that even after bank consolidation is completed, the United States will still have plenty of banks. The banking industry will thus remain highly competitive, probably even more so than it is now, considering that banks that had been protected from competition from out-of-state banks now have to compete with them vigorously to stay in business.

It also does not look as though community banks will disappear. When New York state liberalized its branching laws in 1962, there were fears that community banks upstate would be driven from the market by the big New York City banks. Not only did this not happen, but some of the big boys found that the small banks were able to run rings around them in the local markets. Similarly, California, which has allowed unrestricted statewide branching for a long time, continues to have a thriving population of community banks.

Economists see some important benefits from bank consolidation and nationwide banking. The elimination of geographic restrictions on banking increases competition and drives inefficient banks out of business, increasing the efficiency of the banking sector. The move to larger banking organizations also means that there is some increase in efficiency because these organziations can take advantage of economies of scale and scope. The increased diversification of banks' loan portfolios may lower the probability of a banking crisis in the future. In the 1980s and early 1990s, bank failures were often concentrated in states with weak economies. For example, after the decline in oil prices in 1986, all of the major commercial banks in Texas, which had been very profitable, found themselves in trouble. At that time, banks in New England were doing fine. However, when the 1990–1991 recession hit New England hard, some New England banks started failing. With nationwide banking, a bank could make loans in both New England and Texas and would thus be less likely to fail because when loans went sour in one location, they probably still would be doing well in the other. Thus nationwide banking is seen as a major step toward creating a banking system that is less vulnerable to banking crises.

Two concerns remain about the effects of bank consolidation—that it may lead to a reduction in lending to small businesses and that banks rushing to expand into new geographic markets may take increased risks leading to bank failures. The jury is still out on these concerns, but most economists see the benefits of bank consolidation and nationwide banking as outweighing the costs.

SEPARATION OF BANKING AND OTHER FINANCIAL SERVICE INDUSTRIES

Until recently, an important feature of the structure of the banking industry in the United States was the separation of the banking and other financial services industries—such as securities, insurance, and real estate—mandated by the Glass-Steagall Act of 1933. As pointed out earlier in the chapter, Glass-Steagall allowed commercial banks to sell new offerings of government securities but prohibited them from underwriting corporate securities or from engaging in brokerage activities. It also prevented banks from engaging in insurance and real estate activities. In turn, it prevented investment banks and insurance companies from engaging in commercial banking activities and thus protected banks from competition.

Erosion of Glass-Steagall

Despite the Glass-Steagall prohibitions, the pursuit of profits and financial innovation stimulated both banks and other financial institutions to bypass the intent of the Glass-Steagall Act and encroach on each other's traditional territory. With the development of money market mutual funds and cash management accounts, brokerage firms began to engage in the traditional banking business of issuing deposit instruments. After the Federal Reserve used a loophole in Section 20 of the Glass-Steagall Act in 1987 to allow bank holding companies to underwrite previously prohibited classes of securities, banks began to enter this business. The loophole allowed affiliates of approved commercial banks to engage in underwriting activities as long as the revenue didn't exceed a specified amount, which started at 10% but was raised to 25% of the affiliates' total revenue. After the U.S. Supreme Court validated the Fed's action in July 1988, the Federal Reserve allowed J.P. Morgan, a commercial bank holding company, to underwrite corporate debt securities (in January 1989) and to underwrite stocks (in September 1990), with the privilege later extended to other bank holding companies. The regulatory agencies also allowed banks to engage in some real estate and insurance activities.

The Gramm-Leach-Bliley Financial Services Modernization Act of 1999: Repeal of Glass-Steagall

Because restrictions on commercial banks' securities and insurance activities put American banks at a competitive disadvantage relative to foreign banks, bills to overturn Glass-Steagall appeared in almost every session of Congress in the 1990s. With the merger in 1998 of Citicorp, the second-largest bank in the United States, and Travelers Group, an insurance company that also owned the third-largest securities firm in the country (Salomon Smith Barney), the pressure to abolish Glass-Steagall became overwhelming. Legislation to eliminate Glass-Steagall finally came to fruition in 1999. This legislation, the Gramm-Leach-Bliley Financial Services Modernization Act of 1999, allows securities firms and insurance companies to purchase banks, and allows banks to underwrite insurance and securities and engage in real estate activities. Under this legislation, states retain regulatory authority over insurance activities, while the Securities and Exchange Commission continues to have oversight of securities activities. The Office of the Comptroller of the Currency has the authority to regulate bank subsidiaries engaged in securities underwriting, but the Federal Reserve continues to have the authority to oversee the bank holding companies under which all real estate and insurance activities and large securities operations will be housed.

Implications for Financial Consolidation

As we have seen, the Riegle-Neal Interstate Banking and Branching Efficiency Act of 1994 stimulated consolidation of the banking industry. The financial consolidation process was further hastened by the Gramm-Leach-Bliley Act of 1999, because the way is now open to consolidation not only in terms of the number of banking institutions but also across financial service activities. Given that information technology is increasing economies of scope, mergers of banks with other financial service firms like that of Citicorp and Travelers have become increasingly common, and more mega-mergers are likely to be on the way. Banking institutions are becoming not only larger but also increasingly complex organizations, engaging in the full gamut of financial service activities. The trend toward larger and more complex banking organizations has been accelerated by the global financial crisis of 2007–2009 (see the FYI box, "The Global Financial Crisis and the Demise of Large, Free-Standing Investment Banks").

FYI   **The Global Financial Crisis and the Demise of Large, Free-Standing Investment Banks**

Although the move toward bringing financial service activities into larger, more complex banking organizations was inevitable after the demise of Glass-Steagall, no one expected it to occur as rapidly as it did in 2008. Over a six-month period from March to September 2008, all five of the largest, free-standing investment banks ceased to exist in their old form. When Bear Stearns, the fifth-largest investment bank, revealed its large losses from investments in subprime mortgage-backed securities, it had to be bailed out by the Fed in March 2008; the price it paid was a forced sale to J.P. Morgan for less than one-tenth of its worth only a year or so before. The Bear Stearns bailout made it clear that the government safety net had been extended to investment banks. The tradeoff is that investment banks will be subject to more regulation, along the lines of that of commercial banks, in the future.

Next to go was Lehman Brothers, the fourth-largest investment bank, which declared bankruptcy on September 15. Only one day before, Merrill Lynch, the third-largest investment bank, which also suffered large losses on its holdings of subprime securities, announced its sale to Bank of America for less than half of its year-earlier price. Within a week, Goldman Sachs and Morgan Stanley, the first- and second-largest investment banks, both of which had smaller exposure to subprime securities, nevertheless saw the writing on the wall. They realized that they would soon become regulated on a similar basis and decided to become bank holding companies so that they could access insured deposits, a more stable funding base.

It was the end of an era. Large, free-standing investment banking firms are now a thing of the past.

Separation of Banking and Other Financial Services Industries Throughout the World

In the aftermath of the Great Depression, not many other countries followed the lead of the United States in separating the banking and other financial services industries. In fact, in the past this separation was the most prominent difference between banking regulation in the United States and that in other countries. Around the world, there are three basic frameworks for the banking and securities industries.

The first framework is *universal banking,* which exists in Germany, the Netherlands, and Switzerland. It provides no separation at all between the banking and securities industries. In a universal banking system, commercial banks provide a full range of banking, securities, real estate, and insurance services, all within a single legal entity. Banks are allowed to own sizable equity shares in commercial firms, and often they do.

The *British-style universal banking system,* the second framework, is found in the United Kingdom and countries with close ties to it, such as Canada and Australia, and now the United States. The British-style universal bank engages in securities underwriting, but it differs from the German-style universal bank in three ways: Separate legal subsidiaries are more common, bank equity holdings of commercial firms are less common, and combinations of banking and insurance firms are less common.

The third framework, found in Japan, features some legal separation of the banking and other financial services industries. A major difference between the U.S. and Japanese banking systems is that Japanese banks are allowed to hold substantial equity stakes in commercial firms, whereas American banks are not. In addition, most American banks use a bank holding company structure, but bank holding companies are illegal in Japan. Although the banking and securities industries are legally separated in Japan under Section 65 of the Japanese Securities Act, commercial banks are increasingly being allowed to engage in securities activities and, like U.S. banks, are becoming more like British-style universal banks.

THRIFT INDUSTRY: REGULATION AND STRUCTURE

Not surprisingly, the regulation and structure of the thrift industry (savings and loan associations, mutual savings banks, and credit unions) closely parallel the regulation and structure of the commercial banking industry.

Savings and Loan Associations

Just as there is a dual banking system for commercial banks, savings and loan associations (S&Ls) can be chartered either by the federal government or by the states. Most S&Ls, whether state or federally chartered, are members of the Federal Home Loan Bank System (FHLBS). Established in 1932, the FHLBS was styled after the Federal Reserve System. It has twelve district Federal Home Loan banks, which are supervised by the Office of Thrift Supervision.

Federal deposit insurance up to $250,000 per account for S&Ls is provided by the FDIC. The Office of Thrift Supervision regulates federally insured S&Ls by setting minimum capital requirements, requiring periodic reports, and examining the S&Ls. It is also the chartering agency for federally chartered S&Ls, and for these S&Ls it approves mergers and sets the rules for branching.

The branching regulations for S&Ls were historically more liberal than those for commercial banks: In the past, almost all states permitted branching of S&Ls, and since 1980, federally chartered S&Ls were allowed to branch statewide in all states. Since 1981, mergers of financially troubled S&Ls were allowed across state lines, and nationwide branching of S&Ls is now a reality.

The FHLBS, like the Fed, makes loans to the members of the system (obtaining funds for this purpose by issuing bonds). However, in contrast to the Fed's discount loans, which are expected to be repaid quickly, loans from the FHLBS often need not be repaid for long periods of time. In addition, the rates charged to S&Ls for these loans are often below the rates that the S&Ls must pay when they borrow in the open market. In this way, the FHLBS loan program provides a subsidy to the savings and loan industry (and implicitly to the housing industry, since most S&L loans are for residential mortgages).

The savings and loans industry experienced serious difficulties in the 1980s. Because savings and loans now engage in many of the same activities as commercial banks, many experts view the existence of a separate charter and regulatory apparatus for S&Ls as an anachronism that no longer makes sense.

Mutual Savings Banks

Of the 350 or so mutual savings banks, which are similar to S&Ls but are jointly owned by the depositors, approximately half are chartered by states. Although the mutual savings banks are primarily regulated by the states in which they are located, the majority have their deposits insured by the FDIC up to the limit of $250,000 per account; these banks are also subject to many of the FDIC's regulations for state-chartered banks. As a rule, the mutual savings banks whose deposits are not insured by the FDIC have their deposits insured by state insurance funds.

The branching regulations for mutual savings banks are determined by the states in which they operate. Because these regulations are not particularly restrictive, few mutual savings banks have assets of less than $25 million.

Credit Unions

Credit unions are small cooperative lending institutions organized around a particular group of individuals with a common bond (e.g., union members or employees of a particular firm). They are the only depository institutions that are tax-exempt and can be chartered either by the states or by the federal government; more than half are federally chartered. The National Credit Union Administration (NCUA) issues federal charters and regulates federally chartered credit unions by setting minimum capital requirements, requiring periodic reports, and examining the credit unions. Federal deposit insurance (up to the $250,000-per-account limit) is provided to both federally chartered and state-chartered credit unions by a subsidiary of the NCUA, the National Credit Union Share Insurance Fund (NCUSIF). Because the majority of credit union lending is for consumer loans with fairly short terms to maturity, these institutions did not suffer the financial difficulties of the S&Ls and mutual savings banks in the 1980s.

Because their members share a common bond, credit unions are typically quite small; most hold less than $10 million of assets. In addition, their ties to a particular industry or company make them more likely to fail when large numbers of workers in that industry or company are laid off and have trouble making loan payments. Recent regulatory changes allow individual credit unions to cater to a more diverse group of people by interpreting the common bond requirement less strictly, and this has encouraged an expansion in the size of credit unions that may help reduce credit union failures in the future.

Often a credit union's shareholders are dispersed over many states, and sometimes even worldwide, so branching across state lines and into other countries is permitted for federally chartered credit unions. The Navy Federal Credit Union, for example, whose shareholders are members of the U.S. Navy and Marine Corps, has branches throughout the world.

INTERNATIONAL BANKING

In 1960, only eight U.S. banks operated branches in foreign countries, and their total assets were less than $4 billion. Currently, around 100 American banks have branches abroad, with assets totaling more than $2.5 trillion. The spectacular growth in international banking can be explained by three factors.

First is the rapid growth in international trade and multinational corporations that has occurred since 1960. When American firms operate abroad, they need banking services in foreign countries to help finance international trade. For example, they might need a loan in a foreign currency to operate a factory abroad. And when they sell goods abroad, they need to have a bank exchange the foreign currency they have received for their goods into dollars. Although these firms could use foreign banks to provide them with these international banking services, many of them prefer to do business with the U.S. banks with which they have established long-term relationships and which understand American business customs and practices. As international trade has grown, international banking has grown with it.

Second, American banks have been able to earn substantial profits by being very active in global investment banking, in which they underwrite foreign securities. They also sell insurance abroad, and they derive substantial profits from these investment banking and insurance activities.

Third, American banks have wanted to tap into the large pool of dollar-denominated deposits in foreign countries known as Eurodollars. To understand the structure of U.S. banking overseas, let's first look at the Eurodollar market, an important source of growth for international banking.

Eurodollar Market

Eurodollars are created when deposits in accounts in the United States are transferred to a bank outside the country and are kept in the form of dollars. (For a discussion of the birth of the Eurodollar, see the Global box, "Ironic Birth of the Eurodollar Market.") For example, if Rolls-Royce PLC deposits a $1 million check, written on an account at an American bank, in its bank in London—specifying that the deposit is payable in dollars—$1 million in Eurodollars is created.[2] More than 90% of Eurodollar deposits are time deposits, more than half of them certificates of deposit with maturities of 30 days or more. The Eurodollar market is massive, over $5 trillion, making it one of the most important financial markets in the world economy.

---

[2]Note that the London bank keeps the $1 million on deposit at the American bank, so the creation of Eurodollars has not caused a reduction in the amount of bank deposits in the United States.

Global Ironic Birth of the Eurodollar Market

One of capitalism's great ironies is that the Eurodollar market, one of the most important financial markets used by capitalists, was fathered by the Soviet Union. In the early 1950s, during the height of the Cold War, the Soviets had accumulated a substantial amount of dollar balances held by banks in the United States. Because the Russians feared that the U.S. government might freeze these assets in the United States, they wanted to move the deposits to Europe, where they would be safe from expropriation. (This fear was not unjustified—consider the U.S. freeze on Iranian assets in 1979 and on Iraqi assets in 1990.) However, they also wanted to keep the deposits in dollars so that they could be used in their international transactions. The solution to the problem was to transfer the deposits to European banks but to keep the deposits denominated in dollars. When the Soviets did this, the Eurodollar was born.

Why would companies such as Rolls-Royce want to hold dollar deposits outside the United States? First, the dollar is the most widely used currency in international trade, so Rolls-Royce might want to hold deposits in dollars to conduct its international transactions. Second, Eurodollars are "offshore" deposits—they are held in countries that will not subject them to regulations such as reserve requirements or restrictions (called *capital controls*) on taking the deposits outside the country.[3]

The main center of the Eurodollar market is London, a major international financial center for hundreds of years. Eurodollars are also held outside Europe in locations that provide offshore status to these deposits—for example, Singapore, the Bahamas, and the Cayman Islands.

The minimum transaction in the Eurodollar market is typically $1 million, and approximately 75% of Eurodollar deposits are held by banks. Plainly, you and I are unlikely to come into direct contact with Eurodollars. The Eurodollar market is, however, an important source of funds to U.S. banks. Rather than using an intermediary and borrowing all the deposits from foreign banks, American banks decided that they could earn higher profits by opening their own branches abroad to attract these deposits. Consequently, the Eurodollar market has been an important stimulus to U.S. banking overseas.

Structure of U.S. Banking Overseas

U.S. banks have most of their foreign branches in Latin America, the Far East, the Caribbean, and London. The largest volume of assets is held by branches in London, because it is a major international financial center and the central location for the Eurodollar market. Latin America and the Far East have many branches because of the importance of U.S. trade with these regions. Parts of the Caribbean (especially the Bahamas and the Cayman Islands) have become important as tax havens, with minimal taxation and few restrictive regulations. In actuality, the bank branches in the Bahamas and the Cayman Islands are "shell operations" because they function primarily as bookkeeping centers and do not provide normal banking services.

---

[3]Although most offshore deposits are denominated in dollars, some are denominated in other currencies. Collectively, these offshore deposits are referred to as Eurocurrencies. A Japanese yen-denominated deposit held in London, for example, is called a Euroyen.

An alternative corporate structure for U.S. banks that operate overseas is the **Edge Act corporation**, a special subsidiary engaged primarily in international banking. U.S. banks (through their holding companies) can also own a controlling interest in foreign banks and in foreign companies that provide financial services, such as finance companies. The international activities of U.S. banking organizations are governed primarily by the Federal Reserve's Regulation K.

In late 1981, the Federal Reserve approved the creation of **international banking facilities (IBFs)** within the United States that can accept time deposits from foreigners but are not subject to either reserve requirements or restrictions on interest payments. IBFs are also allowed to make loans to foreigners, but they are not allowed to make loans to domestic residents. States have encouraged the establishment of IBFs by exempting them from state and local taxes. In essence, IBFs are treated like foreign branches of U.S. banks and are not subject to domestic regulations and taxes. The purpose of establishing IBFs is to encourage American and foreign banks to do more banking business in the United States rather than abroad. From this point of view, IBFs are a success: Their assets climbed to nearly $200 billion in the first two years, and are in excess of $1 trillion currently.

Foreign Banks in the United States

The growth in international trade has not only encouraged U.S. banks to open offices overseas, but has also encouraged foreign banks to establish offices in the United States. Foreign banks have been extremely successful in the United States. Currently, they hold more than 6.5% of total U.S. bank assets and do a large portion of all U.S. bank lending, with around a 28% market share for lending to U.S. corporations.

Foreign banks engage in banking activities in the United States by operating an agency office of the foreign bank, a subsidiary U.S. bank, or a branch of the foreign bank. An agency office can lend and transfer funds in the United States, but it cannot accept deposits from domestic residents. Agency offices have the advantage of not being subject to regulations that apply to full-service banking offices (such as requirements for FDIC insurance). A subsidiary U.S. bank is just like any other U.S. bank (it may even have an American-sounding name) and is subject to the same regulations, but it is owned by the foreign bank. A branch of a foreign bank bears the foreign bank's name and is usually a full-service office. Foreign banks may also form Edge Act corporations and IBFs.

Before 1978, foreign banks were not subject to many of the regulations that applied to domestic banks: They could open branches across state lines and were not expected to meet reserve requirements, for example. The passage of the International Banking Act of 1978, however, put foreign and domestic banks on more equal footing. The act stipulated that foreign banks could open new full-service branches only in the state they designated as their home state or in states that allowed the entry of out-of-state banks. Limited-service branches and agency offices in any other state were permitted, however, and foreign banks were allowed to retain any full-service branches opened before the act was ratified.

The internationalization of banking, both by U.S. banks going abroad and by foreign banks entering the United States, has meant that financial markets throughout the world have become more integrated. As a result, there is a growing trend toward international coordination of bank regulation, one example of which is the Basel Accords, discussed in Chapter 10, which were established to standardize minimum bank capital requirements in industrialized countries . Financial market integration has also encouraged

TABLE 3	Ten Largest Banks in the World, 2014
Bank	**Assets (U.S. $ millions)**
1. Industrial and Commercial Bank of China, China	3,181,884
2. HSBC Holdings, UK	2,758,447
3. China Construction Bank Corp, China	2,602,536
4. BNP Paribas SA, France	2,589,191
5. The Bank of Tokyo-Mitsubishi UFJ Ltd, Japan	2,508,839
6. JP Morgan-Chase NA, US	2,476,986
7. Agricultural Bank of China, China	2,470,432
8. Bank of China, China	2,435,485
9. Credit Agricole SA, France	2,346,562
10. Barclays PLC, UK	2,266,815

Source: http://www.relbanks.com/worlds-top-banks/market-cap.

bank consolidation abroad, culminating in the creation of the first trillion-dollar bank with the merger of the Industrial Bank of Japan, Dai-Ichi Kangyo Bank, and Fuji Bank, in 2002. Another development has been the importance of foreign banks in international banking. As is shown in Table 3, in 2014, nine out of ten of the largest banking groups in the world were foreign. The implications of this financial market integration for the operation of our economy are examined further in Chapter 18, where we discuss the international financial system in more detail.

SUMMARY

1. The history of banking in the United States has left us with a dual banking system, with commercial banks chartered by the states and the federal government. Multiple agencies regulate commercial banks: the Office of the Comptroller, the Federal Reserve, the FDIC, and the state banking authorities.

2. A change in the economic environment will stimulate financial institutions to search for financial innovations. Changes in demand conditions, especially an increase in interest-rate risk; changes in supply conditions, especially improvements in information technology; and the desire to avoid costly regulations have been major driving forces behind financial innovation. Financial innovation has caused banks to suffer declines in cost advantages in acquiring funds and in income advantages on their assets. The resulting squeeze has hurt profitability in banks' traditional lines of business and has led to a decline in traditional banking.

3. Restrictive state branching regulations and the McFadden Act, which prohibited branching across state lines, led to a large number of small commercial banks. The large number of commercial banks in the United States reflects the past *lack* of competition, not the presence of vigorous competition. Bank holding companies and ATMs were important responses to branching restrictions that weakened the restrictions' anticompetitive effect.

4. Since the mid-1980s, bank consolidation has been occurring at a rapid pace. The first phase of bank consolidation was the result of bank failures and the reduced effectiveness of branching restrictions. The second phase was stimulated by enhanced information

technology and the Riegle-Neal Interstate Banking and Branching Efficiency Act of 1994, which establishes the basis for a nationwide banking system. Once banking consolidation has settled down, we are likely to be left with a banking system with several thousand banks. Most economists believe that the benefits of bank consolidation and nationwide banking will outweigh the costs.

5. The Glass-Steagall Act separated commercial banking from the securities industry. Legislation in 1999, however, repealed the Glass-Steagall Act, removing the separation of these industries.

6. The regulation and structure of the thrift industry (savings and loan associations, mutual savings banks, and credit unions) parallel closely the regulation and structure of the commercial banking industry. Savings and loans are primarily regulated by the Office of Thrift

Supervision, and deposit insurance is administered by the FDIC. Mutual savings banks are regulated by the states, and federal deposit insurance is provided by the FDIC. Credit unions are regulated by the National Credit Union Administration, and deposit insurance is provided by the National Credit Union Share Insurance Fund.

7. With the rapid growth of world trade since 1960, international banking has grown dramatically. United States banks engage in international banking activities by opening branches abroad, owning controlling interests in foreign banks, forming Edge Act corporations, and operating international banking facilities (IBFs) located in the United States. Foreign banks operate in the United States by owning a subsidiary American bank or by operating branches or agency offices in the United States.

KEY TERMS

automated banking machine (ABM), p. 240
automated teller machine (ATM), p. 240
bank holding companies, p. 237
branches, p. 250
central bank, p. 235
community banks, p. 254
deposit rate ceilings, p. 244
disintermediation, p. 244

dual banking system, p. 236
economies of scope, p. 253
Edge Act corporation, p. 262
financial derivatives, p. 239
financial engineering, p. 237
futures contracts, p. 239
hedge, p. 239
international banking facilities (IBFs), p. 262

national banks, p. 236
originate-to-distribute, p. 243
securitization, p. 242
shadow banking system, p. 237
state banks, p. 236
subprime mortgage, p. 243
superregional banks, p. 253
sweep account, p. 245
virtual bank, p. 240

QUESTIONS

All questions are available in MyEconLab at http://www.myeconlab.com.

1. Why was the United States one of the last major industrialized countries to have a central bank?

2. Why does the United States operate under a dual banking system?

3. What were the motivations for the original Glass-Steagall Act of 1933?

4. Which regulatory agency has the primary responsibility for supervising the following categories of commercial banks?

a. National banks

b. Bank holding companies

c. Non–Federal Reserve member state banks

d. Federal Reserve member state banks

e. Federally chartered savings and loan associations

f. Federally chartered credit unions

5. How does the emergence of interest-rate risk help explain financial innovation?

6. Why did new technology make it harder to enforce limitations on bank branching?

7. "The invention of the computer is the major factor behind the decline of the banking industry." Is this statement true, false, or uncertain? Explain your answer.

8. "If inflation had not risen in the 1960s and 1970s, the banking industry might be healthier today." Is this statement true, false, or uncertain? Explain your answer.

9. How do sweep accounts and money market mutual funds allow banks to avoid reserve requirements?

10. If reserve requirements were eliminated in the future, as some economists advocate, what effects would this have on the size of money market mutual funds?

11. Why is loophole mining so prevalent in the banking industry in the United States?

12. Why have banks been losing cost advantages in acquiring funds in recent years?

13. Why have banks been losing income advantages on their assets in recent years?

14. "The commercial banking industry in Canada is less competitive than the commercial banking industry in the United States because in Canada only a few large banks dominate the industry, while in the United States there are around 5,700 commercial banks." Is this statement true, false, or uncertain? Explain your answer.

15. Why is there a higher percentage of banks with less than $25 million of assets among commercial banks than among savings and loans and mutual savings banks?

16. Unlike commercial banks, savings and loans, and mutual savings banks, credit unions did not have restrictions on setting up branches in other states. Why, then, are credit unions typically smaller than the other depository institutions?

17. Why has the number of bank holding companies dramatically increased?

18. What are the advantages and disadvantages of interstate banking?

19. How did competitive forces lead to the repeal of the Glass-Steagall Act's separation of the banking and securities industries?

20. What has been the likely effect of the Gramm-Leach-Bliley Act on financial consolidation?

21. What factors explain the rapid growth of international banking?

22. What incentives have regulatory agencies created to encourage international banking? Why have they done this?

23. How could the approval of international banking facilities (IBFs) by the Fed in 1981 have reduced employment in the banking industry in Europe?

24. If the bank at which you keep your checking account is owned by foreigners, should you worry that your deposits are less safe than if the bank were owned by Americans?

25. Why is there only one U.S. bank among the ten largest banks in the world?

DATA ANALYSIS PROBLEMS

The Problems update with real-time data in MyEconLab *and are available for practice or instructor assignment.*

 1. Go to the St. Louis Federal Reserve FRED database, and find data on the 30-year conventional mortgage rate (WRMORTG) and the 5/1-year adjustable-rate mortgage (MORTGAGE5US).

   a. What are the mortgage rates reported for the most recent week of data available?

   b. If the principal payment for a given month were $2000, then what would be the interest payment per month (using simple interest) for each of the mortgage types, using the most recent week of data?

   c. Over a one-year period, how much would the difference in interest payments between the two mortgage types amount to?

 2. Go to the St. Louis Federal Reserve FRED database, and find data on the level of money market mutual fund assets (MMMFFAQ027S). Download the data into a spreadsheet.

   a. When did assets start entering money market mutual funds? What was the total worth of assets in money market mutual funds at the end of 1970?

   b. For each decade period, calculate the total percentage change in assets from the beginning of the decade to the end of the decade: 1980:Q1–1990:Q1; 1990:Q1–2000:Q1; 2000:Q1–2010:Q1. For each decade period, divide the total percentage change by 10 to get the average yearly percent increase. Which decade had the largest average yearly growth in money market mutual funds?

c. Calculate the growth rate from the most recent quarter of data available to the same quarter a

year prior. How does this growth rate compare to the highest average yearly growth rate for the decades from part (b)?

WEB EXERCISES

1. Go to http://www2.fdic.gov/hsob/index.asp. Select "Commercial Bank Reports," and then select "Number of Institutions, Branches, and Total Offices." If you look at the trend in the number of bank branches, does the public currently appear to have more or less access to banking facilities? How many banks were there in 1934, and how many are there now? Does the graph indicate that the trend toward consolidation is continuing?

2. Despite the regulations that protect banks from failure, some banks do fail. Go to http://www2.fdic.gov/hsob/index.asp. Select the tab labeled "Failures and Assistance Transactions." How many bank failures occurred in the United States during the most recent complete calendar year? What were the total assets held by the banks that failed? How many banks failed in 1937?

WEB REFERENCES

http://www.fdic.gov/bank/

The FDIC gathers data about individual financial institutions and the banking industry.

http://www2.fdic.gov/hsob/index.asp

Visit this website to gather statistics on the banking industry.

12 Financial Crises

Learning Objectives

- Define the term "financial crisis."
- Identify the key features of the three stages of a financial crisis.
- Describe the causes and consequences of the global financial crisis of 2007–2009.
- Summarize the changes to financial regulation that occurred in response to the global financial crisis of 2007–2009.
- Identify the gaps in current financial regulation and how those gaps may be addressed with future regulatory changes.

Preview

Financial crises are major disruptions in financial markets characterized by sharp declines in asset prices and firm failures. Beginning in August 2007, defaults in the subprime mortgage market (by borrowers with weak credit records) sent a shudder through the financial markets, leading to the worst financial crisis since the Great Depression. In Congressional testimony, Alan Greenspan, former chairman of the Fed, described the financial crisis as a "once-in-a-century credit tsunami." Wall Street firms and commercial banks suffered hundreds of billions of dollars of losses. Households and businesses found they had to pay higher rates on their borrowings—and it was much harder to get credit. All over the world, stock markets crashed, with the U.S market falling by over 50% from its peak. Many financial firms, including commercial banks, investment banks, and insurance companies, went belly up. A recession began in December of 2007, and by the fall of 2008, the economy was in a tailspin. The recession, which ended in June of 2009, was the most severe since World War II and is now known as the "Great Recession."

Why did this financial crisis occur? Why have financial crises been so prevalent throughout U.S. history, as well as in so many other countries, and what insights do they provide on the most recent crisis? Why are financial crises almost always followed by severe contractions in economic activity, as occurred during the Great Recession? We will examine these questions in this chapter by developing a framework with which to understand the dynamics of financial crises. Building on Chapter 8, we make use of agency theory, the economic analysis of the effects of asymmetric information (adverse selection and moral hazard) on financial markets, to see why financial crises occur and why they have such devastating effects on the economy. We then apply our analysis to explain the course of events that led to a number of past financial crises, including the most recent global financial crisis.[1]

WHAT IS A FINANCIAL CRISIS?

In Chapter 8, we saw that a well-functioning financial system solves asymmetric information problems (moral hazard and adverse selection) so that capital is allocated to its most productive uses. These asymmetric information problems, which act as a barrier

[1]Web Chapter 1, "Financial Crises in Emerging Economies," available on the Companion Website, http://www.pearsonhighered.com/mishkin, extends the analysis to financial crises in *emerging market economies,* economies in an early stage of market development that have recently opened up to the flow of goods, services, and capital from the rest of the world.

to efficient allocation of capital, are often described by economists as **financial frictions**. When financial frictions increase, financial markets are less capable of channeling funds efficiently from savers to households and firms with productive investment opportunities, with the result that economic activity declines. A **financial crisis** occurs when information flows in financial markets experience a particularly large disruption, with the result that financial frictions increase sharply and financial markets stop functioning. Then economic activity collapses.

DYNAMICS OF FINANCIAL CRISES

As earth-shaking and headline-grabbing as the most recent financial crisis was, it was only one of a number of financial crises that have hit industrialized countries like the United States over the years. These experiences have helped economists uncover insights into present-day economic turmoil.

Financial crises in advanced economies have progressed in two and sometimes three stages. To understand how these crises have unfolded, refer to Figure 1, which traces the stages and sequence of events in financial crises in advanced economies.

Stage One: Initial Phase

Financial crises can begin in two ways: credit boom and bust, or a general increase in uncertainty caused by failures of major financial institutions.

Credit Boom and Bust   The seeds of a financial crisis are often sown when an economy introduces new types of loans or other financial products, known as **financial innovation**, or when countries engage in **financial liberalization**, the elimination of restrictions on financial markets and institutions. In the long run, financial liberalization promotes financial development and encourages a well-run financial system that allocates capital efficiently. However, financial liberalization has a dark side: In the short run, it can prompt financial institutions to go on a lending spree, called a **credit boom**. Unfortunately, lenders may not have the expertise, or the incentives, to manage risk appropriately in these new lines of business. Even with proper management, credit booms eventually outstrip the ability of institutions—and government regulators—to screen and monitor credit risks, leading to overly risky lending.

As we learned in Chapter 10, government safety nets, such as deposit insurance, weaken market discipline and increase the moral hazard incentive for banks to take on greater risk than they otherwise would. Because lender-savers know that government-guaranteed insurance protects them from losses, they will supply even undisciplined banks with funds. Without proper monitoring, risk-taking grows unchecked.

Eventually, losses on loans begin to mount, and the value of the loans (on the asset side of the balance sheet) falls relative to liabilities, thereby driving down the net worth (capital) of banks and other financial institutions. With less capital, these financial institutions cut back on their lending to borrower-spenders, a process called **deleveraging**. Furthermore, with less capital, banks and other financial institutions become riskier, causing lender-savers and other potential lenders to these institutions to pull out their funds. Fewer funds mean fewer loans to fund productive investments and a credit freeze: The lending boom turns into a lending crash.

When financial institutions stop collecting information and making loans, financial frictions rise, limiting the financial system's ability to address the asymmetric information problems of adverse selection and moral hazard (as shown in the arrow pointing from the first factor, "Deterioration in Financial Institutions' Balance Sheets," in the top row of Figure 1). As loans become scarce, borrower-spenders are no longer able to fund their productive investment opportunities and they decrease their spending, causing economic activity to contract.

Asset-Price Boom and Bust
Prices of assets such as equity shares and real estate can be driven by investor psychology (dubbed "irrational exuberance" by Alan Greenspan when he was chairman of the Federal Reserve) well above their **fundamental economic values**, that is, their values based on realistic expectations of the assets' future income streams. The rise of asset prices above their fundamental economic values is an **asset-price bubble**. Examples of asset-price bubbles are the tech stock market bubble of the late 1990s and the recent housing price bubble that we will discuss later in this chapter. Asset-price bubbles are often also driven by credit booms, in which the large increase in credit is used to fund purchases of assets, thereby driving up their price.

When the bubble bursts and asset prices realign with fundamental economic values, stock and real estate prices tumble, companies see their net worth (the difference between their assets and their liabilities) decline, and the value of collateral these companies can pledge drops. Now these companies have less at stake because they have less "skin in the game," and so they are more likely to make risky investments because they have less to lose, the problem of moral hazard. As a result, financial institutions tighten lending standards for borrower-spenders and lending contracts (as shown by the downward arrow pointing from the second factor, "Asset-Price Decline," in the top row of Figure 1).

The asset-price bust also causes a decline in the value of financial institutions' assets, thereby causing a decline in the institutions' net worth and hence a deterioration in their balance sheets (shown by the arrow from the second factor to the first factor in the top row of Figure 1), which causes them to deleverage, steepening the decline in economic activity.

Increase in Uncertainty
U.S. financial crises have usually begun in periods of high uncertainty, such as just after the start of a recession, a crash in the stock market, or the failure of a major financial institution. Crises began after the failure of Ohio Life Insurance and Trust Company in 1857; the Jay Cooke and Company in 1873; Grant and Ward in 1884; the Knickerbocker Trust Company in 1907; the Bank of the United States in 1930; and Bear Stearns, Lehman Brothers, and AIG in 2008. With information hard to come by in a period of high uncertainty, financial frictions increase, reducing lending and economic activity (as shown by the arrow pointing from the last factor, "Increase in Uncertainty," in the top row of Figure 1).

Stage Two: Banking Crisis

Deteriorating balance sheets and tougher business conditions lead some financial institutions into insolvency, which happens when their net worth becomes negative.

MyEconLab Mini-lecture

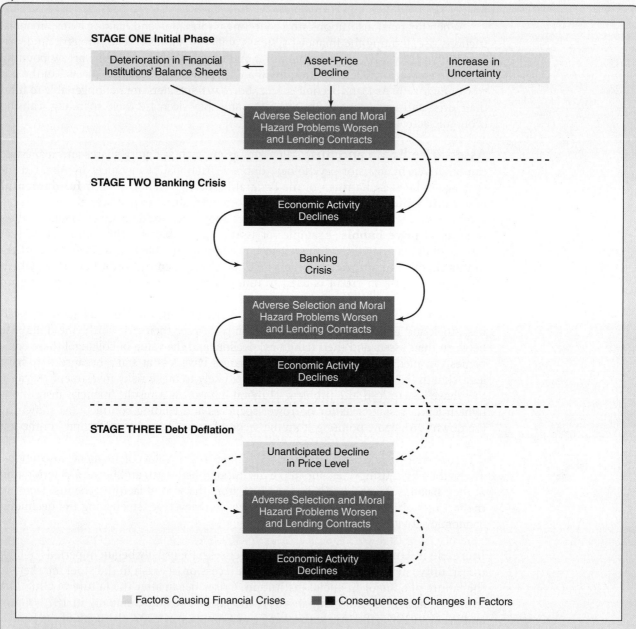

STAGE ONE Initial Phase

STAGE TWO Banking Crisis

STAGE THREE Debt Deflation

Factors Causing Financial Crises   ■ Consequences of Changes in Factors

FIGURE 1   Sequence of Events in Financial Crises in Advanced Economies

The solid arrows trace the sequence of events during a typical financial crisis; the dotted arrows show the additional set of events that occurs if the crisis develops into a debt deflation. The sections separated by the dashed horizontal lines show the different stages of a financial crisis.

Unable to pay off depositors or other creditors, some banks go out of business. If severe enough, these factors can lead to a bank panic in which multiple banks fail simultaneously. The source of the contagion is asymmetric information. In a panic, depositors, fearing for the safety of their deposits (in the absence of or with limited amounts of deposit insurance) and not knowing the quality of banks' loan portfolios, withdraw their deposits to the point that the banks fail. Uncertainty about the health of the banking system in general can lead to runs on banks, both good and bad, which forces banks to sell off assets quickly to raise the necessary funds. These **fire sales** of assets may cause their prices to decline so much that more banks become insolvent and the resulting contagion can then lead to multiple bank failures and a full-fledged bank panic.

With fewer banks operating, information about the creditworthiness of borrower-spenders disappears. Increasingly severe adverse selection and moral hazard problems in financial markets deepen the financial crisis, causing declines in asset prices and the failure of firms throughout the economy that lack funds for productive investment opportunities. Figure 1 represents this progression in the stage two portion. Bank panics were a feature of all U.S. financial crises during the nineteenth and twentieth centuries, occurring every twenty years or so until World War II—1819, 1837, 1857, 1873, 1884, 1893, 1907, and 1930–1933. (The 1933 establishment of federal deposit insurance, which protects depositors from losses, has prevented subsequent bank panics in the United States.)

Eventually, public and private authorities shut down insolvent firms and sell them off or liquidate them. Uncertainty in financial markets declines, the stock market recovers, and balance sheets improve. Financial frictions diminish and the financial crisis subsides. With the financial markets able to operate well again, the stage is set for an economic recovery.

Stage Three: Debt Deflation

If, however, the economic downturn leads to a sharp decline in the price level, the recovery process can be short-circuited. In stage three of Figure 1, **debt deflation** occurs when a substantial unanticipated decline in the price level sets in, leading to a further deterioration in firms' net worth because of the increased burden of indebtedness.

In economies with moderate inflation, which characterizes most advanced countries, many debt contracts with fixed interest rates are typically of fairly long maturity, ten years or more. Because debt payments are contractually fixed in nominal terms, an unanticipated decline in the price level raises the value of borrowing firms' and households' liabilities in real terms (increases the burden of the debt) but does not raise the real value of their assets. The borrowers' net worth in real terms (the difference between assets and liabilities in real terms) thus declines.

To better understand how this decline in net worth occurs, consider what happens if a firm in 2016 has assets of $100 million (in 2016 dollars) and $90 million of long-term liabilities, so that it has $10 million in net worth (the difference between the values of assets and liabilities). If the price level falls by 10% in 2017, the real value of the liabilities would rise to $99 million in 2016 dollars, while the real value of the assets would remain unchanged at $100 million. The result would be that real net worth in 2016 dollars would fall from $10 million to $1 million ($100 million minus $99 million).

The substantial decline in the real net worth of borrowers caused by a sharp drop in the price level creates an increase in adverse selection and moral hazard problems for lenders. Lending and economic activity decline for a long time. The most significant financial crisis that displayed debt deflation was the Great Depression, the worst economic contraction in U.S. history.

APPLICATION The Mother of All Financial Crises: The Great Depression

With our framework for understanding financial crises in place, we are prepared to analyze how a financial crisis unfolded during the Great Depression and how it led to the worst economic downturn in U.S. history.

Stock Market Crash

In 1928 and 1929, prices doubled in the U.S. stock market. Federal Reserve officials viewed the stock market boom as caused by excessive speculation. To curb it, they pursued a tightening of monetary policy to raise interest rates in an effort to limit the rise in stock prices. The Fed got more than it bargained for when the stock market crashed in October 1929, falling by 40% by the end of 1929, as shown in Figure 2.

Bank Panics

By the middle of 1930, stocks had recovered almost half of their losses and credit market conditions had stabilized. What might have been a normal recession turned into something far worse, however, when severe droughts in the Midwest led to a sharp decline in agricultural production, with the result that farmers could not pay back their bank loans. The resulting defaults on farm mortgages led to large loan losses on bank balance sheets in agricultural regions. The general weakness of the economy, and of the banks in agricultural regions in particular, prompted substantial withdrawals from banks, building to a full-fledged panic in November and December of 1930, with the stock market falling sharply. For more than two years, the Fed sat idly by through one bank panic after another, the most severe spate of panics in U.S. history. After what would be the era's final panic in March 1933, President Franklin Delano Roosevelt declared a bank holiday, a temporary closing of all banks. "The only thing we have to

MyEconLab Mini-lecture

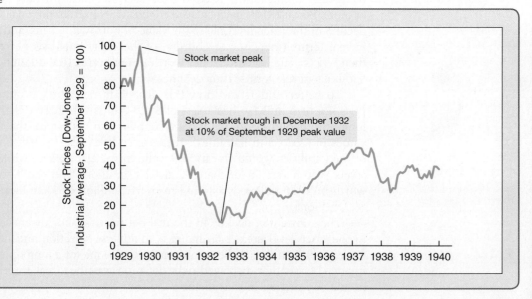

FIGURE 2
Stock Prices During the Great Depression Period
Stock prices crashed in 1929, falling by 40% by the end of 1929, and then continued to fall to only 10% of their peak value by 1932.
Source: Dow-Jones Industrial Average (DJIA). Global Financial Data: http://www .globalfinancialdata.com/ index_tabs.php?action= detailedinfo&id=1165.

fear is fear itself," Roosevelt told the nation. The damage was done, however, and more than one-third of U.S. commercial banks had failed.

Continuing Decline in Stock Prices

Stock prices kept falling. By mid-1932, stocks had declined to 10% of their value at the 1929 peak (as shown in Figure 2), and the increase in uncertainty from the unsettled business conditions created by the economic contraction worsened adverse selection and moral hazard problems in financial markets. With a greatly reduced number of financial intermediaries still in business, adverse selection and moral hazard problems intensified even further. Financial markets struggled to channel funds to borrower-spenders with productive investment opportunities. The amount of outstanding commercial loans fell by half from 1929 to 1933, and investment spending collapsed, declining by 90% from its 1929 level.

A manifestation of the rise in financial frictions is that lenders began charging businesses much higher interest rates to protect themselves from credit losses. The resulting rise in the **credit spread**—the difference between the interest rate on loans to households and businesses and the interest rate on completely safe assets that are sure to be paid back, such as U.S. Treasury securities—is shown in Figure 3, which displays the difference between interest rates on corporate bonds with a Baa (medium-quality) credit rating and rates on similar-maturity Treasury bonds. (Note the credit spread is closely related to the risk premium discussed in Chapter 6.)

Debt Deflation

The ongoing deflation that accompanied declining economic activity eventually led to a 25% decline in the price level. This deflation short-circuited the normal recovery process that occurs in most recessions. The huge decline in prices triggered a debt deflation in which net worth fell because of the increased burden of indebtedness borne by firms

MyEconLab Mini-lecture

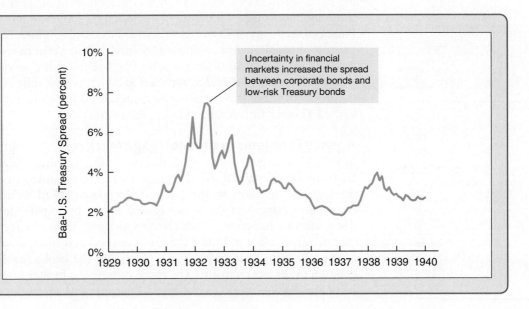

FIGURE 3
Credit Spreads During the Great Depression

Credit spreads (the difference between rates on Baa corporate bonds and U.S. Treasury bonds) rose sharply during the Great Depression.

Source: Federal Reserve Bank of St. Louis FRED database: http://research.stlouisfed.org/fred2/.

and households. The decline in net worth and the resulting increase in adverse selection and moral hazard problems in the credit markets led to a prolonged economic contraction in which unemployment rose to 25% of the labor force. The financial crisis of the Great Depression was the worst ever experienced in the United States, which explains why the economic contraction was also the most severe ever experienced by the nation.

International Dimensions

Although the Great Depression started in the United States, it was not just a U.S. phenomenon. Bank panics in the United States also spread to the rest of the world, and the contraction of the U.S. economy sharply decreased the demand for foreign goods. The worldwide depression caused great hardship, with millions upon millions of people out of work, and the resulting discontent led to the rise of fascism and World War II. The consequences of the Great Depression financial crisis were disastrous. ◆

THE GLOBAL FINANCIAL CRISIS OF 2007–2009

For many years, most economists thought that financial crises of the type experienced during the Great Depression were a thing of the past for advanced countries like the United States. Unfortunately, the financial crisis that engulfed the world in 2007–2009 proved them wrong.

Causes of the 2007–2009 Financial Crisis

We begin our look at the 2007–2009 financial crisis by examining three central factors: financial innovation in mortgage markets, agency problems in mortgage markets, and the role of asymmetric information in the credit-rating process.

Financial Innovation in the Mortgage Markets   As we saw in Chapter 11, starting in the early 2000s advances in information technology made it easier to securitize subprime mortgages, leading to an explosion in subprime mortgage-backed securities. Financial innovation didn't stop there. Financial engineering, the development of new, sophisticated financial instruments, led to **structured credit products** that paid out income streams from a collection of underlying assets, designed to have particular risk characteristics that appealed to investors with differing preferences. The most notorious of these products were collateralized debt obligations (CDOs) (discussed in the FYI box, "Collateralized Debt Obligations).

Agency Problems in the Mortgage Markets   The mortgage brokers who originated the mortgage loans often did not make a strong effort to evaluate whether a borrower could pay off the mortgage, since they planned to quickly sell (distribute) the loans to investors in the form of mortgage-backed securities. This originate-to-distribute business model was exposed to the principal–agent problem of the type discussed in Chapter 8, in which the mortgage brokers acted as agents for investors (the principals) but did not have the investors' best interests at heart. Once the mortgage broker earns his or her fee, why should the broker care if the borrower makes good on his or her payment? The more volume the broker originates, the more money he or she makes.

FYI   **Collateralized Debt Obligations (CDOs)**

The creation of a collateralized debt obligation involves a corporate entity called a *special purpose vehicle (SPV)*, which buys a collection of assets such as corporate bonds and loans, commercial real estate bonds, and mortgage-backed securities. The SPV then separates the payment streams (cash flows) from these assets into a number of buckets that are referred to as *tranches*. The highest-rated tranches, called *super senior tranches*, are the ones that are paid off first and so have the least risk. The super senior CDO is a bond that pays out these cash flows to investors, and because it has the least risk, it also has the lowest interest rate. The next bucket of cash flows, known as the *senior tranche*, is paid out next; the senior CDO has a little more risk and pays a higher interest rate. The next tranche of payment streams, the *mezzanine tranche* of the CDO, is paid out after the super senior and senior tranches and so it bears more risk and has an even higher interest rate. The lowest tranche of the CDO is the *equity tranche*; this is the first set of cash flows that are not paid out if the underlying assets go into

default and stop making payments. This tranche has the highest risk and is often not traded.

If all of this sounds complicated, it is. Tranches also included CDO^2s and CDO^3s that sliced and diced risk even further, paying out the cash flows from CDOs to CDO^2s and from CDO^2s to CDO^3s. Although financial engineering carries the potential benefit of creating products and services that match investors' risk appetites, it also has a dark side. Structured products like CDOs, CDO^2s, and CDO^3s can get so complicated that it becomes hard to value the cash flows of the underlying assets for a security or to determine who actually owns these assets. Indeed, in October 2007, Ben Bernanke, then chairman of the Federal Reserve, joked that he "would like to know what those damn things are worth." In other words, the increased complexity of structured products can actually reduce the amount of information in financial markets, thereby worsening asymmetric information in the financial system and increasing the severity of adverse selection and moral hazard problems.

Not surprisingly, adverse selection became a major problem. Risk-loving real-estate investors lined up to obtain loans to acquire houses that would be very profitable if housing prices went up, knowing they could "walk away" if housing prices went down. The principal–agent problem also created incentives for mortgage brokers to encourage households to take on mortgages they could not afford, or to commit fraud by falsifying information on borrowers' mortgage applications in order to qualify them for mortgages. Compounding this problem was lax regulation of originators, who were not required to disclose information to borrowers that would have helped them assess whether they could afford the loans.

The agency problems went even deeper. Commercial and investment banks, which were earning large fees by underwriting mortgage-backed securities and structured credit products like CDOs, also had weak incentives to make sure that the ultimate holders of the securities would be paid off. **Financial derivatives**, financial instruments whose payoffs are linked to (i.e., derived from) previously issued securities, also were an important source of excessive risk taking. Large fees from writing a type of financial insurance contract called a **credit default swap**, a financial derivative that provides payments to holders of bonds if they default, also drove units of insurance companies like AIG to write hundreds of billions of dollars' worth of these risky contracts.

Asymmetric Information and Credit-Rating Agencies   Credit-rating agencies, who rate the quality of debt securities in terms of the probability of default, were another contributor to asymmetric information in financial markets. The rating agencies advised clients on how to structure complex financial instruments, like CDOs, while at the same time they were rating these identical products. The rating agencies were thus subject to conflicts of interest because the large fees they earned from advising clients on how to structure products that they themselves were rating meant that they did not have sufficient incentives to make sure their ratings were accurate. The result was wildly inflated ratings that enabled the sale of complex financial products that were far riskier than investors recognized.

Effects of the 2007–2009 Financial Crisis

Consumers and businesses alike suffered as a result of the 2007–2009 financial crisis. The impact of the crisis was most evident in five key areas: the U.S. residential housing market, financial institutions' balance sheets, the shadow banking system, global financial markets, and the headline-grabbing failures of major firms in the financial industry.

Residential Housing Prices: Boom and Bust   The subprime mortgage market took off after the recession ended in 2001. By 2007, it had become over a trillion-dollar market. The development of the subprime mortgage market was encouraged by economists and politicians alike because it led to a "democratization of credit" and helped raise U.S. homeownership rates to the highest levels in history. The asset-price boom in housing (see Figure 4), which took off after the 2000–2001 recession was over, also

 MyEconLab Mini-lecture

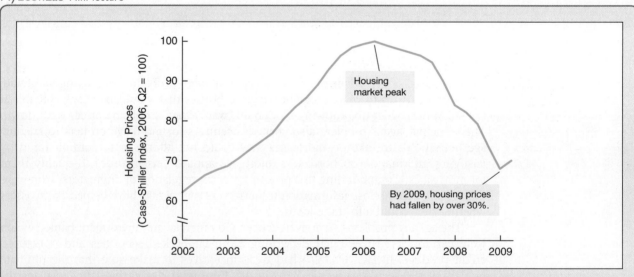

FIGURE 4   **Housing Prices and the Financial Crisis of 2007–2009**

Housing prices boomed from 2002 to 2006, fueling the market for subprime mortgages and forming an asset-price bubble. Housing prices began declining in 2006, falling by more than 30% subsequently, which led to defaults by subprime mortgage holders.

Source: Case-Shiller U.S. National Composite House Price Index from Federal Reserve Bank of St. Louis FRED database: http://research.stlouisfed.org/fred2/.

Inside the Fed   Was the Fed to Blame for the Housing Price Bubble?

Some economists—most prominently, John Taylor of Stanford University—have argued that the low interest rate policy of the Federal Reserve in the 2003–2006 period caused the housing price bubble.[*] Taylor argues that the low federal funds rate led to low mortgage rates that stimulated housing demand and encouraged the issuance of subprime mortgages, both of which led to rising housing prices and a bubble.

In a speech given in January 2010, then-Federal Reserve Chairman Ben Bernanke countered this argument.[†] He concluded that monetary policy was not to blame for the housing price bubble. First, he said, it is not at all clear that the federal funds rate was too low during the 2003–2006 period. Rather, the culprits

were the proliferation of new mortgage products that lowered mortgage payments, a relaxation of lending standards that brought more buyers into the housing market, and capital inflows from countries such as China and India. Bernanke's speech was very controversial, and the debate over whether monetary policy was to blame for the housing price bubble continues to this day.

[*]John Taylor, "Housing and Monetary Policy," in Federal Reserve Bank of Kansas City, *Housing, Housing Finance and Monetary Policy* (Kansas City: Federal Reserve Bank of Kansas City, 2007), 463–476.
[†]Ben S. Bernanke, "Monetary Policy and the Housing Bubble," speech given at the annual meeting of the American Economic Association, Atlanta Georgia, January 3, 2010; http://www.federalreserve.gov/newsevents/speech/bernanke20100103a.htm.

helped stimulate the growth of the subprime mortgage market. High housing prices meant that subprime borrowers could refinance their houses with even larger loans when their homes appreciated in value. With housing prices rising, subprime borrowers were also unlikely to default because they could always sell their house to pay off the loan, making investors happy because the securities backed by cash flows from subprime mortgages had high returns. The growth of the subprime mortgage market, in turn, increased the demand for houses and so fueled the boom in housing prices, resulting in a housing price bubble.

Further stimulus for the inflated housing market came from low interest rates on residential mortgages, which were the result of several different forces. First were the huge capital inflows into the United States from countries like China and India. Second was Congressional legislation that encouraged Fannie Mae and Freddie Mac to purchase trillions of dollars of mortgage-backed securities.[2] Third was Federal Reserve monetary policy that made it easy to lower interest rates. The low cost of financing for housing purchases that resulted from these forces further stimulated the demand for housing, pushing up housing prices. (A highly controversial issue is whether the Federal Reserve was to blame for the housing price bubble, and this is discussed in the Inside the Fed box.)

As housing prices rose and profitability for mortgage originators and lenders grew higher, the underwriting standards for subprime mortgages fell lower and lower. High-risk borrowers were able to obtain mortgages, and the amount of the mortgage relative to the value of the house, the loan-to-value ratio (LTV), rose. Borrowers were often able to get piggyback, second, and third mortgages on top of their original 80% loan-to-value mortgage, so that they had to put almost no money down. When asset

[2]For a discussion of the government's role in encouraging the housing boom, which led to a subsequent bust in the housing market, see Thomas Sowell, *The Housing Boom and Bust*, Revised Edition (New York, Basic Books, 2010).

prices rise too far out of line with fundamentals—in the case of housing, the cost of purchasing a home relative to the cost of renting it, or the cost of houses relative to households' median income—they must come down. Eventually, the housing price bubble burst. With housing prices falling after their peak in 2006 (see Figure 4), the rot in the financial system began to reveal itself. The decline in housing prices led many subprime borrowers to find that their mortgages were "underwater"—that is, the value of the house was below the amount of the mortgage. When this happened, struggling homeowners had tremendous incentives to walk away from their homes and just send the keys back to the lender. Defaults on mortgages shot up sharply, eventually leading to foreclosures on millions of mortgages.

Deterioration of Financial Institutions' Balance Sheets The decline in U.S. housing prices led to rising defaults on mortgages. As a result, the values of mortgage-backed securities and CDOs collapsed, leaving banks and other financial institutions holding those securities with a lower value of assets and thus a lower net worth. With weakened balance sheets, these banks and other financial institutions began to deleverage, selling off assets and restricting the availability of credit to both households and businesses. With no one else able to step in to collect information and make loans, the reduction in bank lending meant that financial frictions increased in financial markets.

Run on the Shadow Banking System The sharp decline in the values of mortgages and other financial assets triggered a run on the shadow banking system, composed of hedge funds, investment banks, and other nondepository financial firms, which are not as tightly regulated as banks. Funds from shadow banks flowed through the financial system and for many years supported the issuance of low-interest-rate mortgages and auto loans.

These securities were funded primarily by **repurchase agreements (repos)**, short-term borrowing that, in effect, uses assets like mortgage-backed securities as collateral. Rising concern about the quality of a financial institution's balance sheet led lenders to require larger amounts of collateral, known as **haircuts**. For example, if a borrower took out a $100 million loan in a repo agreement, the borrower might have to post $105 million of mortgage-backed securities as collateral, for a haircut of 5%.

Rising defaults on mortgages caused the values of mortgage-backed securities to fall, which then led to a rise in haircuts. At the start of the crisis, haircuts were close to zero, but eventually they rose to nearly 50%.[3] The result was that financial institutions could borrow only half as much with the same amount of collateral. Thus, to raise funds, financial institutions had to engage in fire sales and sell off their assets very rapidly. Because selling assets quickly requires lowering their price, the fire sales led to a further decline in financial institutions' asset values. This decline lowered the value of collateral further, raising haircuts and thereby forcing financial institutions to scramble even more for liquidity. The result was similar to the run on the banking system that occurred during the Great Depression, causing massive deleveraging that resulted in a restriction of lending and a decline in economic activity.

---

[3]See Gary Gorton and Andrew Metrick, "Securitized Banking and the Run on Repo," National Bureau of Economic Research Working Paper No. 15223 (August 2009).

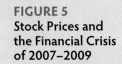

MyEconLab Mini-lecture

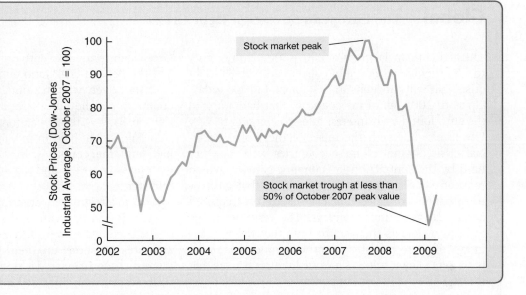

FIGURE 5
Stock Prices and the Financial Crisis of 2007–2009

Stock prices fell by 50% from October 2007 to March 2009.

Source: Dow-Jones Industrial Average (DJIA). Global Financial Data: http://www.globalfinancialdata.com/index_tabs.php?action=detailedinfo&id=1165.

The decline in asset prices in the stock market (which fell by over 50% from October 2007 to March 2009, as shown in Figure 5) and the more than 30% drop in residential house prices (shown in Figure 4), along with the fire sales resulting from the run on the shadow banking system, weakened both firms' and households' balance sheets. This worsening of financial frictions manifested itself in widening credit spreads, causing higher costs of credit for households and businesses and tighter lending standards. The resulting decline in lending meant that both consumption expenditure and investment fell, causing the economy to contract.[4]

Global Financial Markets Although the problem originated in the United States, the wake-up call for the financial crisis came from Europe, a sign of how extensive the globalization of financial markets had become. After Fitch and Standard & Poor's announced ratings downgrades on mortgage-backed securities and CDOs totaling more than $10 billion, on August 7, 2007, a French investment house, BNP Paribas, suspended redemption of shares held in some of its money market funds, which had sustained large losses. The run on the shadow banking system began, only to become worse and worse over time. Despite huge injections of liquidity into the financial system by the European Central Bank and the Federal Reserve, banks began to horde cash and were unwilling to lend to each other. The drying up of credit led to the first major bank failure in the United Kingdom in over 100 years when Northern Rock, which had relied on short-term borrowing in the repo market rather than deposits for its funding, collapsed in September 2007. A string of other European financial institutions then failed as well. Particularly hard hit were countries like Greece, Ireland, Portugal, and Spain. The resulting crisis in markets for government-issued (sovereign) debt in Europe is described in the Global box, "The European Sovereign Debt Crisis."

---

[4]This period was also characterized by a substantial supply shock that occurred when oil and other commodity prices rose sharply until the summer of 2008, but then fell precipitously thereafter. We discuss the aggregate demand and supply analysis of the impact of this supply shock in Chapter 22.

Global The European Sovereign Debt Crisis

The global financial crisis of 2007–2009 led not only to a worldwide recession but also to a sovereign debt crisis that still threatens to destabilize Europe today. Up until 2007, all of the countries that had adopted the euro found their interest rates converging to very low levels, but with the onset of the global financial crisis, several of these countries were hit very hard by the contraction in economic activity, which reduced tax revenues at the same time that government bailouts of failed financial institutions required additional government outlays. The resulting surge in budget deficits then led to fears that the governments of these hard-hit countries would default on their debt. The result was a surge in interest rates that threatened to spiral out of control.[*]

Greece was the first domino to fall in Europe. In September 2009, with an economy weakened by reduced tax revenues and increased spending demands, the Greek government was projecting a budget deficit for the year of 6% and a debt-to-GDP ratio near 100%. However, when a new government was elected in October, it revealed that the budget situation was far worse than anyone had imagined, because the previous government had provided misleading numbers about both the budget deficit, which was at least double the 6% number, and the amount of government debt, which was ten percentage points higher than previously reported. Despite austerity measures aimed at dramatically cutting government spending and raising taxes, interest rates on

Greek debt soared, eventually rising to nearly 40%, and the debt-to-GDP ratio climbed to 160% of GDP in 2012. Even with bailouts from other European countries and liquidity support from the European Central Bank, Greece was forced to write down the value of its debt held in private hands by more than half, and the country was subject to civil unrest, with massive strikes and the resignation of the prime minister.

The sovereign debt crisis spread from Greece to Ireland, Portugal, Spain, and Italy. The governments of these countries were forced to embrace austerity measures to shore up their public finances while interest rates climbed to double-digit levels. Only with a speech in July 2012 by Mario Draghi, the president of the European Central Bank, in which he stated that the ECB was ready to do "whatever it takes" to save the euro, did the markets begin to calm down. Nonetheless, despite a sharp decline in interest rates in these countries, the countries experienced severe recessions, with unemployment rates rising to double-digit levels and Spain's unemployment rate exceeding 25%. The stresses that the European sovereign debt crisis produced for the euro zone, the countries that have adopted the euro, has raised doubts about whether the euro will survive.

[*]For a discussion of the dynamics of sovereign debt crises and case studies of the European debt crisis, see David Greenlaw, James D. Hamilton, Frederic S. Mishkin, and Peter Hooper, "Crunch Time: Fiscal Crises and the Role of Monetary Policy," U.S. *Monetary Policy Forum* (Chicago: Chicago Booth Initiative on Global Markets, 2013).

Failure of High-Profile Firms The impact of the financial crisis on firms' balance sheets forced major players in the financial markets to take drastic action. In March 2008, Bear Stearns, the fifth-largest investment bank in the United States, which had invested heavily in subprime-related securities, had a run on its repo funding and was forced to sell itself to J.P. Morgan for less than one-tenth of its worth just a year earlier. To broker the deal, the Federal Reserve had to take over $30 billion of Bear Stearns's hard-to-value assets. In July, Fannie Mae and Freddie Mac, the two privately-owned, government-sponsored enterprises that together insured over $5 trillion of mortgages or mortgage-backed assets, were propped up by the U.S. Treasury and the Federal Reserve after suffering substantial losses from their holdings of subprime securities. In early September 2008, Fannie Mae and Freddy Mac were put into conservatorship (in effect, run by the government).

On Monday, September 15, 2008, after suffering losses in the subprime market, Lehman Brothers, the fourth-largest investment bank by asset size with over $600 billion in assets and 25,000 employees, filed for bankruptcy, making it the largest bankruptcy filing in U.S. history. The day before, Merrill Lynch, the third-largest investment bank, which had also suffered large losses on its holdings of subprime securities, announced its sale to Bank of America for a price 60% below its value a year earlier. On Tuesday, September 16, AIG, an insurance giant with assets of over $1 trillion, suffered an extreme liquidity crisis when its credit rating was downgraded. It had written over $400 billion of insurance contracts (credit default swaps) that had to make payouts on possible losses from subprime mortgage securities. The Federal Reserve then stepped in with an $85 billion loan to keep AIG afloat (with total government loans later increased to $173 billion).

Height of the 2007–2009 Financial Crisis

The financial crisis reached its peak in September 2008 after the House of Representatives, fearing the wrath of constituents who were angry about the Wall Street bailout, voted down a $700 billion dollar bailout package proposed by the Bush administration. The Emergency Economic Stabilization Act was finally passed nearly a week later. The stock market crash accelerated, with the week beginning October 6, 2008, showing the worst weekly decline in U.S. history. Credit spreads went through the roof over the next three weeks, with the spread between Baa corporate bonds (just above investment grade) and U.S. Treasury bonds going to over 5.5 percentage points (550 basis points), as illustrated by Figure 6.

MyEconLab Mini-lecture

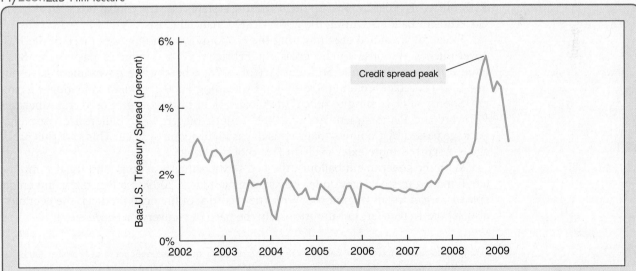

FIGURE 6   Credit Spreads and the 2007–2009 Financial Crisis

Credit spreads (the difference between rates on Baa corporate bonds and U.S. Treasury bonds) rose by more than 4 percentage points (400 basis points) during the crisis. Debate over the bailout package and the stock market crash caused credit spreads to peak in December 2008.

Source: Federal Reserve Bank of St. Louis FRED database: http://research.stlouisfed.org/fred2/.

The impaired financial markets and surging interest rates faced by borrower-spenders led to sharp declines in consumer spending and investment. Real GDP declined sharply, falling at a −1.3% annual rate in the third quarter of 2008 and then at a −5.4% and −6.4% annual rate in the next two quarters. The unemployment rate shot up, going over the 10% level in late 2009. The recession that started in December 2007 became the worst economic contraction in the United States since World War II and as a result is now referred to as the "Great Recession."

Government Intervention and the Recovery

Although the recession produced by the global financial crisis was very severe, the economic contraction was far smaller in magnitude than during the Great Depression because of massive interventions by governments to prop up financial markets and stimulate the economy.

As we will see in Chapter 15, the Federal Reserve took extraordinary actions to contain the crisis, actions involving both monetary policy to stimulate the economy and liquidity provision to support orderly functioning of financial markets. In addition, the U.S. government engaged in massive bailouts, with over $150 billion of loans to AIG and the **Troubled Asset Relief Program (TARP)**, the most important provision of the Bush administration's Emergency Economic Stabilization Act passed in October 2008, which authorized the Treasury to spend $700 billion purchasing subprime mortgage assets from troubled financial institutions or to inject capital into these institutions—the route actually followed. In addition, the Act raised the federal deposit insurance limit temporarily from $100,000 to $250,000 in order to limit withdrawals from banks. Shortly thereafter, the FDIC put in place a guarantee for certain debt newly issued by banks, and the Treasury guaranteed for a year money market mutual fund shares at par value. Similarly, European governments conducted massive bailouts, in excess of $10 trillion, in order to prop up their banking systems (see the Global box, "Worldwide Government Bailouts During the 2007–2009 Financial Crisis").

Fiscal policy aimed at stimulating the economy was another key piece of the U.S. government's response to the crisis. In February 2008, Congress passed the Bush administration's Economic Stimulus Act of 2008, whereby the government gave out one-time tax rebates totaling $78 billion by sending $600 checks to individual taxpayers. Shortly after coming to office, the Obama administration proposed the American Recovery and Reinvestment Act of 2009, a much bigger, $787 billion fiscal stimulus package passed by Congress that to this day is highly controversial. This stimulus package is discussed more extensively in Part 6 of the book.

With the government bailouts, the Fed's extraordinary actions, and fiscal stimulus, a bull market in stocks got under way starting in March 2009 (see Figure 5), and credit spreads began to fall (Figure 6).[5] With the recovery of financial markets, the economy also started to recover, but unfortunately the pace of recovery has been slow.

---

[5]The financial market recovery was aided by the U.S. Treasury's requirement, announced in February 2009, that the nineteen largest banking institutions undergo what became known as the *bank stress tests* (the Supervisory Capital Assessment Program, or SCAP). The stress tests were a supervisory assessment, led by the Federal Reserve in cooperation with the Office of the Comptroller of the Currency and the FDIC, of the balance sheet positions of these banks to ensure that they had sufficient capital to withstand bad macroeconomic outcomes. The Treasury announced the results in early May, and they were well received by market participants, enabling these banks to raise substantial amounts of capital from private capital markets. The stress tests were a key factor that helped increase the amount of information in the marketplace, thereby reducing asymmetric information and adverse selection and moral hazard problems.

Global **Worldwide Government Bailouts During the 2007–2009 Financial Crisis**

The spreading bank failures in Europe in the fall of 2008 led to massive bailouts of financial institutions: the Netherlands, Belgium, and Luxembourg injected $16 billion to prop up Fortis, a major European bank; the Netherlands injected $13 billion into ING, a banking and insurance giant; Germany provided a $50 billion rescue package for Hypo Real Estate Holdings; and Iceland took over its three largest banks after its banking system collapsed. Ireland's government guaranteed all the deposits of its commercial banks as well as interbank lending, as did Greece. Spain implemented a bailout package similar to the United States' to buy up to 50 billion euros ($70 billion) of assets in its banks in order to encourage them to lend. The U.K. Treasury set up a bailout plan with a price tag similar to that of the U.S. Treasury's plan of 400 billion pounds ($699 billion). It guaranteed 250 billion pounds of bank liabilities, added 100 billion pounds to a facility that swaps these assets for government bonds, and allowed the U.K. government to buy up to 50 billion pounds of equity stakes in British banks. Bailout plans to the tune of over $100 billion in South Korea, $200 billion in Sweden, $400 billion in France, and $500 billion in Germany, all of which guaranteed the debt of their banks as well as the injection of capital into them, then followed. Both the scale of these bailout packages and the degree of international coordination was unprecedented.

RESPONSE OF FINANCIAL REGULATION

Given the cost to the economy of the 2007–2009 financial crisis, the size of the bailouts, and the nationalization of so many financial institutions, the system of financial regulation is currently undergoing dramatic changes.

Macroprudential Versus Microprudential Supervision

Before the global financial crisis, regulatory authorities engaged in **microprudential supervision**, which focuses on the safety and soundness of *individual* financial institutions. Microprudential supervision looks at each individual institution separately and assesses the riskiness of its activities and whether it complies with disclosure requirements. Most importantly, microprudential supervision checks whether a particular institution satisfies capital *ratios* and, if it does not, either engages in prompt corrective action to force the institution to raise its capital ratios or the supervisor closes it down, along the lines we have discussed previously.

A focus on microprudential supervision is not enough to prevent financial crises. The run on the shadow banking system illustrates how the problems of one financial institution can harm other financial institutions that are otherwise healthy. When the troubled financial institution is forced to engage in fire sales and sell off assets in order to meet target capital ratios or haircut requirements, this leads to a decline in asset values. The decline in asset values then causes other institutions to engage in fire sales, leading to a rapid deleveraging process and a systemic crisis. In situations like this, even institutions that have high capital ratios and would normally be healthy may find themselves in trouble.

The global financial crisis has therefore made it clear that there is a need for **macroprudential supervision**, which focuses on the safety and soundness of the financial system *in the aggregate*. Rather than focusing on the safety and soundness of individual institutions, macroprudential supervision seeks to mitigate system-wide fire sales and deleveraging by assessing the overall capacity of the financial system to avoid them. In addition, because many institutions that were well capitalized faced liquidity shortages and found that their access to short-term funding was cut off, macroprudential supervision focuses not only on capital adequacy as a whole but also on whether the financial system has sufficient liquidity.

Macroprudential policies can take several forms. The run-up to the global financial crisis included a so-called **leverage cycle**, in which a feedback loop resulted from a boom in issuing credit, which led to higher asset prices, which resulted in higher capital buffers at financial institutions, which supported further lending in the context of unchanging capital requirements, which then raised asset prices further, and so on; in the bust, the value of the capital dropped precipitously, leading to a cut in lending. To short-circuit this leverage cycle, macroprudential policies make capital requirements countercyclical; that is, they are adjusted upward during a boom and downward during a bust. In addition, during the upward swing in the leverage cycle, macroprudential policies might involve forcing financial institutions to tighten credit standards or even direct limits on the growth of credit. In the downward swing, macroprudential supervision might be needed to force the banking system as a whole to raise an aggregate amount of new capital so that banks will not curtail lending in order to reduce the level of their assets and raise capital ratios. To ensure that financial institutions have enough liquidity, macroprudential policies could require that financial institutions have a sufficiently low *net stable funding ratio* (NSFR), which is the percentage of the institution's short-term funding in relation to total funding. Macroprudential policies of the type discussed here are being considered as part of the Basel 3 framework, but have not yet been completely worked out.

Dodd-Frank Wall Street Reform and Consumer Protection Act of 2010

The global financial crisis raised calls for a new regulatory structure that would make a repeat of the crisis less likely. The result was the Dodd-Frank bill, which was passed in July 2010 after more than a year of discussion. It is the most comprehensive financial reform legislation since the Great Depression. The bill addresses five different categories of regulation, which are discussed next.

Consumer Protection　Dodd-Frank created a new Consumer Financial Protection Bureau that is funded and housed within the Federal Reserve, although it is a completely independent agency. It has the authority to examine and enforce regulations on all businesses with more than $10 billion in assets that are engaged in issuing residential mortgage products, as well as on issuers of other financial products marketed to low-income people. The legislation requires lenders to make sure borrowers can repay residential mortgages by requiring verification of their income, credit history, and job status. It also bans payments to brokers for pushing borrowers into higher-priced loans. It allows states to impose stricter consumer protection laws on national banks and gives state attorney generals the power to enforce certain rules issued by the new bureau. It also permanently increased the level of federal deposit insurance to $250,000.

Resolution Authority   Before the new legislation was passed, the FDIC had the authority to seize failing banks and wind them down, but it did not have such resolution authority over the largest financial institutions—those structured as holding companies. Indeed, the U.S. Treasury and the Federal Reserve argued that one reason they were unable to rescue Lehman Brothers, and instead had to let it go into bankruptcy, was that they did not have the legal means with which to take over Lehman and break it up. The Dodd-Frank bill now provides the U.S. government with this authority for financial firms that are deemed systemic—that is, firms that pose a risk to the overall health of the financial system because their failure would cause widespread economic damage. It also gives regulators the right to levy fees on financial institutions with more than $50 billion in assets to recoup any losses.

Systemic Risk Regulation   The Dodd-Frank bill created a Financial Stability Oversight Council, chaired by the Treasury secretary, that monitors markets for asset price bubbles and the buildup of systemic risk. In addition, it designates which financial firms are systemically important and so receive the official designation of **systemically important financial institutions (SIFIs)**. These firms are subject to additional regulation by the Federal Reserve, which includes higher capital standards and stricter liquidity requirements, along with the requirement that such firms draw up a "living will," that is, a plan for orderly liquidation if the firm gets into financial difficulties.

Volcker Rule   Under the new legislation, banks are limited in the extent of their proprietary trading—that is, trading with their own money—and are allowed to own only a small percentage of hedge and private equity funds. These provisions are named after Paul Volcker, a former Chairman of the Board of Governors of the Federal Reserve, who argued that banks should not be allowed to take large trading risks when they receive the benefits of federal deposit insurance.

Derivatives   As discussed in Chapter 11, derivatives such as credit default swaps ended up being "weapons of mass destruction" that helped lead to a financial meltdown when AIG had to be rescued after making overly extensive use of them. To prevent this from happening again, the Dodd-Frank bill requires that many standardized derivative products be traded on exchanges and cleared through clearinghouses to reduce the risk of losses if one counterparty in the derivative transaction goes bankrupt. More customized derivative products are subject to higher capital requirements. Banks are banned from some of their derivative-dealing operations, such as those involving riskier swaps. In addition, the bill imposes capital and margin requirements on firms dealing in derivatives and forces them to disclose more information about their activities.

TOO-BIG-TO-FAIL AND FUTURE REGULATION

The Dodd-Frank bill leaves out many of the details of future regulation, and there are doubts as to whether it has dealt sufficiently with the too-big-to-fail problem, which, as we have seen, was an important factor that contributed to the global financial crisis. Here we discuss some possible measures to reduce the too-big-to-fail problem and explore several areas in which regulation might be heading in the future.

What Can Be Done About the Too-Big-to-Fail Problem?

Three approaches to solving the too-big-to-fail problem have been actively debated.

Break Up Large, Systemically Important Financial Institutions   One way to eliminate the too-big-to-fail problem is to make sure that no financial institution is so large that it can bring down the financial system. Then, regulators will no longer see the need to bail out these institutions if they fail, thereby subjecting them to market discipline. One way to shrink overly-large institutions is to reimpose the restrictions that were in place before Glass-Steagall was repealed, thereby forcing these large SIFIs to break up their different activities into smaller, cohesive companies. Alternatively, regulations could specify that no financial institution can have assets over a specified maximum limit, forcing SIFIs to break up into smaller pieces.

Not surprisingly, both of these approaches have been vehemently opposed by the largest financial institutions. Although breaking up SIFIs would eliminate the too-big-to-fail problem, if there are synergies available that might enable large institutions to manage risk better or to provide financial services at a lower cost, then breaking up SIFIs might decrease the efficiency of the financial system rather than increase it.

Higher Capital Requirements   Because institutions that are "too big to fail" have incentives to take on excessive risk, another way to reduce their risk taking is to impose higher capital requirements on them. With higher capital, not only will these institutions have a larger buffer with which to withstand losses if they occur, but they will also have more to lose and hence have more "skin in the game," thereby reducing moral hazard and giving them less incentive to take on excessive risk. Another way of describing this approach is to say that higher capital requirements reduce the subsidy to risk-taking for institutions that are too big to fail. In addition, because risk taking by SIFIs is far greater during booms, capital requirements could be increased when credit is expanding rapidly and reduced when credit is contracting. Such measures would cause capital requirements to become more countercyclical and could help restrain the boom-bust credit cycle.

The Swiss central bank has been a leader in this kind of approach: It has the highest capital requirements among advanced countries for its largest banks, and it raises them when credit markets become particularly frothy. Legislation has been proposed in the U.S. Congress to double capital requirements for large financial institutions, legislation that these institutions vigorously oppose.

Leave It to Dodd-Frank   Another view is that Dodd-Frank has effectively eliminated the too-big-to-fail problem by making it harder for the Federal Reserve to bail out financial institutions, by imposing stricter regulations on SIFIs, and through application of the Volcker rule. Indeed, the authors of the bill have declared that Dodd-Frank will "end too-big-to-fail as we know it." Although the provisions of Dodd-Frank do take away some of the incentives for excessive risk-taking by large, systemically important financial institutions, there are doubts that this bill completely removes the too-big-to-fail problem.

Other Issues for Future Regulation

The Dodd-Frank bill leaves out many of the details of future regulation and does not address some important regulatory issues at all. Here we examine four areas in which regulation may be heading in the future.

Compensation in the Financial Services Industry   The high fees and executive compensation that so outraged the public created incentives for the financial industry to create securities that turned out to be much riskier than advertised. Regulators are adopting regulations aimed at modifying compensation in the financial services industry to reduce risk taking. For example, regulators are issuing requirements that bonuses be paid out for a number of years after they have been earned, and only if the firm remains in good health. Such "clawbacks" will encourage employees to reduce the riskiness of their activities so that they are more likely to be paid these bonuses in the future.

Government-Sponsored Enterprises (GSEs)

A major gap in the Dodd-Frank bill is that it does not address privately-owned, government-sponsored enterprises, such as Fannie Mae and Freddie Mac. During the global financial crisis, both of these firms got into serious financial trouble and had to be taken over by the government, with massive loans and government guarantees needed to prop them up. To prevent this from occurring again, the government might take any of four routes:

1. Fully privatize GSEs by taking away their government sponsorship, thereby removing the implicit backing for their debt.
2. Completely nationalize them by taking away their private status and making them government agencies.
3. Leave them as privately owned GSEs, but strengthen regulations to restrict the amount of risk they take and to impose higher capital standards.
4. Leave them as privately owned GSEs, but force them to shrink dramatically so that they no longer expose the taxpayer to huge losses or pose a systemic risk to the financial system when they fail.

Credit-Rating Agencies

Regulations to restrict conflicts of interest at credit-rating agencies and to give them greater incentives to provide reliable ratings have already been strengthened in the aftermath of the global financial crisis, but even more regulation is likely to be imposed. The inaccurate ratings provided by credit-rating agencies helped promote risk taking throughout the financial system and led to investors not having the information they needed to make informed choices about their investments. The reliance on credit ratings in the Basel 2 capital requirements may also have to be rethought, given the poor performance of credit-rating agencies in recent years.

The Danger of Overregulation

As a result of the global financial crisis, the world of financial regulation will never be the same. Although it is clear that more regulation is needed to prevent such a crisis from ever occurring again, the danger is substantial that too much or poorly designed regulation could hamper the efficiency of the financial system. If new regulations choke off financial innovation that can benefit both households and businesses, future economic growth will suffer.

SUMMARY

1. A financial crisis occurs when a particularly large disruption to information flows occurs in financial markets, with the result that financial frictions increase sharply, thereby rendering financial markets incapable of channeling funds to households and firms with productive investment opportunities, and causing a sharp contraction in economic activity.

2. Financial crises start in advanced countries like the United States in two ways: credit booms and busts, or a general increase in uncertainty when major financial institutions fail. The result is a substantial increase in adverse selection and moral hazard problems, which leads to a contraction of lending and a decline in economic activity. The worsening business

conditions and deterioration in bank balance sheets then trigger the second stage of the crisis, the simultaneous failure of many banking institutions, a banking crisis. The resulting decrease in the number of banks causes a loss of their information capital, leading to a further decline of lending and a spiraling down of the economy. In some instances, the resulting economic downturn leads to a sharp slide in prices, which increases the real liabilities of firms and households and therefore lowers their net worth, leading to a debt deflation. The further decline in borrowers' net worth worsens adverse selection and moral hazard problems, so that lending, investment spending, and aggregate economic activity remain depressed for a long time.

3. The most significant financial crisis in U.S. history, that which led to the Great Depression, involved several stages: a stock market crash, bank panics, worsening of asymmetric information problems, and finally a debt deflation.

4. The global financial crisis of 2007–2009 was triggered by mismanagement of financial innovations involving subprime residential mortgages and the bursting of a housing price bubble. The crisis spread globally, with substantial deterioration in banks' and other financial institutions' balance sheets, a run on the shadow banking system, and the failure of many high-profile firms.

5. Financial regulation has undergone many changes in the wake of the global financial crisis. First is the shift from microprudential supervision, which focuses on the safety and soundness of individual institutions, to macroprudential supervision, which focuses on the safety and soundness of the financial system in the aggregate. Second is the Dodd-Frank Act of 2010, which is the most comprehensive financial reform legislation since the Great Depression. It makes provisions in five areas: (1) consumer protection, (2) resolution authority, (3) systemic risk regulation, (4) the Volcker rule, and (5) derivatives.

6. Future regulation needs to address five issues: (1) the too-big-to-fail problem, which can be at least partially addressed by either breaking up large financial institutions or by imposing higher capital requirements on them; (2) compensation at financial firms to reduce incentives to take on excessive risk; (3) GSEs to make it less likely that they will require government bailouts in the future; (4) credit-rating agencies to improve incentives for these agencies to provide accurate assessments of credit risk; and (5) the dangers of overregulation, which can decrease the efficiency of the financial system.

KEY TERMS

asset-price bubble, p. 269
credit boom, p. 268
credit default swaps, p. 275
credit spread, p. 273
debt deflation, p. 271
deleveraging, p. 268
financial crisis, p. 268
financial derivatives, p. 275

financial frictions, p. 268
financial innovation, p. 268
financial liberalization, p. 268
fire sales, p. 271
fundamental economic values, p. 269
haircuts, p. 278
leverage cycle, p. 284
macroprudential supervision, p. 284

microprudential supervision, p. 283
repurchase agreements
   (repos), p. 278
structured credit products, p. 274
systemically important financial
   institutions (SIFIs), p. 285
Troubled Asset Relief Program
   (TARP), p. 282

QUESTIONS

All questions are available in MyEconLab at http://www.myeconlab.com.

1. How does the concept of asymmetric information help to define a financial crisis?

2. How can the bursting of an asset-price bubble in the stock market help trigger a financial crisis?

3. How does an unanticipated decline in the price level cause a drop in lending?

4. How can a decline in real estate prices cause deleveraging and a decline in lending?

5. How does a deterioration in balance sheets of financial institutions and the simultaneous failures of these institutions cause a decline in economic activity?

6. How does a general increase in uncertainty as a result of the failure of a major financial institution lead to an increase in adverse selection and moral hazard problems?

7. What is a credit spread? Why do credit spreads rise significantly during a financial crisis?

8. What causes bank panics to occur?

9. Why do bank panics worsen asymmetric information problems in credit markets?

10. How can financial innovation lead to financial crises?

11. What role does weak financial regulation and supervision play in causing financial crises?

12. Describe two similarities and two differences between the United States' experiences during the Great Depression and the financial crisis of 2007–2009.

13. What do you think prevented the financial crisis of 2007–2009 from becoming a depression?

14. What technological innovations led to the development of the subprime mortgage market?

15. Why is the originate-to-distribute business model subject to the principal–agent problem?

16. "Financial engineering always leads to a more efficient financial system." Is this statement true, false, or uncertain?

17. How did a decline in housing prices help trigger the subprime financial crisis that began in 2007?

18. What role did the shadow banking system play in the 2007–2009 financial crisis?

19. Why would haircuts on collateral increase sharply during a financial crisis? How would this lead to fire sales on assets?

20. How did the global financial crisis promote a sovereign debt crisis in Europe?

21. Why is it a good idea for macroprudential policies to require countercyclical capital requirements?

22. How does the process of financial innovation impact the effectiveness of macroprudential regulation?

23. What are the three approaches to limiting the too-big-to-fail problem? Briefly describe the advantages and disadvantages of each of the approaches.

24. Why were consumer protection provisions included in the Dodd-Frank bill, a bill designed to strengthen the financial system?

25. Why is it important for the U.S. government to have resolution authority?

DATA ANALYSIS PROBLEMS

The Problems update with real-time data in MyEconLab *and are available for practice or instructor assignment.*

1. Go to the St. Louis Federal Reserve FRED database, and find data on house prices (SPCS20RSA), stock prices (SP500), a measure of the net wealth of households (TNWBSHNO), and personal consumption expenditures (PCEC). For all four measures, be sure to convert the *frequency* setting to "Quarterly." Download the data into a spreadsheet, and make sure the data align correctly with the appropriate dates. For all four series, for each quarter, calculate the annualized growth rate from quarter to quarter. To do this, take the current-period data minus the previous-quarter data, and then divide by the previous quarter data. Multiply by 100 to change each result to a percent, and multiply by 4 to annualize the data.

   a. For the four series, calculate the average growth rates over the most recent four quarters of data available. Comment on the relationships among house prices, stock prices, net wealth of households, and consumption as they relate to your results.

   b. Repeat part (a) for the four quarters of 2005, and again for the period from 2008:Q3 to 2009:Q2. Comment on the relationships among house prices, stock prices, net wealth of households, and consumption as they relate to your results, before and during the crisis.

   c. How do the current household data compare to the data from the period prior to the financial crisis, and during the crisis? Do you think the current data are indicative of a bubble?

2. Go to the St. Louis Federal Reserve FRED database, and find data on corporate net worth of nonfinancial businesses (TNWMVBSNNCB), private domestic investment (GPDIC1), and a measure of financial frictions, the St. Louis Fed financial stress index (STLFSI). For all three measures, be sure to convert the *frequency* setting to "Quarterly." Download the data into a spreadsheet, and make sure the data align correctly with the appropriate dates. For corporate net worth and private domestic investment, calculate the annualized growth rates from quarter to quarter. To do this, take the current-period data minus the previous-quarter data, then divide by the

previous quarter data. Multiply by 100 to change the results to percentage form, and then multiply by 4 to annualize the data.

a. Calculate the average growth rates over the most recent four quarters of data available for the corporate net worth and private domestic investment variables. Calculate the difference between the value of the stress index during the most recent quarter and the value of the stress index one year earlier. Comment on the relationships among financial stress, net wealth of corporate businesses, and private domestic investment.

b. Repeat part (a) for the four quarters of 2005 and for the period from 2008:Q3 to 2009:Q2.

Comment on the relationships among financial stress, net wealth of corporate businesses, and private domestic investment before and during the crisis as they relate to your results. Assuming the financial stress measure is indicative of heightened asymmetric information problems, comment on how the crisis-period data relate to the typical dynamics of a financial crisis.

c. How do the current investment data compare to the data for the period prior to the financial crisis, and during the crisis? Do you think the current data are indicative of a bubble?

WEB EXERCISES

1. This chapter discusses how an understanding of adverse selection and moral hazard can help us better understand financial crises. The greatest financial crisis faced by the United States was the Great Depression of 1929–1933. Go to http://www.amatecon.com/greatdepression.html. This site contains a brief discussion of the factors that led to the Great Depression. Write a one-page summary explaining how adverse selection and moral hazard contributed to the Great Depression.

2. Go to the International Monetary Fund's Financial Crisis page at http://www.imf.org/external/np/exr/key/finstab.htm. Report on the three countries that most recently received emergency loans from the IMF in response to a financial crisis. According to the IMF, what caused the crisis in each country?

3. One of the countries hardest hit by the global financial crisis of 2008 was Iceland. Go to http://assets.opencrs.com/rpts/RS22988_20081120.pdf and summarize the causes and events that led to the crisis in Iceland.

WEB REFERENCES

http://www.amatecon.com/gd/gdtimeline.html

A time line of the Great Depression.

http://assets.opencrs.com/rpts/RS22988_20081120.pdf

The Congressional Research Service (CRS) report to Congress about Iceland's financial crisis of 2008.

http://freerepublic.com/focus/f-news/2167257/posts

Paper by Carmen Reinhart and Kenneth Rogoff comparing the 2007 subprime crisis to other international crises.

WEB CHAPTER

Please visit the Companion Website at http://www.pearsonhighered.com/mishkin to read Web Chapter 1.

Web Chapter 1: **Financial Crises in Emerging Market Economies**

Central Banking and the Conduct of Monetary Policy

Crisis and Response: The Federal Reserve and the Global Financial Crisis

When the Federal Reserve was confronted with what former Chairman Alan Greenspan described as a "once-in-a-century credit tsunami," it resolved to come to the rescue. Starting in September 2007, the Federal Reserve lowered the federal funds rate target, bringing it down to zero by the end of 2008. At the same time, the Fed implemented large liquidity injections into the credit markets to encourage them to lend again. In mid-August 2007, the Fed lowered the discount rate at which it lent to banks to just 50 basis points above the federal funds rate target, from the normal 100 basis points. Over the course of the crisis, the Fed broadened its provision of liquidity to the financial system well outside its traditional lending to depository institutions. Indeed, after the Fed made loans to assist in the takeover of Bear Stearns by J.P. Morgan in March 2008, Paul Volcker, a former chairman of the Federal Reserve, described the Fed's actions as going to the "very edge of its lawful and implied powers." The number of new Fed lending programs over the course of the crisis spawned a whole new set of acronyms—TAF, TSLF, PDCF, AMLF, CPFF, and MMIFF—making the Fed sound like the Pentagon with code-named initiatives and weapons. Like the Pentagon, the Fed was fighting a war, although its weapons were financial rather than guns, tanks, or aircraft.

The recent global financial crisis demonstrated the importance of central banks like the Federal Reserve to the health of the financial system and the economy. Chapter 13 outlines what central banks are trying to achieve, what motivates them, and how they are set up. Chapter 14 describes how the money supply is determined. In Chapter 15, we look at the tools that central banks like the Fed have at their disposal and how they use them. Chapter 16 extends the discussion of the conduct of monetary policy to focus on the broader picture of central banks' strategies and tactics.

13 Central Banks and the Federal Reserve System

Learning Objectives

- Recognize the historical context of the development of the Federal Reserve System.
- Describe the key features and functions of the Federal Reserve System.
- Assess the degree of independence of the Federal Reserve.
- Summarize the arguments for and against the independence of the Federal Reserve.
- Identify the ways in which the theory of bureaucratic behavior can help explain Federal Reserve actions.
- Identify the similarities and distinctions in structure and independence between the European Central Bank and the Federal Reserve.
- Assess the degree of independence of other major central banks around the world.

Preview

Among the most important players in financial markets throughout the world are central banks, the government authorities in charge of monetary policy. Central banks' actions affect interest rates, the amount of credit available, and the money supply, all of which have direct impacts not only on financial markets but also on aggregate output and inflation. To understand the role that central banks play in financial markets and the overall economy, we need to understand how these organizations work. Who controls central banks and determines their actions? What motivates their behavior? Who holds the reins of power?

In this chapter, we look at the institutional structure of major central banks and focus particularly on the Federal Reserve System, one of the most important central banks in the world. We start by examining the elements of the Fed's institutional structure that determine where the true power within the Federal Reserve System lies. By understanding who makes the decisions, we will have a better idea of how they are made. We then examine the reasons behind central bank behavior and whether it is a good idea to make central banks independent by insulating them from politicians. Finally, we look at the structure and independence of other major central banks, particularly the European Central Bank. With this context in place, we will be prepared to comprehend the actual conduct of monetary policy described in the following chapters.

ORIGINS OF THE FEDERAL RESERVE SYSTEM

Of all the central banks in the world, the Federal Reserve System probably has the most unusual structure. To understand how this structure arose, we must go back to before 1913, when the Federal Reserve System was created.

Before the twentieth century, a major characteristic of American politics was the fear of centralized power, as seen in the checks and balances provisions of the Constitution and the preservation of states' rights. This fear of centralized power was one source of American resistance to the establishment of a central bank. Another source was the traditional American distrust of moneyed interests, the most prominent symbol of which was a central bank. The open hostility of the American public to the existence of a central bank resulted in the demise of the first two experiments in central banking, whose function it was to police the banking system: The First Bank of the United States was disbanded in 1811, and the national charter of the Second Bank of the United States expired in 1836 after its renewal was vetoed in 1832 by President Andrew Jackson.

Inside the Fed   The Political Genius of the Founders of the Federal Reserve System

The history of the United States has been one of public hostility to banks and especially to a central bank. How were the politicians who founded the Federal Reserve able to design a system that has become one of the most prestigious institutions in the United States?

The answer is that the founders recognized that if power was too concentrated in either Washington, DC, or New York, two cities that many Americans loved to hate, an American central bank might not have enough public support to operate effectively. They thus decided to set up a decentralized system with twelve Federal Reserve Banks spread throughout the country, to make sure that all regions of the country were represented in monetary policy deliberations. In addition, they made the Federal Reserve Banks quasi-private institutions overseen by directors from the private sector living in each district. These directors would represent the views of their individual regions and would be in close contact with the president of their Federal Reserve Bank. The unusual structure of the Federal Reserve System ensured that regional issues would be addressed, as is evident in Federal Reserve Bank publications. Without this unusual structure, the Federal Reserve System might have been far less popular with the public, making the institution far less effective.

The termination of the Second Bank's national charter in 1836 created a severe problem for American financial markets because there was no lender of last resort that could provide reserves to the banking system in order to avert a bank panic. Hence, in the nineteenth and early twentieth centuries, nationwide bank panics became a regular event, occurring every twenty years or so, culminating in the panic of 1907. The 1907 panic resulted in such widespread bank failures and such substantial losses to depositors that the public was finally convinced that a central bank was needed to prevent future panics.

The hostility of the American public to banks and centralized authority meant great opposition to the establishment of a single central bank like the Bank of England. Fear was rampant that the moneyed interests on Wall Street (including the largest corporations and banks) would be able to manipulate such an institution to gain control over the economy, and that federal operation of the central bank might result in too much government intervention in the affairs of private banks. Serious disagreements existed over whether the central bank should be a private bank or a government institution. Because of the heated debates on these issues, a compromise was struck. In the great American tradition, Congress wrote an elaborate system of checks and balances into the Federal Reserve Act of 1913, which created the Federal Reserve System with its twelve regional Federal Reserve Banks (see the Inside the Fed box, "The Political Genius of the Founders of the Federal Reserve System").

STRUCTURE OF THE FEDERAL RESERVE SYSTEM

The writers of the Federal Reserve Act wanted to diffuse power along regional lines, between the private sector and the government, and among bankers, business people, and the public. This initial diffusion of power resulted in the evolution of the Federal Reserve System to include the following entities: the **Federal Reserve Banks**, the **Board of Governors of the Federal Reserve System**, the **Federal Open Market**

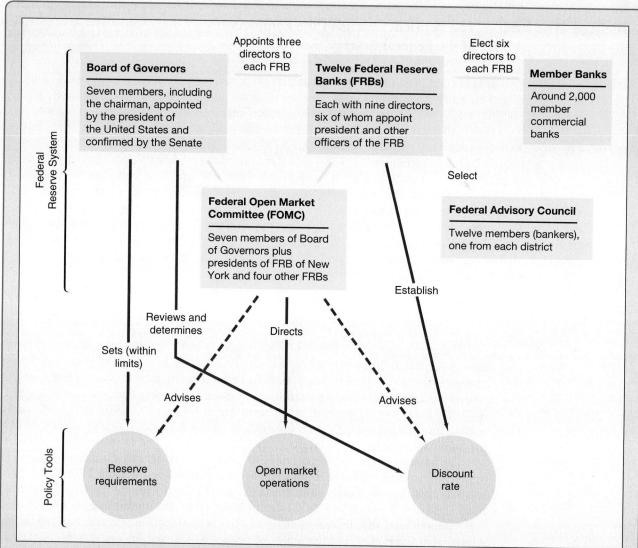

FIGURE 1 **Structure and Responsibility for Policy Tools in the Federal Reserve System**

The relationships of the Federal Reserve Banks, the Board of Governors of the Federal Reserve System, and the FOMC to the three policy tools of the Fed (open market operations, the discount rate, and reserve requirements). Dashed lines indicate that the FOMC "advises" on the setting of reserve requirements and the discount rate.

Committee (FOMC), the Federal Advisory Council, and around 2,000 member commercial banks. Figure 1 outlines the relationships of these entities to one another and to the three policy tools of the Fed (open market operations, the discount rate, and reserve requirements), discussed in Chapters 14 and 15.

Federal Reserve Banks

Each of the twelve Federal Reserve districts defined by the Federal Reserve Act of 1913 has one main Federal Reserve Bank, which may have branches in other cities in the

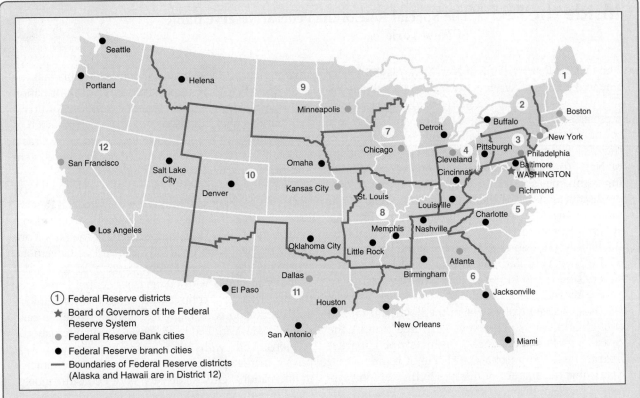

FIGURE 2 **Federal Reserve System**
The locations of the Federal Reserve districts, the Federal Reserve Banks, and their branches.
Source: Federal Reserve *Bulletin.*

district. The locations of these districts, the Federal Reserve Banks, and the Federal Reserve Bank branches are shown in Figure 2. The three largest Federal Reserve Banks in terms of assets are those of New York, Chicago, and San Francisco—combined, they hold more than 50% of the assets (discount loans, securities, and other holdings) of the Federal Reserve System. The New York bank, with around one-quarter of the assets, is the most important of the Federal Reserve Banks (see the Inside the Fed box, "The Special Role of the Federal Reserve Bank of New York").

Each of the Federal Reserve Banks is a quasi-public (part private, part government) institution owned by the private commercial banks in its district that are members of the Federal Reserve System. These member banks have purchased stock in their district Federal Reserve Bank (a requirement of membership), and the dividends paid by that stock are limited by law to 6% annually. The member banks elect six directors for each district bank; three more are appointed by the Board of Governors.

The directors of a district bank are classified into three categories: A, B, and C. The three A directors (elected by the member banks) are professional bankers, and the three B directors (also elected by the member banks) are prominent leaders from industry, labor, agriculture, or the consumer sector. The three C directors, who are appointed by the Board of Governors to represent the public interest, are not allowed to be officers, employees, or stockholders of banks.

Inside the Fed   The Special Role of the Federal Reserve Bank of New York

The Federal Reserve Bank of New York plays a special role in the Federal Reserve System for several reasons. First, its district contains many of the largest commercial banks in the United States, the safety and soundness of which are paramount to the health of the U.S. financial system. The Federal Reserve Bank of New York conducts examinations of bank holding companies and state-chartered member banks in its district, making it the supervisor of some of the most important financial institutions in our financial system. Not surprisingly, given this responsibility, the bank supervision group is one of the largest units of the New York Fed and is by far the largest bank supervision group in the Federal Reserve System.

The second reason for the New York Fed's special role is its active involvement in the bond and foreign exchange markets. The New York Fed houses the open market desk, which conducts open market operations—the purchase and sale of bonds—that determine the amount of reserves in the banking system. Because of this involvement in the Treasury securities market, as well as its walking-distance location near the New York Stock Exchange, the officials at the Federal Reserve Bank of New York are in constant contact with the major domestic financial markets in the United States. In addition, the Federal Reserve Bank of New York houses the foreign exchange desk, which conducts foreign exchange interventions on behalf of the Federal Reserve System and the U.S. Treasury. Its

involvement in these financial markets means that the New York Fed is an important source of information on what is happening in domestic and foreign financial markets, particularly during crisis periods such as the recent subprime mortgage meltdown, as well as a liaison between officials in the Federal Reserve System and private participants in the markets.

The third reason for the Federal Reserve Bank of New York's prominence is that it is the only Federal Reserve Bank to be a member of the Bank for International Settlements (BIS). Thus the president of the New York Fed, along with the chair of the Board of Governors, represents the Federal Reserve System in its regular monthly meetings with other major central bankers at the BIS. This close contact with foreign central bankers and interaction with foreign exchange markets means that the New York Fed has a special role in international relations, both with other central bankers and with private market participants. Adding to its prominence in international circles, the New York Fed is the repository for more than $100 billion of the world's gold, an amount greater than the gold at Fort Knox.

Finally, the president of the Federal Reserve Bank of New York is the only permanent voting member of the FOMC among the Federal Reserve Bank presidents, serving as the vice-chair of the committee. Thus he or she and the chair and vice-chair of the Board of Governors are the three most important officials in the Federal Reserve System.

The directors oversee the activities of the district bank, but their most important job is to appoint the president of the bank (subject to the approval of the Board of Governors). Up until 2010, all nine directors participated in this decision, but the Dodd-Frank legislation passed in July 2010 excluded the three class A directors from involvement in choosing the president of the bank. Congress viewed it as inappropriate for bankers to be involved in choosing the president of the Federal Reserve Bank that would have supervisory oversight of these same banks.

The twelve Federal Reserve Banks are involved in monetary policy in several ways:

- Their directors legally "establish" the discount rate (although the discount rate is in practice set at a fixed amount over the federal funds rate target).
- They decide which banks, member and nonmember alike, can obtain discount loans from the Federal Reserve Bank.

- Their directors select one commercial banker from each bank's district to serve on the Federal Advisory Council, which consults with the Board of Governors and provides information that helps in the conduct of monetary policy.
- Five of the twelve bank presidents each have a vote on the Federal Open Market Committee, which directs **open market operations** (the purchase and sale of government securities that affect both interest rates and the amount of reserves in the banking system). As explained in the Inside the Fed box, "The Special Role of the Federal Reserve Bank of New York," because the president of the New York Fed is a permanent member of the FOMC, he or she always has a vote on the FOMC, making the New York Fed the most important of all the banks; the other four votes allocated to the district banks rotate annually among the remaining eleven presidents.

The twelve Federal Reserve Banks also perform the following functions:

- Clear checks
- Issue new currency and withdraw damaged currency from circulation
- Administer and make discount loans to banks in their districts
- Evaluate proposed mergers and applications for banks to expand their activities
- Act as liaisons between the business community and the Federal Reserve System
- Examine bank holding companies and state-chartered member banks
- Collect data on local business conditions
- Use their staffs of professional economists to research topics related to the conduct of monetary policy

Member Banks

All *national banks* (commercial banks chartered by the Office of the Comptroller of the Currency) are required to be members of the Federal Reserve System. Commercial banks chartered by the states are not required to be members, but they can choose to join. Currently, about a third of the commercial banks in the United States are members of the Federal Reserve System, having declined from a peak figure of 49% in 1947.

Before 1980, only member banks were required to keep reserves as deposits at the Federal Reserve Banks. Nonmember banks were subject to reserve requirements determined by their states, which typically allowed them to hold much of their reserves in interest-bearing securities. Because at the time no interest was paid on reserves deposited at the Federal Reserve Banks, it was costly to be a member of the system, and as interest rates rose, the relative cost of membership rose, and more and more banks left the system.

This decline in Fed membership was a major concern of the Board of Governors; one reason was that it lessened the Fed's control over the money supply, making it more difficult for the Fed to conduct monetary policy. The chair of the Board of Governors repeatedly called for new legislation requiring all commercial banks to be members of the Federal Reserve System. One result of the Fed's pressure on Congress was a provision in the Depository Institutions Deregulation and Monetary Control Act of 1980: All depository institutions became subject (by 1987) to the same requirements to keep deposits at the Fed, so member and nonmember banks would be on equal footing in terms of reserve requirements. In addition, all depository institutions were given equal access to the Federal Reserve facilities, such as the discount window (discussed in Chapter 15) and Fed check clearing. These provisions ended the decline in Fed membership and reduced the distinction between member and nonmember banks.

Board of Governors of the Federal Reserve System

At the head of the Federal Reserve System is the seven-member Board of Governors, headquartered in Washington, DC. Each governor is appointed by the president of the United States and confirmed by the Senate. To limit the president's control over the Fed and insulate the Fed from other political pressures, the governors can each serve one full, nonrenewable, fourteen-year term plus part of another term, with one governor's term expiring every other January.[1] The governors (many are professional economists) are required to come from different Federal Reserve districts, so that the interests of one particular region of the country are not overrepresented. The chair of the Board of Governors is chosen from among the seven governors and serves a four-year, renewable term. It is expected that once a new chair is chosen, the old chair will resign from the Board of Governors, even if many years are left in his or her term as a governor.

The Board of Governors is actively involved in the conduct of monetary policy in the following ways:

- All seven governors are members of the FOMC and vote on the conduct of open market operations. Because only twelve voting members are on this committee (seven governors and five presidents of the district banks), the Board has the majority of the votes.
- It sets reserve requirements (within limits imposed by legislation).
- It effectively controls the fixed amount by which the discount rate exceeds the federal funds rate target by means of the "review and determination" process, whereby it approves or disapproves the discount rate "established" by the Federal Reserve Banks.
- The chair of the Board advises the president of the United States on economic policy, testifies in Congress, and speaks on behalf of the Federal Reserve System to the media.

Through legislation, the Board of Governors has often been given duties not directly related to the conduct of monetary policy, which are as follows:

- Sets margin requirements, the fraction of the purchase price of securities that must be paid for with cash rather than borrowed funds
- Sets the salary of the president and all officers of each Federal Reserve Bank, and reviews each bank's budget
- Approves bank mergers and applications for new activities, specifies the permissible activities of bank holding companies, and supervises the activities of foreign banks in the United States
- Hires a staff of professional economists (larger than the staffs of individual Federal Reserve Banks) who provide economic analysis that the Board of Governors then uses in making its decisions (see the Inside the Fed box, "The Role of the Research Staff")

Federal Open Market Committee (FOMC)

The FOMC usually meets eight times a year (about every six weeks) and makes decisions regarding the conduct of open market operations and the setting of the policy interest rate, the **federal funds rate**, which is the interest rate on overnight loans from

---

[1]Although technically the governor's term is nonrenewable, a governor can resign just before his or her term expires and then be reappointed by the president. This explains how one governor, William McChesney Martin, Jr., served for 28 years. Since Martin, the chair from 1951 to 1970, retired from the board in 1970, the practice of allowing a governor to, in effect, serve a second full term has been eliminated, and this is why Alan Greenspan had to retire from the Board after his fourteen-year term expired in 2006.

Inside the Fed   The Role of the Research Staff

The Federal Reserve System is the largest employer of economists not just in the United States, but in the world. The system's research staff has approximately 1,000 people, about half of whom are economists. Of these 500 economists, about 250 are at the Board of Governors, 100 are at the Federal Reserve Bank of New York, and the remainder are at the other Federal Reserve Banks. What do all these economists do?

The most important task of the Fed's economists is to follow the incoming economic data from government agencies and private sector organizations and provide guidance to the policymakers on the direction in which the economy might be headed and the potential impact of monetary policy actions on the economy. Before each FOMC meeting, the research staff of each Federal Reserve Bank briefs its president and the senior management of the bank on the staff's forecast for the U.S. economy and the issues that are likely to be discussed at the meeting. The research staff also provides briefing materials or a formal briefing on the economic outlook for the bank's region, something that each president discusses at the FOMC meeting. Meanwhile, at the Board of Governors, economists maintain a large econometric model (a model whose equations are estimated using statistical procedures) that helps them produce their forecasts of the national economy, and they, too, brief the governors on the national economic outlook.

The research staffers at the banks and the Board also provide support to the bank supervisory staff by tracking developments in the banking sector and other financial markets and institutions, and by supplying bank examiners with the technical advice they might need in the course of their examinations. Because the Board of Governors has to decide whether to approve bank mergers, the research staffs at both the Board and the bank in whose district the merger is to take place prepare information on the possible effects of the proposed merger on the competitive environment. To ensure compliance with the Community Reinvestment Act, economists also analyze a bank's performance regarding its lending activities in different communities.

Because of the increased influence of developments in foreign countries on the U.S. economy, members of the research staff, particularly those at the New York Fed and the Board, produce reports on the major foreign economies. They also conduct research on developments in the foreign exchange market because of its growing importance in the monetary policy process and to support the activities of the foreign exchange desk. Economists help support the operation of the open market desk by projecting reserve growth and the growth of monetary aggregates.

Staff economists also engage in basic research on the effects of monetary policy on output and inflation, developments in the labor markets, international trade, international capital markets, banking and other financial institutions, financial markets, and the regional economy, among other topics. This research is published widely in academic journals and in Reserve Bank publications. (Federal Reserve Bank reviews are a good source of supplemental material for money and banking students.) Another important activity of the research staff, primarily at the Reserve Banks, is public education. Staff economists are called on frequently to make presentations to the boards of directors at their banks or to make speeches to the public in their districts.

one bank to another. (Details on how the FOMC meeting is conducted are discussed in the Inside the Fed box, "The FOMC Meeting," and the documents produced for the meeting are described in the second Inside the Fed box, "Green, Blue, Teal, and Beige: What Do These Colors Mean at the Fed?") Indeed, the FOMC is often referred to as the "Fed" in the press. For example, when the media report that the Fed is meeting, they actually mean that the FOMC is meeting. The committee consists of the seven members of the Board of Governors, the president of the Federal Reserve Bank of New York, and

Inside the Fed   The FOMC Meeting

The FOMC meeting takes place in the boardroom on the second floor of the main building of the Board of Governors in Washington, DC. The seven governors and the twelve Reserve Bank presidents, along with the secretary of the FOMC, the Board's director of the Research and Statistics Division and his or her deputy, and the directors of the Monetary Affairs and International Finance Divisions, sit around a massive conference table. Although only five of the Reserve Bank presidents have voting rights on the FOMC at any given time, all actively participate in the deliberations. Seated around the sides of the room are the directors of research for each of the Reserve Banks and other senior board and Reserve Bank officials, who, by tradition, do not speak at the meeting.

The meeting starts with a quick approval of the minutes of the previous meeting of the FOMC. The first substantive agenda item is the report by the manager of system open market operations on foreign currency and domestic open market operations, and other issues related to these topics. After the governors and Reserve Bank presidents finish asking questions and discussing these reports, a vote is taken to ratify them.

The next stage of the meeting is a presentation of the Board staff's national economic forecast by the director of the Research and Statistics Division of the Board. After the governors and Reserve Bank presidents have queried the division director about the forecast, the *go-round* occurs: Each bank president presents an overview of economic conditions in his or her district and the bank's assessment of the national outlook, and each governor, including the chair, gives a view of the national outlook. By tradition, remarks avoid the topic of monetary policy at this time.

The agenda then turns to current monetary policy and the domestic policy directive. The Board's director of the Monetary Affairs Division leads off the discussion by outlining the different scenarios for monetary policy actions and may describe an issue relating to

how monetary policy should be conducted. After a question-and-answer period, each of the FOMC members, as well as the nonvoting bank presidents, expresses his or her views on monetary policy and on the monetary policy statement. The chair then summarizes the discussion and proposes specific wording for the monetary policy statement and the directive on the federal funds rate target transmitted to the open market desk, indicating whether the federal funds rate target is to be raised or lowered, say, by 1/4 of a percentage point, or to be left unchanged. The secretary of the FOMC formally reads the proposed statement, and the members of the FOMC vote.[*]

An informal buffet lunch follows, during which, while eating, the participants hear a presentation on the latest developments in Congress on banking legislation and other legislation relevant to the Federal Reserve. At 2:15 p.m., a public announcement is made about the outcome of the meeting: whether the federal funds rate target and discount rate have been raised, lowered, or left unchanged; and an assessment of the "balance of risks" in the future, whether toward higher inflation or a weaker economy. The postmeeting announcement is an innovation initiated in 1994. Before that year, no such announcement was ever made, and the markets had to guess what policy action had been taken. The decision to announce this information was a step in the direction of greater openness by the Fed. A further step in this direction started in April 2011: After the FOMC meetings in April, June, November, and January, the chair of the Federal Reserve gives a press conference in which he or she briefs the press about the FOMC decisions.

---

[*]The decisions expressed in the directive may not be unanimous, and the dissenting views are made public. However, except in extremely rare cases, the chair's vote is always on the winning side.

[†]Half of the meetings have a somewhat different format. Rather than starting on Tuesday morning at 9:00 a.m. like the other meetings, they start in the afternoon on Tuesday and go over into Wednesday, with the usual announcement around 2:15 p.m. In addition to the usual concerns, these longer meetings also consider the longer-term economic outlook and other special topics.

Inside the Fed   Green, Blue, Teal, and Beige: What Do These Colors Mean at the Fed?

Three research documents play an important role in the monetary policy process and at Federal Open Market Committee meetings. Up until 2010, a detailed national forecast for the next three years, generated by the Federal Reserve Board of Governors' Research and Statistics Division, was placed between green covers and was thus known as the "green book." Projections for the monetary aggregates prepared by the Monetary Affairs Division of the Board of Governors, along with typically three alternative scenarios for the stance of monetary policy (labeled A, B, and C), were contained in the "blue book" in blue covers. Both books were distributed to all participants in FOMC meetings. Starting in 2010, the green and blue books were combined into the "teal book" with teal covers: Teal is a combination of green and blue.[*] The "beige book," with beige covers, is produced by the Reserve Banks and details evidence gleaned either from surveys or from talks with key businesses and financial institutions on the state of the economy in each of the Federal Reserve districts. This is the only one of the three books that is distributed publicly, and it often receives a lot of attention in the press.

[*]These FOMC documents are made public after five years, and their contents can be found at http://www.federalreserve.gov/monetarypolicy/fomc_historical.htm.

the presidents of four other Federal Reserve Banks. The chair of the Board of Governors also presides as the chair of the FOMC. Even though only the presidents of five of the Federal Reserve Banks are voting members of the FOMC, the other seven presidents of the district banks attend FOMC meetings and participate in discussions. Hence they have some input into the committee's decisions.

Because in the past open market operations were the most important policy tool the Fed had for controlling the money supply, and because it is where decisions about **tightening of monetary policy** (a rise in the federal funds rate) or **easing of monetary policy** (a lowering of the federal funds rate) are made, the FOMC is necessarily the focal point for policymaking in the Federal Reserve System. Although reserve requirements and the discount rate are not actually set by the FOMC, decisions in regard to these policy tools are effectively made there, and this is why Figure 1 includes dashed lines indicating that the FOMC "advises" on the setting of reserve requirements and the discount rate. The FOMC does not actually carry out securities purchases or sales. Instead, it issues directives to the trading desk at the Federal Reserve Bank of New York, where the manager for domestic open market operations supervises a roomful of people who execute the purchases and sales of the government or agency securities. The manager communicates daily with the FOMC members and their staffs concerning the activities of the trading desk.

Why the Chair of the Board of Governors Really Runs the Show

At first glance, the chair of the Board of Governors is just one of twelve voting members of the FOMC and has no legal authority to exercise control over this body. So why does the media pay so much attention to every word the chair speaks? Does the chair really call the shots at the Fed? If so, why does the chair have so much power?

The chair does indeed run the show. He or she is the spokesperson for the Fed and negotiates with Congress and the president of the United States. The chair also exercises control by setting the agenda of Board and FOMC meetings and by influencing the Board through the forces of stature and personality. Chairs of the Board of Governors (including Marriner S. Eccles, William McChesney Martin, Jr., Arthur Burns, Paul A. Volcker, Alan Greenspan, Ben Bernanke, and Janet Yellen) have typically had strong personalities and have wielded great power.

The chair also exercises power by supervising the Board's staff of professional economists and advisers. Because the staff gathers information for the Board and conducts the analyses the Board uses in its decisions, it has some influence over monetary policy. In addition, in the past, several appointments to the Board itself have come from within the ranks of its professional staff, making the chair's influence even farther-reaching and longer-lasting than a four-year term. The chair's style also matters, as suggested by the Inside the Fed box, "Styles of Federal Reserve Chairs: Bernanke and Yellen versus Greenspan."

Inside the Fed Styles of Federal Reserve Chairs: Bernanke and Yellen Versus Greenspan

Every Federal Reserve chair has a different style, and these styles affect how policy decisions are made at the Fed. There has been much discussion of how two recent chairs of the Fed, former chair Ben Bernanke and current chair Janet Yellen, differ from Alan Greenspan, who was the chair of the Federal Reserve Board for nineteen years, from 1987 until 2006.

Alan Greenspan dominated the Fed like no other prior Federal Reserve chair. His background was very different from that of Bernanke and Yellen, who spent most of the early parts of their careers in academia. Greenspan, a disciple of Ayn Rand, was a strong advocate for laissez-faire capitalism and headed a very successful economic consulting firm, Townsend-Greenspan. Greenspan was never an economic theorist, but rather was famous for immersing himself in the data—literally so, because he was known to review data in his bathtub at the beginning of the day—and often focused on rather obscure data series to come up with his forecasts. As a result, Greenspan did not rely exclusively on the Federal Reserve Board staff's forecast in making his policy decisions. A prominent example occurred during 1997, when the Board staff was forecasting a surge in inflation, which would have required a tightening of monetary policy. Yet Greenspan believed that inflation would not rise and convinced the FOMC not to tighten monetary policy. Greenspan proved to be right and was dubbed the "maestro" by the media.

Bernanke, on the other hand, before going to Washington as a governor of the Fed in 2002, and before becoming the chair of the Council of Economic Advisors in 2005 and the Fed chair in 2006, spent his entire career as a professor, first at Stanford University's Graduate School of Business and then in the Economics Department at Princeton University, where he became chair of the department. Similarly, Janet Yellen was a professor for twenty years at Harvard University and then at the University of California before working for the Federal Reserve System as a member of the Board of Governors from 1994–1997. She served as president of the Federal Reserve Bank of San Francisco from 2004–2010, and then as vice-chair of the Federal Reserve from 2010 to 2014. Because Bernanke and Yellen did not make their names as economic forecasters, the Board staff's forecast now plays a much greater role in decision making at the FOMC. In contrast to Greenspan, Bernanke and Yellen's backgrounds as top academic economists led them to focus on analytics in making their decisions. As a result, model simulations became important tools in guiding policy discussions.

The style of policy discussions also has changed with the more recent chairs. Greenspan exercised extensive control over the discussion at the FOMC. During the Greenspan era, the discussion was formal, with each participant speaking after being put on a list by the secretary of the FOMC. Under Bernanke and now Yellen, there is more give and take. Both chairs have encouraged so-called two-handed interventions. When a participant wants to go out of turn to ask a question or make a point about something another participant has just said, he or she raises two hands and is then acknowledged by the chair and called on to speak.

The order of the discussion at the FOMC has also changed, in a very subtle but extremely important way. Under Greenspan, after the other FOMC participants had expressed their views on the economy, Greenspan would present his views on the state of the economy and then make a recommendation regarding the course of monetary policy action. This protocol required the other participants to just agree or disagree with Greenspan's recommendation during the following round of discussion about monetary policy. In contrast, Bernanke usually did not, and Yellen usually does not, make a recommendation for the course of monetary policy immediately after the other FOMC participants have expressed their views on the economy. Instead, they would summarize what they had heard from the other participants, make some comments of their own, and then wait until after

they had heard the views of all the other participants before making a monetary policy recommendation. Under Greenspan's process, the chair was pretty much making the decision about policy, whereas Bernanke did, and Yellen does, favor procedures that are more democratic and enable participants to have greater influence over the chair's vote.

Another big difference in the chairs' styles is in terms of transparency. Greenspan was famous for being obscure, and even quipped at a Congressional hearing, "I guess I should warn you, if I turn out to be particularly clear, you've probably misunderstood what I've said." Bernanke and Yellen, on the other hand, try to be particularly clear speakers. Although advances in transparency were made under Greenspan, he adopted more transparent communication only reluctantly. Bernanke and Yellen have been much stronger supporters of transparency. They have advocated that the Fed announce its inflation objective (see Chapter 16) and have launched major initiatives in an effort to increase Fed transparency (as discussed in the Inside the Fed box, "The Evolution of the Fed's Communication Strategy," on page 308).

HOW INDEPENDENT IS THE FED?

When we look, in the next three chapters, at how the Federal Reserve conducts monetary policy, we will want to know why the Fed decides to take certain policy actions but not others. To understand its actions, we must understand the incentives that motivate the Fed's behavior. How free is the Fed from presidential and congressional pressures? Do economic, bureaucratic, or political considerations guide it? Is the Fed truly independent of outside pressures?

Stanley Fischer, who was a professor at MIT and is now the vice-chair of the Federal Reserve, has defined two different types of independence of central banks: **instrument independence**, the ability of the central bank to set monetary policy instruments, and **goal independence**, the ability of the central bank to set the goals of monetary policy. The Federal Reserve has both types of independence and is remarkably free of the political pressures that influence other government agencies. Not only are the members of the Board of Governors appointed for a fourteen-year term (and so cannot be ousted from office), but also the term is technically not renewable, eliminating some of the incentive for the governors to curry favor with the president and Congress.

Probably even more important to its freedom from the whims of Congress is the Fed's independent and substantial source of revenue from its holdings of securities and, to a lesser extent, from its loans to banks. In 2013, for example, the Fed had net earnings after expenses of $79 billion—not a bad living if you can find it! Because it returns the bulk of these earnings to the Treasury, it does not get rich from its activities, but this income gives the Fed an important advantage over other government agencies: It is not subject to the appropriations process usually controlled by Congress. Indeed, the General Accounting Office, the auditing agency of the federal government, cannot audit the monetary policy or foreign exchange market functions of the Federal Reserve. Because the power to control the purse strings is usually synonymous with the power of overall control, this feature of the Federal Reserve System contributes to its independence more than any other factor.

Yet the Federal Reserve is still subject to the influence of Congress, because the legislation that structures it is written by Congress and is subject to change at any time. When legislators are upset with the Fed's conduct of monetary policy, they frequently threaten to weaken its independence. A recent example was a bill sponsored by Representative Ron Paul in 2009. The bill advocated subjecting the Fed's monetary policy actions to audits by the General Accounting Office (GAO). Threats like this are a powerful club to wield, and they certainly have some effect in keeping the Fed from straying too far from Congressional wishes.

Congress also has passed legislation to make the Federal Reserve more accountable for its actions. Under the Humphrey-Hawkins Act of 1978 and later legislation, the Federal Reserve is required to issue a *Monetary Policy Report to the Congress* semiannually, with accompanying testimony by the chair of the Board of Governors, to explain how the conduct of monetary policy is consistent with the objectives outlined by the Federal Reserve Act.

The president can also influence the Federal Reserve. Because Congressional legislation can affect the Fed directly or affect its ability to conduct monetary policy, the president can be a powerful ally through his influence on Congress. Second, although ostensibly a president might be able to appoint only one or two members to the Board of Governors during each presidential term, in actual practice the president appoints members far more often. One reason is that most governors do not serve out a full fourteen-year term. (Governors' salaries are substantially below the salaries they could earn in the private sector or even at universities, thus providing an incentive for them to return to academia or take private sector jobs before their term expires.) In addition, the president is able to appoint a new chair of the Board of Governors every four years, and a chair who is not reappointed is expected to resign from the board so that a new member can be appointed.

The power enjoyed by the president through his appointments to the Board of Governors is limited, however. Because the term of the chair is not necessarily concurrent with that of the president, a president may have to deal with a chair of the Board of Governors who was appointed by a previous administration. Alan Greenspan, for example, was appointed chair in 1987 by President Ronald Reagan and was reappointed to another term by a Republican president, George H. W. Bush, in 1992. When Bill Clinton, a Democrat, became president in 1993, Greenspan had several years left to his term. Clinton was put under tremendous pressure to reappoint Greenspan when his term expired, and did so in 1996 and again in 2000, even though Greenspan is a Republican.[2] George W. Bush, a Republican, then reappointed

---

[2]Similarly, William McChesney Martin, Jr., the chair from 1951 to 1970, was appointed by President Truman (Dem.) but was reappointed by Presidents Eisenhower (Rep.), Kennedy (Dem.), Johnson (Dem.), and Nixon (Rep.). Also, Paul Volcker, the chair from 1979 to 1987, was appointed by President Carter (Dem.) but was reappointed by President Reagan (Rep.). Ben Bernanke was appointed by President Bush (Rep.), but was reappointed by President Obama (Dem.).

Greenspan in 2004, while Barack Obama, a Democrat, reappointed Ben Bernanke, a Republican, in 2010.

You can see that the Federal Reserve has extraordinary independence for a government agency. Nonetheless, the Fed is not free from political pressures. Indeed, to understand the Fed's behavior, we must recognize that public support for the actions of the Federal Reserve plays a very important role in its decisions.[3]

SHOULD THE FED BE INDEPENDENT?

As we have seen, the Federal Reserve is probably the most independent government agency in the United States; central banks in most other countries are similarly independent. Every few years, the question arises in Congress whether the independence given the Fed should be curtailed. Politicians who strongly oppose a specific Fed policy often want to bring the Fed under their supervision, in order to impose a policy more to their liking. Should the Fed be independent, or would we be better off with a central bank under the control of the president or Congress?

The Case for Independence

The strongest argument for an independent central bank rests on the view that subjecting it to more political pressures would impart an inflationary bias to monetary policy. In the view of many observers, politicians in a democratic society are short-sighted because they are driven by the need to win their next election. With this as their primary goal, they are unlikely to focus on long-run objectives such as promoting a stable price level. Instead, they will seek short-run solutions to problems such as high unemployment and high interest rates, even if the short-run solutions have undesirable long-run consequences. For example, we saw in Chapter 5 that high money growth can lead initially to a drop in interest rates but might cause an increase later, as inflation heats up. Would a Federal Reserve under the control of Congress or the president be more likely to pursue a policy of excessive money growth when interest rates are high, even though such a policy would eventually lead to inflation and even higher interest rates in the future? The advocates of an independent Federal Reserve say yes. They believe that a politically insulated Fed is more likely to be concerned with long-run objectives and thus more likely to defend a sound dollar and a stable price level.

A variation on the preceding argument is that the political process in America could lead to a **political business cycle**, in which just before an election, expansionary policies are pursued to lower unemployment and interest rates. After the election, the bad effects of these policies—high inflation and high interest rates—come home to roost, requiring contractionary policies that politicians hope the public will forget before the next election. There is some evidence that such a political business cycle exists in the United States, and a Federal Reserve under the control of Congress or the president might make the cycle even more pronounced.

---

[3]To get a further inside view of how the Fed has interacted with the public and politicians, see Bob Woodward, *Maestro: Greenspan's Fed and the American Boom* (New York: Simon and Schuster, 2000) and David Wessel, *In Fed We Trust* (Random House: NY, 2009).

Putting the Fed under the control of the Treasury (and thus making it more subject to influence by the president) is also considered dangerous because the Fed can be used to facilitate Treasury financing of large budget deficits by its purchases of Treasury bonds.[4] Treasury pressure on the Fed to "help out" might lead to more inflation in the economy. An independent Fed is better able to resist this pressure from the Treasury.

Another argument for central bank independence is that control of monetary policy is too important to be left to politicians, a group that has repeatedly demonstrated a lack of expertise at making hard decisions on issues of great economic importance, such as reducing the budget deficit or reforming the banking system. This argument can also be stated in terms of the principal–agent problem discussed in Chapters 8, 10, and 12. Both the Federal Reserve and politicians are agents of the public (the principals), and both politicians and the Fed have incentives to act in their own interest rather than in the interest of the public. The argument supporting Federal Reserve independence is that the principal–agent problem is worse for politicians than for the Fed because politicians have fewer incentives to act in the public interest.

Indeed, some politicians prefer an independent Fed because it can be used as a public "whipping boy" to take some of the heat off their backs. It is possible that a politician who in private opposes an inflationary monetary policy will be forced to support such a policy in public for fear of not being reelected. An independent Fed can pursue policies that are politically unpopular yet ultimately in the public interest.

The Case Against Independence

Proponents of a Fed under the control of the president or Congress argue that it is undemocratic to have monetary policy (which affects almost everyone in the economy) controlled by an elite group responsible to no one. The current lack of accountability of the Federal Reserve has serious consequences: If the Fed performs badly, no provision is in place for replacing members (as there is with politicians). True, the Fed needs to pursue long-run objectives, but elected officials of Congress vote on long-run issues also (foreign policy, for example). If we push the argument further that policy is always performed better by elite groups like the Fed, we end up with such conclusions as "the Joint Chiefs of Staff should determine military budgets" or "the IRS should set tax policies with no oversight by the president or Congress." Would you advocate this degree of independence for the Joint Chiefs or the IRS?

The public holds the president and Congress responsible for the economic well-being of the country, yet it lacks control over the government agency that may well be the most important factor in determining the health of the economy. In addition, to achieve a cohesive program that will promote economic stability, monetary policy must be coordinated with fiscal policy (the management of government spending and taxation). Only by placing monetary policy under the control of the politicians who also control fiscal policy can these two policies be prevented from working at cross-purposes.

Another argument against Federal Reserve independence is that, historically, an independent Fed has not always used its freedom successfully. The Fed failed miserably in its stated role as lender of last resort during the Great Depression, and its independence certainly didn't prevent it from pursuing an overly expansionary monetary policy in the 1960s and 1970s that contributed to rapid inflation in this period.

---

[4]The Federal Reserve Act prohibited the Fed from buying Treasury bonds directly from the Treasury (except to roll over maturing securities); instead, the Fed buys Treasury bonds on the open market. One possible reason for this prohibition is consistent with the foregoing argument: The Fed would find it harder to facilitate Treasury financing of large budget deficits.

Our earlier discussion also suggests that the Federal Reserve is not immune from political pressures. Its independence may encourage it to pursue a course of narrow self-interest rather than actions that are in the public interest.

No consensus has yet been reached on whether central bank independence is a good thing, although public support for independence of the central bank seems to have been growing in both the United States and abroad. As you might expect, people who like the Fed's policies are more likely to support its independence, whereas those who dislike its policies advocate a less independent Fed.

Central Bank Independence and Macroeconomic Performance Throughout the World

We have seen that advocates of an independent central bank believe that macroeconomic performance will be improved by making the central bank more independent. Empirical evidence seems to support this conjecture: When central banks are ranked from least independent to most independent, inflation performance is found to be the best for countries with the most independent central banks. Although a more independent central bank appears to lead to a lower inflation rate, this is not achieved at the expense of poorer real economic performance. Countries with independent central banks are no more likely to have high unemployment or greater output fluctuations than countries with less independent central banks.

EXPLAINING CENTRAL BANK BEHAVIOR

One view of government bureaucratic behavior is that bureaucracies serve the public interest (this is called the *public interest view*). Yet some economists have developed a theory of bureaucratic behavior that emphasizes other factors that influence the operation of bureaucracies. The *theory of bureaucratic behavior* suggests that the objective of a bureaucracy is to maximize its own welfare, just as a consumer's behavior is motivated by the desire to maximize personal welfare and a firm's behavior is motivated by the desire to maximize profits. The welfare of a bureaucracy is related to its power and prestige. Thus this theory suggests that an important factor affecting a central bank's behavior is its wish to increase its power and prestige.

What predictions stem from this particular view of a central bank such as the Fed? One is that the Federal Reserve will fight vigorously to preserve its autonomy, a prediction verified time and time again as the Fed has continually counterattacked Congressional attempts to control its budget. In fact, it is extraordinary how effectively the Fed has been able to mobilize a lobby of bankers and business people to preserve its independence when threatened.

Another prediction is that the Federal Reserve will try to avoid conflict with powerful groups that might threaten to curtail its power and reduce its autonomy. Under this scenario, the Fed's behavior may take several forms. The Fed may be slow to increase interest rates and thus smooth out their fluctuations because it wishes to avoid a conflict with the president and Congress over increases in interest rates. The desire to avoid conflict with Congress and the president may also explain why, in the past, the Fed has not embraced transparency (see the Inside the Fed box, "The Evolution of the Fed's Communication Strategy").

Inside the Fed   The Evolution of the Fed's Communication Strategy

As the theory of bureaucratic behavior predicts, the Fed has incentives to hide its actions from the public and from politicians in order to avoid conflicts with them. In the past, this motivation led to a penchant for secrecy in the Fed. As one former Fed official remarked, "a lot of staffers would concede that [secrecy] is designed to shield the Fed from political oversight."[*] For example, the Fed once actively defended its delay in releasing FOMC directives to Congress and the public. However, as we learned, in 1994 it began to reveal the FOMC directive immediately after each FOMC meeting. In 1999, it also began to immediately announce the "bias" toward the direction in which monetary policy was likely to go, later expressed as the balance of risks in the economy. In 2002, the Fed started to report the roll call vote on the federal funds rate target taken at the FOMC meeting. In December 2004, it moved up the release date of the minutes of FOMC meetings from six weeks after the meeting (its previous policy) to three weeks after the meeting.

The Fed has dramatically increased its transparency in recent years, but was slower to do so than many other central banks. One important trend toward greater transparency is the announcement by a central bank of a specific numerical objective for inflation, often referred to as an inflation target, which will be discussed in Chapter 16. Alan Greenspan was strongly opposed to the Fed's moving in this direction, but former chair Ben Bernanke and present chair Janet Yellen, who was previously the chair of an internal Federal Reserve subcommittee that proposed new communication policies, are much more favorably disposed, having advocated the announcement of a specific numerical inflation objective in their writings and speeches.

In November of 2007, the Federal Reserve announced major enhancements to its communication strategy. First, the forecast horizon for the FOMC's projections under "appropriate policy" for inflation, unemployment, and GDP growth, which were mandated by the Humphrey-Hawkins legislation in 1978, was extended from two calendar years to three, with long-run projections added in 2009. In 2011, the Fed announced a further move toward increased transparency: After the FOMC meetings in April, June, November, and January, the chair of the Federal Reserve would give a press conference outlining the FOMC's decisions. The goal of the press conference would be to enhance the clarity and timeliness of the Federal Reserve's monetary policy communications.

In August of 2011, the Fed provided information on the anticipated target for the federal funds rate with an FOMC statement that "exceptionally low levels for the federal funds rate are likely to be warranted at least through" a specified date. Starting in January of 2012, the FOMC began to provide even more information about the future path of its policy interest rate by adding to its projections the FOMC participants' forecasts for the appropriate level of the target for the federal funds rate. At the same meeting, the FOMC adopted a numerical inflation objective of 2% in an effort to improve the control of inflation by anchoring inflation expectations more firmly.

In December of 2012, the FOMC disclosed that it would modify its target for the federal funds rate in the future by tying the rate to the state of the economy rather than by anticipating a particular date on which the rate would be set. Specifically, the FOMC stated that the federal funds rate would not be raised as long as the unemployment rate remained above 6½ percent and projected inflation one to two years in the future remained below a half percentage point above the Committee's 2 percent longer-run goal. The thresholds of a 6½% unemployment rate and a 2½% inflation rate were abandoned in March of 2014 when the unemployment rate fell to close to 6½%. At its March 2014 meeting, the FOMC indicated that it would assess the best time to raise the federal funds rate by taking into account "a wide range of information, including measures of labor market conditions, indicators of inflation pressures and inflation expectations, and readings on financial developments."

[*]Quoted in "Monetary Zeal: How the Federal Reserve Under Volcker Finally Slowed Down Inflation," *Wall Street Journal*, December 7, 1984, p. 23.

The Fed's desire to hold as much power as possible also explains why it vigorously pursued a campaign to gain control over more banks. The campaign culminated in legislation that expanded jurisdiction of the Fed's reserve requirements to *all* banks (not just the member commercial banks) by 1987.

The theory of bureaucratic behavior seems applicable to the Federal Reserve's actions, but we must recognize that this view of the Fed as being solely concerned with its own self-interest is too extreme. Maximizing one's own welfare does not rule out altruism. (You might give generously to a charity because it makes you feel good about yourself, but in the process you are helping a worthy cause.) The Fed is surely concerned with conducting monetary policy that is in the public interest. However, much uncertainty and disagreement often exist over what that monetary policy should be.[5] When it is unclear what policy will best serve the public interest, other motives may influence the Fed's behavior. In these situations, the theory of bureaucratic behavior can be a useful guide in predicting the motivation behind the actions of the Fed and other central banks.

STRUCTURE AND INDEPENDENCE OF THE EUROPEAN CENTRAL BANK

Until recently, the Federal Reserve had no rivals in terms of its importance in the central banking world. However, this situation changed in January 1999 with the full operational start-up of the European Central Bank (ECB) and European System of Central Banks (ESCB), which now conduct monetary policy for countries that are members of the European Monetary Union. These countries, taken together, have a population that exceeds that of the United States and a GDP comparable to that of the United States. The Maastricht Treaty, which established the ECB and ESCB, patterned these institutions after the Federal Reserve in that the central bank of each member country (referred to as *National Central Banks*, or *NCBs*) has a role similar to that of the Federal Reserve Banks. The European Central Bank, which is housed in Frankfurt, Germany, has an Executive Board that is similar in structure to the Board of Governors of the Federal Reserve; it is made up of the president, the vice president, and four other members, who are appointed to eight-year, nonrenewable terms. The Governing Council, which comprises the Executive Board and the presidents of the National Central Banks, is similar to the FOMC and makes the decisions on monetary policy. While the presidents of the National Central Banks are appointed by their countries' governments, the members of the Executive Board are appointed by a committee consisting of the heads of state of all of the countries that are part of the European Monetary Union.

Differences Between the European System of Central Banks and the Federal Reserve System

In the popular press, the European System of Central Banks is usually referred to as the European Central Bank (ECB), even though it would be more accurate to refer

---

[5]One example of the uncertainty over how best to conduct monetary policy was discussed in Chapter 3: Economists are not sure how to measure money. So even if economists agree that controlling the quantity of money is the appropriate way to conduct monetary policy (a controversial position, as we will see in later chapters), the Fed cannot be sure which monetary aggregate it should control.

to it as the *Eurosystem*, just as it would be more accurate to refer to the Fed as the Federal Reserve System. Although the structure of the Eurosystem is similar to that of the Federal Reserve System, some important differences distinguish the two. First, the budgets of the Federal Reserve Banks are controlled by the Board of Governors, whereas the National Central Banks control their own budgets *and* the budget of the ECB in Frankfurt. The ECB in the Eurosystem therefore has less power than does the Board of Governors in the Federal Reserve System. Second, the monetary operations of the Eurosystem are conducted by the National Central Banks in each country, so monetary operations are not centralized as they are in the Federal Reserve System. Third, in contrast to the Federal Reserve, the ECB is not involved in supervision and regulation of financial institutions; these tasks are left to the individual countries in the European Monetary Union.

Governing Council

Just as there is a focus on meetings of the FOMC in the United States, there is a similar focus in Europe on meetings of the Governing Council, which gathers monthly at the ECB in Frankfurt to make decisions on monetary policy. Currently, eighteen countries are members of the European Monetary Union, and the heads of the eighteen National Central Banks share fifteen votes on the Governing Council; each of the six Executive Board Members has one vote. In contrast to FOMC meetings, which are attended by staff from both the Board of Governors and the individual Federal Reserve Banks, only the twenty-four members of the Governing Council attend its meetings, with no staff present.

The Governing Council has decided that although its members have the legal right to vote, no formal vote will actually be taken; instead, the Council operates by consensus. One reason the Governing Council has decided not to take votes is because of worries that the casting of individual votes might lead the heads of National Central Banks to support a monetary policy that would be appropriate for their individual countries, but not necessarily for the countries of the European Monetary Union as a whole. This problem is less severe for the Federal Reserve: Although Federal Reserve Bank presidents do live in different regions of the country, all have the same nationality and are more likely to take a national view in monetary policy decisions rather than a regional view.

Just as the Federal Reserve releases the FOMC's decision on the setting of the policy interest rate (the federal funds rate) immediately after the meeting is over, the ECB does the same after the conclusion of the monthly Governing Council meeting (by announcing the target for a similar short-term interest rate for interbank loans). In addition, immediately after every monetary policy meeting of the Governing Council, the president and vice president of the ECB hold a press conference in which they take questions from the news media. (A similar press conference is held by the Federal Reserve chair, but it is less frequent, held only four times a year.) The large number of members in the Governing Council presents a particular dilemma. The current size of the Governing Council (twenty-four members) is substantially larger than that of the FOMC (twelve voting members). Many commentators have wondered whether the Governing Council is already too unwieldy—a situation that will get considerably worse as more countries join the European Monetary Union. To deal with this potential problem, the Governing Council decided on a complex system of rotation, somewhat like that of the FOMC, in which National Central Banks from the larger countries will vote more often than National Central Banks from the smaller countries.

How Independent Is the ECB?

Although the Federal Reserve is a highly independent central bank, the Maastricht Treaty, which established the Eurosystem, has made the latter the most independent central bank in the world. Like the Board of Governors, the members of the Executive Board have long terms (eight years), while heads of National Central Banks are required to serve for at least five years. Like the Fed, the Eurosystem determines its own budget, and the governments of the member countries are not allowed to issue instructions to the ECB. These elements of the Maastricht Treaty make the ECB highly independent.

The Maastricht Treaty specifies that the overriding, long-term goal of the ECB is price stability, which means that the goal of the Eurosystem is more clearly specified than it is for the Federal Reserve System. However, the Maastricht Treaty did not specify exactly what "price stability" means. The Eurosystem has defined the quantitative goal of monetary policy to be an inflation rate slightly less than 2%, so from this perspective, the ECB is slightly less goal-independent than the Fed. The Eurosystem is, however, much more goal-independent than the Federal Reserve System in one way: The Eurosystem's charter cannot be changed by legislation; it can be changed only by revision of the Maastricht Treaty—a difficult process because *all* signatories to the treaty must agree to accept any proposed change.

STRUCTURE AND INDEPENDENCE OF OTHER FOREIGN CENTRAL BANKS

Here we examine the structure and degree of independence of three other important foreign central banks: the Bank of Canada, the Bank of England, and the Bank of Japan.

Bank of Canada

Canada was late in establishing a central bank: The Bank of Canada was founded in 1934. Its directors are appointed by the government to three-year terms, and they appoint the governor, who serves a seven-year term. A governing council, consisting of the four deputy governors and the governor, is the policymaking body comparable to the FOMC that makes decisions about monetary policy.

The Bank Act was amended in 1967 to give the ultimate responsibility for monetary policy to the government. So, on paper, the Bank of Canada is not as instrument-independent as the Federal Reserve. In practice, however, the Bank of Canada does essentially control monetary policy. In the event of a disagreement between the bank and the government, the minister of finance can issue a directive that the bank must follow. However, because the directive must be in writing, and must be specific and applicable for a specified period, it would be subject to intense public scrutiny. As a result, it is unlikely that such a directive would be issued, and none has been to date. The goal for monetary policy, a target for inflation, is set jointly by the Bank of Canada and the government, so the Bank of Canada has less goal independence than the Fed.

Bank of England

Founded in 1694, the Bank of England is the second-oldest central bank (the Riksbank of Sweden is the oldest). The Bank Act of 1946 gave the government statutory authority over the Bank of England. The Court (equivalent to a board of directors) of the Bank of England is made up of the governor and two deputy governors, who are appointed for five-year terms, and sixteen non-executive directors, who are appointed for three-year terms.

Until 1997, the Bank of England was the least independent of the central banks examined in this chapter because the decision to raise or lower interest rates resided not within the Bank of England but with the Chancellor of the Exchequer (the equivalent of the U.S. Secretary of the Treasury). All of this changed when a new Labour government came to power in May of 1997 and the Chancellor of the Exchequer, Gordon Brown, made a surprise announcement that the Bank of England would henceforth have the power to set interest rates. However, the Bank was not granted total instrument independence: The government can overrule the Bank and set rates "in extreme economic circumstances" and "for a limited period." Nonetheless, as in Canada, overruling the Bank is likely to be a rare occurrence, because doing so would be highly public and is meant to occur only in highly unusual circumstances and for a limited time.

Because the United Kingdom is not a member of the European Monetary Union, the Bank of England makes its monetary policy decisions independently from the European Central Bank. The power to set interest rates resides with the Monetary Policy Committee, made up of the governor, two deputy governors, two members (normally central bank officials) appointed by the governor after consultation with the chancellor, plus four outside economic experts appointed by the chancellor. (Surprisingly, two of the four outside experts initially appointed to this committee were not British citizens—one was Dutch and the other American—and some later appointments have also not been British citizens, including the current governor, Mark Carney, who is Canadian.) The inflation target for the Bank of England is set by the Chancellor of the Exchequer, so the Bank of England is also less goal-independent than the Fed.

Bank of Japan

The Bank of Japan (Nippon Ginko) was founded in 1882 during the Meiji Restoration. Monetary policy is determined by the Bank's Policy Board, which is composed of the governor; two vice-governors; and six outside members appointed by the cabinet and approved by the parliament, all of whom serve for five-year terms.

Until recently, the Bank of Japan was not formally independent of the government, with the ultimate power residing with the Ministry of Finance. However, the Bank of Japan Law, which took effect in April 1998 and was the first major change in the relative power of the Bank of Japan in 55 years, changed this situation. In addition to stipulating that the objective of monetary policy is to attain price stability, the law granted greater instrument and goal independence to the Bank of Japan. Before this, the government had two voting members on the Policy Board, one from the Ministry of Finance and the other from the Economic Planning Agency. Now the government may send two representatives from these agencies to board meetings, but they no longer have voting rights, although they are allowed to request delays in monetary policy decisions. In addition, the Ministry of Finance lost its authority to oversee many operations of the Bank of Japan, particularly the right to dismiss senior officials. However, the Ministry of Finance continues to have control over the part of the Bank's budget that is unrelated to monetary policy. The recent episode in which Japan's new Abe government put pressure on the Bank of Japan to adopt a 2% inflation target, against the wishes of the Bank's current governor, who then resigned, suggests that the Bank of Japan's independence is limited.

The Trend Toward Greater Independence

As our survey of the structure and independence of the major central banks indicates, in recent years we have been seeing a remarkable trend toward increasing independence of central banks. It used to be that the Federal Reserve was substantially more independent than almost all other central banks, with the exception of those in Germany and Switzerland. Now, the newly established European Central Bank is far more independent than the Fed, and greater independence has been granted to central banks like the Bank of England and the Bank of Japan, putting them more on a par with the Fed, as well as to central banks in such diverse countries as New Zealand, Sweden, and the euro nations. Both theory and experience suggest that more independent central banks produce better monetary policy, thus providing an impetus for this trend.

SUMMARY

1. The Federal Reserve System was created in 1913 to lessen the frequency of bank panics. Because of public hostility to central banks and to the centralization of power in general, the Federal Reserve System was created with many checks and balances aimed at diffusing power.

2. The Federal Reserve System consists of twelve regional Federal Reserve Banks, around 2,000 member commercial banks, the Board of Governors of the Federal Reserve System, the Federal Open Market Committee (FOMC), and the Federal Advisory Council. Although on paper the Federal Reserve System appears to be decentralized, in practice it has come to function as a unified central bank controlled by the Board of Governors, especially the board's chair.

3. The Federal Reserve is more independent than most agencies of the U.S. government, but it is still subject to political pressures because the legislation that structures the Fed is written by Congress and can be changed at any time.

4. The case for an independent Federal Reserve rests on the view that curtailing the Fed's independence and subjecting it to more political pressures would impart an inflationary bias to monetary policy. An independent Fed can afford to take the long view and not respond to short-run problems, which would result in expansionary monetary policy and a political business cycle. The case against an independent Fed holds that it is undemocratic for monetary policy (so important to the public) to be controlled by an elite group that is not accountable to the public. An independent Fed also makes the coordination of monetary and fiscal policy difficult.

5. The theory of bureaucratic behavior suggests that one factor driving central banks' behavior might be their attempt to increase their power and prestige. This view explains many central bank actions, although central banks may also act in the public interest.

6. The European System of Central Banks has a similar structure to that of the Federal Reserve System, with each member country having a National Central Bank, and an Executive Board of the European Central Bank (located in Frankfurt, Germany). The Governing Council, which is made up of the six members of the Executive Board (which includes the president of the European Central Bank) and the presidents of the National Central Banks, makes the decisions on monetary policy. The Eurosystem, which was established under the terms of the Maastricht Treaty, is even more independent than the Federal Reserve System because its charter cannot be changed by legislation. Indeed, it is the most independent central bank in the world.

7. There has been a remarkable trend toward increasing independence of central banks throughout the world. Greater independence has been granted to central banks such as the Bank of England and the Bank of Japan in recent years, as well as to other central banks in such diverse countries as New Zealand and Sweden. Both theory and experience suggest that more independent central banks produce better monetary policy.

KEY TERMS

Board of Governors of the Federal Reserve System, p. 293

easing of monetary policy, p. 301

federal funds rate, p. 298

Federal Open Market Committee (FOMC), p. 293

Federal Reserve Banks, p. 293

goal independence, p. 303

instrument independence, p. 303

open market operations, p. 297

political business cycle, p. 305

tightening of monetary policy, p. 301

QUESTIONS

All questions are available in MyEconLab *at* http://www.myeconlab.com.

1. Why was the Federal Reserve System set up with twelve regional Federal Reserve Banks, rather than one central bank as in other countries?

2. Why is the Twelfth Federal Reserve district (San Francisco) so geographically large, while the Second Federal Reserve district (New York) is so small by comparison?

3. Should the Federal Reserve redraw its district boundaries, similar to the manner in which congressional districts are periodically realigned? Why or why not?

4. "The Federal Reserve System resembles the U.S. Constitution in that it was designed with many checks and balances." Is this statement true, false, or uncertain? Explain your answer.

5. Which entities in the Federal Reserve System control the discount rate? Reserve requirements? Open market operations?

6. In what ways can the regional Federal Reserve Banks influence the conduct of monetary policy?

7. Why is it important for the regional Federal Reserve Bank presidents to attend the FOMC meetings, even if they are nonvoting members?

8. Why is the New York Federal Reserve always a voting member of the FOMC?

9. The presidents of each of the district Federal Reserve Banks (including the New York Federal Reserve Bank) are currently not required to undergo a formal political appointment and approval process. Do you think this is appropriate? Why or why not?

10. Do you think that the fourteen-year, nonrenewable terms for governors effectively insulate the Board of Governors from political pressure?

11. Despite the important role played by the Board of Governors in setting monetary policy, seats to serve on the Board of Governors can sometimes be empty for several years. How might this happen?

12. How is the president of the United States able to exert influence over the Federal Reserve?

13. Why is it unlikely that the policy recommendation put forth by the chair of the Board of Governors would ever be voted down by the rest of the FOMC?

14. In what way does the Federal Reserve have a high degree of instrument independence? If it has a specific mandate from Congress to achieve "maximum employment and low, stable prices," then how does the Fed have goal independence?

15. The Fed is the most independent of all U.S. government agencies. What is the main difference between it and other government agencies that explains the Fed's greater independence?

16. What is the primary tool that Congress uses to exercise some control over the Fed?

17. Should the Federal Reserve be subject to periodic auditing of its policies, procedures, and finances? Why or why not?

18. In the 1960s and 1970s, the Federal Reserve System lost member banks at a rapid rate. How can the theory of bureaucratic behavior explain the Fed's campaign for legislation to require all commercial banks to become members? Was the Fed successful in this campaign?

19. "The theory of bureaucratic behavior indicates that the Fed never operates in the public interest." Is this statement true, false, or uncertain? Explain your answer.

20. Why might eliminating the Fed's independence lead to a more pronounced political business cycle?

21. "The independence of the Fed leaves it completely unaccountable for its actions." Is this statement true, false, or uncertain? Explain your answer.

22. "The independence of the Fed means that it takes the long view and not the short view." Is this statement true, false, or uncertain? Explain your answer.

23. The Fed promotes secrecy by not releasing the minutes of FOMC meetings to Congress or the public immediately. Discuss the arguments for and against this policy.

24. Which is more independent, the Federal Reserve or the European Central Bank? Why?

25. Why did the Bank of England up until 1997 have a low degree of independence?

DATA ANALYSIS PROBLEMS

The Problems update with real-time data in MyEconLab and are available for practice or instructor assignment.

 1. Go to the St. Louis Federal Reserve FRED database, and find data on the unemployment rate in each of the twelve Federal Reserve districts. These are coded as (D1URN), (D2URN), (D3URN), . . . , (D12URN). For the most recent month of data available, determine which district had the highest, and which had the lowest, unemployment rate.

 2. Go to the St. Louis Federal Reserve FRED database, and find data on the federal funds rate target (DFEDTAR, DFEDTARU, and DFEDTARL) and the discount, or primary credit rate (DPCREDIT). When was the last time the federal funds rate target was changed? When was the last time the primary credit rate was changed? Did the rates increase or decrease?

WEB EXERCISES

1. Go to http://www.federalreserve.gov/ and click on "About the Fed." Next click on "The Federal Reserve System" and then on "Structure." According to the Federal Reserve, what is the most important responsibility of the Board of Governors?

2. Go to the site listed in Web Exercise 1 and click on "Monetary Policy." Then click on "Reports" and go to the "beige book." According to the summary of the most recently published book, is the economy weakening or strengthening?

WEB REFERENCES

http://www.federalreserve.gov/pubs/frseries/frseri.htm

Information on the structure of the Federal Reserve System.

http://www.federalreserve.gov/otherfrb.htm

Addresses and phone numbers of Federal Reserve Banks, branches, and RCPCs, and links to the main pages of the twelve Reserve Banks and the Board of Governors.

http://www.federalreserve.gov/bios/boardmembership.htm

Lists all the members of the Board of Governors of the Federal Reserve since its inception.

http://www.federalreserve.gov/fomc

Find general information on the FOMC; its schedule of meetings, statements, minutes, and transcripts; information on its members; and the "beige book."

http://www.ecb.int

The website for the European Central Bank.

http://www.bank-banque-canada.ca/

The website for the Bank of Canada.

http://www.bankofengland.co.uk/index.htm

The website for the Bank of England.

http://www.boj.or.jp/en/index.htm

The website for the Bank of Japan.

14 The Money Supply Process

Learning Objectives

- List and describe the "three players" that influence the money supply.
- Classify the factors affecting the Federal Reserve's assets and liabilities.
- Identify the factors that affect the monetary base and discuss their effects on the Federal Reserve's balance sheet.
- Explain and illustrate the deposit creation process through T-accounts.
- List the factors that affect the money supply.
- Summarize how the "three players" can influence the money supply.
- Calculate and interpret changes in the money multiplier.

Preview

As we saw in Chapter 5 and will see in later chapters on monetary theory, movements in the money supply affect interest rates and inflation and thus affect us all. Because of its far-reaching effects on economic activity, it is important to understand how the money supply is determined. Who controls it? What causes it to change? How might control of it be improved? In this chapter, we start to answer these questions by providing a detailed description of the *money supply process*, the mechanism that determines the level of the money supply.

Because deposits at banks are by far the largest component of the money supply, learning how these deposits are created is the first step in understanding the money supply process. This chapter provides an overview of how the banking system creates deposits and describes the basic principles of the money supply, concepts that will form the foundation for the material presented in later chapters.

THREE PLAYERS IN THE MONEY SUPPLY PROCESS

The "cast of characters" in the money supply story is as follows:

1. The *central bank*—the government agency that oversees the banking system and is responsible for the conduct of monetary policy; in the United States, the Federal Reserve System
2. *Banks* (depository institutions)—the financial intermediaries that accept deposits from individuals and institutions and make loans: commercial banks, savings and loan associations, mutual savings banks, and credit unions
3. *Depositors*—individuals and institutions that hold deposits in banks

Of the three players, the central bank—the Federal Reserve System—is the most important. The Fed's conduct of monetary policy involves actions that affect its balance sheet (holdings of assets and liabilities), to which we turn now.

THE FED'S BALANCE SHEET

The operation of the Fed and its monetary policy involve actions that affect its balance sheet, or its holdings of assets and liabilities. Here we discuss a simplified balance sheet that includes just four items that are essential to our understanding of the money supply process.[1]

Federal Reserve System	
Assets	**Liabilities**
Securities Loans to financial institutions	Currency in circulation Reserves

Liabilities

The two liabilities on the balance sheet, currency in circulation and reserves, are often referred to as the *monetary liabilities* of the Fed. They are an important part of the money supply story, because increases in either or both will lead to an increase in the money supply (everything else held constant). The sum of the Fed's monetary liabilities (currency in circulation and reserves) and the U.S. Treasury's monetary liabilities (Treasury currency in circulation, primarily coins) is called the **monetary base** (also called **high-powered money**). When discussing the monetary base, we will focus only on the monetary liabilities of the Fed, because those of the Treasury account for less than 10% of the base.[2]

1. *Currency in circulation.* The Fed issues currency (those green-and-gray pieces of paper in your wallet that say "Federal Reserve Note" at the top). Currency in circulation is the amount of currency in the hands of the public. Currency held by depository institutions is also a liability of the Fed, but is counted as part of the reserves.

Federal Reserve notes are IOUs from the Fed to the bearer and are also liabilities, but unlike most liabilities, they promise to pay back the bearer solely with Federal Reserve notes; that is, they pay off IOUs with other IOUs. Accordingly, if you bring a $100 bill to the Federal Reserve and demand payment, you will receive two $50s, five $20s, ten $10s, one hundred $1 bills, or some other combination of bills that adds to $100.

People are more willing to accept IOUs from the Fed than from you or me because Federal Reserve notes are a recognized medium of exchange; that is, they are accepted as a means of payment and so function as money. Unfortunately, neither you nor I can convince people that our IOUs are worth anything more than the paper they are written on.[3]

---

[1]A detailed discussion of the Fed's balance sheet and the factors that affect the monetary base can be found in Appendix 1 to this chapter, which you can find on the Companion Website at http://www.pearsonhighered.com/mishkin.

[2]It is also safe to ignore the Treasury's monetary liabilities when discussing the monetary base because legal restrictions prevent the Treasury from actively supplying its monetary liabilities to the economy.

[3]The currency item on our balance sheet refers only to currency *in circulation*—that is, the amount in the hands of the public. Currency that has been printed by the U.S. Bureau of Engraving and Printing is not automatically a liability of the Fed. For example, consider the importance of having $1 million of your own IOUs printed. You give out $100 worth to other people and keep the other $999,900 in your pocket. The $999,900 of IOUs does not make you richer or poorer and does not affect your indebtedness. You care only about the $100 of liabilities from the $100 of circulated IOUs. The same reasoning applies to the Fed in regard to its Federal Reserve notes.

For similar reasons, the currency component of the money supply, no matter how it is defined, includes only currency in circulation. It does not include any additional currency that is not yet in the hands of the public. The fact that currency has been printed but is not circulating means that it is not anyone's asset or liability and thus cannot affect anyone's behavior. Therefore, it makes sense not to include it in the money supply.

2. *Reserves.* All banks have an account at the Fed in which they hold deposits. **Reserves** consist of deposits at the Fed plus currency that is physically held by banks (called *vault cash* because it is stored in bank vaults). Reserves are assets for the banks but liabilities for the Fed, because the banks can demand payment on them at any time and the Fed is required to satisfy its obligation by paying Federal Reserve notes. As you will see, an increase in reserves leads to an increase in the level of deposits and hence in the money supply.

Total reserves can be divided into two categories: reserves that the Fed requires banks to hold (**required reserves**) and any additional reserves the banks choose to hold (**excess reserves**). For example, the Fed might require that for every dollar of deposits at a depository institution, a certain fraction (say, 10 cents) must be held as reserves. This fraction (10%) is called the **required reserve ratio**.

Assets

The two assets on the Fed's balance sheet are important for two reasons. First, changes in the asset items lead to changes in reserves and the monetary base, and consequently to changes in the money supply. Second, because these assets (government securities and Fed loans) earn higher interest rates than the liabilities (currency in circulation, which pays no interest, and reserves), the Fed makes billions of dollars every year—its assets earn income, and its liabilities cost practically nothing. Although it returns most of its earnings to the federal government, the Fed does spend some of it on "worthy causes," such as supporting economic research.

1. *Securities.* This category of assets covers the Fed's holdings of securities issued by the U.S. Treasury and, in unusual circumstances (as discussed in Chapter 15), other securities. As we will see, the primary way in which the Fed provides reserves to the banking system is by purchasing securities, thereby increasing its holdings of these assets. An increase in government or other securities held by the Fed leads to an increase in the money supply.

2. *Loans to financial institutions.* The second way in which the Fed can provide reserves to the banking system is by making loans to banks and other financial institutions. The loans taken out by these institutions are referred to as *discount loans*, or alternatively *borrowings from the Fed* or as *borrowed reserves*. These loans appear as a liability on financial institutions' balance sheets. An increase in loans to financial institutions can also be the source of an increase in the money supply. During normal times, the Fed makes loans only to banking institutions, and the interest rate charged to banks for these loans is called the **discount rate**. (As we will discuss in Chapter 15, during the recent financial crisis, the Fed made loans to other financial institutions.)

CONTROL OF THE MONETARY BASE

The monetary base equals currency in circulation C plus the total reserves in banking system R.[4] The monetary base MB can be expressed as

$$MB = C + R$$

---

[4]Here, currency in circulation includes both Federal Reserve currency (Federal Reserve notes) and Treasury currency (primarily coins).

The Federal Reserve exercises control over the monetary base through its purchases or sales of securities in the open market, called **open market operations**, and through its extension of discount loans to banks.

Federal Reserve Open Market Operations

The primary way in which the Fed causes changes in the monetary base is through its open market operations. A purchase of bonds by the Fed is called an **open market purchase**, and a sale of bonds by the Fed is called an **open market sale**. Federal Reserve purchases and sales of bonds are always done through **primary dealers**, government securities dealers who operate out of private banking institutions.

Open Market Purchase   Suppose the Fed purchases $100 million of bonds from a primary dealer. To understand the consequences of this transaction, we look at *T-accounts*, which list only the changes that occur in balance sheet items, starting from the initial balance sheet position.

When the primary dealer sells the $100 million of bonds to the Fed, the Fed adds $100 million to the dealer's deposit account at the Fed, so that reserves in the banking system go up by $100 million. The banking system's T-account after this transaction is:

Banking System	
Assets	**Liabilities**
Securities −$100 m	
Reserves +$100 m	

The effects on the Fed's balance sheet are shown below. The balance sheet shows an increase of $100 million of securities in its assets column, along with an increase of $100 million of reserves in its liabilities column:

Federal Reserve System	
Assets	**Liabilities**
Securities +$100 m	Reserves +$100 m

As you can see, the Fed's open market purchase of $100 million causes an expansion of reserves in the banking system by an equal amount. Another way of seeing this is to recognize that open market purchases of bonds expand reserves because the central bank pays for the bonds with reserves. Because the monetary base equals currency plus reserves, an open market purchase increases the monetary base by an amount equal to the amount of the purchase.

Open Market Sale.   Similar reasoning indicates that if the Fed conducts an open market sale of $100 million of bonds to a primary dealer, the Fed deducts $100 million from the dealer's deposit account, so the Fed's reserves (liabilities) fall by $100 million (and the monetary base falls by the same amount). The T-account is now:

Federal Reserve System			
Assets		**Liabilities**	
Securities	−$100 m	Reserves	−$100 m

Shifts from Deposits into Currency

Even when the Fed does not conduct open market operations, a shift from deposits to currency will affect the reserves in the banking system. However, such a shift will have no effect on the monetary base. This tells us that the Fed has more control over the monetary base than over reserves.

Let's suppose that during the Christmas season, the public wants to hold more currency to buy gifts and so withdraws $100 million in cash. The effect on the T-account of the nonbank public is:

Nonbank Public			
Assets		**Liabilities**	
Checkable deposits	−$100 m		
Currency	+$100 m		

The banking system loses $100 million of deposits and hence $100 million of reserves:

Banking System			
Assets		**Liabilities**	
Reserves	−$100 m	Checkable deposits	−$100 m

For the Fed, the public's action means that $100 million of additional currency is circulating in the hands of the public, while reserves in the banking system have fallen by $100 million. The Fed's T-account is:

Federal Reserve System			
Assets		**Liabilities**	
		Currency in circulation	+$100 m
		Reserves	−$100 m

The net effect on the monetary liabilities of the Fed is a wash; the monetary base is unaffected by the public's increased desire for cash. But reserves *are* affected. Random fluctuations of reserves can occur as a result of random shifts into currency and out of deposits, and vice versa. The same is not true for the monetary base, making it a more stable variable and more controllable by the Fed.

Loans to Financial Institutions

In this chapter so far, we have seen how changes in the monetary base occur as a result of open market operations. However, the monetary base is also affected when the Fed makes a loan to a financial institution. When the Fed makes a $100 million loan to the First National Bank, the bank is credited with $100 million of reserves from the proceeds of the loan. The effects on the balance sheets of the banking system and the Fed are illustrated by the following T-accounts:

Banking System				Federal Reserve System			
Assets		**Liabilities**		**Assets**		**Liabilities**	
Reserves	+$100 m	Loans (borrowings from the Fed)	+$100 m	Loans (borrowings from the Fed)	+$100 m	Reserves	+$100 m

The monetary liabilities of the Fed have now increased by $100 million, and the monetary base, too, has increased by this amount. However, if a bank pays off a loan from the Fed, thereby reducing its borrowings from the Fed by $100 million, the T-accounts of the banking system and the Fed are as follows:

Banking System				Federal Reserve System			
Assets		**Liabilities**		**Assets**		**Liabilities**	
Reserves	−$100 m	Loans (borrowings from the Fed)	−$100 m	Loans (borrowings from the Fed)	−$100 m	Reserves	−$100 m

The net effect on the monetary liabilities of the Fed, and hence on the monetary base, is a reduction of $100 million. We see that the monetary base changes in a one-to-one ratio with the change in the borrowings from the Fed.

Other Factors That Affect the Monetary Base

So far in this chapter, it seems as though the Fed has complete control of the monetary base through its open market operations and loans to financial institutions. However, the world is a little bit more complicated for the Fed. Two important items that affect the monetary base, but are not controlled by the Fed, are *float* and *Treasury deposits at the Fed.* When the Fed clears checks for banks, it often credits the amount of the check to a bank that has deposited it (increases the bank's reserves) before it debits (decreases the reserves of) the bank on which the check is drawn. The resulting temporary net increase in the total amount of reserves in the banking system (and hence in the monetary base) caused by the Fed's check-clearing process is called **float**. When the U.S. Treasury moves deposits from commercial banks to its account at the Fed, leading to an increase in *Treasury deposits at the Fed,* it causes a deposit outflow at these banks such as that shown in Chapter 9, and thus causes reserves in the banking system and the monetary base to decrease. Thus *float* (affected by random events such as the weather, which influences how quickly checks are presented for payment) and *Treasury deposits at the Fed* (determined by the U.S. Treasury's actions) both affect the monetary base but are not controlled by the Fed at all. Decisions by the U.S. Treasury to have the Fed intervene in the foreign exchange market also affect the monetary base.

Overview of the Fed's Ability to Control the Monetary Base

Our discussion above indicates that two primary features determine the monetary base: open market operations and lending to financial institutions. Whereas the amount of open market purchases or sales is completely controlled by the Fed's placing orders with dealers in bond markets, the central bank cannot unilaterally determine, and therefore cannot perfectly predict, the amount of borrowings from the Fed. The Federal Reserve sets the discount rate (interest rate on loans to banks), and then banks make decisions about whether to borrow. The amount of lending, though influenced by the Fed's setting of the discount rate, is not completely controlled by the Fed; banks' decisions play a role, too.

Therefore, we might want to split the monetary base into two components: one that the Fed can control completely, and another that is less tightly controlled. The less tightly controlled component is the amount of the base that is created by loans from the Fed. The remainder of the base (called the **nonborrowed monetary base**) is under the Fed's control because it results primarily from open market operations.[5] The nonborrowed monetary base is formally defined as the monetary base minus borrowings from the Fed, which are referred to as **borrowed reserves**:

$$MB_n = MB - BR$$

where MB_n = nonborrowed monetary base
MB = monetary base
BR = borrowed reserves from the Fed

Factors not controlled at all by the Fed (for example, float and Treasury deposits with the Fed) undergo substantial short-run variations and can be important sources of fluctuations in the monetary base over time periods as short as a week. However, these fluctuations are usually predictable and so can be offset through open market operations. *Although float and Treasury deposits with the Fed undergo substantial short-run fluctuations, which complicate control of the monetary base, they do not prevent the Fed from accurately controlling it.*

---

[5]Actually, other items on the Fed's balance sheet (discussed in Appendix 1 to Chapter 14 on the website) affect the magnitude of the nonborrowed monetary base. Because their effects on the nonborrowed base relative to open market operations are both small and predictable, these other items do not present the Fed with difficulties in controlling the nonborrowed base.

MULTIPLE DEPOSIT CREATION: A SIMPLE MODEL

With our understanding of how the Federal Reserve controls the monetary base and how banks operate (Chapter 9), we now have the tools necessary to explain how deposits are created. When the Fed supplies the banking system with $1 of additional reserves, deposits increase by a multiple of this amount—a process called **multiple deposit creation**.

Deposit Creation: The Single Bank

Suppose the $100 million open market purchase described earlier was conducted with the First National Bank. After the Fed has bought the $100 million in bonds from the First National Bank, the bank finds that it has an increase in reserves of $100 million. To analyze what the bank will do with these additional reserves, assume that the bank does not want to hold excess reserves because it earns little interest on them. We begin the analysis with the following T-account:

First National Bank			
Assets		**Liabilities**	
Securities	−$100 m		
Reserves	+$100 m		

(handwritten: bonds are now the fed's ← Securities)
(handwritten: result from bonds being bought ← Reserves)

Because the bank has no increase in its checkable deposits, required reserves remain the same, and the bank finds that its additional $100 million of reserves means that its excess reserves have risen by $100 million. Let's say the bank decides to make a loan equal in an amount to the $100 million rise in excess reserves. When the bank makes the loan, it sets up a checking account for the borrower and puts the proceeds of the loan into this account. In this way, the bank alters its balance sheet by increasing its liabilities with $100 million of checkable deposits and at the same time increasing its assets with the $100 million loan. The resulting T-account looks like this:

First National Bank			
Assets		**Liabilities**	
Securities	−$100 m	Checkable deposits	+$100 m
Reserves	+$100 m		
Loans	+$100 m		

The bank has created checkable deposits by its act of lending. Because checkable deposits are part of the money supply, the bank's act of lending has, in fact, created money.

In its current balance sheet position, the First National Bank still has excess reserves and so might want to make additional loans. However, these reserves will not stay at the bank for very long. The borrowers took out loans not to leave $100 million sitting idle in a checking account at the First National Bank but to purchase goods and services from other individuals and corporations. When the borrowers make these purchases by writing checks, the checks will be deposited at other banks, and the $100 million of reserves will leave the First National Bank. *As a result, a bank cannot safely make a loan for an amount greater than the excess reserves that it has before it makes the loan.*

The final T-account of the First National Bank is:

First National Bank			
Assets		**Liabilities**	
Securities	−$100 m		
Loans	+$100 m		

The increase in reserves of $100 million has been converted into additional loans of $100 million at the First National Bank, plus an additional $100 million of deposits that have made their way to other banks. (All the checks written on accounts at the First National Bank are deposited in banks rather than converted into cash, because we are assuming that the public does not want to hold any additional currency.) Now let's see what happens to these deposits at the other banks.

Deposit Creation: The Banking System

To simplify the analysis, let's assume that the $100 million of deposits created by First National Bank's loan is deposited at Bank A, and that this bank and all other banks hold no excess reserves. Bank A's T-account becomes:

Bank A			
Assets		**Liabilities**	
Reserves	+$100 m	Checkable deposits	+$100 m

If the required reserve ratio is 10%, this bank will now find itself with a $10 million increase in required reserves, leaving it $90 million of excess reserves. Because Bank A (like the First National Bank) does not want to hold on to excess reserves, it will make loans for the entire amount. Its loans and checkable deposits will then increase by $90 million, but when the borrowers spend the $90 million of checkable deposits, they and the reserves at Bank A will fall back down by this same amount. The net result is that Bank A's T-account will look like this:

Bank A			
Assets		**Liabilities**	
Reserves	+$10 m	Checkable deposits	+$100 m
Loans	+$90 m		

If the money spent by the borrowers to whom Bank A lent the $90 million is deposited in another bank, such as Bank B, the T-account for Bank B will be:

Bank B			
Assets		**Liabilities**	
Reserves	+$90 m	Checkable deposits	+$90 m

The checkable deposits in the banking system have risen by another $90 million, for a total increase of $190 million ($100 million at Bank A plus $90 million at Bank B). In fact, the distinction between Bank A and Bank B is not necessary to obtain the same result on the overall expansion of deposits. If the borrowers from Bank A write checks to someone who deposits them at Bank A, the same change in deposits occurs. The T-accounts for Bank B would just apply to Bank A, and its checkable deposits would increase by the total amount of $190 million.

Bank B will want to modify its balance sheet further. It must keep 10% of $90 million ($9 million) as required reserves and has 90% of $90 million ($81 million) in excess reserves and so can make loans of this amount. Bank B will make loans totaling $81 million to borrowers, who spend the proceeds from the loans. Bank B's T-account will be:

Bank B			
Assets		**Liabilities**	
Reserves	+$ 9 m	Checkable deposits	+$90 m
Loans	+$81 m		

The $81 million spent by the borrowers from Bank B will be deposited in another bank (Bank C). Consequently, from the initial $100 million increase of reserves in the banking system, the total increase of checkable deposits in the system so far is $271 million (= $100 m + $90 m + $81 m).

Following the same reasoning, if all banks make loans for the full amount of their excess reserves, further increments in checkable deposits will continue (at Banks C, D, E, and so on), as depicted in Table 1. Therefore, the total increase in deposits from the initial $100 increase in reserves will be $1,000 million: The increase is tenfold, the reciprocal of the 10% (0.10) reserve requirement.

If the banks choose to invest their excess reserves in securities, the result is the same. If Bank A had taken its excess reserves and purchased securities instead of making loans, its T-account would have looked like this:

Bank A			
Assets		**Liabilities**	
Reserves	+$10 m	Checkable deposits	+$100m
Securities	+$90 m		

TABLE 1	Creation of Deposits (assuming 10% reserve requirement and a $100 million increase in reserves)		
Bank	**Increase in Deposits ($)**	**Increase in Loans ($)**	**Increase in Reserves ($)**
First National	0.00	100.00 m	0.00
A	100.00 m	90.00 m	10.00 m
B	90.00 m	81.00 m	9.00 m
C	81.00 m	72.90 m	8.10 m
D	72.90 m	65.61 m	7.29 m
E	65.61 m	59.05 m	6.56 m
F	59.05 m	53.14 m	5.91 m
.	.	.	.
.	.	.	.
.	.	.	.
Total for all banks	1,000.00 m	1,000.00 m	100.00 m

When the bank buys $90 million of securities, it writes $90 million in checks to the sellers of the securities, who in turn deposit the $90 million at a bank such as Bank B. Bank B's checkable deposits increase by $90 million, and the deposit expansion process is the same as before. ***Whether a bank chooses to use its excess reserves to make loans or to purchase securities, the effect on deposit expansion is the same.***

You can now see the difference in deposit creation for a single bank versus the banking system as a whole. Because a single bank can create deposits equal only to the amount of its excess reserves, it cannot by itself generate multiple deposit expansion. A single bank cannot make loans greater in amount than its excess reserves, because the bank will lose these reserves as the deposits created by the loan find their way to other banks. However, the banking system as a whole can generate a multiple expansion of deposits, because when a bank loses its excess reserves, these reserves do not leave the banking system, even though they are lost to the individual bank. So as each bank makes a loan and creates deposits, the reserves find their way to another bank, which uses them to make additional loans and create additional deposits. As you have seen, this process continues until the initial increase in reserves results in a multiple increase in deposits.

The multiple increase in deposits generated from an increase in the banking system's reserves is called the **simple deposit multiplier**.[6] In our example, with a 10% required reserve ratio, the simple deposit multiplier is 10. More generally, the simple deposit multiplier equals the reciprocal of the required reserve ratio, expressed

---

[6]This multiplier should not be confused with the Keynesian multiplier, which is derived through a similar step-by-step analysis. That multiplier relates an increase in income to an increase in investment, whereas the simple deposit multiplier relates an increase in deposits to an increase in reserves.

as a fraction (for example, $10 = 1/0.10$). So the formula for the multiple expansion of deposits can be written as follows:

$$\Delta D = \frac{1}{rr} \times \Delta R \tag{1}$$

where ΔD = change in total checkable deposits in the banking system
  rr = required reserve ratio (0.10 in the example)
  ΔR = change in reserves for the banking system ($100 million in the example)

Deriving the Formula for Multiple Deposit Creation

The formula for the multiple creation of deposits can be derived directly using algebra. We obtain the same result for the relationship between a change in deposits and a change in reserves.

Our assumption that banks do not hold on to any excess reserves means that the total amount of required reserves in the banking system RR will equal the total reserves in the banking system R:

$$RR = R$$

The total amount of required reserves equals the required reserve ratio rr times the total amount of checkable deposits D:

$$RR = rr \times D$$

Substituting $rr \times D$ for RR in the first equation,

$$rr \times D = R$$

and dividing both sides of the preceding equation by rr gives

$$D = \frac{1}{rr} \times R$$

Taking the change in both sides of this equation and using delta to indicate a change gives

$$\Delta D = \frac{1}{rr} \times \Delta R$$

which is the same formula for deposit creation given in Equation 1.[7]

---

[7]A formal derivation of this formula follows. Using the reasoning in the text, the change in checkable deposits is $100($= \Delta R \times 1$) plus $90 $[= \Delta R \times (1 - rr)]$ plus $81 $[= \Delta R \times (1 - rr)^2]$ and so on, which can be rewritten as

$$\Delta D = \Delta R \times [1 + (1 - rr) + (1 - rr)^2 + (1 - rr)^3 + \cdots]$$

Using the formula for the sum of an infinite series found in footnote 3 of Chapter 4, this equation can be rewritten as

$$\Delta D = \Delta R \times \frac{1}{1 - (1 - rr)} = \frac{1}{rr} \times \Delta R$$

This derivation provides us with another way of looking at the multiple creation of deposits, because it forces us to examine the banking system as a whole rather than one bank at a time. For the banking system as a whole, deposit creation (or contraction) will stop only when excess reserves in the banking system are zero; that is, the banking system will be in equilibrium when the total amount of required reserves equals the total amount of reserves, as seen in the equation $RR = R$. When $rr \times D$ is substituted for RR, the resulting equation $rr \times D = R$ tells us how high checkable deposits must be for required reserves to equal total reserves. Accordingly, a given level of reserves in the banking system determines the level of checkable deposits when the banking system is in equilibrium (when $ER = 0$); put another way, the given level of reserves supports a given level of checkable deposits.

In our example, the required reserve ratio is 10%. If reserves increase by $100 million, checkable deposits must rise by $1,000 million for total required reserves also to increase by $100 million. If the increase in checkable deposits is less than this—say, $900 million—then the increase in required reserves of $90 million remains below the $100 million increase in reserves, so excess reserves still exist somewhere in the banking system. The banks holding the excess reserves will now make additional loans, thereby creating new deposits; this process will continue until all reserves in the system are used up, which occurs when checkable deposits rise by $1,000 million.

We can also see this by looking at the resulting T-account of the banking system as a whole (including the First National Bank):

Banking System			
Assets		**Liabilities**	
Securities	−$ 100 m	Checkable deposits	+$1,000 m
Reserves	+$ 100 m		
Loans	+$1,000 m		

The procedure of eliminating excess reserves by loaning them out continues until the banking system (First National Bank and Banks A, B, C, D, and so on) has made $1,000 million of loans and created $1,000 million of deposits. In this way, $100 million of reserves supports $1,000 million (ten times the quantity) of deposits.

Critique of the Simple Model

Our model of multiple deposit creation seems to indicate that the Federal Reserve is able to exercise complete control over the level of checkable deposits by setting the required reserve ratio and the level of reserves. The actual creation of deposits is much less mechanical than the simple model indicates. If proceeds from Bank A's $90 million loan are not deposited but are kept in currency, nothing is deposited in Bank B and the deposit creation process ceases. The total increase in the money supply is now the $90 million increase in currency plus the initial $100 million of deposits created by First

National Bank's loans, which were deposited at Bank A, for a total of only $190 million—considerably less than the $1,000 million we calculated using the simple model above. In other words, currency does not lead to multiple deposit expansion, whereas deposits do. Thus, if some proceeds from loans are not deposited in banks but instead are used to raise the holdings of currency, less multiple expansion occurs overall, and the money supply does not increase by the amount predicted by our simple model of multiple deposit creation.

Another situation ignored in our model is one in which banks do not make loans or buy securities in the full amount of their excess reserves. If Bank A decides to hold on to all $90 million of its excess reserves, no deposits will be made in Bank B, and this will stop the deposit creation process. The total increase in deposits will be only $100 million, not the $1,000 million increase in our example. Hence, if banks choose to hold on to all or some of their excess reserves, the full expansion of deposits predicted by the simple model of multiple deposit creation again does not occur.

Our examples indicate that the Fed is not the only player whose behavior influences the level of deposits and therefore the money supply. Depositors' decisions regarding how much currency to hold and banks' decisions regarding the amount of excess reserves to hold also can cause the money supply to change.

FACTORS THAT DETERMINE THE MONEY SUPPLY

Our critique of the simple model shows how we can expand on it to discuss all the factors that affect the money supply. Let's look at changes in each factor in turn, holding all other factors constant.

Changes in the Nonborrowed Monetary Base, MB_n

As shown earlier in the chapter, the Fed's open market purchases increase the nonborrowed monetary base, and its open market sales decrease it. Holding all other variables constant, an increase in MB_n arising from an open market purchase raises the amount of the monetary base and reserves, so that multiple deposit creation occurs and the money supply increases. Similarly, an open market sale that reduces MB_n shrinks the amount of the monetary base and reserves, thereby causing a multiple contraction of deposits and a decrease in the money supply. We have the following result: **The money supply is positively related to the nonborrowed monetary base MB_n.**

Changes in Borrowed Reserves, *BR*, from the Fed

An increase in loans from the Fed provides additional borrowed reserves and thereby increases the amount of the monetary base and reserves, so that multiple deposit creation occurs and the money supply expands. If banks reduce the level of their discount loans, all other variables held constant, the monetary base and amount of reserves fall, and the money supply decreases. The result is this: **The money supply is positively related to the level of borrowed reserves, BR, from the Fed.**

Changes in the Required Reserve Ratio, *rr*

If the required reserve ratio on checkable deposits increases while all other variables, such as the monetary base, stay the same, we have seen that multiple deposit expansion is reduced and hence the money supply falls. If, on the other hand, the required reserve ratio falls, multiple deposit expansion is higher and the money supply rises.

We now have the following result: *The money supply is negatively related to the required reserve ratio rr.* In the past, the Fed sometimes used reserve requirements to affect the size of the money supply. In recent years, however, reserve requirements have become a less important factor in the determination of the money multiplier and the money supply, as we shall see in the next chapter.

Changes in Excess Reserves

When banks increase their holdings of excess reserves, those reserves are no longer being used to make loans, causing multiple deposit creation to stop dead in its tracks, resulting in less expansion of the money supply. If, on the other hand, banks choose to hold fewer excess reserves, loans and multiple deposit creation increase, and the money supply rises. *The money supply is negatively related to the amount of excess reserves.*

Recall from Chapter 9 that the primary benefit to a bank of holding excess reserves is that they provide insurance against losses due to deposit outflows; that is, they enable the bank experiencing deposit outflows to escape the costs of calling in loans, selling securities, borrowing from the Fed or other corporations, or bank failure. If banks fear that deposit outflows are likely to increase (that is, if expected deposit outflows increase), they will seek more insurance against this possibility, and excess reserves will rise.

Changes in Currency Holdings

As shown before, checkable deposits undergo multiple expansion, whereas currency does not. Hence, when checkable deposits are converted into currency, as long as the amount of excess reserves are held constant, a switch is made from a component of the money supply that undergoes multiple expansion to one that does not. The overall level of multiple expansion declines, and the money supply falls. On the other hand, if currency holdings fall, a switch is made into checkable deposits that undergo multiple deposit expansion, so the money supply rises. This analysis suggests the following result: *Holding excess reserves constant, the money supply is negatively related to currency holdings.*

OVERVIEW OF THE MONEY SUPPLY PROCESS

We now have a model of the money supply process in which all three of the players—the Federal Reserve System, depositors, and banks—directly influence the money supply. As a study aid, Summary Table 1 charts the money supply responses to the five factors discussed above and gives a brief synopsis of the reasoning behind them.

The variables are grouped by the player who is the primary influence behind the variable. The Federal Reserve, for example, influences the money supply by controlling the first two variables. Depositors influence the money supply through their decisions about holdings of currency, while banks influence the money supply with their decisions about borrowings from the Fed and excess reserves.

SUMMARY TABLE 1

Money Supply Response

Player	Variable	Change in Variable	Money Supply Response	Reason
Federal Reserve System	Nonborrowed monetary base, MB_n	↑	↑	More MB for deposit creation
	Required reserve ratio, rr	↑	↓	Less multiple deposit expansion
Banks	Borrowed reserves, BR	↑	↑	More MB for deposit creation
	Excess reserves	↑	↓	Less loans and deposit creation
Depositors	Currency holdings	↑	↓	Less multiple deposit expansion

Note: Only increases (↑) in the variables are shown. The effects of decreases on the money supply would be the opposite of those indicated in the "Money Supply Response" column.

THE MONEY MULTIPLIER

The intuition inherent in the preceding section is sufficient for you to understand how the money supply process works. For those of you who are more mathematically inclined, we can derive all of the above results using a concept called the **money multiplier**, denoted by m, which tells us how much the money supply changes for a given change in the monetary base. The relationship between the money supply M, the money multiplier, and the monetary base is described by the following equation:

$$M = m \times MB \tag{2}$$

The money multiplier m tells us what multiple of the monetary base is transformed into the money supply. Because the money multiplier is typically larger than 1, the alternative name for the monetary base, *high-powered money*, is logical: A $1 change in the monetary base typically leads to more than a $1 change in the money supply.

Deriving the Money Multiplier

Let's assume that the desired holdings of currency C and excess reserves ER grow proportionally with checkable deposits D; in other words, we assume that the ratios of these items to checkable deposits are constants in equilibrium, as the braces in the following expressions indicate:

$$c = \{C/D\} = \text{currency ratio}$$

$$e = \{ER/D\} = \text{excess reserves ratio}$$

We will now derive a formula that describes how the currency ratio desired by depositors, the excess reserves ratio desired by banks, and the required reserve ratio set by the Fed affect the multiplier *m*. We begin the derivation of the model of the money supply with the following equation:

$$R = RR + ER$$

which states that the total amount of reserves in the banking system *R* equals the sum of required reserves *RR* and excess reserves *ER*. (Note that this equation corresponds to the equilibrium condition *RR* = *R* given earlier in the chapter, where excess reserves were assumed to be zero.)

The total amount of required reserves equals the required reserve ratio *rr* times the amount of checkable deposits *D*:

$$RR = rr \times D$$

Substituting *rr* × *D* for *RR* in the first equation yields an equation that links reserves in the banking system to the amount of checkable deposits and excess reserves they can support:

$$R = (rr \times D) + ER$$

A key point here is that the Fed sets the required reserve ratio *rr* to less than 1. Thus $1 of reserves can support more than $1 of deposits, and the multiple expansion of deposits can occur.

Let's see how this works in practice. If excess reserves are held at zero (*ER* = 0), the required reserve ratio is set at *rr* = 0.10, and the level of checkable deposits in the banking system is $1,600 billion, then the amount of reserves needed to support these deposits is $160 billion (=0.10 × $1,600 billion). The $160 billion of reserves can support ten times this amount in checkable deposits because multiple deposit creation will occur.

Because the monetary base *MB* equals currency *C* plus reserves *R*, we can generate an equation that links the amount of the monetary base to the levels of checkable deposits and currency by adding currency to both sides of the preceding equation:

$$MB = R + C = (rr \times D) + ER + C$$

Notice that this equation reveals the amount of the monetary base needed to support the existing amounts of checkable deposits, currency, and excess reserves.

To derive the money multiplier formula in terms of the currency ratio *c* = {*C*/*D*} and the excess reserves ratio *e* = {*ER*/*D*}, we rewrite the last equation, specifying *C* as *c* × *D* and *ER* as *e* × *D*:

$$MB = (rr \times D) + (e \times D) + (c \times D) = (rr + e + c) \times D$$

We next divide both sides of the equation by the term inside the parentheses to get an expression linking checkable deposits *D* to the monetary base *MB*:

$$D = \frac{1}{rr + e + c} \times MB \tag{3}$$

Using the M1 definition of the money supply as currency plus checkable deposits (*M* = *D* + *C*) and again specifying *C* as *c* × *D*, we get

$$M = D + (c \times D) = (1 + c) \times D$$

Substituting in this equation the expression for D from Equation 3 yields

$$M = \frac{1+c}{rr+e+c} \times MB \tag{4}$$

We have derived an expression in the form of our earlier Equation 2. As you can see, the ratio that multiplies MB is the money multiplier, which tells how much the money supply changes in response to a given change in the monetary base (high-powered money). The money multiplier m is thus

$$m = \frac{1+c}{rr+e+c} \tag{5}$$

It is a function of the currency ratio set by depositors c, the excess reserves ratio set by banks e, and the required reserve ratio set by the Fed rr.

Intuition Behind the Money Multiplier

To get a feel for what the money multiplier means, let's construct a numerical example with realistic numbers for the following variables:

$$rr = \text{required reserve ratio} = 0.10$$

$$C = \text{currency in circulation} = \$1,\!200 \text{ billion}$$

$$D = \text{checkable deposits} = \$1,\!600 \text{ billion}$$

$$ER = \text{excess reserves} = \$2,\!500 \text{ billion}$$

$$M = \text{money supply (M1)} = C + D = \$2,\!800 \text{ billion}$$

From these numbers we can calculate the values for the currency ratio c and the excess reserves ratio e:

$$c = \frac{\$1,\!200 \text{ billion}}{\$1,\!600 \text{ billion}} = 0.75$$

$$e = \frac{\$2,\!500 \text{ billion}}{\$1,\!600 \text{ billion}} = 1.56$$

The resulting value of the money multiplier is

$$m = \frac{1+0.75}{0.1+1.56+0.75} = \frac{1.75}{2.41} = 0.73$$

The money multiplier of 0.73 tells us that, given the required reserve ratio of 10% on checkable deposits and the behavior of depositors, as represented by $c = 0.75$, and banks, as represented by $e = 1.56$, a \$1 increase in the monetary base leads to a \$0.73 increase in the money supply (M1).

An important characteristic of the money multiplier is that it is far less than the simple deposit multiplier of 10 found earlier in the chapter. There are two reasons for this result. First, *although deposits undergo multiple expansion, currency does not.* Thus, if some portion of the increase in high-powered money finds its way into currency, this portion does not undergo multiple deposit expansion. In our simple model earlier in the chapter, we did not allow for this possibility, and so the increase in reserves led to the maximum amount of multiple deposit creation. However, in our current model of the money multiplier, the level of currency does rise when the monetary base MB and checkable deposits D increase, because c is greater than zero. As previously stated, any increase in MB that goes into an increase in currency is not multiplied, so only part of the increase in MB is available to support checkable deposits that undergo multiple expansion. The overall level of multiple deposit expansion must be lower, meaning that the increase in M, given an increase in MB, is smaller than indicated by the simple model earlier in the chapter.

Second, since e is positive, **any increase in the monetary base and deposits leads to higher excess reserves.** When there is an increase in MB and D, the resulting increase in excess reserves means that the amount of reserves used to support checkable deposits does not increase as much as it otherwise would. Hence the increase in checkable deposits and the money supply are lower, and the money multiplier is smaller.

Prior to 2008, the excess reserves ratio e was almost always very close to zero (less than 0.001), and so its impact on the money multiplier (Equation 5) was essentially irrelevant. When e is close to zero, the money multiplier is always greater than 1, and it was around 1.6 during that period. However, as we will see in the next chapter, nonconventional monetary policy during the global financial crisis caused excess reserves to skyrocket to over $2 trillion. Such an extraordinarily large value of e caused the excess reserves factor in the money multiplier equation to become dominant, and so the money multiplier fell to below 1, as discussed above.

Money Supply Response to Changes in the Factors

By recognizing that the monetary base is $MB = MB_n + BR$, we can rewrite Equation 2 as

$$M = m \times (MB_n + BR) \tag{6}$$

Now we can show algebraically all the results given in Summary Table 1, which shows how the money supply responds to the changes in the factors.

As you can see from Equation 6, a rise in MB_n or BR raises the money supply M because the money multiplier m is always greater than zero. We can see that a rise in the required reserve ratio rr lowers the money supply by calculating the value of the money multiplier (using Equation 5) in our numerical example when rr increases from 10% to 15% (leaving all other variables unchanged). The money multiplier then becomes

$$m = \frac{1 + 0.75}{0.15 + 1.56 + 0.75} = \frac{1.75}{2.46} = 0.71$$

which, as we would expect, is less than 0.73.

Similarly, we can see that a rise in excess reserves lowers the money supply by calculating the money multiplier when e is increased from 1.56 to 3.0. The money multiplier decreases from 0.73 to

$$m = \frac{1 + 0.75}{0.1 + 3.00 + 0.75} = \frac{1.75}{3.85} = 0.45$$

We can also analyze what happens in our numerical example when there is a rise in the currency ratio c from 0.75 to 1.50. In this case, something peculiar happens. Instead of falling, the money multiplier rises from 0.73 to

$$m = \frac{1 + 1.50}{0.1 + 1.56 + 1.50} = \frac{2.50}{3.20} = 0.78$$

At first glance, this result might seem counterintuitive. After all, a dollar of monetary base that goes into currency only increases the money supply by one dollar, whereas a dollar of monetary base that goes into deposits leads to multiple deposit expansion that increases the money supply by a factor of 10. Thus it seems as though the shift from deposits to currency should lower the overall amount of multiple expansion and hence the money supply. This reasoning is correct, but it assumes a small value of the excess reserves ratio. Indeed, that is the case during normal times, when the excess reserves ratio is near zero. However, in our current situation, in which the excess reserves ratio e is abnormally high, when a dollar moves from deposits into currency, the amount of excess reserves falls by a large amount, which releases reserves to support more deposits, causing the money multiplier to rise.[8]

APPLICATION   Quantitative Easing and the Money Supply, 2007–2014

When the global financial crisis began in the fall of 2007, the Fed initiated lending programs and large-scale asset-purchase programs in an attempt to bolster the economy. By June 2014, these purchases of securities had led to a quintupling of the Fed's balance sheet and a 377% increase in the monetary base. These lending and asset-purchase programs, discussed further in Chapter 15, resulted in a huge expansion of the monetary base and have been given the name "quantitative easing." As our analysis in this chapter indicates, such a massive expansion of the monetary base could potentially lead to a large expansion of the money supply. However, as shown in Figure 1, when the monetary base increased by more than 370%, the M1 money supply rose by less than 110%. How can we explain this result using our money supply model?

Figure 2 shows the currency ratio c and the excess reserves ratio e for the 2007–2014. We see that the currency ratio was relatively steady during this period and so was not a major source of changes in the money multiplier and the money supply. Instead, we have to look to the extraordinary rise in the excess reserves ratio e, which climbed by more than a factor of 1,000 during this period.

What explains this substantial increase in the excess reserves ratio e? The Fed's actions created far more reserves than were needed for banks to meet their reserve requirements. Banks were willing to hold the huge increases in excess reserves because, after the Fed began paying interest on these reserves starting in 2008, the interest rate on reserves often exceeded the rate at which the banks could lend them out in the federal funds market. Because excess reserves had a very small or even negative cost,

[8]All the above results can be derived more generally from the Equation 5 formula for m as follows. When rr or e increases, the denominator of the money multiplier increases, and therefore the money multiplier must decrease. As long as $rr + e$ is less than 1 (as is usually the case), an increase in c raises the denominator of the money multiplier proportionally by more than it raises the numerator. The increase in c causes the money multiplier to fall. On the other hand, when $rr + e$ is greater than 1 (the current situation), an increase in c raises the numerator of the money multiplier proportionally by more than it raises the denominator, so the money multiplier rises. For more background on the currency ratio c, consult the third Web appendix to this chapter at http://www.pearsonhighered.com/mishkin. Recall that the money multiplier in Equation 5 is for the M1 definition of money. Appendix 2 to Chapter 14 on the website discusses how the multiplier for M2 is determined.

MyEconLab Mini-lecture   MyEconLab Real-time data

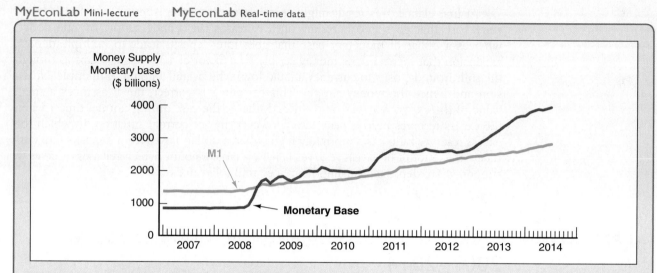

FIGURE 1   M1 and the Monetary Base, 2007–2014
The money supply rose by less than 110% despite the increase in the monetary base by over 370%.
Source: Federal Reserve Bank of St. Louis, FRED database: http://research.stlouisfed.org/fred2/.

banks were willing to tolerate a much higher excess reserves ratio *e*. As predicted by our money supply model, the huge increase in *e* sharply lowered the money multiplier, and so the money supply did not undergo that large an expansion, despite the huge increase in the monetary base. ◆

MyEconLab Mini-lecture   MyEconLab Real-time data

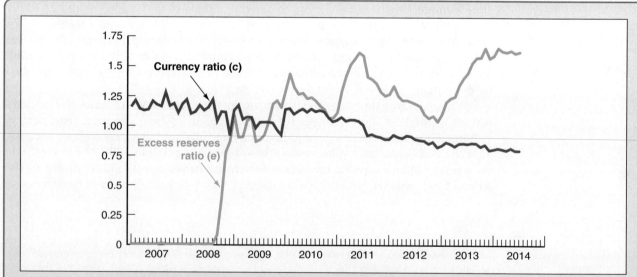

FIGURE 2   Excess Reserves Ratio and Currency Ratio, 2007–2014
The currency ratio *c* was relatively steady, whereas the excess reserves ratio *e* rose by a factor of over 1,000.
Source: Federal Reserve Bank of St. Louis, FRED database: http://research.stlouisfed.org/fred2/.

SUMMARY

1. The three players in the money supply process are the central bank, banks (depository institutions), and depositors.

2. Four items in the Fed's balance sheet are essential to our understanding of the money supply process: the two liability items, currency in circulation and reserves, which together make up the monetary base, and the two asset items, securities and loans to financial institutions.

3. The Federal Reserve controls the monetary base through open market operations and extensions of loans to financial institutions, and has better control over the monetary base than over reserves. Although float and Treasury deposits with the Fed undergo substantial short-run fluctuations, which complicate control of the monetary base, they do not prevent the Fed from accurately controlling it.

4. A single bank can make loans up to the amount of its excess reserves, thereby creating an equal amount of deposits. The banking system can create a multiple expansion of deposits, because as each bank makes a loan and creates deposits, the reserves find their way to another bank, which uses them to make loans and create additional deposits. In the simple model of multiple deposit creation, in which banks do not hold on to excess reserves and the public holds no currency, the multiple increase in checkable deposits (simple deposit multiplier) equals the reciprocal of the required reserve ratio.

5. The simple model of multiple deposit creation has serious deficiencies. Decisions by depositors to increase their holdings of currency or by banks to hold excess reserves will result in a smaller expansion of deposits than is predicted by the simple model. All three players—the Fed, banks, and depositors—are important in the determination of the money supply.

6. The money supply is positively related to the nonborrowed monetary base MB_n, which is determined by open market operations, and the level of borrowed reserves (lending) from the Fed, BR. The money supply is negatively related to the required reserve ratio, rr, and excess reserves. The money supply is also negatively related to holdings of currency, but only if excess reserves do not vary much when there is a shift between deposits and currency. The model of the money supply process takes into account the behavior of all three players in the money supply process: the Fed through open market operations and setting of the required reserve ratio; banks through their decisions to borrow from the Federal Reserve and hold excess reserves; and depositors through their decisions about the holding of currency.

7. The monetary base is linked to the money supply using the concept of the money multiplier, which tells us how much the money supply changes when the monetary base changes.

KEY TERMS

borrowed reserves, p. 322
discount rate, p. 318
excess reserves, p. 318
float, p. 322
high-powered money, p. 317
monetary base, p. 317

money multiplier, p. 331
multiple deposit creation, p. 323
nonborrowed monetary base, p. 322
open market operations, p. 319
open market purchase, p. 319
open market sale, p. 319

primary dealers, p. 319
required reserve ratio, p. 318
required reserves, p. 318
reserves, p. 318
simple deposit multiplier, p. 326

QUESTIONS

All questions are available in MyEconLab at
http://www.myeconlab.com. Unless otherwise noted, the following assumptions are made in all questions: The required reserve ratio on checkable deposits is 10%, banks do not hold any excess reserves, and the public's holdings of currency do not change.

1. Classify each of these transactions as an asset, a liability, or neither for each of the "players" in the money supply process—the Federal Reserve, banks, and depositors.

   a. You get a $10,000 loan from the bank to buy an automobile.

b. You deposit $400 into your checking account at the local bank.

c. The Fed provides an emergency loan to a bank for $1,000,000.

d. A bank borrows $500,000 in overnight loans from another bank.

e. You use your debit card to purchase a meal at a restaurant for $100.

2. The First National Bank receives an extra $100 of reserves but decides not to lend out any of these reserves. How much deposit creation takes place for the entire banking system?

3. Suppose the Fed buys $1 million of bonds from the First National Bank. If the First National Bank and all other banks use the resulting increase in reserves to purchase securities only and not to make loans, what will happen to checkable deposits?

4. If a bank depositor withdraws $1,000 of currency from an account, what happens to reserves, checkable deposits, and the monetary base?

5. If a bank sells $10 million of bonds to the Fed to pay back $10 million on the loan it owes, what is the effect on the level of checkable deposits?

6. If you decide to hold $100 less cash than usual and therefore deposit $100 more cash in the bank, what effect will this have on checkable deposits in the banking system if the rest of the public keeps its holdings of currency constant?

7. "The Fed can perfectly control the amount of reserves in the system." Is this statement true, false, or uncertain? Explain.

8. "The Fed can perfectly control the amount of the monetary base, but has less control over the composition of the monetary base." Is this statement true, false, or uncertain? Explain.

9. The Fed buys $100 million of bonds from the public and also lowers the required reserve ratio. What will happen to the money supply?

10. Describe how each of the following can affect the money supply: (a) the central bank; (b) banks; and (c) depositors.

11. "The money multiplier is necessarily greater than 1." Is this statement true, false, or uncertain? Explain your answer.

12. What effect might a financial panic have on the money multiplier and the money supply? Why?

13. During the Great Depression years from 1930–1933, both the currency ratio c and the excess reserves ratio e rose dramatically. What effect did these factors have on the money multiplier?

14. In October 2008, the Federal Reserve began paying interest on the amount of excess reserves held by banks. How, if at all, might this affect the multiplier process and the money supply?

15. The money multiplier declined significantly during the period 1930–1933 and also during the recent financial crisis of 2008–2010. Yet the M1 money supply *decreased* by 25% in the Depression period but *increased* by more than 20% during the recent financial crisis. What explains the difference in outcomes?

APPLIED PROBLEMS

All applied problems are available in MyEconLab at http://www.myeconlab.com. *Unless otherwise noted, the following assumptions are made in all of the applied problems: The required reserve ratio on checkable deposits is 10%, banks do not hold any excess reserves, and the public's holdings of currency do not change.*

16. If the Fed sells $2 million of bonds to the First National Bank, what happens to reserves and the monetary base? Use T-accounts to explain your answer.

17. If the Fed sells $2 million of bonds to Irving the Investor, who pays for the bonds with a briefcase filled with currency, what happens to reserves and the monetary base? Use T-accounts to explain your answer.

18. If the Fed lends five banks a total of $100 million but depositors withdraw $50 million and hold it as currency, what happens to reserves and the monetary base? Use T-accounts to explain your answer.

19. Using T-accounts, show what happens to checkable deposits in the banking system when the Fed lends $1 million to the First National Bank.

20. Using T-accounts, show what happens to checkable deposits in the banking system when the Fed sells $2 million of bonds to the First National Bank.

21. If the Fed buys $1 million of bonds from the First National Bank, but an additional 10% of any deposit

is held as excess reserves, what is the total increase in checkable deposits? (*Hint:* Use T-accounts to show what happens at each step of the multiple expansion process.)

22. If reserves in the banking system increase by $1 billion because the Fed lends $1 billion to financial institutions, and checkable deposits increase by $9 billion, why isn't the banking system in equilibrium? What will continue to happen in the banking system until equilibrium is reached? Show the T-account for the banking system in equilibrium.

23. If the Fed reduces reserves by selling $5 million worth of bonds to the banks, what will the T-account of the banking system look like when the banking system is in equilibrium? What will have happened to the level of checkable deposits?

24. If the Fed sells $1 million of bonds and banks reduce their borrowings from the Fed by $1 million, predict what will happen to the money supply.

25. Suppose that currency in circulation is $600 billion, the amount of checkable deposits is $900 billion, and excess reserves are $15 billion.

a. Calculate the money supply, the currency deposit ratio, the excess reserve ratio, and the money multiplier.

b. Suppose the central bank conducts an unusually large open market purchase of bonds held by banks of $1400 billion due to a sharp contraction in the economy. Assuming the ratios you calculated in part (a) remain the same, predict the effect on the money supply.

c. Suppose the central bank conducts the same open market purchase as in part (b), except that banks choose to hold all of these proceeds as excess reserves rather than loan them out, due to fear of a financial crisis. Assuming that currency and deposits remain the same, what happens to the amount of excess reserves, the excess reserve ratio, the money supply, and the money multiplier?

d. During the financial crisis in 2008, the Federal Reserve began injecting the banking system with massive amounts of liquidity, and at the same time, very little lending occurred. As a result, the M1 money multiplier was below 1 for most of the time from October 2008 through 2011. How does this scenario relate to your answer to part (c)?

DATA ANALYSIS PROBLEMS

The Problems update with real-time data in MyEconLab and are available for practice or instructor assignment.

 1. Go to the St. Louis Federal Reserve FRED database, and find the most current data available on Currency (CURRNS), Total Checkable Deposits (TCDNS), Total Reserves (RESBALNS), and Required Reserves (RESBALREQ).

a. Calculate the value of the currency deposit ratio *c*.

b. Use RESBALNS and RESBALREQ to calculate the amount of excess reserves, and then calculate the value of the excess reserve ratio *e*. Be sure the units of total and required reserves are the same when you do the calculations.

c. Assuming a required reserve ratio *rr* of 11%, calculate the value of the money multiplier *m*.

 2. Go to the St. Louis Federal Reserve FRED database, and find data on the M1 Money Stock (M1SL) and the Monetary Base (AMBSL).

a. Calculate the value of the money multiplier using the most recent data available and the data from five years prior.

b. Based on your answer to part (a), how much would a $100 million open market purchase of securities affect the M1 money supply today and five years ago?

WEB EXERCISES

1. Go to http://www.federalreserve.gov/boarddocs/hh/ and find the most recent annual report of the Federal Reserve. Read the first section of the annual report, which summarizes Monetary Policy and the Economic Outlook. Write a one-page summary of this section of the report.

2. Go to http://www.federalreserve.gov/releases/h6/hist/ and find the historical report of M1 and M2. Compute the growth rate of each aggregate over each of the past three years (it will be easier to do this if you move the data into Excel, as demonstrated in Chapter 1). Does it appear that the Fed has been increasing or decreasing the rate of growth of the money supply? Is this consistent with your understanding of the needs of the economy? Why?

3. An important aspect of the supply of money is reserve balances. Go to http://www.federalreserve.gov/Releases/h41/ and locate the most recent release. This site reports changes in factors that affect depository reserve balances.

a. What is the current reserve balance?

b. What is the change in reserve balances since a year ago?

c. Based on your results in parts (a) and (b), does it appear that the money supply should be increasing or decreasing?

WEB REFERENCES

http://www.federalreserve.gov/boarddocs/rptcongress/annual04/default.htm

See the most recent Federal Reserve financial statement.

http://www.richmondfed.org/about_us/visit_us/tours/money_museum/index.cfm?WT.si_n=Search&WT.si_x=3

A virtual tour of the Federal Reserve Bank of Richmond's money museum.

http://www.federalreserve.gov/Releases/h3/

The Federal Reserve website reports data about aggregate reserves and the monetary base. This site also reports on the volume of borrowings from the Fed.

http://www.federalreserve.gov/Releases/h6/

This site reports current and historical levels of M1 and M2, as well as other data on the money supply.

WEB APPENDICES

Please visit the Companion Website at http://www.pearsonhighered.com/mishkin to read the Web appendices to Chapter 14.

Appendix 1: **The Fed's Balance Sheet and the Monetary Base**

Appendix 2: **The M2 Money Multiplier**

Appendix 3: **Explaining the Behavior of the Currency Ratio**

Appendix 4: **Application: The Great Depression Bank Panics, 1930–1933, and the Money Supply**

15 Tools of Monetary Policy

Learning Objectives

- Illustrate the market for reserves, and demonstrate how changes in monetary policy can affect the equilibrium federal funds rate.
- Summarize how conventional monetary policy tools are implemented and the relative advantages and limitations of each tool.
- Explain the key monetary policy tools that are used when conventional policy is no longer effective.
- Identify the distinctions and similarities between the monetary policy tools of the Federal Reserve and those of the European Central Bank.

Preview

In this chapter, we examine the tools of monetary policy used by the Fed to control the money supply and interest rates. Because the Fed's use of these policy tools has such an important impact on interest rates and economic activity, it is vital to understand how the Fed wields them in practice and how relatively useful each tool is.

In recent years, the Federal Reserve has increasingly focused on the **federal funds rate** (the interest rate on overnight loans of reserves from one bank to another) as the primary instrument of monetary policy. Since February 1994, the Fed has announced a federal funds rate target at each Federal Open Market Committee (FOMC) meeting, an announcement that is watched closely by market participants because it affects interest rates throughout the economy. Thus, to fully comprehend how the Fed uses its tools in the conduct of monetary policy, we must understand not only their effect on the money supply but also their direct effect on the federal funds rate and how they can be used to help achieve a federal funds rate that is close to the target. The chapter therefore begins with a supply and demand analysis of the market for reserves to explain how the Fed's settings for the four tools of monetary policy—open market operations, discount policy, reserve requirements, and the interest paid on reserves—determine the federal funds rate. We next go on to look in more detail at each of these tools of monetary policy to see how they are used in practice and to gain a sense of their relative advantages. We then examine the nonconventional tools of monetary policy that the Federal Reserve was forced to use during the extraordinary circumstances of the recent financial crisis. The chapter ends with a discussion of the tools of monetary policy used by other central banks besides the Federal Reserve.

THE MARKET FOR RESERVES AND THE FEDERAL FUNDS RATE

In Chapter 14, we saw how open market operations (changes in nonborrowed reserves) and Federal Reserve lending (changes in borrowed reserves) affect the balance sheet of the Fed and the amount of reserves. The market for reserves is where the federal funds rate is determined, and this is why we turn to a supply and demand analysis of this market to analyze how the tools of monetary policy affect the federal funds rate.

Demand and Supply in the Market for Reserves

The analysis of the market for reserves proceeds in a similar fashion to the analysis of the bond market that we conducted in Chapter 5. First, we derive demand and supply curves for reserves. Then, the market equilibrium in which the quantity of reserves demanded equals the quantity of reserves supplied determines the level of the federal funds rate, the interest rate charged on the loans of these reserves.

Demand Curve   To derive the demand curve for reserves, we need to ask what happens to the quantity of reserves demanded by banks, holding everything else constant, as the federal funds rate changes. Recall from Chapter 14 that the amount of reserves can be split up into two components: (1) required reserves, which are equal to the required reserve ratio times the amount of deposits on which reserves are required; and (2) excess reserves, the additional reserves banks choose to hold. Therefore, the quantity of reserves demanded by banks equals required reserves plus the quantity of excess reserves demanded. Excess reserves are insurance against deposit outflows, and the cost of holding these excess reserves is their *opportunity cost*—the interest rate that could have been earned on lending these reserves out minus the interest rate that is earned on these reserves, i_{or}.

Before the fall of 2008, the Federal Reserve did not pay interest on reserves, but since then it has paid interest on reserves at a level that is typically set at a fixed amount below the federal funds rate target and therefore changes when the target changes. When the federal funds rate is above the rate paid on reserves, i_{or}, then as the federal funds rate decreases, the opportunity cost of holding excess reserves falls. Holding everything else constant, including the quantity of required reserves, the quantity of reserves demanded rises. Consequently, the demand curve for reserves, R^d, slopes downward in Figure 1 when the federal funds rate is above i_{or}. If, however, the federal funds rate begins to fall below the interest rate paid on excess reserves i_{or}, banks do not lend in the overnight market at a lower interest rate. Instead, they just keep on adding to their holdings of excess reserves indefinitely. The result is that the demand curve for reserves, R^d, becomes flat (infinitely elastic) at i_{or} in Figure 1.

MyEconLab Mini-lecture

FIGURE 1
Equilibrium in the Market for Reserves

Equilibrium occurs at the intersection of the supply curve R^s and the demand curve R^d, at point 1 and an interest rate of i_{ff}^*.

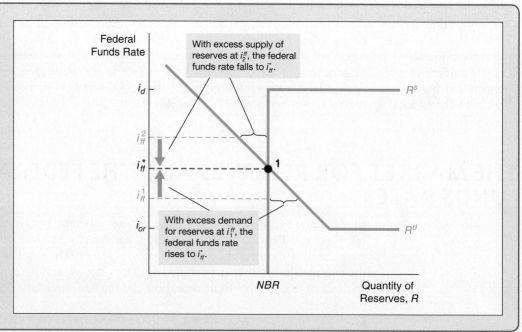

With excess supply of reserves at i_2^{ff}, the federal funds rate falls to i_{ff}^*.

With excess demand for reserves at i_1^{ff}, the federal funds rate rises to i_{ff}^*.

Supply Curve The supply of reserves, R^s, can be broken up into two components: the amount of reserves that are supplied by the Fed's open market operations, called *nonborrowed reserves* (*NBR*), and the amount of reserves borrowed from the Fed, called *borrowed reserves* (*BR*). The primary cost of borrowing from the Fed is the interest rate charged by the Fed on these loans—the discount rate, i_d, which is set at a fixed amount above the federal funds target rate and thus changes when the target changes. Because borrowing federal funds from other banks is a substitute for borrowing (taking out discount loans) from the Fed, if the federal funds rate i_{ff} is below the discount rate i_d, then banks will not borrow from the Fed. Borrowed reserves will be zero because borrowing in the federal funds market is cheaper. Thus, as long as i_{ff} remains below i_d, the supply of reserves will just equal the amount of nonborrowed reserves supplied by the Fed, *NBR*, and so the supply curve will be vertical, as shown in Figure 1. However, as the federal funds rate begins to rise above the discount rate, banks will want to keep borrowing more and more at i_d and then lending out the proceeds in the federal funds market at the higher rate, i_{ff}. The result is that the supply curve becomes flat (infinitely elastic) at i_d, as shown in Figure 1.

Market Equilibrium Market equilibrium occurs when the quantity of reserves demanded equals the quantity supplied, $R^s = R^d$. Equilibrium therefore occurs at the intersection of the demand curve R^d and the supply curve R^s at point 1, with an equilibrium federal funds rate of i_{ff}^*. When the federal funds rate is above the equilibrium rate at i_{ff}^2, more reserves are supplied than are demanded (excess supply), and so the federal funds rate falls to i_{ff}^*, as shown by the downward arrow. When the federal funds rate is below the equilibrium rate at i_{ff}^1, more reserves are demanded than are supplied (excess demand), and so the federal funds rate rises, as shown by the upward arrow. (Note that Figure 1 is drawn so that i_d is above i_{ff}^* because the Federal Reserve now keeps the discount rate substantially above the target for the federal funds rate.)

How Changes in the Tools of Monetary Policy Affect the Federal Funds Rate

Now that we understand how the federal funds rate is determined, we can examine how changes in the four tools of monetary policy—open market operations, discount lending, reserve requirements, and the interest rate paid on reserves—affect the market for reserves and the equilibrium federal funds rate.

Open Market Operations The effect of an open market operation depends on whether the supply curve initially intersects the demand curve in its downward-sloped section or in its flat section. Panel (a) of Figure 2 shows what happens if the intersection initially occurs on the downward-sloped section of the demand curve. We have already seen that an open market purchase leads to a greater quantity of reserves supplied; this is true at any given federal funds rate because of the higher amount of nonborrowed reserves, which rises from NBR_1 to NBR_2. An open market purchase therefore shifts the supply curve to the right from R_1^s to R_2^s and moves the equilibrium from point 1 to point 2, lowering the federal funds rate from i_{ff}^1 to i_{ff}^2.[1] The same reasoning implies that an open market sale decreases the quantity of nonborrowed reserves supplied, shifts the supply curve to the left, and causes the federal funds rate to rise. Because this is the typical situation—since the Fed usually keeps the federal funds rate target above the interest rate paid on reserves—the conclusion is that ***an open market purchase causes the federal funds rate to fall, whereas an open market sale causes the federal funds rate to rise.***

[1]We come to the same conclusion if we use the money supply framework outlined in Chapter 14, along with the liquidity preference framework outlined in Chapter 5. An open market purchase raises reserves and the money supply, and then the liquidity preference framework shows that interest rates fall as a result.

MyEconLab Mini-lecture

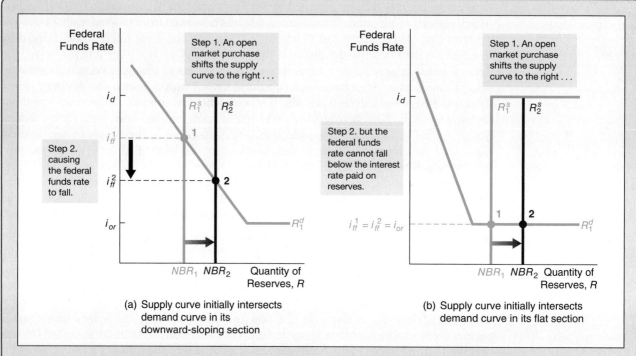

FIGURE 2　**Response to an Open Market Operation**

An open market purchase increases nonborrowed reserves and hence the reserves supplied, and shifts the supply curve from R_1^s to R_2^s. In panel (a), the equilibrium moves from point 1 to point 2, lowering the federal funds rate from i_{ff}^1 to i_{ff}^2. In panel (b), the equilibrium moves from point 1 to point 2, but the federal funds rate remains unchanged, $i_{ff}^1 = i_{ff}^2 = i_{or}$.

However, if the supply curve initially intersects the demand curve on its flat section, as in panel (b) of Figure 2, open market operations have no effect on the federal funds rate. To see this, let's again look at an open market purchase that raises the quantity of reserves supplied, which shifts the supply curve from R_1^s to R_2^s. However, this time we consider the case in which $i_{ff}^1 = i_{or}$ initially. The shift in the supply curve moves the equilibrium from point 1 to point 2, but the federal funds rate remains unchanged at i_{or} because *the interest rate paid on reserves, i_{or}, sets a floor for the federal funds rate.*

Discount Lending　The effect of a discount rate change depends on whether the demand curve intersects the supply curve in its vertical section or its flat section. Panel (a) of Figure 3 shows what happens if the intersection occurs on the vertical section of the supply curve, so that there is no discount lending and borrowed reserves, *BR*, are zero. In this case, when the discount rate is lowered by the Fed from i_d^1 to i_d^2, the horizontal section of the supply curve falls, as in R_2^s, but the intersection of the supply and demand curves remains at point 1. Thus, in this case, no change occurs in the equilibrium federal funds rate, which remains at i_{ff}^1. Because this is the typical situation—since the Fed now usually keeps the discount rate above its target for the federal funds rate—the conclusion is that *most changes in the discount rate have no effect on the federal funds rate.*

However, if the demand curve intersects the supply curve on its flat section, so that there is some discount lending (i.e., *BR* > 0), as in panel (b) of Figure 3, changes in the discount rate do affect the federal funds rate. In this case, initially

MyEconLab Mini-lecture

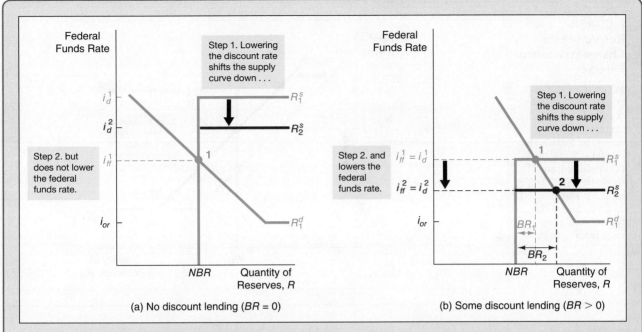

FIGURE 3 **Response to a Change in the Discount Rate**

In panel (a), when the discount rate is lowered by the Fed from i_d^1 to i_d^2, the horizontal section of the supply curve falls, as in R_2^s, and the equilibrium federal funds rate remains unchanged at i_{ff}^1. In panel (b), when the discount rate is lowered by the Fed from i_d^1 to i_d^2, the horizontal section of the supply curve R_2^s falls, and the equilibrium federal funds rate falls from i_{ff}^1 to i_{ff}^2 as borrowed reserves increase.

discount lending is positive and the equilibrium federal funds rate equals the discount rate, $i_{ff}^1 = i_d^1$. When the discount rate is lowered by the Fed from i_d^1 to i_d^2, the horizontal section of the supply curve R_2^s falls, moving the equilibrium from point 1 to point 2, and the equilibrium federal funds rate falls from i_{ff}^1 to i_{ff}^2 ($=i_d^2$), as shown in panel (b). In this case, BR increases from BR_1 to BR_2.

Reserve Requirements   When the required reserve ratio increases, required reserves increase and hence the quantity of reserves demanded increases for any given interest rate. Thus a rise in the required reserve ratio shifts the demand curve to the right from R_1^d to R_2^d in Figure 4, moves the equilibrium from point 1 to point 2, and in turn raises the federal funds rate from i_{ff}^1 to i_{ff}^2. The result is that **when the Fed raises reserve requirements, the federal funds rate rises.**[2]

Similarly, a decline in the required reserve ratio lowers the quantity of reserves demanded, shifts the demand curve to the left, and causes the federal funds rate to fall. **When the Fed decreases reserve requirements, the federal funds rate falls.**

Interest on Reserves   The effect of a change in the interest rate paid by the Fed on reserves depends on whether the supply curve intersects the demand curve in its

[2]Because an increase in the required reserve ratio means that the same amount of reserves is able to support a smaller amount of deposits, a rise in the required reserve ratio leads to a decline in the money supply. Using the liquidity preference framework from Chapter 5, the fall in the money supply results in a rise in interest rates, yielding the same conclusion given in the text—that raising reserve requirements leads to higher interest rates.

MyEconLab Mini-lecture

FIGURE 4
Response to a Change in Required Reserves

When the Fed raises reserve requirements, required reserves increase, which raises the demand for reserves. The demand curve shifts from R_1^d to R_2^d, the equilibrium moves from point 1 to point 2, and the federal funds rate rises from i_{ff}^1 to i_{ff}^2.

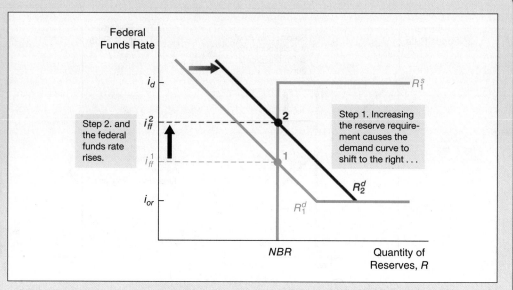

MyEconLab Mini-lecture

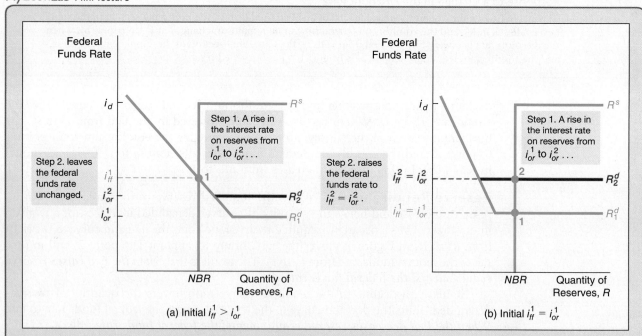

FIGURE 5 **Response to a Change in the Interest Rate on Reserves**

In panel (a), when the equilibrium federal funds rate is above the interest rate paid on reserves, a rise in the interest rate on reserves from i_{or}^1 to i_{or}^2 raises the horizontal section of the demand curve, as in R_1^d, but the equilibrium federal funds rate remains unchanged at i_{ff}^1. In panel (b), when the equilibrium federal funds rate is equal to the interest rate paid on reserves, a rise in the interest rate on reserves from i_{or}^1 to i_{or}^2 raises the equilibrium federal funds rate $i_{ff}^1 = i_{or}^1$ to $i_{ff}^1 = i_{or}^2$.

downward-sloping section or its flat section. Panel (a) of Figure 5 shows what happens if the intersection occurs on the demand curve's downward-sloping section, where the equilibrium federal funds rate is above the interest rate paid on reserves. In this case, when the interest rate on reserves is raised from i_{or}^1 to i_{or}^2, the horizontal section of the demand curves rises, as in R_2^d, but the intersection of the supply and demand curves remains at point 1. However, if the supply curve intersects the demand curve on its flat section, where the equilibrium federal funds rate is equal to the interest rate paid on reserves, as in panel (b) of Figure 5, a rise in the interest rate on reserves from i_{or}^1 to i_{or}^2 moves the equilibrium to point 2, where the equilibrium federal funds rate rises from $i_{ff}^1 = i_{or}^1$ to $i_{ff}^2 = i_{or}^2$. **When the federal funds rate is at the interest rate paid on reserves, a rise in the interest rate on reserves raises the federal funds rate.**

APPLICATION ## How the Federal Reserve's Operating Procedures Limit Fluctuations in the Federal Funds Rate

An important advantage of the Fed's current procedures for operating the discount window and paying interest on reserves is that they limit fluctuations in the federal funds rate. We can use our supply and demand analysis of the market for reserves to see why.

Suppose that, initially, the equilibrium federal funds rate is at the federal funds rate target of i_{ff}^T in Figure 6. If the demand for reserves experiences a large unexpected increase, the demand curve shifts to the right to $R^{d''}$, where it now intersects the supply curve for reserves on the flat portion, where the equilibrium federal funds rate i_{ff}'' equals the discount rate i_d. No matter how far the demand curve shifts to the right, the equilibrium federal funds rate i_{ff}'' will stay at i_d because borrowed reserves will just continue to increase, matching the increase in demand. Similarly, if the demand for reserves experiences a large unexpected decrease, the demand curve shifts to the left to $R^{d'}$, and the supply curve intersects the demand curve on its flat portion, where the equilibrium federal funds rate i_{ff}' equals the interest rate paid on reserves i_{or}. No matter how far left the demand curve shifts, the equilibrium federal funds rate i_{ff}' stays at i_{or} because excess reserves will keep on decreasing so that the quantity demanded of reserves equals the quantity of nonborrowed reserves supplied.[3]

Our analysis therefore shows that the **Federal Reserve's operating procedures limit the fluctuations of the federal funds rate so that it remains between i_{er} and i_d.** If the range between i_{or} and i_d is kept narrow enough, then fluctuations around the target rate will be small. ◆

---

[3]There are times when the federal funds rate might fall below the level of the interest rate on reserves. This situation can occur because some participants in the federal funds market, particularly Fannie Mae and Freddie Mac, are not banks and so cannot keep their funds as deposits at the Federal Reserve. When they have excess funds, they may be forced to accept a lower interest rate than that paid on reserves because they don't have access to this higher rate from the Federal Reserve.

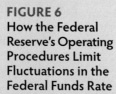

FIGURE 6
How the Federal Reserve's Operating Procedures Limit Fluctuations in the Federal Funds Rate

A rightward shift in the demand curve for reserves to $R^{d''}$ will raise the equilibrium federal funds rate to a maximum of $i_{ff}'' = i_d$, whereas a leftward shift of the demand curve to $R^{d'}$ will lower the federal funds rate to a minimum of $i_{ff}' = i_{or}$.

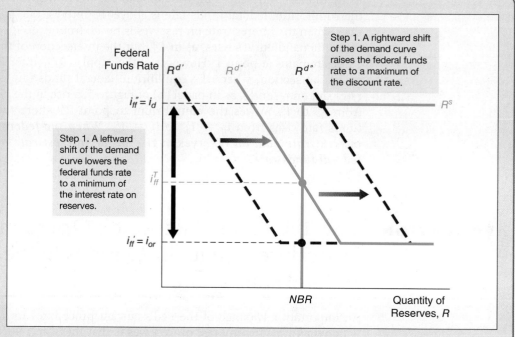

CONVENTIONAL MONETARY POLICY TOOLS

During normal times, the Federal Reserve uses three tools of monetary policy—open market operations, discount lending, and reserve requirements—to control the money supply and interest rates, and these three tools are referred to as **conventional monetary policy tools**. We will look at each of them in turn, and then at the additional tool of paying interest on reserves, to see how the Fed wields them in practice and how relatively useful each tool is.

Open Market Operations

Open market operations are the most important conventional monetary policy tool because they are the primary determinants of changes in interest rates and the monetary base, the main source of fluctuations in the money supply. Open market purchases expand reserves and the monetary base, thereby increasing the money supply and lowering short-term interest rates. Open market sales shrink reserves and the monetary base, decreasing the money supply and raising short-term interest rates. Now that we understand from Chapter 14 the elements of the Fed's balance sheet that influence reserves and the monetary base, we can examine how the Federal Reserve conducts open market operations with the objective of controlling short-term interest rates and the money supply.

Open market operations fall into two categories: **Dynamic open market operations** are intended to change the level of reserves and the monetary base, and **defensive open market operations** are intended to offset movements in other factors that affect reserves and the monetary base, such as changes in Treasury deposits with the Fed or changes in float. The Fed conducts conventional open market operations in U.S.

Treasury and government agency securities, especially U.S. Treasury bills. The Fed conducts most of its open market operations in Treasury securities because the market for these securities is the most liquid and has the largest trading volume. It has the capacity to absorb the Fed's substantial volume of transactions without experiencing excessive price fluctuations that would disrupt the market.

As we saw in Chapter 13, the decision-making authority for open market operations is the Federal Open Market Committee (FOMC), which sets a target for the federal funds rate. The actual execution of these operations, however, is conducted by the trading desk at the Federal Reserve Bank of New York, whose operations are described by the Inside the Fed box, "A Day at the Trading Desk."

Open market operations are conducted electronically through a specific set of dealers in government securities, known as **primary dealers**, by a computer system called TRAPS (Trading Room Automated Processing System). A message is electronically transmitted to all the primary dealers simultaneously over TRAPS, indicating the type and maturity of the operation being arranged. The dealers are given several minutes to respond via TRAPS with their propositions to buy or sell government securities at various prices. The propositions are then assembled and displayed on a computer screen for evaluation. The desk will select all propositions, beginning with the most attractively priced, up to the point at which the desired amount of securities is purchased or sold, and it will then notify each dealer via TRAPS on which of its propositions have been chosen. The entire selection process is typically completed in a matter of minutes.

Defensive open market operations are of two basic types. In a **repurchase agreement** (often called a **repo**), the Fed purchases securities with an agreement that the seller will repurchase them in a short period of time, anywhere from one to fifteen days from the original date of purchase. Because the effects on reserves of a repo are reversed on the day the agreement matures, a repo is actually a temporary open market purchase and is an especially desirable way of conducting a defensive open market purchase that will be reversed shortly. When the Fed wants to conduct a temporary open market sale, it engages in a **matched sale–purchase transaction** (sometimes called a **reverse repo**) in which the Fed sells securities and the buyer agrees to sell them back to the Fed in the near future.

At times, the desk may see the need to address a persistent reserve shortage or surplus and wish to arrange a dynamic open market operation that will have a more permanent impact on the supply of reserves. Outright transactions, which involve a purchase or sale of securities that is not self-reversing, are also conducted over TRAPS.

Discount Policy and the Lender of Last Resort

The facility at which banks can borrow reserves from the Federal Reserve is called the **discount window**. The easiest way to understand how the Fed affects the volume of borrowed reserves is by looking at how the discount window operates.

Operation of the Discount Window
The Fed's discount loans to banks are of three types: primary credit, secondary credit, and seasonal credit.[4] *Primary credit* is the discount lending that plays the most important role in monetary policy. Healthy banks

---

[4]The procedures for administering the discount window were changed in January 2003. The primary credit facility replaced an adjustment credit facility whose discount rate was typically set below market interest rates, so banks were restricted in their access to this credit. In contrast, healthy banks now can borrow all they want from the primary credit facility. The secondary credit facility replaced the extended credit facility, which focused somewhat more on longer-term credit extensions. The seasonal credit facility remains basically unchanged.

Inside the Fed   A Day at the Trading Desk

The manager of domestic open market operations supervises the analysts and traders who execute the purchases and sales of securities in the drive to hit the federal funds rate target. To get a grip on what might happen in the federal funds market that day, the manager's workday starts early in the morning, around 7:30 a.m., when her staff presents a review of developments in the federal funds market the previous day and an update on the actual amount of reserves in the banking system the day before. Then the staff produces updated reports that contain detailed forecasts of what will be happening to some of the short-term factors affecting the supply and demand of reserves (discussed in Chapter 14). For example, if float is predicted to decrease because good weather throughout the country is speeding up check delivery, the manager of domestic open market operations knows that she will have to conduct a defensive open market operation (in this case, a *purchase* of securities) to offset the expected decline in reserves and the monetary base from the decreased float. However, if Treasury deposits with the Fed are predicted to fall, a defensive open market *sale* would be needed to offset the expected increase in reserves. The report also predicts the change in the public's holding of currency. If currency holdings are expected to rise, then, as we saw in Chapter 14, reserves will fall, and an open market purchase is needed to raise reserves back up again.

This information helps the manager of domestic open market operations and her staff decide how large a change in nonborrowed reserves is needed to reach the federal funds rate target. If the amount of reserves in the banking system is too large, many banks will have excess reserves to lend that other banks may have little desire to hold, and the federal funds rate will fall. If the level of reserves is too low, banks seeking to borrow reserves from the few banks that have excess reserves to lend may push the funds rate higher than the desired level. Also during the morning, the staff will monitor the behavior of the federal funds rate and contact some of the major participants in the market for reserves, which may provide independent information about whether a change in reserves is needed to achieve the desired level of the federal funds rate.

Members of the manager's staff also contact several representatives of the primary dealers with whom the open market desk trades. Her staff finds out how the dealers view market conditions to get a feel for what may happen to the prices of the securities they trade in over the course of the day. They also call the Treasury to get updated information on the expected level of Treasury balances at the Fed to refine their estimates of the supply of reserves.

Members of the Monetary Affairs Division at the Board of Governors are then contacted, and the New York Fed's forecasts of reserve supply and demand are compared with the Board's. On the basis of these projections and the observed behavior of the federal funds market, the desk formulates and proposes a course of action to be taken that day, which may involve plans to add reserves to or drain reserves from the banking system through open market operations. If an operation is contemplated, the type, size, and maturity will be discussed.

At about 9 a.m., a daily conference call takes place, linking the desk with the Office of the Director of Monetary Affairs at the Board of Governors and with one of the four voting Reserve Bank presidents outside New York. During the call, a member of the open market operations unit outlines the desk's proposed reserve management strategy for the day. After the plan is approved, it is announced to the markets at 9:30 a.m., and the desk is instructed to execute immediately any temporary open market operations that are planned for that day.

At times, the desk may see the need to address a persistent reserve shortage or surplus and may wish to arrange an operation that will have a more permanent impact on the supply of reserves. These operations, referred to as *outright operations*, involve a straightforward purchase or sale of securities that is not self-reversing, and they are traditionally executed later in the day, when temporary operations are not being conducted. Even when outright operations are not being conducted, the manager of domestic open market operations and her staff do not sit idle for the rest of the day. They are continually monitoring the markets and bank reserves to plan for the next day's operations.

are allowed to borrow all they want at very short maturities (usually overnight) from the primary credit facility, and it is therefore referred to as a **standing lending facility**.[5] The interest rate on these loans is the discount rate, and as we mentioned before, it is set higher than the federal funds rate target, usually by 100 basis points (one percentage point) because the Fed prefers that banks borrow from each other in the federal funds market so that they continually monitor each other for credit risk. As a result, in most circumstances the amount of discount lending under the primary credit facility is very small. If the amount is so small, why does the Fed have this facility?

The answer is that the facility is intended to be a backup source of liquidity for sound banks so that the federal funds rate never rises too far above the federal funds target set by the FOMC. We have already seen how this works in Figure 6. When the demand for reserves experiences a large unexpected increase, no matter how far right the demand curve shifts, the equilibrium federal funds rate i_{ff}^* will stay at i_d because borrowed reserves will just continue to increase, and the federal funds rate can rise no further. The primary credit facility has thus put a ceiling on the federal funds rate at i_d.

Secondary credit is given to banks that are in financial trouble and are experiencing severe liquidity problems. The interest rate on secondary credit is set at 50 basis points (0.5 percentage point) above the discount rate. The interest rate on these loans is set at a higher, penalty rate to reflect the less-sound condition of these borrowers. *Seasonal credit* is given to meet the needs of a limited number of small banks in vacation and agricultural areas that have a seasonal pattern of deposits. The interest rate charged on seasonal credit is tied to the average of the federal funds rate and certificate of deposit rates. The Federal Reserve has questioned the need for the seasonal credit facility because of improvements in credit markets and is thus contemplating eliminating it at some point in the future.

Lender of Last Resort In addition to its use as a tool to influence reserves, the monetary base, and the money supply, discounting is important in preventing and coping with financial panics. When the Federal Reserve System was created, its most important role was intended to be as the **lender of last resort**; to prevent bank failures from spinning out of control, the Fed was to provide reserves to banks when no one else would, thereby preventing bank and financial panics. Discounting is a particularly effective way to provide reserves to the banking system during a banking crisis because reserves are immediately channeled to the banks that need them most.

In performing the role of lender of last resort, the Fed must use the discount tool wisely when attempting to thwart financial panics. This is an extremely important aspect of successful monetary policymaking. Financial panics can severely damage the economy because they interfere with the ability of financial intermediaries and markets to move funds to people with productive investment opportunities (see Chapter 12).

Unfortunately, the discount tool has not always been used by the Fed to prevent financial panics, as the massive bank failures during the Great Depression attest. The Fed learned from its mistakes of that period and has performed admirably in its role of lender of last resort in the post–World War II period. The Fed has used its discount lending weapon several times to avoid bank panics by extending loans to troubled banking institutions, thereby preventing further bank failures.

---

[5]This type of standard lending facility is commonly called a *Lombard facility* in other countries, and the interest rate charged on these loans is often called a *Lombard rate*. (This name comes from Lombardy, a region in northern Italy that was an important center of banking in the Middle Ages.)

At first glance, it might seem that the presence of the FDIC, which insures depositors up to a limit of $250,000 per account from losses due to a bank's failure, would make the lender-of-last-resort function of the Fed superfluous. There are two reasons why this is not the case. First, it is important to recognize that the FDIC's insurance fund amounts to about 1% of the total amount of deposits held by banks. If a large number of bank failures occurred simultaneously, the FDIC would not be able to cover all the depositors' losses. Indeed, the large number of bank failures in the 1980s and early 1990s led to large losses and a shrinkage of the FDIC's insurance fund, which reduced the FDIC's ability to cover depositors' losses. This fact has not weakened the confidence of small depositors in the banking system because the Fed has been ready to stand behind the banks to provide whatever reserves are needed to prevent bank panics. Second, the $1.7 trillion of large-denomination deposits in the banking system are not guaranteed by the FDIC because they exceed the $250,000 limit. A loss of confidence in the banking system could still lead to runs on banks from the large-denomination depositors, and bank panics could still occur despite the existence of the FDIC. The Federal Reserve's role as lender of last resort is, if anything, more important today than ever because of the high number of bank failures experienced in the 1980s and early 1990s, and during the global financial crisis from 2007 to 2009.

Not only can the Fed act as a lender of last resort to banks, but it can also play the same role in the financial system as a whole. The Fed's discount window can help prevent and address financial panics that are not triggered by bank failures, such as the Black Monday stock market crash of 1987 and the terrorist destruction of the World Trade Center in September 2001 (discussed in the Inside the Fed box). Although the Fed's role as the lender of last resort provides the benefit of preventing bank and financial panics, it does come with a cost. If a bank expects that the Fed will provide it with discount loans if it gets into trouble, then it will be willing to take on more risk, knowing that the Fed will come to the rescue if necessary. The Fed's lender-of-last-resort role has thus created a moral hazard problem similar to the one created by deposit insurance (discussed in Chapter 10): Banks take on more risk, thus exposing the deposit insurance agency, and hence taxpayers, to greater losses. The moral hazard problem is most severe for large banks, which may believe that the Fed and the FDIC view them as "too big to fail"; that is, they believe they will always receive Fed loans when they are in trouble because their failure would be likely to precipitate a bank panic.

Similarly, Federal Reserve actions to prevent financial panics may encourage financial institutions other than banks to take on greater risk. They, too, expect that the Fed will bail them out if their failure would cause or worsen a financial panic. When the Fed considers using the discount weapon to prevent a panic, it needs to consider the trade-off between the moral hazard cost of its role as lender of last resort and the benefit of preventing the financial panic. This trade-off explains why the Fed must be careful not to perform its function as lender of last resort too frequently.

Reserve Requirements

As we saw in Chapter 14, changes in reserve requirements affect the money supply by causing the money supply multiplier to change. A rise in reserve requirements reduces the amount of deposits that can be supported by a given level of the monetary base and leads to a contraction of the money supply. A rise in reserve requirements also increases the demand for reserves and raises the federal funds rate. Conversely, a decline in reserve requirements leads to an expansion of the money supply and a fall in the federal funds rate. The Fed has had the authority to vary reserve requirements since the 1930s;

Inside the Fed   Using Discount Policy to Prevent a Financial Panic

The Black Monday Stock Market Crash of 1987 and the Terrorist Destruction of the World Trade Center in September 2001. Although October 19, 1987, dubbed "Black Monday," will go down in the history books as the day of the largest one-day percentage decline in stock prices to date (the Dow Jones Industrial Average decreased by more than 20%), it was on Tuesday, October 20, 1987, that financial markets almost stopped functioning. Felix Rohatyn, one of the most prominent players on Wall Street, stated flatly: "Tuesday was the most dangerous day we had in 50 years."[*] Much of the credit for preventing a market meltdown after Black Monday must be given to the Federal Reserve System and then-Chair of the Board of Governors, Alan Greenspan.

The stress of keeping markets functioning during the sharp decline in stock prices that occurred on Monday, October 19, meant that many brokerage houses and specialists (dealer-brokers who maintain orderly trading on the stock exchanges) were severely in need of additional funds to finance their activities. However, understandably enough, New York banks, as well as foreign and regional U.S. banks, who were growing very nervous about the financial health of securities firms, began to cut back credit to the securities industry at the very time when it was most needed. Panic was in the air. One chair of a large specialist firm commented that on Monday, "from 2 p.m. on, there was total despair. The entire investment community fled the market. We were left alone on the field." It was time for the Fed, like the cavalry, to come to the rescue.

Upon learning of the plight of the securities industry, Alan Greenspan and E. Gerald Corrigan, then president of the Federal Reserve Bank of New York and the Fed official most closely in touch with Wall Street, became fearful of a spreading collapse of securities firms. To prevent this collapse, Greenspan announced before the market opened on Tuesday, October 20, the Federal Reserve System's "readiness to serve as a source of liquidity to support the economic and financial system." In addition to this extraordinary announcement, the Fed made it clear that it would provide discount loans to any bank that

would make loans to the securities industry, although this did not prove to be necessary. As one New York banker said, the Fed's message was, "We're here. Whatever you need, we'll give you."

The outcome of the Fed's timely action was that a financial panic was averted. The markets kept functioning on Tuesday, and a market rally ensued that day, with the Dow Jones Industrial Average climbing over 100 points.

A similar lender-of-last-resort operation was carried out in the aftermath of the destruction of the World Trade Center in New York City on Tuesday, September 11, 2001—the worst terrorist incident in U.S. history. Because of the disruption to the most important financial center in the world, the liquidity needs of the financial system skyrocketed. To satisfy these needs and to keep the financial system from seizing up, within a few hours of the incident, the Fed made an announcement similar to that made after the crash of 1987: "The Federal Reserve System is open and operating. The discount window is available to meet liquidity needs."[†] The Fed then proceeded to provide $45 billion to banks through the discount window, a 200-fold increase over the amount provided during the previous week. As a result of this action, along with the injection of as much as $80 billion of reserves into the banking system through open market operations, the financial system kept functioning. When the stock market reopened on Monday, September 17, trading was orderly, although the Dow Jones Average did decrease 7%.

The terrorists were able to bring down the twin towers of the World Trade Center, causing nearly 3,000 deaths. However, they were unable to bring down the U.S. financial system because of the timely actions of the Federal Reserve.

---

[*]"Terrible Tuesday: How the Stock Market Almost Disintegrated a Day After the Crash," *Wall Street Journal*, November 20, 1987, p. 1. This article provides a fascinating and more detailed view of the events described here and is the source of all the quotations cited.

[†]"Economic Front: How Policy Makers Regrouped to Defend the Financial System," *Wall Street Journal*, September 18, 2001, p. A1, provides more detail on this episode.

this method was once a powerful way of affecting the money supply and interest rates but is rarely used today.

The Depository Institutions Deregulation and Monetary Control Act of 1980 provided a simpler scheme for setting reserve requirements. All depository institutions, including commercial banks, savings and loan associations, mutual savings banks, and credit unions, are subject to the same reserve requirements: Required reserves on all checkable deposits—including non–interest-bearing checking accounts, NOW accounts, super-NOW accounts, and ATS (automatic transfer savings) accounts—are equal to zero for the first $13.3 million of a bank's checkable deposits, 3% on checkable deposits from $13.3 to $89.0 million, and 10% on checkable deposits over $89.0 million.[6] The percentage set at 10% can be varied between 8% and 14%, at the Fed's discretion. In extraordinary circumstances, the percentage can be raised as high as 18%.

Interest on Reserves

Because the Fed started paying interest on reserves only in 2008, this tool of monetary policy does not have a long history. For the same reason the Fed sets the discount rate above the federal funds target—that is, to encourage borrowing and lending in the federal funds market so that banks monitor each other—the Fed to date generally has set the interest rate on reserves below the federal funds target. This means that the Fed has not yet used interest on reserves as a tool of monetary policy, but instead has just used it to help provide a floor under the federal funds rate. However, in the aftermath of the global financial crisis, banks have accumulated huge quantities of excess reserves and, in this situation, increasing the federal funds rate would require massive amounts of open market operations to remove these reserves from the banking system. The interest-on-reserves tool can come to the rescue because it can be used to raise the federal funds rate, as illustrated in panel (b) of Figure 5. Indeed, it is likely that this tool of monetary policy will be used extensively when the Fed wants to raise the federal funds rate and exit from the policy of maintaining it at zero, a policy that started in December 2008.

Relative Advantages of the Different Tools

Open market operations constitute the most important conventional monetary policy tool because they have four basic advantages over the other tools:

1. Open market operations occur at the initiative of the Fed, which has complete control over their volume. This control is not found, for example, in discount operations, in which the Fed can encourage or discourage banks' borrowing of reserves by altering the discount rate but cannot directly control the volume of borrowed reserves.

2. Open market operations are flexible and precise; they can be used to the exact extent desired. No matter how small a change in reserves or the monetary base is required, open market operations can achieve it with a small purchase or sale of securities. Conversely, if the desired change in reserves or the base is very large, the open market operations tool is strong enough to do the job through a very large purchase or sale of securities.

---

[6]These figures are for 2014. Each year, the figures are adjusted upward by 80% of the percentage increase in checkable deposits in the United States.

3. Open market operations are easily reversed. If a mistake is made in conducting an open market operation, the Fed can immediately reverse it. If the trading desk decides that the federal funds rate is too low because it has made too many open market purchases, it can immediately make a correction by conducting open market sales.

4. Open market operations can be implemented quickly; they involve no administrative delays. When the trading desk decides that it wants to change the monetary base or reserves, it just places orders with securities dealers, and the trades are executed immediately. Changes to reserve requirements, on the other hand, take time to implement because banks must be given advance warning so that they can adjust their computer systems to calculate required reserves. Also, since it is costly to adjust computer systems, reversing a change in reserve requirements is burdensome to banks. For these reasons, the policy tool of changing reserve requirements does not have much to recommend it, and it is rarely used.

There are two situations in which the other tools have advantages over open market operations. One is when the Fed wants to raise interest rates after banks have accumulated large amounts of excess reserves. In this case, the federal funds rate can be raised by increasing the interest on reserves, which eliminates the need to conduct massive open market operations to raise the federal funds rate by reducing reserves. The second situation is when discount policy can be used by the Fed to perform its role as lender of last resort. The Black Monday crash, the terrorist attacks of September 11, 2001, and the global financial crisis, which we will discuss next, all indicate that the role of discount policy has become more important in the past couple of decades.

NONCONVENTIONAL MONETARY POLICY TOOLS AND QUANTITATIVE EASING

In normal times, conventional monetary policy tools, which expand the money supply and lower interest rates, are enough to stabilize the economy. However, when the economy experiences a full-scale financial crisis like the one we recently experienced, conventional monetary policy tools cannot do the job, for two reasons. First, the financial system seizes up to such an extent that it becomes unable to allocate capital to productive uses, and so investment spending and the economy collapse, as discussed in Chapter 12. Second, the negative shock to the economy can lead to the **zero-lower-bound problem**, in which the central bank is unable to lower short-term interest rates further because they have hit a floor of zero, as occurred at the end of 2008. The zero-lower-bound problem occurs because people can always earn more from holding bonds than from holding cash, and therefore nominal interest rates cannot be negative. For both of these reasons, central banks need non–interest-rate tools, known as **nonconventional monetary policy tools**, to stimulate the economy. These nonconventional monetary policy tools take three forms: (1) liquidity provision, (2) asset purchases, and (3) commitment to future monetary policy actions.

Liquidity Provision

Because conventional monetary policy actions were not sufficient to heal the financial markets during the recent financial crisis, the Federal Reserve implemented unprecedented increases in its lending facilities to provide liquidity to the financial markets.

1. **Discount Window Expansion:** At the outset of the crisis in mid-August 2007, the Fed lowered the discount rate (the interest rate on loans it makes to banks) to 50 basis points (0.50 percentage point) above the federal funds rate target from the normal 100 basis points. It then lowered it further in March 2008, to only 25 basis points above the federal funds rate target. However, because borrowing from the discount window has a "stigma" attached to it (because such borrowing suggests that the borrowing bank is desperate for funds and thus in trouble), use of the discount window was limited during the crisis.

2. **Term Auction Facility:** To encourage additional borrowing, in December 2007 the Fed set up a temporary Term Auction Facility (TAF), in which it made loans at a rate determined through competitive auctions. The TAF was more widely used than the discount window facility because it enabled banks to borrow at a rate lower than the discount rate, and the rate was determined competitively rather than being set at a penalty rate. The TAF auctions started at amounts of $20 billion, but as the crisis worsened, the Fed raised the amounts dramatically, with a total outstanding of over $400 billion. (The European Central Bank conducted similar operations, with one auction in June 2008 of over 400 billion euros.)

3. **New Lending Programs:** The Fed broadened its provision of liquidity to the financial system well beyond its traditional lending to banking institutions. These actions included lending to investment banks as well as lending to promote purchases of commercial paper, mortgage-backed securities, and other asset-backed securities. In addition, the Fed engaged in lending to J.P. Morgan to assist in its purchase of Bear Stearns and to AIG to prevent its failure. The enlargement of the Fed's lending programs during the 2007–2009 financial crisis was indeed remarkable, expanding the Fed's balance sheet by over $1 trillion by the end of 2008, with the balance-sheet expansion continuing even after 2008. The number of new programs introduced over the course of the crisis spawned a whole new set of abbreviations, including the TAF, TSLF, PDCF, AMLF, MMIFF, CPFF, and TALF. These facilities are described in more detail in the Inside the Fed box, "Fed Lending Facilities During the Global Financial Crisis."

Large-Scale Asset Purchases

The Fed's open market operations normally involve only the purchase of government securities, particularly those that are short-term. However, during the crisis, the Fed started two new, large-scale asset purchase programs (often referred to as LSAPs) to lower interest rates for particular types of credit.

1. In November 2008, the Fed set up a Government Sponsored Entities Purchase Program in which the Fed eventually purchased $1.25 trillion of mortgage-backed securities (MBS) guaranteed by Fannie Mae and Freddie Mac. Through these purchases, the Fed hoped to prop up the MBS market and to lower interest rates on residential mortgages to stimulate the housing market.

2. In November 2010, the Fed announced that it would purchase $600 billion of long-term Treasury securities at a rate of about $75 billion per month. This large-scale purchase program, which became known as QE2 (which stands for Quantitative Easing 2, not the Cunard cruise ship), was intended to lower long-term interest rates. Although *short-term* interest rates on Treasury securities hit a floor of zero during the global financial crisis, *long-term* interest rates did not. Since investment projects have a long life, long-term interest rates are more relevant to investment

Inside the Fed   Fed Lending Facilities During the Global Financial Crisis

During the global financial crisis, the Federal Reserve became very creative in assembling a host of new lending facilities to help restore liquidity to different parts of the financial system. The new facilities, the dates on which they were created, and their functions are listed in the table below.

Lending Facility	Date of Creation	Function
Term Auction Facility (TAF)	December 12, 2007	To increase borrowing from the Fed, the TAF extends loans of fixed amounts to banks at interest rates that are determined by competitive auction rather than set by the Fed as with normal discount lending
Term Securities Lending Facility (TSLF)	March 11, 2008	To provide sufficient Treasury securities to act as collateral in credit markets, the TSLF lends Treasury securities to primary dealers for terms longer than overnight against a broad range of collateral
Swap Lines	March 11, 2008	Lend dollars to foreign central banks in exchange for foreign currencies so that these central banks can in turn make dollar loans to their domestic banks
Loans to J.P. Morgan to buy Bear Stearns	March 14, 2008	Buys $30 billion of Bear Stearns assets through nonrecourse loans to J.P. Morgan to facilitate its purchase of Bear Stearns
Primary Dealer Credit Facility (PDCF)	March 16, 2008	Lends to primary dealers (including investment banks) so that they can borrow on terms similar to those on which banks borrow from the traditional discount window facility
Loans to AIG	September 16, 2008	Loans $85 billion to AIG
Asset-Backed Commercial Paper Money Market Mutual Fund Liquidity Facility (AMLF)	September 19, 2008	Lends to primary dealers so that they can purchase asset-backed commercial paper from money market mutual funds so that these funds can sell this paper to meet redemptions from their investors
Commercial Paper Funding Facility (CPFF)	October 7, 2008	Finances purchase of commercial paper from issuers
Money Market Investor Funding Facility (MMIFF)	October 21, 2008	Lends to special-purpose vehicles that can buy a wider range of money market mutual fund assets
Term Asset-Backed Securities Loan Facility (TALF)	November 25, 2008	Lends to issuers of asset-backed securities against these securities as collateral to improve functioning of this market

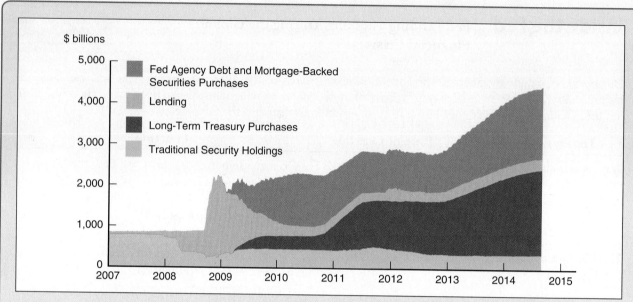

FIGURE 7   **The Expansion of the Federal Reserve's Balance Sheet, 2007–2014**

The shaded areas show the Federal Reserve's holdings of four different categories of assets: traditional security holdings, long-term Treasuries, lending, and agency debt and mortgage-backed securities. The Federal Reserve's lending and asset-purchase programs led to a quadrupling of the Fed's balance sheet.

Source: Federal Reserve Bank of Cleveland: http://www.clevelandfed.org/research/data/redit_easing/index.cfm

decisions than short-term rates. The Fed's purchase of long-term Treasuries was an effort to stimulate investment spending and the economy by lowering long-term interest rates.

3. In September 2012, the Federal Reserve announced a third large-scale asset-purchase program, which became known as *QE3*, that combined elements of QE1 and QE2. Through QE3, the Fed conducted purchases of $40 billion of mortgage-backed securities and $45 billion of long-term Treasuries. However, QE3 differed in one major way from the previous QE programs in that its goal was not to increase assets by a fixed dollar amount but instead was open-ended, with the purchase plan set to continue "if the outlook for the labor market does not improve substantially."

These liquidity-provision and large-scale asset-purchase programs led to an unprecedented quadrupling of the Federal Reserve's balance sheet (shown in Figure 7).

Quantitative Easing Versus Credit Easing

As we just learned, the programs introduced by the Fed in response to the global financial crisis led to an unprecedented expansion of the Federal Reserve's balance sheet. From before the financial crisis began in September 2007 through 2014, the amount of Federal Reserve assets rose from about $800 billion to over $4 trillion. This expansion of the balance sheet is referred to as **quantitative easing** because, as shown in Chapter 14, it leads to a huge increase in the monetary base. Because such an increase in the monetary base would usually result in an expansion of the money supply, it seems as though such an expansion could be a powerful force in stimulating the economy in the near term and possibly producing inflation down the road.

There are reasons to be very skeptical of this hypothesis. First, as we saw in the final application in Chapter 14, the huge expansion in the Fed's balance sheet and the monetary base did not result in a large increase in the money supply, because most of the increase in the monetary base just flowed into holdings of excess reserves. Second, because the federal funds rate had already fallen to the zero lower bound, the expansion of the balance sheet and the monetary base could not lower short-term interest rates any further and thereby stimulate the economy. Third, an increase in the monetary base does not mean that banks will increase lending, because they can just add to their holdings of excess reserves instead of making loans. Indeed, this appears to be exactly what happened during the global financial crisis, when the huge increase in the monetary base led primarily to a massive rise in excess reserves, and bank lending did not increase. A similar phenomenon seems to have occurred when the Bank of Japan engaged in quantitative easing after Japan's stock and real estate market bubbles burst in the 1990s; yet not only did the Japanese economy fail to recover, but inflation even turned negative.

Does skepticism about the merits of quantitative easing mean that the Fed's non-conventional monetary policy actions during the financial crisis were ineffective in stimulating the economy? Former Fed Chair Ben Bernanke has argued that the answer is no, because the Fed's policies were directed not at expanding the Fed's balance sheet but rather at **credit easing**—that is, altering the composition of the Fed's balance sheet in order to improve the functioning of particular segments of the credit markets. Indeed, Bernanke was adamant that the Fed's policies should not be characterized as quantitative easing.

Altering the composition of the Fed's balance sheet can stimulate the economy in several ways. First, when the Fed provides liquidity to a particular segment of the credit markets that has seized up, such liquidity can help unfreeze the market and thereby enable it to allocate capital to productive uses, consequently stimulating the economy. Second, when the Fed purchases particular securities, it increases the demand for those securities and, as we saw in Chapter 6, such an action can lower the interest rates on those securities relative to rates on other securities. Thus, even if short-term interest rates have hit a floor of zero, asset purchases can lower interest rates for borrowers in particular credit markets and thereby stimulate spending. For example, purchases of GSE mortgage-backed securities appear to have lowered the interest rates on these securities, which led to a substantial decrease in residential mortgage rates. Purchases of long-term government securities could also lower their interest rates relative to short-term interest rates, and because long-term interest rates are likely to be more relevant to investment decisions, these asset market purchases could boost investment spending. Recent research appears to support this viewpoint, with estimates of the decline in long-term interest rates following the Fed's asset purchase programs on the order of 100 basis points (one percentage point).[7]

---

[7]See, for example, Joseph Gagnon, Mathew Raskin, Julie Remache, and Brian Sack, "Large Scale Asset Purchases by the Federal Reserve: Did They Work?" *Federal Reserve Bank of New York Economic Policy Review*, Volume 17, Number 1 (May 2011), pp. 41–59.

Forward Guidance and the Commitment to Future Policy Actions

Although short-term interest rates could not be driven below zero in the aftermath of the global financial crisis, the Federal Reserve had the option of taking a different route in its efforts to achieve lower long-term interest rates, which, as we mentioned above, would stimulate the economy. This route involved a commitment by the Fed to keep the federal funds rate at zero for a long period of time. To see how this would work, recall our discussion of the expectations theory of the term structure of interest rates in Chapter 6. There we saw that long-term interest rates will equal an average of the short-term interest rates that markets expect to occur over the life of the long-term bond. By committing to the future policy action of keeping the federal funds rate at zero for an extended period, the Fed could lower the market's expectations of future short-term interest rates, thereby causing the long-term interest rate to fall. Michael Woodford of Columbia University has referred to such a strategy as **management of expectations**, but it is more commonly referred to as **forward guidance**.

The Fed pursued this forward-guidance strategy when it announced, after its FOMC meeting on December 16, 2008, that not only would it lower the federal funds rate target to between zero and ¼%, but also that "the Committee anticipates that weak economic conditions are likely to warrant exceptionally low levels of the federal funds rate for some time." The Fed continued to use this type of language in its FOMC statements for several years afterward, even committing to keep the federal funds rate near zero until an actual date of mid-2013 at its FOMC meeting in August of 2011 (modified to mid-2015 at later meetings). Although long-term interest rates on Treasury securities did subsequently fall, it is not clear how much of this decline was due to the Fed's forward guidance versus the general weakness of the economy.

There are two types of commitments to future policy actions: conditional and unconditional. The commitment to keep the federal funds rate at zero for an extended period starting in 2008 was *conditional* because it stated that the decision was predicated on a weak economy going forward. If economic circumstances changed, the FOMC was indicating that it might abandon the commitment. Alternatively, the Fed could have made an *unconditional* commitment by just stating that it would keep the federal funds rate at zero for an extended period, without indicating that this decision might change depending on the state of the economy. An unconditional commitment is stronger than a conditional commitment because it does not suggest that the commitment will be abandoned and so is likely to have a larger effect on long-term interest rates. Unfortunately, it has the disadvantage that, even if circumstances change in such a way that it would be better to abandon the commitment, the Fed may feel that it cannot go back on its word and therefore cannot abandon the commitment.

The disadvantages of an unconditional commitment are illustrated by the Fed's experience in the 2003–2006 period. In 2003, the Fed became worried that inflation was too low and that the probability of a deflation was significant. At the August 12, 2003, FOMC meeting, the FOMC stated, "In these circumstances, the Committee believes that policy accommodation can be maintained for a considerable period." Then, when the Fed started to tighten policy at its June 30, 2004, FOMC meeting, it changed its statement to "policy accommodation can be removed at a pace that is likely to be measured." For the next ten FOMC meetings, through June 2006, the Fed raised the federal funds rate target by exactly ¼ percentage point at every single meeting. The market interpreted the FOMC's statements as indicating an unconditional commitment, and this is why the Fed may have been constrained not to deviate from a ¼ percentage point move at every FOMC meeting. In retrospect, this commitment led to monetary policy that was too easy for too long, with inflation subsequently rising to well above desirable levels and, as discussed in Chapter 12, may have helped promote the housing bubble whose bursting led to such devastating consequences for the economy.

When the Fed announced a specific date for exiting from exceptionally low rates, many market participants viewed this announcement as an unconditional commitment, despite the Federal Reserve's objections to such an interpretation. To avoid the problems associated with an unconditional commitment, in December of 2012 the Fed changed its statement to be more clearly conditional by indicating that "the exceptionally low range for the federal funds rate will be appropriate at least as long as the unemployment rate remains above 6-1/2 percent, and inflation between one and two years ahead is projected to be no more than a half percentage point above the Committee's 2 percent longer-run goal."

Although it is an improvement over a fixed-date commitment, this type of conditional approach based on thresholds is not without its own problems. First, it may be viewed as a Federal Reserve commitment to achieve a specific unemployment rate, regardless of the monetary stimulus required to reach it. It was exactly this kind of commitment that got the Fed into trouble in the 1970s and produced the escalation in inflation that became known as the "Great Inflation" (discussed in Chapter 23). Second, this approach may be viewed as an increase in the inflation target from 2% to 2.5% and a weakening of the Federal Reserve's credibility with regard to its commitment to keep inflation low and stable. As we will see in Chapter 24, this loss of credibility can result in poorer outcomes in stabilizing not only inflation but also economic activity.

At its March 2014 meeting, with the unemployment rate approaching 6½%, the FOMC dropped forward guidance based on unemployment and inflation thresholds. Instead, it announced that it would assess its commitment to keeping the federal funds rate near zero by taking "into account a wide range of information, including measures of labor market conditions, indicators of inflation pressures and inflation expectations, and readings on financial developments."

MONETARY POLICY TOOLS OF THE EUROPEAN CENTRAL BANK

Like the Federal Reserve, the European System of Central Banks (usually referred to as the European Central Bank) signals the stance of its monetary policy by setting a **target financing rate**, which in turn sets a target for the **overnight cash rate**. Like the federal funds rate, the overnight cash rate is the interest rate for very short-term interbank loans. The monetary policy tools used by the European Central Bank are similar to those used by the Federal Reserve and involve open market operations, lending to banks, and reserve requirements.

Open Market Operations

Like the Federal Reserve, the European Central Bank uses open market operations as its primary tool for conducting monetary policy and setting the overnight cash rate at the target financing rate. **Main refinancing operations** are the predominant form of open market operations and are similar to the Fed's repo transactions. They involve weekly **reverse transactions** (purchase or sale of eligible assets under repurchase or credit operations against eligible assets as collateral) that are reversed within two weeks. Credit institutions submit bids, and the European Central Bank decides which bids to accept. Like the Federal Reserve, the European Central Bank accepts the most attractively priced bids and makes purchases or sales up to the point at which the desired amount of reserves is supplied. In contrast to the Federal Reserve, which conducts open market operations in one location at the Federal Reserve Bank of New York, the European Central Bank decentralizes its open market operations by conducting them through the individual national central banks.

A second category of open market operations is **longer-term refinancing operations**, which are a much smaller source of liquidity for the euro-area banking system and are similar to the Fed's outright purchases or sales of securities. These operations are carried out monthly and typically involve purchases or sales of securities with a maturity of three months. They are not used for signaling the monetary policy stance, but instead are aimed at providing euro-area banks access to longer-term funds.

Lending to Banks

As is the case for the Fed, the next most important tool of monetary policy for the European Central Bank involves lending to banking institutions, which is carried out by the national central banks, just as discount lending is performed by the individual Federal Reserve Banks. This lending takes place through a standing lending facility called the **marginal lending facility**. Through these facilities, banks can borrow (against eligible collateral) overnight loans from the national central banks at the **marginal lending rate**, which is set at 100 basis points above the target financing rate. The marginal lending rate provides a ceiling for the overnight market interest rate in the European Monetary Union, just as the discount rate does in the United States. As in the United States, Canada, Australia, and New Zealand, the Eurosystem has another standing facility, the **deposit facility**, in which banks are paid a fixed interest rate that is 100 basis points below the target financing rate. The prespecified interest rate on the deposit facility provides a floor for the overnight market interest rate, while the marginal lending rate sets a ceiling. This creates a channel/corridor, but with a much wider range of 100 basis points on either side.

Reserve Requirements

Like the Federal Reserve, the European Central Bank imposes reserve requirements such that all deposit-taking institutions are required to hold 2% of the total amount of checking deposits and other short-term deposits in reserve accounts with national central banks. All institutions that are subject to minimum reserve requirements have access to the European Central Bank's standing lending facilities and participate in open market operations.

SUMMARY

1. A supply and demand analysis of the market for reserves yields the following results: When the Fed makes an open market purchase or lowers reserve requirements, the federal funds rate drops. When the Fed makes an open market sale or raises reserve requirements, the federal funds rate rises. Changes in the discount rate and the interest rate paid on reserves may also affect the federal funds rate.

2. Conventional monetary policy tools include open market operations, discount policy, reserve requirements, and interest on reserves. Open market operations are the primary tool used by the Fed to implement monetary policy in normal times because they occur at the initiative of the Fed, are flexible, are easily reversed, and can be implemented quickly. Discount policy has the advantage of enabling the Fed to perform its role of lender of last resort, while raising interest rates on reserves to increase the federal funds rate eliminates the need to conduct massive open market operations to reduce reserves when banks have accumulated large amounts of excess reserves.

3. Conventional monetary policy tools are no longer effective when the zero-lower-bound problem occurs, in which the central bank is unable to lower short-term interest rates because they have hit a floor of zero. In this situation, central banks use nonconventional monetary policy tools, which involve liquidity provision, asset purchases, and commitment to future policy actions. Liquidity provision and asset purchases lead to an expansion of the central bank balance sheet, which is referred to as *quantitative easing*. Expansion of the central bank balance sheet by itself is unlikely to have a large impact on the economy, but changing the composition of the balance sheet, which is accomplished by liquidity provisions and asset purchases and is referred to as *credit easing*, can have a large impact by improving the functioning of credit markets.

4. The monetary policy tools used by the European Central Bank are similar to those used by the Federal Reserve System and involve open market operations, lending to banks, and reserve requirements. Main financing operations—open market operations in repos that are typically reversed within two weeks—are the primary tool used to set the overnight cash rate at the target financing rate. The European Central Bank also operates standing lending facilities, which ensure that the overnight cash rate remains within 100 basis points of the target financing rate.

KEY TERMS

conventional monetary policy tools, p. 348

credit easing, p. 359

defensive open market operations, p. 348

deposit facility, p. 362

discount window, p. 349

dynamic open market operations, p. 348

federal funds rate, p. 341

forward guidance, p. 360

lender of last resort, p. 351

longer-term refinancing operations, p. 362

main refinancing operations, p. 361

management of expectations, p. 360

marginal lending facility, p. 362

marginal lending rate, p. 362

matched sale–purchase transaction (reverse repo), p. 349

nonconventional monetary policy tools, p. 355

overnight cash rate, p. 361

primary dealers, p. 349

quantitative easing, p. 358

repurchase agreement (repo), p. 348

reverse transactions, p. 361

standing lending facility, p. 351

target financing rate, p. 361

zero-lower-bound problem, p. 355

QUESTIONS

All questions are available in MyEconLab *at* http://www.myeconlab.com.

1. If the manager of the open market desk hears that a snowstorm is about to strike New York City, making it difficult to present checks for payment there and so raising the float, what defensive open market operations will the manager undertake?

2. During the holiday season, when the public's holdings of currency increase, what defensive open market operations typically occur? Why?

3. If the Treasury pays a large bill to defense contractors and as a result its deposits with the Fed fall, what defensive open market operations will the manager of the open market desk undertake?

4. If float decreases to below its normal level, why might the manager of domestic operations consider it more desirable to use repurchase agreements to affect the monetary base, rather than an outright purchase of bonds?

5. "The only way that the Fed can affect the level of borrowed reserves is by adjusting the discount rate." Is this statement true, false, or uncertain? Explain your answer.

6. "The federal funds rate can never be above the discount rate." Is this statement true, false, or uncertain? Explain your answer.

7. "The federal funds rate can never be below the interest rate paid on reserves." Is this statement true, false, or uncertain? Explain your answer.

8. Why is paying interest on reserves an important tool for the Federal Reserve in managing crises?

9. Why are repurchase agreements used to conduct most short-term monetary policy operations, rather than the simple, outright purchase and sale of securities?

10. Open market operations are typically repurchase agreements. What does this tell you about the likely volume of defensive open market operations relative to the volume of dynamic open market operations?

11. Following the global financial crisis in 2008, assets on the Federal Reserve's balance sheet increased dramatically, from approximately $800 billion at the end of 2007 to $3 trillion by 2011. Many of the assets held are longer-term securities acquired through various loan programs instituted as a result of the crisis. In this situation, how could reverse repos (matched sale–purchase transactions) help the Fed reduce its assets held in an orderly fashion, while reducing potential inflationary problems in the future?

12. "Discount loans are no longer needed because the presence of the FDIC eliminates the possibility of bank panics." Is this statement true, false, or uncertain?

13. What are the disadvantages of using loans to financial institutions to prevent bank panics?

14. "Considering that raising reserve requirements to 100% makes complete control of the money supply possible, Congress should authorize the Fed to raise reserve requirements to this level." Discuss.

15. Compare the methods of controlling the money supply—open market operations, loans to financial institutions, and changes in reserve requirements—--on the basis of the following criteria: flexibility, reversibility, effectiveness, and speed of implementation.

16. Why was the Term Auction Facility more widely used by financial institutions than the discount window during the global financial crisis?

17. What are the advantages and disadvantages of *quantitative easing* as an alternative to conventional monetary policy when short-term interest rates are at the zero lower bound?

18. Why is the composition of the Fed's balance sheet a potentially important aspect of monetary policy during an economic crisis?

19. What is the main advantage and the main disadvantage of an unconditional policy commitment?

APPLIED PROBLEMS

All applied problems are available in MyEconLab at http://www.myeconlab.com.

20. If a switch occurs from deposits into currency, what happens to the federal funds rate? Use the supply and demand analysis of the market for reserves to explain your answer.

21. Why is it that a decrease in the discount rate does not normally lead to an increase in borrowed reserves? Use the supply and demand analysis of the market for reserves to explain.

22. Using the supply and demand analysis of the market for reserves, indicate what happens to the federal funds rate, borrowed reserves, and nonborrowed reserves, holding everything else constant, under the following situations.

   a. The economy is surprisingly strong, leading to an increase in the amount of checkable deposits.

   b. Banks expect an unusually large increase in withdrawals from checking deposit accounts in the future.

   c. The Fed raises the target federal funds rate.

   d. The Fed raises the interest rate on reserves above the current equilibrium federal funds rate.

   e. The Fed reduces reserve requirements.

   f. The Fed reduces reserve requirements and then offsets this action by conducting an open market sale of securities.

DATA ANALYSIS PROBLEMS

The Problems update with real-time data in MyEconLab and are available for practice or instructor assignment.

1. Go to the St. Louis Federal Reserve FRED database, and find data on nonborrowed reserves (NONBORRES) and the federal funds rate (FEDFUNDS).

   a. Calculate the percent change in nonborrowed reserves and the percentage point change in the federal funds rate for the most recent month of data available and for the same month a year earlier.

   b. Is your answer to part (a) consistent with what you expect from the market for reserves? Why or why not?

2. In December 2008, the Fed switched from a point federal funds target to a range target (and it's possible that it will switch back to a point target in the future). Go to the St. Louis Federal Reserve FRED database, and find data on the federal funds targets/ranges (DFEDTAR, DFEDTARU, DFEDTARL) and the effective federal funds rate (DFF). Download into a spreadsheet the data from the beginning of 2006 through the most current data available.

   a. What is the current federal funds target/range, and how does it compare to the effective federal funds rate?

   b. When was the last time the Fed missed its target or was outside the target range? By how much did it miss?

   c. For each daily observation, calculate the "miss" by taking the absolute value of the difference between the effective federal funds rate and the target (use the abs(.) function). For the periods in which the rate was a range, calculate the absolute value of the "miss" as the amount by which the effective federal funds rate was above or below the range. What was the average daily miss between the beginning of 2006 and the end of 2007? What was the average daily miss between the beginning of 2008 and December 15, 2008? What is the average daily miss for the period from December 16, 2008, to the most current date available? Since 2006, what was the largest single daily miss? Comment on the Fed's ability to control the federal funds rate during these three periods.

WEB EXERCISES

1. Go to http://www.federalreserve.gov/fomc/. This site reports activity by the FOMC. Scroll down to Calendar and click on the statement released after the most recent FOMC meeting. Summarize this statement in one paragraph. Be sure to note what the committee decided to do to the federal funds rate target. Now review the statements from the past two meetings. Has the stance of the committee changed?

2. Go to http://www.federalreserve.gov/releases/h15/update/. What is the current federal funds rate? What is the current Federal Reserve discount rate? (Define this rate as well.) Have short-term rates increased or decreased since the end of 2008?

WEB REFERENCES

http://www.federalreserve.gov/fomc/fundsrate.htm

Historical federal funds rates and discussions about Federal Reserve targets.

http://www.frbdiscountwindow.org/

Information on the operation of the discount window, and data on current and historical interest rates.

http://www.federalreserve.gov/monetarypolicy/reservereq.htm

Historical data and discussions about reserve requirements.

http://www.federalreserve.gov/fomc

A discussion about the Federal Open Market Committee, a list of current members, meeting dates, and other current information.

The Conduct of Monetary Policy: Strategy and Tactics

Learning Objectives

- Define and recognize the importance of a nominal anchor.
- Identify the six potential goals that monetary policymakers may pursue.
- Summarize the distinctions between hierarchical and dual mandates.
- Compare and contrast the advantages and disadvantages of inflation targeting.
- Identify the key changes made over time to the Federal Reserve's monetary policy strategy.
- List the four lessons learned from the global financial crisis, and discuss what they mean for inflation targeting.
- Summarize the arguments for and against central bank policy responses to asset-price bubbles.
- Describe and assess the four criteria for choosing a policy instrument.
- Interpret and assess the performance of the Taylor rule as a hypothetical policy instrument for setting the federal funds rate.

Preview

Getting monetary policy right is crucial to the health of the economy. Overly expansionary monetary policy leads to high inflation, which decreases the efficiency of the economy and hampers economic growth. Monetary policy that is too tight can produce serious recessions in which output falls and unemployment rises. It can also lead to deflation, a fall in the price level such as occurred in the United States during the Great Depression and in Japan more recently. As we saw in Chapter 12, deflation can be especially damaging to an economy because it promotes financial instability and can worsen financial crises.

Now that we understand the tools that central banks such as the Federal Reserve use to conduct monetary policy, we can consider how central banks *should* conduct monetary policy. To explore this subject, we start by looking at the goals of monetary policy and then examine one of the most important strategies for the conduct of monetary policy, inflation targeting. We then discuss tactics—that is, the choice and setting of the monetary policy instrument.

THE PRICE STABILITY GOAL AND THE NOMINAL ANCHOR

Over the past few decades, policymakers throughout the world have become increasingly aware of the social and economic costs of inflation, and more concerned with maintaining a stable price level as a goal of economic policy. Indeed, **price stability**, which central bankers define as low and stable inflation, is increasingly viewed as the most important goal of monetary policy. Price stability is desirable because a rising price level (inflation) creates uncertainty in the economy, and that uncertainty might hamper economic growth. For example, when the overall level of prices is changing, the information conveyed by the prices of goods and services is harder to interpret, which complicates decision making for consumers, businesses, and governments, thereby leading to a less efficient financial system.

Not only do public opinion surveys indicate that the public is hostile to inflation, but a growing body of evidence also suggests that inflation leads to lower economic growth. The most extreme example of unstable prices is *hyperinflation*, such as occurred in Argentina, Brazil, Russia, and Zimbabwe in the recent past. Hyperinflation has proved to be very damaging to the workings of an economy.

Inflation also makes it difficult to plan for the future. For example, it is more difficult to decide how much to put aside to provide for a child's college education in an inflationary environment. Furthermore, inflation can strain a country's social fabric: Conflict might result, because each group in the society may compete with other groups to make sure that its income keeps up with the rising level of prices.

The Role of a Nominal Anchor

Because price stability is so crucial to the long-term health of an economy, a central element in successful monetary policy is the use of a **nominal anchor**—a nominal variable, such as the inflation rate or the money supply, that ties down the price level to achieve price stability. Adherence to a nominal anchor that keeps the nominal variable within a narrow range promotes price stability by directly promoting low and stable inflation expectations. A more subtle reason for a nominal anchor's importance is that it can limit the **time-inconsistency problem**, in which monetary policy conducted on a discretionary, day-by-day basis leads to poor long-term outcomes.

The Time-Inconsistency Problem

The time-inconsistency problem is something we deal with continually in everyday life. We often have a plan that we know will produce a good outcome in the long run, but when tomorrow comes, we just can't help ourselves and we renege on our plan because doing so has short-term gains. For example, we make a New Year's resolution to go on a diet, but soon thereafter we can't resist having one more bite of that rocky road ice cream—and then another bite, and then another bite—and the weight begins to pile back on. In other words, we find ourselves unable to *consistently* follow a good plan over *time*; the good plan is said to be *time-inconsistent* and will soon be abandoned.

Monetary policymakers also face the time-inconsistency problem. They are always tempted to pursue a discretionary monetary policy that is more expansionary than firms or people expect because such a policy would boost economic output (or lower unemployment) in the short run. The best policy, however, is *not* to pursue expansionary policy, because decisions about wages and prices reflect workers' and firms' expectations about policy; when they see a central bank pursuing expansionary policy, workers and firms will raise their expectations about inflation, driving wages and prices up. The rise in wages and prices will lead to higher inflation, but will not result in higher output on average. (We examine this issue more formally in Chapter 24.)

A central bank will have better inflation performance in the long run if it does not try to surprise people with an unexpectedly expansionary policy, but instead keeps inflation under control. However, even if a central bank recognizes that discretionary policy will lead to a poor outcome (high inflation with no gains in output), it still may not be able to pursue the better policy of inflation control because politicians are likely to apply pressure on the central bank to try to boost output with overly expansionary monetary policy.

A clue as to how we should deal with the time-inconsistency problem comes from how-to books on parenting. Parents know that giving in to a child to keep him from acting up will produce a very spoiled child. Nevertheless, when a child throws a tantrum, many parents give him what he wants just to shut him up. Because parents don't stick to their "do not give in" plan, the child expects that he will get what he wants if he behaves badly, so he continues to throw tantrums, over and over again. Parenting books suggest a solution to the time-inconsistency problem (although they don't call it that): Parents should set behavior rules for their children and stick to them.

A nominal anchor is like a behavior rule. Just as rules can help prevent the time-inconsistency problem in parenting by helping adults resist pursuing the discretionary policy of giving in, a nominal anchor can help prevent the time-inconsistency problem in monetary policy by providing an expected constraint on discretionary policy.

OTHER GOALS OF MONETARY POLICY

Although price stability is the primary goal of most central banks, five other goals are continually mentioned by central bank officials when they discuss the objectives of monetary policy: (1) high employment and output stability, (2) economic growth, (3) stability of financial markets, (4) interest-rate stability, and (5) stability in foreign exchange markets.

High Employment and Output Stability

High employment is a worthy goal for two main reasons: (1) the alternative situation—high unemployment—causes much human misery; and (2) when unemployment is high, the economy has both idle workers and idle resources (closed factories and unused equipment), resulting in a loss of output (lower GDP).

Although it is clear that high employment is desirable, how high should it be? At what point can we say that the economy is at full employment? At first, it might seem that full employment is the point at which no worker is out of a job—that is, when unemployment is zero. But this definition ignores the fact that some unemployment, called *frictional unemployment*, which involves searches by workers and firms to find suitable matchups, is beneficial to the economy. For example, a worker who decides to look for a better job might be unemployed for a while during the job search. Workers often decide to leave work temporarily to pursue other activities (raising a family, travel, returning to school), and when they decide to reenter the job market, it may take some time for them to find the right job.

Another reason that unemployment is not zero when the economy is at full employment is *structural unemployment*, a mismatch between job requirements and the skills or availability of local workers. Clearly, this kind of unemployment is undesirable. Nonetheless, it is something that monetary policy can do little about.

This goal of high employment is not an unemployment level of zero but a level above zero that is consistent with full employment, the point at which the demand for labor equals the supply of labor. This level is called the **natural rate of unemployment**.

Although this definition sounds neat and authoritative, it leaves a troublesome question unanswered: What unemployment rate is consistent with full employment? In some cases, it is obvious that the unemployment rate is too high. The unemployment rate in excess of 20% during the Great Depression, for example, was clearly far too high. In the early 1960s, on the other hand, policymakers thought that a reasonable goal for the unemployment rate was 4%, a level that was probably too low, because it led to accelerating inflation. Current estimates of the natural rate of unemployment place it between $4\frac{1}{2}$ and 6%, but even this estimate is subject to much uncertainty and disagreement. It is possible, for example, that appropriate government policy, such as the provision of better information about job vacancies or job training programs, might decrease the natural rate of unemployment.

The high employment goal can be thought of in another way. Because the level of unemployment is tied to the level of economic activity in the economy, a particular level of output is produced at the natural rate of unemployment, which naturally enough is referred to as the **natural rate of output** but is more often referred to as **potential output**.

Trying to achieve the goal of high employment thus means that central banks should try to move the level of output toward the natural rate of output. In other words, they should try to stabilize the level of output around its natural rate.

Economic Growth

The goal of steady economic growth is closely related to the high-employment goal because businesses are more likely to invest in capital equipment to increase productivity and economic growth when unemployment is low. Conversely, if unemployment is high and factories are idle, it does not pay for a firm to invest in additional plants and equipment. Although the two goals are closely related, policies can be aimed specifically at promoting economic growth by directly encouraging firms to invest or by encouraging people to save, which provides more funds for firms to invest. In fact, this approach is the stated purpose of *supply-side economics* policies, which are intended to spur economic growth by providing tax incentives for businesses to invest in facilities and equipment and for taxpayers to save more. Active debate continues over the role that monetary policy should play in boosting growth.

Stability of Financial Markets

As our analysis in Chapter 12 showed, financial crises can interfere with the ability of financial markets to channel funds to people with productive investment opportunities, and can lead to a sharp contraction in economic activity. The promotion of a more stable financial system, in which financial crises are avoided, is thus an important goal for a central bank. Indeed, as we saw in Chapter 13, the Federal Reserve System was created to promote financial stability in the wake of the bank panic of 1907.

Interest-Rate Stability

Interest-rate stability is desirable because fluctuations in interest rates can create uncertainty in the economy and make it harder to plan for the future. Fluctuations in interest rates that affect consumers' willingness to buy houses, for example, make it more difficult for consumers to decide when to purchase a house and for construction firms to plan how many houses to build. A central bank may also want to reduce upward movements in interest rates for the reasons we discussed in Chapter 13: Upward movements in interest rates generate hostility toward central banks and lead to demands that their power be curtailed.

The stability of financial markets is also fostered by interest-rate stability, because fluctuations in interest rates create great uncertainty for financial institutions. An increase in interest rates produces large capital losses on long-term bonds and mortgages, losses that can cause the failures of the financial institutions holding them. In recent years, more pronounced interest-rate fluctuations have been a particularly severe problem for savings and loan associations and mutual savings banks, many of which got into serious financial trouble in the 1980s and early 1990s.

Stability in Foreign Exchange Markets

With the increasing importance of international trade to the U.S. economy, the value of the dollar relative to other currencies has become a major consideration for the Fed. A rise in the value of the dollar makes American industries less competitive with those abroad, and a drop in the value of the dollar stimulates inflation in the United States. In addition, preventing large changes in the value of the dollar makes it easier for firms and individuals purchasing or selling goods abroad to plan ahead. Stabilizing extreme movements in the value of the dollar in foreign exchange markets is thus an important goal of monetary policy. In other countries, which are even more dependent on foreign trade, stability in foreign exchange markets takes on even greater importance.

SHOULD PRICE STABILITY BE THE PRIMARY GOAL OF MONETARY POLICY?

In the long run, no inconsistency exists between the price stability goal and the other goals mentioned earlier. The natural rate of unemployment is not lowered by high inflation, so higher inflation cannot produce lower unemployment or more employment in the long run. In other words, there is no long-run trade-off between inflation and employment. In the long run, price stability promotes economic growth as well as financial and interest-rate stability. Although price stability is consistent with the other goals in the long run, in the short run price stability often conflicts with the goals of output stability and interest-rate stability. For example, when the economy is expanding and unemployment is falling, the economy may become overheated, leading to a rise in inflation. To pursue the price stability goal, a central bank would prevent this overheating by raising interest rates, an action that would initially cause output to fall and increase interest-rate instability. How should a central bank resolve this conflict among goals?

Hierarchical Versus Dual Mandates

Because price stability is crucial to the long-run health of the economy, many countries have decided that price stability should be the primary, long-run goal for central banks. For example, the Maastricht Treaty, which created the European Central Bank, states, "The primary objective of the European System of Central Banks [ESCB] shall be to maintain price stability. Without prejudice to the objective of price stability, the ESCB shall support the general economic policies in the Community," which include objectives such as "a high level of employment" and "sustainable and non-inflationary growth." Mandates of this type, which put the goal of price stability first and then state that other goals can be pursued as long as price stability is achieved, are known as **hierarchical mandates**. They are the directives governing the behavior of such central banks as the Bank of England, the Bank of Canada, and the Reserve Bank of New Zealand, as well as the European Central Bank.

In contrast, the legislation that defines the mission of the Federal Reserve states, "The Board of Governors of the Federal Reserve System and the Federal Open Market Committee shall maintain long-run growth of the monetary and credit aggregates commensurate with the economy's long-run potential to increase production, so as to promote effectively the goals of maximum employment, stable prices, and moderate long-term interest rates." Because, as we learned in Chapter 5, long-term interest rates will be very high if inflation is high, this statement in practice is a **dual mandate** to achieve two coequal objectives: price stability and maximum employment (output stability).

Is it better for an economy to operate under a hierarchical mandate or a dual mandate?

Price Stability as the Primary, Long-Run Goal of Monetary Policy

Because no inconsistency exists between achieving price stability in the long run and the natural rate of unemployment, these two types of mandates are not very different *if maximum employment is defined as the natural rate of employment.* In practice, however, a substantial difference between these two mandates might exist because the public and politicians may believe that a hierarchical mandate puts too much emphasis on inflation control and not enough on stabilizing output.

Because low and stable inflation rates promote economic growth, central bankers have come to realize that price stability should be the primary, long-run goal of monetary policy. Nevertheless, because output fluctuations should also be a concern of monetary policy, the goal of price stability should be seen as primary only in the long run. Attempts to keep inflation at the same level in the short run, no matter what else is happening in the economy, are likely to lead to excessive output fluctuations.

As long as price stability is a long-run, but not short-run, goal, central banks can focus on reducing output fluctuations by allowing inflation to deviate from the long-run goal for short periods and, therefore, can operate under a dual mandate. However, if a dual mandate leads a central bank to pursue short-run expansionary policies that increase output and employment without worrying about the long-run consequences for inflation, the time-inconsistency problem may recur. Concerns that a dual mandate might lead to overly expansionary policy is a key reason why central bankers often favor hierarchical mandates in which the pursuit of price stability takes precedence. Hierarchical mandates can also be a problem if they lead to a central bank behaving as what the Governor of the Bank of England, Mervyn King, referred to as an "inflation nutter"—that is, a central bank that focuses solely on inflation control, even in the short run, and so undertakes policies that lead to large output fluctuations. Deciding which type of mandate is better for a central bank ultimately depends on the subtleties of how the mandate will work in practice. Either type of mandate is acceptable as long as it operates to make price stability the primary goal in the long run, but not in the short run.

INFLATION TARGETING

The recognition that price stability should be the primary long-run goal of monetary policy and that a nominal anchor is a valuable tool in helping to achieve this goal has led to a monetary policy strategy known as *inflation targeting.* **Inflation targeting** involves several elements: (1) public announcement of medium-term numerical objectives (targets) for inflation; (2) an institutional commitment to price stability as the primary, long-run goal of monetary policy and a commitment to achieving the inflation goal; (3) an information-inclusive approach in which many variables (not just monetary aggregates) are used in making decisions about monetary policy; (4) increased transparency of the monetary policy strategy through communication with the public and the markets about the plans and objectives of monetary policymakers; and (5) increased accountability of the central bank for attaining its inflation objectives. New Zealand was the first country to formally adopt inflation targeting in 1990, followed by Canada in 1991, the United Kingdom in 1992, Sweden and Finland in 1993, and Australia and Spain in 1994. Israel, Chile, and Brazil, among other countries, have also adopted a form of inflation targeting.[1]

Inflation Targeting in New Zealand, Canada, and the United Kingdom

We begin our look at inflation targeting with New Zealand, because it was the first country to adopt this strategy. We then go on to examine inflation targeting in Canada and the United Kingdom, which were the next countries to adopt it.

New Zealand   As part of a general reform of the government's role in the economy, the New Zealand parliament passed a new Reserve Bank of New Zealand Act in 1989, which became effective on February 1, 1990. In addition to increasing the independence of the central bank, which transformed it from one of the least independent central banks among developed countries to one of the most independent, the act committed the Reserve Bank to a sole objective of price stability. The act stipulated that the minister of finance and the governor of the Reserve Bank should negotiate and make public a Policy Targets Agreement, a statement that sets out the targets by which monetary policy performance will be evaluated, specifying numerical target ranges for inflation and the dates by which they are to be reached. An unusual feature of the New Zealand legislation is that the governor of the Reserve Bank is held highly accountable for the success of monetary policy. If the goals set forth in the Policy Targets Agreement are not satisfied, the governor is subject to dismissal.

The first Policy Targets Agreement, signed by the minister of finance and the governor of the Reserve Bank on March 2, 1990, directed the Reserve Bank to achieve an annual inflation rate within a 3–5% range. Subsequent agreements lowered the range to 0–2% until the end of 1996, when the range was changed to 0–3%. In 2002, the range was changed again, to 1–3%. Tight monetary policy brought the inflation rate down from above 5% to below 2% by the end of 1992 (see Figure 1, panel (a)), but at the cost of a deep recession and a sharp rise in unemployment. Since then, inflation has typically remained within the targeted range, with the exception of brief periods in 1995, 2000, 2006, 2008, and 2011, when it exceeded the range by a small amount, and in 2013, when it temporarily dropped slightly below the target range. (Under the Reserve Bank Act, the governor could have been dismissed, but after parliamentary debates, the governor retained his job each time.) Since 1992, New Zealand's growth rate has generally been high, with some years exceeding 5%, and unemployment has decreased significantly.

Canada   On February 26, 1991, a joint announcement by the minister of finance and the governor of the Bank of Canada established formal inflation targets. The target ranges were 2–4% by the end of 1992, 1.5–3.5% by June 1994, and 1–3% by December 1996.

---

[1]A precursor to the inflation-targeting strategy is monetary targeting. This strategy is discussed in Appendix 1 to this chapter, "Monetary Targeting," which is available on the Companion Website at http://www.pearsonhighered.com/mishkin.

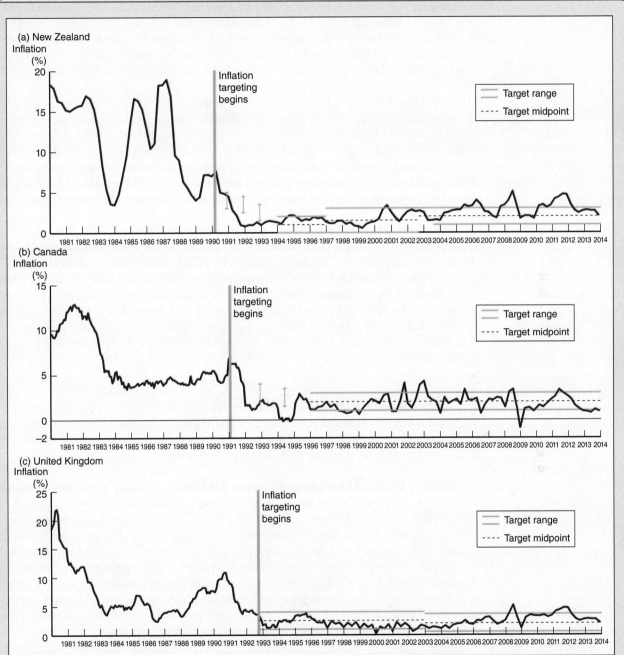

FIGURE 1   **Inflation Rates and Inflation Targets for New Zealand, Canada, and the United Kingdom, 1980–2014**

Inflation-targeting countries have significantly reduced the rate of inflation and over time have achieved their inflation targets.

Sources: Ben S. Bernanke, Thomas Laubach, Frederic S. Mishkin, and Adam S. Poson, *Inflation Targeting: Lessons from the International Experience* (Princeton: Princeton University Press, 1999); and Federal Reserve Bank of St. Louis, FRED database: http://research .stlouisfed.org/fred2/.

After the new government took office in late 1993, the target range was set at 1–3% from December 1995 until December 1998 and has been kept at this level. Canadian inflation has also fallen dramatically since the adoption of inflation targets, from above 5% in 1991, to a 0% rate in 1995, and to around 2% subsequently (see Figure 1, panel (b)). As was the case in New Zealand, however, this decline was not without cost: Unemployment soared to above 10% from 1991 until 1994, but then declined substantially.

United Kingdom   In October 1992, the United Kingdom adopted an inflation target as its nominal anchor, and the Bank of England began to produce an *Inflation Report*, a quarterly report on the progress being made in achieving the target. The inflation target range was initially set at 1–4% until the next election (spring 1997 at the latest), with the intent that the inflation rate should settle down to the lower half of the range (below 2.5%). In May 1997, the inflation target was set at 2.5% and the Bank of England was given the power to set interest rates henceforth, granting it a more independent role in monetary policy.

Before the adoption of inflation targets, inflation had already been falling in the United Kingdom, with a peak of 9% at the beginning of 1991 and a rate of 4% at the time of adoption (see Figure 1, panel (c)). By the third quarter of 1994, it was at 2.2%, within the intended range. Subsequently, inflation rose, climbing slightly above the 2.5% level by the end of 1995, but then fell and has remained close to the target since then, except for the period from 2008 to 2012. In December 2003, the target was changed to 2.0% for a slightly different measure of inflation. Meanwhile, growth of the U.K. economy was strong until 2008, causing a substantial reduction in the unemployment rate.[2]

Advantages of Inflation Targeting

There are a number of benefits associated with inflation targeting: reduction of the time-inconsistency problem, increased transparency, increased accountability, consistency with democratic principles, and improved performance.

Reduction of the Time-Inconsistency Problem   Because an explicit numerical inflation target increases the accountability of the central bank, inflation targeting can reduce the likelihood that the central bank will fall into the time-inconsistency trap of trying to expand output and employment in the short run by pursuing overly expansionary monetary policy. A key advantage of inflation targeting is that it can help focus the political debate on what a central bank can do in the long run—that is, control inflation—rather than what it cannot do, that is, permanently increase economic growth and the number of jobs through expansionary monetary policy. Thus inflation targeting can reduce political pressures on the central bank to pursue inflationary monetary policy and thereby reduce the likelihood of the time-inconsistency problem.

Increased Transparency   Inflation targeting has the advantage that it is readily understood by the public and is thus highly transparent. Indeed, inflation-targeting regimes place great importance on transparency in policymaking and on regular

---

[2]If you are interested in a more detailed discussion of inflation targeting in these and other countries, see Ben S. Bernanke, Thomas Laubach, Frederic S. Mishkin, and Adam S. Posen, *Inflation Targeting: Lessons from the International Experience* (Princeton: Princeton University Press, 1999).

communication with the public. Inflation-targeting central banks have frequent communications with the government, some mandated by law and some in response to informal inquiries, and their officials take every opportunity to make public speeches on their monetary policy strategy. Although these techniques are also commonly used in countries that have not adopted inflation targeting, inflation-targeting central banks have taken public outreach a step further: Not only do they engage in extended public information campaigns, including the distribution of glossy brochures, but they also publish documents like the Bank of England's *Inflation Report*. These documents are particularly noteworthy because, unlike the usual dull-looking, formal reports of central banks, they make use of fancy graphics, boxes, and other eye-catching design elements to engage the public's interest.

The channels of communication just discussed are used by central banks in inflation-targeting countries to explain the following concepts to the general public, financial market participants, and politicians: (1) the goals and limitations of monetary policy, including the rationale for inflation targets; (2) the numerical values of the inflation targets and how they were determined; (3) how the inflation targets are to be achieved, given current economic conditions; and (4) reasons for any deviations from the targets. These communications have improved private sector planning by reducing uncertainty about monetary policy, interest rates, and inflation; they have promoted public debate of monetary policy, in part by educating the public about what a central bank can and cannot achieve; and they have helped clarify the responsibilities of the central bank and of politicians in the conduct of monetary policy.

Increased Accountability   Another key feature of inflation-targeting regimes is the tendency toward increased accountability of the central bank. Indeed, transparency and communication go hand in hand with increased accountability. The strongest case of accountability of a central bank in an inflation-targeting regime is in New Zealand, where the government has the right to dismiss the Reserve Bank's governor if the inflation targets are breached, even for one quarter. In other inflation-targeting countries, the central bank's accountability is less formalized. Nevertheless, the transparency of policy associated with inflation targeting has tended to make the central bank highly accountable to the public and the government. Sustained success in the conduct of monetary policy as measured against a preannounced and well-defined inflation target can be instrumental in building public support for a central bank's independence and for its policies. This building of public support and accountability occurs even in the absence of a rigidly defined and legalistic standard of performance evaluation and punishment.

Consistency with Democratic Principles   Not only is accountability valuable in its own right, but it also makes the institutional framework for the conduct of monetary policy more consistent with democratic principles. The inflation-targeting framework promotes the accountability of the central bank to elected officials, who are given some responsibility for setting the goals of monetary policy and then monitoring the economic outcomes. However, under inflation targeting as it generally has been practiced, the central bank has complete control over operational decisions and so can be held accountable for achieving its assigned objectives.

Improved Performance   The performance of inflation-targeting regimes has been quite good. Inflation-targeting countries seem to have significantly reduced both the rate of inflation and inflation expectations beyond what likely would have occurred in the absence of inflation targets. Furthermore, once lowered, inflation in these countries has stayed low; following disinflations, the inflation rate in inflation-targeting countries has not bounced back up during subsequent cyclical expansions of the economy.

Disadvantages of Inflation Targeting

Critics of inflation targeting cite four disadvantages of this monetary policy strategy: delayed signaling, too much rigidity, the potential for increased output fluctuations, and low economic growth. We look at each in turn and examine the validity of these criticisms.

Delayed Signaling   Inflation is not easily controlled by the monetary authorities. Furthermore, because of the long lags in the effects of monetary policy, inflation outcomes are revealed only after a substantial lag. Thus an inflation target does not send immediate signals to the public and the markets about the stance of monetary policy.

Too Much Rigidity   Some economists criticize inflation targeting because they believe it imposes a rigid rule on monetary policymakers and limits their ability to respond to unforeseen circumstances. However, useful policy strategies exist that are "rule-like" in that they involve forward-looking behavior that limits policymakers from systematically engaging in policies with undesirable long-run consequences. Such policies avoid the time-inconsistency problem and would be best described as "constrained discretion," a term coined by Ben Bernanke and the author of this book.

Indeed, inflation targeting can be described exactly in this way. Inflation targeting, as actually practiced, is far from rigid and is better described as "flexible inflation targeting." First, inflation targeting does not prescribe simple and mechanical instructions on how the central bank should conduct monetary policy. Rather, it requires the central bank to use all available information to determine which policy actions are appropriate to achieve the inflation target. Unlike simple policy rules, inflation targeting never requires the central bank to focus solely on one key variable. Second, inflation targeting, as practiced, contains a substantial degree of policy discretion. Inflation targets have been modified depending on economic circumstances, as we have seen. Moreover, central banks under inflation-targeting regimes have left themselves considerable scope to respond to output growth and fluctuations through several devices.

Potential for Increased Output Fluctuations   An important criticism of inflation targeting is that a sole focus on inflation may lead to monetary policy that is too tight when inflation is above target and thus may result in larger output fluctuations. Inflation targeting does not, however, require a sole focus on inflation—in fact, experience has shown that inflation targeters display substantial concern about output fluctuations. All the inflation targeters have set their inflation targets above zero.[3] For example, New Zealand, Canada, the United Kingdom, and Sweden currently set the midpoints of their inflation targets at 2%, while Australia sets its midpoint at 2.5%.

The decision by inflation targeters to choose inflation targets above zero reflects the concern of monetary policymakers that particularly low inflation can have substantial negative effects on real economic activity. Deflation (negative inflation, in which the

---

[3]Consumer price indexes have been found to have an upward bias in the measurement of true inflation, so it is not surprising that inflation targets are chosen to exceed zero. However, the actual targets have been set to exceed the estimates of this measurement bias, indicating that inflation targeters have decided on targets for inflation that exceed zero even after measurement bias is accounted for.

price level actually falls) is especially to be feared because of the possibility that it may promote financial instability and precipitate a severe economic contraction (as discussed in Chapter 12). The deflation in Japan in recent years has been an important factor in the weakening of the Japanese financial system and economy. Inflation-targeting rates above zero make periods of deflation less likely. This is one reason why some economists, both within and outside of Japan, called on the Bank of Japan to adopt an inflation target at levels of 2%, which the Bank of Japan finally did in 2013.

Inflation targeting also does not ignore traditional stabilization goals. Central bankers in inflation-targeting countries continue to express their concern about fluctuations in output and employment, and the ability to accommodate short-run stabilization goals to some degree is built into all inflation-targeting regimes. All inflation-targeting countries have been willing to minimize output declines by gradually lowering medium-term inflation targets toward the long-run goal.

Low Economic Growth   Another common concern about inflation targeting is that it will lead to low growth in output and employment. Although inflation reduction has been associated with below-normal output during disinflationary phases in inflation-targeting regimes, once low inflation levels were achieved, output and employment returned to levels at least as high as they were before. A conservative conclusion is that once low inflation is achieved, inflation targeting is not harmful to the real economy. Given the strong economic growth after disinflation in many countries (such as New Zealand) that have adopted inflation targets, a case can be made that inflation targeting promotes real economic growth, in addition to controlling inflation.

THE EVOLUTION OF THE FEDERAL RESERVE'S MONETARY POLICY STRATEGY

The Federal Reserve's monetary policy has evolved over time. We first discuss the Fed's monetary policy strategy prior to Ben Bernanke's term as chair of the Federal Reserve, and then see how the monetary policy evolved into a flexible inflation-targeting regime starting in January 2012.

The Fed's "Just Do It" Monetary Policy Strategy

From the 1980s up until the time Ben Bernanke became chair of the Federal Reserve in 2006, the Federal Reserve was able to achieve excellent macroeconomic performance (including low and stable inflation), and it did so without using an explicit nominal anchor such as an inflation target. Although the Federal Reserve did not articulate an explicit strategy, a coherent strategy for the conduct of monetary policy existed nonetheless. This strategy involved an implicit, but not an explicit, nominal anchor in the form of an overriding concern on the part of the Federal Reserve to control inflation in the long run. In addition, it involved forward-looking behavior that included careful monitoring for signs of future inflation, using a wide range of information coupled with periodic "preemptive strikes" by monetary policy against the threat of inflation.

As emphasized by Milton Friedman, monetary policy effects have long lags. In industrialized countries with a history of low inflation, the inflation process seems to have tremendous inertia: Estimates from large macroeconometric models of the U.S. economy, for example, suggest that monetary policy takes over a year to affect output and over two years to have a significant impact on inflation. For countries that have experienced highly variable inflation, and therefore have more flexible prices, the lags may be shorter.

The presence of long lags means that monetary policy cannot wait for inflation to begin before it responds to it. If a central bank waits until overt signs of inflation appear, it will already be too late to maintain stable prices, at least not without a severe tightening of policy: Inflation expectations will already be embedded in the wage- and price-setting process, creating an inflation momentum that will be hard to halt. Inflation becomes much harder to control once it has been allowed to gather momentum, because higher inflation expectations become ingrained in various types of long-term contracts and pricing agreements.

To prevent inflation from getting started, therefore, monetary policy needs to be forward-looking and preemptive. That is, depending on the lags from monetary policy to inflation, monetary policy needs to act long before inflationary pressures are seen in the economy. For example, suppose it takes roughly two years for monetary policy to have a significant impact on inflation. In this case, even if inflation is currently low but policymakers believe inflation will rise over the next two years with an unchanged stance of monetary policy, they must tighten monetary policy *now* to prevent the inflationary surge.

Under Alan Greenspan and Ben Bernanke, the Federal Reserve was successful in pursuing a preemptive monetary policy. For example, the Fed raised interest rates from 1994 to 1995 before a rise in inflation got a toehold. As a result, inflation did not just remain steady; it fell slightly. The Fed also conducted preemptive strikes against economic downturns. For example, the Fed started easing monetary policy in September 2007 at the onset of the global financial crisis, even though the economy was growing strongly at the time and inflation was rising.[4] (However, in this case, the Fed's preemptive policy was not sufficient to overcome the massive negative shock to the economy from the disruption to financial markets.) This preemptive, forward-looking monetary policy strategy is clearly also a feature of inflation-targeting regimes, because monetary policy instruments are adjusted to take into account the long lags in their effects on inflation.

However, the Fed's policy regime prior to the global financial crisis might best be described as a "just do it" policy, and it differed from inflation targeting in that it did not officially set a nominal anchor and was much less transparent. However, because the Fed's "just do it" approach had some of the key elements of inflation targeting, it also had many of its strengths. As with inflation targeting, the central bank used many sources of information to determine the best settings for monetary policy. The Fed's forward-looking behavior and stress on price stability helped discourage overly expansionary monetary policy, thereby ameliorating the time-inconsistency problem.

However, despite its success, the Fed's "just do it" approach had several weaknesses. First was its lack of transparency. The Fed's close-mouthed approach about its intentions gave rise to a constant guessing game about its future actions. This high level of uncertainty led to unnecessary volatility in financial markets and created doubt among producers and the general public about the future course of inflation and output. Furthermore, the opacity of the Fed's policymaking made it hard for Congress and the general public to hold the Federal Reserve accountable: The Fed could not be held accountable for its decisions if there were no predetermined criteria for judging its performance, and this lack of accountability was inconsistent with democratic principles. Low accountability might also make the Fed more susceptible to the time-inconsistency problem, whereby it might pursue short-term objectives at the expense of long-term ones.

---

[4]These episodes are discussed in the brief history of Fed policymaking given in Appendix 2 to this chapter, which is available on the Companion Website at http://www.pearsonhighered.com/mishkin.

The Long Road to Inflation Targeting

Alan Greenspan, chair of the Fed from 1987 until 2006, was not a strong advocate of increased Federal Reserve transparency. Hence, despite the weaknesses of the "just do it" approach and the successes of inflation-targeting regimes from 1991 on, Greenspan was opposed to the adoption of an inflation target and quashed movements in this direction at an FOMC meeting in 1996. When Ben Bernanke became chair of the Fed in 2006, increased Fed transparency and inflation targeting now had a strong advocate (see the Inside the Fed box).

Shortly after becoming Fed chair, Bernanke made it clear that any movement toward inflation targeting must result from a consensus within the FOMC. He then set up an internal subcommittee to discuss Federal Reserve communications, which included discussions about announcing a specific numerical inflation objective. The FOMC made a partial step in the direction of inflation targeting in November 2007 when it announced a new communication strategy that lengthened the horizon for FOMC participants' inflation projections to three years. In many cases, the three-year horizon would be sufficiently long that the projection for inflation under "appropriate policy" would reflect each participant's inflation objective, because at the three-year horizon inflation should converge to the long-run objective.

In July 2008, in his last speech as a governor of the Federal Reserve, the author of this book argued that a few relatively minor modifications to the inflation objective could move the Fed even further toward inflation targeting.[5] The Fed's first goal should be to

[5]See Frederic S. Mishkin, "Whither Federal Reserve Communications," speech given at the Petersen Institute for International Economics, Washington, DC, July 28, 2008, http://www.federalreserve.gov/newsevents/speech/mishkin20080.

Inside the Fed   Ben Bernanke's Advocacy of Inflation Targeting

Ben Bernanke is a world-renowned expert on monetary policy who wrote extensively on inflation targeting while working in academia. While a professor at Princeton, Bernanke, in several articles and in a book co-written with the author of this book, argued that inflation targeting would be a major step forward for the Federal Reserve and would produce better economic outcomes, for many of the reasons outlined earlier.[*]

When Bernanke took his position as a governor of the Federal Reserve from 2002 to 2005, he continued to advocate the adoption of an inflation target. In an important speech given at a conference at the Federal Reserve Bank of St. Louis in 2004, he described how the Federal Reserve might approach a movement toward inflation targeting: The Fed should announce a numerical value for its long-run inflation goal.[†] Bernanke emphasized that announcing such an objective for inflation would be completely consistent with the Fed's dual mandate of achieving price stability and maximum employment, and therefore might be called a *mandate-consistent inflation objective*, since the inflation objective would be set above zero to avoid deflations, which have harmful effects on employment. In addition, the inflation objective would not be intended as a short-run target that might lead to excessively tight control of inflation at the expense of overly high employment fluctuations.

[*]Ben S. Bernanke and Frederic S. Mishkin, "Inflation Targeting: A New Framework for Monetary Policy," *Journal of Economic Perspectives*, vol. 11, no. 2 (1997); Ben S. Bernanke, Frederic S. Mishkin, and Adam S. Posen, "Inflation Targeting: Fed Policy After Greenspan," *Milken Institute Review* (Fourth Quarter, 1999): 48–56; Ben S. Bernanke, Frederic S. Mishkin, and Adam S. Posen, "What Happens When Greenspan Is Gone," *Wall Street Journal*, January 5, 2000, p. A22; and Ben S. Bernanke, Thomas Laubach, Frederic S. Mishkin, and Adam S. Posen, *Inflation Targeting: Lessons from the International Experience* (Princeton, NJ: Princeton University Press, 1999).

[†]Ben S. Bernanke, "Inflation Targeting," Federal Reserve Bank of St. Louis, *Review*, vol. 86, no. 4 (July/August 2004): 165–168.

set a date for its inflation objective that was sufficiently far off that inflation would almost surely converge to its long-run value by that date. In January 2009, the FOMC adopted this modification by adding long-term inflation forecasts under "appropriate policy" to the published FOMC participants' projections. Second, the FOMC participants should be willing to reach a consensus on a single value for the mandate-consistent inflation objective. Third, the FOMC should not modify this inflation objective unless there were valid scientific reasons for doing so. With these two additional modifications, the longer-run inflation projections would, in effect, be an announcement of a specific numerical objective for the inflation rate, and so would serve as a flexible version of inflation targeting. In October 2010, then-chair Bernanke gave a speech advocating exactly this approach.[6] However, he was unable to convince his colleagues on the FOMC to adopt it.

When Janet Yellen left her position as president of the Federal Reserve Bank of San Francisco to become the vice-chair of the Board of Governors of the Federal Reserve System in 2010, Bernanke now had a strong ally for inflation targeting occupying the second-most-powerful position in the Federal Reserve System. In October 2010, Bernanke appointed Yellen as the chair of the internal subcommittee on communications, and the adoption of inflation targeting was not far off. The FOMC finally moved to inflation targeting on January 25, 2012, when it issued its "Statement on Long-Run Goals and Monetary Policy Strategy."[7] In this statement, which is renewed every January, the FOMC agreed to a single numerical value of the inflation objective, 2% on the PCE deflator. However, the statement also made it clear that the Federal Reserve would be pursuing a flexible form of inflation targeting, consistent with its dual mandate, because it would not only seek to achieve its inflation target but would also focus on promoting maximum sustainable employment.

The Federal Reserve is not the only central bank that has moved slowly toward inflation targeting. As the Global box, "The European Central Bank's Monetary Policy Strategy," suggests, the European Central Bank also follows a weak form of inflation targeting.

Global   The European Central Bank's Monetary Policy Strategy

The European Central Bank (ECB) has also been slow to move toward inflation targeting, adopting a hybrid monetary strategy that includes some elements of inflation targeting.* Shortly before the ECB became fully operational in 1999, its governing council defined price stability as an inflation rate below 2%. However, in May 2003, the ECB adopted a goal for inflation over the medium term of "below, but close to, 2%." The ECB's strategy has two key "pillars." First, monetary and credit aggregates are assessed for "their implications for future inflation and economic growth." Second, many other economic variables are used to assess the future economic outlook.

The ECB's strategy is somewhat unclear and has been subject to criticism for this reason. Although the "below, but close to, 2%" goal for inflation sounds like an inflation target, the ECB has repeatedly stated that it does not have an inflation target. This central bank seems to have decided to try to "have its cake and eat it, too" by not committing too strongly to an inflation-targeting strategy. The resulting difficulty in assessing the ECB's strategy has the potential to reduce the accountability of the institution.

*For a description of the ECB's monetary policy strategy, go to the ECB's website at http://www.ecb.int.

---

[6]Ben S. Bernanke, "Monetary Policy Objectives and Tools in a Low-Inflation Environment," speech given at the Federal Reserve Bank of Boston's conference, Revisiting Monetary Policy in a Low-Inflation Environment, October 15, 2010.

[7]These statements can be found at http://www.federalreserve.gov/monetarypolicy/default.htm.

LESSONS FOR MONETARY POLICY STRATEGY FROM THE GLOBAL FINANCIAL CRISIS

Our discussion in previous chapters of the course of events that characterized the global financial crisis suggests four basic lessons for economists and policymakers on how the economy works.[8]

1. *Developments in the financial sector have a far greater impact on economic activity than was earlier realized.* Although before the crisis economists and policymakers generally recognized that financial frictions could play an important role in business cycle fluctuations, as we saw in Chapter 12, the global financial crisis made it abundantly clear that the adverse effects of financial disruptions on economic activity could be far worse than originally anticipated.

2. *The zero lower bound on interest rates can be a serious problem.* As we saw in Chapter 15, the zero lower bound on interest rates has forced the Federal Reserve to use nonconventional monetary policy tools, not only since the crisis but also during the 2003–2006 period. Although these nonconventional tools can help stimulate the economy, they are more complicated to use than conventional tools and their impact on the economy is more uncertain, so they may be harder to use effectively.

3. *The cost of cleaning up after a financial crisis is very high.* As we saw in Chapter 12, financial crises are followed by deep recessions. In addition, recoveries from financial crises are very slow. Carmen Reinhart of the Petersen Institute for International Economics and Vincent Reinhart of the American Enterprise Institute have documented that economic growth is significantly lower during the decade following financial crises, and unemployment rates stay persistently higher for a decade after crisis episodes. In addition, in the aftermath of financial crises, government indebtedness almost always sharply increases and can lead to defaults on government debt, which have become a major concern in Europe in the aftermath of the most recent crisis.[9]

4. *Price and output stability do not ensure financial stability.* Before the recent financial crisis, the common view in both academia and central banks was that achieving price and output stability would promote financial stability. However, the success of central banks in stabilizing inflation and the decreased volatility of business cycle fluctuations before 2007, which became known as the "Great Moderation," did not protect the economy from financial instability. Indeed, it may have promoted it. The low volatility of both inflation and output fluctuations may have lulled market participants into thinking less risk was present in the economic system than was really the case, leading them to take excessive risks, which in turn helped to fuel the global financial crisis.

What implications do these lessons have for monetary policy strategy? We first consider how these lessons might affect our thinking about inflation targeting and then look at how central banks should respond to asset-price bubbles.

---

[8]For a more detailed discussion of the lessons of the global financial crisis for monetary policy strategy, see Frederic S. Mishkin, "Monetary Policy Strategy: Lessons from the Crisis," in Marek Jarocinski, Frank Smets, and Christian Thimann, eds., *Monetary Policy Revisited: Lessons from the Crisis*, Sixth ECB Central Banking Conference (Frankfurt, European Central Bank, 2011), pp. 67–118.

[9]See Carmen M. Reinhart and Vincent R. Reinhart, "After the Fall," *Macroeconomic Challenges: The Decade Ahead*, Federal Reserve Bank of Kansas City Economic Symposium, 2010, manuscript available at http://www.kansascityfed .org; and Carmen M. Reinhart and Kenneth S. Rogoff, *This Time Is Different: Eight Centuries of Financial Folly* (Princeton, NJ: Princeton University Press, 2009).

Implications for Inflation Targeting

Earlier in the chapter, we outlined the arguments for inflation targeting, and none of the lessons listed above contradicts these arguments. Although support for the inflation-targeting strategy is not weakened by the lessons learned from the financial crisis, these lessons do suggest that inflation targeting may need to be more flexible and also may need to be modified on several dimensions. First, we look at what these lessons might mean for the level of the inflation target.

Level of the Inflation Target   As our discussion earlier in the chapter indicated, central banks typically have an inflation target around the 2% level. The seriousness of the zero-lower-bound problem raises the question of whether this target level is too low. A controversial paper written by researchers at the IMF, including its chief economist, suggests that the inflation target might be raised from the 2% level to the 4% level.[10] The paper argues that with expectations of inflation anchored to this 4% target, by lowering the nominal interest rate to zero, the real interest rate, $i_r = i - \pi^e$, could be decreased to as low as -4% ($= 0 - 4\%$), rather than the rate of -2% ($= 0 - 2\%$) associated with the 2% inflation target. Conventional monetary policy, which involves manipulating the nominal policy rate, would then be able to become more expansionary when interest rates fell to a floor of zero than it could with the lower inflation target. In other words, the zero lower bound on the policy rate would be less binding with a higher inflation target.

Although this argument is theoretically sound, and raising the inflation target does have its benefits, we also have to look at its costs. The benefits of a higher inflation target accrue only when the zero-lower-bound problem occurs. Although this was a major problem during the global financial crisis, such episodes have not been very frequent. If the zero-lower-bound problem is rare, then the benefits of a higher inflation target are not so large because they are available only infrequently. However, the costs of higher inflation in terms of the distortions it produces in the economy, mentioned early in the chapter, are ongoing. Thus, although these costs may not be that large in any given year, they add up over time and may outweigh the intermittent benefits of a higher inflation target when the zero lower bound occurs.

Another problem with a higher inflation target is that the history of inflation suggests that it is more difficult to stabilize the inflation rate at a 4% level than at a 2% level. Once inflation starts to rise above this level, the public is likely to believe that price stability is no longer a credible goal of the central bank. The question then arises, if a 4% level of inflation is okay, then why not 6%, or 8%, and so on? Indeed, this is what seems to have happened in the 1960s, when economists such as Paul Samuelson and Robert Solow of MIT, both eventual recipients of the Nobel Prize, argued that policymakers should be willing to tolerate higher inflation rates in the 4–5% range. But when inflation rose to that level, the policy authorities could not contain it at that level, and it kept on rising to double-digit levels by the early 1980s. Getting inflation back down again during the Volcker era was very costly. No central banker wants to go through that cycle again, and this is why central bankers have been so hostile to the IMF researchers' suggestion.

Flexibility of Inflation Targeting   We have seen that inflation targeting as actually practiced would be better described as "flexible inflation targeting." However, before the global financial crisis, this flexibility involved allowing some short-run deviations

---

[10]Olivier Blanchard, Giovanni Dell'Ariccia, and Paolo Mauro, "Rethinking Monetary Policy," *Journal of Money, Credit and Banking*, vol. 42, Issue Supplement S1 (September 2010): 199–217.

of inflation from the inflation target in order to promote output stability as well as price stability. Two lessons from the crisis—that financial instability can have devastating effects on the economy and that achieving price and output stability does not ensure financial stability—have led to a recognition that central banks need to pay more attention to financial stability, not only in designing inflation-targeting regimes but also in any monetary policy framework. Particularly important in this regard is the issue of how central banks should respond to asset-price bubbles, the topic we discuss next.

SHOULD CENTRAL BANKS TRY TO STOP ASSET-PRICE BUBBLES?

Over the centuries, economies have been subject to periodic **asset-price bubbles**, pronounced increases in asset prices, or "bubbles," that depart from fundamental values and that eventually burst resoundingly. The story of the global financial crisis, discussed in Chapter 12, indicates just how costly these bubbles can be. The bursting of the asset-price bubble in the housing market brought down the financial system, leading to an economic downturn, a rise in unemployment, and direct hardship for families who were forced to leave their homes after foreclosures.

The high economic cost of asset-price bubbles raises the following questions: What should central banks do about them? Should they use monetary policy to try to pop the bubbles? Are there regulatory measures they can take to rein in asset-price bubbles? To answer these questions, we need to ask whether there are different kinds of bubbles that require different types of responses.

Two Types of Asset-Price Bubbles

To think about central banks' response to asset-price bubbles, we first need to look at the different types of bubbles and how each might best be addressed. Asset-price bubbles are of two types: one type is driven by credit, and the second type is driven purely by overly optimistic expectations (dubbed "irrational exuberance" by Alan Greenspan).

Credit-Driven Bubbles When a credit boom begins, an asset-price bubble may begin to form. Easier-to-get credit can be used to purchase particular assets and thereby raise their prices. The rise in asset values, in turn, encourages further lending for these assets, either because it increases the value of collateral, making it easier to borrow, or because it raises the value of capital at financial institutions, which gives them more capacity to lend. The lending for these assets can then further increase demand for them and hence raise their prices even more. This feedback loop—in which a credit boom drives up asset prices, which in turn fuels the credit boom, which drives asset prices even higher, and so on—can generate a bubble in which asset prices rise well above their fundamental values.

Credit-driven bubbles are particularly dangerous, as the recent global financial crisis has demonstrated. When asset prices come back down to earth and the bubble bursts, the collapse in asset prices leads to a reversal of the feedback loop: loans go sour, lenders cut back on the credit supply, the demand for assets declines further, and prices drop even more. These were exactly the dynamics that characterized housing markets during the global financial crisis. Driven by a credit boom in subprime lending, housing prices rose way above fundamental values; but when housing prices crashed, credit shriveled up and housing prices plummeted.

The resulting losses on subprime loans and securities eroded the balance sheets of financial institutions, causing a decline in credit (deleveraging) and a sharp fall in business and household spending, and therefore in economic activity. During the global financial crisis, the interaction between housing prices and the health of financial institutions following the collapse of the housing price bubble endangered the operation of the financial system as a whole and had dire consequences for the economy.

Bubbles Driven Solely by Irrational Exuberance   Bubbles that are driven solely by overly optimistic expectations, but that are not associated with a credit boom, pose much less risk to the financial system. For example, the bubble in technology stocks in the late 1990s was not fueled by credit, and the bursting of the tech-stock bubble was not followed by a marked deterioration in financial institutions' balance sheets. The bursting of the tech-stock bubble thus did not have a very severe impact on the economy, and the recession that followed was quite mild. Bubbles driven solely by irrational exuberance are therefore far less dangerous than those driven by credit booms.

The Debate over Whether Central Banks Should Try to Pop Bubbles

Because asset prices are a central element of monetary policy and directly affect its outcomes (the transmission mechanisms of monetary policy are discussed in Chapter 25), monetary policy certainly needs to respond to asset prices in order to obtain good outcomes in terms of inflation and output. Hence, the issue is not whether monetary policy should respond to asset price movements at all, but whether it should respond at a level over and above the level called for in terms of the objectives of stabilizing inflation and employment. Should monetary policy try to pop, or slow, the growth of potential asset-price bubbles to minimize damage to the economy when these bubbles burst? Alternatively, rather than responding directly to possible asset-price bubbles, should the monetary authorities respond only to the asset-price declines that occur after a bubble bursts, to stabilize both output and inflation? These opposing positions have been characterized as *leaning against* asset-price bubbles versus *cleaning up* after the bubbles burst, and so the debate over what to do about asset-price bubbles has been labeled the "lean versus clean" debate.

Whether central banks should try to pop, or prick, bubbles was actively debated before the global financial crisis, with Alan Greenspan arguing against such actions. Greenspan's position held great sway in central banking circles before the crisis. However, the crisis has led economists to reevaluate this viewpoint, and we look at the pro and con arguments below.

Con: Why Central Banks Should Not Try to Prick Asset-Price Bubbles but Should Just Clean Up After They Burst   Alan Greenspan's argument that central banks should not take actions to prick bubbles became known as the "Greenspan doctrine." His position reflected five arguments:

1. Asset-price bubbles are nearly impossible to identify. If central banks or government officials knew that a bubble was in progress, wouldn't market participants know as well? If so, then a bubble would be unlikely to develop, because market participants would know that prices were getting out of line with fundamentals. Unless central

bank or government officials are smarter than market participants, an unlikely situation given the savvy of especially talented (and high-earning) market participants, they will be unlikely to identify when bubbles of this type are occurring. A strong argument, then, exists for not responding to suspected bubbles.

2. Although some economic analysis suggests that raising interest rates can diminish asset price increases, raising interest rates may be very ineffective in restraining bubbles, because market participants expect such high rates of return from buying bubble-driven assets. Furthermore, raising interest rates has often been found to cause a bubble to burst more severely, thereby increasing the damage to the economy. Another way of saying this is that bubbles are departures from normal behavior, and it is unrealistic to expect that the usual tools of monetary policy will be effective in abnormal conditions.

3. Many different asset prices exist, and at any one time a bubble may be present in only a fraction of asset markets. Monetary policy actions are a very blunt instrument in such a case, as such actions would be likely to affect asset prices in general, rather than the specific assets that are experiencing a bubble.

4. Monetary policy actions to prick bubbles can have harmful effects on the aggregate economy. If interest rates are raised significantly in an effort to curtail a bubble, the economy will slow, people will lose jobs, and inflation might fall below its desirable level. Indeed, as arguments 2 and 3 suggest, the rise in interest rates necessary to prick a bubble may be so high that it can be done only at great cost to workers and the economy. This is not to say that monetary policy should not respond to asset prices per se. The level of asset prices does affect aggregate demand (discussed in Chapter 25) and thus the evolution of the economy. Monetary policy should react to fluctuations in asset prices to the extent that they affect inflation and economic activity.

5. As long as policymakers respond in a timely fashion, by easing monetary policy aggressively after an asset bubble bursts, the harmful effects of a bursting bubble can be kept at a manageable level. Indeed, the Greenspan Fed acted in exactly this way after the stock market crash of 1987 and the bursting of the tech bubble in the stock market in 2000. Aggressive easing after the stock market bubbles burst in 1987 and 2000 was highly successful. The economy did not enter a recession after the stock market crash of 1987, and the recession that followed the tech bubble burst in 2000 was very mild.

Pro: Why Central Banks Should Try to Pop Bubbles The recent financial crisis clearly demonstrated that the bursting of credit-driven bubbles can be not only extremely costly but also very hard to clean up. Furthermore, credit-driven bubbles can occur even if price and output stability exist in the period leading up to them. Indeed, as we have seen, price and output stability might actually encourage credit-driven bubbles because they lead market participants to underestimate the amount of risk present in the economy. The global financial crisis has therefore provided a much stronger case for leaning against potential bubbles than for just cleaning up after they burst.

However, the distinction between the two types of bubbles, one of which (credit-driven) is much more costly to the economy than the other, suggests that the lean versus clean debate may have been miscast. Rather than leaning against potential asset-price bubbles, which would include both credit-driven and irrational exuberance-type bubbles, the case is much stronger for leaning against credit *booms*, which would involve leaning against credit-driven asset-price bubbles but not against asset-price bubbles driven by irrational exuberance. It is much easier to identify credit booms than asset-price bubbles. When asset-price bubbles are rising rapidly at the same time that credit is booming, the likelihood is greater that asset prices are deviating from fundamentals because laxer credit standards are driving asset prices upward. In this case, central bank or government officials are more likely to identify that a boom is in progress; this was indeed the case during the housing market bubble in the United States, when central banks and government officials were aware that lenders had weakened lending standards and that credit extension in the mortgage markets was rising at abnormally high rates.

The case for leaning against credit-driven bubbles seems strong, but what policies would be most effective in restraining them?

Macroprudential Policies   First, it is important to recognize that the key principle to consider in designing effective policies to lean against credit booms is that such policies must curb excessive risk taking. Only when risk taking is excessive are credit booms likely to develop, and so it is natural to look to prudential regulatory measures to constrain credit booms. Regulatory policy to affect what is happening in credit markets in the aggregate is referred to as **macroprudential regulation**, and it does seem to be the right tool for reining in credit-driven bubbles.

Financial regulation and supervision, either by central banks or by other government entities, with the usual elements of a well-functioning prudential regulatory and supervisory system, as described in Chapter 10, can prevent the excessive risk taking that can trigger a credit boom, which in turn will lead to an asset-price bubble. These elements include adequate disclosure and capital requirements, prompt corrective action, close monitoring of financial institutions' risk management procedures, and close supervision to enforce compliance with regulations. More generally, regulation should focus on preventing leverage cycles. As the global financial crisis demonstrated, the rise in asset prices that accompanied the credit boom resulted in higher capital buffers at financial institutions, supporting further lending in the context of unchanging capital requirements, which led to higher asset prices, and so on; in the bust, the value of the capital dropped precipitously, leading to a cut in lending. Capital requirements that are countercyclical, that is, adjusted upward during a boom and downward during a bust, might help eliminate the pernicious feedback loops that promote credit-driven bubbles.

A rapid rise in asset prices accompanied by a credit boom provides a signal that market failures or poor financial regulation and supervision might be causing a bubble to form. Central banks and other government regulators can then consider implementing policies to rein in credit growth directly or can implement measures to make sure credit standards are sufficiently high.

Monetary Policy   The fact that the low interest rate policies of the Federal Reserve from 2002 to 2005 were followed by excessive risk taking suggests to many that overly easy monetary policy might promote financial instability, as was discussed in Chapter 12. Although it is far from clear that the Federal Reserve is primarily to blame for the housing bubble, research does suggest that low interest rates can encourage excessive risk taking, in what has been called the "risk-taking channel of monetary policy." Low interest rates may increase the incentives for asset managers in financial institutions to search for higher yields and hence increase risk taking. Low interest rates may also increase the demand for assets, raising their prices and leading to increased valuation of collateral, which in turn encourages lenders to lend to riskier borrowers.

The risk-taking channel of monetary policy suggests that monetary policy should be used to lean against credit booms. However, many of the Greenspan doctrine's objections to using monetary policy to prick booms are still valid, so wouldn't it be better to use macroprudential supervision to constrain credit booms, leaving monetary policy to focus on price and output stability?

This argument would be quite strong if macroprudential policies were able to do the job. However, there are doubts on this score. Prudential supervision is subject to more political pressure than monetary policy because it affects the bottom line of financial institutions more directly. Thus these institutions have greater incentives to lobby politicians to discourage macroprudential policies that would rein in credit booms, particularly during a credit boom, when they are making the most money. In addition, financial institutions are often very good at finding loopholes to avoid regulation, as we discovered in Chapter 11, and so macroprudential supervision may not be effective. The possibility that macroprudential policies may not be implemented sufficiently well to constrain credit booms suggests that monetary policy may have to be used instead.

An important lesson from the global financial crisis is that central banks and other regulators should not have a laissez-faire attitude and let credit-driven bubbles proceed without any reaction. Figuring out how to do this well, however, is indeed a daunting task.

TACTICS: CHOOSING THE POLICY INSTRUMENT

Now that we are familiar with the alternative strategies for implementing monetary policy, let's look at how monetary policy is conducted on a day-to-day basis. Central banks directly control the tools of monetary policy—open market operations, reserve requirements, the discount rate, the interest rate on reserves, large-scale asset purchases, and forward guidance—but knowing the tools and the strategies for implementing a monetary policy does not tell us whether that policy is easy or tight. To ascertain whether policy is easy or tight, we can observe the **policy instrument** (also called an **operating instrument**), a variable that responds to the central bank's tools and indicates the stance (easy or tight) of monetary policy. A central bank like the Fed has at its disposal two basic types of policy instruments: reserve aggregates (total reserves, nonborrowed reserves, the monetary base, and the nonborrowed base) and interest rates (the federal funds rate and other short-term interest rates). (Central banks in small countries can choose another policy instrument, the exchange rate, but we leave this topic to Chapter 18.) The policy instrument might be linked to an **intermediate target**, such as a monetary aggregate like M2 or a long-term interest rate. Intermediate targets stand between the policy instrument and the goals of monetary policy (e.g., price stability, output growth); they are not as directly affected by the tools of monetary policy but might be more closely linked to the goals of monetary policy. As a study aid, Figure 2 shows a schematic of the linkages among the tools of monetary policy, policy instruments, intermediate targets, and the goals of monetary policy.

As an example, suppose the central bank's employment and inflation goals are consistent with a nominal GDP growth rate of 5%. The central bank might believe that the 5% nominal GDP growth rate will be achieved by a 4% growth rate for M2 (an intermediate target), which will in turn be achieved by a growth rate of 3% for nonborrowed reserves (the policy instrument). Alternatively, the central bank might believe that the best way to achieve its objectives would be to set the federal funds rate (a policy instrument) at, say, 4%. Can the central bank choose to target both the nonborrowed reserves

MyEconLab Mini-lecture

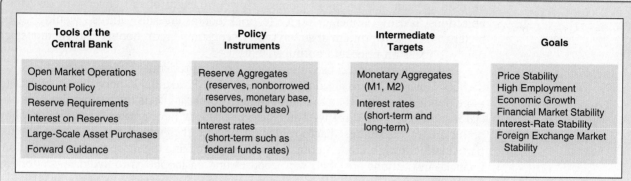

FIGURE 2 **Linkages Among Central Bank Tools, Policy Instruments, Intermediate Targets, and Goals of Monetary Policy**

The tools of the central bank are used to change the policy instruments to achieve the intermediate target and then the goals of monetary policy.

and the federal-funds-rate policy instruments at the same time? The answer is no. The application of supply and demand analysis to the market for reserves, developed in Chapter 15, explains why a central bank must choose one or the other.

Let's first see why choosing an aggregate target involves losing control of the interest rate. Figure 3 contains a supply and demand diagram of the market for reserves. Although the central bank expects the demand curve for reserves to be at R^{d*}, it fluctuates between $R^{d'}$ and $R^{d''}$ because of unexpected fluctuations in deposits (and hence required reserves) and changes in banks' desire to hold excess reserves. If the central bank has a nonborrowed reserves target of NBR^* (say, because it has a target growth rate

MyEconLab Mini-lecture

FIGURE 3

Result of Targeting on Nonborrowed Reserves

Targeting on nonborrowed reserves of NBR^* will lead to fluctuations in the federal funds rate between i'_{ff} and i''_{ff} because of fluctuations in the demand for reserves between $R^{d'}$ and $R^{d''}$.

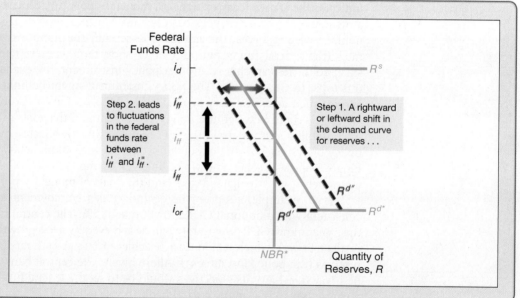

FIGURE 4
Result of Targeting on the Federal Funds Rate

Targeting on the interest rate i_{ff}^* will lead to fluctuations in nonborrowed reserves between NBR' and NBR'' because of fluctuations in the demand for reserves between $R^{d'}$ and $R^{d''}$.

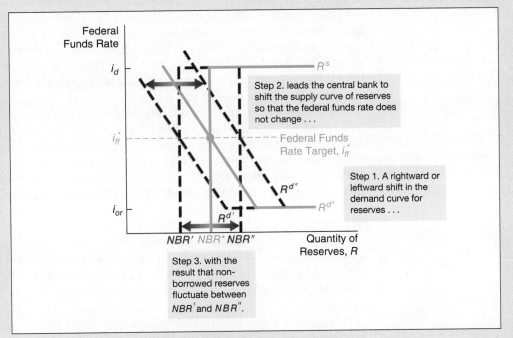

Step 2. leads the central bank to shift the supply curve of reserves so that the federal funds rate does not change . . .

Federal Funds Rate Target, i_{ff}^*

Step 1. A rightward or leftward shift in the demand curve for reserves . . .

Step 3. with the result that non-borrowed reserves fluctuate between NBR' and NBR''.

of the money supply of 4%), it expects that the federal funds rate will be i_{ff}^*. However, as the figure indicates, the fluctuations in the reserves demand curve between $R^{d'}$ and $R^{d''}$ will result in a fluctuation in the federal funds rate between i_{ff}' and i_{ff}''. Pursuing an aggregate target implies that interest rates will fluctuate.

The supply and demand diagram in Figure 4 shows the consequences of an interest-rate target set at i_{ff}^*. Again the central bank expects the reserves demand curve to be at R^{d*}, but it fluctuates between $R^{d'}$ and $R^{d''}$ due to unexpected changes in deposits or banks' desire to hold excess reserves. If the demand curve rises to $R^{d''}$, the federal funds rate will begin to rise above i_{ff}^* and the central bank will engage in open market purchases of bonds until it raises the supply of nonborrowed reserves to NBR'', at which point the equilibrium federal funds rate will return to i_{ff}^*. Conversely, if the demand curve falls to $R^{d'}$ and the federal funds rate drops, the central bank will keep making open market sales until nonborrowed reserves fall to NBR'' and the federal funds rate returns to i_{ff}^*. The central bank's adherence to the interest-rate target thus leads to a fluctuating quantity of nonborrowed reserves and the money supply.

The conclusion from our supply and demand analysis is that interest-rate and reserve (monetary) aggregate targets are incompatible. A central bank can hit one or the other, but not both. Because a choice between them has to be made, we need to examine what criteria should be used to select a policy instrument.

Criteria for Choosing the Policy Instrument

Three criteria apply when choosing a policy instrument: The instrument must be observable and measurable, it must be controllable by the central bank, and it must have a predictable effect on the goals.

Observability and Measurability   Quick observability and accurate measurement of a policy instrument are necessary because such an instrument is useful only if it signals the policy stance rapidly. Reserve aggregates like nonborrowed reserves are easily measured, but some lag in the reporting of reserve aggregates (a delay of two weeks) exists. Short-term interest rates (like the federal funds rate), by contrast, are not only easy to measure but are also immediately observable. Thus, it seems that interest rates are more observable and measurable than reserves and are therefore a better policy instrument.

However, as we learned in Chapter 4, the interest rate that is easiest to measure and observe is the nominal interest rate. It is typically a poor measure of the real cost of borrowing, which indicates with more certainty what will happen to the real GDP. The real cost of borrowing is more accurately measured by the real interest rate—that is, the nominal interest rate adjusted for expected inflation ($i_r = i - \pi^e$). Unfortunately, real interest rates are extremely difficult to measure because we do not have a direct way of measuring expected inflation. Given that both interest rates and aggregates are associated with observability and measurability problems, it is not clear whether one should be preferred over the other as a policy instrument.

Controllability   A central bank must be able to exercise effective control over a variable if the variable is to function as a useful policy instrument. If the central bank cannot control the policy instrument, knowing that it is off track does little good because the central bank has no way of getting it back on track.

Because of shifts into and out of currency, even reserve aggregates, such as nonborrowed reserves, are not completely controllable. Conversely, the Fed can control short-term interest rates, such as the federal funds rate, very tightly. It might appear, therefore, that short-term interest rates would dominate reserve aggregates on the controllability scale. However, a central bank cannot set short-term real interest rates because it does not have control over expectations of inflation. Once again, a clear-cut case cannot be made that short-term interest rates are preferable to reserve aggregates as a policy instrument, or vice versa.

Predictable Effect on Goals   The most important characteristic of a policy instrument is that it must have a predictable effect on a goal such as high employment or price stability. If a central bank can accurately and quickly measure the price of tea in China and can completely control its price, what good does that do? The central bank cannot use the price of tea in China to affect unemployment or the price level in its own country. Because the ability of a policy instrument to affect goals is critical to its usefulness, the strength of the link between reserve or monetary aggregates and the goals (output, employment, and inflation) or, alternatively, between interest rates and these goals, has been the subject of much research and debate. In recent years, most central banks have concluded that the link between interest rates and goals such as stable inflation is stronger than the link between aggregates and inflation. For this reason, central banks throughout the world now generally use short-term interest rates as their policy instrument.

TACTICS: THE TAYLOR RULE

As we have seen, the Federal Reserve and most other central banks currently conduct monetary policy by setting a target for short-term interest rates such as the federal funds rate. But how should this target be chosen?

John Taylor of Stanford University has come up with an answer, called the **Taylor rule**. The Taylor rule indicates that the federal (fed) funds rate should be set equal to the inflation rate plus an "equilibrium" real fed funds rate (the real fed funds rate that is consistent with full employment in the long run) plus a weighted average of two gaps: (1) an inflation gap, current inflation minus a target rate; and (2) an output gap, the percentage deviation of real GDP from an estimate of its potential (natural rate) level.[11]

This rule can be written as follows:

$$\text{Federal funds rate target} = \text{inflation rate} + \text{equilibrium real fed funds rate}$$

$$+ \frac{1}{2}(\text{inflation gap}) + \frac{1}{2}(\text{output gap})$$

Taylor assumed an equilibrium real fed funds rate of 2% and an appropriate target for inflation of 2%, with equal weights of $\frac{1}{2}$ on the inflation and output gaps. For a numerical example of the Taylor rule, suppose the inflation rate is at 3%, leading to a positive inflation gap of 1% (= 3% − 2), and real GDP is 1% above its potential, resulting in a positive output gap of 1%. Then the Taylor rule suggests that the federal funds rate should be set at 6% [= 3% inflation + 2% equilibrium real fed funds rate + $\frac{1}{2}$ (1% inflation gap) + $\frac{1}{2}$ (1% output gap)].

An important feature of the Taylor rule is that the coefficient on the inflation gap, $1/2$, is positive. If the inflation rate rises by 1 percentage point, then the federal funds target is raised by 1.5 percentage points, and so it is raised by more than a one-to-one ratio. In other words, a rise in inflation of 1 percentage point leads to an increase in the *real* federal funds rate of $\frac{1}{2}$ percentage point. The principle that the monetary authorities should raise nominal interest rates by more than the increase in the inflation rate has been named the **Taylor principle**, and it is critical to the success of monetary policy. Suppose that the Taylor principle is not followed and that the rise in nominal rates is *less* than the rise in the inflation rate, so that real interest rates *fall* when inflation rises. Serious instability then results, because a rise in inflation leads to an effective easing of monetary policy, which then leads to even higher inflation in the future. Indeed, this scenario characterizes the monetary policy of the 1970s, which led to a loss of the nominal anchor and the era of the so-called "Great Inflation," when inflation rates climbed to double-digit levels. Fortunately, since 1979, the Taylor principle has become a feature of monetary policy, with much happier outcomes on both the inflation and aggregate output fronts.

Some economists take the view that the presence of an output gap in the Taylor rule indicates that the Fed should care not only about keeping inflation under control but also about minimizing business cycle fluctuations of output around its potential level. Caring about both inflation and output fluctuations is consistent with the Fed's dual mandate and with many statements by Federal Reserve officials that controlling inflation and stabilizing real output are important concerns of the Fed.

An alternative interpretation of the presence of the output gap in the Taylor rule is that the output gap is an indicator of future inflation, as stipulated in **Phillips curve theory**. Phillips curve theory states that changes in inflation are influenced by the state of the economy relative to its productive capacity, as well as by other factors. This productive capacity can be measured by potential GDP, which is a function of the natural rate of unemployment, defined as the rate of unemployment consistent with full

---

[11]The original formulation of the Taylor rule can be found in John B. Taylor, "Discretion Versus Policy Rules in Practice," *Carnegie-Rochester Conference Series on Public Policy* 39 (1993): 195–214. However, a more intuitive discussion with a historical perspective can be found in John B. Taylor, "A Historical Analysis of Monetary Policy Rules," in *Monetary Policy Rules*, ed., John B. Taylor (Chicago: University of Chicago Press, 1999), pp. 319–341.

employment. A related concept is the **NAIRU**, the **nonaccelerating inflation rate of unemployment**, defined as the rate of unemployment at which there is no tendency for inflation to change. Simply put, the theory states that when the unemployment rate is above NAIRU, with output below potential, inflation will fall, but when it is below NAIRU, with output above potential, inflation will rise. Prior to 1995, the NAIRU was thought to reside around 6%. However, with the drop in unemployment to around the 4% level in the late 1990s, with no increase (and even a slight decrease) in inflation, some critics have questioned the value of Phillips curve theory. They either claim that Phillips curve theory just doesn't work any more or, alternatively, they believe that great uncertainty exists about the value of NAIRU, which may have fallen to below 5% for reasons that are not absolutely clear. Phillips curve theory is now highly controversial, and critics question whether it should be used as a guide in the conduct of monetary policy.

As Figure 5 shows, the Taylor rule does a pretty good, but not perfect, job of describing the Fed's setting of the federal funds rate under former Fed chairs Greenspan and Bernanke. (Notice in Figure 5 that the Taylor rule does not accurately describe the movement of the federal funds rate during the 1970s, which reflects the fact that the Taylor principle was not being followed at that time, which in turn explains why monetary policy outcomes were so poor.) Does this mean that the Fed should fire all of its economists and put a computer in charge to simply compute the Taylor rule setting for the federal funds rate? This would certainly save the taxpayers a lot of money. Although the Fed does not use the Taylor rule to directly compute the federal funds rate, it does make use of the Taylor rule in thinking about how to conduct monetary policy (see the Inside the Fed box, "The Fed's Use of the Taylor Rule"). Given the above discussion, it is no surprise that the Taylor rule does not explain all of the movements in the federal funds rate outlined in Figure 5. For this reason, financial institutions hire Fed "watchers," as described in the second Inside the Fed box.

MyEconLab Mini-lecture   MyEconLab Real-time data

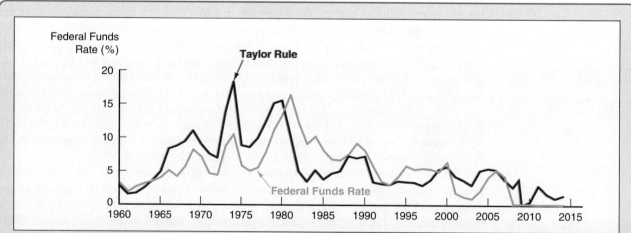

FIGURE 5   The Taylor Rule for the Federal Funds Rate, 1960–2014

The Taylor rule does a pretty good job of describing the Fed's setting of the federal funds rate under former chairs Greenspan and Bernanke, but it does not accurately describe the movement of the federal funds rate during the 1970s.

Source: Federal Reserve Bank of St. Louis, FRED database: http://research.stlouisfed.org/fred2/.

Inside the Fed   The Fed's Use of the Taylor Rule

Why hasn't the Fed put the federal funds rate on Taylor rule autopilot, guided by a computer? There are several reasons why the Fed hasn't taken this drastic action. First and foremost, no perfect model of the economy exists, so even the best and brightest economists do not know the current output gap with certainty at any given moment. Since the economy is changing all the time, the Taylor rule coefficients are unlikely to stay constant in any event.

Even if we could determine the output gap with certainty, monetary policy is by necessity a forward-looking activity, since it takes a long time for monetary policy to affect the economy. Good monetary policy requires that the Fed forecast where inflation and economic activity are headed in the future, and then adjust the policy instrument accordingly. The Fed will therefore look at a much wider range of information than just the current inflation gap and output gap, the variables used in the Taylor rule, when setting its policy. In other words, the conduct of monetary policy is as much an art as it is a science, requiring both careful analytics and human judgment. The Taylor rule leaves out all of the art and so is unlikely to produce the best monetary policy outcomes. For example, financial crises, such as the crisis that occurred from 2007 to 2009, require complex monetary policy actions because changes in credit spreads (the difference between interest rates on securities with credit risk and those without) may alter how the federal funds rate affects investment decisions, and therefore economic activity.

The bottom line is that putting monetary policy on autopilot by using a Taylor rule with fixed coefficients would be a bad idea. The Taylor rule is useful, however, as a *guide* to monetary policy. If the proposed setting of the policy instrument is very different from the setting suggested by the Taylor rule, policymakers should ask whether they have a good reason for deviating from this rule. If they don't, as during the era of the 1970s when Arthur Burns was the chair of the Federal Reserve, then they might be making a mistake. Indeed, the FOMC makes use of Taylor rule estimates in exactly this way—by referring to these estimates to inform their decisions about the federal funds rate target.[*]

[*]For an in-depth discussion of the FOMC's actual use of the Taylor rule in its policy deliberations, see Pier Francesco Asso, George A. Kahn, and Robert Leeson, "The Taylor Rule and the Practice of Central Banking," Federal Reserve Bank of Kansas City Working Paper RWP 10-05 (February 2010).

Inside the Fed   Fed Watchers

As we have seen, the most important player in the determination of U.S. interest rates is the Federal Reserve. When the Fed wants to inject reserves into the system, it conducts open market purchases of bonds, an action that causes bond prices to increase and their interest rates to fall, at least in the short term. If the Fed withdraws reserves from the system, it sells bonds, thereby depressing their price and raising their interest rates. Knowing what actions the Fed might take can thus help investors and financial institutions predict the future course of interest rates with greater accuracy. Because, as we have seen, changes in interest rates have a major impact on investors and financial institutions' profits, these parties are particularly interested in scrutinizing the Fed's behavior. To assist in this task, financial institutions hire *Fed watchers*, experts on Federal Reserve behavior who may have worked in the Federal Reserve System and so have an insider's view of Federal Reserve operations. A Fed watcher who can accurately predict the course of monetary policy is a very valuable commodity, and successful Fed watchers therefore often earn very high salaries, well into the six-figure range and sometimes even higher.

SUMMARY

1. The six basic goals of monetary policy are price stability (the primary goal), high employment (output stability), economic growth, stability of financial markets, interest-rate stability, and stability in foreign exchange markets.

2. A strong nominal anchor is a key element of a successful monetary policy. A strong nominal anchor helps promote price stability by tying down inflation expectations and limiting the time-inconsistency problem, in which monetary policymakers conduct monetary policy in a discretionary way that focuses on short-run objectives but produces poor long-run outcomes.

3. Inflation targeting has several advantages: (1) By focusing the political debate on long-run inflation, it can reduce the likelihood of the time-inconsistency problem; (2) it is readily understood by the public and is highly transparent; (3) it increases accountability of the central bank; and (4) it appears to ameliorate the effects of inflationary shocks. It does have some disadvantages, however: (1) Inflation is not easily controlled by the monetary authorities, and so an inflation target does not send immediate signals to the public and the markets; (2) it might impose a rigid rule on policymakers, although this has not been the case in practice; and (3) a sole focus on inflation may lead to larger output fluctuations, or lower economic growth although this also has not been the case in practice.

4. The Federal Reserve's monetary policy has evolved over time. From the 1980s through 2006, the Federal Reserve set an implicit, not an explicit, nominal anchor. Despite its demonstrated success, this monetary policy lacked transparency and was inconsistent with democratic principles. Under Ben Bernanke, the Federal Reserve moved to a flexible form of inflation targeting that was consistent with the Fed's dual mandate.

5. Four lessons can be learned from the global financial crisis: (1) Developments in the financial sector have a far greater impact on economic activity than was earlier realized; (2) the zero lower bound on interest rates can be a serious problem; (3) the cost of cleaning up after a financial crisis is very high; and (4) price and output stability do not ensure financial stability.

6. The lessons of the global financial crisis provide support for more flexible inflation targeting, possibly with a higher inflation target.

7. The lessons from the crisis also suggest that monetary policy should lean against credit booms but not asset-price bubbles.

8. Because interest-rate and aggregate policy instruments are incompatible, a central bank must choose between them on the basis of three criteria: measurability, controllability, and their ability to affect goal variables predictably. Central banks now typically use short-term interest rates as their policy instrument.

9. The Taylor rule indicates that the federal funds rate should be set equal to the inflation rate plus an "equilibrium" real fed funds rate plus a weighted average of two gaps: (1) an inflation gap, current inflation minus a target rate; and (2) an output gap, the percentage deviation of real GDP from an estimate of its potential (natural rate) level. The output gap in the Taylor rule can be interpreted as an indicator of future inflation, as stipulated in Phillips curve theory. However, this theory is controversial, because high output relative to potential as measured by low unemployment has not seemed to produce higher inflation in recent years.

KEY TERMS

asset-price bubble, p. 383
dual mandate, p. 371
hierarchical mandates, p. 370
inflation targeting, p. 371
intermediate target, p. 387
macroprudential regulation, p. 386
natural rate of output, p. 369

natural rate of unemployment, p. 368
nominal anchor, p. 367
nonaccelerating inflation rate of unemployment (NAIRU), p. 392
operating instrument, p. 387
Phillips curve theory, p. 391
policy instrument, p. 387

potential output, p. 369
price stability, p. 366
Taylor principle, p. 391
Taylor rule, p. 391
time-inconsistency problem, p. 367

QUESTIONS

All questions are available in MyEconLab *at* http://www.myeconlab.com.

1. What are the benefits of using a nominal anchor for the conduct of monetary policy?

2. What incentives arise for a central bank to fall into the time-inconsistency trap of pursuing overly expansionary monetary policy?

3. Why would it be problematic for a central bank to have a primary goal of maximizing economic growth?

4. "Since financial crises can impart severe damage to the economy, a central bank's primary goal should be to ensure stability in financial markets." Is this statement true, false, or uncertain? Explain.

5. "A central bank with a dual mandate will achieve lower unemployment in the long run than a central bank with a hierarchical mandate in which price stability takes precedence." Is this statement true, false, or uncertain? Explain.

6. Why is a public announcement of numerical inflation rate objectives important to the success of an inflation-targeting central bank?

7. How does inflation targeting help reduce the time-inconsistency problem of discretionary policy?

8. What methods have inflation-targeting central banks used to increase communication with the public and to increase the transparency of monetary policymaking?

9. Why might inflation targeting increase support for the independence of the central bank in conducting monetary policy?

10. "Because inflation targeting focuses on achieving the inflation target, it will lead to excessive output fluctuations." Is this statement true, false, or uncertain? Explain.

11. What are the key advantages and disadvantages of the monetary strategy used by the Federal Reserve under Alan Greenspan, in which the nominal anchor was implicit rather than explicit?

12. "The zero lower bound on short-term interest rates is not a problem, since the central bank can just use quantitative easing to lower intermediate and longer-term interest rates instead." Is this statement true, false, or uncertain? Explain.

13. If higher inflation is bad, then why might it be advantageous to have a higher inflation target rather than a lower target that is closer to zero?

14. Why aren't most central banks more proactive in trying to use monetary policy to eliminate asset-price bubbles?

15. Why might it be better to *lean* against credit-driven bubbles rather than just *clean* up after other types of asset bubbles burst?

16. According to the Greenspan doctrine, under what conditions might a central bank respond to a perceived stock market bubble?

17. Classify each of the following as either a policy instrument or an intermediate target, and explain your choice.
    a. The ten-year Treasury bond rate
    b. The monetary base
    c. M1
    d. The fed funds rate

18. "If the demand for reserves did not fluctuate, the Fed could pursue both a reserves target and an interest-rate target at the same time." Is this statement true, false, or uncertain? Explain.

19. What procedures can the Fed use to control the federal funds rate? Why does control of this interest rate imply that the Fed will lose control of nonborrowed reserves?

20. Compare the monetary base to M1 on the grounds of controllability and measurability. Which do you prefer as an intermediate target? Why?

21. "Interest rates can be measured more accurately and quickly than reserve aggregates; hence an interest rate is preferred to the reserve aggregates as a policy instrument." Do you agree or disagree? Explain your answer.

22. How can bank behavior and the Fed's behavior cause money supply growth to be procyclical (rising during booms and falling during recessions)?

23. What does the Taylor rule imply that policymakers should do to the fed funds rate under the following scenarios?
    a. Unemployment rises due to a recession.
    b. An oil price shock causes the inflation rate to rise by 1% and output to fall by 1%.
    c. The economy experiences prolonged increases in productivity growth while actual output growth is unchanged.
    d. Potential output declines while actual output remains unchanged.
    e. The Fed revises its (implicit) inflation target downward.

APPLIED PROBLEMS

All applied problems are available in MyEconLab *at* http://www.myeconlab.com.

24. If the Fed has an interest-rate target, why will an increase in the demand for reserves lead to a rise in the money supply? Use a graph of the market for reserves to explain.

25. Since monetary policy changes made through the fed funds rate occur with a lag, policymakers are usually more concerned with adjusting policy according to changes in the forecasted or expected inflation rate, rather than the current inflation rate. In light of this, suppose that monetary policymakers employ the Taylor rule to set the fed funds rate, where the inflation gap is defined as the difference between expected inflation and the target inflation rate. Assume that the weights on both the inflation and output gaps are ½, the equilibrium real fed funds rate is 2%, the inflation rate target is 2%, and the output gap is 1%.

a. If the expected inflation rate is 4%, then at what target should the fed funds rate be set according to the Taylor rule?

b. Suppose half of Fed economists forecast inflation to be 3%, and half of Fed economists forecast inflation to be 5%. If the Fed uses the average of these two forecasts as its measure of expected inflation, then at what target should the fed funds rate be set according to the Taylor rule?

c. Now suppose half of Fed economists forecast inflation to be 0%, and half forecast inflation to be 8%. If the Fed uses the average of these two forecasts as its measure of expected inflation, then at what target should the fed funds rate be set according to the Taylor rule?

d. Given your answers to parts (a)–(c) above, do you think it is a good idea for monetary policymakers to use a strict interpretation of the Taylor rule as a basis for setting policy? Why or why not?

DATA ANALYSIS PROBLEMS

The Problems update with real-time data in MyEconLab *and are available for practice or instructor assignment.*

 1. The Fed's maximum employment mandate is generally interpreted as an attempt to achieve an unemployment rate that is as close as possible to the natural rate and inflation that is close to its 2% goal for personal consumption expenditure price inflation. Go to the St. Louis Federal Reserve FRED database, and find data on the personal consumption expenditure price index (PCECTPI), the unemployment rate (UNRATE), and a measure of the natural rate of unemployment (NROU). For the price index, adjust the *units* setting to "Percent Change From Year Ago" to convert the data to the inflation rate; for the unemployment rate, change the *frequency* setting to "Quarterly." Download the data into a spreadsheet. Calculate the unemployment gap and inflation gap for each quarter. Then, using the inflation gap, create an average inflation gap measure by taking the average of the current inflation gap and the gaps for the previous three quarters. Now apply the

following (admittedly arbitrary and ad hoc) test to the data from 2000:Q1 through the most recent data available: If the unemployment gap is larger than 1.0 for two or more consecutive quarters, and/or the average inflation gap is larger in absolute value than 0.5 for two or more consecutive quarters, consider the mandate "violated."

a. Based on this ad hoc test, in which quarters has the Fed "violated" the price stability portion of its mandate? In which quarters has the Fed "violated" the maximum employment mandate?

b. Is the Fed currently "in violation" of its mandate?

c. Interpret your results. What do your response to part (a) and the data imply about the challenge that monetary policymakers face in achieving the Fed's mandate perfectly at all times?

 2. Go to the St. Louis Federal Reserve FRED database, and find data on the personal consumption expenditure price index (PCECTPI), real GDP

(GDPC1), an estimate of potential GDP (GDPPOT), and the federal funds rate (DFF). For the price index, adjust the *units* setting to "Percent Change From Year Ago" to convert the data to the inflation rate; for the federal funds rate, change the *frequency* setting to "Quarterly." Download the data into a spreadsheet. Assuming the inflation target is 2%, calculate the inflation gap and the output gap for each quarter, from 2000 until the most recent quarter of data available. Calculate the output gap as the percentage deviation of output from the potential level of output.

a. Use the output and inflation gaps to calculate, for each quarter, the fed funds rate predicted by the Taylor rule. Assume that the weights on inflation stabilization and output stabilization are both ½ (see the formula in the chapter). Compare the current (quarterly average) federal funds rate to the federal funds rate prescribed by the Taylor rule. Does the Taylor rule accurately predict the current rate? Briefly comment.

b. Create a graph that compares the predicted Taylor rule values with the actual quarterly

federal funds rate averages. How well, in general, does the Taylor rule prediction fit the average federal funds rate? Briefly explain.

c. Based on the results from the 2008–2009 period, explain the limitations of the Taylor rule as a formal policy tool. How do these limitations help explain the use of nonconventional monetary policy during this period?

d. Suppose Congress changes the Fed's mandate to a hierarchical one in which inflation stabilization takes priority over output stabilization. In this context, recalculate the predicted Taylor rule value for each quarter since 2000, assuming that the weight on inflation stabilization is ¾ and the weight on output stabilization is ¼. Create a graph showing the Taylor rule prediction calculated in part (a), the prediction using new "hierarchical" Taylor rule, and the fed funds rate. How, if at all, does changing the mandate change the predicted policy paths? How would the fed funds rate be affected by a hierarchical mandate? Briefly explain.

WEB EXERCISES

1. The Federal Open Market Committee (FOMC) meets about every six weeks to assess the state of the economy and to decide what actions the central bank should take. The minutes of this meeting are released three weeks after the meeting; however, a brief press release is made available immediately after the meeting. Find the schedule of minutes and press releases at http://www.federalreserve.gov/fomc/.

   a. When was the last scheduled meeting of the FOMC? When is the next meeting?

   b. Review the press release from the last meeting. What did the committee decide to do about short-term interest rates?

   c. Review the most recently published meeting minutes. What areas of the economy seemed to be of most concern to the committee members?

2. It is possible to access other central bank websites to learn about these banks' structures. One example is the European Central Bank. Go to http://www.ecb.int/index.html. On the ECB home page, find information about the ECB's strategy for monetary policy.

3. Many countries have central banks that are responsible for their nation's monetary policy. Go to http//www.bis.org/cbanks.htm and select one of the central banks (for example, the central bank of Norway). Review that bank's website to determine its policies regarding the application of monetary policy. How does this bank's policies compare to those of the U.S. central bank?

WEB REFERENCES

http://www.federalreserve.gov/pf/pf.htm

The Federal Reserve reports on its primary purposes and functions.

http://www.economagic.com/

A comprehensive listing of sites that offer a wide variety of economic summary data and graphs.

http://www.federalreserve.gov/releases/H3

Historic and current data on the aggregate reserves of depository institutions and the monetary base.

http://www.federalreserve.gov/aboutthefed/relatedWebSites.htm

The Federal Reserve provides links to other central bank Web pages.

WEB APPENDICES

Please visit the Companion Website at http://www.pearsonhighered.com/mishkin to read the Web appendices to Chapter 16.

Appendix 1: **Monetary Targeting**

Appendix 2: **A Brief History of Federal Reserve Policymaking**

International Finance and Monetary Policy

Crisis and Response: Foreign Exchange Market Turmoil and the IMF

From 2002 until 2008, the U.S. dollar steadily declined in value relative to other currencies. Indeed, a major concern of policymakers was that the dollar might crash, with adverse effects on both economic activity and inflation. With the credit markets seizing up in September and October 2008, after the failure of Lehman Brothers, an amazing thing happened. Instead of continuing its decline, the dollar appreciated sharply. The same "flight to quality" that led investors to step up their purchases of U.S. Treasury securities also led them to want to hold more U.S. dollars, thereby bidding up the dollar's value.

The dollar's higher value made imported goods—ranging from flat-screen televisions to wines—cheaper to purchase and traveling abroad more affordable. But this good news for the U.S. dollar was often bad news for other currencies. Many countries in Latin America and Eastern Europe now found their currencies in free fall. The International Monetary Fund (IMF) stepped in and set up a new lending facility to make loans to distressed countries with fewer strings attached than were attached to the IMF's previous lending programs. The IMF started making loans to the tune of billions of dollars. The IMF, which had looked as though it was on the sidelines as the global financial crisis spread worldwide, now was moving to front and center.

The global financial crisis demonstrated that financial events that start in the United States can have worldwide ramifications and that international financial institutions like the IMF have an important role in responding to such events, to make sure that the international financial system continues to work well. Chapter 17 outlines how the foreign exchange market functions and how exchange rates between different countries' currencies are determined. In Chapter 18, we examine how the international financial system operates and how it affects monetary policy.

17 The Foreign Exchange Market

Preview

In the mid-1980s, American businesses became less competitive with their foreign counterparts; subsequently, in the 1990s and 2000s, their competitiveness increased. Did this swing in competitiveness occur primarily because American management fell down on the job in the 1980s and then got its act together afterwards? Not really. American businesses became less competitive in the 1980s because American dollars became worth more in terms of foreign currencies, making American goods more expensive relative to foreign goods. By the 1990s and 2000s, the value of the U.S. dollar had fallen appreciably from its highs in the mid-1980s, making American goods cheaper and American businesses more competitive.

The price of one currency in terms of another is called the **exchange rate**. As you can see in Figure 1, exchange rates are highly volatile. The exchange rate affects the economy and our daily lives, because when the U.S. dollar becomes more valuable relative to foreign currencies, foreign goods become cheaper for Americans, and American goods become more expensive for foreigners. When the U.S. dollar falls in value, foreign goods become more expensive for Americans, and American goods become cheaper for foreigners.

Fluctuations in the exchange rate also affect both inflation and output, and are an important concern to monetary policymakers. When the U.S. dollar falls in value, the higher prices of imported goods feed directly into a higher price level and inflation. At the same time, a declining U.S. dollar, which makes U.S. goods cheaper for foreigners, increases the demand for U.S. goods and leads to higher production and output.

We begin our study of international finance by examining the **foreign exchange market**, the financial market in which exchange rates are determined.

FOREIGN EXCHANGE MARKET

Most countries of the world have their own currencies: The United States has its dollar; the European Monetary Union, its euro; Brazil, its real; and China, its yuan. Trade between countries involves the mutual exchange of different currencies (or, more typically, bank deposits denominated in different currencies). When an American firm buys foreign goods, services, or financial assets, for example, U.S. dollars (typically, bank deposits denominated in U.S. dollars) must be exchanged for foreign currency (bank deposits denominated in the foreign currency).

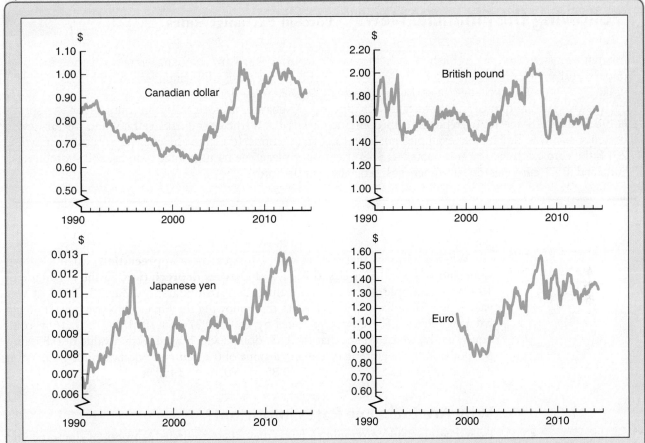

FIGURE 1 **Exchange Rates, 1990–2014**

Exchange rates are highly volatile. Note that exchange rates are quoted as $ per unit of foreign currency, so that a rise in these plots indicates a strengthening of the foreign currency (weakening of the dollar).

Source: Federal Reserve Bank of St. Louis, FRED database: http://research.stlouisfed.org/fred2/.

The trading of currencies and bank deposits denominated in particular currencies takes place in the foreign exchange market. Transactions conducted in the foreign exchange market determine the rates at which currencies are exchanged, which in turn determine the cost of purchasing foreign goods and financial assets.

What Are Foreign Exchange Rates?

There are two kinds of exchange rate transactions. The predominant ones, called **spot transactions**, involve the immediate (two-day) exchange of bank deposits. **Forward transactions** involve the exchange of bank deposits at some specified future date. The **spot exchange rate** is the exchange rate for the spot transaction, and the **forward exchange rate** is the exchange rate for the forward transaction.

Following the Financial News   Foreign Exchange Rates

Foreign exchange rates are published daily in newspapers and on Internet sites such as http://www.finance.yahoo.com. Exchange rates for a currency such as the euro are quoted in two ways: in U.S. dollars per unit of domestic currency and in domestic currency per U.S. dollar. For example, on May 13, 2014, the euro exchange rate was quoted as $1.37 per euro and 0.73 euro per dollar. Americans generally would regard the exchange rate with the euro as $1.37 per euro, while Europeans would think of it as 0.73 euro per dollar.

Exchange rates typically are quoted for the spot transaction (the spot exchange rate) and for forward transactions (the forward exchange rates) that will take place one month, three months, and six months in the future.

When a currency increases in value, it experiences **appreciation**; when it falls in value and is worth fewer U.S. dollars, it undergoes **depreciation**. At the beginning of 1999, for example, the euro was valued at 1.18 dollars; on May 13, 2014, it was valued at 1.37 dollars, as indicated in the Following the Financial News box, "Foreign Exchange Rates." The euro *appreciated* by 16%: (1.37 − 1.18/1.18) = 0.16 = 16%. Equivalently, we could say that the U.S. dollar, which went from a value of 0.85 euro per dollar at the beginning of 1999 to a value of 0.73 euro per dollar on May 13, 2014, *depreciated* by 14%: (0.73 − 0.85)/0.85 = −0.14 = 14%.

Why Are Exchange Rates Important?

Exchange rates are important because they affect the relative prices of domestic and foreign goods. The dollar price of French goods to an American is determined by the interaction of two factors: the price of French goods in euros and the euro/dollar exchange rate.

Suppose that Wanda the Winetaster, an American, decides to buy a bottle of 1961 (a very good year) Château Lafite Rothschild to complete her wine cellar. If the price of the wine in France is 1,000 euros and the exchange rate is $1.37 to the euro, the wine will cost Wanda $1,370 (= 1,000 euros × $1.37/euro). Now suppose that Wanda delays her purchase by two months, at which time the euro has appreciated to $1.70 per euro. If the domestic price of the bottle of Lafite Rothschild remains 1,000 euros, its dollar cost will have risen from $1,370 to $1,700.

The same currency appreciation, however, makes the price of foreign goods in France less expensive. At an exchange rate of $1.37 per euro, a Dell computer priced at $2,000 costs Pierre the Programmer 1,460 euros; if the exchange rate increases to $1.70 per euro, the computer will cost only 1,176 euros.

A depreciation of the euro lowers the cost of French goods in America but raises the cost of American goods in France. If the euro drops in value to $1.00, Wanda's bottle of Lafite Rothschild will cost her only $1,000 instead of $1,370, and the Dell computer will cost Pierre 2,000 euros rather than 1,460 euros.

Such reasoning leads to the following conclusion: **When a country's currency appreciates (rises in value relative to other currencies), the country's goods abroad become more expensive, and foreign goods in that country become cheaper (holding** *domestic prices constant in the two countries). Conversely, when a country's currency depreciates, its goods abroad become cheaper, and foreign goods in that country become more expensive.*

Depreciation of a currency makes it easier for domestic manufacturers to sell their goods abroad and makes foreign goods less competitive in domestic markets. From 2002 to 2014, the depreciated dollar helped U.S. industries sell more goods, but it hurt American consumers because foreign goods were more expensive. The prices of French wine and cheese and the cost of vacationing abroad all rose as a result of the weak dollar.

How Is Foreign Exchange Traded?

You cannot go to a centralized location to watch exchange rates being determined; currencies are not traded on exchanges such as the New York Stock Exchange. Instead, the foreign exchange market is organized as an over-the-counter market in which several hundred dealers (mostly banks) stand ready to buy and sell deposits denominated in foreign currencies. Because these dealers are in constant telephone and computer contact, the market is very competitive; in effect, it functions no differently from a centralized market.

An important point to note is that although banks, companies, and governments talk about buying and selling currencies in foreign exchange markets, they do not take a fistful of dollar bills and sell them for British pound notes. Rather, most trades involve the buying and selling of bank deposits denominated in different currencies. So when we say that a bank is buying dollars in the foreign exchange market, what we actually mean is that the bank is buying *deposits denominated in dollars*. The volume in this market is colossal, exceeding $5 trillion per day.

Trades in the foreign exchange market consist of transactions in excess of $1 million. The market that determines the exchange rates given in the Following the Financial News box is not the market in which we would buy foreign currency for a trip abroad. Instead, we buy foreign currency in the retail market, from dealers such as American Express or from banks. Because retail prices are higher than wholesale prices, when we buy foreign exchange, we obtain fewer units of foreign currency per dollar—that is, we pay a higher price for foreign currency—than the exchange rates quoted in the newspaper.

EXCHANGE RATES IN THE LONG RUN

Like the price of any good or asset in a free market, exchange rates are determined by the interaction of supply and demand. To simplify our analysis of exchange rates in a free market, we divide it into two parts. First, we examine how exchange rates are determined in the long run; then we use our knowledge of the long-run determinants of exchange rates to help us understand how they are determined in the short run.

Law of One Price

The starting point for understanding how exchange rates are determined is a simple idea called the **law of one price**: If two countries produce an identical good, and transportation costs and trade barriers are very low, the price of the good should be the same throughout the world, no matter which country produces it. Suppose that American steel costs $100 per ton and identical Japanese steel costs 10,000 yen per ton. For the law of one price to hold, the exchange rate between the yen and the dollar must be 100 yen per dollar ($0.01 per yen), so that one ton of American steel sells for 10,000 yen in Japan (the price of Japanese steel) and one ton of Japanese steel sells for $100 in the United States (the price of U.S. steel). If the exchange rate were 200 yen to the dollar, Japanese steel would sell for $50 per ton in the United States, or half the price of American steel, and American steel would sell for 20,000 yen per ton in Japan, twice the price of Japanese steel. Because American steel would be more expensive than Japanese steel in both countries and because American steel is identical to Japanese steel, the demand for American steel would go to zero. Given a fixed dollar price for American steel, the resulting excess supply of American steel would be eliminated only if the exchange rate fell to 100 yen per dollar, making the prices of American steel and Japanese steel the same in both countries.

Theory of Purchasing Power Parity

One of the most prominent theories of how exchange rates are determined is the **theory of purchasing power parity (PPP)**. It states that exchange rates between any two currencies will adjust to reflect changes in the price levels of the two countries. The theory of PPP is simply an application of the law of one price to national price levels rather than to individual prices. Suppose that the yen price of Japanese steel rises 10% (to 11,000 yen) relative to the dollar price of American steel (unchanged at $100). For the law of one price to hold, the exchange rate must rise to 110 yen to the dollar, a 10% appreciation of the dollar. By applying the law of one price to the price levels in the two countries, we get the theory of purchasing power parity, which maintains that if the Japanese price level rises 10% relative to the U.S. price level, the dollar will appreciate by 10%.

Another way of thinking about purchasing power parity is through a concept called the **real exchange rate**, the rate at which domestic goods can be exchanged for foreign goods. In effect, the real exchange rate is the price of domestic goods relative to the price of foreign goods denominated in the domestic currency. For example, if a basket of goods in New York costs $50 while the same basket of goods in Tokyo costs $75 (because the basket of goods costs 7500 yen and the exchange rate is 100 yen per dollar), then the real exchange rate is 0.66 (= $50/$75). In our example, the real exchange rate is below 1.0, indicating that it is cheaper to buy the basket of goods in the United States than in Japan. The real exchange rate for the U.S. dollar is currently low against many other currencies, and this is why New York is overwhelmed by so many foreign tourists going on shopping sprees. The real exchange rate indicates whether a currency is relatively cheap or not. The theory of PPP can also be described in terms of the real exchange rate. PPP predicts that the real exchange rate is always equal to 1.0, so that the purchasing power of the dollar is the same as that of other currencies, such as the yen or the euro.

As our U.S./Japanese example demonstrates, the theory of PPP suggests that if one country's price level rises relative to another's, its currency should depreciate (and the other country's currency should appreciate). As you can see in Figure 2, this prediction is borne out in the long run. From 1973 to 2014, the British price level rose 68% relative to the U.S. price level, and as the theory of PPP predicts, the dollar appreciated against the pound—although by 43%, an amount smaller than the 68% increase predicted by PPP.

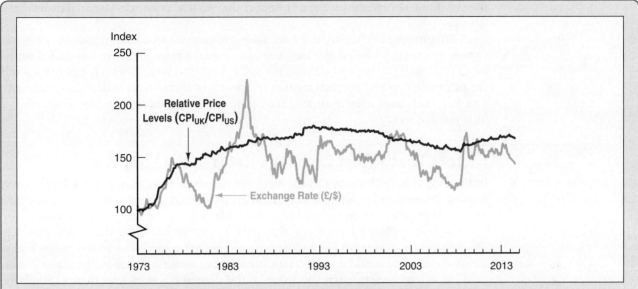

FIGURE 2   **Purchasing Power Parity, United States/United Kingdom, 1973–2014 (Index: March 1973 = 100.)**

Over the whole period shown, the rise in the British price level relative to the U.S. price level is associated with a rise in the value of the dollar, as predicted by PPP. However, the PPP relationship does not hold over shorter periods.

Source: Federal Reserve Bank of St. Louis, FRED database: http://research.stlouisfed.org/fred2/.

Yet, as the same figure indicates, PPP theory often has poor predictive power in the short run. From early 1985 to the end of 1987, for example, the British price level rose relative to that of the United States. Instead of appreciating, as predicted by PPP theory, the U.S. dollar actually depreciated by 40% against the pound. So even though PPP theory provides some guidance as to the long-run movement of exchange rates, it is not perfect and in the short run is a particularly poor predictor. What explains the PPP theory's failure to predict well in the short run?

Why the Theory of Purchasing Power Parity Cannot Fully Explain Exchange Rates

The PPP conclusion that exchange rates are determined solely by changes in relative price levels rests on the assumptions that all goods are identical in both countries and that transportation costs and trade barriers are very low. When these assumptions are true, the law of one price states that the relative prices of all these goods (that is, the relative price level between the two countries) will determine the exchange rate. The assumption that goods are identical may not be unreasonable for American and Japanese steel, but is it a reasonable assumption for American and Japanese cars? Is a Toyota the equivalent of a Chevrolet?

Because Toyotas and Chevys are obviously not identical, their prices do not have to be equal. Toyotas can be more expensive relative to Chevys, and both Americans and Japanese will still purchase Toyotas. Because the law of one price does not hold for all goods, a rise in the price of Toyotas relative to Chevys will not necessarily mean that the yen must depreciate by the amount of the relative price increase of Toyotas over Chevys.

Furthermore, PPP theory does not take into account that many goods and services (whose prices are included in a measure of a country's price level) are not traded across borders. Housing, land, and services such as restaurant meals, haircuts, and golf lessons are not traded goods. So even though the prices of these items might rise, leading to a higher price level relative to another country's, the exchange rate would experience little direct effect.

Factors That Affect Exchange Rates in the Long Run

In the long run, four major factors affect the exchange rate: relative price levels, trade barriers, preferences for domestic versus foreign goods, and productivity. We examine how each of these factors affects the exchange rate while holding the other factors constant.

The basic reasoning proceeds along the following lines: Anything that increases the demand for domestically produced goods that are traded relative to foreign traded goods tends to appreciate the domestic currency, because domestic goods will continue to sell well even when the value of the domestic currency is higher. Similarly, anything that increases the demand for foreign goods relative to domestic goods tends to depreciate the domestic currency, because domestic goods will continue to sell well only if the value of the domestic currency is lower. In other words, *if a factor increases the demand for domestic goods relative to foreign goods, the domestic currency will appreciate; if a factor decreases the relative demand for domestic goods, the domestic currency will depreciate.*

Relative Price Levels   In line with PPP theory, when prices of American goods rise (holding prices of foreign goods constant), the demand for American goods falls, and the dollar tends to depreciate so that American goods can still sell well. By contrast, if prices of Japanese goods rise, causing the relative prices of American goods to fall, the demand for American goods increases, and the dollar tends to appreciate because American goods will continue to sell well even with a higher value of the domestic currency. *In the long run, a rise in a country's price level (relative to the foreign price level) causes its currency to depreciate, and a fall in the country's relative price level causes its currency to appreciate.*

Trade Barriers   Barriers to free trade such as **tariffs** (taxes on imported goods) and **quotas** (restrictions on the quantity of foreign goods that can be imported) can affect the exchange rate. Suppose the United States increases its tariff or puts a lower quota on Japanese steel. These increases in trade barriers increase the demand for American steel, and the dollar tends to appreciate because American steel will still sell well even with a higher value of the dollar. *Increasing trade barriers causes a country's currency to appreciate in the long run.*

Preferences for Domestic Versus Foreign Goods   If the Japanese develop an appetite for American goods—say, for Florida oranges and American movies—the increased demand for American goods (exports) tends to appreciate the dollar, because the American goods will continue to sell well even at a higher value of the dollar. Likewise, if Americans decide that they prefer Japanese cars to American cars, the increased

SUMMARY TABLE 1

Factors That Affect Exchange Rates in the Long Run

Factor	Change in Factor	Response of the Exchange Rate, E*
Domestic price level[†]	↑	↓
Trade barriers[†]	↑	↑
Import demand	↑	↓
Export demand	↑	↑
Productivity[†]	↑	↑

*Units of foreign currency per dollar: ↑ indicates domestic currency appreciation; ↓, depreciation.
†Relative to other countries.
Note: Only increases (↑) in the factors are shown; the effects of decreases in the variables on the exchange rate are the opposite of those indicated in the "Response" column.

demand for Japanese goods (imports) tends to depreciate the dollar. *Increased demand for a country's exports causes its currency to appreciate in the long run; conversely, increased demand for imports causes the domestic currency to depreciate.*

Productivity When productivity in a country rises, it tends to rise in domestic sectors that produce traded goods rather than nontraded goods. Higher productivity, therefore, is associated with a decline in the price of domestically produced traded goods relative to foreign traded goods. As a result, the demand for domestic traded goods rises, and the domestic currency tends to appreciate. If, however, a country's productivity lags behind that of other countries, its traded goods become relatively more expensive, and the currency tends to depreciate. *In the long run, as a country becomes more productive relative to other countries, its currency appreciates.*[1]

Our long-run theory of exchange rate behavior is summarized in Table 1. We use the convention that the exchange rate E is quoted such that an appreciation of the domestic currency corresponds to a rise in the exchange rate. In the case of the United States, this means that we are quoting the exchange rate as units of foreign currency, say, euros, per dollar.[2]

---

[1]A country might be so small that a change in productivity or the preferences for domestic or foreign goods will have no effect on the prices of these goods relative to foreign goods. In this case, changes in productivity or changes in preferences for domestic or foreign goods affect the country's income but do not necessarily affect the value of the currency. In our analysis, we are assuming that changes in productivity or preferences can affect relative prices and consequently the exchange rate.

[2]Exchange rates can be quoted either as units of foreign currency per domestic currency or as units of domestic currency per foreign currency. In professional writing, many economists quote exchange rates as units of domestic currency per foreign currency so that an appreciation of the domestic currency is portrayed as a fall in the exchange rate. The opposite convention is used in this text because it is more intuitive to think of an appreciation of the domestic currency as a rise in the exchange rate.

EXCHANGE RATES IN THE SHORT RUN: A SUPPLY AND DEMAND ANALYSIS

We have developed a theory of the long-run behavior of exchange rates. However, because factors driving long-run changes in exchange rates move slowly over time, if we are to understand why exchange rates exhibit such large changes (sometimes several percentage points) from day to day, we must develop a supply and demand analysis that explains how current exchange rates (spot exchange rates) are determined in the short run.

The key to understanding the short-run behavior of exchange rates is to recognize that an exchange rate is the price of domestic assets (bank deposits, bonds, equities, and so on, denominated in the domestic currency) in terms of foreign assets (similar assets denominated in the foreign currency). Because the exchange rate is the price of one asset in terms of another, the natural way to investigate the short-run determination of exchange rates is with a supply and demand analysis that uses an asset market approach, which relies heavily on the theory of portfolio choice developed in Chapter 5. As you will see, however, the long-run determinants of the exchange rate we have just outlined also play an important part in the short-run asset market approach.

In the past, supply and demand approaches to exchange rate determination emphasized the role of import and export demand. The more modern asset market approach used here emphasizes stocks of assets rather than the flows of exports and imports over short periods, because export and import transactions are small relative to the amounts of domestic and foreign assets held at any given time. For example, the total value of foreign exchange transactions in the United States each year is well over 25 times greater than the amount of U.S. exports and imports. Thus, over short periods, decisions to hold domestic or foreign assets have a much greater role in exchange rate determination than the demand for exports and imports does.

Supply Curve for Domestic Assets

We start by discussing the supply curve. In this analysis we treat the United States as the home country, so domestic assets are denominated in dollars. For simplicity, we use euros to stand for any foreign country's currency, so foreign assets are denominated in euros.

The quantity of dollar assets supplied is primarily the quantity of bank deposits, bonds, and equities in the United States, and for all practical purposes we can take this amount as fixed with respect to the exchange rate. The quantity supplied at any exchange rate is the same, so the supply curve, S, is vertical, as shown in Figure 3.

Demand Curve for Domestic Assets

The demand curve traces out the quantity demanded at each current exchange rate by holding everything else constant, particularly the expected future value of the exchange rate. We write the current exchange rate (the spot exchange rate) as E_t, and the expected exchange rate for the next period as E_{t+1}^e. As suggested by the theory of portfolio choice, the most important determinant of the quantity of domestic (dollar) assets demanded is the relative expected return on domestic assets. Let's see what happens as the current exchange rate E_t falls.

Suppose we start at point A in Figure 3, where the current exchange rate is at E_A. With the future expected value of the exchange rate held constant at E_{t+1}^e, a lower value of the exchange rate—say, at E^*—implies that the dollar is more likely to rise in value, that is, appreciate. The greater the expected rise (appreciation) of the dollar, the higher is

FIGURE 3
Equilibrium in the Foreign Exchange Market

Equilibrium in the foreign exchange market occurs at point *B*, the intersection of the demand curve *D* and the supply curve *S* at an exchange rate of E^*.

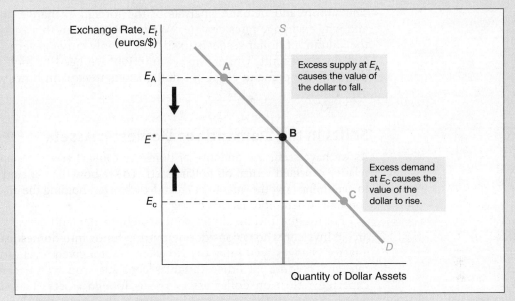

the relative expected return on dollar (domestic) assets. According to the theory of portfolio choice, because dollar assets are now more desirable to hold, the quantity of dollar assets demanded will rise, as shown by point *B* in Figure 3. If the current exchange rate falls even further to E_C, there will be an even higher expected appreciation of the dollar, a higher expected return, and therefore an even greater quantity of dollar assets demanded. This effect is shown at point *C* at Figure 3. The resulting demand curve *D*, which connects these points, is downward-sloping, indicating that at lower current values of the dollar (everything else being equal), the quantity demanded of dollar assets is higher.

Equilibrium in the Foreign Exchange Market

As in the usual supply and demand analysis, the market is in equilibrium when the quantity of dollar assets demanded equals the quantity supplied. In Figure 3, equilibrium occurs at point *B*, the intersection of the demand and supply curves. At point *B*, the exchange rate is E^*.

Suppose the exchange rate is at E_A, which is higher than the equilibrium exchange rate of E^*. As we can see in Figure 3, the quantity of dollar assets supplied is now greater than the quantity demanded, a condition of excess supply. Given that more people want to sell dollar assets than want to buy them, the value of the dollar will fall. As long as the exchange rate remains above the equilibrium exchange rate, an excess supply of dollar assets will continue to be available, and the dollar will fall in value until it reaches the equilibrium exchange rate of E^*.

Similarly, if the exchange rate is less than the equilibrium exchange rate at E_C, the quantity of dollar assets demanded will exceed the quantity supplied, a condition of excess demand. Given that more people want to buy dollar assets than want to sell them, the value of the dollar will rise until the excess demand disappears and the value of the dollar is again at the equilibrium exchange rate of E^*.

EXPLAINING CHANGES IN EXCHANGE RATES

The supply and demand analysis of the foreign exchange market illustrates how and why exchange rates change.[3] We have simplified this analysis by assuming that the amount of dollar assets is fixed: The supply curve is vertical at a given quantity and does not shift. Under this assumption, we need to look at only those factors that shift the demand curve for dollar assets to explain how exchange rates change over time.

Shifts in the Demand for Domestic Assets

As we have seen, the quantity of domestic (dollar) assets demanded depends on the relative expected return on dollar assets. To see how the demand curve shifts, we need to determine how the quantity demanded changes, holding the current exchange rate, E_t, constant, when other factors change.

For insight into the direction in which the demand curve will shift, suppose you are an investor who is considering putting funds into domestic (dollar) assets. When a factor changes, you must decide whether, at a given level of the current exchange rate and holding all other variables constant, you would earn a higher or lower expected return on dollar assets versus foreign assets. This decision will tell you whether you want to hold more or fewer dollar assets and thus whether the quantity demanded will increase or decrease at each level of the exchange rate. The direction of the change in the quantity demanded at each exchange rate indicates which way the demand curve will shift. In other words, if the relative expected return on dollar assets rises, holding the current exchange rate constant, the demand curve will shift to the right. If the relative expected return falls, the demand curve will shift to the left.

Domestic Interest Rate, i^D

Suppose that dollar assets pay an interest rate of i^D. When the domestic interest rate on dollar assets i^D rises, holding the current exchange rate E_t and everything else constant, the return on dollar assets increases relative to the return on foreign assets, and so people will want to hold more dollar assets. The quantity of dollar assets demanded increases at every value of the exchange rate, as shown by the rightward shift of the demand curve from D_1 to D_2 in Figure 4. The new equilibrium is reached at point 2, the intersection of D_2 and S, and the equilibrium exchange rate rises from E_1 to E_2. *An increase in the domestic interest rate i^D shifts the demand curve for domestic assets D to the right and causes the domestic currency to appreciate (E↑).*

Conversely, if i^D falls, the relative expected return on dollar assets falls, the demand curve shifts to the left, and the exchange rate falls. *A decrease in the domestic interest rate i^D shifts the demand curve for domestic assets D to the left and causes the domestic currency to depreciate (E↓).*

---

[3]How and why exchange rates change can also be modeled using the *interest parity condition*, an important concept in international finance that shows the relationships among domestic interest rates, foreign interest rates, and the expected appreciation of domestic currency. The interest parity condition and how it explains the determination of exchange rates is discussed in an appendix to this chapter.

MyEconLab Mini-lecture

FIGURE 4
Response to an Increase in the Domestic Interest Rate, i^D

When the domestic interest rate i^D increases, the relative expected return on domestic (dollar) assets increases and the demand curve shifts to the right. The equilibrium exchange rate rises from E_1 to E_2.

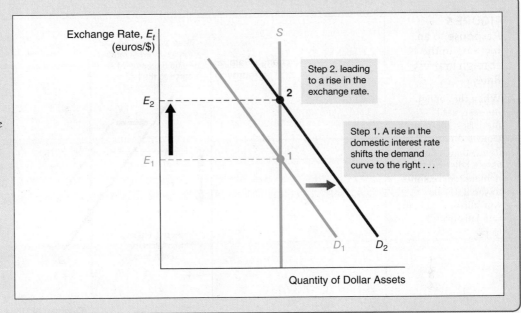

Step 2. leading to a rise in the exchange rate.

Step 1. A rise in the domestic interest rate shifts the demand curve to the right . . .

Foreign Interest Rate, i^F   Suppose foreign assets pay an interest rate of i^F. When the foreign interest rate i^F rises, holding the current exchange rate and everything else constant, the return on foreign assets rises relative to the return on dollar assets. Thus the relative expected return on dollar assets falls. Now people want to hold fewer dollar assets, and the quantity demanded decreases at every value of the exchange rate. This scenario is shown by the leftward shift of the demand curve from D_1 to D_2 in Figure 5. The new equilibrium is reached at point 2, when the value of the dollar has fallen. Conversely, a decrease in i^F raises the relative expected return on dollar assets, shifts the demand curve to the right, and raises the exchange rate. To summarize, *an increase in the foreign interest rate i^F shifts the demand curve D to the left and causes the domestic currency to depreciate; a fall in the foreign interest rate i^F shifts the demand curve D to the right and causes the domestic currency to appreciate.*

Changes in the Expected Future Exchange Rate, E_{t+1}^e   Expectations about the future value of the exchange rate play an important role in shifting the current demand curve because the demand for domestic assets, like that for any physical or financial asset, depends on the future resale price. Given the current exchange rate E_t, any factor that causes the expected future exchange rate E_{t+1}^e to rise increases the expected appreciation of the dollar. The result is a higher relative expected return on dollar assets, which increases the demand for dollar assets at every exchange rate, thereby shifting the demand curve to the right from D_1 to D_2 in Figure 6. The equilibrium exchange rate rises to point 2 at the intersection of the D_2 and S curves. *A rise in the expected future exchange rate E_{t+1}^e shifts the demand curve to the right and causes an appreciation of the domestic currency.* According to the same reasoning, *a fall in the expected future exchange rate E_{t+1}^e shifts the demand curve to the left and causes a depreciation of the currency.*

MyEconLab Mini-lecture

FIGURE 5
Response to an Increase in the Foreign Interest Rate, i^F

When the foreign interest rate i^F increases, the relative expected return on domestic (dollar) assets falls and the demand curve shifts to the left. The equilibrium exchange rate falls from E_1 to E_2.

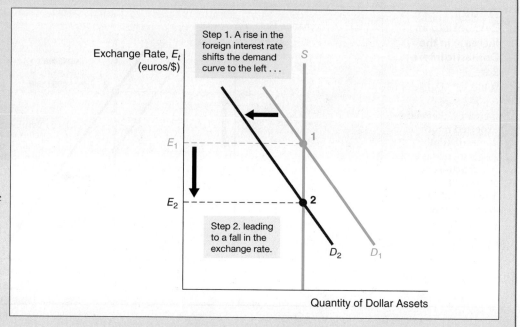

Earlier in the chapter we discussed the determinants of the exchange rate in the long run: the relative price level, relative trade barriers, import and export demand, and relative productivity (refer to Summary Table 1). These four factors influence the expected future exchange rate. The theory of purchasing power parity suggests that if a

MyEconLab Mini-lecture

FIGURE 6
Response to an Increase in the Expected Future Exchange Rate, E_{t+1}^e

When the expected future exchange rate increases, the relative expected return on domestic (dollar) assets rises and the demand curve shifts to the right. The equilibrium exchange rate rises from E_1 to E_2.

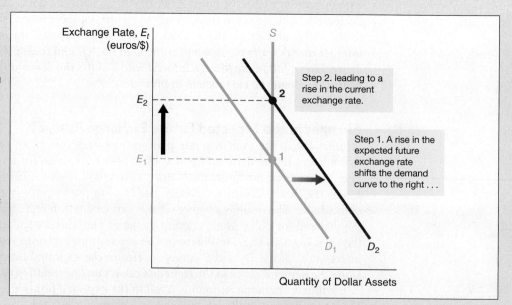

higher American price level relative to the foreign price level is expected to persist, then the dollar will depreciate in the long run. A higher expected relative American price level should thus have a tendency to lower E^e_{t+1}, lower the relative expected return on dollar assets, shift the demand curve to the left, and lower the current exchange rate.

Similarly, the other long-run determinants of the exchange rate can influence the relative expected return on dollar assets and the current exchange rate. Briefly, the following changes, all of which increase the demand for domestic goods relative to foreign goods, will raise E^e_{t+1}: (1) expectations of a fall in the American price level relative to the foreign price level; (2) expectations of higher American trade barriers relative to foreign trade barriers; (3) expectations of lower American import demand; (4) expectations of higher foreign demand for American exports; and (5) expectations of higher American productivity relative to foreign productivity. By increasing E^e_{t+1}, all of these changes increase the relative expected return on dollar assets, shift the demand curve to the right, and cause an appreciation of the domestic currency, the dollar.

Recap: Factors That Change the Exchange Rate

Summary Table 2 outlines all of the factors that shift the demand curve for domestic assets and thereby cause the exchange rate to change. Shifts in the demand curve occur when one factor changes, holding everything else constant, including the current exchange rate. Again, the theory of portfolio choice asserts that changes in the relative expected return on dollar assets are the source of shifts in the demand curve.

Let's review what happens when each of the seven factors in Table 2 changes. Remember that to understand the direction in which the demand curve will shift, we must consider what happens to the relative expected return on dollar assets when the factor changes. If the relative expected return rises, holding the current exchange rate constant, the demand curve shifts to the right. If the relative expected return falls, the demand curve shifts to the left.

1. When the interest rates on domestic assets i^D rise, the expected return on dollar assets rises at each exchange rate and so the quantity demanded increases. The demand curve therefore shifts to the right, and the equilibrium exchange rate rises, as shown in the first row of Table 2.

2. When the foreign interest rate i^F rises, the return on foreign assets rises, and so the relative expected return on dollar assets falls. The quantity demanded of dollar assets then falls, the demand curve shifts to the left, and the exchange rate falls, as shown in the second row of Table 2.

3. When the expected domestic price level rises relative to the foreign price level, our analysis of the long-run determinants of the exchange rate indicates that the value of the dollar will fall in the future. The expected return on dollar assets thus falls, the quantity demanded declines, the demand curve shifts to the left, and the exchange rate falls, as indicated in the third row of Table 2.

4. With higher expected trade barriers, the value of the dollar is higher in the long run and the expected return on dollar assets is higher. The quantity demanded of dollar assets thus rises, the demand curve shifts to the right, and the exchange rate rises, as shown in the fourth row of Table 2.

5. When the expected import demand rises, we expect the exchange rate to depreciate in the long run, so the expected return on dollar assets falls. The quantity demanded of dollar assets at each value of the current exchange rate therefore falls, the demand curve shifts to the left, and the exchange rate falls, as shown in the fifth row of Table 2.

SUMMARY TABLE 2

Factors That Shift the Demand Curve for Domestic Assets and Affect the Exchange Rate

Factor	Change in Factor	Change in Quantity Demanded of Domestic Assets at Each Exchange Rate	Response of Exchange Rate, E_t	
Domestic interest rate, i^D	↑	↑	↑	E_t E_2 E_1 S D_1 D_2 Dollar Assets
Foreign interest rate, i^F	↑	↓	↓	E_t E_1 E_2 S D_2 D_1 Dollar Assets
Expected domestic price level*	↑	↓	↓	E_t E_1 E_2 S D_2 D_1 Dollar Assets
Expected trade barriers*	↑	↑	↑	E_t E_2 E_1 S D_1 D_2 Dollar Assets
Expected import demand	↑	↓	↓	E_t E_1 E_2 S D_2 D_1 Dollar Assets
Expected export demand	↑	↑	↑	E_t E_2 E_1 S D_1 D_2 Dollar Assets
Expected productivity*	↑	↑	↑	E_t E_2 E_1 S D_1 D_2 Dollar Assets

*Relative to other countries.

Note: Only increases (↑) in the factors are shown; the effects of decreases in the variables on the exchange rate are the opposite of those indicated in the "Response" column.

6. When the expected export demand rises, the exchange rate is expected to appreciate in the long run. Thus the expected return on dollar assets rises, the demand curve shifts to the right, and the exchange rate rises, as indicated in the sixth row of Table 2.

7. When expected domestic productivity rises, the exchange rate is expected to appreciate in the long run, so the expected return on domestic assets rises. The quantity demanded at each exchange rate therefore rises, the demand curve shifts to the right, and the exchange rate rises, as shown in the seventh row of Table 2.

APPLICATION Effects of Changes in Interest Rates on the Equilibrium Exchange Rate

Our analysis has revealed the factors that affect the value of the equilibrium exchange rate. Now we use this analysis to take a closer look at the response of the exchange rate to changes in interest rates and money growth.

Changes in domestic interest rates i^D are often cited as a major factor affecting exchange rates. For example, we see headlines in the financial press like this one: "Dollar Recovers as Interest Rates Edge Upward." But is the positive correlation suggested in this headline true in every case?

Not necessarily, because to analyze the effects of interest rate changes, we must carefully distinguish the sources of the changes. The Fisher equation (Chapter 4) states that a nominal interest rate such as i^D equals the *real* interest rate plus expected inflation: $i = i_r + \pi^e$. The Fisher equation thus indicates that the interest rate i^D can change for two reasons: Either the real interest rate i_r changes or the expected inflation rate π^e changes. The effect on the exchange rate is quite different, depending on which of these two factors is the source of the change in the nominal interest rate.

Suppose the domestic real interest rate increases, so that the nominal interest rate i^D rises while expected inflation remains unchanged. In this case, it is reasonable to assume that the expected appreciation of the dollar will be unchanged because expected inflation is unchanged. In this case, the increase in i^D increases the relative expected return on dollar assets, raises the quantity of dollar assets demanded at each level of the exchange rate, and shifts the demand curve to the right. We end up with the situation depicted in Figure 4, which analyzes an increase in i^D, holding everything else constant. Our model of the foreign exchange market produces the following result: **When domestic real interest rates rise, the domestic currency appreciates.**

When the nominal interest rate rises because of an increase in expected inflation, we get a different result from the one shown in Figure 4. The rise in expected domestic inflation leads to a decline in the expected appreciation of the dollar, which is typically found to be larger than the increase in the domestic interest rate i^D. As a result, at any given exchange rate, the relative expected return on domestic (dollar) assets falls, the demand curve shifts to the left, and the exchange rate falls from E_1 to E_2, as shown in Figure 7. Our analysis leads to this conclusion: **When domestic interest rates rise due to an expected increase in inflation, the domestic currency depreciates.**

Because this result is completely different from the result that is obtained when the rise in the domestic interest rate is associated with a higher real interest rate, we must always distinguish between *real* and *nominal* measures when analyzing the effects of interest rates on exchange rates.

MyEconLab Mini-lecture

FIGURE 7
Effect of a Rise in the Domestic Interest Rate as a Result of an Increase in Expected Inflation

Because a rise in domestic expected inflation leads to a decline in expected dollar appreciation that is larger than the increase in the domestic interest rate, the relative expected return on domestic (dollar) assets falls. The demand curve shifts to the left, and the equilibrium exchange rate falls from E_1 to E_2.

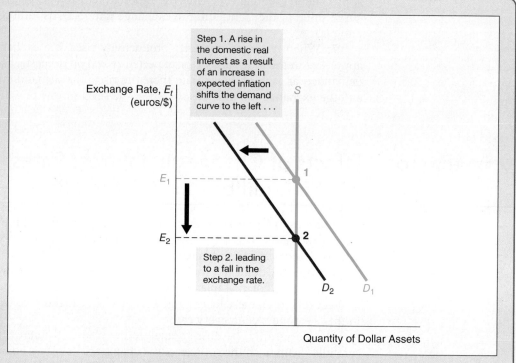

Step 1. A rise in the domestic real interest as a result of an increase in expected inflation shifts the demand curve to the left . . .

Exchange Rate, E_t (euros/\$)

Step 2. leading to a fall in the exchange rate.

Quantity of Dollar Assets

APPLICATION   Why Are Exchange Rates So Volatile?

The high volatility of foreign exchange rates has surprised many people. Thirty or so years ago, economists generally believed that allowing exchange rates to be determined in the free market would not lead to large fluctuations in their values. Recent experience has proved them wrong. If we return to Figure 1, we see that exchange rates over the 1990–2014 period have been very volatile.

The asset market approach to exchange rate determination that we have outlined in this chapter gives a straightforward explanation of the volatility of exchange rates. Because expected appreciation of the domestic currency affects the expected return on domestic assets, expectations about the price level, inflation, trade barriers, productivity, import demand, export demand, and the money supply play important roles in determining the exchange rate. When expectations about any of these variables change, as they do—and often, at that—our model indicates that the expected return on domestic assets, and therefore the exchange rate, will be immediately affected. Because expectations on all of these variables change with just about every bit of news that is reported, it is not surprising that the exchange rate is volatile. Because earlier models of exchange rate behavior focused on goods markets rather than asset markets, they did not emphasize changing expectations as a source of exchange rate movements, and so these earlier models did not predict substantial fluctuations in exchange rates. The failure of earlier models to explain volatility is one reason why they are no longer so popular. The more modern approach developed here emphasizes that the foreign exchange market is like any other asset market in which expectations of the future matter. The foreign exchange market, like other asset markets such as the stock market, displays substantial price volatility, and foreign exchange rates are notoriously hard to forecast.

APPLICATION The Dollar and Interest Rates

In the chapter preview, we mentioned that the value of the dollar was weak in the late 1970s, rose substantially from 1980 to 1985, and declined thereafter. We can use our analysis of the foreign exchange market to understand exchange rate movements and help explain the dollar's rise in value in the early 1980s and its fall in value thereafter.

Some important information that will enable us to trace the dollar's changing value is presented in Figure 8, which plots measures of real and nominal interest rates and the value of the dollar in terms of a basket of foreign currencies (called an **effective exchange rate index**). We can see that the value of the dollar and the measure of real

MyEconLab Mini-lecture   MyEconLab Real-time data

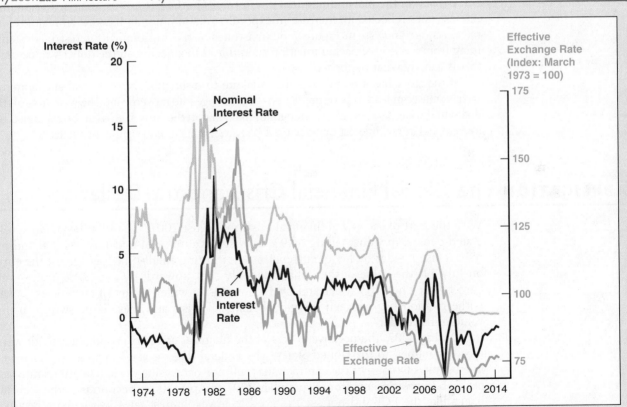

FIGURE 8   Value of the Dollar and Interest Rates, 1973–2014

The correspondence between nominal interest rates and exchange rate movements is not nearly as close as that between *real* interest rates and exchange rate movements.

Source: Federal Reserve Bank of St. Louis, FRED database: http://research.stlouisfed.org/fred2/.

interest rates tend to rise and fall together. In the late 1970s, real interest rates were at low levels, and so was the value of the dollar. Beginning in 1980, however, real interest rates in the United States began to climb sharply, and at the same time, so did the value of the dollar. After 1984, the real interest rate declined substantially, as did the value of the dollar.

Our model of exchange rate determination helps explain the rise in the value of the dollar in the early 1980s and its fall in value thereafter. As Figure 4 indicates, a rise in the U.S. real interest rate raises the relative expected return on dollar assets, which leads to purchases of dollar assets that raise the exchange rate. This is exactly what happened in the 1980–1984 period. The subsequent fall in U.S. real interest rates then reduced the relative expected return on dollar assets, which lowered the demand for them and thus lowered the exchange rate.

The plot of nominal interest rates in Figure 8 also demonstrates that the correspondence between nominal interest rates and exchange rate movements is not nearly as close as that between *real* interest rates and exchange rate movements. This is also exactly what our analysis predicts. The rise in nominal interest rates in the late 1970s was not reflected in a corresponding rise in the value of the dollar; indeed, the value of the dollar actually fell in the late 1970s. Figure 8 explains why the rise in nominal rates in the late 1970s did not produce a rise in the value of the dollar. As is indicated by a comparison of the real and nominal interest rates in the late 1970s, the rise in nominal interest rates reflected an increase in expected inflation, not an increase in real interest rates. As our analysis in Figure 7 demonstrates, a rise in nominal interest rates stemming from a rise in expected inflation should lead to a decline in the dollar's value, and that is exactly what happened.

If the story has a moral, it is that a failure to distinguish between real and nominal interest rates can lead to poor predictions of exchange rate movements. The weakness of the dollar in the late 1970s and the strength of the dollar in the early 1980s can be explained by movements in *real* interest rates, but not by movements in *nominal* interest rates.

APPLICATION The Global Financial Crisis and the Dollar

With the start of the global financial crisis in August 2007, the dollar began an accelerated decline in value, falling by 9% against the euro until mid-July of 2008 and by 6% against a wider basket of currencies. After hitting an all-time low against the euro on July 11, the value of the dollar suddenly shot upward, by over 20% against the euro by the end of October and by 15% against a wider basket of currencies. What is the relationship between the global financial crisis and these large swings in the value of the dollar?

During 2007, the negative effects of the financial crisis on economic activity were mostly confined to the United States. The Federal Reserve acted aggressively to lower interest rates to counter the contractionary effects, decreasing the federal funds rate target by 325 basis points from September 2007 to April 2008. In contrast, other central banks like the ECB did not see the need to lower interest rates, particularly because high energy prices had led to a surge in inflation. The relative expected return on dollar assets thus declined, shifting the demand curve for dollar assets to the left, as in Figure 5, and leading to a decline in the equilibrium exchange rate. Our analysis of the foreign exchange market thus explains why the early phase of the global financial crisis led to a decline in the value of the dollar.

We now turn to the rise in the value of the dollar. Starting in the summer of 2008, the effects of the global financial crisis on economic activity began to spread more widely throughout the world. Foreign central banks started to cut interest rates, with the expectation that further rate cuts would follow, as indeed did occur. The expected decline in foreign interest rates then increased the relative expected return on dollar assets, leading to a rightward shift in the demand curve and a rise in the value of the dollar, as shown in Figure 4. Another factor driving the dollar upward was the "flight to quality" that occurred when the global financial crisis reached a particularly virulent stage in September and October. Both Americans and foreigners now wanted to put their money into the safest assets possible: U.S. Treasury securities. The resulting increase in the demand for dollar assets provided an additional reason for the demand curve for dollar assets to shift out to the right, thereby helping to produce a sharp appreciation of the dollar. ◆

SUMMARY

1. Foreign exchange rates (the price of one country's currency in terms of another's) are important because they affect the price of domestically produced goods sold abroad and the cost of foreign goods bought domestically.

2. The theory of purchasing power parity suggests that long-run changes in the exchange rate between the currencies of two countries are determined by changes in the relative price levels in the two countries. Other factors that affect exchange rates in the long run are tariffs and quotas, import demand, export demand, and productivity.

3. In the short run, exchange rates are determined by changes in the relative expected return on domestic assets, which cause the demand curve to shift. Any factor that changes the relative expected return on domestic assets will lead to changes in the exchange rate. Such factors include changes in the interest rates on domestic and foreign assets, as well as changes in any of the factors that affect the long-run exchange rate and hence the expected future exchange rate.

4. The asset market approach to exchange rate determination can explain the volatility of exchange rates, the rise in the value of of the dollar during the 1980–1984 period and its subsequent fall in value, and changes in the value of the dollar during the global financial crisis.

KEY TERMS

appreciation, p. 402
capital mobility, p. 425
depreciation, p. 402
effective exchange rate index, p. 417
exchange rate, p. 400
foreign exchange market, p. 400

forward exchange rate, p. 401
forward transaction, p. 401
interest parity condition, p. 425
law of one price, p. 403
quotas, p. 406
real exchange rate, p. 404

spot exchange rate, p. 401
spot transaction, p. 401
tariffs, p. 406
theory of purchasing power parity (PPP), p. 404

QUESTIONS

All questions are available in MyEconLab *at* http://www.myeconlab.com.

1. When the euro appreciates, are you more likely to drink California wine or French wine?

2. "A country is always worse off when its currency is weak (falls in value)." Is this statement true, false, or uncertain? Explain your answer.

3. When the U.S. dollar depreciates, what happens to exports and imports in the United States?

4. If the Japanese price level rises by 5% relative to the price level in the United States, what does the theory of purchasing power parity predict will happen to the value of the Japanese yen in terms of dollars?

5. If the demand for a country's exports falls at the same time that tariffs on imports are raised, will the country's currency tend to appreciate or depreciate in the long run?

6. When the Federal Reserve conducts an expansionary monetary policy, what happens to the money supply? How does this affect the supply of dollar assets?

7. From 2009 to 2011, the economies of Australia and Switzerland suffered relatively mild effects from the global financial crisis. At the same time, many countries in the euro area were hit hard by high unemployment and burdened with unsustainably high government debts. How should this have affected the euro/Swiss franc and euro/Australian dollar exchange rates?

8. In the mid- to late 1970s, the yen appreciated in value relative to the dollar, even though Japan's inflation rate was higher than America's. How can this be explained by improvements in the productivity of Japanese industry relative to American industry?

9. Suppose the president of the United States announces a new set of reforms that includes a new anti-inflation program. Assuming the announcement is believed by the public, what will happen to the exchange rate on the U.S. dollar?

10. If the British central bank lowers interest rates to reduce unemployment, what will happen to the value of the pound in the short run and in the long run?

11. If the Indian government unexpectedly announces that it will be imposing higher tariffs on foreign goods one year from now, what will happen to the value of the Indian rupee today?

12. If nominal interest rates in America rise but real interest rates fall, predict what will happen to the U.S. dollar exchange rate.

13. If American auto companies make a breakthrough in automobile technology and are able to produce a car that gets 200 miles to the gallon, what will happen to the U.S. dollar exchange rate?

14. If Mexicans go on a spending spree and buy twice as much French perfume and twice as many Japanese TVs, English sweaters, Swiss watches, and bottles of Italian wine, what will happen to the value of the Mexican peso?

15. Through the summer and fall of 2008, as the global financial crisis began to take hold, international financial institutions and sovereign wealth funds significantly increased their purchases of U.S. Treasury securities as a safe haven investment. How should this have affected U.S. dollar exchange rates?

16. In September 2012, the Federal Reserve announced a large-scale asset-purchase program (known as QE3) designed to lower intermediate and longer-term interest rates. What effect should this have had on the dollar/euro exchange rate?

APPLIED PROBLEMS

All applied problems are available in MyEconLab *at* http://www.myeconlab.com.

17. A German sports car is selling for 70,000 euros. What is the dollar price in the United States of the German car if the exchange rate is 0.90 euro per dollar?

18. If the Canadian dollar to U.S. dollar exchange rate is 1.28 and the British pound to U.S. dollar exchange rate is 0.62, what must be the Canadian dollar to British pound exchange rate?

19. The New Zealand dollar to U.S. dollar exchange rate is 1.36, and the British pound to U.S. dollar exchange rate is 0.62. If you find that the British pound to New Zealand dollar is trading at 0.49, what can you do to earn a riskless profit?

20. In 1999, the euro was trading at $0.90 per euro. If the euro is now trading at $1.16 per euro, what is the percentage change in the euro's value? Is this an appreciation or a depreciation?

21. The Mexican peso is trading at 10 pesos per dollar. If the expected U.S. inflation rate is 2% while the expected Mexican inflation rate is 23% over the next year, given PPP, what is the expected exchange rate in one year?

22. If the price level recently increased by 20% in England while falling by 5% in the United States, by how much must the exchange rate change if PPP holds? Assume that the current exchange rate is 0.55 pound per dollar.

For Problems 23–25, use a graph of the foreign exchange market for dollars to illustrate the effects described in each problem.

23. If expected inflation drops in Europe, so that interest rates fall there, what will happen to the exchange rate on the U.S. dollar?

24. If the European Central Bank decides to pursue a contractionary monetary policy to fight inflation, what will happen to the value of the U.S. dollar?

25. If a strike takes place in France, making it harder to buy French goods, what will happen to the value of the U.S. dollar?

DATA ANALYSIS PROBLEMS

The Problems update with real-time data in MyEconLab and are available for practice or instructor assignment.

1. Go to the St. Louis Federal Reserve FRED database, and find data on the exchange rate of U.S. dollars per British pound (DEXUSUK). A Mini Cooper can be purchased in London, England, for £17,865 or in Boston, United States, for $23,495.

   a. Use the most recent exchange rate available to calculate the real exchange rate of the London Mini per Boston Mini.

   b. Based on your answer to part (a), are Mini Coopers relatively more expensive in Boston or in London?

   c. What price in British pounds would make the Mini Cooper equally expensive in both locations, all else being equal?

2. Go to the St. Louis Federal Reserve FRED database, and find data on the daily dollar exchange rates for the euro (DEXUSEU), British pound (DEXUSUK),

and Japanese yen (DEXJPUS). Also find data on the daily three-month London Interbank Offer Rate, or LIBOR, for the United States dollar (USD3M-TD156N), euro (EUR3MTD156N), British pound (GBP3MTD156N), and Japanese yen (JPY3M-TD156N). LIBOR is a measure of interest rates denominated in each country's respective currency.

   a. Calculate the difference between the LIBOR rate in the United States and the LIBOR rates in the three other countries using the data from one year ago and the most recent data available.

   b. Based on the changes in interest rate differentials, do you expect the dollar to depreciate or appreciate against the other currencies?

   c. Report the percentage change in the exchange rates over the past year. Are the results you predicted in part (b) consistent with the actual exchange rate behavior?

WEB EXERCISES

1. The Federal Reserve maintains a website that lists the exchange rates between the U.S. dollar and many other currencies. Go to http://www.newyorkfed.org/markets/foreignex.html . Go to the historical data for 1999 and afterward, and find the data on the euro.

   a. Calculate the percentage change in the euro–dollar exchange rate from the time the euro was introduced until now.

   b. Calculate the annual percentage change in the euro–dollar exchange rate for each year since the euro's introduction.

2. International travelers and business people frequently need to accurately convert from one currency to another. It is often easy to find the rate needed to convert the U.S. dollar into another currency. It can be more difficult to find exchange rates between two non-U.S. currencies. Go to http://www.oanda.com/convert/classic. This site lets you convert from any currency into any other currency. How many Lithuanian litas can you currently buy with one Chilean peso?

WEB REFERENCES

http://www.newyorkfed.org/markets/foreignex.html

Get detailed information about the foreign exchange market in the United States.

http://quotes.ino.com/chart/

Go to this website and click on Exchange List to get market rates and time charts for the exchange rate of the U.S. dollar to major world currencies.

http://www.oecd.org/general/searchresults/
?q=purchasing%20power%20parities

The purchasing power parities home page includes the PPP program overview, statistics, research, publications, and OECD meetings on PPP.

http://www.federalreserve.gov/releases/

The Federal Reserve reports current and historical exchange rates for many countries.

http://fx.sauder.ubc.ca

The Pacific Exchange Rate Service at the University of British Columbia's Sauder School of Business provides information on how market conditions are affecting exchange rates and allows easy plotting of exchange rate data.

17 The Interest Parity Condition

All of the results stated in the text can be derived using a concept that is widely used in international finance. The *interest parity condition* gives the relationships among domestic interest rates, foreign interest rates, and the expected appreciation of the domestic currency. To derive this condition, we examine how expected returns on domestic and foreign assets are compared.

COMPARING EXPECTED RETURNS ON DOMESTIC AND FOREIGN ASSETS

As in the chapter, we treat the United States as the home country, so domestic assets are denominated in dollars. For simplicity, we use euros to stand for any foreign country's currency, so foreign assets are denominated in euros. Suppose that dollar assets pay an interest rate of i^D and do not have any possible capital gains, so that they have an expected return payable in dollars of i^D. Similarly, suppose that foreign assets have an interest rate of i^F and an expected return payable in the foreign currency, euros, of i^F. To compare the expected returns on dollar assets and foreign assets, investors must convert the returns into the currency unit that they use.

First, let us examine how François the Foreigner compares the returns on dollar assets and foreign assets denominated in his currency, the euro. When he considers the expected return on dollar assets in terms of euros, he recognizes that it does not equal i^D; instead, the expected return must be adjusted for any expected appreciation or depreciation of the dollar. If François expects the dollar to appreciate by 3%, for example, the expected return on dollar assets in terms of euros would be 3% higher than i^D because the dollar is expected to become worth 3% more in terms of euros. Thus, if the interest rate on dollar assets is 4%, with an expected 3% appreciation of the dollar, the expected return on dollar assets in terms of euros is 7%: the 4% interest rate plus the 3% expected appreciation of the dollar. Conversely, if the dollar is expected to depreciate by 3% over the year, the expected return on dollar assets in terms of euros will be only 1%: the 4% interest rate minus the 3% expected depreciation of the dollar.

Writing the current exchange rate (the spot exchange rate) as E_t and the expected exchange rate for the next period as E_{t+1}^e, the expected rate of appreciation of the dollar is $(E_{t+1}^e - E_t)/E_t$. Our reasoning indicates that the expected return on dollar assets

R^D in terms of foreign currency can be written as the sum of the interest rate on dollar assets plus the expected appreciation of the dollar.[1]

$$R^D \text{ in terms of euros} = i^D + \frac{E_{t+1}^e - E_t}{E_t}$$

However, François's expected return on foreign assets R^F in terms of euros is just i^F. Thus, in terms of euros, the relative expected return on dollar assets (that is, the difference between the expected returns on dollar assets and euro assets) is calculated by subtracting i^F from the expression above to yield

$$\text{Relative } R^D = i^D - i^F + \frac{E_{t+1}^e - E_t}{E_t} \tag{1}$$

As the relative expected return on dollar assets increases, foreigners will want to hold more dollar assets and fewer foreign assets.

Next let us look at the decision to hold dollar assets versus euro assets from Al the American's point of view. Following the same reasoning we used in François's case, we know that the expected return on foreign assets R^F in terms of dollars is the interest rate on foreign assets i^F plus the expected appreciation of the foreign currency, which is equal to minus the expected appreciation of the dollar, $(E_{t+1}^e - E_t)/E_t$:

$$R^F \text{ in terms of dollars} = i^F - \frac{E_{t+1}^e - E_t}{E_t}$$

If the interest rate on euro assets is 5%, for example, and the dollar is expected to appreciate by 3%, then the expected return on euro assets in terms of dollars is 2%. Al earns the 5% interest rate, but he expects to lose 3% because he expects the euro to be worth 3% less in terms of dollars as a result of the dollar's appreciation.

Al's expected return on the dollar assets R^D in terms of dollars is just i^D. Hence, in terms of dollars, the relative expected return on dollar assets is calculated by subtracting the expression just given from i^D to obtain

$$\text{Relative } R^D = i^D - \left(i^F - \frac{E_{t+1}^e - E_t}{E_t} \right) = i^D - i^F + \frac{E_{t+1}^e - E_t}{E_t}$$

---

[1]This expression is actually an approximation of the expected return in terms of euros, which can be calculated more precisely by thinking about how a foreigner invests in dollar assets. Suppose that François decides to put one euro into dollar assets. First he buys $1/E_t$ of U.S. dollar assets (recall that E_t, the exchange rate between dollar and euro assets, is quoted in euros per dollar), and at the end of the period he is paid $(1 + i^D)(1/E_t)$ in dollars. To convert this amount into the number of euros he expects to receive at the end of the period, he multiplies this quantity by E_{t+1}^e. François's expected return on his initial investment of one euro can thus be written as $(1 + i^D)(E_{t+1}^e/E_t)$ minus his initial investment of one euro:

$$(1 + i^D)\left(\frac{E_{t+1}^e}{E_t}\right) - 1$$

This expression can be rewritten as

$$i^D\left(\frac{E_{t+1}^e}{E_t}\right) + \frac{E_{t+1}^e - E_t}{E_t}$$

which is approximately equal to the expression in the text because E_{t+1}^e/E_t is typically close to 1. To see this, consider the example in the text in which $i^D = 0.04$; $(E_{t+1}^e - E_t)/E_t = 0.03$, so $E_{t+1}^e/E_t = 1.03$. Then François's expected return on dollar assets is $(0.04 \times 1.03) + 0.03 = 0.0712 = 7.12\%$, rather than the 7% reported in the text.

This equation is the same as Equation 1 describing François's relative expected return on dollar assets (calculated in terms of euros). The key point here is that the relative expected return on dollar assets is the same whether it is calculated by François in terms of euros or by Al in terms of dollars. Thus, as the relative expected return on dollar assets increases, both foreigners and domestic residents respond in exactly the same way—both will want to hold more dollar assets and fewer foreign assets.

INTEREST PARITY CONDITION

We currently live in a world in which **capital mobility** exists: Foreigners can easily purchase American assets, and Americans can easily purchase foreign assets. If few impediments to capital mobility are present and we are looking at assets that have similar risk and liquidity—say, foreign and American bank deposits—then it is reasonable to assume that the assets are perfect substitutes (that is, equally desirable). When capital is mobile and assets are perfect substitutes, if the expected return on dollar assets is greater than that on foreign assets, both foreigners and Americans will want to hold only dollar assets and will be unwilling to hold foreign assets. Conversely, if the expected return on foreign assets is higher than that on dollar assets, both foreigners and Americans will not want to hold dollar assets and will want to hold only foreign assets. Therefore, for existing supplies of both dollar assets and foreign assets to be held, it must be the case that no difference exists in their expected returns; that is, the relative expected return in Equation 1 must equal zero. This condition can be rewritten as

$$i^D = i^F - \frac{E^e_{t+1} - E_t}{E_t} \tag{2}$$

This equation, called the **interest parity condition**, states that the domestic interest rate equals the foreign interest rate minus the expected appreciation of the domestic currency. Equivalently, this condition can be stated in a more intuitive way: The domestic interest rate equals the foreign interest rate plus the expected appreciation of the foreign currency. If the domestic interest rate is higher than the foreign interest rate, there is a positive expected appreciation of the foreign currency, which compensates for the lower foreign interest rate. A domestic interest rate of 5% versus a foreign interest rate of 3% means that the expected appreciation of the foreign currency must be 2% (or, equivalently, that the expected depreciation of the dollar must be 2%).

The interest parity condition can be looked at in several ways. First, recognize that interest parity simply means that the expected returns are the same on both dollar assets and foreign assets. To see this, note that the left side of the interest parity condition (Equation 2) is the expected return on dollar assets, while the right side is the expected return on foreign assets, both calculated in terms of a single currency, the U.S. dollar. Given our assumption that domestic and foreign assets are perfect substitutes (equally desirable), the interest parity condition is an equilibrium condition for the foreign exchange market. Only when the exchange rate is such that expected returns on domestic and foreign assets are equal—that is, when interest parity holds—will investors be willing to hold both domestic and foreign assets.

With some algebraic manipulation, we can rewrite the interest parity condition in Equation 2 as

$$E_t = \frac{E_{t+1}^e}{i^F - i^D + 1}$$

This equation produces exactly the same results that we derived in the supply and demand analysis given in the text: If i^D rises, the value of the denominator decreases and so E_t rises. If i^F rises, the value of the denominator increases and so E_t falls. If E_{t+1}^e rises, the value of the numerator increases and so E_t rises.

The International Financial System

Learning Objectives

- Use graphs and T-accounts to illustrate the distinctions between the effects of sterilized and unsterilized interventions on foreign exchange markets.
- Interpret the relationships among the current account, the capital account, and the official reserve transaction balance.
- Identify the mechanisms for maintaining a fixed exchange rate, and assess the challenges faced by fixed exchange rate regimes.
- Summarize the advantages and disadvantages of capital controls.
- Assess the role of the IMF as an international lender of last resort.
- Identify the ways in which international monetary policy and exchange rate arrangements can affect domestic monetary policy operations.
- Summarize the advantages and disadvantages of exchange-rate targeting.

Preview

As the U.S. economy and the economies of the rest of the world grow more interdependent, a country's monetary policy can no longer be conducted without taking international considerations into account. In this chapter, we examine how international financial transactions and the structure of the international financial system affect monetary policy. We also examine the evolution of the international financial system during the past half century and consider where it may be headed in the future.

INTERVENTION IN THE FOREIGN EXCHANGE MARKET

In Chapter 17, we analyzed the foreign exchange market as if it were a completely free market that responds to all conventional market pressures. Like many other markets, however, the foreign exchange market is not free of government intervention; central banks regularly engage in international financial transactions, called **foreign exchange interventions**, to influence exchange rates. In our current international environment, exchange rates fluctuate from day to day, but central banks attempt to influence their countries' exchange rates by buying and selling currencies. We can use the exchange rate analysis we developed in Chapter 17 to explain the impact of central bank intervention on the foreign exchange market.

Foreign Exchange Intervention and the Money Supply

The first step in understanding how central bank intervention in the foreign exchange market affects exchange rates is to explore the impact on the monetary base of a central bank sale in the foreign exchange market of some of its holdings of assets denominated in a foreign currency (called **international reserves**). Suppose the Fed decides to sell $1 billion of its foreign assets in exchange for $1 billion of U.S. currency. (This type of transaction is conducted at the foreign exchange desk at the Federal Reserve Bank of New York—see the Inside the Fed box.) The Fed's purchase of dollars has two effects. First, it reduces the Fed's holdings of international reserves by $1 billion. Second, because the Fed's purchase of currency removes it from the hands of the public, currency in circulation falls by $1 billion. We can see this in the following T-account for the Federal Reserve:

Inside the Fed   A Day at the Federal Reserve Bank of New York's Foreign Exchange Desk

Although the U.S. Treasury holds primary responsibility for foreign exchange policy, decisions to intervene in the foreign exchange market are made jointly by the U.S. Treasury and the Federal Reserve's FOMC (Federal Open Market Committee). The actual conduct of foreign exchange intervention is the responsibility of the foreign exchange desk at the Federal Reserve Bank of New York, which is right next to the open market desk.

The manager of foreign exchange operations at the New York Fed supervises the traders and analysts, who follow developments in the foreign exchange market. Every morning at 7:30, a trader on staff who has arrived at the New York Fed in the predawn hours speaks on the telephone with counterparts at the U.S. Treasury and provides an update on overnight activity in overseas financial and foreign exchange markets. Later in the morning, at 9:30, the manager and his or her staff hold a conference call with the senior staff members at the Board of Governors of the Federal Reserve in Washington. In the afternoon, at 2:30, the manager and staff hold a second conference call, which is a joint briefing of officials at the Board and at the Treasury. Although by statute the Treasury has the lead role in setting foreign exchange policy, it strives to reach a consensus among all three parties—the Treasury, the Board of Governors, and the Federal Reserve Bank of New York. If the three parties decide that a foreign exchange intervention is necessary that day—an unusual occurrence, as a year may go by without a U.S. foreign exchange intervention—the manager instructs his traders to carry out the agreed-on purchase or sale of foreign currencies. Because funds for exchange rate intervention are held separately by the Treasury (in its Exchange Stabilization Fund) and the Federal Reserve, the manager and his or her staff are not trading the funds of the Federal Reserve Bank of New York; rather, they act as an agent for the Treasury and the FOMC in conducting these transactions.

As part of their duties, before every FOMC meeting, the staff help prepare a lengthy document full of data for the FOMC members, other Reserve Bank presidents, and Treasury officials, a task that keeps them especially busy. The document describes developments in the domestic and foreign markets over the previous five or six weeks.

Federal Reserve System			
Assets		**Liabilities**	
Foreign assets (international reserves)	−$1 billion	Currency in circulation	−$1 billion

Because the monetary base is made up of currency in circulation plus reserves, this decline in currency implies that the monetary base has fallen by $1 billion.

If, as is more likely, the persons buying the foreign assets pay for them with checks written on accounts at domestic banks rather than with currency, then the Fed deducts the $1 billion from the reserve deposits it holds for these banks. The result is that deposits with the Fed (reserves) decline by $1 billion, as shown in the following T-account:

Federal Reserve System			
Assets		**Liabilities**	
Foreign assets (international reserves)	−$1 billion	Deposits with the Fed (reserves)	−$1 billion

In this case, the outcome of the Fed sale of foreign assets and the purchase of dollar deposits is a $1 billion decline in reserves and, as before, a $1 billion decline in the monetary base, because reserves are also a component of the monetary base.

We now see that the outcome for the monetary base is exactly the same when a central bank sells foreign assets to purchase domestic bank deposits or domestic currency. This is why, when we say that a central bank has purchased its domestic currency, we do not have to distinguish between currency and bank deposits denominated in the domestic currency. We have thus reached an important conclusion: *A central bank's purchase of domestic currency and corresponding sale of foreign assets in the foreign exchange market leads to an equal decline in its international reserves and the monetary base.*

We could have reached the same conclusion by a more direct route. A central bank sale of a foreign asset is no different from an open market sale of a government bond. We learned in our exploration of the money supply process that an open market sale leads to an equal decline in the monetary base; therefore, a sale of foreign assets also leads to an equal decline in the monetary base. By similar reasoning, a central bank purchase of foreign assets paid for by selling domestic currency, like an open market purchase, leads to an equal rise in the monetary base. Thus we reach the following conclusion: *A central bank's sale of domestic currency to purchase foreign assets in the foreign exchange market results in an equal rise in its international reserves and the monetary base.*

The intervention we have just described, in which a central bank allows the purchase or sale of domestic currency to have an effect on the monetary base, is called an **unsterilized foreign exchange intervention**. But what if the central bank does not want the purchase or sale of domestic currency to affect the monetary base? All it has to do is counteract the effect of the foreign exchange intervention by conducting an offsetting open market operation in the government bond market. For example, in the case of a $1 billion purchase of dollars by the Fed and a corresponding $1 billion sale of foreign assets, which, as we have seen, would decrease the monetary base by $1 billion, the Fed can conduct an open market purchase of $1 billion of government bonds, which will increase the monetary base by $1 billion. The resulting T-account for the foreign exchange intervention and the offsetting open market operation leaves the monetary base unchanged:

Federal Reserve System			
Assets		**Liabilities**	
Foreign assets (international reserves)	−$1 billion	Monetary base	0
Government bonds	+$1 billion		

MyEconLab Mini-lecture

FIGURE 1
Effect of an Unster-ilized Purchase of Dollars and Sale of Foreign Assets

A purchase of dollars and the consequent open market sale of foreign assets decrease the monetary base and the money supply. The resulting fall in the money supply leads to a rise in domestic interest rates, which raises the relative ex-pected return on dollar assets. The demand curve shifts to the right from D_1 to D_2, and the equilibrium exchange rate rises from E_1 to E_2.

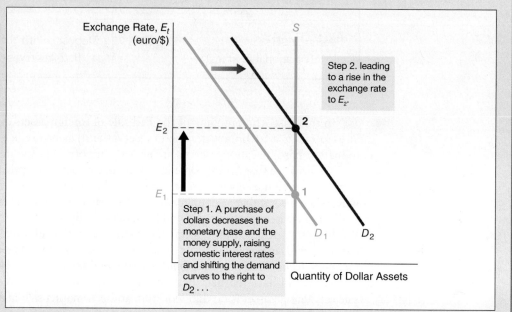

Step 2. leading to a rise in the exchange rate to E_2.

Step 1. A purchase of dollars decreases the monetary base and the money supply, raising domestic interest rates and shifting the demand curves to the right to D_2 . . .

A foreign exchange intervention with an offsetting open market operation that leaves the monetary base unchanged is called a **sterilized foreign exchange intervention**.

Now that we understand that there are two types of foreign exchange interventions—unsterilized and sterilized—let's look at how each affects the exchange rate.

Unsterilized Intervention

Intuition might lead you to suspect that if a central bank wants to raise the value of the domestic currency, it should buy its currency in the foreign exchange market and sell foreign assets. Indeed, this intuition is correct in the case of an unsterilized intervention.

Recall that in an unsterilized intervention, if the Federal Reserve decides to buy dollars and therefore sells foreign assets in exchange for dollar assets, this exchange works just like an open market sale of bonds to decrease the monetary base. Hence the purchase of dollars leads to a decrease in the money supply, which raises the domestic interest rate and increases the relative expected return on dollar assets. As a result, the demand curve shifts to the right from D_1 to D_2, as shown in Figure 1, and the exchange rate rises to E_2.[1]

Our analysis leads us to the following conclusion about unsterilized interventions in the foreign exchange market: *An unsterilized intervention in which domestic currency is bought and foreign assets are sold leads to a fall in international reserves, a fall in the money supply, and an appreciation of the domestic currency.*

---

[1]An unsterilized intervention in which the Fed buys dollars decreases the amount of dollar assets slightly because it leads to a decrease in the monetary base while leaving the amount of government bonds in the hands of the public unchanged. The curve depicting the supply of dollar assets thus shifts to the left slightly, which also works toward raising the exchange rate, yielding the same conclusion derived in Figure 1. Because the resulting increase in the monetary base is only a minuscule fraction of the total amount of dollar assets outstanding, the supply curve shifts by an imperceptible amount. This is why Figure 1 is drawn with the supply curve unchanged.

The reverse result is found for an unsterilized intervention in which domestic currency is sold and foreign assets are purchased. The sale of domestic currency and purchase of foreign assets (which increases international reserves) work like an open market purchase to increase the monetary base and the money supply. The increase in the money supply lowers the interest rate on dollar assets. The resulting decrease in the relative expected return on dollar assets means that people will buy less dollar assets, so the demand curve shifts to the left and the exchange rate falls. *An unsterilized intervention in which domestic currency is sold and foreign assets are purchased leads to a rise in international reserves, a rise in the money supply, and a depreciation of the domestic currency.*

Sterilized Intervention

The key point to remember about a sterilized intervention is that the central bank engages in offsetting open market operations, and so there is no impact on the monetary base and the money supply. In the context of the model of exchange rate determination we have developed here, it is a straightforward task to show that a sterilized intervention has almost *no effect* on the exchange rate. A sterilized intervention leaves the money supply unchanged and thus has no direct way of affecting interest rates.[2] Because the relative expected return on dollar assets is unaffected, the demand curve remains at D_1 in Figure 1, and the exchange rate remains unchanged at E_1.

At first it might seem puzzling that a central bank purchase or sale of domestic currency that is sterilized does not lead to a change in the exchange rate. A central bank–sterilized purchase of domestic currency cannot raise the exchange rate because, with no effect on the domestic money supply or interest rates, any resulting rise in the exchange rate would lead to an excess supply of dollar assets. With more people willing to sell dollar assets than willing to buy them, the exchange rate would fall back to its initial equilibrium level, where the demand and supply curves intersect.

BALANCE OF PAYMENTS

Because international financial transactions such as foreign exchange interventions have considerable effects on monetary policy, it is worth knowing how these transactions are measured. The **balance of payments** is a bookkeeping system used to record all receipts and payments (both private sector and government) that have a direct bearing on the movement of funds between a nation and foreign countries. Here we examine the key items in the balance of payments, items that you often hear about in the media.

---

[2]A sterilized intervention changes the amount of foreign securities relative to domestic securities in the hands of the public, called a *portfolio balance effect*. Through this effect, the central bank might be able to influence the interest differential between domestic and foreign assets, which in turn affects the relative expected return on domestic assets. Empirical evidence has not revealed this portfolio balance effect to be significant. However, a sterilized intervention *could* indicate what central banks want to happen to the future exchange rate and so might provide a signal about the course of future monetary policy. In this way, a sterilized intervention could lead to a shift in the demand curve for domestic assets and ultimately affect the exchange rate. However, the future change in monetary policy—not the sterilized intervention—is the source of the exchange rate effect. For a further discussion of the signaling and portfolio balance effects and the possible differential effects of sterilized versus unsterilized intervention, see Paul Krugman, Maurice Obstfeld, and Mark Melitz, *International Economics: Theory and Policy*, 9th ed. (Boston: Addison-Wesley, 2012).

The **current account** shows international transactions that involve currently produced goods and services. The difference between merchandise exports and imports, the net receipts from trade, is called the **trade balance**. When merchandise imports are greater than exports (by $701.7 billion in 2013), the result is a trade deficit; if exports are greater than imports, the result is a trade surplus.

Additional items included in the current account are the net receipts (cash flows received from abroad minus cash flows sent abroad) from three categories: investment income, service transactions, and unilateral transfers (gifts, pensions, and foreign aid). In 2013, for example, net investment income was $199.7 billion for the United States because Americans received more investment income from abroad than they paid out. Americans bought less in services from foreigners than foreigners bought from Americans, so net services generated $225.3 billion in receipts. Because Americans made more unilateral transfers to foreign countries than foreigners made to the United States, net unilateral transfers were −$123.5 billion. The sum of the previous three items plus the trade balance gives the current account balance, which in 2013 showed a deficit of $400.3 billion (−$701.7 + $199.7 + $225.3 − $123.5 = −$400.3). Another important item in the balance of payments is the **capital account**, the net receipts from capital transactions (e.g., purchases of stocks and bonds, bank loans, etc.). In 2013, the capital account was −$0.4 billion, indicating that $0.4 billion more capital flowed out of the United States than came in.[3] The sum of the current account and the capital account equals the **official reserve transactions balance** (net change in government international reserves), which was −$400.7 billion in 2013 (−$400.3 − 0.4 = −$400.7 billion). When economists refer to a surplus or deficit in the balance of payments, they actually mean a surplus or deficit in the official reserve transactions balance.

Because the balance of payments must balance, the official reserve transactions balance, which equals the current account plus the capital account, gives the net amount of international reserves that must move between governments (as represented by their central banks) in order to finance international transactions; that is,

$$\text{Current account} + \text{capital account} = \text{net change in government international reserves}$$

This equation shows us why the current account receives so much attention from economists and the media. The current account balance tells us whether the United States (private sector and government combined) is increasing or decreasing its claims on foreign wealth. A surplus indicates that America is increasing its claims on foreign wealth and thus is increasing its holdings of foreign assets (both good things for Americans); a deficit (as in 2013) indicates that the United States is reducing its holdings of foreign assets and foreign countries are increasing their claims on the United States.[4] The large U.S. current account deficit in recent years, which in 2013 was over

[3]The capital account balance number reported here includes a statistical discrepancy item that represents errors due to unrecorded transactions involving smuggling and other capital flows (−$30 billion in 2013). Many experts believe that the statistical discrepancy item, which keeps the balance of payments in balance, is primarily the result of large hidden capital flows, and this is why it is included in the capital account balance.

[4]The current account balance can also be viewed as showing the amount by which total saving exceeds private sector and government investment in the United States. Total U.S. saving equals the increase in total wealth held by the U.S. private sector and government. Total investment equals the increase in the U.S. capital stock (wealth physically in the United States). The difference between them is the increase in U.S. claims on foreign wealth.

The large U.S. current account deficit in recent years, which in 2013 was 2.4% of GDP, worries economists for several reasons. First, it indicates that at current exchange rate values, foreigners' demand for U.S. exports is far less than Americans' demand for imports. As we saw in the previous chapter, low demand for U.S. exports and high U.S. demand for imports may lead to a future decline in the value of the U.S. dollar.

Second, the current account deficit means that foreigners' claims on U.S. assets are growing, and these claims will have to be paid back at some point. Americans are mortgaging their future to foreigners;

when the bill comes due, Americans will be poorer. Furthermore, if Americans have a greater preference for dollar assets than foreigners do, the movement of American wealth to foreigners could decrease the demand for dollar assets over time, also causing the dollar to depreciate.

The hope is that the eventual decline in the dollar resulting from the large U.S. current account deficit will be a gradual one, occurring over a period of several years. If the decline is precipitous, however, it could potentially disrupt financial markets and hurt the U.S. economy.

$400 billion, has raised serious concerns that these large deficits may have negative consequences for the U.S. economy (see the Global box, "Why the Large U.S. Current Account Deficit Worries Economists").

EXCHANGE RATE REGIMES IN THE INTERNATIONAL FINANCIAL SYSTEM

Exchange rate regimes in the international financial system are classified into two basic types: fixed and floating. In a **fixed exchange rate regime**, the value of a currency is pegged relative to the value of another currency (called the **anchor currency**) so that the exchange rate is fixed in terms of the anchor currency. In a **floating exchange rate regime**, the value of a currency is allowed to fluctuate against all other currencies. When countries intervene in foreign exchange markets in an attempt to influence their exchange rates by buying and selling foreign assets, the regime is referred to as a **managed float regime** (or a **dirty float**).

In examining past exchange rate regimes, we start with the gold standard of the late nineteenth and early twentieth centuries.

Gold Standard

Before World War I, the world economy operated under the **gold standard**, a fixed exchange rate regime in which the currencies of most countries were convertible directly into gold at fixed rates, so that exchange rates between currencies were also fixed. One American dollar bill, for example, could be turned in to the U.S. Treasury and exchanged for approximately $\frac{1}{20}$ ounce of gold. Likewise, the British Treasury would exchange $\frac{1}{4}$ ounce of gold for £1 sterling. Because an American could convert

$20 into 1 ounce of gold, which could be used to buy £4, the exchange rate between the pound and the dollar was effectively fixed at $5 to the pound. The fixed exchange rates under the gold standard had the important advantage of encouraging world trade by eliminating the uncertainty that occurs when exchange rates fluctuate.

One problem with the gold standard was that monetary policy throughout the world was greatly influenced by the production of gold and gold discoveries. When gold production was low in the 1870s and 1880s, the money supply throughout the world grew slowly and did not keep pace with the growth of the world economy. The result was deflation (falling price levels). Gold discoveries in Alaska and South Africa in the 1890s greatly expanded gold production, causing money supplies to increase rapidly and price levels to rise (inflation) until World War I.

The Bretton Woods System

After World War II, the victors set up a fixed exchange rate system that became known as the **Bretton Woods system**, after the New Hampshire town in which the agreement was negotiated in 1944. The Bretton Woods system remained in effect until 1971.

The Bretton Woods agreement created the **International Monetary Fund (IMF)**, headquartered in Washington, DC, which had 30 original member countries in 1945 and currently has over 180. The IMF was given the task of promoting the growth of world trade by setting rules for the maintenance of fixed exchange rates and by making loans to countries that were experiencing balance-of-payments difficulties. In addition to monitoring the compliance of member countries with its rules, the IMF also took on the job of collecting and standardizing international economic data.

The Bretton Woods agreement also set up the International Bank for Reconstruction and Development, commonly referred to as the **World Bank**. Headquartered in Washington, DC, it provides long-term loans to help developing countries build dams, roads, and other physical capital that will contribute to their economic development. The funds for these loans are obtained primarily by the issuance of World Bank bonds, which are sold in the capital markets of the developed countries. In addition, the General Agreement on Tariffs and Trade (GATT), headquartered in Geneva, Switzerland, was set up to monitor rules for the conduct of trade between countries (tariffs and quotas). The GATT has since evolved into the **World Trade Organization (WTO)**.

Because the United States emerged from World War II as the world's largest economic power, with over half of the world's manufacturing capacity and the greater part of the world's gold, Bretton Woods put in place a system of fixed exchange rates that was based on the convertibility of U.S. dollars into gold (for foreign governments and central banks only) at $35 per ounce. The fixed exchange rates were to be maintained by intervention in the foreign exchange market by central banks in countries besides the United States that bought and sold dollar assets, which these countries held as international reserves. The U.S. dollar, which was used by other countries to denominate the assets that they held as international reserves, was called the **reserve currency**. Thus an important feature of the Bretton Woods system was the establishment of the United States as the reserve currency country. Even after the breakup of the Bretton Woods system, the U.S. dollar kept its position as the reserve currency in which most international financial transactions are conducted. The fixed exchange rate, which was a feature of the Bretton Woods system, was finally abandoned in 1973. From 1979 to 1990, the European Union instituted among its members its own fixed exchange rate system, called the European Monetary System (EMS). In theory, in the *exchange rate mechanism (ERM)* of this system, the exchange rate between any pair of currencies of

MyEconLab Mini-lecture

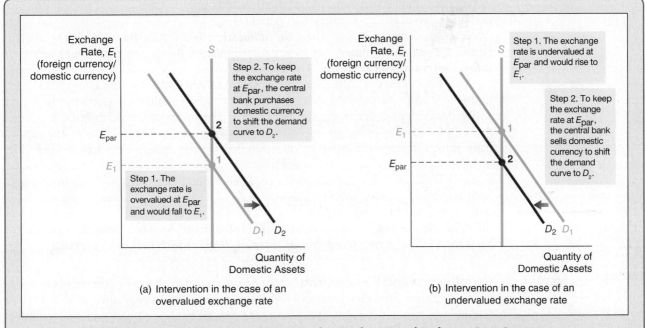

FIGURE 2   Intervention in the Foreign Exchange Market Under a Fixed Exchange Rate Regime
In panel (a), the exchange rate at E_{par} is overvalued. To keep the exchange rate at E_{par} (point 2), the central bank must purchase domestic currency to shift the demand curve to D_2. In panel (b), the exchange rate at E_{par} is undervalued, so the central bank must sell domestic currency to shift the demand curve to D_2 and keep the exchange rate at E_{par} (point 2).

the participating countries was not supposed to fluctuate outside narrow limits, called the "snake." In practice, all of the countries in the EMS pegged their currencies to the German mark.

How a Fixed Exchange Rate Regime Works

Figure 2 uses the supply and demand analysis of the foreign exchange market that we learned in the previous chapter to show how a fixed exchange rate regime works in practice. Panel (a) describes a situation in which the domestic currency is fixed relative to an anchor currency at E_{par}, while the demand curve has shifted left to D_1, perhaps because foreign interest rates have risen, thereby lowering the relative expected return on domestic assets. At E_{par}, the exchange rate is now *overvalued:* The demand curve D_1 intersects the supply curve at an exchange rate E_1 that is lower than the fixed (par) value of the exchange rate E_{par}. To keep the exchange rate at E_{par}, the central bank must intervene in the foreign exchange market and purchase domestic currency by selling foreign assets. This action, like an open market sale, causes both the monetary base and the money supply to decrease, driving up the interest rate on domestic assets, i^D.[5] This increase in the domestic interest rate raises the relative expected return on

---

[5]Because the exchange rate will continue to be fixed at E_{par}, the expected future exchange rate remains unchanged and so is not addressed in the analysis.

domestic assets, shifting the demand curve to the right. The central bank will continue to purchase domestic currency until the demand curve reaches D_2 and the equilibrium exchange rate is at E_{par}, at point 2 in panel (a).

We thus conclude that ***when the domestic currency is overvalued, the central bank must purchase domestic currency to keep the exchange rate fixed, but as a result it loses international reserves.***

Panel (b) in Figure 2 describes the situation in which the demand curve has shifted to the right to D_1 because the relative expected return on domestic assets has risen and hence the exchange rate at E_{par} is *undervalued*: The initial demand curve D_1 intersects the supply curve at exchange rate E_1, which is above E_{par}. In this situation, the central bank must sell domestic currency and purchase foreign assets. This action works like an open market purchase; it increases the money supply and lowers the interest rate on domestic assets i^D. The central bank keeps selling domestic currency and lowering i^D until the demand curve shifts all the way to D_2, where the equilibrium exchange rate is at E_{par}—point 2 in panel (b). Our analysis thus leads us to the following result: ***When the domestic currency is undervalued, the central bank must sell domestic currency to keep the exchange rate fixed, but as a result, it gains international reserves.***

Devaluation and Revaluation   As we have seen, if a country's currency is overvalued, its central bank's attempts to keep the currency from depreciating will result in a loss of international reserves. If the country's central bank eventually runs out of international reserves, it cannot keep its currency from depreciating, and a **devaluation**, in which the par exchange rate is reset at a lower level, must occur.

If, by contrast, a country's currency is undervalued, its central bank's intervention to keep the currency from appreciating leads to a gain of international reserves. As we will see shortly, the central bank might not want to acquire these international reserves, and so it might want to reset the par value of its exchange rate at a higher level (a **revaluation**).

Perfect Capital Mobility   If perfect capital mobility exists—that is, if there are no barriers to domestic residents purchasing foreign assets or to foreigners purchasing domestic assets—then a sterilized exchange rate intervention cannot keep the exchange rate at E_{par} because, as we saw earlier in the chapter, the relative expected return on domestic assets is unaffected. For example, if the exchange rate is overvalued, a sterilized purchase of domestic currency will leave the relative expected return and the demand curve unchanged, so pressure for a depreciation of the domestic currency is not removed. If the central bank keeps purchasing its domestic currency but continues to sterilize, it will just keep losing international reserves until it finally runs out of them and is forced to let the value of the currency seek a lower level.

Speculative Attacks

A serious shortcoming of fixed exchange rate systems such as the Bretton Woods system and the European Monetary System is that such systems can lead to foreign exchange crises involving a **speculative attack** on a currency. A speculative attack involves massive sales of a weak currency or purchases of a strong currency that cause a sharp change in the exchange rate. In the following application, we use our model of exchange rate determination to understand how the September 1992 exchange rate crisis that rocked the European Monetary System came about.

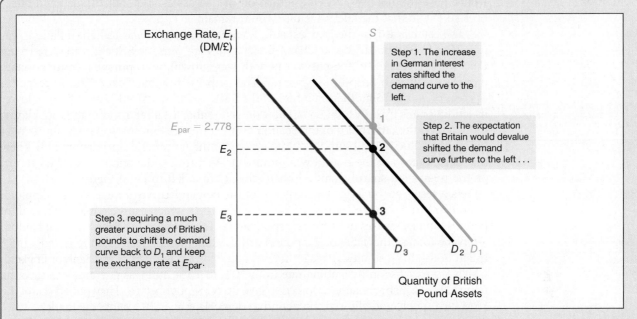

FIGURE 3   Foreign Exchange Market for British Pounds in 1992

The realization by speculators that the United Kingdom would soon devalue the pound decreased the relative expected return on British pound assets, resulting in a leftward shift of the demand curve from D_2 to D_3. As a result, the British central bank was forced to purchase a large amount of pounds in an effort to raise the interest rate, so that the demand curve would shift back to D_1 and the exchange rate E_{par} would remain at 2.778 German marks per pound.

APPLICATION   The Foreign Exchange Crisis of September 1992

In the aftermath of German reunification in October 1990, the German central bank, the Bundesbank, faced rising inflationary pressures, with inflation having accelerated from below 3% in 1990 to near 5% by 1992. To get monetary growth under control and to dampen inflation, the Bundesbank raised German interest rates to near double-digit levels. Figure 3 shows the consequences of these actions by the Bundesbank in the foreign exchange market for British pounds. Note that in the diagram, the pound is the domestic currency and the German mark (deutsche mark, DM, Germany's currency before the advent of the euro in 1999) is the foreign currency.

The increase in German interest rates i^F lowered the relative expected return on British pound assets and shifted the demand curve to D_2, as shown in Figure 3. The intersection of the supply and demand curves at point 2 was now below the lower exchange rate limit at that time (2.778 marks per pound, denoted E_{par}). To increase the value of the pound relative to the mark and to restore the mark/pound exchange rate to within the exchange rate mechanism limits, one of two things had to happen. In the first option, the Bank of England would have to pursue a contractionary monetary policy, thereby raising British interest rates sufficiently to shift the demand curve back to D_1, so that the equilibrium would remain at point 1 and the exchange rate would remain at E_{par}. Alternatively, the Bundesbank would have to pursue an expansionary monetary policy, thereby lowering German interest rates. Lower German interest rates would raise the relative expected return on British assets and shift the demand curve back to D_1, so that the exchange rate would remain at E_{par}.

The catch was that the Bundesbank, whose primary goal was to fight inflation, was unwilling to pursue an expansionary monetary policy, and the British, who were facing their worst recession in the postwar period, were unwilling to pursue a contractionary monetary policy to prop up the pound. This impasse became clear when, in response to great pressure from other members of the EMS, the Bundesbank was willing to lower its lending rates by only a token amount on September 14 after a speculative attack was mounted on the currencies of the Scandinavian countries. So, at some point in the near future, the value of the pound would have to decline to point 2. Speculators now knew that depreciation of the pound was imminent. As a result, the relative expected return on the pound fell sharply, shifting the demand curve left to D_3 in Figure 3.

As a result of the large leftward shift of the demand curve, a huge excess supply of pound assets now existed at the par exchange rate E_{par}, which caused a massive sell-off of pounds (and purchases of marks) by speculators. The need for the British central bank to intervene to raise the value of the pound now became much greater and required a huge rise in British interest rates. A major intervention effort on the part of the Bank of England, which led to a rise in its lending rate from 10% to 15%, still wasn't enough to save the pound. The British were finally forced to give up on September 16: They pulled out of the ERM indefinitely and allowed the pound to depreciate by 10% against the mark.

Speculative attacks on other currencies forced devaluation of the Spanish peseta by 5% and of the Italian lira by 15%. To defend its currency, the Swedish central bank was forced to raise its daily lending rate to the astronomical level of 500%! By the time the crisis was over, the British, French, Italian, Spanish, and Swedish central banks had intervened to the tune of $100 billion; the Bundesbank alone had laid out $50 billion for foreign exchange intervention. Because foreign exchange crises lead to large changes in central banks' holdings of international reserves and thus significantly affect the official reserve asset items in the balance of payments, these crises are also referred to as **balance-of-payments crises**.

The attempt to prop up the European Monetary System was not cheap for these central banks. It is estimated that they lost $4 to $6 billion as a result of exchange rate intervention during the crisis. What the central banks lost, the speculators gained. A speculative fund run by George Soros ran up $1 billion of profits during the crisis, and Citibank traders reportedly made $200 million. When an exchange rate crisis arises, life certainly can be sweet for exchange rate speculators. ◆

The Policy Trilemma

An important implication of the foregoing analysis is that a country that ties its exchange rate to an anchor currency of a larger country loses control of its monetary policy. If the larger country pursues a more contractionary monetary policy and raises interest rates, this action will lead to lower expected inflation in the larger country, thus causing an appreciation of the larger country's currency and a depreciation of the smaller country's currency. The smaller country, having locked its exchange rate to the anchor currency, will now find its currency overvalued and will therefore have to sell the anchor currency and buy its own to keep its currency from depreciating. The result of this foreign exchange intervention will be a decline in the smaller country's international reserves, a contraction of its monetary base, and a rise in interest rates. Sterilization of this foreign exchange intervention is not an option because this course

FIGURE 4
The Policy Trilemma

A country (or monetary union) cannot pursue the following three policies at the same time: (1) free capital mobility, (2) a fixed exchange rate, and (3) an independent monetary policy. Instead, it must choose two of the three policies denoted by the sides of the triangle.

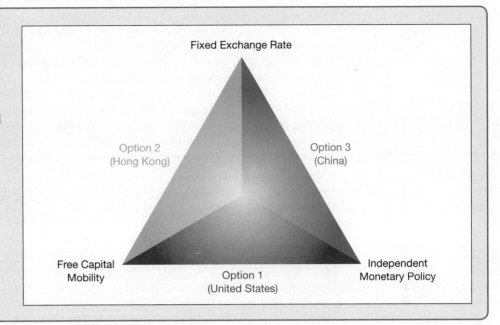

of action would just lead to a continuing loss of international reserves, until the smaller country was forced to devalue its currency. The smaller country no longer controls its monetary policy because movements in its interest rates are completely determined by movements in the larger country's interest rates.

Our analysis therefore indicates that a country (or a monetary union like the Eurozone) can't pursue the following three policies at the same time: (1) free capital mobility, (2) a fixed exchange rate, and (3) an independent monetary policy. Economists call this result the **policy trilemma** (or, more graphically, the **impossible trinity**). Figure 4 illustrates the policy trilemma. A country can choose only two of the three options, which are denoted by the sides of the triangle. In option 1, a country (or monetary union) chooses to have capital mobility and an independent monetary policy, but not a fixed exchange rate. The Eurozone and the United States have made this choice. Hong Kong and Belize have chosen option 2, in which there is free capital mobility and the exchange rate is fixed, but the country does not have an independent monetary policy. Other countries, like China, have chosen option 3, in which the country has a fixed exchange rate and pursues an independent monetary policy but does not have free capital mobility because of **capital controls**, or restrictions on the free movement of capital across the borders.

The policy trilemma thus leaves countries with a difficult choice. Do they accept exchange rate volatility (option 1), give up an independent monetary policy (option 2), or restrict capital flows (option 3)?

APPLICATION   ## How Did China Accumulate $4 Trillion of International Reserves?

By 2014, China had accumulated $4 trillion of international reserves. How did the Chinese get their hands on this vast amount of foreign assets? After all, China is not yet a rich country.

The answer is that in 1994, China pegged its exchange rate to the U.S. dollar at a fixed rate of 12 cents to the yuan (also called the renminbi). China's rapidly growing productivity, accompanied by an inflation rate lower than that of the United States, caused the long-run value of the yuan to increase, leading to a higher relative expected return on yuan assets and a rightward shift of the demand curve for yuan assets. As a result, the Chinese found themselves in the situation depicted in panel (b) of Figure 2, a situation in which the yuan is undervalued. To keep the yuan from appreciating above E_{par} to E_1 in the figure, the Chinese central bank has engaged in massive purchases of U.S. dollar assets. Today the Chinese government is one of the largest holders of U.S. government bonds in the world.

The pegging of the yuan to the U.S. dollar has created several problems for Chinese authorities. First, the Chinese now own a lot of U.S. assets, particularly U.S. Treasury securities, which have very low returns. Second, the undervaluation of the yuan has caused Chinese goods abroad to become so cheap that many countries have threatened to erect trade barriers against these goods if the Chinese government does not allow an upward revaluation of the yuan. Third, as we learned earlier in the chapter, the Chinese purchase of dollar assets has resulted in a substantial increase in the Chinese monetary base and money supply, which could lead to high inflation in the future. Because the Chinese authorities have created substantial roadblocks to capital mobility, they have been able to sterilize most of their exchange rate interventions while maintaining the exchange-rate peg. Nevertheless, they still worry about inflationary pressures. In July 2005, China finally made its peg somewhat more flexible by letting the value of the yuan rise 2.1%, and China subsequently allowed the yuan to appreciate at a gradual pace. The Chinese central bank also indicated that it would no longer fix the value of the yuan to the U.S. dollar, but would instead maintain its value relative to a basket of currencies.

Why did the Chinese authorities maintain this exchange-rate peg for so long, despite the associated problems? One answer is that China wanted to keep its export sector humming by keeping the prices of its export goods low. A second answer might be that China wanted to accumulate a large amount of international reserves as a "war chest" that could be sold to buy yuan in the event of a speculative attack against the currency at some future date. Given the pressure from government officials in the United States and Europe on the Chinese government to further revalue its currency, future adjustments to China's exchange rate policy are likely. ◆

Monetary Unions

A variant of a fixed exchange rate regime is a **monetary** (or **currency**) **union**, in which a group of countries decides to adopt a common currency, thereby fixing the countries' exchange rates in relation to each other. One of the earliest monetary unions was formed in 1787, when the thirteen American colonies formed the United States of America and gave up their individual currencies for the U.S. dollar. The most recently formed monetary union is the European Monetary Union (EMU), which was formed in January of 1999, when eleven initial member countries adopted a new joint currency, the euro.

The key economic advantage of a monetary union is that it makes trade across borders easier because goods and services in all of the member countries are now priced in the same currency. However, as with any fixed exchange rate regime and free capital mobility, a currency union means that individual countries no longer have their own independent monetary policies with which to address shortfalls of aggregate demand. This disadvantage of a currency union has raised questions about whether the Eurozone will break up, as discussed in the Global box, "Will the Euro Survive?"

Global   Will the Euro Survive?

The global financial crisis of 2007–2009 led to economic contraction throughout Europe, with the countries in the southern part of the Eurozone hit especially hard. Unemployment in the hard-hit southern countries climbed much faster than in the northern countries such as Germany. Furthermore, with the contraction of their economies, many of the southern countries began to experience large government budget deficits and sovereign debt crises, as described in Chapter 12, in which investors pulled back from purchasing these countries' bonds, sending interest rates to extremely high levels. The resulting collapse of the southern countries' economies could have been alleviated by easier monetary policy that would have stimulated economic activity, but this option was unavailable to these countries because the European Central Bank had to conduct monetary policy for the Eurozone as a whole, which was not suffering as badly as the individual southern countries.

This "straightjacket" effect of the euro has weakened support for the euro in the southern countries, leading to increased talk of abandoning the euro. Support for the euro has also weakened in the stronger, northern countries, since they have been called upon to provide bailouts to the weaker member countries. Because the stronger countries might wish to abandon their commitment to the euro in order to limit their transfers of funds to the weaker countries, and the weaker countries might wish to abandon their commitment to the euro so that they can boost their economies through more expansionary monetary policy and depreciation of their currencies, there are doubts that the European Monetary Union will survive. However, the euro is still seen by many as an important step in the creation of a more united and powerful Europe, and this political consideration has created strong support for retaining the monetary union.

Managed Float

With the demise of the Bretton Woods system, most exchange rates now change daily in response to market forces, but central banks have not been willing to give up the option of intervening in the foreign exchange market. The ability to prevent large changes in exchange rates makes it easier for firms and individuals purchasing or selling goods abroad to plan for the future. Furthermore, countries with surpluses in their balances of payments frequently do not want to see their currencies appreciate, because it makes their goods more expensive abroad and foreign goods cheaper in the home country. Because an appreciation might hurt sales for domestic businesses and increase unemployment, countries with balance-of-payments surpluses often have sold their currencies in the foreign exchange market and acquired international reserves.

Countries with balance-of-payments deficits do not want to see their currencies lose value because it makes foreign goods more expensive for domestic consumers and can stimulate inflation. To keep the value of the domestic currency high, countries with deficits have often bought their own currencies in the foreign exchange market and given up international reserves.

The current international financial system is a hybrid of a fixed and a flexible exchange rate system. Rates fluctuate in response to market forces but are not determined solely by them. Furthermore, many countries continue to keep the value of their currency fixed against other currencies, as was the case in the European Monetary System before the introduction of the euro and China from 1994 until 2005.

CAPITAL CONTROLS

Emerging market countries are countries that have recently opened up to flows of goods, services, and capital from the rest of the world. Politicians and some economists have advocated that these countries avoid financial instability by restricting capital mobility. Are capital controls a good idea?

Controls on Capital Outflows

Capital outflows can promote financial instability because, when domestic residents and foreigners pull their capital out of a country, the resulting capital outflow forces the country to devalue its currency. Because they want to avoid such instability, politicians in emerging market countries may find capital controls particularly attractive.

Although these controls sound like a good idea, they suffer from several disadvantages. First, empirical evidence indicates that controls on capital outflows are seldom effective during a crisis, because the private sector will find ingenious ways to evade them and will have little difficulty in moving funds out of the country. Second, the evidence suggests that capital flight may actually increase after controls are put into place because confidence in the government is weakened. Third, controls on capital outflows can lead to corruption, since government officials are often paid to look the other way while domestic residents try to move funds abroad. Fourth, controls on capital outflows may lull governments into thinking they do not have to act to reform their financial systems to deal with the crisis, and so opportunities to improve the functioning of the economy are lost.

Controls on Capital Inflows

Although most economists find the arguments against controls on capital outflows persuasive, the idea of controls on capital inflows receives more support. Supporters reason that if speculative capital cannot come in, then it cannot go out suddenly. Thus a potential crisis is averted. Our analysis of financial crises in Chapter 12 provides support for this view by suggesting that capital inflows can lead to credit booms and excessive risk taking on the parts of banks, factors that can help trigger a financial crisis.

However, controls on capital inflows have the undesirable feature that they might block funds that could be used for productive investment opportunities from entering a country. Although controls on capital inflows may limit the amount of fuel supplied to lending booms through capital flows, over time they produce substantial distortions and misallocations of resources as households and businesses try to get around them. Indeed, as with controls on capital outflows, controls on capital inflows can lead to corruption. Serious doubts exist over whether capital controls can be effective in today's environment, in which trade is open and in which the variety of financial instruments makes it easier to get around these controls.

On the other hand, a strong case can be made for improving bank regulation and supervision so that capital inflows are less likely to produce a lending boom that would encourage excessive risk taking by banking institutions. For example, restrictions on the growth of bank borrowing might substantially limit capital inflows. Supervisory controls that focus on the sources of financial fragility, rather than the symptoms, can enhance the efficiency of the financial system rather than hamper it.

THE ROLE OF THE IMF

The International Monetary Fund (IMF) was originally set up under the Bretton Woods system to help countries deal with balance-of-payments problems and stand by the fixed exchange rates by lending to deficit countries. When the Bretton Woods system of fixed exchange rates collapsed in 1971, the IMF took on new roles.

The IMF continues to function as a data collector and continues to provide technical assistance to its member countries. Although the IMF no longer attempts to encourage fixed exchange rates, its role as an international lender has become more important in recent years. This role first came to the fore in the 1980s during the Third World debt crisis, during which the IMF assisted developing countries in repaying their loans. During the financial crises in Mexico from 1994–1995 and in East Asia from 1997–1998, the IMF made huge loans to these and other affected countries to help them recover financially and to prevent the spread of the crises to other countries. Then, starting in 2010, the IMF made large loans to Greece, Ireland, and Portugal to help these countries avoid defaults on their government debt. This role of the IMF, in which it acts as an international lender of last resort and helps countries cope with financial instability, is indeed highly controversial.

Should the IMF Act as an International Lender of Last Resort?

We have seen that when a central bank engages in a lender-of-last-resort operation, as the Federal Reserve did during the recent global financial crisis, such an action can minimize the severity of the financial crisis and sometimes even prevent it from happening. When the IMF acts as an international lender of last resort, this role can have similar benefits, particularly when the central bank of the country it is lending to does not have the capacity to cope with the crisis.

However, when the IMF acts as an international lender of last resort, it can lead to serious moral hazard problems. First, knowing that the IMF is willing to take on this role may encourage governments to be profligate, because they know they are likely to be bailed out by the IMF if things get out of hand. Second, governments use IMF funds to protect depositors and other creditors of banking institutions from losses. This safety net creates the moral hazard problem discussed in Chapter 10, because depositors and other creditors have less incentive to monitor these banking institutions and to withdraw their deposits if the institutions are taking on too much risk.

An international lender of last resort must find ways to limit these two moral hazard problems or it can actually make the situation worse. The international lender of last resort can make it clear that it will extend liquidity only to governments that both put their fiscal houses in order and implement measures to prevent excessive risk taking by financial institutions. Critics of the IMF, however, believe that the IMF has not put enough pressure on the governments to which it lends to contain these two moral hazard problems, and for this reason they believe the IMF should abandon its role as an international lender of last resort. The IMF has also been criticized for imposing so-called austerity programs that force borrowing governments to cut government spending, raise taxes, and raise interest rates. These austerity programs can be highly contractionary (see Chapter 22) and can lead to high unemployment and even political instability.

The debate as to whether the world would be better off with the IMF operating as an international lender of last resort is currently a hot one. Much attention is being focused on efforts to make the IMF more effective in performing this role, and redesign of the IMF is at the center of proposals for a new international financial architecture that will help reduce international financial instability.

INTERNATIONAL CONSIDERATIONS AND MONETARY POLICY

Our analysis in this chapter so far has suggested several ways in which monetary policy can be affected by international matters. Awareness of these effects can have significant implications for the way in which monetary policy is conducted.

Direct Effects of the Foreign Exchange Market on Monetary Policy

When central banks intervene in the foreign exchange market, they acquire or sell off international reserves, and their monetary base is affected. When a central bank intervenes in the foreign exchange market, it gives up some control of its monetary policy. For example, in the early 1970s, the German central bank faced a dilemma. In attempting to keep the German mark from appreciating too much against the U.S. dollar, the Germans acquired huge quantities of international reserves, leading to a high rate of money growth and lower interest rates that the German central bank considered inflationary.

The Bundesbank could have stopped its intervention in the foreign exchange market, thereby reasserting control over its own monetary policy. Such a strategy has a major drawback when a central bank is under pressure not to allow its currency to appreciate: The lower price of imports and higher price of exports that result from an appreciation of its currency will hurt domestic producers and increase unemployment.

Because the U.S. dollar has been a reserve currency, the U.S. monetary base and money supply have not been greatly affected by developments in the foreign exchange market. As long as foreign central banks, rather than the Fed, intervene to keep the value of the dollar from changing, American holdings of international reserves will remain unaffected. Conducting monetary policy is typically easier when a country's currency is a reserve currency.[6]

Balance-of-Payments Considerations

Balance-of-payments considerations were more important under the Bretton Woods system than they are under the current managed float regime. When a nonreserve currency country is running balance-of-payments deficits, it necessarily gives up international reserves. Under the Bretton Woods system, to keep from running out of these reserves, a nonreserve currency country had to implement contractionary monetary policy to strengthen its currency. This is exactly what occurred in the United Kingdom before its devaluation of the pound in 1967. When policy became expansionary, the balance of payments deteriorated, and the British were forced to "slam on the brakes" by implementing a contractionary policy. Once the balance of payments had improved, policy became more expansionary, until the deteriorating balance of payments again forced the British to pursue a contractionary policy. Such on-again, off-again actions became known as a "stop-go" policy, and the domestic instability it created was criticized severely.

---

[6]However, the central bank of a reserve currency country must worry about a shift away from the use of its currency for international reserves.

Because the United States is a major reserve currency country, it can run large balance-of-payments deficits without losing huge amounts of international reserves. This does not mean, however, that the Federal Reserve is never influenced by developments in the U.S. balance of payments. Current account deficits in the United States suggest that American businesses may be losing some of their ability to compete because the value of the dollar is too high. In addition, large U.S. balance-of-payments deficits lead to balance-of-payments surpluses in other countries, which can in turn lead to large increases in their holdings of international reserves (this was especially true under the Bretton Woods system). Because such increases put a strain on the international financial system and may stimulate world inflation, the Fed worries about U.S. balance-of-payments and current account deficits. To help shrink these deficits, the Fed might pursue a more contractionary monetary policy.

Exchange Rate Considerations

Unlike balance-of-payments considerations, which have become less important under the current managed float system, exchange rate considerations now play a greater role in the conduct of monetary policy. If a central bank does not want to see its currency fall in value, it may pursue a more contractionary monetary policy to raise the domestic interest rate, thereby strengthening its currency. Similarly, if a country experiences an appreciation in its currency, its domestic industry may suffer from increased foreign competition and may pressure the central bank to ease monetary policy in order to lower the exchange rate.

TO PEG OR NOT TO PEG: EXCHANGE-RATE TARGETING AS AN ALTERNATIVE MONETARY POLICY STRATEGY

In Chapter 16, we discussed two monetary policy strategies that could be used to promote price stability: inflation targeting and the Federal Reserve's "just do it" strategy. Another strategy that uses a strong nominal anchor to promote price stability is called **exchange-rate targeting** (sometimes referred to as an **exchange-rate peg**).

Targeting the exchange rate is a monetary policy strategy with a long history. It can take the form of fixing the value of the domestic currency to a commodity such as gold, the key feature of the gold standard described earlier in the chapter. More recently, fixed exchange rate regimes have involved fixing the value of the domestic currency to that of a large, low-inflation country like the United States (the *anchor country*). Another alternative is to adopt a *crawling target* or *peg*, in which a currency is allowed to depreciate at a steady rate so that the inflation rate of the pegging country can be higher than that of the anchor country.

Advantages of Exchange-Rate Targeting

Exchange-rate targeting has several advantages. First, the nominal anchor of an exchange-rate target directly contributes to the goal of keeping inflation under control by tying the inflation rate for internationally traded goods to the rate in the anchor country. The exchange-rate target is able to do this because the foreign price of internationally traded goods is set by the world market, whereas the domestic price of these goods is fixed by the exchange-rate target. For example, until 2002, the exchange rate for the Argentine peso was exactly one to the dollar, so that a bushel of wheat traded internationally at five dollars had its price set at five pesos. If the exchange-rate target is credible (i.e., expected to be adhered to), the exchange-rate target has the added benefit of anchoring inflation expectations to the inflation rate in the anchor country.

Second, an exchange-rate target provides an automatic rule for the conduct of monetary policy that helps mitigate the time-inconsistency problem described in Chapter 16. As we saw earlier in the chapter, an exchange-rate target forces a tightening of monetary policy when there is a tendency for the domestic currency to depreciate and a loosening of policy when there is a tendency for the domestic currency to appreciate, so that discretionary monetary policy is less of an option. The central bank will therefore be constrained from falling into the time-inconsistency trap of trying to expand output and employment in the short-run by pursuing overly expansionary monetary policy.

Third, an exchange-rate target has the advantage of simplicity and clarity, which makes it easily understood by the public. A "sound currency" is an easy-to-understand rallying cry for monetary policy. In the past, for example, this aspect of simplicity was important in France, where an appeal to the "franc fort" (strong franc) was often used to justify tight monetary policy.

Given its advantages, it is not surprising that exchange-rate targeting has been used successfully to control inflation in industrialized countries. Both France and the United Kingdom, for example, successfully used exchange-rate targeting to lower inflation by tying the values of their currencies to the German mark. In 1987, when France first pegged its exchange rate to the mark, its inflation rate was 3%, two percentage points above the German inflation rate. By 1992, its inflation rate had fallen to 2%, a level that can be argued is consistent with price stability and that was actually below the German inflation rate. By 1996, the French and German inflation rates had converged to a number slightly below 2%. Similarly, after pegging its currency to the German mark in 1990, the United Kingdom was able to lower its inflation rate from 10% to 3% by 1992, when it was forced to abandon the exchange rate mechanism (ERM).

Exchange-rate targeting has also been an effective means of reducing inflation quickly in emerging market countries. For example, before the devaluation in Mexico in 1994, its exchange-rate target enabled it to bring inflation down from levels above 100% in 1988 to levels below 10% in 1994.

Disadvantages of Exchange-Rate Targeting

Despite the inherent advantages of exchange-rate targeting, several serious criticisms of this strategy can be made. The problem (as we saw earlier in the chapter) is that with capital mobility, the targeting country can no longer pursue its own independent monetary policy and use it to respond to domestic shocks that are independent of those hitting the anchor country. Furthermore, an exchange-rate target means that shocks to the anchor country are directly transmitted to the targeting country, because changes in interest rates in the anchor country lead to corresponding changes in interest rates in the targeting country.

A striking example of these weaknesses occurred when Germany was reunified in 1990. In response to concerns about inflationary pressures arising from reunification and the massive fiscal expansion required to rebuild East Germany, long-term German interest rates rose until February 1991, and short-term rates rose until December 1991. This shock to the anchor country in the exchange rate mechanism (ERM) was transmitted directly to the other countries in the ERM whose currencies were pegged to the mark, and their interest rates rose in tandem with the German rates. Continued adherence to the exchange-rate target slowed economic growth and increased unemployment in countries such as France that remained in the ERM exchange-rate peg.

A second problem with exchange-rate targets is that they leave countries open to speculative attacks on their currencies. Indeed, one aftermath of German reunification was the foreign exchange crisis of September 1992. As we saw earlier, the tight monetary policy practiced in Germany following reunification subjected the countries of the ERM to a negative demand shock that led to declines in economic growth and increases in unemployment. It was certainly feasible for the governments of these countries to keep their exchange rates fixed relative to the mark under these circumstances, but speculators began to question whether these countries' commitment to the exchange-rate peg would eventually weaken. Speculators reasoned that these countries would not tolerate the rise in unemployment that resulted from keeping interest rates high enough to fend off attacks on their currencies.

At this stage, speculators were, in effect, presented with a one-way bet, because the currencies of countries like France, Spain, Sweden, Italy, and the United Kingdom could go in only one direction and depreciate against the mark. Selling these currencies before the likely depreciation occurred gave speculators an attractive profit opportunity with potentially high expected returns. The result was the speculative attack of September 1992. Only in France was the commitment to the fixed exchange rate strong enough that France did not devalue. The governments of the other ERM countries were unwilling to defend their currencies at all costs and eventually allowed their currencies to fall in value.

The different responses of France and the United Kingdom after the September 1992 exchange rate crisis illustrate the potential cost of an exchange-rate target. France, which continued to peg its currency to the mark and thus was unable to use monetary policy to respond to domestic conditions, found that economic growth remained slow after 1992, and unemployment increased. The United Kingdom, on the other hand, which dropped out of the ERM exchange-rate peg and adopted inflation targeting, enjoyed much better economic results: Economic growth was higher, the unemployment rate fell, and yet the inflation rate was not much worse than France's.

In contrast to industrialized countries, emerging market countries (including the transition countries of Eastern Europe) may not lose all that much by giving up an independent monetary policy when they target exchange rates. Because many emerging market countries have not developed the political or monetary institutions that are necessary for the successful use of discretionary monetary policy, they may have little to gain but a lot to lose from an independent monetary policy. Thus they are better off if they adopt, in effect, the monetary policy of a country like the United States through targeting exchange rates than if they pursue their own independent policy. This is one of the reasons so many emerging market countries have adopted exchange-rate targeting.

Nonetheless, exchange-rate targeting is highly dangerous for these countries because it leaves them open to speculative attacks that can have far more serious consequences for their economies than for those of industrialized countries. Indeed, the successful speculative attacks on Mexico in 1994, East Asia in 1997, and Argentina in 2002 plunged their economies into full-scale financial crises that devastated their countries.

An additional disadvantage of an exchange-rate target is that it can weaken the accountability of policymakers, particularly in emerging market countries. Because exchange-rate targeting fixes the exchange rate, it eliminates an important signal that can help constrain monetary policy from becoming too expansionary and thereby limit the time-inconsistency problem. In industrialized countries, particularly in the

United States, the bond market provides an important signal about the stance of monetary policy. Overly expansionary monetary policy or strong political pressure to engage in overly expansionary monetary policy produces an inflation scare, in which inflation expectations surge, interest rates rise (because of the Fisher effect, described in Chapter 5), and long-term bond prices decline sharply. Because both central banks and politicians want to avoid this kind of scenario, overly expansionary monetary policy is less likely.

In many countries, particularly emerging market countries, the long-term bond market is essentially nonexistent. Under a floating exchange rate regime, however, if monetary policy is too expansionary, the exchange rate will depreciate. In these countries, the daily fluctuations of the exchange rate can, like the bond market in the United States, provide an early warning signal that monetary policy is too expansionary. Just as the fear of a visible inflation scare in the bond market constrains central bankers from pursuing overly expansionary monetary policy and constrains politicians from putting pressure on the central bank to do so, fear of exchange rate depreciations can make overly expansionary monetary policy, and therefore the time-inconsistency problem, less likely.

The need for signals from the foreign exchange market may be even more acute for emerging market countries because the balance sheets and actions of their central banks are not as transparent as those of industrialized countries. Targeting the exchange rate can make it even harder to ascertain the central bank's policy actions. The public is less able to keep a watch on the central bank and the politicians pressuring it, which makes it easier for monetary policy to become too expansionary.

When Is Exchange-Rate Targeting Desirable for Industrialized Countries?

Given the above disadvantages of exchange-rate targeting, when might it make sense? In industrialized countries, the biggest cost to exchange-rate targeting is the loss of an independent monetary policy to deal with domestic considerations. If an independent, domestic monetary policy can be conducted responsibly, the loss of such a policy can be a serious cost indeed, as the comparison between the post-1992 experiences of France and the United Kingdom indicates. However, not all industrialized countries are capable of conducting their own monetary policies successfully, either because the central bank is not independent or because political pressures on the central bank lead to an inflationary bias in monetary policy. In these cases, giving up independent control of domestic monetary policy may not be such a great loss, while the advantages of having monetary policy determined by a better-performing central bank in the anchor country can be substantial.

Italy provides a good example. It is not a coincidence that the Italian public had the most favorable attitude of all the European countries toward the European Monetary Union. The past record of Italian monetary policy was not good, and the Italian public recognized that a monetary policy controlled by more responsible outsiders had benefits that far outweighed the costs to the country of losing the ability to focus monetary policy on domestic considerations.

A second reason why industrialized countries might find exchange-rate targeting useful is that it encourages integration of the domestic economy with the economies of neighboring countries. Clearly, this was the rationale for the long-standing pegging of the exchange rate to the deutsche mark by countries such as Austria and the

Netherlands, and the more recent exchange-rate pegs that preceded the formation of the European Monetary Union.

To sum, exchange-rate targeting for industrialized countries is probably not the best monetary policy strategy for controlling the overall economy unless (1) domestic monetary and political institutions are not conducive to good monetary policymaking or (2) an exchange-rate target has other important benefits that have nothing to do with monetary policy.

When Is Exchange-Rate Targeting Desirable for Emerging Market Countries?

In countries with particularly weak political and monetary institutions that have experienced continued bouts of hyperinflation, a characterization that applies to many emerging market (including transition) countries, exchange-rate targeting may be the only way to break inflationary psychology and stabilize the economy. In this situation, exchange-rate targeting is the stabilization policy of last resort. However, if the exchange-rate targeting regimes in emerging market countries are not transparent, they are more likely to break down, often resulting in disastrous financial crises.

Are there exchange rate strategies that will make it less likely that the exchange rate regime will break down in an emerging market country? Two such strategies, currency boards and dollarization, have received increased attention in recent years.

Currency Boards

A **currency board** is an arrangement in which the domestic currency is backed 100% by a foreign currency (say, dollars), and the note-issuing authority, whether it be the central bank or the government, establishes a fixed exchange rate to this foreign currency and stands ready to exchange domestic currency for the foreign currency at this rate whenever the public so requests. A currency board is just a variant of a fixed exchange-rate target in which the commitment to the fixed exchange rate is especially strong because the conduct of monetary policy is, in effect, put on autopilot and taken completely out of the hands of the central bank and the government. In contrast, the typical fixed or pegged exchange rate regime does allow the monetary authorities some discretion in their conduct of monetary policy, because they can still adjust interest rates or print money.

A currency board arrangement thus has important advantages over a monetary policy strategy that just uses an exchange-rate target. First, the money supply can expand only when foreign currency is exchanged for domestic currency at the central bank. Therefore, the increased amount of domestic currency is matched by an equal increase in foreign exchange reserves. The central bank no longer has the ability to print money and thereby cause inflation. Second, the currency board setup involves a stronger commitment by the central bank to the fixed exchange rate and may therefore be effective in bringing inflation down quickly and in decreasing the likelihood of a successful speculative attack against the currency.

Although currency boards solve the transparency and commitment problems inherent in an exchange-rate target regime, they suffer from some of the same shortcomings: the loss of an independent monetary policy, increased exposure of the economy to shocks from the anchor country, and the loss of the central bank's ability to create money and act as a lender of last resort. Other means must therefore be used to cope with potential banking crises. In addition, if a speculative attack on a currency board occurs, the exchange of domestic currency for foreign currency leads to a sharp contraction of the money supply, which can be highly damaging to the economy.

Currency boards have been established in the territory of Hong Kong (1983) and in countries such as Argentina (1991), Estonia (1992), Lithuania (1994), Bulgaria (1997), and Bosnia (1998). Argentina's currency board, which operated from 1991 until 2002 and required the central bank to exchange U.S. dollars for new pesos at a fixed exchange rate of 1 to 1, is one of the most interesting. For more on this subject, see the Global box, "Argentina's Currency Board."

Global   Argentina's Currency Board

Argentina has a long history of monetary instability, with inflation rates fluctuating dramatically over the years, sometimes surging to beyond 1,000% per year. To end this cycle of inflationary surges, Argentina decided to adopt a currency board in April of 1991. The Argentine currency board worked as follows. Under Argentina's convertibility law, the peso/dollar exchange rate was fixed at 1 to 1, and a member of the public could go to the Argentine central bank and exchange a peso for a dollar, or vice versa, at any time.

The early years of Argentina's currency board looked stunningly successful. Inflation, which was running at an 800% annual rate in 1990, fell to less than 5% by the end of 1994, and economic growth was rapid, averaging almost 8% per year from 1991 to 1994. In the aftermath of the Mexican peso crisis, however, concern about the health of the Argentine economy led the public to pull money out of the banks (deposits fell by 18%) and exchange pesos for dollars, thus causing a contraction of the Argentine money supply. The result was a sharp drop in Argentine economic activity, with real GDP shrinking by more than 5% in 1995 and the unemployment rate jumping above 15%. Only in 1996 did the economy begin to recover.

Because the central bank of Argentina had no control over monetary policy under the currency board system, it was virtually helpless to counteract the contractionary monetary effects stemming from the public's behavior. Furthermore, because the currency board did not allow the central bank to create pesos and lend them to the banks, it had very little capability to act as a lender of last resort. With help from international agencies such as the IMF, the World Bank, and the Inter-American Development Bank, which lent Argentina more than $5 billion in 1995 to help shore up its banking system, the currency board survived.

In 1998, however, Argentina entered another recession, one that was both severe and very long-lasting. By the end of 2001, unemployment had reached nearly 20%, a level comparable to that experienced in the United States during the Great Depression of the 1930s. The result was civil unrest and the fall of the elected government, as well as a major banking crisis and a default on nearly $150 billion of government debt. Because the Central Bank of Argentina had no control over monetary policy under the currency board system, it was unable to use monetary policy to expand the economy and get Argentina out of its recession. In addition, because the currency board limited the central bank's ability to create pesos and act as a lender of last resort, the central bank was unable to help banks weather the banking crisis. In January 2002, the currency board finally collapsed, the peso depreciated by more than 70%, and inflation shot through the roof. The result was a full-scale financial crisis that led to an extremely severe depression. Clearly, the Argentine public is not as enamored of its currency board as it once was.[*]

[*]The Argentine financial crisis is described in detail in Web Chapter 1, "Financial Crises in Emerging Market Economies," which can be found on the Companion Website at http://www.pearsonhighered.com/mishkin.

Dollarization

Another solution to the transparency problem and doubts about commitment to the exchange-rate target is **dollarization**, the adoption of a sound currency, like the U.S. dollar, as a country's money. Indeed, dollarization is just another variant of a fixed exchange-rate target, but with an even stronger commitment mechanism than that provided by a currency board. A currency board can be abandoned, allowing a change in the value of the currency, but a change of value is impossible with dollarization: A dollar bill is always worth one dollar, whether it is held in the United States or outside it.

Dollarization has been advocated as a monetary policy strategy for emerging market countries: It was discussed actively by Argentine officials in the aftermath of the devaluation of the Brazilian real in January 1999 and was adopted by Ecuador in March 2000. Dollarization's key advantage is that it completely eliminates the possibility of a speculative attack on the domestic currency (because there is no such currency). (Such an attack is still a danger under a currency board arrangement.)

Dollarization is subject to the usual weaknesses of an exchange-rate target (the loss of an independent monetary policy, increased exposure of the economy to shocks from the anchor country, and the inability of the central bank to create money and act as a lender of last resort). Dollarization has one additional weakness not characteristic of currency boards or other exchange-rate target regimes. Because a country adopting dollarization no longer has its own currency, it loses the revenue that a government receives by issuing money, which is called **seignorage**. Because governments (or their central banks) do not have to pay interest on their domestic currency, they earn revenue (seignorage) by using this currency to purchase income-earning assets such as bonds. In the case of the Federal Reserve in the United States, this revenue is usually in excess of $30 billion per year. If an emerging market country dollarizes and gives up its currency, it needs to make up this loss of revenue somehow, and this is not always easy for a poor country.

SUMMARY

1. An unsterilized central bank intervention in which the domestic currency is sold to purchase foreign assets leads to a gain in international reserves, an increase in the money supply, and a depreciation of the domestic currency. Available evidence suggests, however, that sterilized central bank interventions have little long-term effect on the exchange rate.

2. The balance of payments is a bookkeeping system used to record all payments that have a direct bearing on the movement of funds between a country and foreign countries. The official reserve transactions balance is the sum of the current account balance plus the items in the capital account. It indicates the amount of international reserves that must be moved between countries to finance international transactions.

3. Before World War I, the gold standard was predominant. Currencies were convertible into gold, thus fixing exchange rates between them. After World War II, the

Bretton Woods system and the IMF were established to promote a fixed exchange rate system in which the U.S. dollar, the reserve currency, was convertible into gold. The Bretton Woods system collapsed in 1971. We now have an international financial system that has elements of a managed float and a fixed exchange rate system. Some exchange rates fluctuate from day to day, even though central banks intervene in the foreign exchange market, while other exchange rates are fixed.

4. Controls on capital outflows receive support because they may prevent domestic residents and foreigners from pulling capital out of a country during a crisis and thereby make devaluation less likely. Controls on capital inflows make sense under the theory that, if speculative capital cannot flow in, then it also cannot go out suddenly. Thus a crisis is averted. However, capital controls suffer from several disadvantages:

They are seldom effective, they often lead to corruption, and they may encourage governments to avoid taking the steps that are necessary to reform their financial systems to deal with the crisis.

5. The IMF's role as an international lender of last resort can help lessen the severity of financial crises. However, the IMF's role as an international lender of last resort also creates serious moral hazard problems because it encourages governments to be profligate and also encourages excessive risk taking by financial institutions, making a financial crisis more likely.

6. Three international considerations affect the conduct of monetary policy: direct effects of the foreign exchange market on monetary policy, balance-of-payments considerations, and exchange rate considerations. Inasmuch as the United States has been a reserve currency country in the post–World War II period, U.S. monetary policy has been less affected than that of other countries by developments in the foreign exchange market and its balance of payments. However, in recent years, exchange rate considerations have played a more prominent role in influencing U.S. monetary policy.

7. Exchange-rate targeting has the following advantages as a monetary policy strategy: (1) It directly keeps inflation under control by tying the inflation rate for internationally traded goods to that found in the anchor country to which the targeting country's currency is pegged; (2) it provides an automatic rule for the conduct of monetary policy that helps mitigate the time-inconsistency problem; and (3) it is simple and clear. Exchange-rate targeting also has some serious disadvantages: (1) It results in a loss of independent monetary policy in the pegging country; (2) it leaves the pegging country open to speculative attacks; and (3) it can weaken the accountability of policymakers because the exchange rate signal is lost. Two strategies that make it less likely that the exchange rate regime will break down are currency boards, in which the central bank stands ready to automatically exchange domestic currency for foreign currency at a fixed rate, and dollarization, in which a sound currency like the U.S. dollar is adopted as a country's money.

KEY TERMS

anchor currency, p. 433
balance of payments, p. 431
balance-of-payments crisis, p. 438
Bretton Woods system, p. 434
capital account, p. 432
capital controls, p. 439
currency board, p. 449
current account, p. 432
devaluation, p. 436
dollarization, p. 451
emerging market countries, p. 442
exchange-rate peg, p. 445

exchange-rate targeting, p. 445
fixed exchange rate regime, p. 433
floating exchange rate regime, p. 433
foreign exchange interventions, p. 427
gold standard, p. 433
impossible trinity, p. 439
International Monetary Fund (IMF), p. 434
international reserves, p. 427
managed float regime (dirty float), p. 433
monetary (or currency) union, p. 440
official reserve transactions balance, p. 432
policy trilemma, p. 439

reserve currency, p. 434
revaluation, p. 436
seignorage, p. 451
speculative attack, p. 436
sterilized foreign exchange intervention, p. 430
trade balance, p. 432
unsterilized foreign exchange intervention, p. 429
World Bank, p. 434
World Trade Organization (WTO), p. 434

QUESTIONS

All questions are available in MyEconLab at http://www.myeconlab.com.

1. If the Federal Reserve buys dollars in the foreign exchange market but conducts an offsetting open market operation to sterilize the intervention, what will be the impact on international reserves, the money supply, and the exchange rate?

2. If the Federal Reserve buys dollars in the foreign exchange market but does not sterilize the intervention, what will be the impact on international reserves, the money supply, and the exchange rate?

3. For each of the following, identify in which part of the balance-of-payments account the transaction is recorded (current account, capital account, or net change in international reserves) and whether it is a receipt or a payment.

a. A British subject's purchase of a share of Johnson & Johnson stock

b. An American citizen's purchase of an airline ticket from Air France

c. The Swiss government's purchase of U.S. Treasury bills

d. A Japanese citizen's purchase of California oranges

e. $50 million of foreign aid to Honduras

f. A loan by an American bank to Mexico

g. An American bank's borrowing of Eurodollars

4. Why does a balance-of-payments deficit for the United States have a different effect on its international reserves than a balance-of-payments deficit for the Netherlands?

5. How can a large balance-of-payments surplus contribute to a country's inflation rate?

6. Why can balance-of-payments deficits force some countries to implement contractionary monetary policies?

7. Under the gold standard, if Britain became more productive relative to the United States, what would happen to the money supply in the two countries? Why would the changes in the money supply help preserve a fixed exchange rate between the United States and Britain?

8. What is the exchange rate between dollars and Swiss francs if one dollar is convertible into 1/20 ounce of gold and one Swiss franc is convertible into 1/40 ounce of gold?

9. "Inflation is not possible under the gold standard." Is this statement true, false, or uncertain? Explain your answer.

10. What are some of the disadvantages of China's pegging the yuan to the dollar?

11. If a country's par exchange rate was undervalued during the Bretton Woods fixed exchange rate regime, what kind of intervention would that country's central bank be forced to undertake, and what effect would the intervention have on the country's international reserves and money supply?

12. "The abandonment of fixed exchange rates after 1973 has led countries to pursue more independent monetary policies." Is this statement true, false, or uncertain? Explain your answer.

13. "If a country wants to keep its exchange rate from changing, it must give up some control over its money supply." Is this statement true, false, or uncertain? Explain your answer.

14. Why is it that in a pure, flexible exchange rate system, the foreign exchange market has no direct effect on the money supply? Does this mean that the foreign exchange market has no effect on monetary policy?

15. Why did the exchange-rate peg lead to difficulties for the countries in the ERM after the German reunification?

16. How can exchange-rate targets lead to a speculative attack on a currency?

17. What are the advantages and disadvantages of having the IMF as an international lender of last resort?

18. How can the long-term bond market help reduce the time-inconsistency problem for monetary policy? Can the foreign exchange market also perform this role?

19. "Balance-of-payments deficits always cause a country to lose international reserves." Is this statement true, false, or uncertain? Explain your answer.

20. How can persistent U.S. balance-of-payments deficits stimulate world inflation?

21. What are the key advantages of exchange-rate targeting as a monetary policy strategy?

22. When is exchange-rate targeting likely to be a sensible strategy for industrialized countries? When is exchange-rate targeting likely to be a sensible strategy for emerging market countries?

23. What are the advantages and disadvantages of currency boards and dollarization over a monetary policy that uses only an exchange-rate target?

APPLIED PROBLEMS

All applied problems are available in MyEconLab *at* http://www.myeconlab.com.

24. Suppose the Federal Reserve purchases $1,000,000 worth of foreign assets.

a. If the Federal Reserve purchases the foreign assets with $1,000,000 in currency, show the effect of this open market operation, using T-accounts. What happens to the monetary base?

   b. If the Federal Reserve purchases the foreign assets by selling $1,000,000 in T-bills, show the effect of this open market operation, using T-accounts. What happens to the monetary base?

25. Suppose the Mexican central bank chooses to peg the peso to the U.S. dollar and commits to a fixed peso/dollar exchange rate. Use a graph of the market for peso assets (foreign exchange) to show and explain how the peg must be maintained if a shock in the U.S. economy forces the Fed to pursue contractionary monetary policy. What does this say about the ability of central banks to address domestic economic problems while maintaining a pegged exchange rate?

DATA ANALYSIS PROBLEMS

The Problems update with real-time data in MyEconLab *and are available for practice or instructor assignment.*

1. Go to the St. Louis Federal Reserve FRED database, and find data on the capital account (BOPCAT) and the current account (BOPBCA). Calculate the net change in government international reserves for the most recent quarter of data available and for the same quarter five years prior. What do the numbers imply about the net wealth of the United States relative to the net wealth of the rest of the world? How does the fact that the dollar is used as an international reserve currency affect your interpretation?

2. Go to the St. Louis Federal Reserve FRED database, and find data on the monthly U.S. dollar exchange rate to the Chinese yuan (EXCHUS), the Canadian dollar (EXCAUS), and the South Korean won (EXKOUS). Download the data into a spreadsheet.

   a. For the most recent five-year period of data available, use the average, max, min, and stdev functions in Excel to calculate the average, highest, and lowest exchange rate values, as well as the standard deviation of the exchange rate to the dollar (this is an absolute measure of the volatility of the exchange rate).

   b. Using the maximum and minimum values of each exchange rate over the last five years, calculate the ratio of the difference between the maximum and minimum values to the average level of the exchange rate (expressed as a percentage by multiplying by 100). This value gives an indication of how tightly the exchange rate moves. Based on your results, which of the three countries is most likely to peg its currency to the U.S. dollar? How does this country's currency compare with the other two?

   c. Calculate the ratio of the standard deviation to the average exchange rate over the last five years (expressed as a percentage by multiplying by 100). This value gives an indication of how volatile the exchange rate is. Based on your results, which of the three currencies is most likely to be pegged to the U.S. dollar? How does this currency compare with the other two?

WEB EXERCISES

1. The International Monetary Fund stands ready to help nations facing monetary crises. Go to http://www.imf.org. Click on the tab labeled "About the IMF." What is the stated purpose of the IMF? How many nations participate, and when was it established?

WEB REFERENCES

http://research.stlouisfed.org/fred2

This website contains exchange rates, balance of payments data, and trade data.

http://www.imf.org/

Find information about the structure and operations of the International Monetary Fund.

Monetary Theory

Crisis and Response: The Perfect Storm of 2007–2009

In 2007 and 2008, the U.S. economy was hit by a perfect storm of formidable shocks. By the end of 2007, oil prices had risen from $60 per barrel at the beginning of the year to $100, reaching a peak of over $140 per barrel in July 2008. The oil price shock was both contractionary and inflationary, and as a result led to both higher inflation and higher unemployment—not to mention many unhappy drivers at the gas pumps.

If this supply shock were not bad enough, the global financial crisis hit the economy starting in August 2007 and caused a contraction in both household and business spending. This shock led to a further rise in unemployment, with some weakening of inflationary pressure further down the road.

The result of this perfect storm of adverse shocks was the most severe economic contraction since the Great Depression, with unemployment rising from the 4.6% level in 2006 and 2007 to the 10% level by the end of 2009. Inflation also accelerated from 2.5% in 2006 to over 5% by the middle of 2008, but with the increase in the unemployment rate and the decline of oil and other commodity prices by the fall of 2008, inflation rapidly came back down again.

Although the Fed's aggressive monetary policy attempted to address the contractionary forces in the economy, lawmakers wanted additional action. In February 2008 and then again in February 2009, the U.S. Congress passed economic stimulus packages, first of $150 billion and then of $787 billion. However, although both stimulus packages helped boost GDP, they were overwhelmed by the continued worsening of the financial crisis, and the economy went into a tailspin.

The impact of the perfect storm of adverse shocks highlights the need to understand how monetary and other government policies affect inflation and economic activity. Chapter 19 discusses how the quantity theory of money explains inflation in the long run and how theories of the demand for money have evolved. Aggregate supply and demand analysis, the basic framework that will enable us to study the effects of monetary policy on output and inflation, is then developed in Chapters 20–23. In Chapter 24, we expand on aggregate supply and demand analysis in order to understand how monetary policy can be used to stabilize the economy and inflation. Chapter 25 outlines the transmission mechanisms through which monetary policy affects the aggregate economy.

19 Quantity Theory, Inflation, and the Demand for Money

Learning Objectives

- Assess the relationship between money growth and inflation in the short run and the long run, as implied by the quantity theory of money.
- Identify the circumstances under which budget deficits can lead to inflationary monetary policy.
- Summarize the three motives underlying the liquidity preference theory of money demand.
- Identify the factors underlying the portfolio choice theory of money demand.
- Assess and interpret the empirical evidence on the validity of the liquidity preference and portfolio theories of money demand.

Preview

In earlier chapters, we spent a lot of time and effort learning what the money supply is, how it is determined, and what part the Federal Reserve System plays in it. Now we are ready to explore the role of the money supply and monetary policy in determining inflation and total production of goods and services (aggregate output) in the economy. The study of the effects of money and monetary policy on the economy is called **monetary theory**, and we examine this branch of economics in the chapters of Part 6.

When economists mention *supply*, the word *demand* is sure to follow, and the discussion of money is no exception. Understanding the supply of money is an essential building block in understanding how monetary policy affects the economy, because understanding the supply of money suggests the factors that influences the quantity of money in the economy. Not surprisingly, another essential part of monetary theory is the demand for money.

After discussing the quantity theory of money and its link to the demand for money, we delve more deeply into the factors that determine the demand for money. A central question in monetary theory is whether or to what extent the quantity of money demanded is affected by changes in interest rates. Because this issue is crucial to how we view money's effects on aggregate economic activity, we will focus on the role of interest rates in the demand for money.

QUANTITY THEORY OF MONEY

Developed by the classical economists in the nineteenth and early twentieth centuries, the quantity theory of money explains how the nominal value of aggregate income is determined. Because the theory also tells us how much money is held for a given amount of aggregate income, it is a theory of the demand for money. The most important feature of this theory is that it suggests that interest rates have no effect on the demand for money.

Velocity of Money and Equation of Exchange

The clearest exposition of the classical quantity theory approach is found in the work of the American economist Irving Fisher, in his influential book *The Purchasing Power of*

Money, published in 1911. Fisher wanted to examine the link between the total quantity of money M (the money supply) and the total amount of spending on final goods and services produced in the economy $P \times Y$, where P is the price level and Y is aggregate output (income). (Total spending $P \times Y$ is also thought of as aggregate nominal income for the economy or as nominal GDP.) The concept that provides the link between M and $P \times Y$ is called the **velocity of money** (often abbreviated to *velocity*), the average number of times per year (turnover) that a dollar is spent in buying the total amount of goods and services produced in the economy. Velocity V is defined more precisely as total spending $P \times Y$ divided by the quantity of money M:

$$V = \frac{P \times Y}{M} \tag{1}$$

If, for example, nominal GDP ($P \times Y$) in a year is $10 trillion and the quantity of money (M) is $2 trillion, we can calculate velocity as follows:

$$V = \frac{\$10 \text{ trillion}}{\$2 \text{ trillion}} = 5$$

The value of 5 for velocity means that the average dollar bill is spent five times in purchasing final goods and services in the economy.

By multiplying both sides of Equation 1 by M, we obtain the **equation of exchange**, which relates nominal income to the quantity of money and velocity:

$$M \times V = P \times Y \tag{2}$$

The equation of exchange thus states that the quantity of money multiplied by the number of times this money is spent in a given year must equal nominal income (the total nominal amount spent on goods and services in that year).[1]

As it stands, Equation 2 is nothing more than an identity—a relationship that is true by definition. It does not tell us, for instance, that when the money supply M changes, nominal income ($P \times Y$) changes in the same direction; a rise in M, for example, might be offset by a fall in V, leaving $M \times V$ (and therefore $P \times Y$) unchanged. To convert the equation of exchange (an *identity*) into a *theory* of how nominal income is determined, we must first understand the factors that determine velocity.

Determinants of Velocity
Irving Fisher reasoned that velocity is determined by the institutions within an economy that affect the ways in which individuals conduct transactions. If people use charge accounts and credit cards to conduct their transactions, as they often do today, and consequently use money less often when making purchases, less money is required to conduct the transactions generated by nominal income

---

[1]Fisher actually first formulated the equation of exchange in terms of the nominal value of transactions in the economy PT:

$$MV_T = PT$$

where P = average price per transaction
          T = number of transactions conducted in a year
          $V_T = PT/M$ = transactions velocity of money

Because the nominal value of transactions T is difficult to measure, the quantity theory has been formulated in terms of aggregate output Y as follows: T is assumed to be proportional to Y so that $T = vY$, where v is a constant of proportionality. Substituting vY for T in Fisher's equation of exchange yields $MV_T = vPY$, which can be written as Equation 2 in the text, in which $V = V_T/v$.

(M falls relative to $P \times Y$), and so velocity $(P \times Y)/M$ increases. Conversely, if it is more convenient for purchases to be paid for with cash, checks, or debit cards (all of which are money), more money is used to conduct the transactions generated by the same level of nominal income, and so velocity falls. Fisher took the view that the institutional and technological features of the economy would affect velocity only slowly over time, so velocity would normally be reasonably constant in the short run.

Demand for Money   Fisher's quantity theory can also be interpreted in terms of the **demand for money**, the quantity of money that people want to hold.

Because the quantity theory of money tells us how much money is held for a given amount of nominal spending, it is, in fact, a theory of the demand for money. To illustrate, let's first divide both sides of the equation of exchange (Equation 2) by V to yield the following:

$$M = \frac{1}{V} \times PY$$

When the money market is in equilibrium, money supply equals money demand, so we can replace M in the equation by M^d. In addition, since velocity is assumed to be constant in the quantity theory of money, we can replace $1/V$ with a constant k. Substituting k for $1/V$ and M^d for M, we can rewrite the equation as

$$M^d = k \times PY \tag{3}$$

Equation 3 tells us that because k is constant, the level of transactions generated by a fixed level of nominal income PY determines the quantity of money M^d that people will demand. Therefore, Fisher's theory suggests that the demand for money is purely a function of income, and interest rates have no effect on the demand for money.[2]

From the Equation of Exchange to the Quantity Theory of Money

Fisher's view that velocity is fairly constant in the short run, so that $V = \overline{V}$ transforms the equation of exchange into the **quantity theory of money**, which states that nominal income (spending) is determined solely by movements in the quantity of money M.

$$P \times Y = M \times \overline{V} \tag{4}$$

The quantity theory equation above indicates that when the quantity of money M doubles, $M \times \overline{V}$ doubles, and so must $P \times Y$, the value of nominal income. To illustrate, let's assume that velocity is 5, nominal income (GDP) is initially $10 trillion, and the money supply is $2 trillion. If the money supply doubles to $4 trillion, the quantity theory of money suggests that nominal income will double to $20 trillion ($= 5 \times \$4$ trillion).

---

[2]While Fisher was developing his quantity theory approach to the demand for money, a group of classical economists in Cambridge, England, led by Alfred Marshall and A. C. Pigou, came to similar conclusions, although via slightly different reasoning. They derived Equation 3 by recognizing that two properties of money motivate people to hold it: its utility as a medium of exchange, and its value as a store of wealth.

Quantity Theory and the Price Level

Because the classical economists (including Fisher) thought that wages and prices were completely flexible, they believed that the level of aggregate output Y produced in the economy during normal times would remain at the full-employment level. Hence Y in the equation of exchange could be treated as reasonably constant in the short run and thus could be assigned a fixed value of $\overline{Y}$ in Equation 4. Dividing both sides of Equation 4 by $\overline{Y}$, we can write the price level as follows:

$$P = \frac{M \times \overline{V}}{\overline{Y}} \tag{5}$$

The quantity theory of money as represented by Equation 5 implies that if M doubles, P must also double in the short run, because $\overline{V}$ and $\overline{Y}$ are constant. In our example, if aggregate output is \$10 trillion, velocity is 5, and the money supply is \$2 trillion, then the price level equals 1.0.

$$P = \frac{\$2 \text{ trillion} \times 5}{\$10 \text{ trillion}} = \frac{\$10 \text{ trillion}}{\$10 \text{ trillion}} = 1.0$$

When the money supply doubles to \$4 trillion, the price level must also double, to 2.0, because

$$P = \frac{\$4 \text{ trillion} \times 5}{\$10 \text{ trillion}} = \frac{\$20 \text{ trillion}}{\$10 \text{ trillion}} = 2.0$$

Classical economists relied on the quantity theory of money to explain movements in the price level. In their view, **changes in the quantity of money lead to proportional changes in the price level.**

Quantity Theory and Inflation

We now transform the quantity theory of money into a theory of inflation. You might recall from high school the mathematical fact that the percentage change ($\%\Delta$) of a product of two variables is approximately equal to the sum of the percentage changes of the individual variables. In other words,

$$\text{Percentage Change in } (x \times y) = (\text{Percentage Change in } x)$$
$$+ (\text{Percentage Change in } y)$$

Using this mathematical fact, we can rewrite the equation of exchange as follows:

$$\%\Delta M + \%\Delta V = \%\Delta P + \%\Delta Y$$

Subtracting $\%\Delta Y$ from both sides of the preceding equation, and recognizing that the inflation rate π is equal to the growth rate of the price level $\%\Delta P$, we can write:

$$\pi = \%\Delta P = \%\Delta M + \%\Delta V - \%\Delta Y$$

Since we assume velocity is constant, its growth rate is zero, and so the quantity theory of money is also a theory of inflation:

$$\pi = \%\Delta M - \%\Delta Y \tag{6}$$

Because the percentage change in a variable at an annual rate is the same as the growth rate of that variable, Equation 6 can be stated in words as follows: ***the quantity theory of inflation indicates that the inflation rate equals the growth rate of the money supply minus the growth rate of aggregate output.*** For example, if the aggregate output is growing at 3% per year and the growth rate of money is 5%, then inflation is 2% (= 5% − 3%). If the Federal Reserve increases the money growth rate to 10%, then the quantity theory of inflation given by Equation 6 indicates that the inflation rate will rise to 7% (= 10% − 3%).

APPLICATION   Testing the Quantity Theory of Money

Now that we have fully outlined the quantity theory of money, let's put it to the test with actual data over the long and short runs.

The Quantity Theory of Money in the Long Run   The quantity theory of money provides a long-run theory of inflation because it is based on the assumption that wages and prices are flexible. Panel (a) of Figure 1 plots ten-year averages of U.S. inflation rates against the ten-year average rate of U.S. money growth (M2) from 1870 through 2013. Because the growth rate of aggregate output Y over ten-year periods does not vary very much, Equation 6 indicates that the ten-year inflation rate should be the ten-year money growth rate minus a constant (the rate of aggregate output growth). Thus a strong positive relationship should exist between inflation and money growth rates—and this relationship is borne out in panel (a). Decades with higher growth rates of the U.S. money supply typically see higher average inflation rates.

Does the quantity theory also explain differing long-run inflation rates across countries? It certainly does. Panel (b) of Figure 1 plots the average inflation rate over the ten-year period from 2003 to 2013 against the ten-year money growth rate for several countries. Note that countries with high money growth rates, such as Turkey, Ukraine, and Zambia, tend to have higher inflation rates.

The Quantity Theory of Money in the Short Run   Does the quantity theory of money provide a good explanation of short-run inflation fluctuations as well? Figure 2 provides evidence of the link between money growth and inflation in the short run by plotting the annual U.S. inflation rate from 1965 to 2014 against the annual money (M2) growth rate from two years before. (The money growth rate lags by two years to allow for the time it takes for changes in money growth to affect inflation.) The relationship between inflation and money growth on an annual basis is not strong at all. There were many years—such as 1963–1967, 1985–1986, 2003–2005, 2010–2011, and 2013–2014—in which money growth was high but inflation was low. Indeed, it is hard to see any positive correlation at all between money growth and inflation in Figure 2.

The conclusion from that data given in Figure 2 is that ***the quantity theory of money is a good theory of inflation in the long run but not in the short run.*** We could also say that ***Milton Friedman's statement that "inflation is always and everywhere a monetary phenomenon" (mentioned in Chapter 1) is accurate in the long run, but is not supported by the data for the short run.*** This insight tells us that the classical assumption that wages and prices are completely flexible may not apply in the case of short-run fluctuations in inflation and aggregate output. For this reason, we relax this assumption in the following chapters of the book when we develop models of short-run inflation and output fluctuations. ◆

MyEconLab Mini-lecture

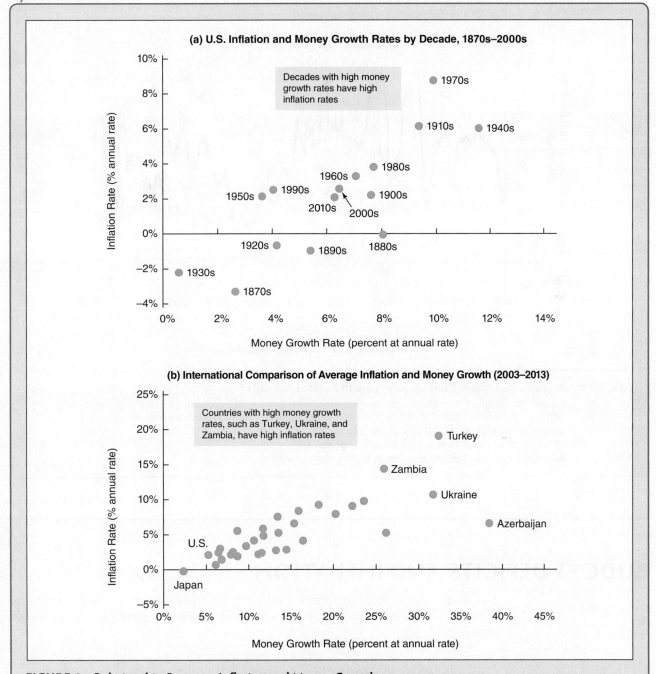

FIGURE 1 **Relationship Between Inflation and Money Growth**
In panel (a), decades with higher money growth rates (the 1910s, the 1940s, and the 1970s) typically have a higher average inflation rate. This relationship also holds in panel (b), where we examine the ten-year inflation and money growth rates from 2003–2013 for various countries.

Sources: For panel (a), Milton Friedman and Anna Schwartz, Monetary Trends in the United States and the United Kingdom: Their Relation to Income, Prices, and Interest Rates, 1867–1975; Federal Reserve Bank of St. Louis, FRED database: http://research.stlouisfed .org/fred2/. For panel (b), International Financial Statistics. International Monetary Fund, http://www.imfstatistics.org/imf/.

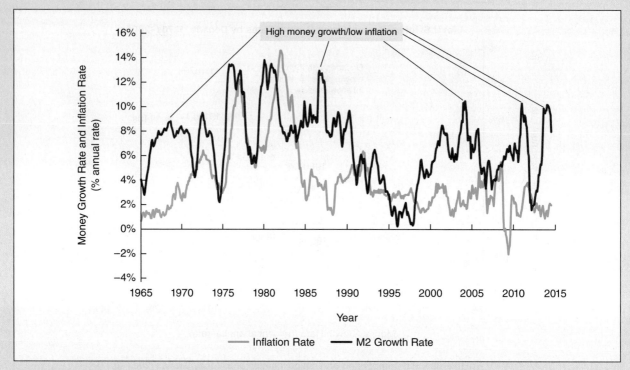

FIGURE 2 **Annual U.S. Inflation and Money Growth Rates, 1965–2013**

Plots of the annual U.S. inflation rate against the annual money (M2) growth rate from two years earlier (to allow for lag effects from money growth to inflation) do not support a short-run link between inflation and money growth. There were many years (1963–1967, 1983–1985, 2001–2002, 2008–2009, and 2011–2012) in which money growth was high yet inflation was low.

Sources: Federal Reserve Bank of St. Louis, FRED database: http://research.stlouisfed.org/fred2/.

BUDGET DEFICITS AND INFLATION

Budget deficits can be an important source of inflationary monetary policy. To see why this is the case, we need to look at the ways in which a government finances its budget deficits.

Government Budget Constraint

Because the government has to pay its bills just as we do, it has a budget constraint. We can pay for our spending in two ways: we can raise revenue (by working), or we can borrow. The government also enjoys these two options: it can raise revenue by levying taxes, or it can go into debt by issuing government bonds. Unlike us, however, it has a third option: The government can create money and use it to pay for the goods and services it buys.

The methods used to finance government spending are described by an expression called the **government budget constraint**, which states the following: The government budget deficit *DEF*, which equals the excess of government spending *G* over tax revenue *T*, must equal the sum of the change in the monetary base ΔMB and the change in government bonds held by the public ΔB. Algebraically, this expression can be written as follows:

$$DEF = G - T = \Delta MB + \Delta B \tag{7}$$

To see what the government budget constraint means in practice, let's look at the case in which the only government purchase is a $100 million supercomputer. If the government convinces the electorate that such a computer is worth paying for, it will probably be able to raise the $100 million in taxes to pay for it, and the budget deficit will equal zero. According to the government budget constraint, no issue of money or bonds is needed to pay for the computer because the budget is balanced. If taxpayers think the supercomputer is too expensive and refuse to pay taxes to sponsor its purchase, the budget constraint indicates that the government must pay for the computer by selling $100 million of new bonds to the public or by, in effect, printing $100 million of currency. In either case, the budget constraint is satisfied. The $100 million deficit is balanced by the change in the stock of government bonds held by the public (ΔB = $100 million) or by the change in the monetary base (ΔMB = $100 million).

The government budget constraint thus reveals two important facts: *If the government deficit is financed by an increase in bond holdings by the public, there is no effect on the monetary base and hence no effect on the money supply. But if the deficit is not financed by increased bond holdings by the public, both the monetary base and the money supply increase.*

There are several ways to understand why a deficit leads to an increase in the monetary base when the public's bond holdings do not increase. The simplest case is the case in which a government's treasury has the legal right to issue currency to finance its deficit. Financing the deficit is then very straightforward: The government just pays for the spending that is in excess of its tax revenues by issuing new currency. Because this increase in currency adds directly to the monetary base, the monetary base rises, and the money supply rises with it through the process of multiple deposit creation described in Chapter 14.

In the United States, however, and in many other countries, the government does not have the right to issue currency to pay for its bills. In this case, the government must finance its deficit by first issuing bonds to the public. If these bonds do not actually end up in the hands of the public, however, the only alternative is for the central bank to purchase them. To keep the newly-issued government bonds from ending up in the hands of the public, the central bank must conduct an open market purchase, which, as we saw in Chapter 14, leads to an increase in the monetary base and in the money supply. This method of financing government spending is called **monetizing the debt** because, as indicated by the two-step process just described, government debt issued to finance government spending has been removed from the hands of the public and has been replaced by high-powered money. This method of financing is somewhat inaccurately referred to as **printing money** because high-powered money (the monetary base) is created in the process. The use of the word *printing* is misleading because no new currency is actually printed; instead, the monetary base increases when the central bank conducts open market purchases, just as it would increase if more currency were put into circulation.

We thus see that a budget deficit can lead to an increase in the money supply if it is financed by the creation of high-powered money. However, because the quantity theory of money explains inflation only in the long run, in order to produce inflation, the budget deficit must be *persistent*—that is, it must last for a substantial period of time. This leads us to the following conclusion: ***The financing of a persistent deficit by means of money creation will lead to sustained inflation.***

Hyperinflation

The analysis here can be used to explain **hyperinflations**, periods of extremely high inflation of more than 50% per month. Many economies—both poor and developed—have experienced hyperinflation over the past century, but the United States has been spared such turmoil. One of the most extreme examples of hyperinflation throughout world history occurred in Zimbabwe in the 2000s, and it is discussed in the application that follows.

APPLICATION | # The Zimbabwean Hyperinflation

We now use our analysis of the quantity theory of money to explain the Zimbabwean hyperinflation that started in the early 2000s.

After the government expropriation of farms in 2000, which were redistributed to supporters of Robert Mugabe, the president of the country, Zimbabwean agricultural output plummeted, and, along with it, tax revenue. As a result, the government's expenditures now massively exceeded revenues. The government could have obtained revenues to cover its expenditures by raising taxes, but given the depressed state of the economy, generating revenue in this way was both hard to do and would have been politically unpopular. Alternatively, the government could have tried to finance its expenditure by borrowing from the public, but given the public's distrust of the government, this was not an option. There was only one route left: the printing press. The government could pay for its expenditures by simply printing more currency (increasing the money supply) and using it to make payments to individuals and businesses. This is exactly what the Zimbabwean government did, and the money supply began to increase rapidly.

As predicted by the quantity theory, the surge in the money supply led to a rapidly rising price level. In February 2007, the Reserve Bank of Zimbabwe, the central bank, outlawed price increases on many commodities. Although this tactic has been tried before by governments in countries experiencing hyperinflations, it has never worked: Criminalizing inflation cannot stop inflation when the central bank keeps on printing money. In March 2007, the inflation rate hit a record of over 1,500%. By 2008, Zimbabwe's official inflation rate was officially over 2 million percent (but unofficially over 10 million percent). In July 2008, the Zimbabwean central bank issued a new $100 billion bank note and shortly later issued a $100 trillion dollar bill, the highest denomination dollar note on record. That's a lot of zeros, but don't be too impressed. Although holding one of these bills made you a trillionaire, such a bill could not even buy you a bottle of beer. Zimbabwean currency became worth less than toilet paper.

In 2009, the Zimbabwean government allowed the use of foreign currencies like the U.S. dollar for all transactions, but the damage had already been done. The hyperinflation wreaked havoc on the economy, and an extremely poor country became even poorer. ◆

KEYNESIAN THEORIES OF MONEY DEMAND

In his famous 1936 book *The General Theory of Employment, Interest and Money*, John Maynard Keynes abandoned the quantity theory view that velocity is a constant and developed a theory of money demand that emphasized the importance of interest rates. In his theory of the demand for money, which he called the **liquidity preference theory**, Keynes presented three motives behind the demand for money: the transactions motive, the precautionary motive, and the speculative motive.

Transactions Motive

In the quantity theory approach, individuals are assumed to hold money because it is a medium of exchange that can be used to carry out everyday transactions. Keynes initially accepted the quantity theory view that the transactions component is proportional to income. Later, he and other economists recognized that new methods of payment, referred to as **payment technology**, could also affect the demand for money. For example, credit cards enable consumers to make even very small purchases without needing to hold money. Electronic payments that can be made from investors' brokerage accounts also reduce money demand. In Keynes's view, as payment technology advanced, the demand for money would be likely to decline relative to income.

Precautionary Motive

Keynes also recognized that people hold money as a cushion against unexpected opportunities. Suppose you have been thinking about buying a new Wii entertainment system and now see that it is on sale at 25% off. If you are holding money as a precaution for just such an occurrence, you can immediately buy it. Keynes argued that the precautionary money balances people would want to hold would also be proportional to income.

Speculative Motive

Keynes also believed that people choose to hold money as a store of wealth, which he called the *speculative motive*. Because the definition of money in Keynes's analysis includes currency (which earns no interest) and checking account deposits (which typically earn little interest), he assumed that money earns no interest and hence its opportunity cost relative to holding other assets, such as bonds, is the nominal interest rate on bonds, i. As the interest rate i rises, the opportunity cost of money rises (it becomes more costly to hold money relative to bonds), and the quantity of money demanded falls.

Putting the Three Motives Together

In combining the three motives for holding money balances into a demand-for-money equation, Keynes was careful to distinguish between nominal quantities and real quantities. Money is valued in terms of what it can buy. If, for example, all prices in the economy doubled (the price level doubled), the same nominal quantity of money would be able to buy only half as many goods. Keynes thus reasoned that people want to hold a certain amount of **real money balances** (the quantity of money in real terms). By combining the three motives for holding money balances into a demand for real money balances, Keynes formulated what is called the liquidity preference function, which is written as follows:

$$\frac{M^d}{P} = L(\underset{-}{i}, \underset{+}{Y}) \tag{8}$$

Equation 8 states that the demand for real money balances is negatively related to the nominal interest rate and is positively related with real income.

Later Keynesian economists, such as Nobel Prize winner James Tobin, expanded the analysis and showed that interest rates play a more important role in money demand than even Keynes supposed. These economists demonstrated that even the transactions and precautionary demands for money would be negatively related to the interest rate.[3]

An important implication of Keynesian theories of money demand is that velocity is not a constant but will fluctuate with changes in interest rates. To illustrate, we write the liquidity preference function as follows:

$$\frac{P}{M^d} = \frac{1}{L(i,Y)}$$

Multiplying both sides of this equation by Y and recognizing that we can replace M^d by M (because they must be equal in money market equilibrium), we can solve for velocity:

$$V = \frac{PY}{M} = \frac{Y}{L(i,Y)} \tag{9}$$

We know that the demand for money is negatively related to interest rates; when i goes up, $L(i,Y)$ declines, and therefore velocity rises. Because interest rates undergo substantial fluctuations, Keynesian theories of the demand for money indicate that velocity undergoes substantial fluctuations as well. Thus Keynesian theories cast doubt on the classical quantity theory view that nominal income is determined primarily by movements in the quantity of money.

PORTFOLIO THEORIES OF MONEY DEMAND

Related to Keynes's analysis of the demand for money are so-called portfolio theories of money demand, in which people decide how much of an asset such as money they want to hold as part of their overall portfolio of assets.[4]

---

[3]Three famous papers that elaborated on Keynes's approach to the demand for money are as follows: William J. Baumol, "The Transactions Demand for Cash: An Inventory Theoretic Approach," *Quarterly Journal of Economics* 66 (1952): 545–556; James Tobin, "The Interest Elasticity of the Transactions Demand for Cash," *Review of Economics and Statistics* 38 (1956): 241–247; and James Tobin, "Liquidity Preference as Behavior Towards Risk," *Review of Economic Studies* 25 (1958): 65–86. For further discussion of the models outlined in these papers, see the first appendix to this chapter, which can be found on the Companion Website at http://www.pearsonhighered.com/mishkin.

[4]This is the approach taken by Milton Friedman in his famous paper, "The Quantity Theory of Money: A Restatement," in *Studies in the Quantity Theory of Money*, ed. Milton Friedman (Chicago: University of Chicago Press, 1956), 3–21.

Theory of Portfolio Choice and Keynesian Liquidity Preference

In Chapter 5, we developed the theory of portfolio choice, which stated that the demand for an asset is positively related to wealth, the expected return on the asset relative to other assets, and relative liquidity, whereas it is negatively related to its risk relative to other assets. This theory of portfolio choice can justify the conclusion from the Keynesian liquidity preference function that the demand for real money balances is positively related to income and negatively related to the nominal interest rate.

Because income and wealth tend to move together, when income is higher, wealth is likely to be as well. Hence, higher income means greater wealth, and the theory of portfolio choice then indicates that the demand for the money assets will rise and the demand for real money balances will be higher.

As interest rates rise, the expected return on money does not change. However, the return on bonds, an alternative asset, goes up. Thus, although the expected *absolute* return on money did not change, money's expected return *relative* to bonds went down. In other words, as the theory of portfolio choice indicates, higher interest rates make money less desirable, and the demand for real money balances falls.

Other Factors That Affect the Demand for Money

The theory of portfolio choice indicates that other factors besides income and the nominal interest rate can affect the demand for money. We look at each of these in turn.

Wealth   The theory of portfolio choice posits that as wealth increases, investors have more resources with which to purchase assets, increasing the demand for money. However, when income is held constant, greater wealth has only a small effect on the demand for money. In general, investors will hold only a small amount of money in their investment portfolio, preferring interest-bearing assets with similar risk and liquidity profiles, such as money market mutual funds, that are not included in measures of money such as M1. Currency and checkable deposits are sometimes said to be **dominated assets**, because investors can hold other assets that pay higher returns and yet are perceived to be just as safe.

Risk   It's hard to imagine an asset less risky than money. Currency will always be accepted, unless there's a revolution and the new government does not accept the old government's currency. And bank deposits are safe as long as deposit insurance exists. In the theory of portfolio choice, however, risk is always measured relative to another asset. Thus, if the stock market becomes more volatile, money can become less risky relative to stocks and demand for it will increase. In addition, although money is extremely safe on a nominal basis, its real return (the nominal return minus expected inflation) can become highly variable when inflation becomes very variable. Higher variability in the real return of money lowers the demand for money, as people shift into alternative assets known as **inflation hedges**, whose real returns are less affected than that of money when inflation varies. Popular inflation hedges include TIPS (Treasury Inflation Protected Securities), gold, and real estate.

Liquidity of Other Assets   In recent years, financial innovation has led to the development of new liquid assets, such as money market mutual funds or home equity lines of credit, that allow households to write checks that are backed by their homes. As these alternative assets become more liquid, the relative liquidity of money falls, and so the demand for money falls as well.

SUMMARY TABLE 1

Factors That Determine the Demand for Money

Variable	Change in Variable	Money Demand Response	Reason
Interest rates	↑	↓	Opportunity cost of money rises
Income	↑	↑	Higher value of transactions
Payment technology	↑	↓	Less need for money in transactions
Wealth	↑	↑	More resources to put into money
Riskiness of other assets	↑	↑	Money relatively less risky and so more desirable
Inflation risk	↑	↓	Money relatively more risky and so less desirable
Liquidity of other assets	↑	↓	Money relatively less liquid and so less desirable

Note: Only increases (↑) in the factors are shown; the effects of decreases in the variables on the exchange rate are the opposite of those indicated in the "Response" column.

Summary

Our analysis of the demand for money using Keynesian and portfolio theories indicates that seven factors affect the demand for money: interest rates, income, payment technology, wealth, riskiness of other assets, inflation risk, and liquidity of other assets. As a study aid, Summary Table 1 indicates the response of money demand to changes in each of these factors and gives a brief synopsis of the reasoning behind each response.

EMPIRICAL EVIDENCE FOR THE DEMAND FOR MONEY

Here we examine the empirical evidence on the two key issues that distinguish different theories of money demand and affect their conclusions about whether the quantity of money is the primary determinant of aggregate spending: Is the demand for money sensitive to changes in interest rates, and is the demand-for-money function stable over time?[5]

Interest Rates and Money Demand

We have established that if interest rates do not affect the demand for money, velocity is more likely to be constant—or at least predictable—and so the quantity

---

[5]If you are interested in a more detailed discussion of the empirical research on the demand for money, you can find it in a second appendix to this chapter on the Companion Website, http://www.pearsonhighered.com/mishkin.

theory view that aggregate spending is determined by the quantity of money is more likely to be true. However, the more sensitive to interest rates the demand for money is, the more unpredictable velocity will be, and the less clear the link between the money supply and aggregate spending becomes. Indeed, there exists an extreme case of ultrasensitivity of the demand for money to interest rates, called the **liquidity trap**, in which conventional monetary policy has no direct effect on aggregate spending because a change in the money supply has no effect on interest rates.[6]

The evidence for the interest sensitivity of the demand for money is remarkably consistent. Neither extreme case is supported by the data: In situations in which nominal interest rates have not hit a floor of zero, the demand for money is sensitive to interest rates, and little evidence is present that a liquidity trap has ever existed. However, when nominal interest rates fall to zero, they can go no lower. In this situation, a liquidity trap occurs because the demand for money is now completely flat. Indeed, this is exactly the situation that has occurred in the United States in recent years, which is why the Federal Reserve has had to resort to nonconventional monetary policy.

Stability of Money Demand

If the money demand function, like the one in Equation 8, is unstable and undergoes substantial, unpredictable shifts, as Keynes believed, then velocity is unpredictable, and the quantity of money may not be tightly linked to aggregate spending as it is in the quantity theory. The stability of the money demand function is crucial to whether the Federal Reserve should target interest rates or the money supply. If the money demand function is unstable and so the money supply is not closely linked to aggregate spending, then the level of interest rates set by the Fed will provide more information about the stance of monetary policy than will the money supply.

Until the early 1970s, the evidence strongly supported the stability of the money demand function. However, after 1973, the rapid pace of financial innovation, which changed the items that could be used as money, led to substantial instability in estimated money demand functions. The instability of the money demand function calls into question whether our theories and empirical analyses are adequate. It also has important implications for the conduct of monetary policy, because it casts doubt on the usefulness of the money demand function as a tool for providing guidance to policymakers. In particular, because the money demand function has become unstable, velocity is now harder to predict. Monetary policymakers have found that the money supply does not provide reliable information on the future course of the economy, leading them to think of monetary policy in terms of the setting of interest rates. The instability of money demand has thus led to a downgrading of the focus on money supply in the conduct of monetary policy.

---

[6]If the demand for money is ultrasensitive to interest rates, a tiny change in interest rates produces a very large change in the quantity of money demanded. Hence, in this case, the demand for money would be completely flat in the supply and demand diagrams of Chapter 5. Therefore, a change in the money supply that shifts the money supply curve to the right or left causes it to intersect the flat money demand curve at the same unchanged interest rate.

SUMMARY

1. The quantity theory of money as expressed by the equation of exchange, $M \times V = P \times Y$, indicates that nominal spending is determined solely by movements in the quantity of money. The quantity theory indicates that (1) changes in the quantity of money lead to proportional changes in the price level, because $P = (M \times \overline{V})/\overline{Y}$, and (2) the inflation rate is the growth rate of the money supply minus the growth rate of aggregate output—that is, $\pi = \%\Delta M - \%\Delta Y$. These implications of the quantity theory are borne out by the data in the long run, but not in the short run.

2. The government budget constraint indicates that a deficit must be financed by either money creation or by the issuance of government bonds. That is, $DEF = G - T = \Delta MB + \Delta B$. Combining this fact with the quantity theory indicates that financing a persistent deficit by money creation will lead to sustained inflation. This analysis helps explain hyperinflations, in which inflation and money growth rise to extremely high levels because of massive budget deficits.

3. John Maynard Keynes suggested three motives for holding money: the transactions motive, the precautionary motive, and the speculative motive. His resulting liquidity preference theory views the transactions and precautionary components of money demand as proportional to income. However, the speculative component of money demand is viewed as sensitive to interest rates as well as to expectations about the future movements of interest rates. This theory, then, implies that velocity is unstable and cannot be treated as a constant.

4. Portfolio theories of money demand indicate that the demand for money is determined not only by interest rates, income, and payment technology, as in the Keynesian analysis, but also by wealth, riskiness of other assets, inflation risk, and liquidity of other assets.

5. Two main conclusions can be reached from the research on the demand for money: The demand for money is sensitive to interest rates, but little evidence exists that it is or ever has been ultrasensitive (liquidity trap). Since 1973, money demand has been found to be unstable, with the most likely source of the instability being the rapid pace of financial innovation. Because the money demand function is found to be both unstable and sensitive to interest rates, velocity cannot be viewed as constant and is not easily predicted. These conclusions have led to a downgrading of the focus on money supply and a greater emphasis on interest rates in the conduct of monetary policy.

KEY TERMS

demand for money, p. 458
dominated assets, p. 467
equation of exchange, p. 457
government budget constraint, p. 463
hyperinflations, p. 464

inflation hedges, p. 467
liquidity preference theory, p. 465
liquidity trap, p. 469
monetary theory, p. 456
monetizing the debt, p. 463

payment technology, p. 465
printing money, p. 463
quantity theory of money, p. 458
real money balances, p. 465
velocity of money, p. 457

QUESTIONS

All questions are available in MyEconLab at http://www.myeconlab.com.

1. How would you expect velocity to typically behave over the course of the business cycle?

2. If velocity and aggregate output are reasonably constant (as the classical economists believed), what will happen to the price level when the money supply increases from $1 trillion to $4 trillion?

3. If credit cards were made illegal by congressional legislation, what would happen to velocity? Explain your answer.

4. "If nominal GDP rises, velocity must rise." Is this statement true, false, or uncertain? Explain your answer.

5. Why would a central bank be concerned about persistent, long-term budget deficits?

6. "Persistent budget deficits always lead to higher inflation." Is this statement true, false, or uncertain? Explain your answer.

7. Suppose a new "payment technology" allows individuals to make payments using U.S. Treasury bonds (i.e., U.S. Treasury bonds are immediately cashed when needed to make a payment, and that balance is transferred to the payee). How do you think this payment technology would affect the transaction components of the demand for money?

8. Some payment technologies require infrastructure (e.g., merchants need to have access to credit card swiping machines). In most developing countries, this infrastructure is either nonexistent or very costly. Everything else being equal, would you expect the transaction component of the demand for money to be greater or smaller in a developing country than in a rich country?

9. What three motives for holding money did Keynes consider in his liquidity preference theory of the demand for real money balances? On the basis of these motives, what variables did he think determined the demand for money?

10. In many countries, people hold money as a cushion against unexpected needs arising from a variety of potential scenarios (e.g., banking crises, natural disasters, health problems, unemployment, etc.) that are not usually covered by insurance markets. Explain the effect of such behavior on the precautionary component of the demand for money.

11. In Keynes's analysis of the speculative demand for money, what will happen to money demand if people suddenly decide that the normal level of the interest rate has fallen? Why?

12. Why is Keynes's analysis of the speculative demand for money important to his view that velocity will undergo substantial fluctuations and thus cannot be treated as constant?

13. According to the portfolio theories of money demand, what are the four factors that determine money demand? What changes in these factors can increase the demand for money?

14. Explain how the following events will affect the demand for money according to the portfolio theories of money demand:

    a. The economy experiences a business cycle contraction.

    b. Brokerage fees decline, making bond transactions cheaper.

    c. The stock market crashes. (*Hint:* Consider both the increase in stock price volatility following a market crash and the decrease in wealth of stockholders.)

15. Suppose a given country experienced low and stable inflation rates for quite some time, but then inflation picked up and over the past decade has been relatively high and quite unpredictable. Explain how this new inflationary environment would affect the demand for money according to portfolio theories of money demand. What would happen if the government decided to issue inflation-protected securities?

16. Consider the portfolio choice theory of money demand. How do you think the demand for money would be affected during a hyperinflation (i.e., monthly inflation rates in excess of 50%)?

17. Both the portfolio choice and Keynes's theories of the demand for money suggest that as the relative expected return on money falls, demand for it will fall. Why does the portfolio choice approach predict that money demand is affected by changes in interest rates? Why did Keynes think that money demand *is* affected by changes in interest rates?

18. Why does the Keynesian view of the demand for money suggest that velocity is unpredictable?

19. What evidence is used to assess the stability of the money demand function? What does the evidence suggest about the stability of money demand, and how has this conclusion affected monetary policymaking?

20. Suppose that a plot of the values of M2 and nominal GDP for a given country over 40 years shows that these two variables are very closely related. In particular, a plot of their ratio (nominal GDP/M2) yields very stable and easy-to-predict values. On the basis of this evidence, would you recommend that the monetary authorities of this country conduct monetary policy by focusing mostly on the money supply rather than on setting interest rates? Explain.

APPLIED PROBLEMS

All applied problems are available in MyEconLab *at*
http://www.myeconlab.com.

21. Suppose the money supply *M* has been growing at
10% per year, and nominal GDP, *PY*, has been growing
at 20% per year. The data are as follows (in billions of
dollars):

	2015	2016	2017
M	100	110	121
PY	1,000	1,200	1,440

Calculate the velocity for each year. At what rate is the
velocity growing?

22. Calculate what happens to nominal GDP if velocity
remains constant at 5 and the money supply increases
from $200 billion to $300 billion.

23. What happens to nominal GDP if the money supply
grows by 20% but velocity declines by 30%?

24. If velocity and aggregate output remain constant at 5
and $1,000 billion, respectively, what happens to the
price level if the money supply declines from $400 bil-
lion to $300 billion?

25. Suppose the liquidity preference function is given by

$$L(i,Y) = \frac{Y}{8} - 1,000i$$

Use the money demand equation, along with the following
table of values, to calculate the velocity for each period.

	Period 1	Period 2	Period 3	Period 4	Period 5	Period 6	Period 7
Y (in billions)	12,000	12,500	12,250	12,500	12,800	13,000	13,200
Interest rate	0.05	0.07	0.03	0.05	0.07	0.04	0.06

DATA ANALYSIS PROBLEMS

The Problems update with real-time data in MyEconLab *and
are available for practice or instructor assignment.*

 1. Go to the St. Louis Federal Reserve FRED database,
and find data on the M1 Money Stock (M1SL), M1
Money Velocity (M1V), and Real GDP (GDPC1).
Convert the M1SL data series to "quarterly" using
the *frequency* setting, and for all three series, use the
"Percent Change from Year Ago" setting for *units*.

   a. Calculate the average percentage change in real
GDP, the M1 money stock, and velocity since
2000:Q1.

   b. Based on your answer to part (a), calculate the
average inflation rate since 2000 as predicted by
the quantity theory of money.

   c. Next, find the data on the GDP deflator price
index (GDPDEF), download the data using the
'Percent Change from Year Ago' setting, and
calculate the average inflation rate since 2000:Q1.
Comment on the value relative to your answer in
part (b).

 2. Go to the St. Louis Federal Reserve FRED database,
and find data on the budget deficit (FYFSD), the
amount of federal debt held by the public
(FYGFDPUN), and the amount of federal debt held
by the Federal Reserve (FDHBFRBN). Convert
the two "debt held" series to "Annual" using the
frequency setting. Download all three series into a
spreadsheet. Make sure that the rows of data align
properly to the correct dates. Note that for the
deficit series, a negative number indicates a deficit;
multiply the series by −1 so that a deficit is indicated
by a positive number. Manipulate the three series
so that all data are given in terms of the same units
(either millions or billions of dollars). To do this,
if a series is in millions and you are converting it to
billions, divide the series by 1000. Finally, for each
year, convert the two "debt held" series into one
"changes in debt holdings by the public and the
Federal Reserve" series by calculating, for each year, the
difference in bond holdings from the preceding year.

a. Create a scatter plot showing the deficit on the horizontal axis and the change in bond holdings by the public on the vertical axis, using the data from 1980 through the most recent period of data available. Insert a fitted line into the scatter plot, and comment on the relationship between the deficit and the change in public bond holdings.

b. Create a scatter plot showing the deficit on the horizontal axis and the change in bond holdings by the Federal Reserve on the vertical axis, using

the data from 1980 through the most recent period of data available. Insert a fitted line into the scatter plot, and comment on the relationship between the deficit and the change in Federal Reserve bond holdings.

c. Based on your results in parts (a) and (b), comment on how, if at all, the monetizing of the debt is exhibited in the data. Do you think the relationship between the deficit and the change in bond holdings of the Federal Reserve has changed since 2008? Why or why not?

WEB EXERCISES

1. John Maynard Keynes is among the most well-known economic theorists. Go to http://en.wikipedia.org/wiki/ John_Maynard_Keynes and write a one-page summary of his life and contributions.

WEB REFERENCES

http://www.usagold.com/gildedopinion/puplava/20020614 .html

A summary of how various factors affect the velocity of money.

WEB APPENDICES

Please visit the Companion Website at http://www .pearsonhighered.com/mishkin to read the Web appendices to Chapter 19.

Appendix 1: **The Baumol-Tobin and the Tobin Mean-Variance Models of the Demand for Money**

Appendix 2: **Empirical Evidence for the Demand for Money**

20 The *IS* Curve

Preview

During the Great Depression of the 1930s, aggregate output fell precipitously, by 30%, with unemployment rising to 25%. Although the recession of 2007–2009 was not as severe, the contraction in economic activity led unemployment to rise to over 10%. To understand why these contractions in economic activity occur, economists make use of the concept of *aggregate demand*, the total amount of output demanded in the economy. This concept was developed by John Maynard Keynes in his revolutionary book, *The General Theory of Employment, Interest, and Money*, published in 1936, in which he argued that short-run changes in aggregate output, such as the decline in output that occurred during the Great Depression, are determined by changes in aggregate demand. The concept of aggregate demand is a central element in the *aggregate demand–aggregate supply (AD/AS) model*, the basic macroeconomic model used to explain short-run fluctuations in aggregate output.

In this chapter, we develop the first building block in understanding aggregate demand, the *IS curve*, which describes the relationship between real interest rates and aggregate output when the market for goods and services (more simply referred to as the *goods market*) is in equilibrium. We begin by deriving the *IS* curve and then go on to explain what factors cause the *IS* curve to shift. With our understanding of the *IS* curve, we can examine why fluctuations in economic activity occur and how the fiscal stimulus package of 2009 affected the economy. Then, in the next chapter, we make use of the *IS* curve to understand the role played by monetary policy in economic fluctuations.

PLANNED EXPENDITURE AND AGGREGATE DEMAND

We start our analysis by discussing the concept of **planned expenditure**, the total amount that households, businesses, the government, and foreigners want to spend on domestically produced goods and services. In contrast, *actual expenditure* is the amount that these entities actually do spend, which equals the total amount of output produced in the economy. Note that all of the analysis in this chapter refers to expenditure in real terms, that is, in terms of actual physical amounts of goods and services. Keynes viewed **aggregate demand**, the total amount of output demanded in the economy, as being the same as planned expenditure. As we shall see shortly, planned expenditure—and hence aggregate demand—explains the level of aggregate output when the good market is in equilibrium, that is, when aggregate demand for goods and services is equal to the actual amount of goods and services produced.

The total amount of aggregate demand (planned expenditure) is the sum of four types of spending:

1. **Consumption expenditure** (C), the total demand for consumer goods and services (e.g., hamburgers, iPods, rock concerts, visits to the doctor, etc.)
2. **Planned investment spending** (I), the total planned spending by businesses on new physical capital (e.g., machines, computers, factories), plus planned spending on new homes
3. **Government purchases** (G), the spending by all levels of government on goods and services (e.g., aircraft carriers, salaries of government employees, red tape), not including transfer payments
4. **Net exports** (NX), the net foreign spending on domestic goods and services, equal to exports minus imports

We represent the total aggregate demand (Y^{ad}) with the following equation:

$$Y^{ad} = C + I + G + NX \tag{1}$$

THE COMPONENTS OF AGGREGATE DEMAND

To understand what determines aggregate demand (total planned expenditure) in the economy, let's look at each of its components in detail.

Consumption Expenditure

What determines how much you spend on consumer goods and services? Your income is likely the most important factor; if your income rises, you most likely will be willing to spend more. Keynes reasoned similarly that consumption expenditure is related to **disposable income** (denoted by Y_D), the total amount of income available for spending, equal to aggregate output Y minus taxes T ($Y - T$).[1]

Consumption Function Keynes called the relationship between disposable income Y_D and consumption expenditure C the **consumption function**, and expressed it as follows:

$$C = \overline{C} + mpc \times Y_D \tag{2}$$

or, alternatively,

$$C = \overline{C} + mpc \times (Y - T) \tag{3}$$

The term $\overline{C}$ stands for **autonomous consumption expenditure**, the amount of consumption expenditure that is **exogenous** (independent of variables in the model, such as disposable income). Autonomous consumption is related to consumers' optimism about their future income and household wealth, a factor that induces consumers to increase spending.

---

[1]More precisely, taxes T refers to taxes minus net transfers (government payments to households and businesses that are, in effect, negative taxes). Examples of government transfers include Social Security payments and unemployment insurance payments.

FYI   **Meaning of the Word *Investment***

Economists use the word *investment* somewhat differently than other people do. When noneconomists say that they are making an investment, they are normally referring to the purchase of common stocks or bonds, purchases that do not necessarily involve newly produced goods and services. But when economists speak of investment spending, they are referring to the purchases of *new* physical assets, such as new machines or new houses—purchases that add to aggregate demand.

The term *mpc*, the **marginal propensity to consume**, reflects the change in consumption expenditure that results from an additional dollar of disposable income. Keynes assumed that *mpc* was a constant between the values of 0 and 1. If, for example, a $1.00 increase in disposable income leads to an increase in consumption expenditure of $0.60, then *mpc* = 0.6.

Planned Investment Spending

Investment spending is another key component of total expenditure. There are two types of investment spending: *fixed* and *inventory*. (Note that economists' use of the word *investment* differs from the everyday use of the term, as explained in the FYI box.)

Fixed Investment   **Fixed investment** is planned spending by firms on equipment (machines, computers, airplanes) and structures (factories, office buildings, shopping centers), plus planned spending on new residential housing.

Inventory Investment   **Inventory investment** is spending by firms on additional holdings of raw materials, parts, and finished goods, calculated as the change in holdings of these items in a given time period—say, a year.

Inventory investment is a much smaller component of investment than fixed investment. We discuss inventory investment in detail at this juncture because it plays an important role in the determination of aggregate output. To illustrate, consider the following scenarios:

1. Suppose that Ford Motor Company has 100,000 cars sitting in its factory lots on December 31, 2016, ready to be shipped to dealers. If each car has a wholesale price of $20,000, Ford has an inventory worth $2 billion. If by December 31, 2017, its inventory of cars has risen to 150,000, with a value of $3 billion, its inventory investment in 2017 is $1 billion, the *change* in the level of its inventory over the course of the year ($3 billion in 2017 minus $2 billion in 2016).
2. Now suppose that by December 31, 2017, Ford's inventory of cars has dropped to 50,000, with a value of $1 billion. Its inventory investment in 2017 is now –$1 billion, the *change* in the level of its inventory over the course of the year ($1 billion in 2017 minus $2 billion in 2016).
3. Ford will have additional inventory investment if the level of raw materials and parts that it is holding to produce these cars increases over the course of the year. If on December 31, 2016, it holds $50 million of steel to be used to produce its cars, and on December 31, 2017, it holds $100 million of steel, it has an additional $50 million of inventory investment in 2017.

An important feature of inventory investment is that some inventory investment can be unplanned (in contrast, fixed investment is always planned). Suppose that the reason Ford finds itself with an additional $1 billion of cars on December 31, 2017, is because it sold $1 billion less of its cars than expected in 2017. This $1 billion of inventory investment in 2017 was unplanned. In this situation, Ford is producing more cars than it can sell, and it will cut production to avoid accumulating unsold goods. The act of adjusting production to eliminate unplanned inventory investment plays a key role in the determination of aggregate output, as we shall see.

Planned Investment Spending and Real Interest Rates   Planned investment spending, a component of aggregate demand Y^{ad}, is equal to planned fixed investment plus the amount of inventory investment *planned* by firms. Keynes considered the level of the real interest rate for investments as a key determinant of planned investment spending.

To understand Keynes's reasoning, we need to recognize that businesses make investments in physical capital (machines and factories) as long as they expect to earn more from the physical capital than the interest cost of a loan to finance the investment. When the real interest rate for investments is high—say, at 10%—few investments in physical capital will earn more than the 10% interest cost of borrowing funds, and so planned investment spending will be low. When the real interest rate for investments is low—say, 1%—many investments in physical capital will earn more than the 1% interest cost of borrowing funds. Therefore, when the real interest rate for investments and hence the cost of borrowing are low, business firms are more likely to undertake investments in physical capital, and planned investment spending increases.

Even if a company has surplus funds and does not need to borrow to undertake an investment in physical capital, its planned investment spending still will be affected by the real interest rate for investments. Instead of investing in physical capital, the company could purchase a corporate bond. If the real interest rate on this security were high—say, 10%—the opportunity cost (forgone interest earnings) of an investment in physical capital would be high. Planned investment spending would then be low, because the firm probably would prefer to purchase the security and earn the high 10% return than to invest in physical capital. As the real interest rate for investments and the opportunity cost of investing fall—say, to 1%—planned investment spending will increase because investments in physical capital are likely to earn greater income for the firm than the measly 1% that would be earned by investing in the security.

Planned Investment and Business Expectations   Keynes also believed that planned investment spending is heavily influenced by business expectations about the future. Businesses that are optimistic about future profit opportunities are willing to spend more, whereas pessimistic businesses cut back their spending. Thus Keynes posited a component of planned investment spending, which he called **autonomous investment**, $\bar{I}$, that is completely exogenous and so is unexplained by variables in his model, such as output or interest rates.

Keynes believed that changes in autonomous spending are dominated by these unstable exogenous fluctuations in planned investment spending, which are influenced by emotional waves of optimism and pessimism—factors he labeled **"animal spirits."** His view was colored by the collapse in investment spending during the Great Depression, which he saw as the primary reason for the economic contraction.

Investment Function   By combining the two factors that Keynes theorized drive investment, we can derive an investment function that describes how planned investment spending is related to autonomous investment and the real interest rate for investments. We write this function as follows:

$$I = \bar{I} - dr_i \tag{4}$$

where d is a parameter reflecting the responsiveness of investment to the real interest rate for investments, which is denoted by r_i.

However, the real interest rate for investments reflects not only the real interest rate r on short-term, safe, debt instruments, which is controlled by the central bank, but also **financial frictions**, denoted by $\bar{f}$, which are additions to the real cost of borrowing caused by barriers to the efficient functioning of financial markets. (We discussed the origins of these frictions–the asymmetric information problems of adverse selection and moral hazard–in detail in Chapter 8.) Financial frictions make it harder for lenders to ascertain the creditworthiness of a borrower. Lenders need to charge a higher interest rate to protect themselves against the possibility that the borrower may not pay back the loan, which leads to a *credit spread*, the difference between the interest rate on loans to businesses and the interest rate on completely safe assets that are sure to be paid back. Hence financial frictions add to the real interest rate for investments, and we can write:

$$r_i = r + \bar{f} \tag{5}$$

Substituting in Equation 4 the real cost of borrowing from Equation 5 yields:

$$I = \bar{I} - d(r + \bar{f}) \tag{6}$$

Equation 6 states that investment is positively related to business optimism as represented by autonomous investment, and negatively related to the real interest rate and financial frictions.

Net Exports

As with planned investment spending, we can think of net exports as being made up of two components: *autonomous net exports* and the part of net exports that is affected by changes in real interest rates.

Real Interest Rates and Net Exports   Real interest rates influence the amount of net exports through the **exchange rate**. Recall that the exchange rate is the price of one currency, say, the dollar, in terms of another currency, say, the euro.[2] We examined a model that explains the link between the exchange rate and real interest rates in Chapter 17, but here we will only outline the intuition. When U.S. real interest rates rise, U.S. dollar assets earn higher returns relative to foreign assets. People then want to hold more dollars, so they bid up the value of a dollar and thereby increase its value relative to the values of other currencies. Thus a rise in U.S. real interest rates leads to a higher value of the dollar.

---

[2]If a government pegs the exchange rate to another country's currency, so that the rate is fixed in what is called a *fixed exchange rate regime* (see Chapter 18), then real interest rates do not directly affect net exports as in Equation 5, and $NX = \overline{NX}$. Taking out the response of net exports to the real interest rates does not change the basic analysis of the chapter but does lead to a slightly different Equation 12 later in the chapter.

A rise in the value of the dollar makes U.S. exports more expensive in foreign currencies, so foreigners will buy less of these exports, thereby driving down net exports. A rise in the value of the dollar also makes foreign goods less expensive in terms of dollars, so U.S. imports will rise, also causing a decline in net exports. We therefore see that a rise in the real interest rate, which leads to an increase in the value of the dollar, in turn leads to a decline in net exports.

Autonomous Net Exports   The amount of exports is also affected by the demand by foreigners for domestic goods, while the amount of imports is affected by the demand by domestic residents for foreign goods. For example, if the Chinese have a poor harvest and want to buy more U.S. wheat, U.S. exports will rise. If the Brazilian economy is booming, then Brazilians will have more money to spend on U.S. goods, and U.S. exports will rise. On the other hand, if U.S. consumers discover how good Chilean wine is and want to buy more, then U.S. imports will rise. Thus we can think of net exports as being determined by real interest rates as well as by a component called **autonomous net exports**, $\overline{NX}$, which is the level of net exports that is treated as exogenous (outside the model).[3]

Net Export Function   Putting these two components of net exports together, we can write a net export function:

$$NX = \overline{NX} - xr \tag{7}$$

where x is a parameter that indicates how net exports respond to the real interest rate. This equation tells us that net exports are positively related to autonomous net exports and are negatively related to the level of real interest rates.

Government Purchases and Taxes

Now we bring the government into the picture. The government affects aggregate demand in two ways: through its purchases and through taxes.

Government Purchases   As we saw in the aggregate demand equation, Equation 1, government purchases add directly to aggregate demand. Here we assume that government purchases are exogenous, and we write government purchases as follows:

$$G = \overline{G} \tag{8}$$

Equation 8 states that government purchases are set at a fixed amount $\overline{G}$.

Taxes   The government affects spending through taxes because, as discussed earlier, disposable income is equal to income minus taxes, $Y - T$, and disposable income affects consumption expenditure. Higher taxes T reduce disposable income for a given level of

---

[3]Foreign aggregate output is outside the model, and so its effect on net exports is exogenous and hence is a factor that affects autonomous net exports. U.S. domestic output, Y, could also affect net exports because greater domestic disposable income would increase spending on imports and thus would lower net exports. To build this factor into the *IS* curve, we could modify the net export function given in Equation 7 as follows:

$$NX = \overline{NX} - xr - iY$$

where i is the marginal propensity to spend on imports. This change would lead to a modification of Equation 12 later in the chapter, in which the *mpc* term would be replaced by $mpc - i$.

income and hence cause consumption expenditure to fall. The tax laws in a country like the United States are very complicated, so to keep the model simple, we assume that government taxes are exogenous and are set at a fixed amount $\bar{T}$:[4]

$$T = \bar{T} \tag{9}$$

GOODS MARKET EQUILIBRIUM

Keynes recognized that equilibrium will occur in the economy when the total quantity of output is equal to the total amount of aggregate demand (planned expenditure). That is,

$$Y = Y^{ad} \tag{10}$$

When this equilibrium condition is satisfied, planned spending for goods and services is equal to the amount that is produced. Producers are able to sell all of their output and have no reason to change their production levels, because there is no unplanned inventory investment. By examining the factors that affect each component of planned spending, we can understand why aggregate output goes to a certain level.

Solving for Goods Market Equilibrium

With our understanding of the factors that drive the components of aggregate demand, we can see how aggregate output is determined by using Equation 1, the aggregate demand equation, to rewrite the equilibrium condition given in Equation 10 as follows:

$$Y = C + I + G + NX \tag{11}$$

Aggregate Output = Consumption Expenditure + Planned Investment Spending

+ Government Purchases + Net Exports

Now we can use our consumption, investment, and net export functions in Equations 3, 6, and 7, along with Equations 8 and 9, to determine aggregate output. Substituting all of these equations into the equilibrium condition given by Equation 11 yields the following:

$$Y = \bar{C} + mpc \times (Y - \bar{T}) + \bar{I} - d(r + \bar{f}) + \bar{G} + \overline{NX} - xr$$

Collecting terms, we can rewrite this equation as follows:

$$Y = \bar{C} + \bar{I} - d\bar{f} + \bar{G} + \overline{NX} + mpc \times Y - mpc \times \bar{T} - (d + x)r$$

Subtracting $mpc \times Y$ from both sides of the equation, we have

$$Y - mpc \times Y = Y(1 - mpc) = \bar{C} + \bar{I} - d\bar{f} + \bar{G} + \overline{NX} - mpc \times \bar{T} - (d + x)r$$

---

[4]For simplicity, we assume here that taxes are unrelated to income. However, because taxes increase with income, we can describe taxes more realistically with the following tax function:

$$T = \bar{T} + tY$$

Using this equation instead of Equation 9 in the derivation of Equation 12 later in the chapter would lead to mpc being replaced by $mpc(1 - t)$ in Equation 12.

Then, dividing both sides of the equation by $1 - mpc$, we obtain an equation that gives us a means of determining aggregate output when the goods market is in equilibrium:[5]

$$Y = [\overline{C} + \overline{I} - d\overline{f} + \overline{G} + \overline{NX} - mpc \times \overline{T}] \times \frac{1}{1 - mpc} - \frac{d + x}{1 - mpc} \times r \quad (12)$$

Deriving the *IS* Curve

We refer to Equation 12 as the **IS curve**, and it shows the relationship between aggregate output and the real interest rate when the goods market is in equilibrium. Equation 12 is made up of two terms. Since mpc is between 0 and 1, $1/(1 - mpc)$ is positive, so the first term tells us that an increase in autonomous consumption, investment, government purchases, or net exports, or a decrease in taxes or financial frictions, leads to an increase in output at any given real interest rate. In other words, the first term tells us about shifts in the *IS* curve. The second term tells us that an increase in real interest rates results in a decrease in output, which can be shown as a movement along the *IS* curve.

UNDERSTANDING THE *IS* CURVE

To gain a deeper understanding of the *IS* curve, we will proceed in several steps. In this section, we begin by looking at the intuition behind the *IS* curve, and then we discuss a numerical example. Then, in the following section, we outline the factors that shift the *IS* curve.

What the *IS* Curve Tells Us: Intuition

The *IS* curve traces out the points at which the goods market is in equilibrium. For each given level of the real interest rate, the *IS* curve tells us the level of aggregate output that is necessary for the goods market to be in equilibrium. As the real interest rate rises, planned investment spending and net exports fall, which in turn lowers aggregate demand; aggregate output must be lower if it is to equal aggregate demand and satisfy goods market equilibrium. Hence the *IS* curve is downward-sloping.

What the *IS* Curve Tells Us: Numerical Example

We can analyze the *IS* curve with the following numerical example, which gives specific values for the exogenous variables and the parameters in Equation 12.

$$\overline{C} = \$1.4 \text{ trillion}$$
$$\overline{I} = \$1.2 \text{ trillion}$$
$$\overline{G} = \$3.0 \text{ trillion}$$
$$\overline{T} = \$3.0 \text{ trillion}$$
$$\overline{NX} = \$1.3 \text{ trillion}$$
$$\overline{f} = 1$$
$$mpc = 0.6$$
$$d = 0.3$$
$$x = 0.1$$

[5]Note that the term $1/(1 - mpc)$ that multiplies $\overline{G}$ is known as the *expenditure multiplier*, and the term $-mpc/(1 - mpc)$ that multiplies $\overline{T}$ is called the *tax multiplier*. The tax multiplier is smaller in absolute value than the expenditure multiplier because $mpc < 1$.

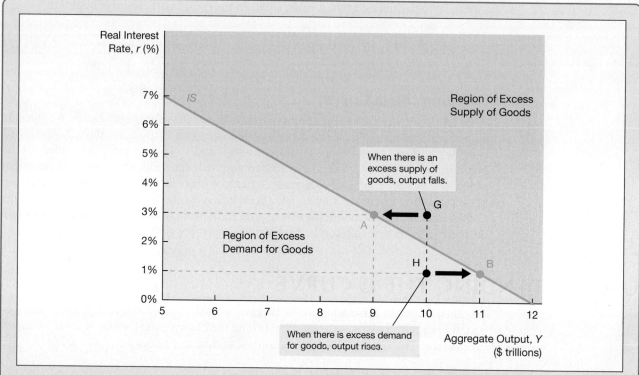

FIGURE 1 The *IS* Curve

The downward-sloping *IS* curve represents points at which the goods market is in equilibrium—for example, points *A* and *B*. Notice that output changes as necessary to return the market to equilibrium. For example, at point *G* in the orange shaded area, an excess supply of goods exists and firms will cut production, decreasing aggregate output to the equilibrium level at point *A*. At point *H* in the blue shaded area, an excess demand for goods exists, so firms will increase production, and aggregate output will increase toward the equilibrium level at point *B*.

Using these values, we can rewrite Equation 12 as follows:

$$Y = \left[1.4 + 1.2 - 0.3 + 3.0 + 1.3 - 0.6 \times 3.0\right] \times \frac{1}{1 - 0.6} - \frac{0.3 + 0.1}{1 - 0.6} \times r$$

Plugging these values into Equation 12 yields the equation of the *IS* curve shown in Figure 1:

$$Y = \frac{4.8}{0.4} - \frac{0.4}{0.4} \times r = 12 - r \tag{13}$$

At a real interest rate of $r = 3\%$, the equilibrium output Y is equal to $12 trillion − $3 trillion = $9 trillion. We plot this combination of the real interest rate and equilibrium output as point *A* in Figure 1. At a real interest rate of $r = 1\%$, the equilibrium output Y is equal to $12 trillion − $1 trillion = $11 trillion, which we plot as point *B*. The line connecting these points is the *IS* curve and, as you can see, it is downward-sloping.

Why the Economy Heads Toward Equilibrium

The concept of equilibrium is useful only if there is a tendency for the economy to settle there. Let's first consider what happens if the economy is located to the right of the *IS* curve (the orange shaded area), where an excess supply of goods exists. In Figure 1 at point *G*, actual output is above aggregate demand, and firms are saddled with unsold inventory. To keep from accumulating unsold goods, firms will continue cutting production. As long as production is above the equilibrium level, output will exceed aggregate demand and firms will continue cutting production, sending aggregate output toward the equilibrium level, as indicated by the leftward arrow from point *G* to point *A*. Only when the economy moves to point *A* on the *IS* curve will there be no further tendency for output to change.

What happens if aggregate output is below the equilibrium level of output (the blue shaded area to the left of the *IS* curve), where an excess demand for goods exists? At point *H* in Figure 1, actual output is below aggregate demand, so firms will want to increase production because inventories are declining more than they desire, and aggregate output will increase, as shown by the rightward arrow. When the economy has moved to point *B* on the *IS* curve, there will again be no further tendency for output to change.

FACTORS THAT SHIFT THE *IS* CURVE

You have now learned that the *IS* curve describes equilibrium points in the goods market—the combinations of the real interest rate and equilibrium output. The *IS* curve shifts whenever change occurs in autonomous factors (factors independent of aggregate output and the real interest rate). Note that a change in the real interest rate that affects equilibrium aggregate output causes only a *movement along* the *IS* curve. A *shift* in the *IS* curve, by contrast, occurs when equilibrium output changes *at each given real interest rate*.

In Equation 12, we identified six autonomous factors that can shift aggregate demand and hence affect the level of equilibrium output. Although Equation 12 directly tells us how these factors shift the *IS* curve, we will develop some intuition as to how each autonomous factor does so.

Changes in Government Purchases

Let's look at what happens if government purchases rise from $3 trillion to $4 trillion in Figure 2. IS_1 represents the same *IS* curve that we developed in Figure 1. We determine the equation for IS_2 by substituting the $4 trillion value into Equation 12:

$$Y = [1.4 + 1.2 - 0.3 + 4.0 + 1.3 - 0.6 \times 3.0] \times \frac{1}{1 - 0.6} - \frac{0.3 + 0.1}{1 - 0.6} \times r = \frac{5.8}{0.4} - r$$

$$= 14.5 - r$$

On the basis of these results, at a real interest rate of $r = 3\%$, equilibrium output Y is equal to $14.5 trillion $- $3 trillion $= $11.5 trillion, which we mark as point *C* on Figure 2. At a real interest rate of $r = 1\%$, equilibrium output has increased to $Y = $14.5 trillion $- $1 trillion $= $13.5 trillion, which we mark as point *D*. The increase in government purchases therefore shifts the *IS* curve to the right from IS_1 to IS_2.

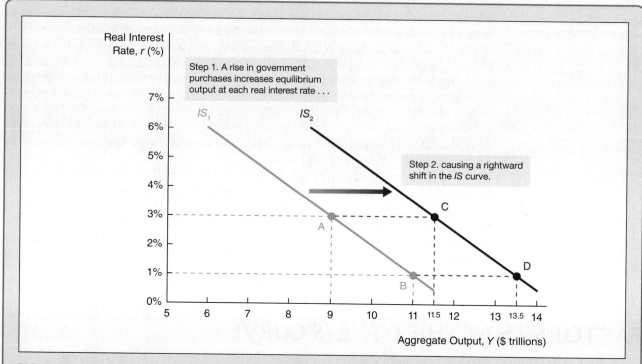

FIGURE 2 **Shift in the *IS* Curve from an Increase in Government Purchases**

IS_1 represents the *IS* curve we derived in Figure 1. IS_2 reflects a $1.0 trillion increase in government purchases. The increase in government purchases causes aggregate output to rise, shifting the *IS* curve to the right by $2.5 trillion, from IS_1 to IS_2.

Intuitively, we can see why an increase in government purchases leads to a rightward shift of the *IS* curve by recognizing that an increase in government purchases causes aggregate demand to increase at any given real interest rate. Since aggregate output equals aggregate demand when the goods market is in equilibrium, *an increase in government purchases that causes aggregate demand to rise also causes equilibrium output to rise, thereby shifting the IS curve to the right. Conversely, a decrease in government purchases causes aggregate demand to fall at any given real interest rate and leads to a leftward shift of the IS curve.*

Application   The Vietnam War Buildup, 1964–1969

The United States' involvement in Vietnam began to escalate in the early 1960s. After 1964, the United States was fighting a full-scale war. Beginning in 1965, the resulting increases in military expenditure raised government purchases. When government purchases are rising rapidly, central banks will usually raise real interest rates to keep the economy from overheating. The Vietnam War period, however, was unusual in that the Federal Reserve decided to keep real interest rates constant. Hence, this period provides an excellent example of how policymakers might make use of *IS* curve analysis to inform policy.

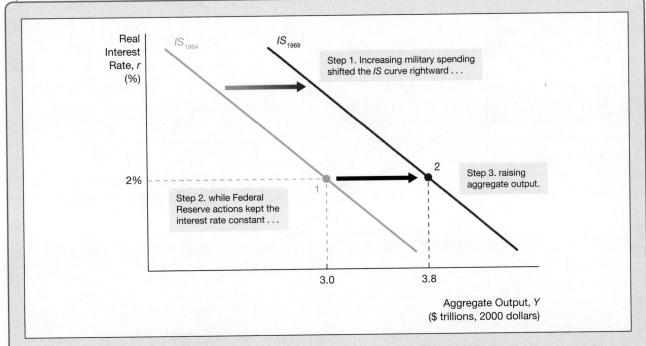

FIGURE 3   Vietnam War Buildup

Increases in military spending beginning in 1965 caused the *IS* curve to shift from IS_{1964} to IS_{1969}. Because the Federal Reserve decided to keep real interest rates constant at 2% during this period, equilibrium output rose from $3.0 trillion (in 2000 dollars) in 1964 to $3.8 trillion in 1969, setting the stage for an increase in inflation.

The rise in government purchases shifted the *IS* curve to the right, from IS_{1964} to IS_{1969} in Figure 3. Because the Federal Reserve decided to keep real interest rates constant at 2% during this period, equilibrium output rose from $3.0 trillion (in 2000 dollars) in 1964 to $3.8 trillion by 1969, with the unemployment rate falling steadily from 5% in 1964 to 3.4% in 1969. However, all was not well for the economy: The combination of an increase in government purchases and a constant real interest rate led to an overheating of the economy that eventually resulted in high inflation. (We will discuss the link between an overheating economy and inflation in the coming chapters.) ◆

Changes in Taxes

Now let's look at Figure 4 to see what happens if the government raises taxes from $3 trillion to $4 trillion. IS_1 represents the same *IS* curve that we developed in Figure 1. We determine the equation for IS_2 by substituting the $4 trillion value into Equation 12:

$$Y = [1.4 + 1.2 - 0.3 + 3.0 + 1.3 - 0.6 \times 4.0] \times \frac{1}{1 - 0.6} - \frac{0.3 + 0.1}{1 - 0.6} \times r = \frac{4.2}{0.4} - r$$

$$= 10.5 - r$$

MyEconLab Mini-lecture

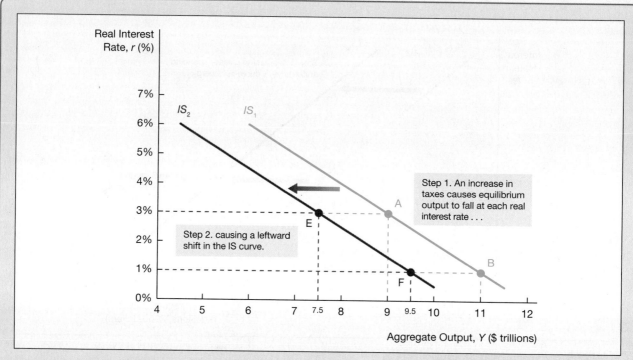

FIGURE 4   Shift in the *IS* Curve from an Increase in Taxes

IS_1 represents the *IS* curve we derived in Figure 1. IS_2 reflects a $1.0 trillion increase in government tax revenues. The increase in taxes decreases aggregate output levels by $1.5 trillion, shifting the *IS* curve to the left, from IS_1 to IS_2.

At a real interest rate of $r = 3\%$, equilibrium output $Y = \$10.5$ trillion $- \$3$ trillion $= \$7.5$ trillion, which we mark as point *E* in Figure 4. At this real interest rate, equilibrium output has decreased from point *A* to point *E*, as shown by the leftward arrow. Similarly, at a real interest rate of $r = 1\%$, equilibrium output has decreased to $Y = \$10.5$ trillion $- \$1$ trillion $= \$9.5$ trillion, causing a leftward shift from point *B* to point *F*. The *IS* curve shifts to the left, from IS_1 to IS_2, as a result of the increase in taxes.

We have the following result: ***At any given real interest rate, a rise in taxes causes aggregate demand and hence equilibrium output to fall, thereby shifting the IS curve to the left. Conversely, a cut in taxes at any given real interest rate increases disposable income and causes aggregate demand and equilibrium output to rise, shifting the IS curve to the right.***

Policymakers use both tax and government purchase policies to stimulate the economy when it enters a recession, as illustrated in the following Application.

APPLICATION   The Fiscal Stimulus Package of 2009

In the fall of 2008, the U.S. economy was in crisis. By the time the new Obama administration took office, the unemployment rate had risen from 4.7% just before the recession began in December 2007 to 7.6% in January 2009. To stimulate the economy, the Obama administration proposed a fiscal stimulus package that, when passed by Congress, included $288 billion in tax cuts for households and businesses and $499 billion in increased federal spending, including transfer payments. What does our *IS* curve analysis suggest should have happened to the economy?

As the analyses in Figure 2 and Figure 4 indicate, these tax cuts and spending increases should have increased aggregate demand, thereby raising the equilibrium level of aggregate output at any given real interest rate and so shifting the *IS* curve to the right. Unfortunately, things didn't work out quite as the Obama administration had planned. Most of the government purchases did not kick in until after 2010, while the declines in autonomous consumption and investment were much larger than anticipated. The fiscal stimulus was more than offset by the weak consumption and investment caused by an increase in financial frictions and worries about the economy. As a result, aggregate demand ended up contracting rather than rising, and the *IS* curve did not shift to the right as hoped. Despite the good intentions of the fiscal stimulus package, the unemployment rate ended up rising to 10% in 2009. Without the fiscal stimulus package, however, the *IS* curve likely would have shifted even further to the left, resulting in even more unemployment. ◆

Changes in Autonomous Spending

As you can see from Equation 12, autonomous consumption, investment, and net exports—$\overline{C}$, $\overline{I}$, and $\overline{NX}$, respectively—all are multiplied by the term $1/(1 - mpc)$ in the same way the $\overline{G}$ term is. Thus an increase in any of these variables has the same impact on the *IS* curve as an increase in government purchases. For this reason, we can lump these variables together as **autonomous spending**, exogenous spending that is unrelated to variables in the model such as output or real interest rates. We look intuitively at how changes in each of these variables affect the *IS* curve in turn.

Autonomous Consumption   Suppose consumers find that their wealth has increased courtesy of a stock market boom, or that they have become increasingly optimistic about their future income prospects because a positive productivity shock to the economy has occurred. Both of these events are autonomous; that is, they are not affected by the level of the real interest rate. *The resulting rise in autonomous consumption would raise aggregate demand and equilibrium output at any given interest rate, shifting the IS curve to the right. Conversely, a decline in autonomous consumption expenditure would cause aggregate demand and equilibrium output to fall, shifting the IS curve to the left.*

Autonomous Investment Spending   Earlier in the chapter, we learned that changes in the real interest rate affect planned investment spending and hence the equilibrium level of output. This change in investment spending merely causes a movement along the *IS* curve, not a shift. An autonomous rise in planned investment spending unrelated to the real interest rate—say, because companies become more confident about investment profitability after the stock market rises—increases aggregate demand. *An increase in autonomous investment spending therefore increases equilibrium output at any given interest rate, shifting the IS curve to the right. On the other hand, a decrease in autonomous investment spending causes aggregate demand and equilibrium output to fall, shifting the IS curve to the left.*

SUMMARY TABLE 1

Shifts in the *IS* Curve from Autonomous Changes in $\overline{C}, \overline{I}, \overline{G}, \overline{T}, \overline{NX}$, and $\overline{f}$

Variable	Change in Variable	Shift in IS Curve	Reason
Autonomous consumption expenditure, $\overline{C}$	↑		$C\uparrow Y\uparrow$
Autonomous investment, $\overline{I}$	↑		$I\uparrow Y\uparrow$
Government spending, $\overline{G}$	↑		$G\uparrow Y\uparrow$
Taxes, $\overline{T}$	↑		$T\uparrow \Rightarrow C\downarrow Y\downarrow$
Autonomous net exports, $\overline{NX}$	↑		$\overline{NX}\uparrow Y\uparrow$
Financial frictions, $\overline{f}$	↑		$I\downarrow Y\downarrow$

Note: Only increases (↑) in the variables are shown; the effects of decreases in the variables on aggregate output would be the opposite of those indicated in the last two columns.

Autonomous Net Exports   An autonomous rise in net exports unrelated to the real interest rate—say, because American-made handbags become more chic than French-made handbags, or because foreign countries have a boom and thus buy more U.S. goods—causes aggregate demand to rise. ***An autonomous increase in net exports thus leads to an increase in equilibrium output at any given interest rate and shifts the IS curve to the right. Conversely, an autonomous fall in net exports causes aggregate demand and equilibrium output to decline, shifting the IS curve to the left.***

Changes in Financial Frictions

An increase in financial frictions, as occurred during the financial crisis of 2007–2009, raises the real interest rate for investments and hence causes investment spending and aggregate demand to fall. *An increase in financial frictions leads to a decline in equilibrium output at any given real interest rate and shifts the IS curve to the left. Conversely, a decrease in financial frictions causes aggregate demand and equilibrium output to rise, shifting the IS curve to the right.*

Summary of Factors That Shift the *IS* Curve

As a study aid, Summary Table 1 shows how each factor shifts the *IS* curve and the reason the shift occurs. Now that we have a full understanding of the *IS* curve, we can use this building block to examine the relationship between monetary policy and the aggregate demand curve in the following chapter.

SUMMARY

1. Planned expenditure, the total amount of goods demanded in the economy, is the same as aggregate demand, which is the sum of four types of spending: consumption expenditure, planned investment spending, government purchases, and net exports. We represent the total aggregate demand (Y^{ab}) with Equation 1: $Y^{ad} = C + I + G + NX$.

2. Consumption expenditure is described by the consumption function, which indicates that consumption expenditure will rise as disposable income increases. Planned expenditure and hence aggregate demand are negatively related to the real interest rate because a rise in the real interest rate reduces both planned investment spending and net exports. An increase in financial frictions raises the real interest rate for investments and hence lowers investment spending and aggregate demand. The government also affects planned expenditure via spending, which directly changes aggregate demand, or via taxes, which indirectly affect aggregate demand by influencing disposable income and hence consumption expenditure.

3. The level of aggregate output when the goods market is in equilibrium is determined by the condition that aggregate output equals aggregate demand.

4. The *IS* curve traces out the combinations of the real interest rate and aggregate output at which the goods market is in equilibrium. The *IS* curve slopes downward because higher real interest rates lower planned investment spending and net exports and so lower equilibrium output.

5. The *IS* curve shifts to the right when there is a rise in autonomous consumption, a rise in autonomous investment, a rise in government purchases, a rise in autonomous net exports, a fall in taxes, or a decline in financial frictions. Movements of these six factors in the opposite direction will shift the *IS* curve to the left.

KEY TERMS

aggregate demand, p. 474
"animal spirits," p. 477
autonomous consumption
   expenditure, p. 475
autonomous investment, p. 477
autonomous net exports, p. 479
autonomous spending, p. 487

consumption expenditure, p. 475
consumption function, p. 475
disposable income, p. 475
exchange rate, p. 478
exogenous, p. 475
financial frictions, p. 478
fixed investment, p. 476

government purchases, p. 475
inventory investment, p. 476
IS curve, p. 481
marginal propensity to consume, p. 476
net exports, p. 475
planned expenditure, p. 474
planned investment spending, p. 475

QUESTIONS

All questions are available in MyEconLab at http://www.myeconlab.com.

1. "When the stock market rises, investment spending is increasing." Is this statement true, false, or uncertain? Explain your answer.

2. Why is inventory investment counted as part of aggregate spending if it isn't actually sold to the final end user?

3. "Since inventories can be costly to hold, firms' planned inventory investment should be zero, and firms should acquire inventory only through unplanned inventory accumulation." Is this statement true, false, or uncertain? Explain your answer.

4. During and in the aftermath of the financial crisis of 2007–2009, planned investment fell substantially despite significant decreases in the real interest rate. What factors related to the planned investment function could explain this?

5. If households and firms believe the economy will be in a recession in the future, will this necessarily cause a recession, or have any impact on output at all?

6. Why do increases in the real interest rate lead to decreases in net exports, and vice versa?

7. Why does equilibrium output increase as the marginal propensity to consume increases?

8. If firms suddenly become more optimistic about the profitability of investment and planned investment spending rises by $100 billion, while consumers become more pessimistic and autonomous consumer spending falls by $100 billion, what happens to aggregate output?

9. In each of the cases below, what happens to equilibrium output? Briefly explain how it affects the relevant component(s) of planned spending.

    a. The real interest rate rises.

    b. The marginal propensity to consume falls.

    c. Financial frictions increase.

    d. Autonomous consumption decreases.

    e. Both taxes and government spending decrease by the same amount.

    f. The sensitivity of net exports to changes in the real interest rate decreases.

    g. The government provides tax incentives for research and development programs for firms.

10. If an increase in autonomous consumer expenditure is matched by an equal increase in taxes, will aggregate output rise or fall?

11. If a change in the interest rate has no effect on planned investment spending or net exports, what does this imply about the slope of the *IS* curve?

12. Why do companies cut production when they find that their unplanned inventory investment is greater than zero? If they didn't cut production, what effect would this have on their profits? Why?

13. "Firms will increase production when planned investment is less than (actual) total investment." Is this statement true, false, or uncertain? Explain your answer.

14. In each of the cases below, determine whether the *IS* curve shifts to the right or left, does not shift, or is indeterminate in the direction of shift.

    a. The real interest rate rises.

    b. The marginal propensity to consume declines.

    c. Financial frictions increase.

    d. Autonomous consumption decreases.

    e. Both taxes and government spending decrease by the same amount.

    f. The sensitivity of net exports to changes in the real interest rate decreases.

    g. The government provides tax incentives for research and development programs for firms.

15. "The fiscal stimulus package of 2009 caused the *IS* curve to shift to the left, since output decreased and unemployment increased after the policies were implemented." Is this statement true, false, or uncertain? Explain your answer.

16. When the Federal Reserve reduces its policy interest rate, how, if at all, is the *IS* curve affected? Briefly explain.

17. Suppose you read that prospects for stronger future economic growth have led the dollar to strengthen and stock prices to increase.

    a. What effect does the strengthened dollar have on the *IS* curve?

    b. What effect does the increase in stock prices have on the *IS* curve?

    c. What is the combined effect of these two events on the *IS* curve?

APPLIED PROBLEMS

All applied problems are available in MyEconLab at
http://www.myeconlab.com.

18. Calculate the value of the consumption function at each level of income in the table below if autonomous consumption = 300, taxes = 200, and $mpc = 0.9$.

Income Y	Disposable Income Y^D	Consumption C
0		
100		
200		
300		
400		
500		
600		

19. Assume that autonomous consumption is $1,625 billion and disposable income is $11,500 billion. Calculate consumption expenditure if an increase of $1,000 in disposable income leads to an increase of $750 in consumption expenditure.

20. Suppose that Dell Corporation has 20,000 computers in its warehouses on December 31, 2016, ready to be shipped to merchants (each computer is valued at $500). By December 31, 2017, Dell Corporation has 25,000 computers ready to be shipped, each valued at $450.

   a. Calculate Dell's inventory on December 31, 2016.

   b. Calculate Dell's inventory investment in 2017.

   c. What happens to inventory spending during the early stages of an economic recession?

21. If the consumption function is $C = 100 + 0.75Y_D$, $I = 200$, government spending is 200, and net exports are zero, what will be the equilibrium level of output? What will happen to aggregate output if government spending rises by 100?

22. If the marginal propensity to consume is 0.75, by how much would government spending have to rise to increase output by $1,000 billion? By how much would taxes need to decrease to increase output by $1,000 billion?

23. Assuming both taxes and government spending increase by the same amount, derive an expression for the effect on equilibrium output.

24. Consider an economy described by the following data:

$$\overline{C} = \$3.25 \text{ trillion}$$
$$\overline{I} = \$1.3 \text{ trillion}$$
$$\overline{G} = \$3.5 \text{ trillion}$$
$$\overline{T} = \$3.0 \text{ trillion}$$
$$\overline{NX} = -\$1.0 \text{ trillion}$$
$$\overline{f} = 1$$
$$mpc = 0.75$$
$$d = 0.3$$
$$x = 0.1$$

   a. Derive simplified expressions for the consumption function, the investment function, and the net export function.

   b. Derive an expression for the IS curve.

   c. If the real interest rate is $r = 2$, what is equilibrium output? If $r = 5$, what is equilibrium output?

   d. Draw a graph of the IS curve showing the answers from part (c) above.

   e. If government purchases increase to $4.2 trillion, what will happen to equilibrium output at $r = 2$? What will happen to equilibrium output at $r = 5$? Show the effect of the increase in government purchases in your graph from part (d).

25. Consider an economy described by the following data:

$$\overline{C} = \$4 \text{ trillion}$$
$$\overline{I} = \$1.5 \text{ trillion}$$
$$\overline{G} = \$3.0 \text{ trillion}$$
$$\overline{T} = \$3.0 \text{ trillion}$$
$$\overline{NX} = \$1.0 \text{ trillion}$$
$$\overline{f} = 0$$
$$mpc = 0.8$$
$$d = 0.35$$
$$x = 0.15$$

   a. Derive an expression for the IS curve.

   b. Assume that the Federal Reserve controls the interest rate and sets the interest rate at $r = 4$. What is the equilibrium level of output?

c. Suppose that a financial crisis begins, and $\bar{f}$ increases to $\bar{f} = 3$. What will happen to equilibrium output? If the Federal Reserve can set the interest rate, then at what level should the interest rate be set to keep output from changing?

d. Suppose the financial crisis causes $\bar{f}$ to increase as indicated in part (c) and also causes

planned autonomous investment to decrease to $\bar{I} = \$1.1$ trillion. Will the change in the interest rate implemented by the Federal Reserve in part (c) be effective in stabilizing output? If not, what additional monetary or fiscal policy changes could be implemented to stabilize output at the original equilibrium output level given in part (b)?

DATA ANALYSIS PROBLEMS

The Problems update with real-time data in MyEconLab *and are available for practice or instructor assignment.*

1. Go to the St. Louis Federal Reserve FRED database, and find data on Personal Consumption Expenditures (PCEC), Personal Consumption Expenditures: Durable Goods (PCDG), Personal Consumption Expenditures: Nondurable Goods (PCND), and Personal Consumption Expenditures: Services (PCESV).

a. Using the most recent data: What percentage of total household expenditures is devoted to the consumption of goods (both durable and nondurable goods)?

b. Given these data, which specific component of household expenditures would be most impacted by a reduction in overall household spending? Explain.

2. Go to the St. Louis Federal Reserve FRED database, and find data on Real Private Domestic Investment (GPDIC1), a measure of the real interest rate; the 10-year Treasury Inflation-Indexed Security, *TIIS* (FII10); and the spread between Baa corporate bonds and the 10-year U.S. treasury (BAA10YM), a measure of financial frictions. For (FII10) and (BAA10YM), convert the *frequency* setting to "quarterly," and download the data into a spreadsheet. For each quarter, add the (FII10) and (BAA10YM)

series to create r_i, the real interest rate for investments for that quarter. Then calculate the change in both investment and r_i as the change in each variable from the previous quarter.

a. For the eight most recent quarters of data available, calculate the change in investment from the previous quarter, and then calculate the average change over the eight most recent quarters.

b. Assume there is a one-quarter lag between movements in r_i and changes in investment; in other words, if r_i changes in the current quarter, it will affect investment in the next quarter. For the eight most recent lagged quarters of data available, calculate the one-quarter-lagged average change in r_i.

c. Take the ratio of your answer from part (a) divided by your answer from part (b). What does this value represent? Briefly explain.

d. Repeat parts (a) through (c) for the period 2008:Q3 to 2009:Q2. How do financial frictions help explain the behavior of investment during the financial crisis? How do the coefficients on investment compare between the current period and the financial crisis period? Briefly explain.

WEB EXERCISES

1. Go to http://www.eurmacro.unisg.ch/Tutor/ islm.html. Set the policy instruments to $G = 80$, $t = 0.20$, $c = 0.75$, and $b = 40$. Now increase government spending, G, from 80 to 160. By how much does the *IS* curve shift horizontally to the right? Why is the amount of shift greater than the increase in G? Now increase the marginal propensity to consume, c, from 0.75 to 0.90. In which direction does the *IS* curve shift, and why? By how much does it shift? Now increase the tax rate, t, from 0.20 to 0.28. In which direction does the *IS* curve shift, and why? By how much does it shift?

2. Go to http://www.eurmacro.unisg.ch/Tutor/ islm.html. Set the policy instruments to $G = 80$, $t = 0.20$, $c = 0.75$, and $b = 40$. Now increase the sensitivity of investment to the interest rate, b, from 40 to 80. What happens to the slope of the *IS* curve? Why?

WEB REFERENCE

http://research.stlouisfed.org/fred2/

Information about the macroeconomic variables discussed in this chapter.

21 The Monetary Policy and Aggregate Demand Curves

Learning Objectives

- Recognize the impact of changes in the nominal federal funds rate on short-term real interest rates.
- Define and illustrate the monetary policy (*MP*) curve, and explain shifts in the *MP* curve.
- Explain why the aggregate demand (*AD*) curve slopes downward, and explain shifts in the *AD* curve.

Preview

At the height of the financial crisis in December 2008, the Federal Open Market Committee of the Federal Reserve announced a surprisingly bold policy decision that sent the markets into a frenzy. The committee lowered the federal funds rate, the interest rate charged on overnight loans between banks, by 75 basis points (0.75 percentage point), moving the federal funds rate almost all the way to zero.

To see how a monetary policy action like the one described above affects the economy, we need to analyze how monetary policy affects aggregate demand. We start this chapter by explaining why monetary policymakers set interest rates higher when inflation increases, leading to a positive relationship between real interest rates and inflation that can be illustrated using the *monetary policy (MP) curve*. Then, by combining the *MP* curve with the *IS* curve we developed in the previous chapter, we derive the *aggregate demand curve*, a key element in the aggregate demand/aggregate supply model framework used in the rest of this book to discuss short-run economic fluctuations.

THE FEDERAL RESERVE AND MONETARY POLICY

Central banks throughout the world use a very short-term interest rate as their primary policy tool. In the United States, the Federal Reserve conducts monetary policy via its setting of the federal funds rate. For example, after the FOMC meeting of July 30, 2014, the Federal Reserve issued a statement that the Committee would "maintain the current 0 to ¼ percent target for the federal funds rate."

As we saw in Chapter 15, the Federal Reserve controls the federal funds rate by varying the reserves it provides to the banking system. When it provides more reserves, banks have more money to lend to each other, and this excess liquidity causes the federal funds rate to fall. When the Fed drains reserves from the banking system, banks have less to lend, and the lack of liquidity leads to a rise in the federal funds rate.

The federal funds rate is a *nominal* interest rate, but as we learned in the previous chapter, it is the *real* interest rate that affects net exports and business spending, thereby determining the level of equilibrium output. How does the Federal Reserve's control of the federal funds rate enable it to control the real interest rate, through which monetary policy impacts the economy?

Recall from Chapter 4 that the real interest rate, r, is the nominal interest rate, i, minus expected inflation, π^e.

$$r = i - \pi^e$$

Changes in nominal interest rates can change the real interest rate only if actual and expected inflation remain unchanged in the short run. Because prices typically are slow to move—that is, they are *sticky*—changes in monetary policy will not have an immediate effect on inflation and expected inflation. As a result, **when the Federal Reserve lowers the federal funds rate, real interest rates fall; when the Federal Reserve raises the federal funds rate, real interest rates rise.**

THE MONETARY POLICY CURVE

We have seen how the Federal Reserve can control real interest rates in the short run. The next step in our analysis is to examine how monetary policy reacts to inflation. The **monetary policy (MP) curve** indicates the relationship between the real interest rate set by the central bank and the inflation rate. We can write the equation of this curve as follows:

$$r = \bar{r} + \lambda\pi \tag{1}$$

where $\bar{r}$ is the autonomous (exogenous) component of the real interest rate set by the monetary policy authorities, which is unrelated to the current level of the inflation rate or any other variable in the model, and λ is the responsiveness of the real interest rate to the inflation rate.

To make our discussion of the monetary policy curve more concrete, Figure 1 shows an example of a monetary policy curve MP in which $\bar{r} = 1.0$ and $\lambda = 0.5$:

$$r = 1.0 + 0.5\pi \tag{2}$$

At point A, where inflation is 1%, the Federal Reserve sets the real interest rate at 1.5%; at point B, where inflation is 2%, the Fed sets the real interest rate at 2%; and at point C, where inflation is 3%, the Fed sets the real interest rate at 2.5%. The line going through points A, B, and C is the monetary policy curve MP, and it is upward-sloping, indicating that monetary policymakers raise real interest rates when the inflation rate rises.

The Taylor Principle: Why the Monetary Policy Curve Has an Upward Slope

To see why the MP curve has an upward slope, we need to recognize that central banks seek to keep inflation stable. To stabilize inflation, monetary policymakers tend to follow the **Taylor principle**, named after John Taylor of Stanford University: They raise *nominal* rates by more than any rise in expected inflation so that *real* interest rates will rise when there is a rise in inflation, as illustrated by the MP curve.[1]

---

[1]Note that the Taylor principle differs from the Taylor rule, described in Chapter 16, in that it does not provide a rule for how monetary policy should react to conditions in the economy, whereas the Taylor rule does.

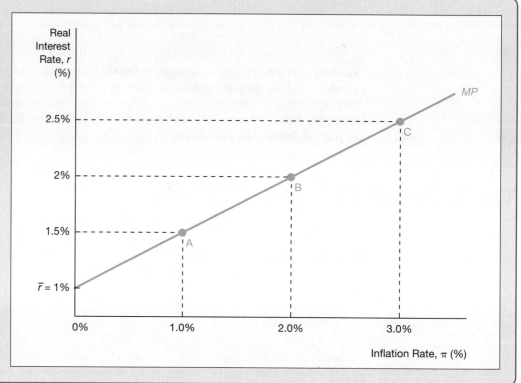

FIGURE 1
The Monetary Policy Curve

The upward slope of the *MP* curve indicates that the central bank reacts to higher inflation by raising real interest rates, because monetary policy follows the Taylor principle.

To see why monetary policymakers follow the Taylor principle, reacting to rising inflation by raising real interest rates, consider what would happen if monetary policymakers instead allowed the real interest rate to fall when inflation rose. In this case, an increase in inflation would lead to a decline in the real interest rate, which, as we saw in the previous chapter, would increase aggregate output, which would in turn cause inflation to rise further, which would then cause the real interest rate to fall even more, increasing aggregate output again. Schematically, we can write this chain of events as follows:[2]

$$\pi \uparrow \Rightarrow r \downarrow \Rightarrow Y \uparrow \Rightarrow \pi \uparrow \Rightarrow r \downarrow \Rightarrow Y \uparrow \Rightarrow \pi \uparrow$$

Under these conditions, inflation would keep rising and eventually spin out of control. Indeed, this is exactly what happened in the 1970s, when the Federal Reserve did not raise nominal interest rates by as much as inflation rose, so that real interest rates fell. Inflation accelerated to over 10%.[3]

---

[2]The liquidity preference framework developed in Chapter 5 gives another rationale for using the Taylor principle when the path of the money supply curve and inflation expectations are unchanged. A rise in inflation means that the price level will be higher than it otherwise would be, and so the money demand curve shifts to the right, causing both nominal and real interest rates to rise (because inflation expectations are unchanged). Schematically, this can be written as follows:

$$\pi \uparrow \Rightarrow P \uparrow \Rightarrow M^d \text{ to the right} \Rightarrow i \uparrow \Rightarrow r \uparrow$$

[3]In Web Appendix D to Chapter 22 we formally demonstrate the instability of inflation when central banks do not follow the Taylor principle.

Shifts in the *MP* Curve

In common parlance, the Federal Reserve is said to "tighten" monetary policy when it raises real interest rates and to "ease" it when it lowers real interest rates. It is important, however, to distinguish between changes in monetary policy that shift the monetary policy curve, which we call *autonomous* changes, and the Taylor principle–driven changes that are reflected in movements along the monetary policy curve, which are called *automatic* adjustments to interest rates.

Central banks may make autonomous changes to monetary policy for various reasons. They may wish to change the inflation rate from its current value. For example, to lower inflation, they could increase $\bar{r}$ by one percentage point and so raise the real interest rate at any given inflation rate, a move that we will refer to as an **autonomous tightening of monetary policy**. This autonomous monetary tightening would shift the monetary policy curve upward by one percentage point, from MP_1 to MP_2 in Figure 2, thereby causing the economy to contract and inflation to fall. Or, the central banks may have other information, unrelated to inflation, suggesting that interest rates must be adjusted to achieve good economic outcomes. For example, if the economy is going into a recession, monetary policymakers will want to lower real interest rates at any given inflation rate, an **autonomous easing of monetary policy**, in order to stimulate the economy and to prevent inflation from falling. This autonomous easing of monetary policy would result in a downward shift of the monetary policy curve by, say, one percentage point, from MP_1 to MP_3 in Figure 2.

MyEconLab Mini-lecture

FIGURE 2
Shifts in the Monetary Policy Curve

Autonomous changes in monetary policy—for example, when a central bank changes the real interest rate at any given inflation rate—shift the *MP* curve. An autonomous tightening of monetary policy that increases the real interest rate shifts the *MP* curve up to MP_2, whereas an autonomous easing of monetary policy that lowers the real interest rate shifts the *MP* curve down to MP_3.

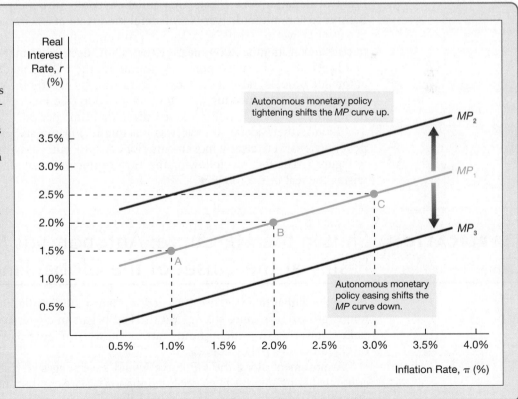

Movements Along Versus Shifts in the *MP* Curve

A stumbling block for many students studying the aggregate demand/aggregate supply (*AD/AS*) framework is understanding the distinction between *shifts in* the *MP* curve versus *movements along* the *MP* curve. Movements along the *MP* curve—that is, movements from point *A* to *B* to *C* in Figure 1—should be viewed as a central bank's normal response (also known as an endogenous response) of raising interest rates when inflation is rising. Thus we can think of a movement along the *MP* curve as an *automatic* response of the central bank to a change in inflation. Such an automatic response does not involve a shift in the *MP* curve.

On the other hand, when the central bank raises interest rates *at a given level of the inflation rate*, this action is not an automatic response to higher inflation but is instead an autonomous tightening of monetary policy that shifts the *MP* curve up, from MP_1 to MP_2 in Figure 2.

The distinction between autonomous monetary policy changes and movements along the monetary policy curve is illustrated by the two applications below, which describe the monetary policy actions taken by the Federal Reserve in the period from 2004–2006 and at the onset of the global financial crisis in the fall of 2007. ◆

APPLICATION Movement Along the *MP* Curve: The Rise in the Federal Funds Rate Target, 2004–2006

Fears of deflation—i.e., fears that inflation could turn negative—led the Federal Reserve to commit to the very low federal funds rate of 1% from June of 2003 to June of 2004. However, with the economy growing rapidly, inflationary pressures began to rise, and at its June 2004 meeting the FOMC decided to increase the federal funds rate by ¼ of a percentage point. Furthermore, the FOMC made this increase a very automatic process, raising the federal funds rate by exactly the same amount at every subsequent FOMC meeting through June of 2006 (see Figure 3). What does this tell us about the monetary policy curve during that time period?

Because the Federal Reserve was reacting to inflationary pressures, its monetary policy actions were clearly movements along the *MP* curve, say, from point *A* to *B* to *C* in Figure 1. The Fed was following the Taylor principle, reacting to higher inflation by raising the real interest rate. ◆

APPLICATION Shift in the *MP* Curve: Autonomous Monetary Easing at the Onset of the Global Financial Crisis

When the global financial crisis started in August 2007, inflation was rising and economic growth was quite strong. Yet the Fed began an aggressive easing of monetary policy, lowering the federal funds rate as shown in Figure 3. What were the effects on the monetary policy curve?

A movement along the *MP* curve would have suggested that the Fed planned to continue hiking interest rates because inflation was rising, but instead the Fed did the opposite. The Fed's actions thus shifted the monetary policy curve down, from MP_1 to MP_3, as shown in Figure 2. The Fed pursued this autonomous monetary policy

FIGURE 3
The Federal Funds Rate and Inflation Rate, 2003–2014

From June of 2004 through June of 2006, because of pressures from rising inflation, the Fed increased its policy rate, the federal funds rate, by 1/4 of a percentage point at every FOMC meeting. These Fed actions were a movement along the MP curve. In contrast, the Fed began an autonomous easing of monetary policy in September 2007, bringing down the federal funds rate despite the continuing high inflation.

Source: Federal Reserve Bank of St. Louis FRED database. http://research.stlouisfed.org/fred2/

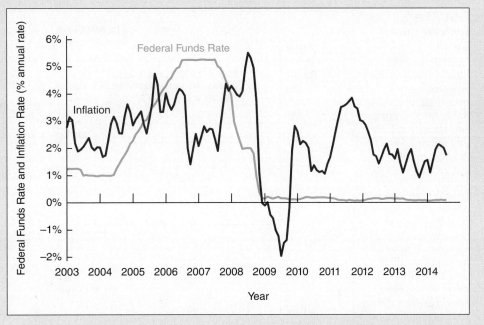

easing because the negative shock to the economy caused by the disruption to financial markets (discussed in Chapter 12) indicated that, despite the high inflation rates at the time, the economy was likely to weaken in the near future, and the inflation rate would then fall. Indeed, this is exactly what came to pass, with the economy going into a recession in December 2007 and the inflation rate falling sharply after July 2008. ◆

THE AGGREGATE DEMAND CURVE

We are now ready to derive the relationship between the inflation rate and aggregate output when the goods market is in equilibrium: the **aggregate demand curve**. The *MP* curve that we just developed demonstrates how central banks respond to changes in inflation by changing the interest rate in line with the Taylor principle. The *IS* curve we developed in Chapter 20 showed that changes in real interest rates, in turn, affect equilibrium output. With these two curves, we can now link the quantity of aggregate output demanded with the inflation rate, given the public's expectations of inflation and the stance of monetary policy. The aggregate demand curve is central to the aggregate demand and supply analysis we will develop further in the next chapter, which will enable us to explain short-run fluctuations in both aggregate output and inflation.

Deriving the Aggregate Demand Curve Graphically

Using the hypothetical *MP* curve from Equation 2, we know that when the inflation rate rises from 1% to 2% to 3%, the Federal Reserve reacts by raising the real interest rate from 1.5% to 2% to 2.5%. We plot these points in panel (a) of Figure 4 as the

MyEconLab Mini-lecture

FIGURE 4
Deriving the *AD* Curve

The *MP* curve in panel (a) shows that as inflation rises from 1.0% to 2.0% to 3.0%, the real interest rate rises from 1.5% to 2.0% to 2.5%. The *IS* curve in panel (b) then shows that higher real interest rates lead to lower planned investment spending and net exports, and hence aggregate output falls from $10.5 trillion to $10.0 trillion to $9.5 trillion. Finally, panel (c) plots the level of equilibrium output corresponding to each of the three inflation rates: the line that connects these points is the *AD* curve, and it is downward-sloping.

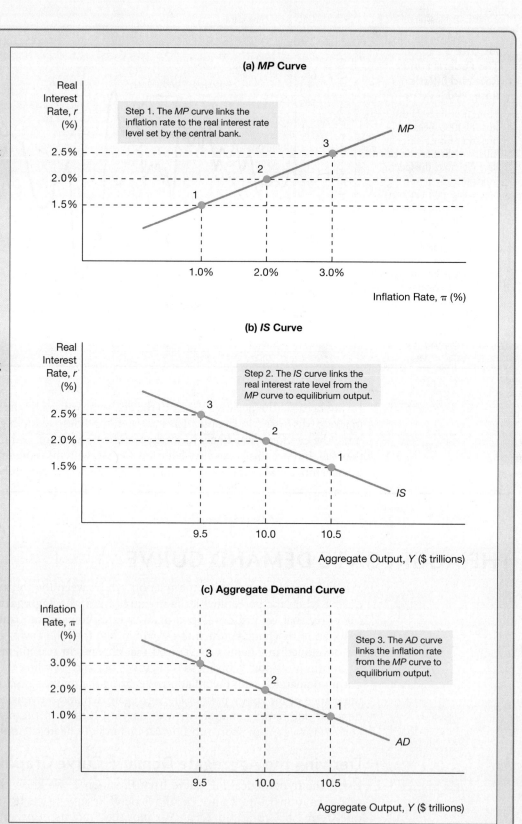

MP curve. In panel (b), we graph the *IS* curve described in Equation 13 of Chapter 20 ($Y = 12 - r$). As the real interest rate rises from 1.5% to 2% to 2.5%, the equilibrium moves from point 1 to point 2 to point 3, and aggregate output falls from $10.5 trillion to $10 trillion to $9.5 trillion. In other words, as real interest rates rise, investment and net exports decline, leading to a reduction in aggregate demand. Using the information from panels (a) and (b), we can create the curve shown in panel (c). As inflation rises from 1% to 2% to 3%, the equilibrium moves from point 1 to point 2 to point 3 in panel (c), and aggregate output falls from $10.5 trillion to $10 trillion to $9.5 trillion.

The line that connects the three points shown in panel (c) is the aggregate demand curve, *AD*, and it indicates the level of aggregate output corresponding to each of the three real interest rates consistent with equilibrium in the goods market for any given inflation rate. The aggregate demand curve has a downward slope because a higher inflation rate leads the central bank to raise the real interest rate, thereby lowering planned spending and hence lowering the level of equilibrium aggregate output.

By using some algebra (see the FYI box, "Deriving the Aggregate Demand Curve Algebraically"), the *AD* curve in Figure 4 can be written numerically as follows:

$$Y = 11 - 0.5\pi \tag{3}$$

Factors That Shift the Aggregate Demand Curve

Movements along the aggregate demand curve describe how the equilibrium level of aggregate output changes when the inflation rate changes. When factors other than the inflation rate change, however, the aggregate demand curve shifts. We first review the factors that shift the *IS* curve, and then consider the factors that shift the *AD* curve.

FYI   Deriving the Aggregate Demand Curve Algebraically

To derive a numerical *AD* curve, we start by taking the numerical *IS* curve given by Equation 13 in Chapter 20:

$$Y = 12 - r$$

We then use the numerical *MP* curve given in Equation 2, $r = 1.0 + 0.5\pi$, to substitute for *r*, yielding

$$Y = 12 - (1.0 + 0.5\pi)$$
$$= (12 - 1) - 0.5\pi$$
$$= 11 - 0.5\pi$$

which is the same as Equation 3 in the text.

Similarly, we can derive a more general version of the *AD* curve by using the algebraic version of the *IS* curve given by Equation 12 in Chapter 20:

$$Y = [\overline{C} + \overline{I} - d\overline{f} + \overline{G} + \overline{NX} - mpc \times \overline{T}]$$
$$\times \frac{1}{1 - mpc} - \frac{d + x}{1 - mpc} \times r$$

We then substitute for *r* using the algebraic *MP* curve given in Equation 1, $r = \overline{r} + \lambda\pi$, to get the more general equation of the *AD* curve:

$$Y = [\overline{C} + \overline{I} - d\overline{f} + \overline{G} + \overline{NX} - mpc \times \overline{T}]$$
$$\times \frac{1}{1 - mpc} - \frac{d + x}{1 - mpc} \times (\overline{r} + \lambda\pi)$$

Shifts in the *IS* Curve

We saw in the preceding chapter that there are six factors that cause the *IS* curve to shift. It turns out that these same factors will cause the aggregate demand curve to shift as well:

1. Autonomous consumption expenditure
2. Autonomous investment spending
3. Government purchases
4. Taxes
5. Autonomous net exports
6. Financial frictions

We examine how changes in these factors lead to a shift in the aggregate demand curve, as shown in Figure 5.

Suppose that inflation is at 2.0%, and so the *MP* curve in panel (a) of Figure 5 shows that the real interest rate is at 2.0%. The IS_1 curve in panel (b) then shows that the equilibrium level of output is at $10 trillion at point A_1, which corresponds to an equilibrium level of output of $10 trillion at point A_1 on the AD_1 curve in panel (c). Now suppose there is a rise in, for example, government purchases of $1 trillion. Panel (b) shows that with both the inflation rate and the real interest rate held constant at 2.0%, the equilibrium moves from point A_1 to point A_2, with output rising to $12.5 trillion,[4] and so the *IS* curve shifts to the right from IS_1 to IS_2. The rise in output to $12.5 trillion means that, holding inflation and the real interest rate constant, the equilibrium in panel (c) also moves from point A_1 to point A_2, and so the *AD* curve also shifts to the right, from AD_1 to AD_2.

Figure 5 shows that ***any factor that shifts the IS curve shifts the aggregate demand curve in the same direction.*** Therefore, any factor that shifts the *IS* curve to the right—a rise in autonomous consumption expenditure or planned investment spending encouraged by "animal spirits," a rise in government purchases, an autonomous rise in net exports, a fall in taxes, or a decline in financial frictions—will also shift the aggregate demand curve to the right. Conversely, any factor that shifts the *IS* curve to the left—a fall in autonomous consumption expenditure, a fall in planned investment spending, a fall in government purchases, a fall in net exports, a rise in taxes, or a rise in financial frictions—will shift the aggregate demand curve to the left.

Shifts in the *MP* Curve

We now examine what happens to the aggregate demand curve when the *MP* curve shifts. Suppose the Federal Reserve is worried about the economy overheating and so decides to autonomously tighten monetary policy by raising the real interest rate by one percentage point at any given level of the inflation rate. At an inflation rate of 2.0%, the real interest rate rises from 2.0% to 3.0% in Figure 6. The *MP* curve shifts up from MP_1 to MP_2 in panel (a). Panel (b) shows that when the inflation rate is at 2.0%, the higher real interest rate of 3.0% causes the equilibrium to move from point A_1 to point A_2 on the *IS* curve, with output falling from $10 trillion to $9 trillion. The lower output of $9 trillion occurs because the higher real interest leads to a decline in investment and net exports, which lowers aggregate demand. The lower output of $9 trillion then decreases the equilibrium output level from point A_1 to point A_2 in panel (c), and so the *AD* curve shifts to the left, from AD_1 to AD_2.

---

[4]As we saw in the numerical example in Chapter 20, a rise in government purchases of $1 trillion leads to a $2.5 trillion increase in equilibrium output at any given real interest rate, and this is why output rises from $10 trillion to $12.5 trillion when the real interest rate is at 2.0%.

FIGURE 5
Shift in the *AD* Curve from Shifts in the *IS* Curve

At a 2% inflation rate in panel (a), the monetary policy curve indicates that the real interest rate is 2%. An increase in government purchases shifts the *IS* curve to the right in panel (b). At a given inflation rate and real interest rate of 2.0%, equilibrium output rises from $10 trillion to $12.5 trillion, which is shown as a movement from point A_1 to point A_2 in panel (c), shifting the aggregate demand curve to the right from AD_1 to AD_2. Any factor that shifts the *IS* curve shifts the *AD* curve in the same direction.

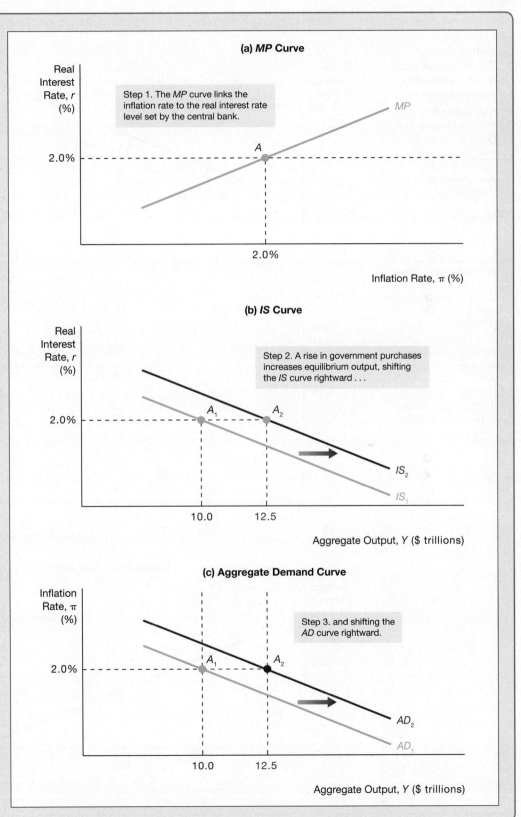

(a) MP Curve

Real Interest Rate, r (%)

Step 1. The *MP* curve links the inflation rate to the real interest rate level set by the central bank.

MP

2.0%

A

2.0%

Inflation Rate, π (%)

(b) IS Curve

Real Interest Rate, r (%)

Step 2. A rise in government purchases increases equilibrium output, shifting the *IS* curve rightward . . .

A_1 A_2

2.0%

IS_2

IS_1

10.0   12.5

Aggregate Output, Y ($ trillions)

(c) Aggregate Demand Curve

Inflation Rate, π (%)

Step 3. and shifting the *AD* curve rightward.

A_1 A_2

2.0%

AD_2

AD_1

10.0   12.5

Aggregate Output, Y ($ trillions)

MyEconLab Mini-lecture

FIGURE 6
Shift in the *AD* Curve from Autonomous Monetary Policy Tightening

Autonomous monetary tightening that raises real interest rates by one percentage point at any given inflation rate shifts the *MP* curve up, from MP_1 to MP_2 in panel (a). With the inflation rate at 2.0%, the higher 3% interest rate results in a movement from point A_1 to A_2 on the *IS* curve, with output falling from $10 trillion to $9 trillion. This change in equilibrium output leads to movement from point A_1 to point A_2 in panel (c), shifting the aggregate demand curve to the left, from AD_1 to AD_2.

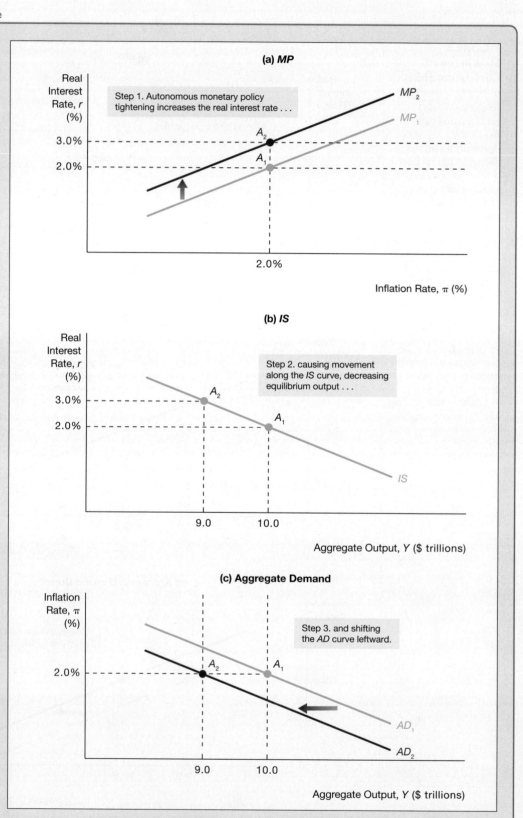

Our conclusion from Figure 6 is that *an autonomous tightening of monetary policy—that is, a rise in the real interest rate at any given inflation rate—shifts the aggregate demand curve to the left. Conversely, an autonomous easing of monetary policy shifts the aggregate demand curve to the right.*

We have now derived and analyzed the aggregate demand curve, an essential element in the aggregate demand and supply framework that we will examine in the next chapter. We will use the aggregate demand curve in this framework to determine both aggregate output and inflation, as well as to examine events that cause these variables to change.

SUMMARY

1. When the Federal Reserve lowers the federal funds rate by providing more liquidity to the banking system, real interest rates fall in the short run; when the Federal Reserve raises the federal funds rate by reducing the amount of liquidity in the banking system, real interest rates rise in the short run.

2. The monetary policy (*MP*) curve shows the relationship between inflation and the real interest rate that arises from monetary authorities' actions. Monetary policy follows the Taylor principle, in which higher inflation results in higher real interest rates, represented by upward movements along the monetary policy curve. An autonomous tightening of monetary policy occurs when monetary policymakers raise the real interest rate at any given inflation rate, resulting in an upward shift of the monetary policy curve. An autonomous easing of monetary policy and a downward shift of the monetary policy curve occur when monetary

policymakers lower the real interest rate at any given inflation rate.

3. The aggregate demand curve gives the level of equilibrium aggregate output (which equals the total quantity of output demanded) for any given inflation rate. It slopes downward because a higher inflation rate leads the central bank to raise real interest rates, which leads to a lower level of equilibrium output. The aggregate demand curve will shift in the same direction as the *IS* curve; hence the *AD* curve shifts to the right when government purchases increase, taxes decrease, "animal spirits" encourage consumer and business spending, autonomous net exports increase, or financial frictions decrease. An autonomous tightening of monetary policy—that is, an increase in the real interest rate at any given inflation rate—leads to a decline in aggregate demand, and the aggregate demand curve shifts to the left.

KEY TERMS

aggregate demand curve, p. 499
autonomous easing of monetary
  policy, p. 497

autonomous tightening of monetary
  policy, p. 497

monetary policy (*MP*) curve, p. 495
Taylor principle, p. 495

QUESTIONS

All questions are available in MyEconLab at
http://www.myeconlab.com.

1. When the inflation rate increases, what happens to the federal funds rate? Operationally, how does the Fed adjust the federal funds rate?

2. What is the key assumption underlying the Fed's ability to control the real interest rate?

3. Why does the *MP* curve necessarily have an upward slope?

4. If $\lambda = 0$, what does this imply about the relationship between the nominal interest rate and the inflation rate?

5. How does an autonomous tightening or easing of monetary policy by the Fed affect the *MP* curve?

6. How is an autonomous tightening or easing of monetary policy different from a change in the real interest rate caused by a change in the current inflation rate?

7. Suppose that a new Fed chair is appointed and that his or her approach to monetary policy can be summarized by the following statement: "I care only about increasing employment. Inflation has been at very low levels for quite some time; my priority is to ease monetary policy to promote employment." How would you expect the monetary policy curve to be affected, if at all?

8. "The Fed decreased the fed funds rate in late 2007, even though inflation was increasing. This action demonstrated a violation of the Taylor principle." Is this statement true, false, or uncertain? Explain your answer.

9. What factors affect the slope of the aggregate demand curve?

10. "Autonomous monetary policy is more effective at changing output when λ is higher." Is this statement true, false, or uncertain? Explain your answer.

11. If net exports were not sensitive to changes in the real interest rate, would monetary policy be more or less effective in changing output?

12. How does an autonomous tightening or easing of monetary policy by the Fed affect the aggregate demand curve?

13. For each of the following situations, describe how (if at all) the *IS*, *MP*, and *AD* curves are affected.

a. A decrease in financial frictions

b. An increase in taxes and an autonomous easing of monetary policy

c. An increase in the current inflation rate

d. A decrease in autonomous consumption

e. Firms become more optimistic about the future of the economy.

f. The new Federal Reserve chair begins to care more about fighting inflation.

14. What would be the effect of an increase in U.S. net exports on the aggregate demand curve? Would an increase in net exports affect the monetary policy curve? Explain.

15. Why does the aggregate demand curve shift when "animal spirits" change?

16. If government spending increases and taxes are raised to keep the budget balanced, what happens to the aggregate demand curve?

17. Suppose that government spending is increased at the same time that an autonomous monetary policy tightening occurs. What will happen to the position of the aggregate demand curve?

18. "If $\bar{f}$ increases, then the Fed can keep output constant by reducing the real interest rate by the same amount as the increase in financial frictions." Is this statement true, false, or uncertain? Explain your answer.

APPLIED PROBLEMS

All applied problems are available in MyEconLab *at* http://www.myeconlab.com.

19. Assume that the monetary policy curve is given by $r = 1.5 + 0.75\pi$.

a. Calculate the real interest rate when the inflation rate is 2%, 3%, and 4%.

b. Draw a graph of the *MP* curve, labeling the points from part (a).

c. Assume now that the monetary policy curve is given by $r = 2.5 + 0.75\pi$. Does the new monetary policy curve represent an autonomous tightening or loosening of monetary policy?

d. Calculate the real interest rate when the inflation rate is 2%, 3%, and 4%, and draw the new *MP* curve, showing the shift from part (b).

20. Use an *IS* curve and an *MP* curve to derive graphically the *AD* curve.

21. Suppose the monetary policy curve is given by $r = 1.5 + 0.75\pi$, and the *IS* curve is given by $Y = 13 - r$.

a. Calculate an expression for the aggregate demand curve.

b. Calculate the real interest rate and aggregate output when the inflation rate is 2%, 3%, and 4%.

c. Draw graphs of the *IS*, *MP*, and *AD* curves, labeling the points from part (b) on the appropriate graphs.

22. Consider an economy described by the following:

$\overline{C}$ = $4 trillion
$\overline{I}$ = $1.5 trillion
$\overline{G}$ = $3.0 trillion
$\overline{T}$ = $3.0 trillion
$\overline{NX}$ = $1.0 trillion
$\overline{f}$ = 0
mpc = 0.8
d = 0.35
x = 0.15
λ = 0.5
$\overline{r}$ = 2

a. Derive expressions for the *MP* curve and the *AD* curve.

b. Calculate the real interest rate and aggregate output when $\pi = 2$ and $\pi = 4$.

c. Draw a graph of the *MP* curve and the *AD* curve, labeling the points given in part (b).

23. Consider an economy described by the following:

$\overline{C}$ = $3.25 trillion
$\overline{I}$ = $1.3 trillion
$\overline{G}$ = $3.5 trillion
$\overline{T}$ = $3.0 trillion
$\overline{NX}$ = −$1.0 trillion
$\overline{f}$ = 1
mpc = 0.75
d = 0.3
x = 0.1
λ = 1
$\overline{r}$ = 1

a. Derive expressions for the *MP* curve and the *AD* curve.

b. Assume that $\pi = 1$. Calculate the real interest rate, the equilibrium level of output, consumption, planned investment, and net exports.

c. Suppose the Fed increases $\overline{r}$ to $\overline{r} = 2$. Calculate the real interest rate, the equilibrium level of output, consumption, planned investment, and net exports at this new level of $\overline{r}$.

d. Considering that output, consumption, planned investment, and net exports all decreased in part (c), why might the Fed choose to increase $\overline{r}$?

24. Consider the economy described in Applied Problem 23.

a. Derive expressions for the *MP* curve and the *AD* curve.

b. Assume that $\pi = 2$. What are the real interest rate and the equilibrium level of output?

c. Suppose government spending increases to $4 trillion. What happens to equilibrium output?

d. If the Fed wants to keep output constant, then what monetary policy change should it make?

25. Suppose the *MP* curve is given by $r = 2 + \pi$, and the *IS* curve is given by $Y = 20 - 2r$.

a. Derive an expression for the *AD* curve, and draw a graph labeling points at $\pi = 0$, $\pi = 4$, and $\pi = 8$.

b. Suppose that λ increases to $\lambda = 2$. Derive an expression for the new *AD* curve, and draw the new *AD* curve using the graph from part (a).

c. What does your answer to part (b) imply about the relationship between a central bank's distaste for inflation and the slope of the *AD* curve?

DATA ANALYSIS PROBLEMS

The Problems update with real-time data in MyEconLab *and are available for practice or instructor assignment.*

1. A measure of real interest rates can be approximated by the Treasury Inflation-Indexed Security, or *TIIS*. Go to the St. Louis Federal Reserve FRED database, and find data on the five-year *TIIS* (FII5) and the personal consumption expenditure price index (PCECTPI), a measure of the price index. Choose "Quarterly" for the *frequency* setting of the *TIIS*, and download both

data series. Convert the price index data to annualized inflation rates by taking the quarter-to-quarter percent change in the price index and multiplying it by 4. Be sure to multiply by 100 so that your results are percentages.

a. Calculate the average inflation rate and the average real interest rate over the most recent four quarters of data available, and the four quarters prior to that.

b. Calculate the change in the average inflation rate between the most recent annual period and the year prior. Then calculate the change in the average real interest rate over the same period.

c. Using your answers to part (b), compute the ratio of the change in the average real interest rate to the change in the average inflation rate. What does this ratio represent? Comment on how it relates to the Taylor principle.

2. A measure of real interest rates can be approximated by the Treasury Inflation-Indexed Security, or *TIIS*.

Go to the St. Louis Federal Reserve FRED database, and find data on the five-year *TIIS* (FII5) and the personal consumption expenditure price index (PCECTPI), a measure of the price index. Choose "Quarterly" for the *frequency* setting for the *TIIS*, and choose "Percent Change From Year Ago" for the *units* setting on (PCECTPI). Plot both series on the same graph, using data from 2007 through the most current data available. Use the graph to identify periods of autonomous monetary policy changes. Briefly explain your reasoning.

WEB EXERCISES

1. Go to http://www.federalreserve.gov/pf/pdf/pf_2.pdf. Review the FOMC's document, "Longer-Run Goals and Monetary Policy Strategy." Explain why these goals are consistent with the Taylor principle.

2. Go to http://www.federalreserve.gov/fomc/. Read the latest FOMC statement and the minutes of the most recent FOMC meeting. Are the statement and the discussion in the minutes consistent with the Taylor principle?

WEB REFERENCES

http://www.federalreserve.gov/pf/pf.htm

Describes the purposes and functions of the Federal Reserve System and its rationale for the conduct of monetary policy.

http://www.federalreserve.gov/fomc

Provides information on all the FOMC's actions, including the statement and minutes for each meeting.

22 Aggregate Demand and Supply Analysis

Learning Objectives

- Summarize and illustrate the aggregate demand curve and the factors that shift it.
- Illustrate and interpret the short-run and long-run aggregate supply curves.
- Illustrate and interpret shifts in the short-run and long-run aggregate supply curves.
- Illustrate and interpret the short-run and long-run equilibria, and the role of the self-correcting mechanism.
- Illustrate and interpret the short-run and long-run effects of a shock to aggregate demand.
- Illustrate and interpret the short-run and long-run effects of temporary and permanent supply shocks.
- Explain business cycle fluctuations in major economies during the 2007–2009 financial crisis.

Preview

In earlier chapters, we focused considerable attention on monetary policy because it touches our everyday lives by affecting both inflation and the quantity of jobs available. In this chapter , we develop aggregate demand and supply analysis, a basic tool that will enable us to study the effects of monetary policy on output and inflation. *Aggregate demand* is the total amount of output demanded at different inflation rates. *Aggregate supply* is the total amount of output that firms in an economy want to sell at different inflation rates. As was the case in the supply and demand analysis from your earlier economics courses, equilibrium occurs at the intersection of the aggregate demand and aggregate supply curves.

Aggregate demand and supply analysis will enable us to explore how aggregate output and inflation are determined. (The Following the Financial News box indicates where and how often data on aggregate output and the inflation rate are published.) Not only will the analysis help us interpret the past, but it also will help us understand recent episodes in the business cycle, such as the severe recession of 2007–2009, and predict how future events may affect aggregate output and inflation.

AGGREGATE DEMAND

The first building block of aggregate supply and demand analysis is the **aggregate demand curve**, which describes the relationship between the quantity of aggregate output demanded and the inflation rate when all other variables are held constant.

Aggregate demand is made up of four component parts: **consumption expenditure**, the total demand for consumer goods and services; **planned investment spending**,[1] the total planned spending by business firms on new machines, factories, and other capital goods, plus planned spending on new homes; **government purchases**, spending by all levels of government (federal, state, and local) on goods and services (paper clips, computers, computer programming, missiles, government employees, and so on); and **net exports**, the net foreign spending on domestic goods and services, equal to exports minus

---

[1]Recall that economists restrict the definition of the word *investment* to mean the purchase of new physical capital, such as a new machine or a new house, which adds to spending on newly produced goods or services. This differs from the everyday use of the term by noneconomists, who use the word *investment* to describe purchases of common stocks or bonds, purchases that do not necessarily involve newly produced goods and services. When economists speak of investment spending, they are referring to purchases that add to aggregate demand.

Following the Financial News Aggregate Output, Unemployment, and Inflation

Newspapers and Internet sites periodically report data that provide information on the level of aggregate output, unemployment, and the inflation rate. Here is a list of the relevant data series, their frequencies of publication, and the times at which they are published.

Aggregate Output and Unemployment

Real GDP: Quarterly (January–March, April–June, July–September, October–December); published three to four weeks after the end of a quarter.

Industrial production: Monthly. Industrial production is not as comprehensive a measure of aggregate output as real GDP because it measures only manufacturing output; the estimate for the previous month is reported in the middle of the following month.

Unemployment rate: Monthly. The previous month's figure is usually published on the Friday of the first week of the following month.

Inflation Rate

There are several different measures of the inflation rate that are calculated from different measures of the price level.

GDP deflator: Quarterly. This comprehensive measure of the price level (described in the appendix to Chapter 1) is published at the same time as the real GDP data.

Consumer price index (CPI): Monthly. The CPI is a measure of the price level for consumers (also described in the appendix to Chapter 1); the value for the previous month is published in the third or fourth week of the following month.

PCE deflator: Quarterly. This is another measure of the price level for consumers. It is calculated in a similar way to the GDP deflator, but applies only to the items that are in the personal consumption expenditure category of GDP. It is published at the same time as the real GDP data.

Producer price index (PPI): Monthly. The PPI is a measure of the average level of wholesale prices charged by producers and is published at the same time as industrial production data.

imports. Using the symbols C for consumption expenditure, I for planned investment spending, G for government spending, and NX for net exports, we can write the following expression for aggregate demand Y^{ad}:

$$Y^{ad} = C + I + G + NX \tag{1}$$

Deriving the Aggregate Demand Curve

The first step in deriving the aggregate demand curve is to recognize that when the inflation rate rises ($\pi\uparrow$), the monetary authorities react by raising the real interest rate ($r\uparrow$). They do this to keep inflation from spiraling out of control. Next we can examine the effects of the higher real interest rate on the individual components of aggregate demand. When the real interest rate is higher, the cost of financing purchases of new physical capital becomes higher, making investment less profitable and causing planned investment spending to decline ($I\downarrow$). Because, as shown in Equation 1, planned investment spending is included in aggregate demand, the decline in planned investment spending causes aggregate demand to fall ($Y^{ad}\downarrow$). A higher inflation rate therefore leads to a lower level of the quantity of aggregate output demanded ($\pi\uparrow \Rightarrow Y^{ad}\downarrow$), and so the

FIGURE 1
Leftward Shift in the Aggregate Demand Curve

The aggregate demand curve shifts to the left from AD_1 to AD_2 when there is an autonomous tightening of monetary policy ($\bar{r}\uparrow$), a decrease in government purchases ($\bar{G}\downarrow$), an increase in taxes ($\bar{T}\uparrow$), a decrease in autonomous net exports ($\overline{NX}\downarrow$), a decrease in autonomous consumption expenditure ($\bar{C}\downarrow$), a decrease in autonomous investment ($\bar{I}\downarrow$), or an increase in financial frictions ($\bar{f}\uparrow$).

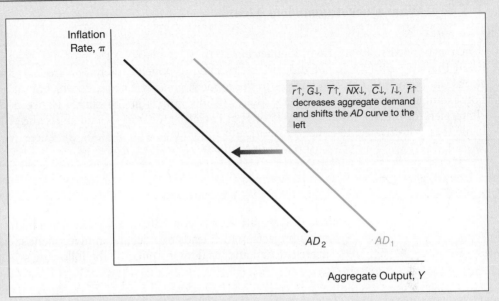

$\bar{r}\uparrow, \bar{G}\downarrow, \bar{T}\uparrow, \overline{NX}\downarrow, \bar{C}\downarrow, \bar{I}\downarrow, \bar{f}\uparrow$ decreases aggregate demand and shifts the *AD* curve to the left

aggregate demand curve slopes downward, as in Figure 1. Schematically, we can write the mechanism just described as follows:[2]

$$\pi\uparrow \Rightarrow r\uparrow \Rightarrow I\downarrow \Rightarrow Y^{ad}\downarrow$$

Factors That Shift the Aggregate Demand Curve

Seven basic factors (often referred to as **demand shocks**) can shift the aggregate demand curve to a new position: (1) autonomous monetary policy, (2) government purchases, (3) taxes, (4) autonomous net exports, (5) autonomous consumption expenditure, (6) autonomous investment, and (7) financial frictions. (The use of the term *autonomous* in the factors listed above sometimes confuses students, and so it is discussed in the FYI box, "What Does *Autonomous* Mean?") As we examine each case, we ask what happens to the aggregate demand curve when each of these factors changes while the inflation rate is held constant.

1. *Autonomous monetary policy.* We have already noted that when inflation rises, the central bank will raise the real interest rate to keep inflation from spiraling out of control. However, there are central-bank movements in the real interest rate that are autonomous, denoted by $\bar{r}$, which are movements unrelated to the variables in the model, such as the current level of the inflation rate. When the Federal Reserve decides to increase this autonomous component of the real interest rate, $\bar{r}$, the higher

---

[2]If you have already read Chapters 20 and Chapter 21, this discussion of aggregate demand is just a recap of the analysis given in those chapters. Note that an additional mechanism for a downward-sloping aggregate demand curve operates through net exports, as discussed in Chapters 20 and 21.

real interest rate at any given inflation rate leads to a higher cost of financing investment projects, which leads to a decline in investment spending and the quantity of aggregate demand, as demonstrated by the following schematic:

$$\bar{r}\uparrow \Rightarrow I\downarrow \Rightarrow Y^{ad}\downarrow$$

Therefore, aggregate demand falls at any given inflation rate, and the aggregate demand curve shifts to the left as in Figure 1.

2. *Government purchases.* An increase in government purchases at any given inflation rate adds directly to aggregate demand expenditure, and hence aggregate demand rises:

$$\overline{G}\uparrow \Rightarrow Y^{ad}\uparrow$$

Aggregate demand, therefore, rises at any given inflation rate, and the aggregate demand curve shifts to the right as in Figure 2.

3. *Taxes.* At any given inflation rate, an increase in taxes lowers disposable income, which leads to lower consumption expenditure and aggregate demand, so that aggregate demand falls:

$$\overline{T}\uparrow \Rightarrow C\downarrow \Rightarrow Y^{ad}\downarrow$$

Aggregate demand falls at any given inflation rate, and the aggregate demand curve shifts to the left as in Figure 1.

4. *Autonomous net exports.* An autonomous increase in net exports at any given inflation rate adds directly to aggregate demand and so raises aggregate demand:

$$\overline{NX}\uparrow \Rightarrow Y^{ad}\uparrow$$

Aggregate demand rises at any given inflation rate, and the aggregate demand curve shifts to the right as in Figure 2.

5. *Autonomous consumption expenditure.* When consumers become more optimistic, autonomous consumption expenditure rises, and so consumers spend more at any given inflation rate. Aggregate demand therefore rises:

$$\overline{C}\uparrow \Rightarrow Y^{ad}\uparrow$$

Aggregate demand rises at any given inflation rate, and the aggregate demand curve shifts to the right as in Figure 2.

FIGURE 2
Rightward Shift in the Aggregate Demand Curve

The aggregate demand curve shifts to the right, from AD_1 to AD_2, when there is an autonomous easing of monetary policy ($\bar{r}\downarrow$), an increase in government purchases($\overline{G}\uparrow$), a decrease in taxes ($\overline{T}\downarrow$), an increase in autonomous net exports ($\overline{NX}\uparrow$), an increase in autonomous consumption expenditure ($\overline{C}\uparrow$), an increase in autonomous investment ($\overline{I}\uparrow$), or a decrease in financial frictions ($\bar{f}\downarrow$).

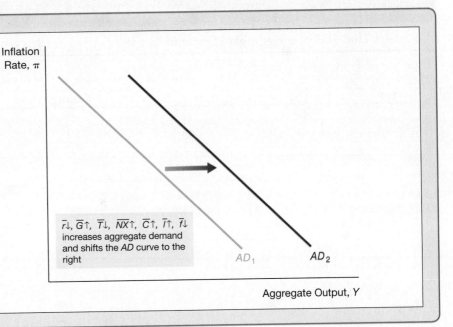

$\bar{r}\downarrow, \overline{G}\uparrow, \overline{T}\downarrow, \overline{NX}\uparrow, \overline{C}\uparrow, \overline{I}\uparrow, \bar{f}\downarrow$ increases aggregate demand and shifts the *AD* curve to the right

Inflation Rate, π

Aggregate Output, Y

AD_1 AD_2

6. *Autonomous investment.* When businesses become more optimistic, autonomous investment rises and businesses spend more at any given inflation rate. Planned investment increases and aggregate demand rises:

$$\overline{I}\uparrow \Rightarrow Y^{ad}\uparrow$$

Aggregate demand rises at any given inflation rate, and the aggregate demand curve shifts to the right as in Figure 2.

7. *Financial frictions.* The real cost of borrowing reflects not only the real interest rate on default-free debt instruments, r, but also financial frictions, denoted by $\bar{f}$, which are additions to the real cost of borrowing caused by asymmetric information problems in financial markets (described in Chapter 8). When financial frictions increase, the real cost of borrowing increases, so that planned investment spending falls at any given inflation rate, and aggregate demand falls:

$$\bar{f}\uparrow \Rightarrow I\downarrow \Rightarrow Y^{ad}\downarrow$$

Aggregate demand falls at any given inflation rate, and the aggregate demand curve shifts to the left as in Figure 1.

The conclusion from our analysis is as follows: *Aggregate demand increases at any given inflation rate, and the aggregate demand curve shifts to the right when there is: (1) an autonomous easing of monetary policy ($\bar{r}\downarrow$), (2) an increase in government purchases ($\overline{G}\uparrow$), (3) a decrease in taxes ($\overline{T}\downarrow$), (4) an increase in autonomous net exports ($\overline{NX}\uparrow$), (5) an increase in autonomous consumption expenditure ($\overline{C}\uparrow$), (6) an increase in autonomous investment $\overline{I}\uparrow$, or (7) a decrease in financial frictions ($\bar{f}\downarrow$). Conversely, the aggregate demand curve shifts to the left when any of these factors change in the opposite direction.* As a study aid, Summary Table 1 summarizes the shifts in the aggregate demand curve that occur with changes in each of these seven factors.

SUMMARY TABLE 1

Factors That Shift the Aggregate Demand Curve

Factor	Change	Shift in Aggregate Demand Curve
Autonomous monetary policy, $\bar{r}$	↑	π, Y; AD_2 AD_1
Government purchases, $\overline{G}$	↑	π, Y; AD_1 AD_2
Taxes, $\overline{T}$	↑	π, Y; AD_2 AD_1
Autonomous net exports, $\overline{NX}$	↑	π, Y; AD_1 AD_2
Autonomous consumption expenditure, $\overline{C}$	↑	π, Y; AD_1 AD_2
Autonomous investment, $\bar{I}$	↑	π, Y; AD_1 AD_2
Financial frictions, $\bar{f}$	↑	π, Y; AD_2 AD_1

Note: Only increases (↑) in the factors are shown. The effect of decreases in the factors would be the opposite of those indicated in the "Shift" column.

AGGREGATE SUPPLY

To complete our analysis, we need to derive an **aggregate supply curve**, a curve that shows the relationship between the quantity of output supplied and the inflation rate. In the typical supply and demand analysis, we have only one supply curve, but because prices and wages take time to adjust to their long-run levels, the aggregate supply curve differs in the short and long runs. First we examine the long-run aggregate supply curve; then we derive the short-run aggregate supply curve. Finally, we look at how both of these curves shift over time and at how the economy moves from the short run to the long run.

Long-Run Aggregate Supply Curve

The amount of output that can be produced in the economy in the long run is determined by the amount of capital in the economy, the amount of labor supplied at full employment, and the available technology. As discussed in Chapter 16, some unemployment cannot be helped because it is either frictional or structural. Thus, at full employment, unemployment is not at zero but is rather at a level above zero at which the demand for labor equals the supply of labor. This **natural rate of unemployment** is the rate to which the economy gravitates in the long run.[3] Many economists believe that the natural rate of unemployment is currently between 5% and 6%.

The level of aggregate output produced at the natural rate of unemployment is called the **natural rate of output** but is more often referred to as **potential output**: It is the level at which the economy settles in the long run for any inflation rate. Suppose potential output is at $10 trillion. The long-run aggregate supply curve (*LRAS*) is then vertical at the $10 trillion of potential output, denoted by Y^P, as drawn in Figure 3.

Short-Run Aggregate Supply Curve

The short-run aggregate supply curve is based on the idea that three factors drive inflation: (1) expectations of inflation, (2) the output gap, and (3) inflation (supply) shocks.

Expected Inflation, π^e Workers and firms care about wages in real terms—that is, in terms of the goods and services that wages can buy. When workers expect a positive inflation rate, they will adjust nominal wages upward one-to-one with the expected inflation rate, so that the real wage rate does not decrease. Thus, holding everything else constant, wage inflation will rise one-to-one with rises in expected inflation. Because wages are the most important cost of producing goods and services, overall inflation will also rise on a one-to-one basis with increases in expected inflation.

Output Gap The **output gap** is defined as the percentage difference between aggregate output and potential output, $Y - Y^P$. When output exceeds its potential level and the output gap is high, there is very little slack in the economy. Workers will demand higher wages, and firms will take the opportunity to raise prices. The end result

---

[3]A more detailed derivation of the short-run aggregate supply curve, based on the Phillips curve (which gives the relationship between unemployment and inflation), can be found in the appendix to this chapter .

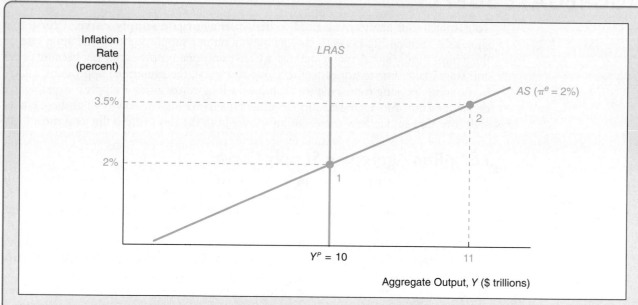

FIGURE 3   Long- and Short-Run Aggregate Supply Curves

The amount of aggregate output supplied at any given inflation rate is at potential output in the long run, $10 trillion, so that the long-run aggregate supply curve *LRAS* is a vertical line at $Y^P = \$10$ trillion. The short-run aggregate supply curve, *AS*, where $\pi^e = 2\%$, is upward-sloping because as Y rises relative to Y^P, labor markets get tighter and inflation rises. *AS* intersects *LRAS* at point 1, where current inflation equals expected inflation of 2%.

will be higher inflation. Conversely, when the output gap is negative, there will be a lot of slack in the economy. Thus workers will accept smaller increases in wages, and firms will need to lower prices to sell their goods, resulting in lower inflation.

Inflation (Supply) Shocks   **Supply shocks** occur when there are shocks to the supply of goods and services produced in the economy that translate into **Inflation shocks**, that is, shifts in inflation that are independent of the amount of slack in the economy or expected inflation. For example, when the supply of oil is restricted, as has occurred several times when Middle East countries were at war, the resulting rise in the price of oil leads firms to raise prices more to reflect the increased costs of production, thus driving up inflation. Energy inflation shocks can also occur when demand increases—for example, increased demand from developing countries like China such as occurred in 2007–2008—again driving up inflation. Inflation shocks can also come from rises in import prices or from **cost-push shocks** in which workers push for wages that are higher than productivity gains, thereby driving up costs and inflation.

Short-Run Aggregate Supply Curve   Putting all of our analysis together, we can write the following equation for the short-run aggregate supply curve:

$$\pi = \pi^e + \gamma(Y - Y^P) + \rho$$

Inflation = Expected $+ \gamma \times$ Output   + Inflation   (2)
Inflation   Gap   Shock

where

$$\pi = \text{inflation}$$
$$\pi^e = \text{expected inflation}$$
$$Y - Y^P = \text{the output gap}$$
$$\gamma = \text{the sensitivity of inflation to the output gap}$$
$$\rho = \text{the inflation shock}$$

The short-run aggregate supply curve given in Equation 2 tells us that inflation is driven by three factors: (1) expectations of inflation, (2) output gaps, and (3) inflation shocks.

Why the Short-Run Aggregate Supply Cuve Is Upward-Sloping   To see why the short-run aggregate supply curve, *AS*, in Figure 3 is upward-sloping, let's assume that expected inflation is at 2% and that there are no inflation shocks. When actual output equals potential output at $10 trillion, the output gap, $Y - Y^P$, is zero, and so Equation 2 indicates that the inflation rate will equal the expected inflation rate of 2%. The combination of $10 trillion of aggregate output and a 2% inflation rate is shown by point 1 on the *AS* curve. (Note that the short-run aggregate supply curve in Figure 3 is marked as *AS* ($\pi^e = 2\%$) to indicate it is drawn assuming $\pi^e = 2\%$.)

Now suppose that aggregate output rises to $11 trillion. Because there is a positive output gap ($Y = \$11$ trillion $> Y^P = \$10$ trillion), Equation 2 indicates that inflation will rise above 2%, say to 3.5%, marked as point 2. The curve connecting points 1 and 2 is the short-run aggregate supply curve, *AS*, and it is upward-sloping. When *Y* rises relative to Y^P and $Y > Y^P$, the labor market is tighter and firms raise their prices at a more rapid rate, causing the inflation rate to rise. Thus the *AS* curve is upward-sloping.

Price Stickiness and the Short-Run Aggregate Supply Curve

If wages and prices are sticky, inflation adjusts slowly over time. The more flexible wages and prices are, the more rapidly they, and inflation, respond to deviations of output from potential output; that is, more flexible wages and prices imply that the absolute value of γ is higher, which in turn implies that the short-run aggregate supply curve is steeper. If wages and prices are completely flexible, then γ becomes so large that the short-run aggregate supply curve becomes vertical and is identical to the long-run aggregate supply curve.

SHIFTS IN THE AGGREGATE SUPPLY CURVES

Now that we have examined the long-run and short-run aggregate supply curves, we can look at why each of these curves shift.

Shifts in the Long-Run Aggregate Supply Curve

The quantity of output supplied in the long run is determined by the three factors that cause potential output to change and thus shift the long-run aggregate supply curve: (1) the total amount of capital in the economy, (2) the total amount of labor supplied in the economy, and (3) the available technology that puts labor and capital together to produce goods and services. When any of these three factors increases, potential output rises, say, from $Y_1^P = \$10$ trillion to $Y_2^P = \$11$ trillion, and the long-run aggregate supply curve shifts to the right, from $LRAS_1$ to $LRAS_2$ in Figure 4.

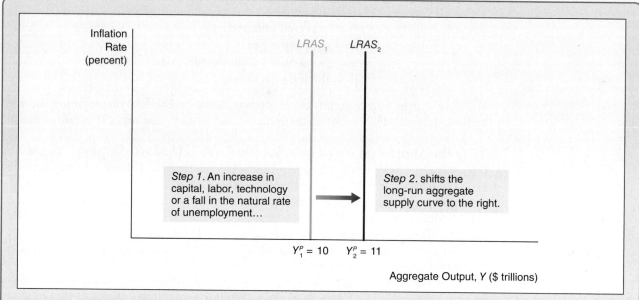

FIGURE 4   **Shift in the Long-Run Aggregate Supply Curve**
The long-run aggregate supply curve shifts to the right from $LRAS_1$ to $LRAS_2$ when there is (1) an increase in the total amount of capital in the economy, (2) an increase in the total amount of labor supplied in the economy, (3) an increase in the available technology, or (4) a decline in the natural rate of unemployment. An opposite movement in these variables shifts the $LRAS$ curve to the left.

Because all three of these factors typically grow fairly steadily over time, Y^P and the long-run aggregate supply curve will keep shifting to the right at a steady pace. To keep things simple in later diagrams in this and following chapters, when Y^P is growing at a steady rate, we will represent Y^P and the long-run aggregate supply curve as fixed.

Another source of shifts in the long-run aggregate supply curve is changes in the natural rate of unemployment. If the natural rate of unemployment declines, it means that labor is being more heavily utilized, and so potential output will increase. A decline in the natural rate of unemployment thus shifts the long-run aggregate supply curve to the right, from $LRAS_1$ to $LRAS_2$ in Figure 4. A rise in the natural rate of unemployment would have the opposite effect, shifting the long-run aggregate supply curve to the left.

The conclusion from our analysis is as follows: *The long-run aggregate supply curve shifts to the right when there is (1) an increase in the total amount of capital in the economy, (2) an increase in the total amount of labor supplied in the economy, (3) an increase in available technology, or (4) a decline in the natural rate of unemployment. An opposite movement in these variables shifts the LRAS curve to the left.*

Shifts in the Short-Run Aggregate Supply Curve

The three terms on the right-hand side of Equation 2 suggest that three factors can shift the short-run aggregate supply curve: (1) expected inflation, (2) a persistent output gap, and (3) inflation shocks.

Expected Inflation   What if a newly appointed chair of the Federal Reserve does not think that inflation is costly and so is willing to tolerate an inflation rate that is two percentage points higher than the current rate? Households and firms will then expect that the Fed will pursue policies that will let inflation rise by, say, two percentage points in the future, and will want to raise wages and prices by this additional amount. In such a situation, expected inflation will jump by two percentage points, and the short-run aggregate supply curve will shift upward and to the left, from AS_1 to AS_2 in Figure 5. *A rise in expected inflation causes the short-run aggregate supply curve to shift upward and to the left. Conversely, a fall in expected inflation causes the short-run aggregate supply curve to shift down and to the right. The larger the change in expected inflation, the larger is the shift.*

Inflation Shock   Suppose that energy prices suddenly shoot up because terrorists destroy a number of oil fields. This supply restriction (an unfavorable supply shock) causes the inflation-shock term in Equation 2 to increase, and so the short-run aggregate supply curve shifts up and to the left, from AS_1 to AS_2 in Figure 5. A favorable supply shock, which drives down inflation, will have the opposite effect and cause the short-run aggregate supply curve to shift down and to the right. *Unfavorable supply shocks that drive up inflation cause the short-run aggregate supply curve to shift up and to the left, while favorable supply shocks that lower inflation cause the short-run aggregate supply curve to shift down and to the right.* As a study aid, Summary Table 2 summarizes the shifts in the short-run aggregate supply curve caused by each of these three factors.

SUMMARY TABLE 2

Factors That Shift the Short-Run Aggregate Supply Curve

Factor	Change	Shift in Supply Curve
Expected inflation, π^e	↑	AS_1 shifts up and to the left to AS_2
Inflation shock, ρ	↑	AS_1 shifts up and to the left to AS_2
Persistent output gap, $(Y - Y^P)$	↑	AS_1 shifts up and to the left to AS_2

Note: Only increases (↑) in the factors are shown. The effect of decreases in the factors would be the opposite of those indicated in the "Shift" column.

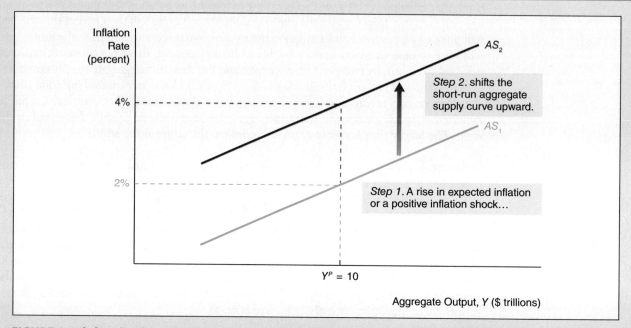

FIGURE 5 **Shift in the Short-Run Aggregate Supply Curve from Changes in Expected Inflation and Inflation Shocks**

A rise in expected inflation or a positive inflation shock shifts the short-run aggregate supply curve upward from AS_1 to AS_2. (A decrease in expected inflation or a negative inflation shock would lead to a downward shift of the AS curve.)

Persistent Output Gap We have already seen that a higher output gap leads to higher inflation, causing a movement along the short-run aggregate supply curve. We can represent this scenario by the movement from point 1 to point 2 on the initial short-run aggregate supply curve AS_1 in Figure 6. A persistent output gap, however, will cause the short-run aggregate supply curve to shift by affecting expected inflation. To see this, consider what happens if the aggregate output stays at $11 trillion, which is greater than the potential output of $Y^P = 10 trillion, so that the output gap remains persistently positive. At point 2 on the initial short-run aggregate supply curve, AS_1, output has risen to $11 trillion and inflation has risen from 2% to 3.5%. This higher level of inflation will cause expected inflation to rise during the next period, and so the short-run aggregate supply curve for the next period, AS_2, will shift upward. If output remains above potential output at point 3, inflation will rise further, to 5.0%. This higher inflation will then lead to higher expected inflation and, as the vertical arrow indicates, the short-run aggregate supply curve will shift upward to AS_3 during the next period.

When will the short-run aggregate supply curve stop rising? It will stop only when output returns to its potential level and the output gap disappears. At this point, there is no longer a reason for actual and hence expected inflation to rise. Suppose this happens when inflation is at 10% and aggregate output $Y = 10 trillion $= Y^P$. Because the output gap is now zero, the aggregate supply curve drawn through point 4, AS_4, has no reason to shift because inflation and expected inflation have stopped rising.

The same reasoning indicates that if aggregate output is kept below potential for a period of time, $Y < Y^P$, then the short-run aggregate supply curve will shift downward

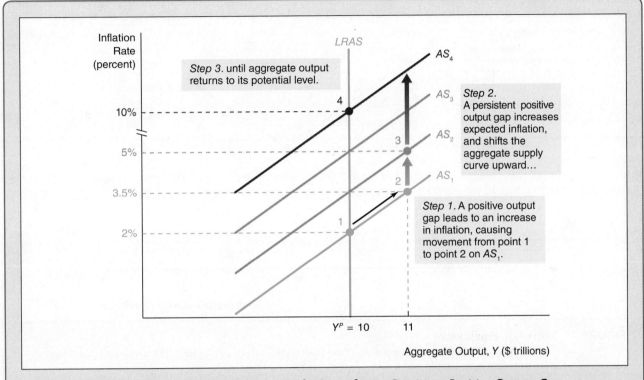

FIGURE 6 **Shift in the Short-Run Aggregate Supply Curve from a Persistent Positive Output Gap**
When output is above potential, the economy moves along the AS_1 curve from point 1 to point 2, and inflation rises to 3.5%. If output continues to remain above potential output, where the output gap is positive, the short-run aggregate supply curve will shift upward, to AS_2 and then to AS_3. The short-run aggregate supply curve stops shifting upward when the economy reaches point 4 on the short-run aggregate supply curve AS_4, where the output gap is once again zero.

and to the right. This downward shift of the aggregate supply curve will stop only when output returns to its potential level and the economy is back on the long-run aggregate supply curve.

Our analysis yields the following conclusion: ***When aggregate output is above potential output, so that a persistent positive output gap exists, the short-run aggregate supply curve shifts up and to the left. Conversely, when aggregate output falls below potential output, the short-run aggregate supply curve shifts down and to the right. Only when aggregate output returns to potential output does the short-run aggregate supply curve stop shifting.***

EQUILIBRIUM IN AGGREGATE DEMAND AND SUPPLY ANALYSIS

We can now put the aggregate demand and supply curves together to describe **general equilibrium** in the economy, the point at which all markets are simultaneously in equilibrium and the quantity of aggregate output demanded equals the quantity of

MyEconLab Mini-lecture

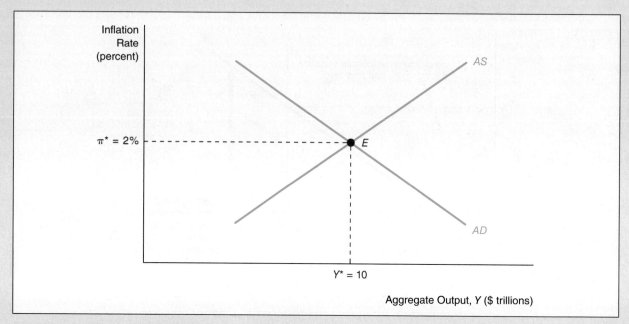

FIGURE 7 **Short-Run Equilibrium**

Short-run equilibrium occurs at point *E*, at the intersection of the aggregate demand curve *AD* and the short-run aggregate supply curve *AS*.

aggregate output supplied. We represent general equilibrium graphically as the point at which the aggregate demand curve intersects the aggregate supply curve. However, recall that we have two aggregate supply curves: one for the short run and one for the long run. Consequently, in the context of aggregate supply and demand analysis, there are short-run and long-run equilibriums. In this section, we illustrate equilibrium in the short and long runs. In following sections, we examine aggregate demand and aggregate supply shocks that lead to changes in equilibrium.

Short-Run Equilibrium

Figure 7 illustrates a short-run equilibrium in which the quantity of aggregate output demanded equals the quantity of output supplied. In Figure 7, the short-run aggregate demand curve *AD* and the short-run aggregate supply curve *AS* intersect at point *E*, with an equilibrium level of aggregate output at $Y^* = \$10$ trillion and an equilibrium inflation rate at $\pi^* = 2\%$.

How the Short-Run Equilibrium Moves to the Long-Run Equilibrium over Time

In supply and demand analysis, once we find the equilibrium point at which the quantity demanded equals the quantity supplied, additional analysis typically is not needed.

In *aggregate* supply and demand analysis, however, that is not the case. Even when the quantity of aggregate output demanded equals the quantity supplied at the intersection of the aggregate demand curve and the short-run aggregate supply curve, if output differs from its potential level ($Y^* \neq Y^P$), the short-run equilibrium will move over time. To understand why, recall that if the current level of inflation changes from its initial level, the short-run aggregate supply curve will shift as wages and prices adjust to a new expected rate of inflation.

We look at how the short-run equilibrium changes over time in response to two situations: when short-run equilibrium output is initially above potential output (the natural rate of output), and when it is initially below potential output.

In panel (a) of Figure 8, the initial equilibrium occurs at point 1, the intersection of the aggregate demand curve AD and the initial short-run aggregate supply curve AS_1. The level of equilibrium output, $Y_1 = \$11$ trillion, is greater than the potential output, $Y^P = \$10$ trilllion, and there is excessive tightness in the labor market. Hence, the positive output gap at Y_1 drives wages up and causes firms to raise their prices at a more rapid rate. Inflation then rises above the initial inflation rate, π_1. At this higher inflation rate, firms and households adjust their expectations next period, and expected inflation becomes higher. Wages and prices then rise more rapidly, and the aggregate supply curve shifts up and to the left, from AS_1 to AS_2.

The new short-run equilibrium at point 2 is an upward movement along the aggregate demand curve, and output falls to Y_2. However, because aggregate output Y_2 is still above potential output Y^P, inflation again rises above its value last period. Expected inflation rises further, eventually shifting the aggregate supply curve up and to the left to AS_3. The economy reaches long-run equilibrium at point 3 on the vertical long-run aggregate supply curve ($LRAS$), at $Y^P = \$10$ trillion. Because output is at potential, there is no further pressure on inflation to rise and thus no further tendency for the aggregate supply curve to shift.

The movements in panel (a) indicate that the economy will not remain at a level of output higher than potential output of $10 trillion over time. Specifically, the short-run aggregate supply curve will shift up and to the left, raising the inflation rate and causing the economy (equilibrium) to move upward along the aggregate demand curve until it comes to rest at a point on the long-run aggregate supply curve ($LRAS$) that is at potential output $Y^P = \$10$ trillion.

In panel (b), at the initial equilibrium at point 1, output $Y_1 = \$9$ trillion is below the level of potential output of $10 trillion. Because unemployment is now above its natural rate, there is excess slack in the labor markets. This slack at $Y_1 = \$9$ trillion decreases inflation, which decreases expected inflation and shifts the short-run aggregate supply curve in the next period down and to the right, to AS_2.

The equilibrium now moves to point 2, and output rises to Y_2. However, because aggregate output Y_2 is still below potential output Y^P, inflation again declines from its value last period, causing expected inflation to fall. This decline in expected inflation shifts the aggregate supply curve down until it comes to rest at AS_3. The economy (equilibrium) moves downward along the aggregate demand curve until it reaches the long-run equilibrium at point 3, at the intersection of the aggregate demand curve (AD) and the long-run aggregate supply curve ($LRAS$) at $Y^P = \$10$ trillion. Here, as in panel (a), the economy comes to rest when output has again returned to its potential level.

MyEconLab Mini-lecture

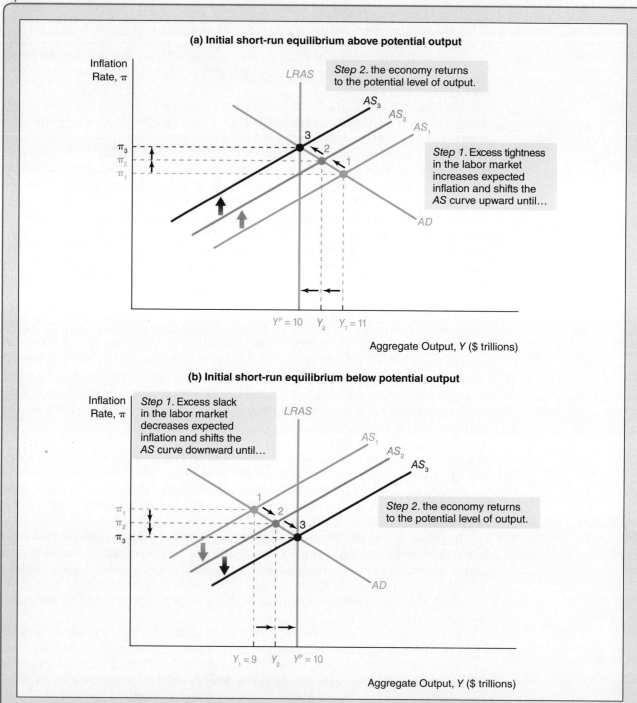

FIGURE 8 **Adjustment to Long-Run Equilibrium in Aggregate Supply and Demand Analysis**
In both panels, the initial short-run equilibrium is at point 1, at the intersection of *AD* and AS_1. In panel (a), initial short-run equilibrium is above potential output, the long-run equilibrium, and so the short-run aggregate supply curve shifts upward until it reaches AS_3, where output returns to Y^P. In panel (b), initial short-run equilibrium is below potential output, and so the short-run aggregate supply curve shifts downward until output returns to Y^P. In both panels, the economy's self-correcting mechanism returns the economy to the level of potential output.

Self-Correcting Mechanism

Notice that in both panels of Figure 8, regardless of where output is initially, it returns eventually to potential output, a feature we call the **self-correcting mechanism**. The self-correcting mechanism occurs because the short-run aggregate supply curve shifts up or down to restore the economy to the long-run equilibrium at full employment (aggregate output at potential) over time.

CHANGES IN EQUILIBRIUM: AGGREGATE DEMAND SHOCKS

With an understanding of the distinction between the short-run and long-run equilibria, we are now ready to analyze what happens when the economy experiences **demand shocks**, shocks that cause the aggregate demand curve to shift. Figure 9 depicts the effects of a rightward shift in the aggregate demand curve due to positive demand shocks, which may be caused by the following:

- An autonomous easing of monetary policy ($\bar{r}\downarrow$, a lowering of the real interest rate at any given inflation rate)
- An increase in government purchases ($\overline{G}\uparrow$)
- A decrease in taxes ($\overline{T}\downarrow$)
- An increase in autonomous net exports ($\overline{NX}\uparrow$)
- An increase in autonomous consumption expenditure ($\overline{C}\uparrow$)
- An increase in autonomous investment ($\bar{I}\uparrow$)
- A decrease in financial frictions ($\bar{f}\downarrow$)

Figure 9 shows the economy initially in long-run equilibrium at point 1, where the initial aggregate demand curve AD_1 intersects the short-run aggregate supply AS_1 curve at $Y^P = \$10$ trillion and the inflation rate is 2%. Suppose that consumers and businesses become more optimistic and that the resulting increases in autonomous consumption and investment create a positive demand shock that shifts the aggregate demand curve to the right to AD_2. The economy moves up the short-run aggregate supply curve AS_1 to point 2, and output and inflation rise to $11 trillion and 3.5%, respectively. However, the economy will not remain at point 2 in the long run because output at $11 trillion is above potential output. Expected inflation will rise, and the short-run aggregate supply curve will eventually shift upward to AS_3. The economy (equilibrium) thus will move up the AD_2 curve from point 2 to point 3, which is the point of long-run equilibrium at which inflation equals 5% and output returns to $Y^P = \$10$ trillion. *Although the initial short-run effect of the rightward shift in the aggregate demand curve is a rise in both inflation and output, the ultimate long-run effect is a rise in inflation only, because output returns to its initial level at Y^P.*[4]

---

[4]The analysis here assumes that each of these positive demand shocks occurs while everything else is held constant, the usual *ceteris paribus* ("other things being equal") assumption that is standard in supply and demand analysis. Specifically, this means that the central bank is assumed not to be responding to demand shocks. In the next chapter, we relax this assumption and allow monetary policymakers to respond to these shocks. As we will see, if monetary policymakers want to keep inflation caused by a positive demand shock from rising, they will respond by autonomously tightening monetary policy.

MyEconLab Mini-lecture

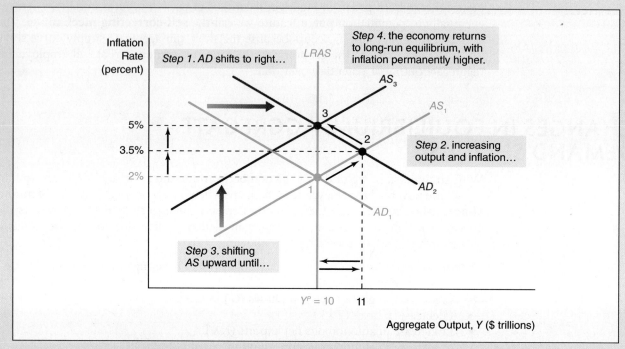

FIGURE 9 **Positive Demand Shock**

A positive demand shock shifts the aggregate demand curve upward from AD_1 to AD_2 and moves the economy from point 1 to point 2, resulting in higher inflation at 3.5% and higher output of $11 trillion. Because output is greater than potential output and therefore expected inflation increases, the short-run aggregate supply curve begins to shift up, eventually reaching AS_3. At point 3, the economy returns to long-run equilibrium, with output at $Y^P = 10 trillion and the inflation level rising to 5%.

We now apply the aggregate demand and supply model to demand shocks, as a payoff for our hard work in constructing the model. Throughout the remainder of this chapter, we will apply aggregate supply and demand analysis to a number of business cycle episodes, both in the United States and in foreign countries, over the past 40 years. To simplify our analysis, we will assume in all examples that aggregate output is initially at the level of potential output.

APPLICATION The Volcker Disinflation, 1980–1986

When Paul Volcker became the chair of the Federal Reserve in August 1979, inflation had spun out of control and the inflation rate exceeded 10%. Volcker was determined to get inflation down. By early 1981, the Federal Reserve had raised the federal funds rate to over 20%, which led to a sharp increase in real interest rates. Volcker was indeed successful in bringing inflation down, as illustrated in panel (b) of Figure 10, with the inflation rate falling from 13.5% in 1980 to 1.9% in 1986. But the decline in inflation came at a high cost: The economy experienced its worst recession since World War II, with the unemployment rate averaging 9.7% in 1982.

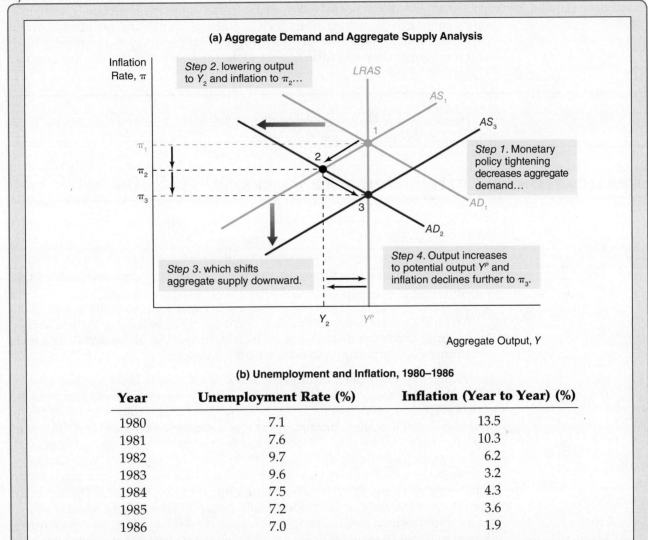

(a) Aggregate Demand and Aggregate Supply Analysis

(b) Unemployment and Inflation, 1980–1986

Year	Unemployment Rate (%)	Inflation (Year to Year) (%)
1980	7.1	13.5
1981	7.6	10.3
1982	9.7	6.2
1983	9.6	3.2
1984	7.5	4.3
1985	7.2	3.6
1986	7.0	1.9

FIGURE 10 The Volcker Disinflation
Panel (a) shows that former Fed chair Volcker's actions to decrease inflation were successful but costly: The autonomous monetary policy tightening caused a negative demand shock that decreased aggregate demand and in turn inflation, resulting in soaring unemployment rates. The data in panel (b) support this analysis: Note the decline in the inflation rate from 13.5% in 1980 to 1.9% in 1986, while the unemployment rate increased to as high as 9.7% in 1982.
Source: Economic Report of the President.

This outcome is exactly the outcome predicted by our aggregate demand and supply analysis. The autonomous tightening of monetary policy decreased aggregate demand and shifted the aggregate demand curve to the left, from AD_1 to AD_2 in panel (a) of Figure 10. The economy moved to point 2, indicating that unemployment was rising and inflation was falling. With unemployment above the natural rate and output below potential, the short-run aggregate supply curve shifted downward and to the right, to AS_3. The economy moved toward long-run equilibrium at point 3, with inflation continuing to fall, output rising back to potential output, and the unemployment rate moving toward its natural rate level. Panel (b) of Figure 10 shows that by 1986, the unemployment rate had fallen to 7% and the inflation rate was 1.9%, just as would be predicted by our aggregate demand and supply analysis. ◆

The next period we will examine, 2001–2004, again illustrates the effects of negative demand shocks—this time, three at once.

APPLICATION ## Negative Demand Shocks, 2001–2004

In 2000, the U.S. economy was expanding when it was hit by a series of negative shocks to aggregate demand.

1. The "tech bubble" burst in March 2000, and the stock market fell sharply.
2. The September 11, 2001, terrorist attacks weakened both consumer and business confidence.
3. The Enron bankruptcy in late 2001 and other corporate accounting scandals in 2002 revealed that corporate financial data were not to be trusted. Interest rates on corporate bonds rose as a result of the increase in financial frictions, making it more expensive for corporations to finance their investments.

All three of these negative demand shocks led to a decline in household and business spending, decreasing aggregate demand and shifting the aggregate demand curve to the left, from AD_1 to AD_2 in panel (a) of Figure 11. At point 2, as predicted by our aggregate demand and supply analysis, unemployment rose and inflation fell. Panel (b) of Figure 11 shows that the unemployment rate, which had been at 4% in 2000, rose to 6% in 2003, while the annual rate of inflation fell from 3.4% in 2000 to 1.6% in 2002. With unemployment above the natural rate (estimated to be around 5%) and output below potential, the short-run aggregate supply curve shifted downward, to AS_3 in panel (a) of Figure 11. The economy moved to point 3, with inflation falling, output rising back to potential output, and the unemployment rate returning to its natural rate level. By 2004, the self-correcting mechanism feature of aggregate demand and supply analysis had begun to come into play, with the unemployment rate dropping back to 5.5% (see Figure 11, panel (b)). ◆

CHANGES IN EQUILIBRIUM: AGGREGATE SUPPLY (INFLATION) SHOCKS

Shifts in the aggregate supply curve can be caused by temporary supply (inflation) shocks, in which the long-run aggregate supply curve does not shift, or permanent supply shocks, in which the long-run aggregate supply curve does shift. We will look at these two types of supply shocks in turn.

Temporary Supply Shocks

In our discussion earlier in the chapter of the short-run aggregate supply curve, we showed that inflation will rise independently of tightness in the labor markets or

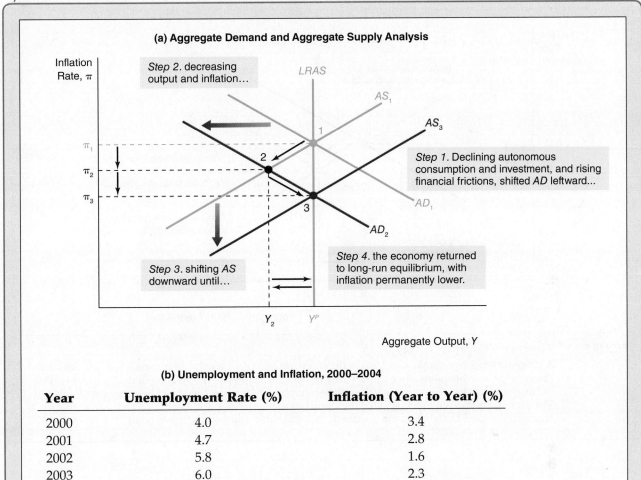

(a) Aggregate Demand and Aggregate Supply Analysis

Step 2. decreasing output and inflation...

Step 1. Declining autonomous consumption and investment, and rising financial frictions, shifted *AD* leftward...

Step 3. shifting *AS* downward until...

Step 4. the economy returned to long-run equilibrium, with inflation permanently lower.

(b) Unemployment and Inflation, 2000–2004

Year	Unemployment Rate (%)	Inflation (Year to Year) (%)
2000	4.0	3.4
2001	4.7	2.8
2002	5.8	1.6
2003	6.0	2.3
2004	5.5	2.7

FIGURE 11   Negative Demand Shocks, 2001–2004

Panel (a) shows that the negative demand shocks from 2001–2004 decreased consumption expenditure and investment, shifting the aggregate demand curve to the left from AD_1 to AD_2. The economy moved to point 2, where output fell, unemployment rose, and inflation declined. The large negative output gap that occurred when output was less than potential caused the short-run aggregate supply curve to begin falling to AS_3. The economy moved toward point 3, where output would return to potential: Inflation declined further to π_3, and unemployment fell back to its natural rate level of around 5%. The data in panel (b) support this analysis, with inflation declining to around 2% and the unemployment rate dropping back to 5.5% by 2004.

Source: Economic Report of the President.

increases in expected inflation caused by temporary supply shocks, such as a decrease in the supply of oil that causes prices to rise. When the temporary shock involves a restriction in supply, we refer to this type of supply shock as a *negative* (or *unfavorable*) *supply shock*, and it results in a rise in commodity prices. Examples of temporary negative supply shocks include a disruption in oil supplies, a rise in import prices when

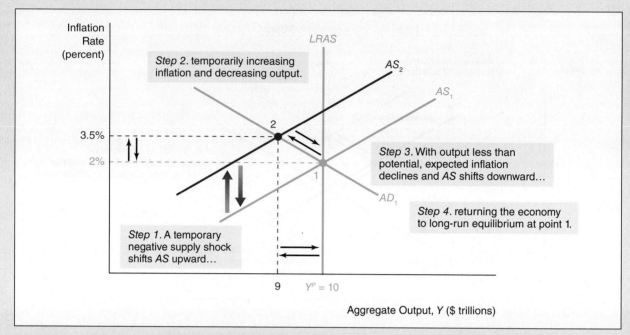

FIGURE 12 **Temporary Negative Supply Shock**
A temporary negative supply shock shifts the short-run aggregate supply curve from AS_1 to AS_2, and the economy moves from point 1 to point 2, where inflation increases to 3.5% and output declines to $9 trillion. Because output is less than potential, the negative output gap lowers inflation and hence expected inflation. The decline in expected inflation shifts the short-run aggregate supply curve back down, and eventually it returns to AS_1, where the economy is again at the initial long-run equilibrium at point 1.

a currency declines in value, or a cost-push shock from workers pushing for higher wages that outpace productivity growth, driving up costs and inflation. When the supply shock involves an increase in supply, it is called a *positive* (or *favorable*) *supply shock*. Temporary positive supply shocks include a particularly good harvest or a fall in import prices.

To see how a temporary supply shock affects the economy, we can use our aggregate supply and demand analysis. We start by assuming that output is at its potential level of $10 trillion and inflation is at 2%, at point 1 in Figure 12. Suppose that a war in the Middle East causes a temporary negative supply shock. When the negative supply shock hits the economy and oil prices rise, the change in the price shock term ρ indicates that inflation will rise to above 2%, and the short-run aggregate supply curve will shift up and to the left, from AS_1 to AS_2.

The economy then will move up the aggregate demand curve, from point 1 to point 2, where inflation rises to 3.5% but aggregate output *falls* below $10 trillion. We use the term **stagflation** (a combination of the words *stagnation* and *inflation*) to describe a situation defined by rising inflation but a falling level of aggregate output, as pictured in Figure 12. Because the supply shock is temporary, productive capacity in the economy does not change, and so Y^P and the long-run aggregate supply curve *LRAS* remain stationary at $10 trillion. At point 2, output is therefore below its potential level (say, at $9 trillion), and so inflation falls. The decline in inflation causes expected inflation to fall and shifts the short-run aggregate supply curve back down to where it was initially, at AS_1. The economy (equilibrium) slides down the aggregate demand curve AD_1 (assuming the aggregate demand curve remains in the same position) and returns to the long-run equilibrium at point 1, where output is again at $10 trillion and inflation is again at 2%.

Although a temporary negative supply shock leads to an upward and leftward shift of the short-run aggregate supply curve, which initially raises inflation and lowers output, the ultimate long-run effect is that output and inflation are unchanged.

A favorable (positive) supply shock—say, an excellent harvest of wheat in the Midwest—moves all the curves in Figure 12 in the opposite direction and so has the opposite effects. *A temporary positive supply shock shifts the short-run aggregate supply curve downward and to the right, initially leading to a fall in inflation and a rise in output. In the long run, however, output and inflation are unchanged (holding the aggregate demand curve constant).*

We now will once again apply the aggregate demand and supply model, this time to temporary supply shocks. We begin by studying the negative supply shocks of 1973–1975 and 1978–1980. (Recall we assume that aggregate output is initially at its potential level.)

APPLICATION   Negative Supply Shocks, 1973–1975 and 1978–1980

In 1973, the U.S. economy was hit by a series of negative supply shocks:

1. As a result of the oil embargo stemming from the Arab–Israeli war of 1973, the Organization of Petroleum Exporting Countries (OPEC) engineered a quadrupling of oil prices by restricting oil production.
2. A series of crop failures throughout the world led to a sharp increase in food prices.
3. The termination of U.S. wage and price controls in 1973 and 1974 led to a push by workers to obtain wage increases that had been prevented by the controls.

The triple thrust of these events shifted the short-run aggregate supply curve sharply upward and to the left, from AS_1 to AS_2 in panel (a) of Figure 13, and the economy moved to point 2. As predicted by the aggregate demand and supply diagram in Figure 13, both inflation and unemployment rose (inflation by 3 percentage points and unemployment by 3.5 percentage points), as per panel (b) of Figure 13.

The 1978–1980 period was almost an exact replay of the 1973–1975 period. By 1978, the economy had just about fully recovered from the 1973–1975 supply shocks when poor harvests and a doubling of oil prices (resulting from the overthrow of the Shah of Iran) led to another sharp upward and leftward shift of the short-run aggregate supply curve in 1979. The pattern predicted by Figure 13 played itself out again—inflation and unemployment both shot upward. ◆

Permanent Supply Shocks and Real Business Cycle Theory

But what if a supply shock is not temporary? A permanent negative supply shock—such as an increase in ill-advised regulations that cause the economy to become less efficient, thereby reducing supply—would decrease potential output from, say, Y_1^P to

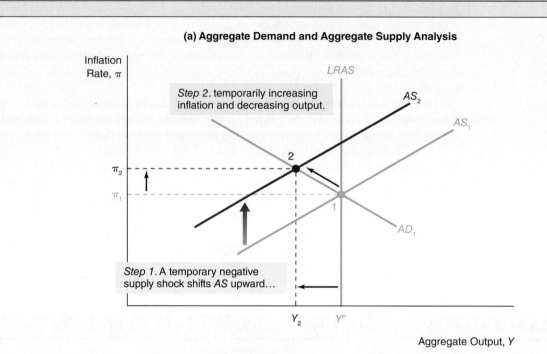

(a) Aggregate Demand and Aggregate Supply Analysis

Step 2. temporarily increasing inflation and decreasing output.

Step 1. A temporary negative supply shock shifts *AS* upward...

(b) Unemployment and Inflation, 1973–1975 and 1978–1980

Year	Unemployment Rate (%)	Inflation (Year to Year) (%)
1973	4.8	6.2
1974	5.5	11.0
1975	8.3	9.1
1978	6.0	7.6
1979	5.8	11.3
1980	7.1	13.5

FIGURE 13 Negative Supply Shocks, 1973–1975 and 1978–1980
Panel (a) shows that the temporary negative supply shocks in 1973 and 1979 led to an upward shift in the short-run aggregate supply curve, from AS_1 to AS_2. The economy moved to point 2, where output fell and both unemployment and inflation rose. The data in panel (b) support this analysis: Note the increase in the inflation rate from 6.2% in 1973 to 9.1% in 1975 and the increase in the unemployment rate from 4.8% in 1973 to 8.3% in 1975. During the 1978–1980 shock, inflation increased from 7.6% in 1978 to 13.5% in 1980, while the unemployment rate increased from 6.0% in 1978 to 7.1% in 1980.
Source: Economic Report of the President.

Y_2^P and shift the long-run aggregate supply curve to the left, from $LRAS_1$ to $LRAS_2$ in Figure 14.

Because the permanent supply shock will lead to higher prices, there will be an immediate rise in inflation—say, to 3% from its previous level of 2%—and so the short-run aggregate supply curve will shift up and to the left, from AS_1 to AS_2. Although output at point 2 has fallen to $9 trillion, it is still above $Y_2^P = $8 trillion. The positive output gap indicates that the aggregate supply curve will shift up and to the left. It will continue to do so until it reaches AS_3, at the intersection of the aggregate demand curve AD and the long-run aggregate supply curve $LRAS_2$. Now, because output is at $Y_2^P = \$8$ trillion at point 3, the output gap is zero and, at an inflation rate of 5%, there is no further upward pressure on inflation.

One group of economists, led by Nobel Prize winner Edward Prescott of Arizona State University, believes that business cycle fluctuations result from permanent supply shocks alone. Their theory of aggregate economic fluctuations is called **real business cycle theory**. This theory views shocks to tastes (workers' willingness to work, for example) and technology (productivity) as the major driving forces behind short-run fluctuations in the business cycle because these shocks lead to substantial short-run fluctuations in Y^P. By contrast, shifts in the aggregate demand curve, perhaps caused by changes in monetary policy, are not viewed as being particularly important to aggregate output fluctuations. Because real business cycle theory views most business cycle fluctuations as resulting from fluctuations in the level of potential of output, it does not see much need for policies aimed at eliminating high unemployment. Real business cycle theory is highly controversial and is the subject of intensive research.

When we hold the aggregate demand curve constant, we generate the following result, as shown in Figure 14: *A permanent negative supply shock initially leads to both a decline in output and a rise in inflation. However, in contrast to a temporary supply shock, in the*

MyEconLab Mini-lecture

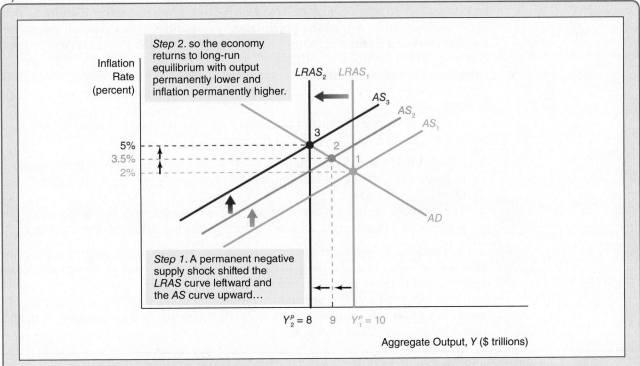

FIGURE 14   Permanent Negative Supply Shock
A permanent negative supply shock initially leads to a decline in output and a rise in inflation. In the long run, it leads to a permanent decline in output and a permanent rise in inflation, as indicated by point 3, where inflation has risen to 5% and output has fallen to $8 trillion.

long run a permanent negative supply shock, which results in a fall in potential output, leads to a permanent decline in output and a permanent rise in inflation.[5]

The opposite conclusion follows if we consider a positive supply shock—say, from the development of new technology that raises productivity. *A permanent positive supply shock lowers inflation and raises output in both the short run and the long run*.

To this point, we have assumed that potential output Y^P and hence the long-run aggregate supply curve are given. Over time, however, economic growth will cause the potential level of output to increase. If the productive capacity of the economy is growing at a steady rate of 3% per year, for example, every year Y^P will grow by 3% and the long-run aggregate supply curve at Y^P will shift to the right by 3%. To simplify the analysis, when Y^P grows at a steady rate, we represent Y^P and the long-run aggregate supply curve as fixed in the aggregate demand and supply diagrams. Keep in mind, however, that the level of aggregate output pictured in these diagrams is actually best thought of as the level of aggregate output relative to its normal rate of growth (trend).

The 1995–1999 period serves as an illustration of permanent positive supply shocks, as indicated in the following application.

APPLICATION Positive Supply Shocks, 1995–1999

In February 1994, the Federal Reserve began to raise interest rates. It believed that the economy would be reaching potential output and the natural rate of unemployment in 1995 and that the economy might become overheated thereafter, with output climbing above potential and inflation rising. As we can see in panel (b) of Figure 15, however, the economy continued to grow rapidly, with the unemployment rate falling to below 5% in 1997. Yet inflation continued to fall, declining to around 1.6% in 1998.

Can we use aggregate demand and supply analysis to explain what happened? Two permanent, positive supply shocks hit the economy in the late 1990s:

1. Changes in the health care industry, such as the emergence of health maintenance organizations (HMOs), reduced medical care costs substantially relative to the costs of other goods and services.
2. The computer revolution finally began to impact productivity favorably, raising the potential growth rate of the economy (which journalists dubbed the "new economy").

In addition, demographic factors, such as an increase in the relative number of older workers who were less likely to be unemployed, led to a fall in the natural rate of unemployment. These factors led to a rightward shift in the long-run aggregate supply curve to $LRAS_2$, and a downward and rightward shift in the short-run aggregate supply curve from AS_1 to AS_2, as shown in panel (a) of Figure 15. Aggregate output rose, and unemployment and inflation fell. ◆

---

[5]Our conclusion about the effects of a permanent supply shock assumes that monetary policy is not changing, and so the aggregate demand curve remains unchanged. Monetary policymakers, however, might want to shift the aggregate demand curve in an attempt to keep inflation at the same level. For further discussion, see the following chapter.

MyEconLab Mini-lecture

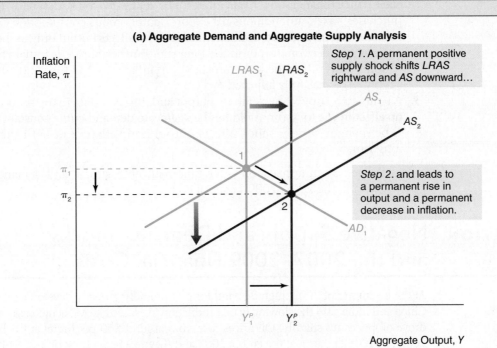

(a) Aggregate Demand and Aggregate Supply Analysis

Step 1. A permanent positive supply shock shifts *LRAS* rightward and *AS* downward…

Step 2. and leads to a permanent rise in output and a permanent decrease in inflation.

(b) Unemployment and Inflation, 1995–1999

Year	Unemployment Rate (%)	Inflation (Year to Year) (%)
1995	5.6	2.8
1996	5.4	3.0
1997	4.9	2.3
1998	4.5	1.6
1999	4.2	2.2

FIGURE 15   Positive Supply Shocks, 1995–1999

Panel (a) shows that the positive supply shocks from lower health care costs and the rise in productivity from the computer revolution led to a rightward shift in the long-run aggregate supply curve, from $LRAS_1$ to $LRAS_2$, and a downward shift in the short-run aggregate supply curve, from AS_1 to AS_2. The economy moved to point 2, where aggregate output rose, and unemployment and inflation fell. The data in panel (b) support this analysis: Note that the unemployment rate fell from 5.6% in 1995 to 4.2% in 1999, while the inflation rate fell from 2.8% in 1995 to 2.2% in 1999.

Source: Economic Report of the President.

Conclusions

Aggregate demand and supply analysis leads us to the following conclusions.[6]

1. The economy has a self-correcting mechanism that returns it to potential output and the natural rate of unemployment over time.

---

[6]Aggregate demand and supply analysis also can be used to understand the effects of macroeconomic shocks on asset prices. This analysis can be found in the first web appendix to this chapter, which can be found on the Companion Website at http://www.pearsonhighered.com/mishkin.

2. A shift in the aggregate demand curve—caused by changes in autonomous monetary policy (changes in the real interest rate at any given inflation rate), government purchases, taxes, autonomous net exports, autonomous consumption expenditure, autonomous investment, or financial frictions—affects output only in the short run, and has no effect on output in the long run. Furthermore, the initial change in inflation is lower than the long-run change in inflation when the short-run aggregate supply curve has fully adjusted.

3. A temporary supply shock affects output and inflation only in the short run and has no effect in the long run (holding the aggregate demand curve constant).

4. A permanent supply shock affects output and inflation in both the short and long run.

Now let's look at an application—this time with both supply and demand shocks at play—featuring the 2007–2009 financial crisis.

APPLICATION **Negative Supply and Demand Shocks and the 2007–2009 Financial Crisis**

At the beginning of 2007, high demand for oil in rapidly growing developing countries like China and India, and the slowing of oil production in places like Mexico, Russia, and Nigeria, drove oil prices up sharply. Oil prices rose from around $60 per barrel at the beginning of 2007 to $100 per barrel at the end of 2007 and they reached a peak of over $140 per barrel in July 2008. The rise in oil prices, along with increases in other commodity prices, led to a negative supply shock that shifted the short-run aggregate supply curve sharply upward, from AS_1 to AS_2 in panel (a) of Figure 16. To make matters worse, a financial crisis hit the economy starting in August 2007, causing a sharp increase in financial frictions, which led to contraction in both household and business spending (discussed in Chapter 12). This negative demand shock shifted the aggregate demand curve to the left, from AD_1 to AD_2 in panel (a) of Figure 16, and moved the economy to point 2. These shocks led to a rise in the unemployment rate, a rise in the inflation rate, and a decline in output, as indicated by point 2. As predicted by our aggregate demand and supply analysis, this perfect storm of negative shocks led to a recession starting in December 2007, with the unemployment rate rising from 4.6% in 2006 and 2007 to 5.5% by June 2008, and the inflation rate rising from 2.5% in 2006 to 5% in June 2008 (see panel (b) of Figure 16).

After July 2008, oil prices fell sharply, shifting short-run aggregate supply back downward to AS_1. However, in the fall of 2008, the financial crisis entered a particularly virulent phase following the bankruptcy of Lehman Brothers, decreasing aggregate demand sharply to AD_3. As a result, the economy moved to point 3, with the unemployment rate rising to 10% and the inflation rate falling to 2.8% by the end of 2009 (see panel (b) of Figure 16). ◆

AD/AS ANALYSIS OF FOREIGN BUSINESS CYCLE EPISODES

Our aggregate demand and supply analysis can help us understand business cycle episodes in foreign countries. Here we look at two such episodes: the business cycle experience of the United Kingdom during the 2007–2009 global financial crisis, and the quite different experience of China during the same time period.

MyEconLab Mini-lecture

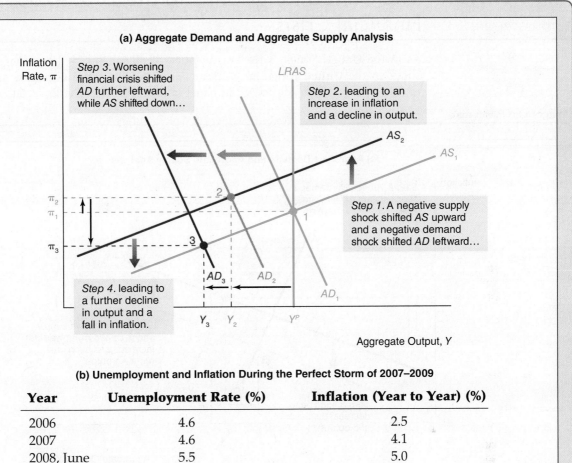

(a) Aggregate Demand and Aggregate Supply Analysis

Step 3. Worsening financial crisis shifted *AD* further leftward, while *AS* shifted down...

Step 2. leading to an increase in inflation and a decline in output.

Step 1. A negative supply shock shifted *AS* upward and a negative demand shock shifted *AD* leftward...

Step 4. leading to a further decline in output and a fall in inflation.

(b) Unemployment and Inflation During the Perfect Storm of 2007–2009

Year	Unemployment Rate (%)	Inflation (Year to Year) (%)
2006	4.6	2.5
2007	4.6	4.1
2008, June	5.5	5.0
2008, Dec.	7.2	0.1
2009, June	9.5	–1.2
2009, Dec.	10.0	2.8

FIGURE 16   Negative Supply and Demand Shocks and the 2007–2009 Crisis

Panel (a) shows that the negative supply shock caused by a rise in the price of oil shifted the short-run aggregate supply curve up, from AS_1 to AS_2, while the negative demand shock caused by the financial crisis led to a sharp contraction in spending, moving the aggregate demand curve from AD_1 to AD_2. The economy thus moved to point 2, leading to a sharp contraction in aggregate output, which fell to Y_2, a rise in unemployment, and a rise in inflation to π_2. The subsequent fall in oil prices shifted the short-run aggregate supply curve back down to AS_1, while the deepening financial crisis shifted the aggregate demand curve to AD_3. As a result, the economy moved to point 3, where inflation fell to π_3 and output to Y_3. The data in panel (b) support this analysis: Note that unemployment rose from 4.6% in 2006 to 5.5% in June 2008, while inflation rose from 2.5% to 5.0% during the same period. In the aftermath of the financial crisis, and with the decline in oil prices, the unemployment rate rose to 10% and inflation fell to 2.8% by the end of 2009.

Source: Economic Report of the President.

APPLICATION   The United Kingdom and the 2007–2009 Financial Crisis

As in the United States, a rise in the price of oil in 2007 led to a negative supply shock in the United Kingdom, which caused the short-run aggregate supply curve to shift upward, from AS_1 to AS_2 in panel (a) of Figure 17. The financial crisis initially

MyEconLab Mini-lecture

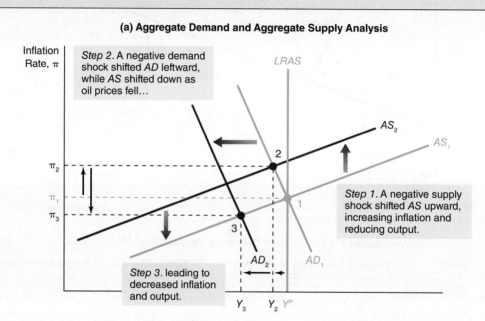

(a) Aggregate Demand and Aggregate Supply Analysis

Inflation Rate, π

Step 2. A negative demand shock shifted *AD* leftward, while *AS* shifted down as oil prices fell...

LRAS

AS_2

AS_1

Step 1. A negative supply shock shifted *AS* upward, increasing inflation and reducing output.

π_2

π_1

π_3

Step 3. leading to decreased inflation and output.

AD_2 AD_1

Y_3 Y_2 Y^P

Aggregate Output, Y

(b) Unemployment and Inflation, 2006–2009

Year	Unemployment Rate (%)	Inflation (Year to Year) (%)
2006	5.4	2.3
2007	5.3	2.3
2008, June	5.3	3.4
2008, Dec.	6.4	3.9
2009, June	7.8	2.1
2009, Dec.	7.8	2.1

FIGURE 17   U.K. Financial Crisis, 2007–2009

Panel (a) shows that a supply shock in 2007 caused by rising oil prices shifted the short-run aggregate supply curve in the United Kingdom up and to the left, from AS_1 to AS_2. The economy moved to point 2. With output below potential and oil prices falling after July 2008, the short-run aggregate supply curve began to shift downward to AS_1. A negative demand shock, caused by an escalation in the global financial crisis after Lehman Brothers declared bankruptcy, shifted the aggregate demand curve to the left to AD_2. The economy now moved to point 3, where output fell to Y_3, unemployment rose, and inflation decreased to π_3. The data in panel (b) support this analysis: Note that the unemployment rate increased from 5.4% in 2006 to 7.8% in December 2009, while the inflation rate rose from 2.3% to 3.9% and then fell to 2.1% over this same time period.

Source: Office of National Statistics, UK. http://www.statistics.gov.uk/statbase/tsdtimezone.asp.

did not have a large impact on spending, and so the aggregate demand curve did not shift and instead equilibrium moved from point 1 to point 2 on AD_1. Our aggregate demand and supply framework indicates that inflation should have risen, which is exactly what occurred (see the increase in the inflation rate from 2.3% in 2007 to 3.9% in December 2008, shown in panel (b) of Figure 17). With output below potential and oil prices falling after July 2008, the short-run aggregate supply curve shifted downward to AS_1. At the same time, the worsening of the financial crisis after Lehman Brothers declared bankruptcy impacted spending worldwide, causing a negative demand shock that shifted the aggregate demand curve to the left to AD_2. The economy now moved to point 3, with a further fall in output, a rise in unemployment, and a fall in inflation. As predicted by aggregate demand and supply analysis, the U.K. unemployment rate rose to 7.8% by the end of 2009, with the inflation rate falling to 2.1%.

APPLICATION China and the 2007–2009 Financial Crisis

The global financial crisis that began in August 2007 at first had very little impact on China.[7] In the fall of 2008, with the collapse of Lehman Brothers and the subsequent escalation of the financial crisis in the United States, things began to change. China's economy had been driven by an extremely strong export market, which up until September of 2008 had been growing at an annual rate of over 20%. Starting in October 2008, Chinese exports collapsed, falling at around a 20% annual rate through August 2009.

The negative demand shock caused by the collapse in exports led to a decline in aggregate demand, shifting the aggregate demand curve to AD_2 and moving the economy from point 1 to point 2 in panel (a) of Figure 18. As predicted by aggregate demand and supply analysis, China's economic growth slowed from over 11% in the first half of 2008 to under 5% in the second half, while inflation declined from 7.9% to 3.9% and became negative thereafter (see panel (b) of Figure 18).

Instead of relying solely on the economy's self-correcting mechanism, the Chinese government proposed a massive fiscal stimulus package of $580 billion in 2008, which at 12.5% of GDP was three times larger than the U.S. fiscal stimulus package relative to GDP. In addition, the People's Bank of China, the central bank, began taking measures to autonomously ease monetary policy. These decisive actions shifted the aggregate demand curve back to AD_1, and the Chinese economy very quickly moved back to point 1. The Chinese economy thus weathered the financial crisis remarkably well, with output growth rising rapidly in 2009 and inflation becoming positive thereafter. ◆

---

[7]Note that China, just like the rest of the world, experienced an increase in energy prices that initially shifted the short-run aggregate supply curve upward. Hence, as in the United Kingdom, in 2007 the Chinese economy experienced a rise in inflation and a slight slowing of growth. These events are not depicted in Figure 18 because including them would have made Figure 18 too complex.

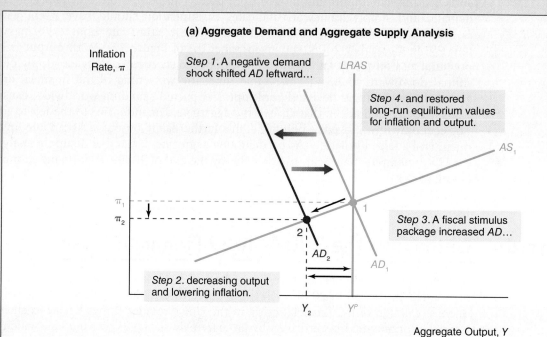

(a) Aggregate Demand and Aggregate Supply Analysis

Step 1. A negative demand shock shifted *AD* leftward…

Step 4. and restored long-run equilibrium values for inflation and output.

Step 3. A fiscal stimulus package increased *AD*…

Step 2. decreasing output and lowering inflation.

(b) Chinese Output Growth and Inflation, 2006–2009

Year	Output Growth (%)	Inflation (Year to Year) (%)
2006	11.8	1.5
2007	12.4	4.8
2008, June	11.2	7.9
2008, Dec.	4.4	3.9
2009, June	11.1	−1.1
2009, Dec.	10.4	−0.3

FIGURE 18   **China and the Financial Crisis, 2007–2009**

Panel (a) shows that the collapse of Chinese exports starting in 2008 led to a negative demand shock that shifted the aggregate demand curve to AD_2, moving the economy to point 2, where output growth fell below potential and inflation declined. A massive fiscal stimulus package and autonomous easing of monetary policy shifted the aggregate demand curve back to AD_1, and the economy very quickly moved back to long-run equilibrium at point 1. The data in panel (b) support this analysis: Note that output growth slowed but then bounced back again, and inflation began to fall at a less rapid rate.

Source: International Monetary Fund. 2010. International Financial Statistics. Country Tables, http://www.imf.org/external/data.htm.

SUMMARY

1. The aggregate demand curve indicates the quantity of aggregate output demanded at each inflation rate, and it is downward-sloping. The primary sources of shifts in the aggregate demand curve are (1) autonomous monetary policy, (2) government purchases, (3) taxes, (4) autonomous net exports, (5) autonomous consumption expenditure, (6) autonomous investment, and (7) financial frictions.

2. The long-run aggregate supply curve is vertical at potential output. The long-run aggregate supply curve shifts when technology changes, when there are long-run changes to the amount of labor or capital, or when the natural rate of unemployment changes. The short-run aggregate supply curve slopes upward because inflation rises as output rises relative to potential output. The short-run supply curve shifts when there are changes in expected inflation, inflation shocks, or persistent output gaps.

3. Equilibrium in the short run occurs at the point at which the aggregate demand curve intersects the short-run aggregate supply curve. Although this is the level to which the economy heads temporarily, the self-correcting mechanism leads the economy to settle permanently at the long-run equilibrium, the point at which the aggregate demand curve intersects the long-run aggregate supply curve and aggregate output is at its potential. Shifts in either the aggregate demand curve or the short-run aggregate supply curve can produce changes in aggregate output and inflation.

4. A positive demand shock shifts the aggregate demand curve to the right and initially leads to a rise in both inflation and output. However, in the long run, such a shock leads only to a rise in inflation, because output returns to its initial level of Y^P.

5. A temporary positive supply shock leads to a downward and rightward shift in the short-run aggregate supply curve, which initially lowers inflation and raises output. However, in the long-run, output and inflation are unchanged. A permanent positive supply shock initially leads to a rise in output and a decline in inflation. However, in contrast to a temporary supply shock, in the long run a permanent positive supply shock, which causes a rise in potential output, leads to a permanent rise in output and a permanent decline in inflation.

6. Aggregate supply and demand analysis can be used to analyze foreign business cycle episodes as well as domestic business cycle episodes.

KEY TERMS

aggregate demand curve, p. 509
aggregate supply curve, p. 515
consumption expenditure, p. 509
cost-push shocks, p. 516
demand shocks, p. 511
general equilibrium, p. 521

government purchases, p. 509
inflation shocks, p. 516
natural rate of output, p. 515
natural rate of unemployment, p. 515
net exports, p. 509
output gap, p. 515

planned investment spending, p. 509
potential output, p. 515
real business cycle theory, p. 533
self-correcting mechanism, p. 525
stagflation, p. 530
supply shocks, p. 516

QUESTIONS

All questions are available in MyEconLab at http://www.myeconlab.com.

1. Explain why the aggregate demand curve slopes downward and the short-run aggregate supply curve slopes upward.

2. Identify three factors that can shift the aggregate demand curve to the right and three different factors that can shift the aggregate demand curve to the left.

3. "The depreciation of the dollar from February 2009 to February 2014 had a positive effect on aggregate demand in the United States." Is this statement true, false, or uncertain? Explain your answer.

4. What determines the unemployment rate when output is at potential?

5. As the labor force becomes more productive over time, how is the long-run aggregate supply curve affected?

6. Why are central banks so concerned with inflation expectations?

7. "If prices and wages are perfectly flexible, then $\gamma = 0$ and changes in aggregate demand have a smaller effect on output." Is this statement true, false, or uncertain? Explain your answer.

8. What factors shift the short-run aggregate supply curve? Do any of these factors shift the long-run aggregate supply curve? Why?

9. If large budget deficits cause the public to think there will be higher inflation in the future, what is likely to happen to the short-run aggregate supply curve when budget deficits rise?

10. Internet sites that enable people to post their resumes online reduce the costs of job searches. How do you think the Internet has affected the natural rate of unemployment?

11. When aggregate output is below the natural rate of output, what happens to the inflation rate over time if the aggregate demand curve remains unchanged? Why?

12. Suppose the public believes that a newly announced anti-inflation program will work and so lowers its expectations of future inflation. What will happen to aggregate output and the inflation rate in the short run?

13. If the unemployment rate is above the natural rate of unemployment, holding other factors constant, what will happen to inflation and output?

14. What happens to inflation and output in the short run and the long run when government spending increases?

15. What factors led to decreases in both the unemployment and inflation rates in the 1990s?

16. Are there any "good" supply shocks?

17. Why did the Federal Reserve pursue inherently recessionary policies in the early 1980s?

18. In what ways is the Volcker disinflation considered a success? In what ways is it considered a failure?

19. Why did China fare much better than the United States and the United Kingdom during the 2007–2009 financial crisis?

APPLIED PROBLEMS

All applied problems are available in MyEconLab *at* http://www.myeconlab.com.

20. Using an aggregate demand and supply graph, show and describe the effects in both the short run and the long run of the following:

    a. A temporary negative supply shock.

    b. A permanent negative supply shock.

21. Suppose the President gets Congress to pass legislation that encourages investment in research and the development of new technologies. Assuming this policy leads to a positive productivity change for the U.S. economy, use aggregate demand and supply analysis to predict the effects on inflation and output. Demonstrate these effects on a graph.

22. Proposals advocating the implementation of a national sales tax have been presented before Congress. Predict the effects of such a tax on the aggregate supply and demand curves, showing the effects on output and inflation. Use a graph of aggregate supply and demand to demonstrate these effects.

23. Suppose the inflation rate remains relatively constant while output decreases and the unemployment rate increases. Using an aggregate demand and supply graph, show how this scenario is possible.

24. Classify each of the following as a supply shock or a demand shock. Use a graph to show the effects on inflation and output in the short run and in the long run.

    a. Financial frictions increase.

    b. Households and firms become more optimistic about the economy.

    c. Favorable weather produces a record crop of wheat and corn in the Midwest.

    d. Auto workers go on strike for four months.

25. During 2014, some Fed officials discussed the possibility of increasing interest rates as a way of fighting potential increases in expected inflation. If the public came to expect higher inflation rates in the future, what would be the effect on the short-run aggregate supply curve? Use an aggregate demand and supply graph to illustrate your answer.

DATA ANALYSIS PROBLEMS

The Problems update with real-time data in MyEconLab *and are available for practice or instructor assignment.*

1. Go to the St. Louis Federal Reserve FRED database, and find data on real government spending (GCEC1), real GDP (GDPC1), taxes (W006RC-1Q027SBEA), and the personal consumption expenditure price index (PCECTPI), a measure of the price level. Download all of the data into a spreadsheet, and convert the tax data series into real taxes. To do this, for each quarter, divide taxes by the price index and then multiply by 100.

a. Calculate the level change in real GDP over the four most recent quarters of data available, and the four quarters prior to that.

b. Calculate the level change in real government spending and real taxes over the four most recent quarters of data available, and the four quarters prior to that.

c. Are your results consistent with what you would expect? How do your answers to part (b) help explain, if at all, your answer to part (a)? Explain using the *IS* and *AD* curves.

2. Go to the St. Louis Federal Reserve FRED database, and find data on the personal consumption expenditure price index (PCECTPI), a measure of the price level; real compensation per hour (COMPRNFB); the nonfarm business sector real output per hour (OPHNFB), a measure of worker productivity; the price of a barrel of oil (MCOILWTICO); and the University of Michigan survey of inflation expectations (MICH). Use the *frequency* setting to convert the oil price and inflation expectations data series to "Quarterly," and use the *units* setting to convert the price index to "Percent Change from Year Ago." Download all of the data into a spreadsheet, and convert the compensation and productivity measures to a single indicator. To do this, for each quarter, take the compensation number and subtract the productivity number. Call this difference "Net Wages Above Productivity."

a. Calculate the change in the inflation rate over the four most recent quarters of data available, and the four quarters prior to that.

b. Calculate the changes in net wages above productivity, the price of oil, and inflation expectations over the four most recent quarters of data available, and the four quarters prior to that.

c. Are your results consistent with what you would expect? How do your answers to part (b) help explain, if at all, your answer to part (a)? Explain using the short-run aggregate supply curve.

WEB EXERCISES

1. The financial crisis of 2007–2009 sent the United States into its worst recession since the end of World War II, with the unemployment rate rising to above 10%. Go to http://research.stlouisfed.org/fred2/ and click on the Series ID link "UNRATE" (Civilian Unemployment Rate). What has happened to the unemployment rate since the time of the last reported value in Figure 16?

2. In its statement dated April 20, 2014, the Federal Open Market Committee indicated that "inflation has been running below the Committee's longer-run objective." Go to http://research.stlouisfed.org/fred2/ and click on the Series ID link "CPIAUCSL" (Consumer Price Index for All Urban Consumers: All Items-SA). Then click on the link "Percent Change from Year Ago." What has happened to the inflation rate since the time of the last reported value in Figure 16?

WEB REFERENCES

http://www.bls.gov

The home page of the Bureau of Labor Statistics lists information on unemployment and price levels.

http://www.census.gov/compendia/statab

Statistics on the U.S. economy are provided in an easy-to-understand format.

http://www.research.stlouisfed.org/fred2/

A database of U.S. economic data hosted by the Federal Reserve Bank of St. Louis.

WEB APPENDICES

Please visit the Companion Website at http://www.pearsonhighered.com/mishkin to read the Web appendices to Chapter 22.

Appendix 1: **The Effects of Macroeconomic Shocks on Asset Prices**

Appendix 2: **Aggregate Demand and Supply: A Numerical Example**

Appendix 3: **The Algebra of the Aggregate Demand and Supply Model**

Appendix 4: **The Taylor Principle and Inflation Stability**

22 The Phillips Curve and the Short-Run Aggregate Supply Curve

This appendix discusses the *Phillips curve*, which describes the relationship of unemployment and inflation and shows how this relationship can be used to derive the short-run aggregate supply curve presented in the chapter.

THE PHILLIPS CURVE

In 1958, New Zealand economist A.W. Phillips published a famous empirical paper that examined the relationship between unemployment and wage growth in the United Kingdom.[1] For the years 1861 to 1957, he found that periods of low unemployment were associated with rapid rises in wages, whereas periods of high unemployment were associated with low growth in wages. Other economists soon discovered that this relationship extended to many other countries. Because inflation is more central to macroeconomic issues than wage growth, these economists studied the relationship between unemployment and inflation. The negative correlation between unemployment and inflation that they found in many countries became known, naturally enough, as the *Phillips curve*.

The idea behind the Phillips curve is quite intuitive. When labor markets are *tight*—that is, the unemployment rate is low—firms may have difficulty hiring qualified workers and may even have a hard time keeping their present employees. Because of the shortage of workers in the labor market, firms will raise wages to attract workers and also raise their prices at a more rapid rate.

Phillips Curve Analysis in the 1960s

Because wage inflation feeds directly into overall inflation, in the 1960s the Phillips curve became extremely popular as a model for inflation fluctuations because it seemed to fit the data so well. Panel (a) of Figure 1 shows a plot of the U.S. inflation rate against the unemployment rate from 1950 to 1969. From this plot, we can see that a very clear negative correlation exists between unemployment and

---

[1]A.W. Phillips, "The Relationship Between Unemployment and the Rate of Change of Money Wages in the United Kingdom, 1861–1957," *Economica* 25 (November 1958): 283–299.

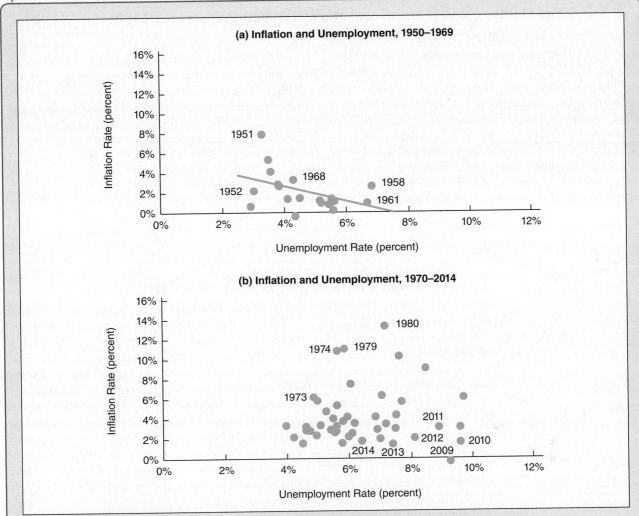

FIGURE 1   **Inflation and Unemployment in the United States, 1950–1969 and 1970–2014**

The plot of inflation against unemployment over the 1950–1969 period in panel (a) shows that a higher inflation rate was generally associated with a lower rate of unemployment. Panel (b) shows that after 1970, the negative correlation between inflation and unemployment disappeared.

Source: Economic Report of the President http://www.gpo.gov/erp.

inflation. The Phillips curve for this period seems to imply that there is a long-run tradeoff between unemployment and inflation—that is, policymakers can choose policies that will lead to a higher rate of inflation and end up with a lower unemployment rate on a sustained basis. This apparent tradeoff was very influential in policy circles in the 1960s, as we can see in the FYI box, "The Phillips Curve Tradeoff and Macroeconomic Policy in the 1960s."

FYI   The Phillips Curve Tradeoff and Macroeconomic Policy in the 1960s

In 1960, Paul Samuelson and Robert Solow published a paper outlining how policymakers could exploit the Phillips curve tradeoff. The policymaker could choose between two competing goals—inflation and unemployment—and decide how high an inflation rate he or she would be willing to accept to attain a lower unemployment rate.[2] Indeed, Samuelson and Solow even stated that policymakers could achieve a "nonperfectionist" goal of a 3% unemployment rate at what they considered to be a tolerable inflation rate of 4–5% per year. This thinking was influential in the Kennedy and then Johnson administrations, and contributed to the adoption of policies in the mid-1960s to stimulate the economy and bring the unemployment rate down to low levels. At first, these policies seemed to be successful because the subsequent higher inflation rates were accompanied by lower unemployment rates. However, the good times were not to last: From the late 1960s through the 1970s, inflation accelerated yet the unemployment rate remained stubbornly high.

The Friedman-Phelps Phillips Curve Analysis

In 1967 and 1968, Nobel Prize winners Milton Friedman and Edmund Phelps pointed out a severe theoretical flaw in the Phillips curve analysis.[3] Phillips curve analysis was inconsistent with the view that workers and firms care about *real* wages, the amount of real goods and services that wages can purchase, not *nominal* wages. Thus when workers and firms expect the price level to be rising, they will adjust nominal wages upward so that the real wage rate does not decrease. In other words, wages and overall inflation will rise on a one-to-one basis with increases in expected inflation, as well as respond to tightness in the labor market. In addition, the Friedman-Phelps analysis suggested that in the long run the economy would reach the level of unemployment that would occur if all wages and prices were flexible, which they called the *natural rate of unemployment*.[4] The natural rate of unemployment is the full-employment level of unemployment, because some unemployment will still exist even when wages and prices are flexible.

The Friedman-Phelps reasoning suggested a Phillips curve that we can write as follows:

$$\pi = \pi^e - \omega(U - U_n) \tag{1}$$

where π represents inflation, π^e expected inflation, U the unemployment rate, U_n the natural rate of unemployment, and ω the sensitivity of inflation to $U - U_n$. The

---

[2]Paul A. Samuelson and Robert M. Solow, "Analytical Aspects of Anti-Inflation Policy," *American Economic Review* 50 (May 1960, Papers and Proceedings): 177–194.

[3]Milton Friedman outlined his criticism of the Phillips curve in his 1967 presidential address to the American Economic Association: Milton Friedman, "The Role of Monetary Policy," *American Economic Review* 58 (1968): 1–17. Phelps's reformulation of the Phillips curve analysis was outlined in Edmund Phelps, "Money-Wage Dynamics and Labor-Market Equilibrium," *Journal of Political Economy* 76 (July/August 1968, Part 2): 687–711.

[4]As we discussed in Chapter 16, there will always be some unemployment—either *frictional unemployment*, unemployment that occurs because workers are searching for jobs, or *structural unemployment*, unemployment that arises from a mismatch of skills with available jobs and is a structural feature of the labor markets. Thus even when wages and prices are fully flexible, the natural rate of unemployment is at a level above zero.

MyEconLab Mini-lecture

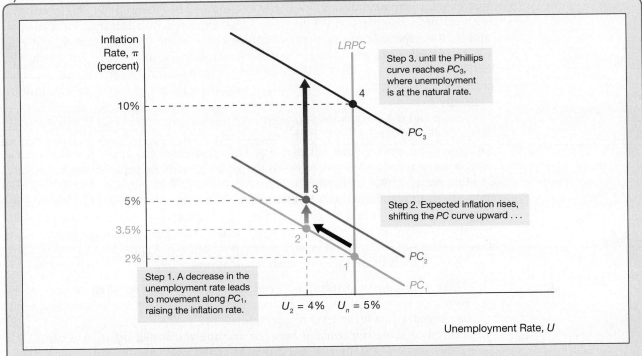

FIGURE 2   The Short- and Long-Run Phillips Curve
The expectations-augmented Phillips curve is downward-sloping because a lower unemployment rate results in a higher inflation rate for any given level of expected inflation. If the economy moves, due to a decline in the unemployment rate, from point 1 to point 2 on PC_1, the inflation rate rises. If unemployment remains at 4%, inflation rises further, shifting the short-run expectations-augmented Phillips curve upward to PC_2 and to point 3. Eventually, when the economy reaches point 4, where $\pi^e = \pi = 10\%$, the expectations-augmented Phillips curve PC_3 stops shifting because unemployment is at the natural rate of unemployment. The line connecting points 1 and 4 is the long-run Phillips curve, *LRPC*, and shows that long-run unemployment is at the natural rate of unemployment for any inflation rate.

presence of the π^e term explains why Equation 1 is also referred to as the *expectations-augmented Phillips curve*: It indicates that inflation is negatively related to the difference between the unemployment rate and the natural rate of unemployment $(U - U_n)$, a measure of tightness in the labor markets called the *unemployment gap*.

The expectations-augmented Phillips curve implies that long-run unemployment will be equal to the natural rate level, as Friedman and Phelps theorized. Recognize that in the long run, expected inflation must gravitate to actual inflation, and Equation 1 therefore indicates that U must be equal to U_n.

The Friedman-Phelps expectations-augmented version of the Phillips curve displays no long-run tradeoff between unemployment and inflation. To show this, Figure 2 presents the expectations-augmented Phillips curve, marked as PC_1, for a given expected inflation rate of 2% and a natural rate of unemployment of 5%. (PC_1 goes through point 1 because Equation 1 indicates that when $\pi = \pi^e = 2\%$, $U = U_n = 5\%$, and the curve's slope is $-\omega$.) Suppose the economy is initially at point 1, where the unemployment rate is at the natural rate level of 5%, but then government policies to stimulate the economy cause the unemployment rate to fall to 4%, a level that is below the natural rate level. The economy then moves along PC_1 to point 2, with inflation rising above 2% to, say, 3.5%. Expected inflation then rises as well, and so the expectations-augmented Phillips curve shifts upward from PC_1 to PC_2. Continued efforts to stimulate the economy and keep the unemployment rate at 4%, below the natural rate level, will cause further increases in the actual and expected inflation rates, causing the expectations-augmented Phillips curve to continue to shift upward.

When will the expectations-augmented Phillips curve stop rising? It will stop only when unemployment is back at the natural rate level, that is, when $U = U_n = 5\%$. Suppose this happens when inflation is at 10%; then expected inflation will also be at 10% because inflation has settled down to that level, with the expectations-augmented Phillips curve at PC_3 in Figure 2. The economy will now move to point 4, where $\pi = \pi^e = 10\%$ and unemployment is at the natural rate $U = U_n = 5\%$. We thus see that in the long run, when the expectations-augmented Phillips curve has stopped shifting, the economy will be at points such as 1 and 4. The line connecting these points is thus the *long-run Phillips curve*, which we mark as *LRPC* in Figure 2.

Figure 2 leads us to three important conclusions:

1. *There is no long-run tradeoff between unemployment and inflation* because, as the shown by the vertical long-run Phillips curve, a higher long-run inflation rate is not associated with a lower level of unemployment.
2. *There is a short-run tradeoff between unemployment and inflation* because, at a given expected inflation rate, policymakers can attain a lower unemployment rate at the expense of a somewhat higher inflation rate, as indicated by point 2 in Figure 2.
3. *There are two types of Phillips curves, long-run and short-run.* The expectations-augmented Phillips curves—PC_1, PC_2, and PC_3—are actually short-run Phillips curves: They are drawn for given values of expected inflation and will shift if deviations of unemployment from the natural rate cause inflation and expected inflation to change.

The Phillips Curve After the 1960s

As indicated in Figure 2, the expectations-augmented Phillips curve shows that the negative correlation between unemployment and inflation breaks down when the unemployment rate remains below the natural rate of unemployment for any extended period of time. This prediction of the Friedman and Phelps analysis turned out to be exactly right. Starting in the 1970s, after a period of very low unemployment rates, the negative correlation between unemployment and inflation that was so visible in the 1950s and 1960s disappeared, as shown in panel (b) of Figure 1. Not surprisingly, given the brilliance of Friedman's and Phelps's work, they were both awarded Nobel Prizes.

The Modern Phillips Curve

Inflation jumped up sharply with the sharp rise in oil prices in 1973 and 1979 (see panel (b) of Figure 1), and Phillips-curve theorists realized that they had to add one more feature to the expectations-augmented Phillips curve. *Supply shocks* are shocks to supply that change the amount of output an economy can produce from the same amount of capital and labor. These supply shocks translate into *inflation shocks*, that is, shifts in inflation that are independent of the tightness of the labor markets or of expected inflation. For example, when the supply of oil was restricted following the war between the Arab states and Israel in 1973, the price of oil more than quadrupled, and firms had to raise prices to reflect their increased costs of production, thus driving up inflation. Adding inflation shocks (ρ) to the expectations-augmented Phillips curve leads to the modern form of the short-run Phillips curve:

$$\pi = \pi^e - \omega(U - U_n) + \rho \qquad (2)$$

The modern, short-run Phillips curve implies that wages and prices are sticky. The more flexible wages and prices are, the more they, and inflation, respond to deviations of unemployment from the natural rate. That is, more flexible wages and prices imply that the absolute value of ω is higher, which in turn implies that the short-run Phillips curve is steeper. If wages and prices are completely flexible, then ω becomes so large that the short-run Phillips curve is vertical and identical to the long-run Phillips curve. In this case, there is no long-run or short-run tradeoff between unemployment and inflation.

The Modern Phillips Curve with Adaptive (Backward-Looking) Expectations

To complete our analysis of the Phillips curve, we need to understand how firms and households form expectations about inflation. One simple model assumes that they do so by looking at past inflation:

$$\pi^e = \pi_{-1}$$

where π_{-1} is the inflation rate for the previous period. This form of expectations is known as *adaptive expectations* or *backward-looking expectations* because expectations are formed by looking at the past and therefore change only slowly over time.[5] Substituting π_{-1} for π^e in Equation 2 yields the following short-run Phillips curve:

$$\pi \quad = \quad \pi_{-1} \quad - \quad \omega(U - U_n) \quad + \quad \rho$$

$$\text{Inflation} = \text{Expected} \quad - \ \omega \times \text{Unemployment} + \text{Inflation} \qquad (3)$$
$$\text{Inflation} \qquad\qquad\quad \text{Gap} \qquad\quad \text{Shock}$$

This form of the Phillips curve has two advantages over the more general formulation given in Equation 2. First, it takes on a very simple mathematical form that is convenient to use. Second, it provides two additional, realistic reasons why inflation might be sticky. One reason is that inflation expectations adjust only slowly as inflation changes over time. Inflation expectations are therefore sticky, which results in some inflation stickiness. Another reason is that the presence of past inflation in the Phillips curve formulation can reflect the fact that some wage and price contracts might be backward-looking, that is, tied to past inflation, and so inflation might not fully adjust to changes in inflation expectations in the short run.

There is, however, one important weakness of the adaptive-expectations form of the Phillips curve given in Equation 3: It takes a very mechanical view of how

---

[5]An alternative, modern form of expectations makes use of the concept *rational expectations*, whereby expectations are formed using all available information and so may react more quickly to new information. We discuss rational expectations and their role in macroeconomic analysis in Chapter 24.

inflation expectations are formed. More sophisticated analysis of expectations formation has important implications for the conduct of macroeconomic policy and is discussed in Chapter 24. For the time being, we will make use of the simple form of the Phillips curve with adaptive expectations, keeping in mind that the π_{-1} term represents expected inflation.

There is another convenient way of looking at the adaptive-expectations form of the Phillips curve. By subtracting π_{-1} from both sides of Equation 3, we can rewrite it as follows:

$$\Delta\pi = \pi - \pi_{-1} = -\omega(U - U_n) + \rho \tag{4}$$

Written in this form, the Phillips curve indicates that a negative unemployment gap (tight labor market) causes the inflation rate to rise, or *accelerate*. Thus the Equation 4 version of the Phillips curve is often referred to as an *accelerationist Phillips curve*. In this formulation, the term U_n has another interpretation. Since inflation stops accelerating (changing) when the unemployment rate is at U_n, we can refer to this term as the *nonaccelerating inflation rate of unemployment* or, more commonly, *NAIRU*.

THE SHORT-RUN AGGREGATE SUPPLY CURVE

To complete our aggregate demand and supply model, we need to use our analysis of the Phillips curve to derive a *short-run aggregate supply curve,* which represents the relationship between the total quantity of output that firms are willing to produce and the inflation rate.

We can translate the modern Phillips curve into a short-run aggregate supply curve by replacing the unemployment gap $(U - U_n)$ with the *output gap*, the difference between output and potential output $(Y - Y^P)$. To do this, we need to make use of a relationship between unemployment and aggregate output that was discovered by the economist Arthur Okun, once the chair of the Council of Economic Advisors and later an economist with the Brookings Institution.[6] *Okun's law* describes the negative relationship between the unemployment gap and the output gap.

Okun's Law   We show Okun's law in Figure 3, which plots the unemployment gap against the output gap. A tight negative relationship exists between the two variables. When output is above potential, so that the output gap is positive, the unemployment rate is below the natural rate of unemployment; that is, the unemployment gap is negative. The line through the data points in Figure 3 describes this negative relationship, which is given algebraically as follows:[7]

$$U - U_n = -0.5 \times (Y - Y^P) \tag{5}$$

---

[6]Arthur M. Okun, "Potential GNP: Its Measurement and Significance," in *Proceeding of the Business and Economics Section: American Statistical Association* (Washington, D.C.: American Statistical Association, 1962), pp. 98–103; reprinted in Arthur M. Okun, *The Political Economy of Prosperity* (Washington, D.C.: Brookings Institution, 1970), pp. 132–145.

[7]The output gap, $Y - Y^P$, in Okun's law is most accurately expressed in percentage terms, so the units of Y and Y^P would be in logarithims. However, to keep the algebra simple in this and later chapters, we will treat Y and Y^P as levels and not logarithms in both the Okun's law equation and the short-run aggregate supply curve developed here.

MyEconLab Mini-lecture   MyEconLab Real-time data

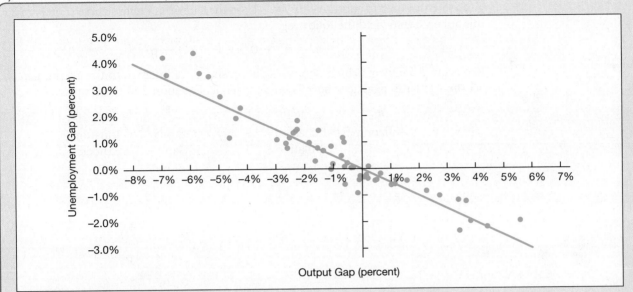

FIGURE 3   Okun's Law, 1960–2014

The plot of the unemployment gap and the output gap reveals a linear relationship, represented by the solid line with a slope of $-\frac{1}{2}$.

Source: Federal Reserve Bank of St. Louis, FRED database: http://research.stlouisfed.org/fred2/.

Okun's law thus states that for each percentage point that output is above potential, the unemployment rate is one-half of a percentage point below the natural rate of unemployment. Alternatively, for every percentage point that unemployment is above its natural rate, output is two percentage points below potential output.

Another way of thinking about Okun's law is to realize that a one percentage point increase in output leads to a one-half percentage point decrease in unemployment.[8] Why is the decrease in the unemployment rate only half the increase in the output rate? When output rises, firms do not increase employment commensurately with the increase in output, a phenomenon that is known as *labor hoarding*. Rather, firms work their employees harder, increasing their hours. Furthermore, when the economy is expanding, more people enter the labor force because job prospects are better, and so the unemployment rate does not fall by as much as employment increases.

---

[8]To see this algebraically, take the differences of Equation 5 and assume that U_n remains constant (a reasonable assumption because the natural rate of unemployment changes only very slowly over time). Then,

$$\%\Delta U = -0.5 \times (\%\Delta Y - \%\Delta Y^P)$$

where $\%\Delta$ indicates a percentage point change. Since potential output grows at a fairly steady rate of around three percent per year, $\%\Delta Y^P = 3\%$, we can also write Okun's law as follows:

$$\%\Delta U = -0.5 \times (\%\Delta Y - 3)$$

or

$$\%\Delta Y = 3 - 2 \times \%\Delta U$$

Hence we can state Okun's law in the following way: for every percentage point rise in output (real GDP), unemployment falls by one-half of a percentage point. Alternatively, for every percentage point rise in unemployment, real GDP falls by two percentage points.

Deriving the Short-Run Aggregate Supply Curve

We can use Okun's law as given in Equation 5 to substitute for $U - U_n$ in the short-run Phillips curve (Equation 2 of this appendix) to yield the following:

$$\pi = \pi^e + 0.5\omega(Y - Y^P) + \rho$$

Replacing 0.5ω by γ, which describes the sensitivity of inflation to the output gap, we get the short-run aggregate supply curve given as Equation 2 in the chapter:

$$\pi \quad = \quad \pi^e \quad + \quad \gamma(Y - Y^P) \quad + \quad \rho$$

Inflation $=$ Expected $+$ $\gamma \times$ Output $+$ Inflation
Inflation   Gap   Shock

23

Monetary Policy Theory

Learning Objectives

- Illustrate and explain the policy choices that monetary policymakers face under the conditions of aggregate demand shocks, temporary supply shocks, and permanent supply shocks.
- Identify the lags in the policy process, and summarize why they weaken the case for an activist policy approach.
- Explain why monetary policymakers can target any inflation rate in the long run but cannot target a level of aggregate output in the long run.
- Identify the sources of inflation and the role of monetary policy in propagating inflation.
- Explain the unique challenges that monetary policymakers face at the zero lower bound, and illustrate how nonconventional monetary policy can be effective under such conditions.

Preview

Between September 2007 and December 2008, the Federal Reserve lowered the target for its policy interest rate, the federal funds rate, from $5\frac{1}{4}\%$ all the way down to zero, and continued to keep it there for more than five years afterward. Why did the Fed lower interest rates so aggressively and continue to keep them so low?

Could this monetary policy easing spark undesirable inflation? Many commentators in the media think so. Starting in the early 1960s, when the inflation rate hovered between 1% and 2%, the economy began to suffer from higher and more variable rates of inflation. By the late 1960s, the inflation rate had climbed to beyond 5%, and by 1974, it reached the double-digit level. After moderating somewhat during the 1975–1978 period, it shot above 10% in 1979 and 1980, decreased to around 5% from 1982 to 1990, declined further to around 2% in the late 1990s, and then climbed above the 5% level in 2008. Inflation has become a major concern of politicians and the public, and how best to control it is an issue that frequently dominates the discussion of economic policy.

In this chapter, we will use the aggregate demand/aggregate supply (*AD/AS*) framework developed in Chapter 22 to develop a theory of monetary policy. Specifically, we will examine the role of monetary policy in creating inflation and stabilizing the economy. We apply the theory to four big questions: What are the roots of inflation? Does stabilizing inflation stabilize output? Should policy be *activist*, responding aggressively to fluctuations in economic activity, or passive and *nonactivist*? How can monetary policy work when interest rates hit a floor of zero?

RESPONSE OF MONETARY POLICY TO SHOCKS

As we saw in Chapter 16, the primary goal of central banks is price stability: that is, they try to maintain inflation, π, close to a target level (π^T), referred to as an **inflation target**, that is slightly above zero. Most central banks set π^T between 1% and 3%. In other words, central banks pursue price stability through monetary policy that aims to minimize the difference between inflation and the inflation target ($\pi - \pi^T$), a difference economists refer to as the **inflation gap**.

In Chapter 16, we learned that central banks also care about stabilizing economic activity. Because economic activity can be sustained only at potential output, we can describe this objective of monetary policy by saying that monetary policymakers want aggregate output to be close to its potential level, Y^P. Central banks want to minimize the difference between aggregate output and potential output $(Y - Y^P)$, i.e., the *output gap*. In our analysis of aggregate demand and supply in Chapter 22, we examined three categories of economic shocks—demand shocks, temporary supply shocks, and permanent supply shocks—and the effects of each on inflation and output. In this section, we describe a central bank's policy responses, given its objectives, to each of these types of shocks. In the case of both demand shocks and permanent supply shocks, policymakers can simultaneously pursue price stability and stability of economic activity. In the aftermath of a temporary supply shock, however, policymakers can achieve either price stability or economic activity stability, but not both. This tradeoff poses a thorny dilemma for central banks with dual mandates.

Response to an Aggregate Demand Shock

We begin by considering the effects of an aggregate demand shock, illustrated in Figure 1. The disruption to financial markets that began in August 2007 increased financial frictions and caused both consumer and business spending to fall. In the figure, the economy is initially at point 1, where output is at Y^P and inflation is at π^T. The negative demand shock decreases aggregate demand, shifting AD_1 to the left to AD_2. Policymakers can respond to this shock in two possible ways.

MyEconLab Mini-lecture

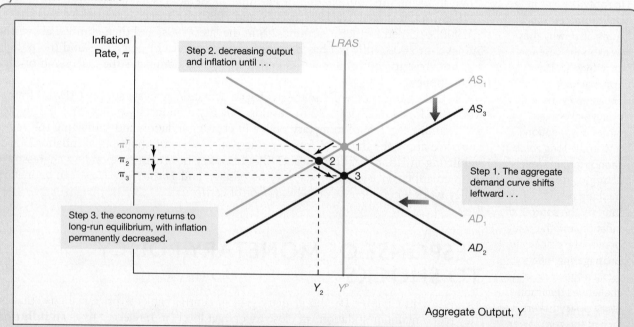

FIGURE 1 **Aggregate Demand Shock: No Policy Response**
An aggregate demand shock shifts the aggregate demand curve leftward from AD_1 to AD_2 and moves the economy from point 1 to point 2, where aggregate output falls to Y_2 and inflation falls to π_2. With output below potential, the short-run aggregate supply curve shifts down to AS_3 and the economy moves to point 3, where output is back at Y^P but inflation has fallen to π_3.

No Policy Response

If the central bank does not respond by changing the autonomous component of monetary policy, the aggregate demand curve remains at AD_2, and so the economy moves to the intersection of AS_1 and AD_2. Here, aggregate output falls to Y_2, below potential output Y^P, and inflation falls to π_2, below the inflation target of π^T. With inflation falling and output below potential, expected inflation will decline and the short-run aggregate supply curve will shift down and to the right until it reaches AS_3, and the economy will move to point 3. Output will be back to its potential level and inflation will fall to a lower level of π_3. At first glance, this outcome looks favorable—inflation is lower and output is back at its potential. But aggregate output will remain below potential for some time, and if inflation was initially at its target level, the fall in inflation is undesirable for the reasons outlined in Chapters 12 and 16.

Policy Stabilizes Economic Activity and Inflation in the Short Run

Policymakers can eliminate both the output gap and the inflation gap in the short run by pursuing policies aimed at increasing aggregate demand to its initial level and returning the economy to its preshock state. The central bank does this by autonomously easing monetary policy by cutting the real interest rate at any given inflation rate. This action stimulates investment spending and increases the quantity of aggregate output demanded at any given inflation rate, thereby shifting the AD curve to the right. As a result, the aggregate demand curve shifts from AD_2 back to AD_1 in Figure 2, and the economy returns to point 1. (The Federal Reserve took exactly these steps by lowering the federal funds rate from 5% to $\frac{1}{4}$% to zero over fifteen months starting in September 2007.)

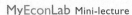 MyEconLab Mini-lecture

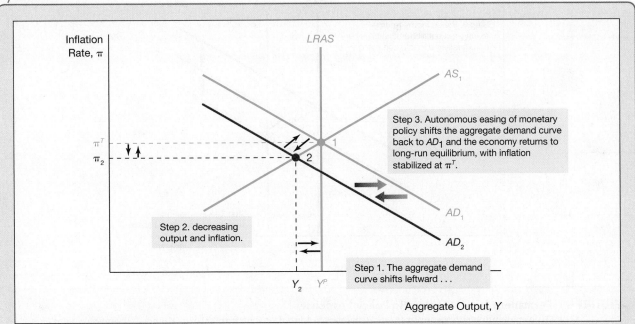

FIGURE 2   Aggregate Demand Shock: Policy Stabilizes Output and Inflation in the Short Run

An aggregate demand shock shifts the aggregate demand curve leftward from AD_1 to AD_2 and moves the economy from point 1 to point 2, where aggregate output falls to Y_2 and inflation falls to π_2. An autonomous easing of monetary policy lowers the real interest rate at any given inflation rate and shifts the AD curve back to AD_1. Aggregate output returns to potential at point 1, and inflation returns to its target level.

Our analysis of this monetary policy response shows that *in the case of aggregate demand shocks, there is no tradeoff between the pursuits of price stability and economic activity stability.* A monetary policy response that focuses on stabilizing inflation is exactly the monetary policy response that will stabilize economic activity. No conflict exists between the dual objectives of stabilizing inflation and stabilizing economic activity, a result that Olivier Blanchard (formerly of MIT but now at the International Monetary Fund) referred to as the **divine coincidence**.

Response to a Permanent Supply Shock

We illustrate a permanent supply shock in Figure 3. Again the economy starts out at point 1, where aggregate output is at the natural rate of Y_1^P and inflation is at π^T. Suppose the economy suffers a permanent negative supply shock when an increase in regulations permanently reduces the level of potential output. Potential output falls from Y_1^P to Y_3^P, and the long-run aggregate supply curve shifts leftward from $LRAS_1$ to $LRAS_3$. The permanent supply shock triggers an inflation shock that shifts the short-run aggregate supply curve upward, from AS_1 to AS_2. Two possible policy responses to this permanent supply shock are possible.

MyEconLab Mini-lecture

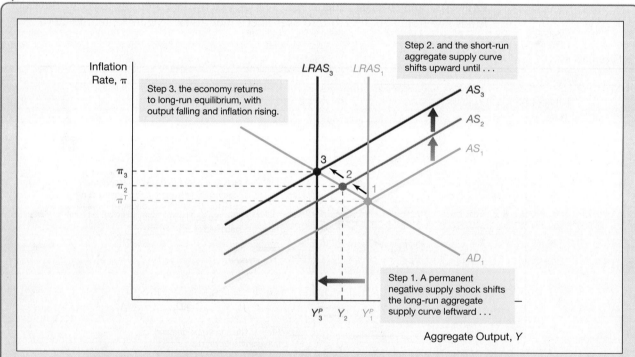

FIGURE 3   Permanent Supply Shock: No Policy Response

A permanent negative supply shock decreases potential output from Y_1^P to Y_3^P, and the long-run aggregate supply curve shifts to the left from $LRAS_1$ to $LRAS_3$, while the short-run aggregate supply curve shifts upward from AS_1 to AS_2. The economy moves to point 2, with inflation rising to π_2 and output falling to Y_2. Because aggregate output is still above potential, the short-run aggregate supply curve will keep on shifting until the output gap is zero when it reaches AS_3. The economy moves to point 3, where inflation rises to π_3 and output falls to Y_3^P.

MyEconLab Mini-lecture

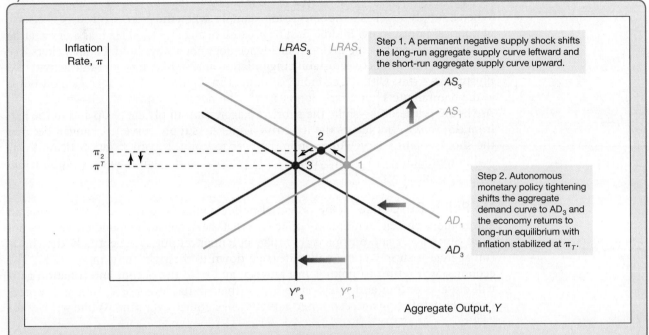

Step 1. A permanent negative supply shock shifts the long-run aggregate supply curve leftward and the short-run aggregate supply curve upward.

Step 2. Autonomous monetary policy tightening shifts the aggregate demand curve to AD_3 and the economy returns to long-run equilibrium with inflation stabilized at π_T.

FIGURE 4   Permanent Supply Shock: Policy Stabilizes Inflation

A permanent negative supply shock decreases potential output from Y_1^P to Y_3^P, and the long-run aggregate supply curve shifts to the left from $LRAS_1$ to $LRAS_3$, while the short-run aggregate supply curve shifts upward from AS_1 to AS_3. An autonomous tightening of monetary policy shifts the aggregate demand curve to the left to AD_3, thereby keeping the inflation rate at π^T at point 3.

No Policy Response   If policymakers leave autonomous monetary policy unchanged, the economy will move to point 2, with inflation rising to π_2 and output falling to Y_2. Because this level of output is still higher than potential output, Y_3^P, the short-run aggregate supply curve will keep shifting up and to the left until it reaches AS_3, where it intersects AD_1 on $LRAS_3$. The economy moves to point 3, eliminating the output gap but leaving inflation higher at π_3 and output lower at Y_3^P.

Policy Stabilizes Inflation   According to Figure 4, monetary authorities can keep inflation at the target inflation rate and thereby stabilize inflation by decreasing aggregate demand. The goal is to shift the aggregate demand curve leftward to AD_3, where it will intersect the long-run aggregate supply curve $LRAS_3$ at the target inflation rate of π^T. To shift the aggregate demand to AD_3, the monetary authorities would autonomously tighten monetary policy by increasing the real interest rate at any given inflation rate, thus causing investment spending to fall, leading to lower aggregate demand at any given inflation rate. The economy thus will go to point 3, where the output gap is zero and inflation is at the target level of π^T.

Here again, keeping the inflation gap at zero leads to a zero output gap, so by stabilizing inflation the policy response has also stabilized economic activity. ***The divine coincidence still holds true when a permanent supply shock occurs: There is no tradeoff between the dual objectives of stabilizing inflation and stabilizing economic activity.***

Response to a Temporary Supply Shock

When a supply shock is temporary—for example, when the price of oil surges because of political unrest in the Middle East or because of an act of God such as a devastating hurricane in Florida—the divine coincidence does not always hold. Policymakers face a short-run tradeoff between stabilizing inflation and stabilizing economic activity. To illustrate, we start with the economy at point 1 in Figure 5, where aggregate output is at the natural rate Y^P and inflation is at π^T. The negative supply shock—from, say, a rise in the price of oil—shifts the short-run aggregate supply curve up and to the left, from AS_1 to AS_2, but leaves the long-run aggregate supply curve unchanged because the shock is temporary. The economy moves to point 2, with inflation rising to π_2 and output falling to Y_2. Policymakers can respond to the temporary supply shock in three possible ways.

No Policy Response   One potential policy choice is to refrain from making an autonomous change in monetary policy, so that the aggregate demand curve does not shift. Since aggregate output is less than potential output Y^P, eventually the short-run aggregate supply curve will shift back down to the right, returning to AS_1. The economy will return to point 1 in Figure 5, and both the output and inflation gaps will close as output and inflation return to their initial levels of Y^P and π^T, respectively. Both inflation and economic activity will stabilize over time. While we wait for

MyEconLab Mini-lecture

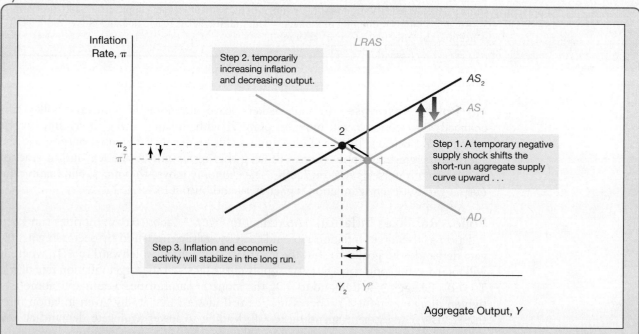

FIGURE 5   **Response to a Temporary Supply Shock: No Policy Response**
A temporary negative supply shock shifts the short-run aggregate supply curve upward from AS_1 to AS_2, moving the economy to point 2, with inflation rising to π_2 and output falling to Y_2. If the autonomous monetary policy remains unchanged, the short-run aggregate supply curve will shift back down and to the right in the long run, eventually returning to AS_1, and the economy will move back to point 1.

MyEconLab Mini-lecture

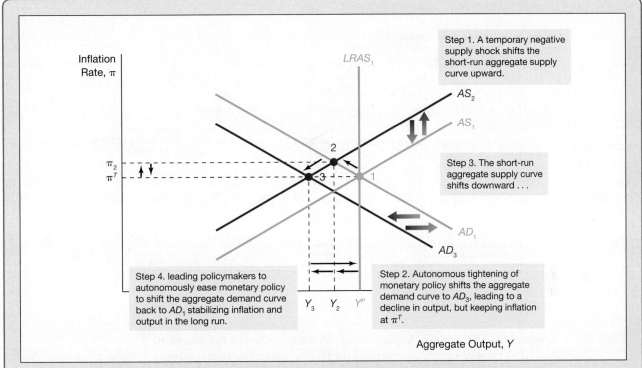

Step 1. A temporary negative supply shock shifts the short-run aggregate supply curve upward.

Step 3. The short-run aggregate supply curve shifts downward . . .

Step 4. leading policymakers to autonomously ease monetary policy to shift the aggregate demand curve back to AD_1 stabilizing inflation and output in the long run.

Step 2. Autonomous tightening of monetary policy shifts the aggregate demand curve to AD_3, leading to a decline in output, but keeping inflation at π^T.

FIGURE 6   Response to a Temporary Supply Shock: Short-Run Inflation Stabilization

A temporary negative supply shock shifts the short-run aggregate supply curve from AS_1 to AS_2, moving the economy to point 2, with inflation rising to π_2 and output falling to Y_2. Autonomous tightening of monetary policy shifts the aggregate demand curve to the left to AD_3, and the economy moves to point 3, where inflation is at π^T. With output below potential at point 3, the short-run aggregate supply curve shifts back to AS_1. To keep the inflation rate at π^T, the autonomous tightening of monetary policy is reversed, shifting the aggregate demand curve back to AD_1 and the economy back to point 1.

the long run, however, the economy will undergo a painful period of reduced output and higher inflation rates. To avoid this period of reduced output and high inflation, monetary policymakers might decide to try to stabilize economic activity or inflation in the short run.

Policy Stabilizes Inflation in the Short Run   A second policy choice for monetary authorities is to keep inflation at the target level of π^T in the short run by autonomously tightening monetary policy and raising the real interest rate at any given inflation rate. Doing so will cause investment spending and aggregate demand to fall at each inflation rate, shifting the aggregate demand curve to the left to AD_3 in Figure 6. The economy now will move to point 3, where the aggregate demand curve AD_3 intersects the short-run aggregate supply curve AS_2 at an inflation rate of π^T. Because output is below potential at point 3 the short-run aggregate supply curve will shift back down to AS_1. To keep the inflation rate at π^T, the monetary authorities will need to move the

MyEconLab Mini-lecture

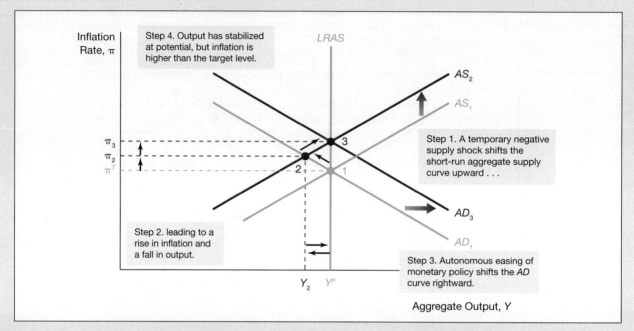

Inflation Rate, π

Step 4. Output has stabilized at potential, but inflation is higher than the target level.

LRAS

AS_2

AS_1

π_3
π_2
π^T

3

2

1

Step 1. A temporary negative supply shock shifts the short-run aggregate supply curve upward . . .

AD_3

AD_1

Step 2. leading to a rise in inflation and a fall in output.

Step 3. Autonomous easing of monetary policy shifts the *AD* curve rightward.

Y_2 Y^P

Aggregate Output, *Y*

FIGURE 7   Response to a Temporary Supply Shock: Short-Run Output Stabilization

A temporary negative supply shock shifts the short-run aggregate supply curve from AS_1 to AS_2, moving the economy to point 2, with inflation rising to π_2 and output falling to Y_2. To stabilize output, autonomous monetary policy easing shifts the aggregate demand curve rightward to AD_3. At point 3, the monetary policy action has stabilized economic activity, but inflation at π_3 is greater than the target level π^T.

short-run aggregate demand curve back to AD_1 by reversing the autonomous tightening, and eventually the economy will return to point 1.

As Figure 6 illustrates, stabilizing inflation reduces aggregate output to Y_3 in the short run, and only over time will output return to potential output at Y^P. ***Stabilizing inflation in response to a temporary supply shock leads to a larger deviation of aggregate output from potential, so this action does not stabilize economic activity.***

Policy Stabilizes Economic Activity in the Short Run   A third policy choice is for monetary policymakers to stabilize economic activity rather than inflation in the short run by increasing aggregate demand. According to Figure 7, this policy decision will shift the aggregate demand curve to the right to AD_3, where it intersects the short-run aggregate supply curve AS_2 and the long-run aggregate supply curve *LRAS* at point 3. To achieve this result, policymakers will have to autonomously ease monetary policy by lowering the real interest rate at any given inflation rate. At point 3, the output gap returns to zero, so monetary policy has stabilized economic activity. However, inflation has risen to π_3, which is greater than π^T, and so inflation has *not* been stabilized. ***Stabilizing economic activity in response to a temporary supply shock results in a larger deviation of inflation from the inflation target rather than a stabilization of inflation.***

The Bottom Line: The Relationship Between Stabilizing Inflation and Stabilizing Economic Activity

We can draw the following conclusions from our analysis:

1. *If most shocks to the economy are aggregate demand shocks or permanent aggregate supply shocks, then policy that stabilizes inflation will also stabilize economic activity, even in the short run.*
2. *If temporary supply shocks are the most common type of shock, then a central bank must choose between the two stabilization objectives in the short run.*

HOW ACTIVELY SHOULD POLICYMAKERS TRY TO STABILIZE ECONOMIC ACTIVITY?

All economists have similar policy goals (to promote high employment and price stability), yet they often disagree on the best approach for achieving these goals. Suppose policymakers confront an economy that has high unemployment resulting from a negative demand or supply shock that has reduced aggregate output. **Nonactivists** believe that wages and prices are very flexible and that the self-correcting mechanism works very rapidly. They argue that the short-run aggregate supply curve will shift downward quickly, returning the economy to full employment rapidly. They thus believe that government action to eliminate unemployment is unnecessary. **Activists**, many of whom are followers of Keynes and are thus referred to as **Keynesians**, regard the self-correcting mechanism, which works through wage and price adjustment, as a very slow-working mechanism because of the stickiness of wages and prices. Thus they believe it will take the economy a very long time to reach the long run, agreeing with Keynes's famous adage that "In the long-run, we are all dead." Activists therefore believe that the government should pursue active policies to increase aggregate demand and eliminate high unemployment when it develops.

Lags and Policy Implementation

If policymakers could shift the aggregate demand curve instantaneously, activist policies could be used to move the economy immediately to the full-employment level, as we saw in the previous section. However, several types of lags prevent this immediate shift from occurring, and there are differences in the lengths of these lags for monetary versus fiscal policy.

1. The **data lag** is the time it takes for policymakers to obtain the data that describe what is happening in the economy. Accurate data on GDP, for example, are not available until several months after a given quarter is over.
2. The **recognition lag** is the time it takes for policymakers to feel confident about the signals the data are sending about the future course of the economy. For example, to minimize errors, the National Bureau of Economic Research (the private organization that officially dates business cycles) will not declare the economy to be in recession until at least six months after it has determined that a recession has begun.
3. The **legislative lag** represents the time it takes to get legislation passed to implement a particular policy. The legislative lag does not apply to most monetary policy actions, such as the lowering of interest rates. It is, however, important in the

implementation of fiscal policy, because it can sometimes take six months to a year to get legislation passed to change taxes or government purchases.

4. The **implementation lag** is the time it takes for policymakers to change policy instruments once they have decided on a new policy. Again, this lag is less important for the conduct of monetary policy, because the Federal Reserve can immediately change its policy interest rate, while it is more important for the implementation of fiscal policy. The implementation of new fiscal policy can take substantial time; for example, getting government agencies to change their spending habits takes time, as does changing tax tables.

5. The **effectiveness lag** is the time it takes for the policy to have a real impact on the economy. The effectiveness lag is both long (often a year long or longer) and variable (that is, substantial uncertainty exists about the length of this lag).

The existence of these lags makes the policymakers' job far more difficult and therefore weakens the case for activism. When unemployment is high, activist policy aimed at shifting the aggregate demand curve rightward to restore the economy to full employment may not produce desirable outcomes. Indeed, if the policy lags described above are very long, then by the time the aggregate demand curve shifts to the right, the self-correcting mechanism may have already returned the economy to full employment. Then, when the activist policy kicks in, it may cause output to rise above potential, leading to a rise in inflation. In situations in which policy lags are longer than the time it takes the self-correcting mechanism to work, a policy of nonactivism may produce better outcomes.

The activist/nonactivist debate came to the fore when the Obama administration advocated a fiscal stimulus package early in its administration in 2009 (see the FYI box, "The Activist/Nonactivist Debate Over the Obama Fiscal Stimulus Package"). In Chapter 24, we will return to the issue of just how active policy should be when we look at the role that expectations play in monetary policy.

INFLATION: ALWAYS AND EVERYWHERE A MONETARY PHENOMENON

Milton Friedman is famous for his adage that in the long run, "Inflation is always and everywhere a monetary phenomenon." This adage is supported by our aggregate demand and supply analysis, which asserts that monetary policymakers can target any inflation rate in the long run by shifting the aggregate demand curve through autonomous monetary policy. As an illustration, look at Figure 8, where the economy is at point 1, with aggregate output at potential output Y^P and inflation at an initial inflation target of π_1^T.

Suppose the central bank believes that this inflation target is too low and chooses to raise it to π_3^T. The central bank eases monetary policy autonomously by lowering the real interest rate at any given inflation rate, thereby increasing investment spending and aggregate demand. In Figure 8, the aggregate demand curve shifts to AD_3. The economy then moves to point 2, at the intersection of AD_3 and AS_1, with inflation rising to π_2. Because aggregate output is above potential output, $Y_2 > Y^P$, the short-run aggregate supply curve shifts up and to the left, eventually stopping at AS_3. The economy moves to point 3, where inflation is at the higher target level of π_3^T and the output gap is back at zero.

The Activist/Nonactivist Debate Over the Obama Fiscal Stimulus Package

When President Obama took office in January 2009, he faced a very serious recession, with unemployment at over 7% and rising rapidly. Although policymakers had been using monetary policy aggressively to stabilize the economy (see Chapters 12 and 15), many activists argued that the government needed to do more by implementing a massive fiscal stimulus package. They argued that without the stimulus package, monetary policy, which had already lowered the federal funds rate to close to zero and so could not lower nominal interest rates further, would be unable to increase aggregate demand to the full-employment level. On the other hand, nonactivists opposed the fiscal stimulus package, arguing that fiscal stimulus would take too long to work because of long implementation lags. They cautioned that if the fiscal stimulus kicked in after the economy had already recovered, the result would be increased volatility in inflation and economic activity.

The economics profession was split over the desirability of fiscal stimulus. Approximately 200 economists who opposed fiscal stimulus signed a petition published in the *Wall Street Journal* and the *New York Times* on January 28, 2009. An opposing petition, also signed by about 200 economists, was sent to the U.S. Congress on February 8. The Obama administration came down squarely on the side of the activists and proposed the American Recovery and Reinvestment Act of 2009, a $787 billion fiscal stimulus package that was passed by Congress on February 13, 2009. In the House, the vote in favor of the stimulus package was 244 to 188, with 177 Republicans and 11 Democrats opposing the bill. In the Senate, the vote was 61 to 37, with all 58 Democrats and 3 Republicans supporting the bill. Even after the fact, the value of the 2009 stimulus package is still hotly debated, with some believing it helped stabilize the economy and others believing it was not effective.

The analysis in Figure 8 demonstrates the following key points:

1. *The monetary authorities can target any inflation rate in the long run with autonomous monetary policy adjustments.*
2. *Potential output—and therefore the quantity of aggregate output produced in the long run—is independent of monetary policy.*

CAUSES OF INFLATIONARY MONETARY POLICY

If everyone agrees that high inflation is bad for an economy, why do we see so much of it? Do governments pursue inflationary monetary policies intentionally? We know that monetary authorities can set the inflation rate in the long run, so it must be that in trying to achieve other goals, governments end up with overly expansionary monetary policies and high inflation. In this section, we will examine the government policies that are the most common sources of inflation.

High Employment Targets and Inflation

The primary goal of most governments is high employment, and the pursuit of this goal can bring on high inflation. The U.S. government is committed by law (the Employment Act of 1946 and the Humphrey-Hawkins Act of 1978) to engage in activist policy

MyEconLab Mini-lecture

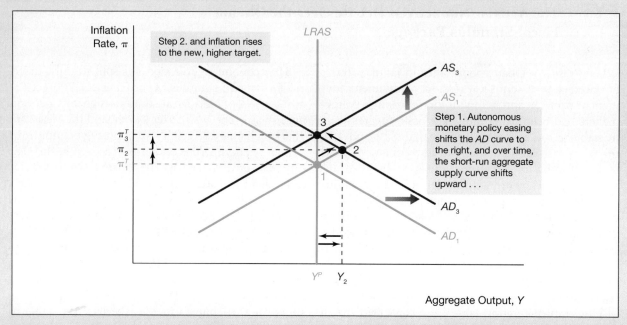

FIGURE 8   A Rise in the Inflation Target

To raise the inflation target to π_3^T, the central bank undertakes an autonomous monetary policy easing by lowering the real interest rate at any given inflation rate, thereby shifting the aggregate demand curve rightward to AD_3. The economy then moves to point 2, and the short-run aggregate supply curve shifts up and to the left, eventually stopping at AS_3. The economy then moves to point 3, with the output gap at zero and inflation at π_3^T.

to promote high employment. Both laws require a commitment to a high level of employment consistent with stable inflation—yet in practice, the U.S. government and the Federal Reserve have often pursued a high employment target with little concern for the inflationary consequences of such a policy. This tendency was especially apparent in the mid-1960s and 1970s, when the government and the Fed began taking an active role in attempting to stabilize unemployment.

Two types of inflation can result from an activist stabilization policy aimed at promoting high employment:

1. **Cost-push inflation** results from either a temporary negative supply shock or a push by workers for wage hikes that are beyond those justified by productivity gains.
2. **Demand-pull inflation** results when policymakers pursue policies that increase aggregate demand.

We will now use aggregate demand and supply analysis to examine the effects of a high employment target on both types of inflation.

Cost-Push Inflation   Consider the economy shown in Figure 9, which is initially at point 1, the intersection of the aggregate demand curve AD_1 and the short-run aggregate supply curve AS_1. Suppose workers succeed in pushing for higher wages, either because

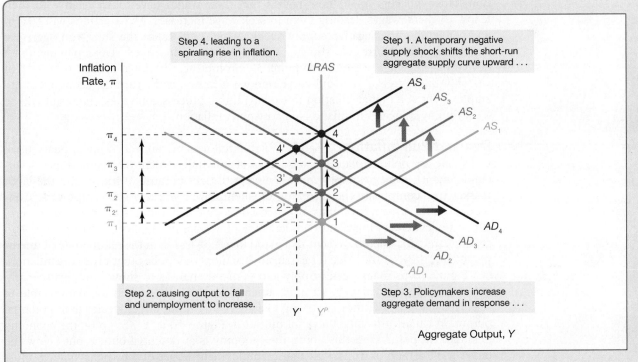

Step 4. leading to a spiraling rise in inflation.

Step 1. A temporary negative supply shock shifts the short-run aggregate supply curve upward . . .

Step 2. causing output to fall and unemployment to increase.

Step 3. Policymakers increase aggregate demand in response . . .

FIGURE 9   Cost-Push Inflation

A cost-push shock (which acts like a temporary negative supply shock) shifts the short-run aggregate supply curve up and to the left to AS_2, and the economy moves to point $2'$. To keep aggregate output at Y^P and to lower the unemployment rate, policymakers shift the aggregate demand curve to AD_2 so that the economy will return quickly to potential output at point 2 and an inflation rate of π_2. Further upward and leftward shifts of the short-run aggregate supply curve, to AS_3 and beyond, lead the policymakers to continue increasing aggregate demand, leading to a continuing increase in inflation—a cost-push inflation.

they want to increase their real wages (their wages in terms of the goods and services they can buy) above the level justified by productivity gains or because they expect inflation to increase and therefore want their wages to increase accordingly. This cost-push shock, which acts like a temporary negative supply shock, raises the inflation rate and shifts the short-run aggregate supply curve up and to the left, to AS_2. If the central bank takes no action to change the equilibrium interest rate and the monetary policy curve remains unchanged, the economy will move to point $2'$, at the intersection of the new short-run aggregate supply curve AS_2 and the aggregate demand curve AD_1. Output will decline to Y', below potential output, and the inflation rate will rise to $\pi_{2'}$, leading to an increase in unemployment.

In contrast, activist policymakers with a high employment target would implement policies to increase aggregate demand, such as tax cuts, increases in government purchases, or an autonomous easing of monetary policy. These policies would shift the aggregate demand curve in Figure 9 to AD_2, quickly returning the economy to potential output at point 2 and increasing the inflation rate to π_2. The workers would fare quite well, earning both higher wages and government protection against excessive unemployment.

The workers' success might encourage them to seek even higher wages. In addition, other workers might now realize that their wages have fallen relative to their fellow workers' wages, leading them to seek wage increases. These actions will lead to another temporary negative supply shock, which will cause the short-run aggregate supply curve in Figure 9 to shift up and to the left again, to AS_3. Unemployment will develop again when we move to point 3′, prompting additional activist policies that will shift the aggregate demand curve rightward to AD_3 and return the economy to full employment at a higher inflation rate of π_3. If this process continues, the result will be a continuing increase in inflation—a cost-push inflation.

Demand-Pull Inflation   A goal of high employment can lead to inflationary fiscal and monetary policy in another way. Even at full employment (the natural rate of unemployment), some unemployment is always present because of frictions in the labor market that complicate the matching of unemployed workers with employers. Consequently, the unemployment rate when employment is full is still greater than zero. When policymakers mistakenly underestimate the natural rate of unemployment and so set a target for unemployment that is too low (i.e., less than the natural rate of unemployment), they set the stage for expansionary monetary policy that produces inflation.

Figure 10 uses aggregate supply and demand analysis to show how this scenario can unfold. If policymakers set a 4% unemployment target when the natural rate of unemployment is 5%, they are trying to achieve an output target greater than potential output. We mark this target level of output in Figure 10 as Y^T. Suppose the economy is initially at point 1: At this point, the economy is at potential output but below the target level of output Y^T. To hit the unemployment target of 4%, policymakers must enact policies, such as expansionary fiscal policy or an autonomous easing of monetary policy, to increase aggregate demand. The aggregate demand curve in Figure 10 shifts to the right until it reaches AD_2 and the economy moves to point 2′, where output is at Y^T and policymakers have achieved the 4% unemployment rate goal. But there is more to the story. At Y^T, the 4% unemployment rate is below the natural rate level and output is above potential, causing wages to rise. The short-run aggregate supply curve will now shift up and to the left, eventually reaching AS_2 and moving the economy from point 2′ to point 2, where it is back at potential output but at a higher inflation rate of π_2. Because unemployment is again higher than the target level, policymakers will once more shift the aggregate demand curve rightward to AD_3 in order to hit the output target at point 3′—and the whole process will continue to drive the economy to point 3 and beyond. The overall result is a steadily rising inflation rate.

Pursuing too low an unemployment rate target or, equivalently, too high an output target thus leads to inflationary monetary or fiscal policy. Policymakers fail on two counts: They have not achieved their unemployment target, and they have caused higher inflation. If the target rate of unemployment is below the natural rate, the process we see in Figure 10 will be well under way before the policymakers realize their mistake.

Cost-Push Versus Demand-Pull Inflation.   When inflation occurs, how do we know whether it is demand-pull inflation or cost-push inflation? We would normally expect to see demand-pull inflation when unemployment is below the natural rate level, and to see cost-push inflation when unemployment is above the natural rate level. Unfortunately, economists and policymakers still struggle with accurately measuring the natural rate of unemployment. Complicating matters further, a cost-push inflation can be initiated by a demand-pull inflation, blurring the distinction. When a

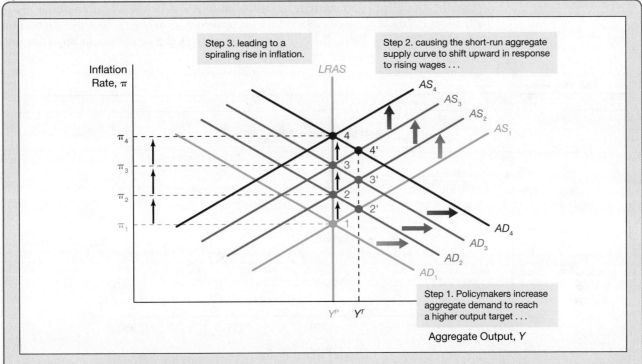

FIGURE 10   Demand-Pull Inflation

Too low an unemployment target (too high an output target of Y^T) causes the government to increase aggregate demand, shifting the AD curve rightward from AD_1 to AD_2 to AD_3 and so on. Because at Y^T the unemployment rate is below the natural rate level, wages will rise and the short-run aggregate supply curve will shift up and leftward, from AS_1 to AS_2 to AS_3 and so on. The result is a continuing rise in inflation known as a demand-pull inflation.

demand-pull inflation produces higher inflation rates, expected inflation will eventually rise and workers will demand higher wages (cost-push inflation) so that their real wages do not fall. Finally, expansionary monetary and fiscal policies produce both kinds of inflation, so we cannot distinguish between the two types of inflation on the basis of their source.

In the United States, as we will see in the following application, the primary reason for inflationary policy has been policymakers' adherence to a high employment target. As we saw in Chapter 19, high inflation can also be caused by persistent government budget deficits that are financed by increases in the monetary base.

APPLICATION   The Great Inflation

Now that we have examined the roots of inflationary monetary policy, we can investigate the causes of the rise in U.S. inflation that occurred from 1965 to 1982, a period dubbed the "Great Inflation."

Panel (a) of Figure 11 documents the rise in inflation during these years. Just before the Great Inflation started, the inflation rate was below 2% at an annual rate; by the late 1970s, it averaged around 8%. It peaked at nearly 14% in 1980 after an oil price shock in 1979. Panel (b) of Figure 11 compares the actual unemployment rate

MyEconLab Mini-lecture

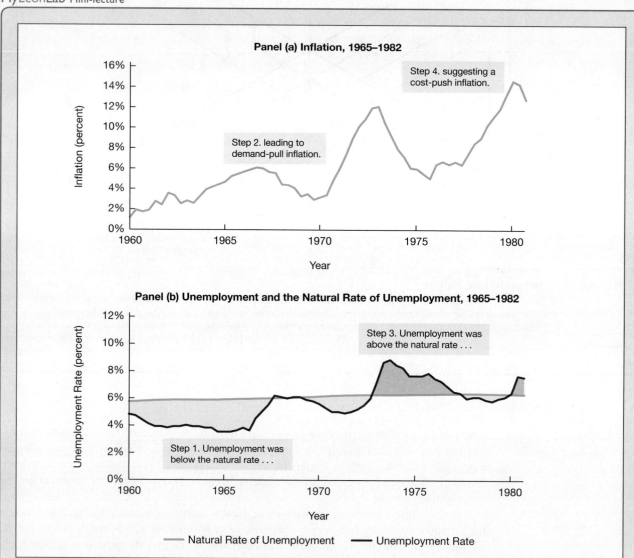

FIGURE 11 **Inflation and Unemployment, 1965–1982**

As shown in panel (a), the CPI inflation rate was below 2% at an annual rate in the early 1960s, but by the late 1970s, it was averaging around 8%. It peaked at over 14% in 1980 following an oil price shock in 1979. As shown in panel (b), the economy experienced unemployment below the natural rate in every year but one between 1960 and 1973, suggesting a demand-pull inflation as described in Figure 10. After 1975, the unemployment rate was regularly above the natural rate of unemployment, suggesting a cost-push inflation as delineated in Figure 9.

Source: Economic Report of the President.

to estimates of the natural rate of unemployment. Notice that the economy experienced unemployment below the natural rate in every year but one between 1960 and 1973, as represented by the shaded areas. This insight suggests that from 1960–1973, the U.S. economy experienced the demand-pull inflation we described in Figure 10. That is, in trying to achieve an output target that was too high, policymakers pursued a policy of autonomous monetary policy easing that shifted the aggregate demand curve to the right and created a positive output gap, thereby increasing inflation. Policymakers, economists, and politicians were committed in the mid-1960s to a target unemployment rate of 4%, a level of unemployment they believed to be consistent with price stability. In hindsight, most economists today agree that the natural rate of unemployment was substantially higher in the 1960s and 1970s, between 5% and 6%, as shown in panel (b) of Figure 11. The inappropriate 4% unemployment target initiated the most sustained inflationary episode in U.S. history.

Panel (b) of Figure 11 shows that after 1974, the unemployment rate remained above the natural rate of unemployment (see shaded area), with the exception of a brief period in 1978 and 1979, and yet inflation continued, as per panel (a), indicating a cost-push inflation such as we described in Figure 9 (the impetus for which was the earlier demand-pull inflation). The public's knowledge that government policy was aimed squarely at high employment explains the persistence of inflation. The higher rate of expected inflation from the demand-pull inflation shifted the short-run aggregate supply curve in Figure 9 upward and to the left, causing a rise in unemployment that policymakers tried to eliminate by autonomously easing monetary policy, shifting the aggregate demand curve to the right. The result was a continuing rise in inflation.

Only when the Federal Reserve, under Fed chair Paul Volcker, committed to an anti-inflationary monetary policy, which involved hiking the federal funds rate to the 20% level, did inflation come down, ending the Great Inflation. ◆

MONETARY POLICY AT THE ZERO LOWER BOUND

So far we have assumed that a central bank can continue to lower the real interest rate as inflation falls by lowering its policy rate—say, the federal funds rate—so that the *MP* curve is always upward-sloping. However, because the federal funds rate is a nominal interest rate, it can never fall below a value of zero. A negative federal funds rate would imply that you are willing to earn a lower return by lending in the federal funds market than you could earn by holding cash, with its zero rate of return. As discussed in Chapter 15, the zero floor on the policy rate is referred to as the *zero lower bound*, and it creates a particular problem for the conduct of monetary policy.

Deriving the Aggregate Demand Curve with the Zero Lower Bound

To understand more deeply the problems created by the zero lower bound with regard to the conduct of monetary policy, let's look at what happens to the aggregate demand curve when a central bank cannot lower its policy rate below zero. Panel (a) of Figure 12 shows an *MP* curve that hits the zero lower bound. For our purposes, let's assume that expected inflation moves closely with the actual inflation rate (as it usually does), as indicated on the horizontal axis in panel (a). Let's start at point 3 on the *MP* curve, where inflation is at 3% and the real interest rate is

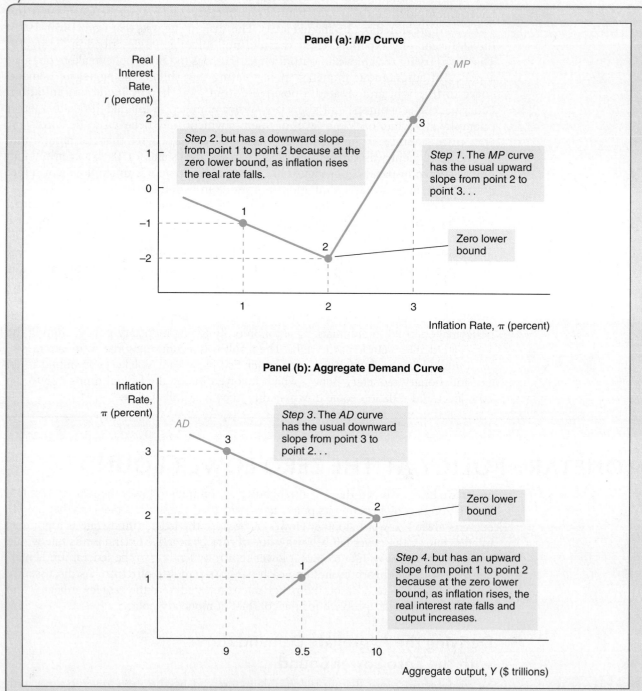

Panel (a): *MP* Curve

Step 2. but has a downward slope from point 1 to point 2 because at the zero lower bound, as inflation rises the real rate falls.

Step 1. The *MP* curve has the usual upward slope from point 2 to point 3. . .

Zero lower bound

Panel (b): Aggregate Demand Curve

Step 3. The *AD* curve has the usual downward slope from point 3 to point 2. . .

Zero lower bound

Step 4. but has an upward slope from point 1 to point 2 because at the zero lower bound, as inflation rises, the real interest rate falls and output increases.

FIGURE 12 **Derivation of the Aggregate Demand Curve with a Zero Lower Bound**

In panel (a), the *MP* curve has the usual upward slope in going from point 2 to point 3, but it slopes downward in the segment from point 1 to point 2 because, with the policy rate at the floor of zero, as inflation and expected inflation fall, the real interest rate rises. This produces a kink in the aggregate demand curve as shown in panel (b).

at 2%. Now let's see happens as inflation falls from 3% to 2%. At this inflation level, the monetary authorities, following the Taylor principle, will want to lower the real interest rate to, say, −2% (point 2 in panel (a)), which will require them to lower the policy rate to zero ($r = 0 − 2\% = −2\%$). At point 2 in panel (a), the zero lower bound has been reached on the *MP* curve. So far, our analysis is identical to the analysis given in Chapter 21, with the *MP* curve having the usual upward slope.

Now, what happens if the inflation rate falls even further—say, to 1%? The monetary authorities would like to lower the real interest rate by lowering the policy rate again, but they can't because the policy rate has already hit the floor of zero. Indeed, as indicated by point 1 on the *MP* curve, the real interest rate at an inflation rate of 1% has now risen to −1% ($r = 0 − 1\% = −1\%$). Hence, we see that the segment of the *MP* curve that connects point 2 to point 1 is downward-sloping, the opposite of what we found in Chapter 21.

Now let's see what happens to the aggregate demand curve, shown in panel (b) of Figure 12. At a 3% inflation rate and a real interest rate of 2% (point 3 on the *MP* curve in panel (a)), the equilibrium level of output is at $9 trillion, marked as point 3 on the aggregate demand curve in panel (b). Now, when inflation falls to 2% and the real interest rate is at −2%, as indicated by point 2 on the *MP* curve in panel (a), aggregate output rises to $10 trillion because planned investment spending rises with the lower real interest rate. The inflation rate of 2% and level of output of $10 trillion is marked as point 2 on the *AD* curve in panel (b). This point is also the zero lower bound. The *AD* curve has the usual downward slope from point 3 to point 2.

However, if inflation falls to 1%, point 1 on the *MP* curve indicates that the real interest rate will rise to −1% because, at the zero lower bound, the decrease in both inflation and expected inflation will raise the real interest rate. The rise in the real interest rate will cause aggregate demand to fall, to $9.5 trillion at point 1 on the *AD* curve in panel (b). Therefore, in going from point 1 to point 2, the aggregate demand curve slopes upward rather than downward. The presence of the zero lower bound thus can produce a kinked aggregate demand curve of the type seen in panel (b).

The Disappearance of the Self-Correcting Mechanism at the Zero Lower Bound

Now let's analyze what happens in our aggregate demand and supply diagram when the economy is hit by a large negative shock, such as the shock that occurred during the global financial crisis (see Chapter 12), so that the zero lower bound becomes binding. In this situation, the initial short-run aggregate supply curve intersects the upward-sloping part of the aggregate demand curve at point 1 in Figure 13, where aggregate output is below potential output. Because $Y_1 < Y^P$, there is slack in the economy, and so the short-run aggregate supply curve will fall to AS_2 and the economy will move to point 2, at the intersection of the AS_2 and *AD* curves, where inflation and output will have declined to π_2 and Y_2, respectively. Now, Y_2 is even lower than Y_1 relative to Y^P, so the short-run aggregate supply curve will shift down even further, to AS_3, and the economy will move to point 3, where inflation and output have fallen even further, to π_3 and Y_3, respectively.

Our analysis of Figure 13 reveals two key results:

- First, the self-correcting mechanism is no longer operational. When the economy is in a situation in which equilibrium output is below potential output and the zero lower bound on the policy rate has been reached, output is not restored to

MyEconLab Mini-lecture

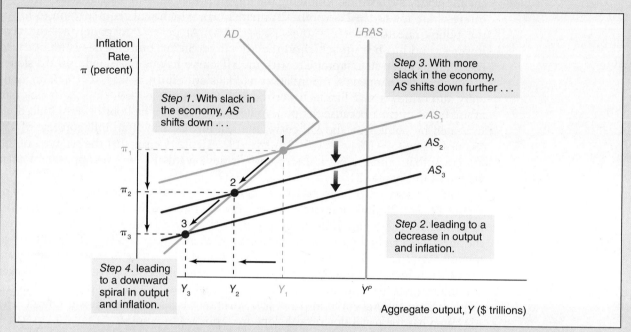

FIGURE 13 **The Absence of the Self-Correcting Mechanism at the Zero Lower Bound**

At the initial equilibrium at point 1, $Y_1 < Y^P$, so the short-run aggregate supply curve shifts down to AS_2 and the economy moves to point 2, where output and inflation have fallen to Y_2 and π_2, respectively. Because Y_2 is even lower than Y_1 relative to Y^P, the short-run aggregate supply curve shifts down even further to AS_2, and the economy moves to point 3, where output and inflation have fallen even further, to Y_3 and π_3, respectively. Both output and inflation therefore experience downward spirals.

its potential level if policymakers do nothing. Indeed, the opposite occurs—the economy goes into a downward spiral.

- Second, in this situation, the economy goes into a deflationary spiral, characterized by continually falling inflation and output.

The intuition behind these two results is fairly straightforward. When output is below potential and the policy rate has hit the floor of zero, the resulting fall in inflation leads to higher real interest rates, which depress output further, which causes inflation to fall further, and so on. Schematically, this chain of events can be expressed as follows:

$$Y < Y^P \Rightarrow \pi\downarrow \Rightarrow r\uparrow \Rightarrow Y\downarrow \Rightarrow Y << Y^P \Rightarrow \pi\downarrow \Rightarrow r\uparrow \Rightarrow Y\downarrow$$

The final outcome is that both output and inflation go into downward spirals.

APPLICATION Nonconventional Monetary Policy and Quantitative Easing

At the zero lower bound, conventional expansionary monetary policy is no longer an option because the monetary policy authorities are unable to lower the policy rate. As a result, the central bank has to turn to the nonconventional policies discussed in Chapter 15 to stimulate the economy. Here we will analyze how these different nonconventional policies lead to economic expansion while avoiding the downward spirals in output and inflation that characterized the situation described in Figure 13.

Recall that nonconventional monetary policy takes three forms: liquidity provision, asset purchases (quantitative easing), and management of expectations. To see how each of these forms works, recall from Chapter 20 that the real interest rate for investments r_i reflects not only the short-term real interest rate set by the central bank, r, but also an additional term $\bar{f}$, which we referred to previously as financial frictions. This relationship can be written mathematically as follows

$$r_i = r + \bar{f} \tag{1}$$

Each of these nonconventional monetary policy measures helps raise aggregate output and inflation by lowering $\bar{f}$ in the *AD/AS* model. Let's look at each of these measures in turn.

Liquidity Provision

The zero lower bound situation depicted in Figure 14 often arises when credit markets seize up and there is a sudden shortage of liquidity, as occurred during the recent global financial crisis. The shortage of liquidity results in a sharp rise in

MyEconLab Mini-lecture

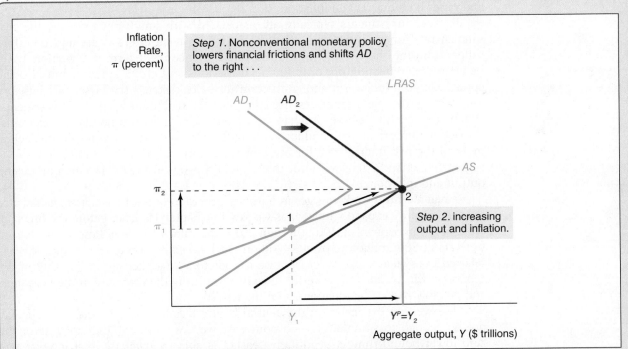

FIGURE 14   Response to Nonconventional Monetary Policy

Nonconventional monetary policy, whether it involves liquidity provision, asset purchases, or management of expectations, lowers $\bar{f}$, which in turn lowers the real interest rate for investments at any given inflation rate and shifts the aggregate demand curve to AD_2. The economy moves to point 2, where output and inflation have risen to Y_2 and π_2, respectively.

financial frictions, which shifts the aggregate demand curve AD_1 in Figure 14 to point 1, where it intersects the aggregate supply curve and where the policy rate has hit a floor of zero and output is below potential. A central bank can bring down financial frictions directly by increasing its lending facilities in order to provide more liquidity to impaired markets so that they can return to their normal functions, thereby bringing down the $\bar{f}$ term. As we saw in Chapter 22, this decline in financial frictions lowers the real interest rate for investments, $r_i = r + \bar{f}$, and so increases investment spending and the quantity of aggregate output demanded at any given inflation rate. The aggregate demand curve then shifts to the right to AD_2 and the economy moves to point 2, where both output and inflation have risen. Indeed, if liquidity provisions are sufficiently successful, the economy can move back to its full employment level, where output will return to potential, as indicated by point 2 in the figure.

Asset Purchases and Quantitative Easing

The monetary authorities can also lower the $\bar{f}$ term by lowering credit spreads through the purchase of private assets. When the monetary authorities purchase a private security, such a purchase raises the security's price and therefore lowers its interest rate, thereby lowering the credit spread and hence $\bar{f}$ and the real interest rate for investments. The decline in the real interest rate for investments at any given inflation rate then causes the aggregate demand curve to shift to the right, as shown in Figure 14, and raises both output and inflation.

Because investments typically are associated with long-term projects, the real interest rate for investments is likely to be a long-term interest rate and therefore differs from the short-term real interest rate r. Hence the $\bar{f}$ term in Equation 1 can be viewed as reflecting not only financial frictions and credit spreads, but also the spread between long-term and short-term rates. This means that asset purchases of long-term government securities also can lower the real interest rate for investments. When the Federal Reserve purchases long-term U.S. Treasury bonds, for example, this action raises their price and lowers long-term interest rates. The result is a decline in $\bar{f}$ and the real interest rate for investments at any given inflation rate, and so the aggregate demand curve will shift to the right, to AD_2 in Figure 14, thereby raising output and inflation.

When a central bank engages in liquidity provision or asset purchases, its balance sheet necessarily expands. Indeed, as we saw in Chapter 15, from before the financial crisis began in September 2007 through 2014, the value of Federal Reserve assets rose from about $800 billion to over $4 trillion. Such an expansion of the balance sheet is referred to as *quantitative easing* because it leads to a huge increase in liquidity in the economy, which can be a powerful force in stimulating the economy in the near term and possibly producing inflation down the road.

However, an expansion in the central bank's balance sheet in and of itself may not be enough to stimulate the economy. As we saw in our *AD/AS* analysis of the zero lower bound, unless quantitative easing is able to lower the real interest rate for investments, in what former Fed chair Ben Bernanke referred to as a *credit easing*, there will be no impact on the aggregate demand curve and hence no impact on output and inflation. If the asset purchase program involves only the purchase of short-term government securities, the program is unlikely to affect credit spreads or the spread between long- and short-term interest rates, and so $\bar{f}$ and the real interest rate for investments will remain unchanged. The result will be a minimal impact on the aggregate economy.[1] Indeed, this was the experience in Japan when the Bank of Japan pursued a large-scale asset-purchase program that primarily involved purchases of short-term government bonds. Not only did the economy fail to recover, but inflation even turned negative.

Management of Expectations

Forward guidance in which the central bank commits to keeping the policy rate low for a long period of time is another way of lowering long-term interest rates relative to short-term rates and thereby lowering $\bar{f}$ and the real interest rate for investments. Because investors can choose to invest in a long-term bond rather than investing in a sequence of short-term bonds, as we saw in Chapter 6, the interest rate on long-term bonds will be closely related to an average of the short-term interest rates that markets expect to occur over the life of the long-term bond. By committing to the future policy action of keeping the federal funds rate at zero for an extended period, a central bank can lower the market's expectations of future short-term interest rates, thereby causing the long-term interest rate to fall. The result will be a decline in $\bar{f}$ and the real interest rate for investments, which will shift the aggregate demand curve to the right as in Figure 14, raising both output and inflation.

So far, the mechanisms for the efficacy of nonconventional monetary policies have operated through the $\bar{f}$ term and rightward shifts in the aggregate demand curve as in Figure 14. However, management of expectations can also operate through shifts in the short-run aggregate supply curve that can be achieved by raising expectations of inflation, as shown in Figure 15. Recall from Chapter 22 that a rise in inflation expectations—say, because the central bank commits to doing whatever it takes to raise inflation in the future—will shift the short-run aggregate supply curve up, to AS_2 in Figure 15, moving the economy to point 2, where output and inflation rise to Y_2 and π_2, respectively. The intuition behind this result is straightforward: With the policy rate set at zero, the rise in expected inflation will lead to a decline in the real interest rate, which will cause investment spending and aggregate output to rise as the economy slides up the aggregate demand curve from point 1 to point 2, as shown in the figure. One problem with this strategy, however, is that the public must believe that inflation will actually rise in the future. If the central bank's commitment to raising inflation is not credible, then inflation expectations may not rise and this particular type of management of expectations will not work.

[1]There are two other reasons that quantitative easing in and of itself will not necessarily be stimulative. First, large expansions in a central bank's balance sheet do not necessarily result in large increases in the money supply. As indicated in the application in Chapter 14, "Quantitative Easing and the Money Supply, 2007–2014," this was exactly the case in the United States from 2007–2014, when huge expansions in the Fed's balance sheet and the monetary base did not result in a large increase in the money supply because most of the increase in the monetary base just flowed into holdings of excess reserves. Second, an increase in the monetary base does not mean that banks will increase lending, because they have the option of just adding to their holdings of excess reserves instead of making loans. This is exactly what happened during the global financial crisis, when a huge increase in the monetary base led primarily to a massive rise in excess reserves, and bank lending did not increase.

MyEconLab Mini-lecture

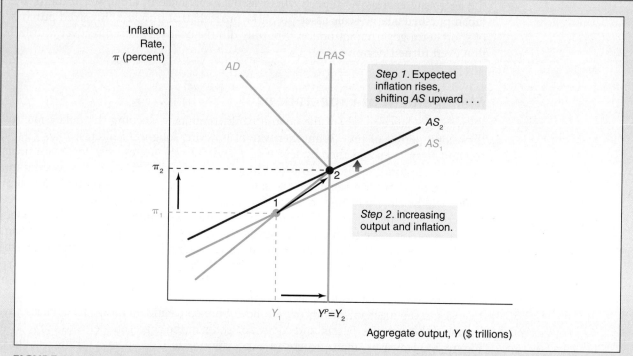

FIGURE 15 **Response to a Rise in Inflation Expectations**
A rise in inflation expectations causes the short-run aggregate supply curve to shift up to AS_2 and the economy to move to point 2, where output and inflation rise to Y_2 and π_2, respectively.

APPLICATION Abenomics and the Shift in Japanese Monetary Policy in 2013

By 2012, the Japanese economy had been in a funk for well over ten years, with very low growth, the policy rate stuck at the zero lower bound, and the economy experiencing deflation. With this scenario as his backdrop, Shinzo Abe won the general election for Prime Minister of Japan in December of 2012, and after taking office he promoted a major shift in economic policy aimed at stimulating economic growth, a policy that the media has since dubbed "Abenomics." A key element of Abenomics was a sea change in monetary policy. First, Abe pressured the Bank of Japan to double its inflation target from 1% to 2% in January of 2013, over the objections of the former Governor of the Bank of Japan, Masaaki Shirakawa, who then resigned in March. After taking over the former governor's position in March of 2013, the new Bank of Japan Governor, Haruhiko Kuroda, announced a major change in the way the Bank of Japan would conduct monetary policy in the future. First, in contrast to the previous governor, who never formally commited to achieving the 1% inflation target, Kuroda committed to achieving the higher 2% inflation objective within two years. Second, he indicated that the Bank of Japan would now engage in a massive asset-purchase (quantitative easing) program that would not only double the size of the Bank of Japan's balance sheet but would also involve the purchase of a very different set of assets. Specifically, rather than purchasing short-term government bonds, the Bank of Japan would now purchase long-term bonds, including private securities such as real estate investment trusts.

We can use our analysis from the previous section to predict how this shift in monetary policy might affect the Japanese economy. First, in contrast to the previous quantitative easing, the Abenomics program sought to lower $\bar{f}$ through the purchase of long-term assets. Specifically, the program would lower $\bar{f}$ by lowering credit spreads through the purchase of private securities and also by lowering long-term interest rates through the purchase of long-term government bonds. As we have seen, with the policy rate at the zero lower bound, a lower $\bar{f}$ would lead to a lower real interest rate for investments, thereby shifting the aggregate demand curve to the right, to AD_2 in Figure 16.

Second, the higher inflation target, and even more importantly the stronger commitment by Kuroda to achieving this higher target, should, according to our analysis, raise expected inflation and hence shift the short-run aggregate supply curve to AS_2. As we can see in Figure 16, the economy would then move to point 2, where both output and inflation would rise.

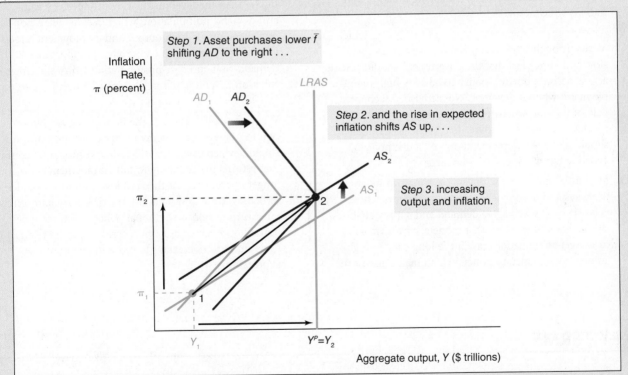

FIGURE 16   Response to the Shift in Japanese Monetary Policy in 2013
The Bank of Japan's revised asset purchase program lowers $\bar{f}$, which lowers the real interest rate on investments at any given inflation rate and shifts the aggregate demand curve to the right, from AD_1 to AD_2. The rise in inflation expectations causes the short-run aggregate supply curve to shift upward from AS_1 to AS_2. The economy moves to point 2, where output and inflation rise to Y_2 and π_2, respectively.

In other words, the new monetary policy's two-pronged attack would both lower the real interest rate for investments directly through the asset-purchase program and also directly raise inflation expectations, providing another factor that would drive down the real interest rate. Both of these mechanisms would then operate to promote an economic expansion and an exit from the deflationary environment that the Japanese had been experiencing for the past fifteen years. This new policy strategy seems to be working, with the Japanese economy growing at a substantial pace in 2013 and 2014 and inflation rising, but the jury is still out. ◆

SUMMARY

1. For aggregate demand shocks and permanent supply shocks, the price stability and economic activity stability objectives are consistent: Stabilizing inflation stabilizes economic activity, even in the short run. For temporary supply shocks, however, there is a tradeoff between stabilizing inflation and stabilizing economic activity in the short run. In the long run, however, there is no conflict between stabilizing inflation and stabilizing economic activity.

2. Activists regard the self-correcting mechanism, which works through wage and price adjustment, as very slow and hence feel that the government should pursue active, accommodating policy to address high unemployment when it develops. Nonactivists, by contrast, believe that the self-correcting mechanism works quickly and therefore advocate that the government should avoid the implementation of active policies aimed at eliminating unemployment.

3. Milton Friedman's view that in the long run inflation is always and everywhere a monetary phenomenon is borne out by aggregate demand and supply analysis: Such analysis shows that monetary policymakers can target any inflation rate in the long run through autonomous monetary policy, which makes use of the federal funds rate policy tool to change the level of aggregate demand and thereby adjust the equilibrium inflation rate.

4. Two types of inflation can result from an activist stabilization policy aimed at promoting high employment: cost-push inflation, which is caused by negative supply shocks or a push by workers for wages that are higher than the level justified by productivity gains; and demand-pull inflation, which results when policymakers pursue high output and employment targets through policies that increase aggregate demand. Both demand-pull and cost-push inflation led to the Great Inflation that occurred in the United States from 1965 to 1982.

5. When the policy rate hits the floor of the zero lower bound, the aggregate demand curve becomes upward sloping, which means that the self-correcting mechanism that returns the economy to full employment is no longer operational. At the zero lower bound, in order to boost output and inflation, the monetary authorities must turn to nonconventional policies of three types: liquidity provision, asset purchases (typically referred to as quantitative easing), and management of expectations.

KEY TERMS

activists, p. 561
cost-push inflation, p. 564
data lag, p. 561
demand-pull inflation, p. 564
divine coincidence, p. 556

effectiveness lag, p. 562
implementation lag, p. 562
inflation gap, p. 553
inflation target, p. 553

Keynesians, p. 561
legislative lag, p. 561
nonactivists, p. 561
recognition lag, p. 561

QUESTIONS

All questions are available in MyEconLab *at*
http://www.myeconlab.com.

1. What does it mean when we say that the inflation gap is negative?

2. "If autonomous spending falls, the central bank should lower its inflation target in order to stabilize inflation." Is this statement true, false, or uncertain? Explain your answer.

3. For each of the following shocks, describe how monetary policymakers would respond (if at all) to stabilize economic activity. Assume the economy starts at a long-run equilibrium.

    a. Consumers reduce autonomous consumption.

    b. Financial frictions decrease.

    c. Government spending increases.

    d. Taxes increase.

    e. The domestic currency appreciates.

4. During the global financial crisis, how was the Fed able to help offset the sharp increase in financial frictions without the option of lowering interest rates further? Did the Fed's plan work?

5. Why does the divine coincidence simplify the job of policymakers?

6. Why do temporary negative supply shocks pose a dilemma for policymakers?

7. In what way is a permanent negative supply shock worse than a temporary negative supply shock?

8. Suppose three economies are hit with the same temporary negative supply shock. In country A, inflation initially rises and output falls; then inflation rises more and output increases. In country B, inflation initially rises and output falls; then both inflation and output fall. In country C, inflation initially rises and output falls; then inflation falls and output eventually increases. What type of stabilization approach did each country take?

9. "Policymakers would never respond by stabilizing output in response to a temporary positive supply shock." Is this statement true, false, or uncertain? Explain your answer.

10. The fact that it takes a long time for firms to get new plants and equipment up and running is an illustration of what policy problem?

11. If someone told you, "Congress and the Senate couldn't vote themselves out of a phone booth," what type of policy lag would that person be referring to?

12. Is stabilization policy more likely to be conducted through monetary policy or through fiscal policy? Why?

13. "If the data and recognition lags could be reduced, activist policy probably would be more beneficial to the economy." Is this statement true, false, or uncertain? Explain your answer.

14. Why do activists believe that the economy's self-correcting mechanism works slowly?

15. If the economy's self-correcting mechanism works slowly, should the government necessarily pursue discretionary policy to eliminate unemployment? Why or why not?

16. Suppose one could measure the welfare gains derived from eliminating output (and unemployment) fluctuations in the economy. Assuming these gains are relatively small for the average individual, how do you think this measurement would affect the activist/nonactivist debate?

17. Given a relatively steep and a relatively flat short-run aggregate supply curve, which curve would support the case for nonactivist policy? Why?

18. "Because government policymakers do not consider inflation desirable, their policies cannot be the source of inflation." Is this statement true, false, or uncertain? Explain your answer.

19. How can monetary authorities target any inflation rate they wish?

20. What will happen if policymakers erroneously believe that the natural rate of unemployment is 7% when it is actually 5% and therefore pursue stabilization policy?

21. How can demand-pull inflation lead to cost-push inflation?

22. How does the policy rate hitting a floor of zero lead to an upward-sloping aggregate demand curve?

23. Why does the self-correcting mechanism stop working when the policy rate hits the zero lower bound?

24. What nonconventional monetary policies shift the aggregate demand curve, and how do they work?

APPLIED PROBLEMS

All applied problems are available in MyEconLab at
http://www.myeconlab.com.

25. Suppose the current administration decides to decrease government expenditures as a means of cutting the existing government budget deficit.

    a. Using a graph of aggregate demand and supply, show the effects of such a decision on the economy in the short run. Describe the effects on inflation and output.

    b. What will be the effect on the real interest rate, the inflation rate, and the output level if the Federal Reserve decides to stabilize the inflation rate?

26. Use a graph of aggregate demand and supply to demonstrate how lags in the policy process can result in undesirable fluctuations in output and inflation.

27. As monetary policymakers become more concerned with inflation stabilization, the slope of the aggregate demand curve becomes flatter. How does the resulting change in the slope of the aggregate demand curve help stabilize inflation when the economy is hit with a temporary negative supply shock? How does this affect output? Use a graph of aggregate demand and supply to demonstrate.

28. Many developing countries suffer from endemic corruption. How does this help explain why these countries' economies typically have high inflation and economic stagnation? Use a graph of aggregate demand and supply to demonstrate.

29. In 2003, as the U.S. economy finally seemed poised to exit its ongoing recession, the Fed began to worry about a "soft patch" in the economy, in particular the possibility of a deflation. As a result, the Fed proactively lowered the federal funds rate from 1.75% in late 2002 to 1% by mid-2003, the lowest federal funds rate on record up to that point in time. In addition, the Fed committed to keeping the federal funds rate at this level for a considerable period of time. This policy was considered highly expansionary and was seen by some as potentially inflationary and unnecessary.

    a. How might fears of a zero lower bound justify such a policy, even if the economy was not actually in a recession?

    b. Show the impact of these policies on the *MP* curve and the *AD/AS* graph. Be sure to show the initial conditions in 2003 and the impact of the policy on the deflation threat.

30. Suppose that $\bar{f}$ is determined by two factors: financial panic and asset purchases.

    a. Using an *MP* curve and an *AS/AD* graph, show how a sufficiently large financial panic can pull the economy below the zero lower bound and into a destabilizing deflationary spiral.

    b. Using an *MP* curve and an *AS/AD* graph, show how a sufficient amount of asset purchases can reverse the effects of the financial panic depicted in part (a).

DATA ANALYSIS PROBLEMS

The Problems update with real-time data in MyEconLab and are available for practice or instructor assignment.

1. On January 28, 2014, the Federal Reserve released a special statement that clarified its goals of "price stability" and "maximum employment." Specifically, it stated that "the Committee judges that inflation at the rate of 2 percent, as measured by the annual change in the price index for personal consumption expenditures, is most consistent over the longer run with the Federal Reserve's statutory mandate" and that "FOMC participants' estimates of the longer-run normal rate of unemployment had a central tendency of 5.2 percent to 6.0 percent." Assume this statement implies that the natural rate of unemployment is believed to be 5.6%. Go to the St. Louis Federal Reserve FRED database, and find data on the personal consumption expenditure price index (PCECTPI), the unemployment rate (UNRATE), real GDP (GDPC1), and real potential gross domestic product (GDPPOT), an estimate of potential GDP. For the price index, adjust the *units* setting to "Percent Change From Year Ago." Download the data into a spreadsheet.

    a. For the most recent four quarters of data available, calculate the average inflation gap using the 2% target referenced by the Fed. Calculate this value as the average of the inflation gaps over the four quarters.

b. For the most recent four quarters of data available, calculate the average output gap using the GDP measure and the potential GDP estimate. Calculate the gap as the percentage deviation of output from the potential level of output. Calculate the average value over the most recent four quarters of data available.

c. For the most recent 12 months of data available, calculate the average unemployment gap, using 5.6% as the presumed natural rate of unemployment. Based on your answers to parts (a) through (c), does the divine coincidence apply to the current economic situation? Why or why not? What does your answer imply about the sources of shocks that have impacted the current economy? Briefly explain.

 2. Go to the St. Louis Federal Reserve FRED database, and find data on the personal consumption expenditure price index (PCECTPI), the unemployment rate (UNRATE), and an estimate of the natural rate of unemployment (NROU). For the price index, adjust the *units* setting to "Percent Change From Year Ago." Select the data from 2000 through the most current data available, download the data, and plot all three variables on the same graph. Using your graph, identify periods of demand-pull or cost-push movements in the inflation rate. Briefly explain your reasoning.

WEB EXERCISES

1. It can be an interesting exercise to compare the purchasing power of the dollar over different periods in history. Go to http://www.bls.gov/cpi/ and scroll down to the link to the inflation calculator. Use this calculator to answer the following questions.

a. If a new home cost $125,000 in 2014, what would it have cost in 1950?

b. The average annual household income in 2014 was about $50,000. What would this income have been in 1945?

c. An average new car cost about $25,000 in 2014. What would this car have cost in 1945?

d. Using your results from parts (b) and (c), did the purchase of a new car consume more or less of an average household's income in 2014 than in 1945?

WEB REFERENCES

http://www.gpoaccess.gov/eop

The *Economic Report of the President* reports debt levels and gross domestic product, along with many other economic statistics.

24 The Role of Expectations in Monetary Policy

Learning Objectives

- Summarize the Lucas critique.
- Compare and contrast the use of policy rules versus discretionary policy.
- Summarize and illustrate the benefits of a credible central bank.
- Identify the ways in which central banks can establish and maintain credibility.

Preview

After World War II, economists, armed with models like the ones we developed in Chapters 20–23, felt that discretionary policies could reduce the severity of business cycle fluctuations without creating inflation. In the 1960s and 1970s these economists got their chance to put their policies into practice, but the results were not what they had anticipated. The economic record for that period is not a happy one. Inflation accelerated, with the inflation rate often climbing to above 10%, and unemployment figures deteriorated from those of the 1950s.[1]

In the 1970s and 1980s, economists, including Nobel Prize winners Robert Lucas of the University of Chicago and Thomas Sargent, now at New York University, used the rational expectations theory discussed in Chapter 7 to examine why discretionary policies appear to have performed so poorly. Their analysis cast doubt on whether macroeconomic models can be used to evaluate the potential effects of policy and on whether policy can be effective when the public *expects* that it will be implemented. Because the analysis of Lucas and Sargent has such strong implications for the way in which policy should be conducted, it has been labeled the *rational expectations revolution*.[2]

This chapter examines the analysis behind the rational expectations revolution. We start first with the Lucas critique, which indicates that because expectations are an important part of economic behavior, it may be quite difficult to predict what the outcome of a discretionary policy will be. We then discuss the effect of rational expectations on the aggregate demand and supply analysis we developed in Chapter 22, and explore how this theoretical breakthrough has shaped current policymaking models and debates.

LUCAS CRITIQUE OF POLICY EVALUATION

Economists have long used **macroeconometric models** to forecast economic activity and to evaluate the potential effects of policy options. In essence, the models are collections of equations that describe statistical relationships among many economic variables. Economists can feed data into such models, which then churn out a forecast or prediction

---

[1]Some of the deterioration can be attributed to supply shocks in 1973–1975 and 1978–1980.

[2]Other economists who have been active in promoting the rational expectations revolution are Robert Barro of Harvard University, Bennett McCallum of Carnegie-Mellon University, Nobel Prize winner Edward Prescott of Arizona State University, and Neil Wallace of Pennsylvania State University.

In his famous paper "Econometric Policy Evaluation: A Critique," Robert Lucas spurred the rational expectations revolution by presenting a devastating argument against the use of the macroeconometric models used at the time for evaluating policy.[3]

Econometric Policy Evaluation

To understand Lucas's argument, we must first understand how econometric policy evaluation is done. Say, for example, that the Federal Reserve wants to evaluate the potential effects of changes in the federal funds rate from the existing level of, say, 5%. Using conventional methods, the Fed economists would feed different fed funds rate options—say, 4% and 6%—into a computer version of a model. The model would then predict how unemployment and inflation would change under the different scenarios. Then, the policymakers would select the policy that the model predicted would have the most desirable outcomes.

Relying on rational expectations theory, Lucas identified faulty reasoning in this approach if the model did not incorporate rational expectations, as was true for the macroeconometric models used by policymakers at the time: When policies change, public expectations shift as well. For example, if the Fed raises the federal funds rate to 6%, this action might change the way the public forms expectations about where interest rates will head in the future. Those changing expectations, as we've seen, can have a real effect on economic behavior and outcomes. Yet econometric models that do not incorporate rational expectations ignore the effects of changing expectations and thus are unreliable for evaluating policy options.

APPLICATION ## The Term Structure of Interest Rates

Let's now apply Lucas's argument to a concrete example involving only one equation typically found in econometric models: the term structure equation. The equation relates the long-term interest rate to current and past values of the short-term interest rate. It is one of the most important equations in macroeconometric models because the long-term interest rate, not the short-term rate, is the one believed to have the larger impact on aggregate demand.

In Chapter 6, we learned that the long-term interest rate is related to an average of expected future short-term interest rates. Suppose that in the past, when the short-term rate rose, it quickly fell back down again; that is, any increase was temporary. Because rational expectations theory suggests that any rise in the short-term interest rate is expected to be only temporary, such a rise should have only a minimal effect on the average of expected future short-term rates. Therefore, the rise in the short-term rate should cause the long-term interest rate to rise by only a negligible amount. The term structure relationship as estimated using past data thus indicates that changes in the short-term interest rate will have only a weak effect on the long-term interest rate.

Suppose the Fed wants to evaluate the effects on the economy of a policy that is likely to raise the short-term interest rate from its existing level of, say, 5%, to a higher level of 6% for the foreseeable future. The term structure equation, which has been estimated using past data, will indicate that just a small change in the long-term inter-

[3]*Carnegie-Rochester Conference Series on Public Policy* 1 (1976): 19–46.

est rate will occur. However, if the public expects that the short-term rate is rising to a permanently higher level, rational expectations theory indicates that people will no longer expect a rise in the short-term rate to be temporary. Instead, when they see the interest rate rise to 6%, they will expect the average of future short-term interest rates to rise substantially, and so the long-term interest rate will rise greatly, not minimally as suggested by the term structure equation. You can see that using an econometric model to evaluate the likely outcome of the change in Fed policy can lead to highly misleading information.

The term structure application demonstrates another aspect of the Lucas critique. The effects of a particular policy depend critically on the public's expectations about the policy. If the public expects the rise in the short-term interest rate to be merely temporary, then the response of long-term interest rate, as we have seen, will be negligible. If, however, the public expects the rise to be more permanent, the response of the long-term rate will be far greater. ***The Lucas critique points out not only that conventional econometric models cannot be used for policy evaluation, but also that the public's expectations about a policy will influence the response to that policy.***

The term structure equation discussed here is only one of many equations in the econometric models to which the Lucas critique applies. In fact, Lucas uses examples of consumption and investment equations in his paper. One attractive feature of the term structure example is that it deals with expectations in the financial market, a sector of the economy for which the empirical evidence supporting rational expectations is much stronger. The Lucas critique should also apply, however, to sectors of the economy with regard to which rational expectations theory is more controversial, because the basic principle of the Lucas critique is not that expectations are always rational but rather that the formation of expectations changes when the behavior of a forecasted variable changes. This less stringent principle is supported by the evidence in sectors of the economy other than financial markets. ◆

POLICY CONDUCT: RULES OR DISCRETION?

The Lucas critique exposed the need for new policy models that reflected the insights of rational expectations theory. Here, we explore the implications of the critique on a long-running debate among economists: whether monetary policymakers should have the flexibility to adapt their policies to a changing situation, or whether they should adopt **rules**, binding plans that specify how policy will respond (or not respond) to particular data such as unemployment and inflation data.

Discretion and the Time-Inconsistency Problem

We say that policymakers operate with **discretion** when they make no commitment to future actions but instead make what they believe in that moment to be the right policy decision for the situation. Complexities are introduced when policymakers are empowered to shape policy "on the fly." The *time-inconsistency problem* discussed in Chapter 16 reveals the potential limitations of discretionary policy. Recall that the time-inconsistency problem is the tendency of policymakers to deviate from good long-run plans when making short-run decisions. Policymakers are always tempted to pursue policies that are more expansionary than firms or people expect because such a policy will boost economic output (and lower unemployment) in the short run. The best policy, however, is *not* to pursue expansionary policy, because decisions about wages and prices reflect workers' and firms' expectations about policy (an implication of the rational expectations revolution). For example, when workers and firms see a central bank pursuing discretionary expansionary policy, they will recognize that this policy is likely to lead to higher inflation in the future. They will therefore raise their expectations of inflation, driving wages and prices up. The rise in wages and prices will lead to higher inflation but may not result in higher output on average.

Policymakers will promote better inflation performance in the long run if they do not try to surprise people with an unexpectedly expansionary policy but instead keep inflation under control. One way of doing this is to abandon discretion and adopt rules to govern policymaking.

Types of Rules

In contrast to discretion, rules are essentially automatic. One famous type of rule, advocated by Milton Friedman and his followers, who are known as **monetarists**, is the **constant-money-growth-rate rule**, whereby policymakers keep the money supply growing at a constant rate regardless of the state of the economy. Other monetarists, such as Bennett McCallum and Alan Meltzer, have proposed variants of this rule that allow the rate of money supply growth to be adjusted for shifts in velocity, nominal income divided by the quantity of money, which has often been found to be unstable in the short run. Rules of this type are deemed nonactivist because they do not "react" to economic conditions. Monetarists advocate rules of this type because they believe that money is the sole source of fluctuations in aggregate demand and that long and variable lags in the effects of monetary policy will lead to greater volatility in economic activity and inflation if policy actively responds to unemployment (as discussed in Chapter 23).

Activist rules, in contrast, specify that monetary policy should react to the level of output as well as to inflation. The most famous rule of this type is the *Taylor rule*, discussed in Chapter 16. It specifies that the Fed should set its federal funds rate target by using a formula that considers both the output gap $(Y - Y^P)$ and the inflation gap $(\pi - \pi^T)$.

The Case for Rules

As suggested by our discussion of the time-inconsistency problem, discretionary monetary policy can lead to poor economic outcomes. If monetary policymakers operate with discretion, they will be tempted to pursue overly expansionary monetary policies that will boost employment in the short run but generate higher inflation (but not higher employment) in the long run. A commitment to a policy rule like the Taylor rule or the constant-money-growth-rate rule solves the time-inconsistency problem because policymakers are forced to follow a set plan that does not allow them to exercise discretion and therefore prevents them from exploiting the short-run tradeoff between inflation and employment. With their hands bound by a policy rule, policymakers can achieve desirable long-run outcomes.

Another argument in support of rules posits that policymakers and politicians simply cannot be trusted to make good decisions. Milton Friedman and Anna Schwartz's monumental work, *A Monetary History of the United States*,[4] documents numerous instances in which the Federal Reserve made serious policy errors, with the worst

---

[4]Milton Friedman and Anna Jacobson Schwartz, *A Monetary History of the United States, 1867–1960* (Princeton, NJ: Princeton University Press, 1963).

FYI   The Political Business Cycle and Richard Nixon

You might know that Richard Nixon and his aides took some extraordinary actions to ensure a landslide victory in the 1972 presidential election, such as breaking into the offices of political rivals at the Watergate Hotel. Less well known are similar actions on the economic front prior to the election. Before the 1972 election, the Nixon administration imposed wage and price controls on the economy, which temporarily lowered the inflation rate. After the election, those same actions contributed to a surge in inflation. Nixon also pursued expansionary fiscal policy by cutting taxes. And it has been rumored that the chair of the Federal Reserve at the time, Arthur Burns, succumbed to direct pressure from Nixon to maintain low interest rates through election day. The aftermath was ugly. The economy overheated and inflation rose to over 10% by the late 1970s, a rate that was abetted by the negative supply shocks during that period (see Chapter 22).

The Nixon episode led economists and political scientists to theorize that politicians will take steps to make themselves look good during election years. Specifically, the theory went, they will take steps to stimulate the economy prior to the election, in the hopes of stimulating a boom and low unemployment, outcomes that will increase their electoral chances. Unfortunately, the result of these actions will be higher inflation down the road, which then will require contractionary policies to get inflation under control, leading to a recession in the future. The resulting ups and downs of the economy would be the direct result of political machinations and so could be characterized as a political business cycle. Although the Nixon episode provided support for the existence of a political business cycle, the research has not led to a definitive answer regarding whether this phenomenon is a general one.[*]

[*]The paper that launched research on the political business cycle was William Nordhaus, "The Political Business Cycle," *Review of Economic Studies* 42 (1975): 169–190.

occurring during the Great Depression, when the Fed just stood by and let the banking system and the economy collapse (Chapter 12 discusses the Fed's actions during the Great Depression). Proponents of this argument believe that the politicians who make fiscal policy are not to be trusted because they have strong incentives to pursue policies that will help them win the next election. They are therefore more likely to focus on increasing employment in the short run without worrying that their actions might lead to higher inflation further down the road. Their advocacy for expansionary policies can lead to a so-called **political business cycle**, in which fiscal and monetary policy are expansionary right before elections, with higher inflation following later. (For an example, see the FYI box, "The Political Business Cycle and Richard Nixon.")

The Case for Discretion

Although policy rules have important advantages, they also have serious drawbacks. First, rules can be too rigid because they cannot account for every contingency. For example, almost no one could have predicted that problems in one small part of the financial system, subprime mortgage lending, would lead to the worst financial crisis in over 70 years, with such devastating effects on the world economy. The unprecedented steps taken by the Federal Reserve during this crisis to prevent the crisis from causing a depression (described in Chapters 12 and 15) could not have been written into a policy rule ahead of time. The ability to act flexibly through discretion can thus be a key factor in a successful monetary policy.

The second problem with policy rules is that they do not easily incorporate the tool of judgment. Monetary policy is as much an art as it is a science. Monetary policymakers must look at a wide range of information in order to decide on the best course for monetary policy, and some of this information is not easily quantifiable. Judgment is thus an essential element of good monetary policy, and it is very hard to write it into a rule. Only through discretion can monetary policy bring judgment to bear.

Third, no one really knows what the true model of the economy is, and so any policy rule that is based on a particular model will prove to be wrong if the model is flawed. Discretion avoids the straightjacket that would lock in the wrong policy if the model that was used to derive the policy rule proved to be a poor one.

Fourth, even if the model is a good one, any structural changes in the economy will necessitate changes in the coefficients of the model. For example, the Lucas critique points out that the structural shifts caused by changes in policies can lead to changes in the coefficients of macroeconometric models. Another example of structural economic change occurred in the 1980s, when the relationship between monetary aggregates, such as M1 and M2, and aggregate spending broke down as a result of financial innovation. Following a rule that assumed a constant growth rate in one of these aggregates would have produced bad outcomes. Indeed, this is what happened in Switzerland in the late 1980s and early 1990s when adherence to a rule that assumed a particular growth rate of monetary aggregates led to a surge in inflation (as discussed in the Global box, "The Demise of Monetary Targeting in Switzerland"). Discretion enables policymakers to change policy settings when an economy undergoes structural changes.

Constrained Discretion

The tug-of-war between rules and discretion has strongly influenced academic debates about monetary policy for many decades. But either choice may be too rigid. As we have

Global   The Demise of Monetary Targeting in Switzerland

In 1975, the Swiss National Bank (Switzerland's central bank) adopted monetary targeting in which it announced a growth rate target for the monetary aggregate M1. In 1980, the Swiss switched their growth rate target to an even narrower monetary aggregate, the monetary base. Although monetary targeting had been quite successful in Switzerland for many years, the Swiss economy ran into serious problems with the introduction of a new interbank payment system, the Swiss Interbank Clearing (SIC), and a wide-ranging revision of commercial banks' liquidity requirements in 1988. These structural changes caused a severe drop in banks' desired holdings of deposits at the Swiss National Bank, and these holdings were the major component of the monetary base. A smaller amount of the monetary base was now needed to conduct transactions, altering the relationship between the monetary base and aggregate spending, and so the 2% target growth rate for the monetary base was suddenly far too expansionary. Inflation subsequently rose to over 5%, well above that in other European countries.

High inflation rates horrified the Swiss, who had always prided themselves on maintaining a low-inflation environment even when the rest of Europe did not. These problems with monetary targeting led the Swiss to abandon it in the 1990s and adopt a much more flexible framework for the conduct of monetary policy.[*]

[*]For a further discussion of monetary targeting in Switzerland, see Chapter 4 of Ben S. Bernanke, Thomas Laubach, Frederic S. Mishkin, and Adam S. Posen, *Inflation Targeting: Lessons from the International Experience* (Princeton, NJ: Princeton University Press, 1999).

seen, both rules and discretion are subject to problems, and so the dichotomy between rules and discretion may be too simple to capture the realities that macroeconomic policymakers face. Discretion can be a matter of degree. Discretion can be a relatively undisciplined approach that leads to policies that change with the personal views of policymakers or with the direction of political winds, or it might operate within a more clearly articulated framework in which the general objectives and tactics of the policymakers—although not their specific actions—are committed to in advance. Ben Bernanke, former chair of the Federal Reserve, along with the author of this textbook, came up with a name for this type of framework: **constrained discretion**.[5] Constrained discretion imposes a conceptual structure and inherent discipline on policymakers, but without eliminating all flexibility. It combines some of the advantages ascribed to rules with those ascribed to discretion.

THE ROLE OF CREDIBILITY AND A NOMINAL ANCHOR

An important way to constrain discretion, as discussed in Chapter 16, is to commit to a *nominal anchor*, a nominal variable—such as the inflation rate, the money supply, or an exchange rate— that ties down the price level or inflation to achieve price stability. For example, if a central bank has an explicit target for the inflation rate—say, 2%—and takes steps to achieve this target, then the inflation target becomes a nominal anchor. Alternatively, a government could commit to a fixed exchange rate between its currency and a sound currency like the dollar and use this as its nominal anchor. If the commitment to a nominal anchor has **credibility**—that is, it is believed by the public—then it has important benefits.

Benefits of a Credible Nominal Anchor

First, a credible nominal anchor has elements of a behavior rule. Just as rules help to prevent the time-inconsistency problem in parenting by helping adults resist pursuit of the discretionary policy of giving in, a nominal anchor can help overcome the time-inconsistency problem by providing an expected constraint on discretionary policy. For example, if monetary policymakers commit to a nominal anchor of achieving a specific inflation objective—say, a 2% inflation rate—then they know that they will be subject to public scrutiny and criticism if they miss this objective or pursue policies that are clearly inconsistent with this objective, such as an interest rate target that is too low. Because policymakers wish to avoid embarrassment and possibly legal punishment, they will be less tempted to pursue overly expansionary, discretionary policies in the short run, policies that would be inconsistent with their commitment to the nominal anchor.

Second, a credible commitment to a nominal anchor helps to anchor inflation expectations, which leads to smaller fluctuations in inflation. Such a commitment thus contributes to price stability and also helps stabilize aggregate output. The credibility of a commitment to a nominal anchor is therefore a critical element in enabling monetary policy to achieve both of its objectives, price stability and stabilization of economic activity. In other words, a credible nominal anchor helps make monetary policy more efficient.

---

[5]See Ben S. Bernanke and Frederic S. Mishkin, "Inflation Targeting: A New Framework for Monetary Policy?" *Journal of Economic Perspectives* 11 (Spring 1997): 97–116.

We will use the aggregate demand and supply framework to show analytically why a credible nominal anchor helps produce this desirable outcome. First we will look at the effectiveness of stabilization policy when it is responding to an aggregate demand shock, and then we will look at its effectiveness when it is responding to an aggregate supply shock. We will also look at the benefits of credibility for anti-inflation policy.

Credibility and Aggregate Demand Shocks

We now examine the importance of credibility in the short run when positive and negative demand shocks are present.

Positive Demand Shock   Let's first look at what happens in the short run when a positive aggregate demand shock occurs. For example, suppose businesses suddenly get new information that makes them more optimistic about the future, and so they increase their investment spending. As a result of this positive demand shock, the aggregate demand curve shifts to the right from AD_1 to AD_2, moving the economy from point 1 to point 2 in panel (a) of Figure 1. Aggregate output rises to Y_2 and inflation rises above the inflation target of π^T to π_2. As we saw in Chapter 23, the appropriate response, if the monetary authorities wish to stabilize inflation and economic activity, is to tighten monetary policy and shift the short-run aggregate demand curve back down to AD_1 in order to move the economy back to point 1. However, because of the long lags between monetary policy actions and their effects on aggregate demand, it will take some time before the short-run aggregate demand curve shifts back to AD_1.

Now let's look at what happens to the short-run aggregate supply curve. Recall from Chapter 22 that the short-run aggregate supply curve can be expressed as follows:

$$\pi = \pi^e + \gamma(Y - Y^P) + \rho$$
$$\text{Inflation} = \text{Expected Inflation} + \gamma \times \text{Output Gap} + \text{Inflation Shock}$$

If the commitment to the nominal anchor is credible, then the public's expected inflation rate π^e will remain unchanged and the short-run aggregate supply curve will remain at AS_1. Inflation therefore will not go higher than π_2, and over time, as the short-run aggregate demand curve shifts back down to AD_1, inflation will fall back down to the inflation target of π^T.

But what if monetary policy is not credible? The public will worry that the monetary authorities are willing to accept a higher inflation rate than π^T and are not willing to drive the short-run aggregate demand curve back to AD_1 quickly. In this case, the weak credibility of the monetary authorities will cause expected inflation π^e to rise and so the short-run aggregate supply curve will rise, shifting from AS_1 to AS_3 and sending the economy to point 3 in the short run, where inflation has risen further to π_3. Even if the monetary authorities tighten monetary policy and return the aggregate demand curve to AD_1, the damage is done: Inflation has risen more than it would have if the central bank had credibility. Our aggregate demand and supply analysis thus yields the following conclusion: ***Monetary policy credibility has the benefit of stabilizing inflation in the short run when faced with positive demand shocks.***

Negative Demand Shock   Panel (b) of Figure 1 illustrates a negative demand shock. For example, suppose consumer confidence dips and consumer spending declines. The aggregate demand curve shifts left from AD_1 to AD_2, and the economy moves to point 2 in the short run, where aggregate output has fallen to Y_2, which is below potential output Y^P, and inflation has fallen to π_2, which is below the target level of π^T. To stabilize output

FIGURE 1
Credibility and Aggregate Demand Shocks

In panel (a), the positive aggregate demand shock shifts the aggregate demand curve to the right from AD_1 to AD_2, moving the economy from point 1 to point 2. If monetary policy is not credible, expected inflation will rise and so the short-run aggregate supply curve will rise and shift to the left to AS_3, sending the economy to point 3, where inflation has risen further to π_3. In panel (b), the negative aggregate demand shock shifts the aggregate demand curve left from AD_1 to AD_2, and the economy moves to point 2. If the central bank is not credible, inflation expectations might increase, and the short-run aggregate supply curve will rise and shift to the left to AS_3. Monetary policy easing then will move the economy to point 3, where aggregate output at Y_3 is still below potential output at Y^P.

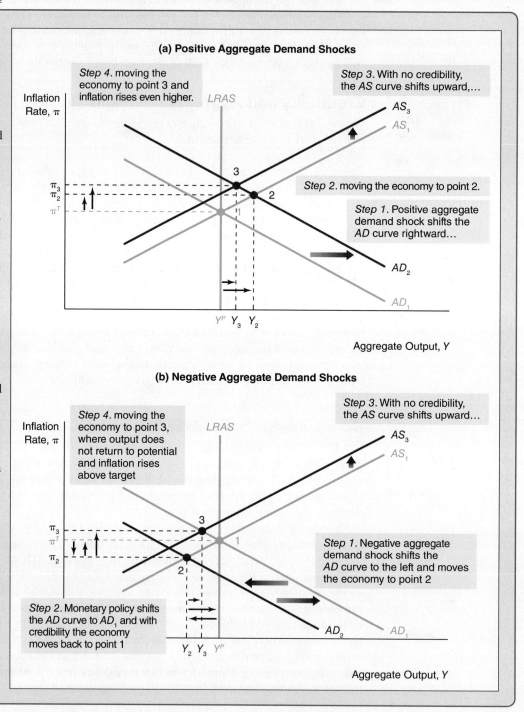

and inflation, the central bank will ease monetary policy to move the aggregate demand curve back to AD_1. If the central bank has high credibility, expected inflation will remain unchanged, the short-run aggregate supply curve will remain at AS_1, and the economy will return to point 1, where output is back at its potential level Y^P.

However, what if the central bank's credibility is weak? When the public sees an easing of monetary policy, it might become concerned that the central bank is weakening its commitment to the nominal anchor and intends to pursue inflationary policy in the future. In this situation, inflation expectations might increase, and so the short-run aggregate supply curve will rise to AS_3, sending the economy to point 3, where aggregate output will rise only from Y_2 to Y_3, leaving output below potential output Y^P. Weak credibility in the face of a negative demand shock will keep output below potential output for a longer period than would occur if credibility was strong. We have the following additional result: ***Monetary policy credibility has the benefit of stabilizing economic activity in the short run when faced with negative demand shocks.***

Credibility and Aggregate Supply Shocks

Now let's look at what happens in Figure 2 if a negative aggregate supply shock occurs. If energy prices increase, the short-run aggregate supply curve will shift up and to the left. How much the aggregate supply curve will shift, however, depends

MyEconLab Mini-lecture

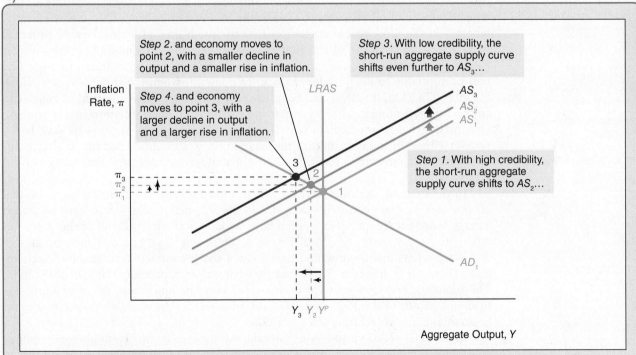

FIGURE 2 **Credibility and Aggregate Supply Shocks**

If the credibility of monetary policy is high, the negative aggregate supply shock will shift the short-run aggregate supply curve only to AS_2 and the economy will move to point 2, where the rise in inflation to π_2 will be minor and the fall in output to Y_2 will also be minor. If credibility is weak, then inflation expectations will rise substantially and the upward shift of the short-run aggregate supply curve will be much larger, moving the curve up and to the left to AS_3. The economy will move to point 3, with worse outcomes for both inflation and output—inflation will be higher at π_3 and output will be lower at Y_3.

on the amount of credibility the monetary authorities have. If the credibility of the nominal anchor is strong, inflation expectations will not rise, and so the upward and leftward shift of the short-run aggregate supply curve to AS_2 will be small. When the economy moves to point 2 in the short run, the rise in inflation to π_2 will then be minor, and the fall in output to Y_2 will also be minor. If, on the other hand, the central bank's commitment to the nominal anchor is perceived as weak, then inflation expectations will rise substantially and the upward and leftward shift of the short-run aggregate supply curve will be much larger, moving the curve up to AS_3. Now the economy will move to point 3 in the short run, with worse outcomes for both inflation and output—inflation will be higher at π_3 and output will be lower at Y_3. We reach the following conclusion: ***Monetary policy credibility has the benefit of producing better outcomes for both inflation and output in the short run when faced with negative supply shocks.***

The theoretical benefits of credibility when the economy is hit by negative supply shocks are confirmed by the data, as illustrated in the following application.

APPLICATION　# A Tale of Three Oil Price Shocks

In 1973, 1979, and 2007, the U.S. economy was hit by major negative supply shocks when the price of oil rose sharply; yet in the first two episodes inflation rose sharply, whereas in the most recent episode it rose by much less, as we can see in panel (a) of Figure 3. In the case of the first two episodes, monetary policy credibility was extremely weak because the economy was suffering from high inflation that the Fed had been unable to keep under control. In contrast, when the third oil price shock hit in 2007–2008, inflation had been low and stable for quite a period of time, and so the Fed had more credibility regarding its intent to keep inflation under control. One reason that might explain why the third oil price shock appears to have had a smaller effect on inflation is that monetary policy was more credible at that point in time. Our aggregate demand and supply analysis provides the reasoning behind this view.

In the first two episodes, during which both the Fed's commitment to a nominal anchor and the Fed's credibility were weak, the oil price shocks would have produced a surge in inflation expectations and a large upward and leftward shift of the short-run aggregate supply curve, to AS_3 in Figure 2. Thus, our aggregate demand and supply analysis predicts that there would have been a sharp contraction in economic activity and a sharp rise in inflation. This is exactly what we see in panels (a) and (b) of Figure 3. The economic contractions were very severe, with unemployment rising to above 8% in the aftermath of the 1973 and 1979 oil price shocks. In addition, inflation shot up to double-digit levels during these periods.

In the 2007–2008 episode, the outcome was quite different. Through greater policy credibility established over many years, inflation expectations remained grounded when the oil price shock occurred. As a result, the short-run aggregate supply curve shifted up and to the left by much less, to only AS_2 in Figure 2. Our aggregate demand and supply analysis predicts that a much smaller increase in inflation would result from the negative supply shock and that the contraction in economic activity also would be less. Indeed, this is exactly what transpired until the global financial crisis entered its virulent phase in the fall of 2008. Inflation rose by much less than in the previous episodes, and the economy held up fairly well until the financial crisis took a disastrous

FIGURE 3
Inflation and Unemployment, 1970–2014

During the 1973 and 1979 oil shock episodes, inflation was initially high and the Fed's commitment to a nominal anchor was weak, whereas during the 2007 episode, inflation was initially low and the Fed's credibility was high. As a result, inflation and unemployment rose more in the first two episodes than in the last episode, with unemployment rising sharply in the third episode only after the 2007–2009 global financial crisis took a disastrous turn in October 2008.

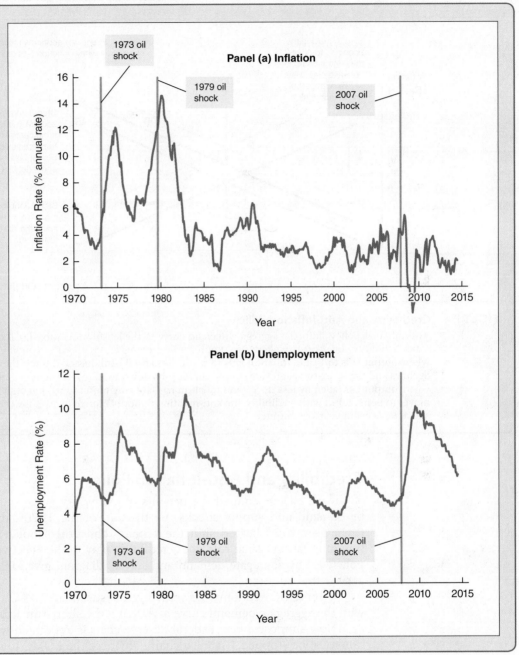

turn in October 2008 (see Chapter 12). Only then did the economy go into a tailspin, but it is clear that this economic contraction was not the result of the negative supply shock. Inflation actually fell quite dramatically, indicating that a massive negative demand shock was the source of the sharp contraction in economic activity. ◆

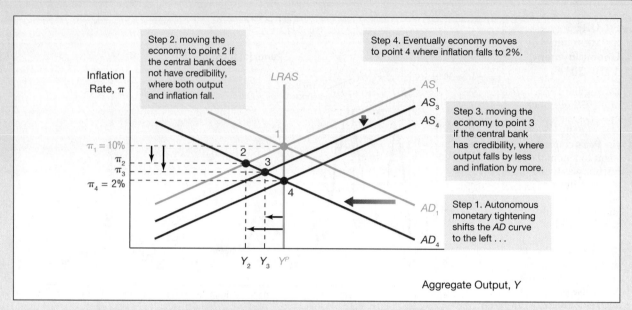

FIGURE 4   Credibility and Anti-Inflation Policy

Anti-inflation policy shifts the aggregate demand curve to the left from AD_1 to AD_4. If the central bank lacks credibility, the short-run aggregate supply curve remains at AS_1 and the economy moves to point 2, where output falls to Y_2 and inflation falls to π_2. If the central bank has credibility, then expected inflation declines and the short-run aggregate supply curve shifts down to AS_3. The economy moves to point 3, where output has fallen by less, to Y_3, and inflation has fallen by more, to π_3. Eventually the economy moves to point 4, but with credibility, the anti-inflation policy is more effective, lowering inflation faster and at less cost in terms of output.

Credibility and Anti-Inflation Policy

So far we have examined the benefits of credibility when the economy is buffeted by demand and supply shocks. By the end of the 1970s, the high inflation rate (then over 10%) helped shift the primary concern of policymakers to the reduction of inflation. What role does credibility play in the effectiveness of anti-inflation policies? The aggregate demand and supply diagram given in Figure 4 will help us answer this question.

Suppose the economy has settled into a sustained 10% inflation rate at point 1, with the aggregate demand curve at AD_1 and the short-run aggregate supply curve at AS_1. Now suppose a new Federal Reserve chair is appointed who decides that inflation must be stopped. The new chair convinces the FOMC to autonomously tighten monetary policy so that the aggregate demand curve is shifted to the left to AD_4, which in the long run will move the economy to point 4 and slow inflation down to the 2% inflation objective.

If the central bank has very little credibility, then the public will not be convinced that the central bank will stay the course to reduce inflation and therefore they will not revise their inflation expectations down from the 10% level. As a result, the short-run aggregate supply curve will remain at AS_1 and the economy will move to point 2. Although inflation will fall to π_2, output will decline to Y_2.

Now consider what will happen if, instead, the central bank has high credibility and so the public believes that the central bank will do whatever it takes to lower inflation. In this case, expectations of inflation will fall, the short-run aggregate supply curve will fall to AS_3, and the economy will move to point 3. Inflation then will fall even further to π_3, and output will decline by less, to Y_3. Indeed, in the extreme case in which the central bank is perfectly credible, there is even a possibility that inflation expectations will immediately decline to the 2% level and that the short-run aggregate supply curve will shift all the way down to AS_4. In this case, the economy will immediately move to point 4, where inflation has declined to the 2% inflation objective, and yet output will remain at Y^P. In this case, the anti-inflation policy will be costless because it will not require any loss of output. Although this last scenario is unlikely, we have shown the following result to be true: *The greater the credibility of the central bank as an inflation fighter, the more rapid the decline in inflation and the lower the loss of output will be in the attempt to achieve the inflation objective.*

Evidence that credibility plays an important role in successful anti-inflation policies is provided by the dramatic end of the Bolivian hyperinflation in 1985 (see the Global box). But establishing credibility is easier said than done. You might think that an announcement by policymakers at the Federal Reserve that they plan to pursue an anti-inflation policy might do the trick. The public will expect that this policy will be adhered to and will act accordingly. However, this conclusion assumes that the public will believe the policymakers' announcement. Unfortunately, that is not how the real world works.

The history of Federal Reserve policymaking suggests that the Fed has not always done what it set out to do. In fact, during the 1970s, the chair of the Federal Reserve

---

Global   Ending the Bolivian Hyperinflation: A Successful Anti-Inflation Program

The most remarkable anti-inflation program of recent times was implemented in Bolivia. In the first half of 1985, Bolivia's inflation rate was running at 20,000% and rising. Indeed, the inflation rate was so high that the price of a movie ticket often rose while people waited in line to buy it. In August 1985, Bolivia's new president announced his anti-inflation program, the New Economic Policy. To rein in money growth and establish credibility, the new government took drastic actions to slash the budget deficit by shutting down many state-owned enterprises, eliminating subsidies, freezing public sector salaries, and collecting a new wealth tax. The finance ministry was put on new footing; the budget was balanced on a day-by-day basis. Without exception, the finance minister would not authorize spending in excess of the amount of tax revenue that had been collected the day before. The Bolivian inflation was stopped in its tracks within one month, and the output loss was minor (less than 5% of GDP).

Certain hyperinflations before World War II were also ended with small losses of output through the implementation of policies similar to Bolivia's,[*] and a more recent anti-inflation program in Israel, which also involved substantial reductions in budget deficits, sharply reduced inflation without any clear loss of output. Without a doubt, credible anti-inflation policies can be highly successful in eliminating inflation.

[*]For an excellent discussion of the end of four hyperinflations in the 1920s, see Thomas Sargent, "The Ends of Four Big Inflations," in *Inflation: Causes and Consequences,* ed. Robert E. Hall (Chicago: University of Chicago Press, 1982), pp. 41–98.

Board at the time, Arthur Burns, repeatedly announced that the Fed would pursue a vigorous anti-inflation policy, yet instead of raising real interest rates when inflation rose, he actually lowered them. Such episodes reduced the credibility of the Federal Reserve in the eyes of the public and, as predicted in Figure 4, the resulting lack of credibility had serious consequences. The reduction of inflation that occurred from 1981 to 1984 was bought at a very high cost; the 1981–1982 recession that helped bring down the inflation rate was one of the most severe recessions of the post–World War II period.

The U.S. government can play an important role in establishing the credibility of anti-inflation policy. We have seen that large budget deficits may help stimulate inflationary monetary policy, and when the government and the Fed announce that they will pursue a restrictive anti-inflation policy, they are unlikely to be believed *unless* the federal government demonstrates fiscal responsibility. This is a good economic example of the old adage, "Actions speak louder than words." When the government takes actions that will help the Fed adhere to an anti-inflation policy, the policy becomes more credible. Unfortunately, this lesson has sometimes been ignored by politicians in the United States and in other countries.

APPLICATION   ## Credibility and the Reagan Budget Deficits

The Reagan administration was strongly criticized for creating huge budget deficits by cutting taxes in the early 1980s. In the aggregate supply and demand framework, we usually think of tax cuts as stimulating aggregate demand and increasing aggregate output. Could the expectation of large budget deficits have helped create a more severe recession in 1981–1982 after the Federal Reserve implemented an anti-inflation monetary policy?

Some economists answer yes, using a diagram like Figure 4. They claim that the prospect of large budget deficits made it harder for the public to believe that an anti-inflationary policy would actually be pursued when the Fed announced its intention to do so. Consequently, the short-run aggregate supply curve remained at AS_1 instead of falling to AS_3, with the result that the economy moved to point 2 rather than point 3 in Figure 4. As our analysis in Figure 4 and the data in Figure 3 show, the result of the Fed's anti-inflation policy was a slowing in the inflation rate to below 5% by the end of 1982, but this outcome was very costly: Unemployment reached a peak of 10.7%.

If the Reagan administration had actively tried to reduce deficits instead of raising them by cutting taxes, what might have been the outcome of the anti-inflation policy? Instead of moving to point 2, the economy might have moved to point 3, leading to an even more rapid reduction in inflation and a smaller loss of output.

Reagan is not the only head of state who ran large budget deficits while espousing an anti-inflation policy. Britain's Prime Minister Margaret Thatcher preceded Reagan in this approach, and economists such as Thomas Sargent assert that the reward for her policy was a climb of unemployment in Britain to unprecedented levels.

Although many economists agree that the Fed's anti-inflation program lacked credibility, especially in its initial phases, not all of them agree that the Reagan budget deficits were the cause of that lack of credibility. The conclusion that the Reagan budget deficits helped create a more severe recession in 1981–1982 is controversial. ◆

APPROACHES TO ESTABLISHING CENTRAL BANK CREDIBILITY

Our analysis has demonstrated that a credible nominal anchor that anchors inflation expectations is a key element in the success of monetary policy. But how do the monetary authorities achieve this credibility? We discussed several approaches in earlier chapters. One approach to credibility, discussed in Chapter 16, is through continued success at keeping inflation under control through concerted policy actions. This approach proved successful for the Federal Reserve during the Greenspan and Bernanke years. An approach that has been growing in popularity in recent years, also discussed in Chapter 16, is *inflation targeting*, which involves the public announcement of a medium-term numerical target for inflation and a commitment to achieving it. Some countries have successfully kept inflation under control by pegging their currency's exchange rate to the currency of an anchor country that already has a strong nominal anchor. We discussed this strategy, sometimes called *exchange-rate targeting*, in Chapter 18. Another way to increase central bank credibility is to give the central bank more independence from the political process, as discussed in Chapter 13. Two additional approaches, not discussed in earlier chapters but discussed below, are nominal GDP targeting and the appointment of "conservative" central bankers.

Nominal GDP Targeting

A variant of inflation targeting that recently has received increased attention is **nominal GDP targeting**, in which the central bank announces an objective of hitting a particular level of nominal GDP growth (recall that nominal GDP is real GDP times the price level). For example, if the inflation objective for the central bank were 2% and potential GDP were expected to grow at an annual rate of 3%, then nominal GDP targeting would mean a commitment by the central bank to keeping nominal GDP growing at 5% per year. Nominal GDP targeting has elements of an inflation targeting regime because the targeted growth rate of nominal GDP is tied to the chosen numerical inflation objective. In addition, nominal GDP targeting implies that the central bank will respond to slowdowns in the real economy even if inflation is not falling. To see this, note that with inflation unchanged, a slowdown in real GDP will result in a slowdown in nominal GDP, and so the monetary authorities will be prompted to pursue more expansionary monetary policy.

A potential advantage of nominal GDP targeting is that it focuses not only on controlling inflation but also explicitly on stabilizing real GDP. Another potential advantage is that with nominal GDP targeting, real GDP growth that is below potential or inflation that is below the inflation objective will encourage more expansionary monetary policy, because actual nominal GDP will fall further below its target. Expectations of this more expansionary policy will help stimulate aggregate demand, which will be particularly useful if the zero-lower-bound problem occurs and the monetary authorities are unable to lower the policy interest rate.

Ctitics cite two major weaknesses of nominal GDP targeting. First, nominal GDP targeting requires accurate estimates of potential GDP growth, which are not easy to achieve. Second, nominal GDP targeting is more complicated to explain to the public than inflation targeting and thus the public might be confused about the objectives of the central bank. At this time, no central bank has adopted nominal GDP targeting, but this may change in the future.

Inside the Fed   The Appointment of Paul Volcker, Anti-Inflation Hawk

President Jimmy Carter appointed Paul Volcker as chair of the Federal Reserve in August 1979. Prior to that, inflation had been climbing steadily, and at the time of Volcker's appointment, the annual CPI inflation rate had reached 11.8%. Volcker was the quintessential "conservative" central banker, a well-known inflation hawk who had made it clear to the president that he would take on inflation and wring it out of the system. In October 1979, shortly after Volcker took the helm of the Fed, the FOMC began to raise interest rates dramatically, increasing the federal funds rate by over eight percentage points to nearly 20% by April 1980. However, with the sharp economic contraction that began in January 1980, Volcker blinked and took his foot off the brake, allowing the federal funds rate to decline to around the 10% level by July, at which time the economy started to recover. Unfortunately, this monetary medicine had not done the trick, and inflation remained very high, with CPI inflation above 13%. Volcker then showed his anti-inflation, hawkish mettle: The Fed raised the federal funds rate to the 20% level by January 1981 and kept it there until July of the same year. Then, in the face of the most severe recession of the post–World War II period up to that point, the Fed kept the federal funds rate at a level of around 15% from July 1981 until July 1982, despite a rise in the unemployment rate to nearly 10%. Finally, only with the inflation rate starting to fall in July of 1982 did the Fed begin to lower the federal funds rate.

Volcker's anti-inflation credentials had now been fully established, and by 1983 inflation had fallen to below 4% and remained around that level for the rest of Volcker's tenure at the Fed through 1987. Volcker had reestablished the credibility of the Fed as an inflation fighter, with the result that inflation expectations had now stabilized, ending the period of high inflation in the United States that became known as the "Great Inflation." Volcker became a monetary policy hero and has been lauded ever since as one of the greatest central bankers of all time. Indeed, even after he left the Fed, he continued to play a prominent role in policy discussions. For example, he served on the Economic Advisory Board under President Obama and authored the so-called "Volcker rule" (discussed in Chapter 10) that restricted banks from trading with their own money (proprietary trading).

Appoint "Conservative" Central Bankers

Kenneth Rogoff of Harvard University suggested that another way of establishing central bank credibility is for the government to appoint central bankers who have a strong aversion to inflation.[6] He characterized these central bankers as "conservative," although a better description would be "tough" or "hawkish on inflation." (See the Inside the Fed box, "The Appointment of Paul Volcker, Anti-Inflation Hawk," to read about the appointment of a "conservative" central banker.)

When the public sees the appointment of a "conservative" central banker, it will expect that he or she will be less tempted to pursue expansionary monetary policy to exploit the short-run tradeoff between inflation and unemployment and will do whatever it takes to keep inflation under control. As a result, inflation expectations and realized inflation are likely to be more stable, with the benefits outlined previously.

The problem with this approach to solving the credibility problem is that it is not clear that it will continue to work over time. If a central banker has more "conservative" preferences than the public, won't the public demand the appointment of central bankers who are more in tune with their preferences? After all, in a democratic society, government officials are supposed to represent the will of the people.

[6]Kenneth Rogoff, "The Optimal Degree of Commitment to an Intermediary Monetary Target," *Quarterly Journal of Economics* (November 1985): 169–189.

SUMMARY

1. The simple principle (derived from rational expectations theory) that the manner in which expectations are formed changes when the behavior of forecasted variables changes led to the famous Lucas critique of econometric policy evaluation. Lucas argued that when policy changes, the method of expectations formation changes; hence the relationships in an econometric model will change. An econometric model that has been created on the basis of past data will no longer be a valid model for evaluating the effects of a policy change and may prove to be highly misleading. The Lucas critique also points out that the effects of a particular policy depend critically on the public's expectations of the policy.

2. Advocates of rules for the conduct of monetary policy believe that rules solve the time-inconsistency problem because policymakers are forced to follow a set plan, which eliminates the temptation to deviate from the plan and ensures the achievement of desirable long-run outcomes. Advocates of discretion believe that rules are much too rigid because they cannot predict every contingency and do not allow for the use of judgment. Constrained discretion imposes a conceptual structure and inherent discipline on policymakers, but it does so without eliminating all flexibility, so that it combines some of the advantages ascribed to rules with those ascribed to discretion.

3. An important way for the monetary authorities to constrain discretion is by committing to a credible nominal anchor—a nominal variable, such as the inflation rate, the money supply, or an exchange rate, that ties down the price level or inflation to achieve price stability. A credible nominal anchor helps solve the time-inconsistency problem and helps anchor inflation expectations. Credibility has the benefit of stabilizing both output and inflation fluctuations and also enables anti-inflation policies to lower inflation at a lower cost in terms of lost output.

4. Approaches to establishing credibility include implementing actual policies to keep inflation low, inflation targeting, exchange-rate targeting, and the promotion of central bank independence. Another approach to establishing central bank credibility is the appointment of a "conservative" central banker (like Paul Volcker) who is hawkish on controlling inflation.

KEY TERMS

constant-money-growth-rate rule, p. 585
constrained discretion, p. 588
credibility, p. 588

discretion, p. 584
macroeconometric models, p. 582
monetarists, p. 585

nominal GDP targeting, p. 597
political business cycle, p. 586
rules, p. 584

QUESTIONS

All questions are available in MyEconLab *at*
http://www.myeconlab.com.

1. What does the Lucas critique state about the limitations of our current understanding of the way in which the economy works?

2. "The Lucas critique by itself casts doubt on the ability of discretionary stabilization policy to be beneficial." Is this statement true, false, or uncertain? Explain your answer.

3. Suppose an econometric model based on past data predicts a small decrease in domestic investment when the Federal Reserve increases the federal funds rate.

Assume the Federal Reserve is considering an increase in the federal funds rate target to fight inflation and promote a low inflation environment that will encourage investment and economic growth.

a. Discuss the implications of the econometric model's predictions if individuals interpret the increase in the federal funds rate target as a sign that the Fed will keep inflation at low levels in the long run.

b. What would be Lucas's critique of this model?

4. If the public expects the Fed to pursue a policy that is likely to raise short-term interest rates permanently to 5%, but the Fed does not go through with this policy

change, what will happen to long-term interest rates? Explain your answer.

5. In what sense can greater central bank independence make the time-inconsistency problem worse?

6. What are the arguments for and against policy rules?

7. If, in a surprise victory, a new administration that the public believes will pursue inflationary policy is elected to office, predict what might happen to the level of output and inflation even before the new administration comes into power.

8. Many economists are worried that a high level of budget deficits may lead to inflationary monetary policies in the future. Could these budget deficits have an effect on the current rate of inflation?

9. In some countries, the president chooses the head of the central bank. The same president can fire the head of the central bank and replace him or her with another director at any time. Explain the implications of such a situation for the conduct of monetary policy. Do you think the central bank will follow a monetary policy rule, or will it engage in discretionary policy?

10. Outline the benefits and costs of sticking to a set of rules in each of the following cases. How does each of these situations relate to the conduct of economic policy?

    a. Going on a diet

    b. Raising children

11. How does Switzerland's monetary targeting strategy as described in this chapter demonstrate the case against monetary policy rules?

12. How is *constrained discretion* different from *discretion* in monetary policy? How are the outcomes of these policies likely to differ?

13. In general, how does credibility (or lack thereof) affect the aggregate supply curve?

14. As part of its response to the global financial crisis, the Fed lowered the federal funds rate target to nearly zero by December 2008 and quadrupled the monetary base between 2008 and 2014, a considerable easing of monetary policy. However, survey-based measures of five- to ten-year inflation expectations remained low throughout most of this period. Comment on the Fed's credibility in fighting inflation.

15. "The more credible the policymakers who pursue an anti-inflation policy, the more successful that policy will be." Is this statement true, false, or uncertain? Explain your answer.

16. Why did the oil price shocks of the 1970s affect the economy differently than the oil price shocks of 2007?

17. Central banks that engage in inflation targeting usually announce the inflation target and time period for which that target will be relevant. In addition, central bank officials are held accountable for their actions (e.g., they could be fired if the target is not reached), and their success or lack thereof is also public information. Explain why transparency is such a fundamental ingredient of inflation targeting.

18. Suppose the statistical office of a country does a poor job in measuring inflation and reports an annualized inflation rate of 4% for a few months, while the true inflation rate has been around 2.5%. What will happen to the central bank's credibility if it is engaged in inflation targeting and its target is 2%, plus or minus 0.5%?

19. What are the purposes of inflation targeting, and how does this monetary policy strategy achieve them?

20. How can the establishment of an exchange-rate target bring credibility to a country with a poor record of inflation stabilization?

21. What traits characterize a "conservative" central banker?

APPLIED PROBLEMS

All applied problems are available in MyEconLab *at* http://www.myeconlab.com.

22. Suppose the central bank is following a constant-money-growth-rate rule and the economy is hit with a severe economic downturn. Use an aggregate supply and demand graph to show the possible effects on the economy. How does this situation reflect on the credibility of the central bank if it maintains the money growth rule? How does it reflect on the central bank's credibility if it abandons the money growth rule to respond to the downturn?

23. Suppose country A has a central bank with full credibility, and country B has a central bank with no credibility. How does the credibility of each country's central bank affect the speed of adjustment of the aggregate supply curve to policy announcements? How does this result affect output stability? Use an aggregate supply and demand diagram to demonstrate.

24. Suppose two countries have identical aggregate demand curves and potential levels of output, and γ is the same in both countries. Assume that in 2016, both countries are hit with the same negative supply shock. Given the table of values below for inflation in each country, what can you say, if anything, about the credibility of each country's central bank? Explain your answer.

	Country A	Country B
2015	3.0%	3.0%
2016	3.8%	5.5%
2017	3.5%	5.0%
2018	3.2%	4.3%
2019	3.0%	3.8%

25. How does a credible nominal anchor help improve the economic outcomes that result from a positive aggregate demand shock? How does a credible nominal anchor help if a negative aggregate supply shock occurs? Use graphs of aggregate supply and demand to demonstrate.

DATA ANALYSIS PROBLEMS

The Problems update with real-time data in MyEconLab *and are available for practice or instructor assignment.*

 1. Go to the St. Louis Federal Reserve FRED database, and find data on the personal consumption expenditure price index (PCECTPI). Convert the *units* setting to "Percent Change from Year Ago," and download the data. Beginning in January 2012, the Fed formally announced a 2% inflation goal over the "longer-term."

   a. Calculate the average inflation rate over the last four and the last eight quarters of data available. How does it compare to the 2% inflation goal?

   b. What, if anything, does your answer to part (a) imply about Federal Reserve credibility?

 2. Go to the St. Louis Federal Reserve FRED database, and find data on the GDP deflator (GDPDEF) and the price of a barrel of oil (MCOILWTICO). For the GDP deflator, convert

the *units* setting to "Percent Change from Year Ago," and download the data.

   a. Calculate the average percent change in the price of oil over the most recent five years of data available. To do this, calculate the percentage change from the beginning of the period to the end, and divide this number by 5. What is the change in the inflation rate over the same time period?

   b. Calculate the average percent change in the price of oil from October 1986 to October 1990. To do this, calculate the percentage change from the beginning of the period to the end, and divide this number by 4. What is the change in the inflation rate over the same time period?

   c. Based on your answers to parts (a) and (b) above, what can you conclude about credibility of current monetary policy compared to its credibility in the earlier periods?

WEB EXERCISES

1. Robert Lucas won the Nobel Prize in economics. Go to http://nobelprize.org/nobel_prizes/economics/ and locate the press release on Robert Lucas. What was his Nobel Prize awarded for? When was it awarded?

25 Transmission Mechanisms of Monetary Policy

Learning Objectives

- List and summarize the transmission mechanisms through which monetary policy can affect the real economy.
- Summarize and apply the four lessons outlined in this chapter for the conduct of monetary policy.

Preview

Since 1980, the U.S. economy has been on a roller coaster, with output, unemployment, and inflation undergoing drastic fluctuations. At the start of the 1980s, inflation was running at double-digit levels, and the recession of 1980 was followed by one of the shortest economic expansions on record. After a year, the economy plunged into the 1981–1982 recession, with the unemployment rate climbing to over 10%, and only then did the inflation rate begin to come down to below the 5% level. The 1981–1982 recession was followed by a long economic expansion that reduced the unemployment rate to below 6% during the 1987–1990 period. With Iraq's invasion of Kuwait and a rise in oil prices in the second half of 1990, the economy again plunged into recession. Subsequent growth in the economy was sluggish at first but eventually sped up, and the unemployment rate fell to below 5% in the late 1990s. In March 2001, after a 10-year expansion, the longest in U.S. history, the economy slipped into a recession, with the unemployment rate climbing to around 6%. By 2007, an economic recovery had brought the unemployment rate below 5%, but with the onset of the global financial crisis, the economy entered a recession in December 2007, with the unemployment rate rising to 10%. Only in July of 2009 did the economy start to recover, making the recession of 2007–2009 the longest recession since World War II. In light of large fluctuations in aggregate output (reflected in the unemployment rate) and inflation, and the economic instability that accompanies them, policymakers face the following dilemma: What policy or policies, if any, should be implemented to reduce fluctuations in output and inflation in the future?

To answer this question, monetary policymakers must be able to accurately assess the timing and effect of their policies on the economy. To make this assessment, they need to understand the mechanisms through which monetary policy affects the economy. In this chapter, we examine the transmission mechanisms of monetary policy and evaluate the empirical evidence on these mechanisms to better understand the role that monetary policy plays in the economy. We will see that these monetary transmission mechanisms emphasize the link between the financial system (which we studied in the first three parts of this book) and monetary theory, the subject of this part of the book.

TRANSMISSION MECHANISMS OF MONETARY POLICY

In this section, we examine the ways in which monetary policy affects aggregate demand and the economy, which are referred to as **transmission mechanisms of monetary policy**. We start with interest-rate channels because they are the key monetary transmission mechanism of the *AD/AS* model developed in Chapters 20, 21, and 22 and applied to monetary policy in Chapters 23 and 24.

Traditional Interest-Rate Channels

The traditional view of the monetary transmission mechanism can be characterized by the following schematic, which shows the effect of an easing of monetary policy accomplished by lowering the real interest rate:

$$r\downarrow \Rightarrow I\uparrow \Rightarrow Y^{ad}\uparrow \tag{1}$$

This schematic shows that an easing of monetary policy leads to a fall in real interest rates ($r\downarrow$), which in turn lowers the real cost of borrowing, causing a rise in investment spending ($I\uparrow$), thereby leading to an increase in aggregate demand ($Y^{ad}\uparrow$).

Although Keynes originally emphasized this channel as operating through businesses' decisions about investment spending, the search for new monetary transmission mechanisms led economists to recognize that consumers' decisions about housing and **consumer durable expenditure** (spending by consumers on durable items such as automobiles and refrigerators) also are investment decisions. Thus the interest-rate channel of monetary transmission outlined in Equation 1 applies equally to consumer spending, and in this case *I* represents investments in residential housing and consumer durable expenditure.

An important feature of the interest-rate transmission mechanism is its emphasis on the *real* (rather than the nominal) interest rate as the rate that affects consumer and business decisions. In addition, it is often the real *long-term* interest rate (not the real short-term interest rate) that is viewed as having the major impact on spending. How is it that a change in the short-term nominal interest rate induced by a central bank results in a corresponding change in the real interest rate on both short- and long-term bonds? We have already seen that the answer lies in the phenomenon of *sticky prices*—the fact that the aggregate price level adjusts slowly over time, so that expansionary monetary policy, which lowers the short-term nominal interest rate, also lowers the short-term real interest rate. The expectations hypothesis of the term structure described in Chapter 6, which states that the long-term interest rate is an average of expected future short-term interest rates, suggests that a lower real short-term interest rate, as long as it is expected to persist, leads to a fall in the real long-term interest rate. These lower real interest rates then lead to increases in business fixed investment, residential housing investment, inventory investment, and consumer durable expenditure, all of which produce the rise in aggregate demand.

The fact that the real interest rate rather than the nominal rate affects spending suggests an important mechanism through which monetary policy can stimulate the economy, even if nominal interest rates hit a floor of zero during a deflationary episode. With nominal interest rates at a floor of zero, a commitment to future expansionary monetary policy can raise expected inflation (π^e), thereby lowering the real interest rate ($r = i - \pi^e$) even when the nominal interest rate is fixed at zero and stimulating spending through the interest-rate channel:

$$\pi^e\uparrow \Rightarrow r\downarrow \Rightarrow I\uparrow \Rightarrow Y^{ad}\uparrow \tag{2}$$

This mechanism thus indicates that monetary policy can still be effective even when nominal interest rates have already been driven down to zero by the monetary authorities. Indeed, this mechanism explains why the Federal Reserve resorted in December 2008 to the nonconventional monetary policy of committing to keep the federal funds rate at zero for an extended period of time. By so doing, the Fed was trying to keep inflation expectations from falling in order to make sure that real interest rates remained low, so as to stimulate the economy. In addition, the commitment to keep interest rates low for an extended period of time would help lower long-term interest rates, which would also induce greater spending.

Some economists, such as John Taylor of Stanford University, take the position that strong empirical evidence exists for substantial interest-rate effects on consumer and investment spending through the real cost of borrowing, making the interest-rate monetary transmission mechanism a strong one. His position is highly controversial, and many researchers, including Ben Bernanke, former chair of the Fed, and Mark Gertler of New York University, believe that the empirical evidence does not support strong interest-rate effects that operate through the real cost of borrowing.[1] Indeed, these researchers see the empirical failure of traditional interest-rate monetary transmission mechanisms as having provided the stimulus for the search for other transmission mechanisms of monetary policy.

These other transmission mechanisms fall into two basic categories: those operating through asset prices other than interest rates, and those operating through asymmetric information effects on credit markets (the **credit view**). These mechanisms are summarized in the schematic diagram in Figure 1.

Other Asset Price Channels

One drawback of the aggregate demand analysis in previous chapters is that it focuses on only one asset price, the interest rate, rather than on many asset prices. In addition to bond prices, two other asset prices receive substantial attention as channels for monetary policy effects: foreign exchange rates and the prices of equities (stocks).

Exchange Rate Effects on Net Exports
With the growing internationalization of economies throughout the world and the advent of flexible exchange rates, more attention has been paid to how monetary policy affects exchange rates, which in turn affect net exports and aggregate demand.

The foreign exchange rate channel also involves interest-rate effects because, as we saw in Chapter 17, when domestic real interest rates fall, domestic dollar assets become less attractive relative to assets denominated in foreign currencies. As a result, the value of dollar assets relative to other currency assets falls, and the dollar depreciates (denoted by $E\downarrow$). The lower value of the domestic currency makes domestic goods cheaper than foreign goods, thereby causing a rise in net exports ($NX\uparrow$) and hence in aggregate demand($Y^{ad}\uparrow$). The schematic for the monetary transmission mechanism that operates through the exchange rate is

$$r\downarrow \Rightarrow E\downarrow \Rightarrow NX\uparrow \Rightarrow Y^{ad}\uparrow \tag{3}$$

Tobin's q Theory
Nobel Prize winner James Tobin developed a theory, referred to as *Tobin's q theory*, that explains how monetary policy can affect the economy through its effects on the valuation of equities (stock). Tobin defines q as the market value of firms divided by the replacement cost of capital. If q is high, the market price of firms

[1]See John Taylor, "The Monetary Transmission Mechanism: An Empirical Framework," *Journal of Economic Perspectives* 9 (Fall 1995): 11–26, and Ben Bernanke and Mark Gertler, "Inside the Black Box: The Credit Channel of Monetary Policy Transmission," *Journal of Economic Perspectives* 9 (Fall 1995): 27–48.

MyEconLab Mini-lecture

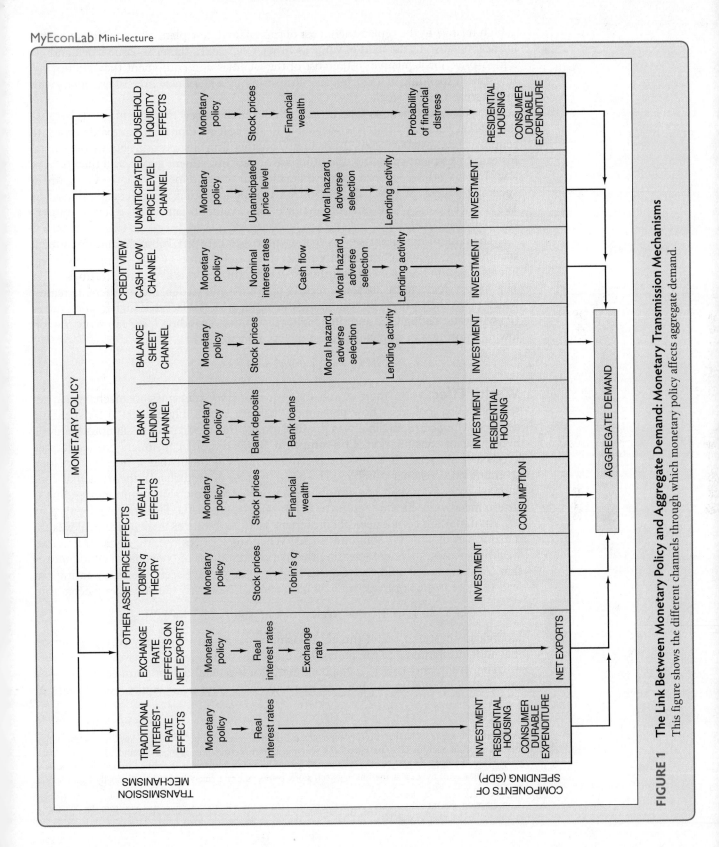

FIGURE 1 The Link Between Monetary Policy and Aggregate Demand: Monetary Transmission Mechanisms

This figure shows the different channels through which monetary policy affects aggregate demand.

is high relative to the replacement cost of capital, and new plant and equipment capital is cheap relative to the market value of firms. Companies then can issue stock and get a high price for it relative to the cost of the facilities and equipment they are buying. Investment spending will rise because firms can buy a lot of new investment goods with only a small issue of stock.

Conversely, when q is low, firms will not purchase *new* investment goods because the market value of firms is low relative to the cost of capital. If companies want to acquire capital when q is low, they can buy another firm cheaply and acquire old capital instead. Investment spending, the purchase of new investment goods, will then be very low. Tobin's q theory gives a good explanation for the extremely low rate of investment spending during the Great Depression. In that period, stock prices collapsed, and by 1933, stocks were worth only one-tenth of their value in late 1929; q fell to unprecedentedly low levels.

The crux of this discussion is that a link exists between Tobin's q and investment spending. But how might monetary policy affect stock prices? Quite simply, lower real interest rates on bonds mean that the expected return on this alternative to stocks falls. This makes stocks more attractive relative to bonds, and so demand for them increases, which raises their price.[2] By combining this result with the fact that higher stock prices (P_s) will lead to a higher q and thus higher investment spending I, we can write the following transmission mechanism of monetary policy:

$$r\downarrow \Rightarrow P_s\uparrow \Rightarrow q\uparrow \Rightarrow I\uparrow \Rightarrow Y^{ad}\uparrow \tag{4}$$

Wealth Effects In their search for new monetary transmission mechanisms, researchers also looked at how consumers' balance sheets might affect their spending decisions. Franco Modigliani was the first to take this tack, using his famous life cycle hypothesis of consumption. **Consumption** is spending by consumers on nondurable goods and services.[3] It differs from *consumer expenditure* in that it does not include spending on consumer durables. The basic premise of Modigliani's theory is that consumers smooth out their consumption over time. Therefore, consumption spending is determined by the lifetime resources of consumers, not just today's income.

An important component of consumers' lifetime resources is their financial wealth, a major part of which is common stocks. When stock prices rise, the value of financial wealth increases, thereby increasing the lifetime resources of consumers, which means that consumption should rise. Considering that, as we have seen, monetary easing can lead to a rise in stock prices, we now have another monetary transmission mechanism:

$$r\downarrow \Rightarrow P_s\uparrow \Rightarrow \text{wealth}\uparrow \Rightarrow \text{consumption}\uparrow \Rightarrow Y^{ad}\uparrow \tag{5}$$

Modigliani's research found this relationship to be an extremely powerful mechanism that adds substantially to the potency of monetary policy.

The wealth and Tobin's q channels allow for a general definition of equity, so they can also be applied to the housing market, where housing is equity. An increase in

[2]An alternative way of looking at this transmission mechanism is to use the model discussed in Chapter 7 in which a decrease in the real interest rate lowers the required return on investments in stocks and so increases stock prices. Then the lower yield on stocks reduces the cost of financing investment spending through the issuance of equity. This way of looking at the link between stock prices and investment spending is formally equivalent to Tobin's q theory.

[3]Consumption also includes another small component, the services that a consumer receives from the ownership of housing and consumer durables.

home prices, which raises their prices relative to replacement cost, leads to a rise in Tobin's *q* for housing, thereby stimulating its production. Similarly, housing prices are extremely important components of wealth, so rises in these prices increase wealth, thereby increasing consumption. Monetary expansion, which raises housing prices through the Tobin's *q* and wealth mechanisms described here, thus leads to a rise in aggregate demand.

Credit View

Dissatisfaction with the conventional story that interest-rate effects explain the impact of monetary policy on spending on durable assets has led to a new explanation that is based on the concept of asymmetric information, a problem that leads to financial frictions in financial markets (see Chapter 8). This explanation, referred to as the *credit view*, proposes that two types of monetary transmission channels arise as a result of financial frictions in credit markets: those that operate through effects on bank lending, and those that operate through effects on firms' and households' balance sheets.

Bank Lending Channel   The concept of the bank lending channel is based on the analysis in Chapter 8, which demonstrated that banks play a special role in the financial system because they are especially well suited to solving asymmetric information problems in credit markets. Because of banks' special role, certain borrowers will not have access to the credit markets unless they borrow from banks. As long as there is no perfect substitutability of retail bank deposits with other sources of funds, the bank lending channel of monetary transmission operates as follows: Expansionary monetary policy, which increases bank reserves and bank deposits, raises the quantity of bank loans available. Because many borrowers are dependent on bank loans to finance their activities, this increase in loans causes investment (and possibly consumer) spending to rise. Schematically, the monetary policy effect is written as follows:

$$\text{Bank reserves} \uparrow \Rightarrow \text{bank deposits} \uparrow \Rightarrow \text{bank loans} \uparrow \Rightarrow I \uparrow \Rightarrow Y^{ad} \uparrow \qquad (6)$$

An important implication of the credit view is that monetary policy will have a greater effect on expenditure by smaller firms, which are more dependent on bank loans, than it will on large firms, which can get funds directly through the stock and bond markets (and not only through banks).

Although this mechanism has been confirmed by researchers, doubts about the influence of the bank lending channel have been raised in the literature, and there are reasons to suspect that the bank lending channel in the United States may not be as powerful as it once was. The first reason this channel is less powerful than it once was is that current U.S. regulations no longer impose restrictions on banks that hinder their ability to raise funds (see Chapter 11). Prior to the mid-1980s, certificates of deposit (CDs) were subjected to reserve requirements and Regulation Q deposit rate ceilings, which made it hard for banks to replace deposits that flowed out of the banking system during a monetary contraction. With these regulatory restrictions abolished, banks can more easily respond to a decline in bank reserves and a loss of retail deposits by issuing CDs at market interest rates that do not have to be backed up by required reserves. Second, the worldwide decline of the traditional bank lending business (also discussed in Chapter 11) has rendered the bank lending channel less potent. Nonetheless, many economists believe that the bank lending channel played an important role in the slow recovery of the United States from the 2007–2009 recession.

Balance Sheet Channel Even though the bank lending channel may be declining in importance, it is by no means clear that this is the case for the other credit channel, the balance sheet channel. Like the bank lending channel, the balance sheet channel arises from the presence of financial frictions in credit markets. In Chapter 8, we saw that the lower the net worth of business firms, the more severe the adverse selection and moral hazard problems in lending to these firms become. Lower net worth means that lenders in effect have less collateral for their loans, so their potential losses from adverse selection are higher. A decline in firms' net worth, which raises the adverse selection problem, thus leads to decreased lending to finance investment spending. The lower net worth of businesses also increases the moral hazard problem because it means that owners have a lower equity stake in their firms, giving them more incentive to engage in risky investment projects. When borrowers take on more risky investment projects, it is more likely that lenders will not be paid back, and so a decrease in businesses' net worth leads to a reduction in lending and hence in investment spending.

Monetary policy can affect firms' balance sheets in several ways. Easing of monetary policy, which causes a rise in stock prices ($P_s\uparrow$) along the lines described earlier, raises the net worth of firms and so leads to higher investment spending ($I\uparrow$) and higher aggregate demand ($Y^{ad}\uparrow$) because of the decrease in adverse selection and moral hazard problems. This leads to the following schematic for this particular balance sheet channel of monetary transmission:

$$r\downarrow \Rightarrow P_s\uparrow \Rightarrow \text{firms' net worth}\uparrow \Rightarrow \text{adverse selection}\downarrow,$$
$$\text{moral hazard}\downarrow \Rightarrow \text{lending}\uparrow \Rightarrow I\uparrow \Rightarrow Y^{ad}\uparrow \qquad (7)$$

Cash Flow Channel Another balance sheet channel operates by affecting *cash flow*, the difference between firms' cash receipts and cash expenditures. An easing of monetary policy, which lowers nominal interest rates, also causes an improvement in firms' balance sheets because it raises cash flow. The increase in cash flow increases the liquidity of the firm (or household) and thus makes it easier for lenders to know whether the firm (or household) will be able to pay its bills. The result is that adverse selection and moral hazard problems become less severe, leading to an increase in lending and economic activity. The following schematic describes this alternative balance sheet channel:

$$i\downarrow \Rightarrow \text{firms' cash flow}\uparrow \Rightarrow \text{adverse selection}\downarrow,$$
$$\text{moral hazard}\downarrow \Rightarrow \text{lending}\uparrow \Rightarrow I\uparrow \Rightarrow Y^{ad}\uparrow \qquad (8)$$

An important feature of this transmission mechanism is that *nominal* interest rates affect firms' cash flow. Thus this interest-rate mechanism differs from the traditional interest-rate mechanism discussed earlier in which the real interest rate affects investment. Furthermore, the short-term interest rate plays a special role in this transmission mechanism because interest payments on short-term (rather than long-term) debt typically have the greatest impact on the cash flow of households and firms.

A related transmission mechanism involving adverse selection is the credit-rationing phenomenon. Through this mechanism, expansionary monetary policy that lowers interest rates can stimulate aggregate demand. As discussed in Chapter 9, credit rationing occurs when borrowers are denied loans even though they are willing to pay a higher interest rate. The loans are denied because individuals and firms with the riskiest investment projects are exactly the ones who are willing to pay the highest interest rates because, if the high-risk investment succeeds, they will be the primary beneficiaries. Thus higher interest rates increase the adverse selection problem, and lower interest rates reduce it. When expansionary monetary policy lowers interest rates, risk-prone borrowers make up a smaller fraction of those demanding loans, and so lenders are more willing to lend, raising both investment and aggregate demand, along the lines of parts of the schematic given in Equation 8.

Unanticipated Price Level Channel   A third balance sheet channel operates through monetary policy effects on the general price level. Because in industrialized countries debt payments are contractually fixed in nominal terms, an unanticipated rise in the price level lowers the value of firms' liabilities in real terms (decreases the burden of the debt) but should not lower the real value of the firms' assets. An easing of monetary policy, which raises inflation and hence leads to an unanticipated rise in the price level ($P\uparrow$), therefore raises real net worth, which lowers adverse selection and moral hazard problems, thereby leading to a rise in investment spending and aggregate demand, as in the following schematic:

$$r\downarrow \Rightarrow \pi\uparrow \Rightarrow \text{unanticipated } P\uparrow \Rightarrow \text{firms' real net worth}\uparrow$$
$$\Rightarrow \text{adverse selection}\downarrow, \text{moral hazard}\downarrow \Rightarrow \text{lending}\uparrow \Rightarrow I\uparrow \Rightarrow Y^{ad}\uparrow \tag{9}$$

The view that unanticipated movements in the price level affect aggregate demand has a long tradition in economics: It is the key feature in the debt-deflation view of the Great Depression, outlined in Chapter 12.

Household Liquidity Effects   Although most literature on the credit channel focuses on spending by businesses, the credit view should apply equally well to consumer spending, particularly spending on consumer durables and housing. Declines in bank lending induced by a monetary contraction should cause corresponding declines in durable and housing purchases by consumers who do not have access to other sources of credit. Similarly, increases in interest rates should cause deteriorations in household balance sheets, because consumers' cash flow is adversely affected.

The balance sheet channel also operates through liquidity effects on consumer durable and housing expenditures. These effects were found to be important factors during the Great Depression (see the FYI box, "Consumers' Balance Sheets and the Great Depression"). In the liquidity effects view, balance sheet effects work through

---

FYI   Consumers' Balance Sheets and the Great Depression

The years between 1929 and 1933 witnessed the worst deterioration in consumers' balance sheets ever seen in the United States. The stock market crash in 1929, which caused an economic slump that lasted until 1933, reduced the value of consumers' wealth by $836 billion (in 2005 dollars), and as expected, consumption dropped sharply (by over $100 billion). Because of the decline in the price level during that period, the level of real debt that consumers owed also increased sharply (by over 20%). Consequently,

the value of financial assets relative to the amount of debt declined sharply, increasing the likelihood of financial distress. Not surprisingly, spending on consumer durables and housing fell precipitously: From 1929 to 1933, consumer durable expenditure declined by over 50%, while expenditure on housing declined by 80%.[*]

[*]For further discussion of the effect of consumers' balance sheets on spending during the Great Depression, see Frederic S. Mishkin, "The Household Balance Sheet and the Great Depression," *Journal of Economic History* 38 (1978): 918–937.

their impact on consumers' desire to spend rather than on lenders' desire to lend. Because of asymmetric information regarding their quality, consumer durables and housing are very illiquid assets. If, as a result of a severe income shock, consumers needed to sell their consumer durables or housing immediately to raise money, they would expect to suffer a big financial loss because they would not be able to get the full value of these assets in a distress sale. (This is just a manifestation of the lemons problem described in Chapter 8.) In contrast, if consumers held financial assets (such as money in the bank, stocks, or bonds), they could sell them quickly and easily for their full market value and raise the cash. Hence, if consumers expect that they are likely to find themselves in financial distress, they will prefer to hold fewer illiquid consumer durable and housing assets and a greater amount of liquid financial assets.

A consumer's balance sheet should be an important influence on his or her estimate of the likelihood of future suffering from financial distress. Specifically, when consumers have a large amount of financial assets relative to their debts, their estimate of the probability of financial distress is low, and they are more willing to purchase consumer durables or housing. When stock prices rise, the value of financial assets increases as well; consumer durable expenditure will also rise because consumers have a more secure financial position and therefore a lower estimate of the likelihood of future financial distress. This leads to another transmission mechanism for monetary policy, one that operates through the link between money and stock prices:

$$r\downarrow \Rightarrow P_s\uparrow \Rightarrow \text{value of households' financial assets}\uparrow$$
$$\Rightarrow \text{likelihood of financial distress}\downarrow \qquad (10)$$
$$\Rightarrow \text{consumer durable and housing expenditure}\uparrow \Rightarrow Y^{ad}\uparrow$$

The illiquidity of consumer durable and housing assets provides another reason why a monetary easing, which lowers interest rates and thereby increases cash flow to consumers, leads to a rise in spending on consumer durables and housing. An increase in consumer cash flow decreases the likelihood of financial distress, which increases the desire of consumers to hold durable goods and housing, thus increasing spending on these items and hence increasing aggregate demand. The only difference between this view of cash flow effects and that outlined in Equation 8 is that in this view, it is not the willingness of lenders to lend to consumers that causes expenditure to rise, but the willingness of consumers to spend.

Why Are Credit Channels Likely to Be Important?

There are three reasons to believe that credit channels are important monetary transmission mechanisms. First, a large body of evidence on the behavior of individual firms supports the view that financial frictions of the type crucial to the operation of credit channels do affect firms' employment and spending decisions. Second, evidence shows that small firms (which are more likely to be credit-constrained) are hurt more by tight monetary policy than large firms, which are unlikely to be credit-constrained. Third, and maybe most compelling, the asymmetric information view of financial frictions, which is at the core of credit channel analysis, is a theoretical construct that has proved useful in explaining many other important economic phenomena, such as why many of our financial institutions exist, why our financial system has the structure that it has, and why financial crises are so damaging to the economy (topics discussed in Chapters 8 and 12). The best support for a theory is its demonstrated usefulness in a wide range of applications. By this standard, the asymmetric information theory, which supports the existence of credit channels as an important monetary transmission mechanism, has much to recommend it.

APPLICATION ## The Great Recession

With the advent of the financial crisis in the summer of 2007, the Fed began a very aggressive easing of monetary policy. The Fed dropped the target federal funds rate from $5\frac{1}{4}$% to $\frac{1}{4}$% to 0% over a fifteen-month period from September 2007 to December 2008. At first, it appeared that the Fed's actions would keep the growth slowdown mild and prevent a recession. However, the economy proved to be weaker than the Fed or private forecasters expected, with the most severe recession of the post-World War II period beginning in December 2007. Why did the economy become so weak despite this unusually rapid reduction in the Fed's policy instrument?

The financial meltdown led to negative effects on the economy from many of the channels we have outlined above. The rising level of subprime mortgage defaults, which led to a decline in the value of mortgage-backed securities and CDOs, led to large losses on the balance sheets of financial institutions. With weaker balance sheets, these financial institutions began to deleverage and cut back on their lending. With no one else available to collect information and make loans, adverse selection and moral hazard problems, and hence financial frictions, increased in credit markets, leading to a slowdown of the economy. Credit spreads also went through the roof with the increase in uncertainty caused by the failure of so many financial markets. The declines in the stock market and housing prices also weakened the economy because they lowered household wealth. The decrease in household wealth led to a drop in Tobin's q, which led to restrained consumer spending and weaker investment spending.

With all these channels operating, it is no surprise that despite the Fed's aggressive lowering of the federal funds rate, the economy still took a big hit. ◆

LESSONS FOR MONETARY POLICY

What useful lessons regarding the appropriate conduct of monetary policy can we draw from the analysis in this chapter? Four basic lessons can be learned.

1. *It is dangerous to consistently associate an easing or tightening of monetary policy with a fall or rise in short-term nominal interest rates.* Because most central banks use short-term nominal interest rates—typically, the interbank rate—as the key operating instrument in their monetary policies, the danger exists that central banks and the public will focus too much on short-term nominal interest rates as an indicator of the stance of monetary policy. Indeed, it is quite common to see statements that always associate monetary tightenings with a rise in the interbank rate and monetary easings with a decline in the interbank rate. We do not make this mistake in this book because we have been careful to associate monetary easing or tightening with changes in *real* and not *nominal* interest rates.

2. *Other asset prices besides those on short-term debt instruments contain important information about the stance of monetary policy because they are* *important elements in various monetary policy transmission mechanisms.* As we have seen in this chapter, economists have come a long way in understanding that other asset prices besides interest rates have major effects on aggregate demand. As we saw in Figure 1, asset prices such as stock prices, foreign exchange rates, and housing prices play an important role in monetary transmission mechanisms. Furthermore, additional channels, such as those that operate through the exchange rate, Tobin's q, and wealth effects, provide additional evidence that other asset prices play an important role in monetary transmission mechanisms. Although economists strongly disagree among themselves about which channels of monetary transmission are the most important—not surprising, given that economists, particularly those in academia, always enjoy a good debate—they do concur that asset prices other than those on short-term debt instruments play an important role in the effects of monetary policy on the economy.

The view that asset prices other than short-term interest rates matter has important implications for monetary policy. When we try to assess the stance of policy, it is critical that we look at other asset prices in addition to short-term interest rates. For example, if short-term interest rates are low or even zero and yet stock prices are low, housing prices are low, and the value of the domestic currency is high, monetary policy is clearly tight, not easy.

3. *Monetary policy can be effective in reviving a weak economy even if short-term interest rates are already near zero.* We have recently entered a world in which inflation is not always the norm. Japan, for example, recently experienced a period of deflation during which the price level was actually falling. In the United States, the federal funds rate hit a floor of zero by the end of 2008. One common view is that when a central bank has driven down short-term nominal interest rates to nearly zero, monetary policy can do nothing more to stimulate the economy. The transmission mechanisms of monetary policy described here indicate that this view is false. As indicated in our discussion of the factors that affect the monetary base in Chapter 14, expansionary monetary policy aimed at increasing liquidity in the economy can be conducted through open market purchases, which do not have to be solely in short-term government securities. For example, purchases of private securities, as the Federal Reserve made in 2009, can reduce financial frictions by lowering credit spreads and stimulating investment spending. In addition, a commitment to future expansionary monetary policy helps revive the economy by raising general price-level expectations and by reflating other asset prices, which then stimulate aggregate demand through the channels outlined here. The nonconventional monetary policies we discussed in Chapter 15 are policies of this type. Nonconventional monetary policies can be a potent force in reviving economies that are undergoing deflation and that have short-term interest rates near zero. Indeed, as we saw in Chapter 12, aggressive nonconventional monetary policy during the recent financial crisis helped prevent the Great Recession from turning into a Great Depression and also helped the economy avoid a deflationary episode like the one that occurred during the Great Depression era.

4. *Avoiding unanticipated fluctuations in the price level is an important objective of monetary policy, thus providing a rationale for price stability as the primary long-run goal of monetary policy.* As we saw in Chapter 16, central banks in recent years have been placing greater emphasis on price stability as the primary long-run goal of monetary policy. Several rationales for this goal have been proposed, including the undesirable effects of uncertainty about the future price level on business decisions and hence on productivity, distortions associated with the interaction of nominal contracts and the tax system with inflation, and increased social conflict stemming from inflation. Our discussion of monetary transmission mechanisms provides an additional reason why price stability is so important. As we have seen, unanticipated movements in the inflation rate can cause unanticipated fluctuations in output, an undesirable outcome. Particularly important in this regard is the knowledge that, as we saw in Chapter 12, price deflation can be an important factor leading to a prolonged financial crisis, as occurred during the Great Depression. An understanding of the monetary transmission mechanisms thus makes it clear that the goal of price stability is desirable because it reduces uncertainty about the future price level. The price stability goal implies that a negative inflation rate is at least as undesirable as too high an inflation rate. Indeed, because of the threat of financial crises, central banks must work very hard to prevent price deflation.

APPLICATION   # Applying the Monetary Policy Lessons to Japan's Two Lost Decades

Until 1990, it looked as if Japan might overtake the United States in per capita income. From the early 1990s until 2012, during the years that have become known as the "two lost decades," the Japanese economy stagnated, with deflation and low growth. As a result, Japanese living standards fell further and further behind those of the United States. Many economists take the view that Japanese monetary policy is in part to blame for the poor performance of the Japanese economy during this period. Could Japanese monetary policy have performed better if Japan had applied the four lessons outlined in the previous section?

The first lesson suggests that it is dangerous to think that declines in interest rates always mean that monetary policy has been easing. In the mid-1990s, when short-term interest rates began to decline, falling to nearly zero in the late 1990s and early 2000s, the monetary authorities in Japan took the view that monetary policy was sufficiently expansionary. Now it is widely recognized that this view was incorrect, because the falling and eventually negative inflation rates in Japan meant that real interest rates were actually quite high and that monetary policy was tight, not easy. If the monetary authorities in Japan had followed the advice of the first lesson, they might have pursued a more expansionary monetary policy, which would have helped boost the economy.

The second lesson suggests that monetary policymakers should pay attention to other asset prices, in addition to those on short-term debt instruments, in assessing the stance of monetary policy. At the same time that interest rates were falling in Japan, stock and real estate prices were collapsing, thus providing another indication that Japanese monetary policy was not easy. Knowledge of the second lesson might have led Japanese monetary policymakers to recognize sooner that they needed a more expansionary monetary policy.

The third lesson indicates that monetary policy can still be effective even if short-term interest rates are near zero. Officials at the Bank of Japan frequently claimed that they were helpless to stimulate the economy because short-term interest rates had fallen to nearly zero. By recognizing that monetary policy can be effective even when interest rates are near zero, as suggested by the third lesson, the Japanese monetary authorities could have taken monetary policy actions that would have stimulated aggregate demand by raising other asset prices and inflationary expectations.

The fourth lesson indicates that unanticipated fluctuations in the price level should be avoided. If the Japanese monetary authorities had adhered to this lesson, they might have recognized that allowing deflation to occur could be very damaging to the economy and that such deflation was inconsistent with the goal of price stability.

These four lessons of monetary policy have finally been taken to heart by the Bank of Japan. As we discussed in Chapter 23, monetary policy in Japan has undergone a dramatic shift since 2013, to a highly expansionary, nonconventional monetary policy with a higher inflation target. Hopefully, this shift in policy will lead to better economic outcomes for Japan in future years. ◆

SUMMARY

1. The transmission mechanisms of monetary policy include traditional interest-rate channels that operate through the real cost of borrowing and affect investment; other asset price channels such as exchange rate effects, Tobin's q theory, and wealth effects; and the credit view channels—the bank lending channel, the balance sheet channel, the cash flow channel, the unanticipated price level channel, and household liquidity effects.

2. Four lessons for monetary policy can be drawn from this chapter: (1) It is dangerous to consistently associate monetary policy easing or tightening with a fall or rise in short-term nominal interest rates; (2) other asset prices besides those on short-term debt instruments contain important information about the stance of monetary policy because they are important elements in the monetary policy transmission mechanisms; (3) monetary policy can be effective in reviving a weak economy even if short-term interest rates are already near zero; and (4) avoiding unanticipated fluctuations in the price level is an important objective of monetary policy, thus providing a rationale for price stability as the primary long-run goal of monetary policy.

KEY TERMS

consumer durable expenditure, p. 603

consumption, p. 606
credit view, p. 604

transmission mechanisms of monetary policy, p. 602

QUESTIONS

All questions are available in MyEconLab at http://www.myeconlab.com.

1. In 2009, in the wake of the global financial crisis and when interest rates were at their lowest, the U.S. government instituted a "cash for clunkers" program and later a "cash for appliances" program. Both rebate programs were designed in part to stimulate new spending on automobiles and major appliances. What does the implementation of these programs imply about the government's views of the health of the interest rate channel during that time?

2. "Considering that consumption accounts for nearly two-thirds of total GDP, this means that the interest rate, wealth, and household liquidity channels are the most important monetary policy channels in the U.S."

Is this statement true, false, or uncertain? Explain your answer.

3. How can the interest rate channel still function when short term nominal interest rates are at the zero lower bound?

4. Lars Svensson, a former Princeton professor and deputy governor of the Swedish central bank, proclaimed that when an economy is at risk of falling into deflation, central bankers should be "responsibly irresponsible" with monetary expansion policies. What does this mean, and how does it relate to the monetary transmission mechanism?

5. Describe an advantage and a disadvantage of the fact that monetary policy has so many different channels through which it can operate.

6. "If countries fix their exchange rate, the exchange rate channel of monetary policy does not exist." Is this statement true, false, or uncertain? Explain your answer.

7. During the 2007–2009 recession, the value of common stocks in real terms fell by more than 50%. How might this decline in the stock market have affected aggregate demand and thus contributed to the severity of the recession? Be specific about the mechanisms through which the stock market decline affected the economy.

8. "The costs of financing investment are related only to interest rates; therefore, the only way that monetary policy can affect investment spending is through its effects on interest rates." Is this statement true, false, or uncertain? Explain your answer.

9. Predict what will happen to stock prices after a monetary easing. Explain your prediction.

10. From mid-2008 to early 2009, the Dow Jones Industrial Average declined by more than 50%, while real interest rates were low or falling. What does this scenario suggest should have happened to investment?

11. Nobel Prize winner Franco Modigliani found that the most important transmission mechanisms of monetary policy involve consumer expenditure. Describe how at least two of these mechanisms work.

12. In the late 1990s, the stock market was rising rapidly, the economy was growing, and the Federal Reserve kept interest rates relatively low. Comment on how this policy stance would affect the economy as it relates to the Tobin q transmission mechanisms.

13. During and after the global financial crisis, the Fed reduced the fed funds rate to nearly zero. At the same time, the stock market fell dramatically and housing market values declined sharply. Comment on the effectiveness of monetary policy during this period with regard to the wealth channel.

14. During and after the global financial crisis, the Fed provided banks with large amounts of liquidity. Banks' excess reserves increased sharply, while credit extended to households and firms decreased sharply. Comment

on the effectiveness of the bank lending channel during this time.

15. Why does the credit view imply that monetary policy has a greater effect on small businesses than on large firms?

16. Why might the bank lending channel be less effective today than it once was?

17. One of the classic features of the global financial crisis was the failure of high-profile investment banks and financial firms such as Lehman Brothers, Bear Stearns, and AIG. These firms experienced sharp contractions in the values of their balance sheets due to risky asset holdings. Comment on how this would affect the economy as it relates to the balance sheet channel.

18. If adverse selection and moral hazard increase, how does this affect the ability of monetary policy to address economic downturns?

19. How does the Great Depression demonstrate the unanticipated price level channel?

20. How are the wealth effect and the household liquidity effect similar? How are they different?

21. Following the global financial crisis, mortgage rates reached record-low levels in 2011.

    a. What effect should this have had on the economy, according to the household liquidity effect channel?

    b. During the same time, most banks raised their credit standards significantly, making it much more difficult to qualify for home loans and to refinance existing loans. How does this information alter your answer to part (a)?

22. What evidence exists to support the credit view of monetary policy?

23. "A decrease in short-term nominal interest rates necessarily implies a stance of monetary easing." Is this statement true, false, or uncertain? Explain your answer.

24. How does the experience of Japan during the "two lost decades" lend support to the four lessons for monetary policy outlined in this chapter?

APPLIED PROBLEMS

All applied problems are available in MyEconLab *at* http://www.myeconlab.com.

25. Suppose the economy is in recession and the monetary policymakers lower interest rates in an effort to stabilize the economy. Use an aggregate supply and demand

diagram to demonstrate the effects of a monetary easing when the transmission mechanisms are functioning normally and when the transmission mechanisms are weak, such as during a deep downturn or when significant financial frictions are present.

DATA ANALYSIS PROBLEMS

The Problems update with real-time data in MyEconLab and are available for practice or instructor assignment.

1. A "rate cycle" is a period of monetary policy during which the federal funds rate moves from its low point toward its high point, or vice versa, in response to business cycle conditions. Go to the St. Louis Federal Reserve FRED database, and find data on the federal funds rate (FEDFUNDS), real business fixed investment (PNFIC96), real residential investment (PRFIC96), and consumer durable expenditures (PCDGCC96). Use the *frequency* setting to convert the federal funds rate data to "quarterly," and download the data.

   a. When did the last rate cycle begin and end? (Note: If a rate cycle is currently in progress, use the current period as the end.) Is this rate cycle a contractionary or an expansionary rate cycle?

   b. Calculate the percentage change in business fixed investment, residential (housing) investment, and consumer durable expenditures over this rate cycle.

   c. Based on your answers to parts (a) and (b), how effective was the traditional interest rate channel of monetary policy over this rate cycle?

2. As defined in Exercise 1, a "rate cycle" is a period of monetary policy during which the federal funds rate moves from its low point toward its high point, or vice versa, in response to business cycle conditions. Go to the St. Louis Federal Reserve FRED database, and find data on the federal funds rate (FEDFUNDS), bank reserves (TOTRESNS), bank deposits (TCDSL), commercial and industrial loans (BUSLOANS), real estate loans (REALLN), real business fixed investment (PNFIC96), and real residential investment (PRFIC96). Use the *frequency* setting to convert the federal funds rate, bank reserves, bank deposits, commercial and industrial loans, and real estate loans data to "quarterly," and download the data.

   a. When did the last rate cycle begin and end? (Note: if a rate cycle is currently in progress, use the current period as the end.) Is this rate cycle a contractionary or an expansionary rate cycle?

   b. Calculate the percentage change in bank deposits, bank lending, real business fixed investment, and real residential (housing) investment over this rate cycle.

   c. Based on your answers to parts (a) and (b), how effective was the bank lending channel of monetary policy over this rate cycle?

WEB EXERCISES

1. Go to http://www.econlib.org/library/Enc1/Recessions.html and review the material on recessions.

   a. What is the formal definition of a recession?

   b. What are the problems with the definition?

   c. What are the three D's used by the National Bureau of Economic Research (NBER) to define a recession?

   d. Review Chart 1. What trend is apparent regarding the length of recessions?

WEB REFERENCES

http://www.martincapital.com/
Click on "U.S. Financial Data," then on "U.S. Financial Charts," and then on "nominal versus real market rates" to find up-to-the-minute data showing the spread between real rates and nominal rates.

http://www.conference-board.org/ A site containing extensive data on the factors that define business cycles.

WEB APPENDIX

Please visit the Companion Website at http://www.pearsonhighered.com/mishkin to read the Web appendix to Chapter 25.

Appendix: **Evaluating Empirical Evidence: The Debate Over the Importance of Money in Economic Fluctuations**

Glossary

activists Economists who regard the self-correcting mechanism, which works through wage and price adjustment, as very slow because wages and prices are sticky. Activists see the need to pursue active policy to eliminate high unemployment when it develops. **561**

adaptive expectations Expectations for the value of a variable that are based on an average of past values of the variable. **146**

adverse selection The problem created by asymmetric information prior to a financial transaction: The party that is the most undesirable from the other party's point of view is the one who is most likely to want to engage in the financial transaction. **36**

agency theory The analysis of how asymmetric information problems affect economic behavior. **167**

aggregate demand The total quantity of output demanded in an economy at different price levels. **474**

aggregate demand curve The curve showing the relationship between the price level and the quantity of aggregate output demanded when the goods and money markets are in equilibrium. **499, 509**

aggregate income The total income of factors of production (land, labor, capital) in an economy. **19**

aggregate output The total production of final goods and services in an economy. **7**

aggregate price level The average price of goods and services in an economy. **8**

aggregate supply curve The curve showing the relationship between the quantity of output supplied and the price level. **515**

anchor currency A currency to which other countries' currencies are pegged. **433**

"animal spirits" Waves of optimism and pessimism that affect consumers' and businesses' willingness to spend. **477**

appreciation Increase in a currency's value. **402**

arbitrage Elimination of a riskless profit opportunity in a market. **150**

asset A financial claim or piece of property that is a store of value. **3**

asset management The acquisition of assets that have a low rate of default and the diversification of asset holdings to increase profits. **193**

asset market approach An approach to determining asset prices that makes use of stocks of assets rather than flows. **91**

asset price bubbles Occur when asset prices in the stock and real estate markets are driven well above the assets' fundamental economic values by investor psychology. **269, 383**

asset transformation The process of turning risky assets into safer assets, accomplished by creating and selling assets with risk characteristics that people are comfortable with and then using the funds acquired by selling these assets to purchase other assets that have far more risk. **36, 190**

asymmetric information The unequal knowledge that each party to a transaction has about the other party. **36**

automated banking machine (ABM) One location that provides an automated teller machine (ATM), an Internet connection to the bank's website, and a telephone link to customer service. **240**

automated teller machine (ATM) An electronic machine that provides banking services 24 hours a day. **240**

autonomous consumption expenditure The amount of consumer expenditure that is independent of disposable income. **475**

autonomous easing of monetary policy The lowering of real interest rates at any given inflation rate. **497**

autonomous investment A component of planned investment spending that is completely exogenous and so is unexplained by the variables in a model. **477**

autonomous net exports The level of net exports that is treated as exogenous (outside the model). **479**

autonomous spending Exogenous spending that is unrelated to variables in the model such as output or the real interest rate. **487**

autonomous tightening of monetary policy The raising of real interest rates at any given inflation rate. **505**

balance of payments A bookkeeping system for recording all payments that have a direct bearing on the movement of funds between a country and other countries. **431**

balance-of-payments crisis A foreign exchange crisis stemming from problems in a country's balance of payments. **438**

balance sheet A balanced list of the assets and liabilities of a bank (or firm): Total assets equal total liabilities plus capital. **186**

bank failure A situation in which a bank cannot satisfy its obligations to pay its depositors and other creditors and so goes out of business. **215**

bank holding companies Companies that own one or more banks. **237**

bank panic The simultaneous failure of many banks, as during a financial crisis. **216**

banks Financial institutions (such as commercial banks, savings and loan associations, and credit unions) that accept money deposits and make loans. **6**

Basel Accord An agreement that required that banks hold as capital at least 8% of their risk-weighted assets. **221**

Basel Committee on Banking Supervision An international committee of bank supervisors that meets under the auspices of the Bank for International Settlements in Basel, Switzerland. **221**

behavioral finance A subfield of finance that applies concepts from other social sciences, such as anthropology, sociology, and particularly psychology, to explain the behavior of securities prices. **156**

Board of Governors of the Federal Reserve System A board with seven governors (including the chair) that plays an essential role in decision making within the Federal Reserve System. **293**

bond A debt security that promises to make periodic payments to the holder for a specified period of time. **3**

borrowed reserves A bank's borrowings from the Fed. **322**

branches A main bank's additional offices in which banking operations are conducted. **250**

Bretton Woods system The international monetary system, in use from 1945 to 1971, in which exchange rates were fixed and the U.S. dollar was freely convertible into gold (by foreign governments and central banks only). **434**

brokers Agents for investors; brokers match buyers with sellers. **26**

bubble A situation in which the price of an asset differs from its fundamental market value. **155**

budget deficit Government expenditures in excess of tax revenues. **11**

budget surplus Tax revenues in excess of government expenditures. **11**

business cycles The upward and downward movement of aggregate output produced in an economy. **7**

capital Wealth, either financial or physical in form, that is employed to produce more wealth. **24**

capital account An account that describes the flow of capital between a country and other countries. **432**

capital adequacy management A bank's decisions about the amount of capital it should maintain and the best ways to acquire the needed capital. **193**

capital controls Restrictions on the free movement of capital across borders. **439**

capital market A financial market in which longer-term debt (generally with an original maturity of greater than one year) and equity instruments are traded. **27**

capital mobility A situation in which foreigners can easily purchase a country's assets, and the country's residents can easily purchase foreign assets. **425**

cash flows Cash payments to the holder of a security. **64, 140**

central bank The government agency that oversees a country's banking system and is responsible for the amount of money and credit supplied in the economy; in the United States, the Federal Reserve System. **10, 235**

collateral Property that is pledged to the lender to guarantee payment in the event that the borrower is unable to make debt payments. **165**

commodity money Money made up of precious metals or another valuable commodity. **53**

common stock A security that is a claim on the earnings and assets of a company. **3**

community banks Small banks with local roots. **254**

compensating balance The required minimum amount of funds that a firm receiving a loan must keep in a checking account at the lending bank. **204**

conflicts of interest A manifestation of the moral hazard problem. Conflicts of interest occur when a financial institution provides multiple services with conflicting goals, a situation that may lead the firm to conceal important information or disseminate misleading information. **38**

consol A perpetual bond with no maturity date and no repayment of principal, and that makes periodic, fixed coupon payments. **73**

constant-money-growth-rate rule Monetary policy rule, advocated by monetarists, in which policymakers keep the money supply growing at a constant rate, regardless of the state of the economy. **585**

constrained discretion A framework in which the general objectives and tactics of policymakers—but not specific actions—are committed to in advance; this framework imposes a conceptual structure and inherent discipline on policymakers without eliminating all flexibility. **588**

consumer durable expenditure Spending by consumers on durable items such as automobiles and household appliances. **603**

consumption Spending by consumers on nondurable goods and services (including services related to the ownership of homes and consumer durables). **606**

consumption expenditure The total demand for consumer goods and services. **475, 509**

consumption function The relationship between disposable income and consumer expenditure. **475**

conventional monetary policy tools The classic tools of monetary policy that the Federal Reserve uses to control the money supply and interest rates: open market operations, discount lending, and reserve requirements. **348**

cost-push inflation Inflation that occurs when workers push to obtain higher wages. **564**

cost-push shocks Price shocks that occur when workers push for wages that are higher than productivity gains, thereby driving up costs and inflation. **516**

costly state verification Monitoring of a firm's activities, an expensive process in terms of both time and money. **174**

coupon bond A credit market instrument that pays the owner a fixed interest payment every year until the maturity date, at which time a specified final amount is repaid. **67**

coupon rate The dollar amount of the yearly coupon payment expressed as a percentage of the face value of a coupon bond. **67**

credibility A commitment to policy actions that is believed by the public. **588**

credit boom A lending spree in which financial institutions expand their lending at a rapid pace. **268**

credit default swaps Financial insurance contracts that provide payments to holders of bonds if they default. **275**

credit easing Altering the composition of the Fed's balance sheet in order to improve the functioning of particular segments of the credit markets. **359**

credit rationing Occurs when a lender refuses to make loans even though borrowers are willing to pay the stated interest rate or even a higher rate, or when a lender restricts the sizes of loans so that the loans are made for less than the full amount sought. **205**

credit risk The risk arising from the possibility that the borrower will default. **193**

credit spread The difference between the interest rate on loans to households and businesses and the interest rate on completely safe assets that are sure to be paid off, such as U.S. Treasury securities. **273**

credit view Monetary transmission mechanisms that operate through asymmetric information effects on credit markets. **604**

credit-rating agencies Investment advisory firms that rate the quality of corporate and municipal bonds in terms of the probability of default. **119**

currency Paper money (such as dollar bills) and coins. **28, 49**

currency board A monetary regime in which the domestic currency is backed 100% by a foreign currency (say, dollars) and in which the note-issuing authority, whether it be the central bank or the government, establishes a fixed exchange rate to this foreign currency and stands ready to exchange domestic currency at this rate whenever the public so requests. **449**

current account An account that shows international transactions involving currently produced goods and services. **432**

current yield An approximation of the yield to maturity; equal to the yearly coupon payment divided by the price of a coupon bond. **74**

data lag The time it takes for policymakers to obtain data on the state of the economy. **561**

dealers People who link buyers with sellers by buying and selling securities at stated prices. **26**

debt deflation A situation in which a substantial decline in the price level sets in, leading to a further deterioration in firms' net worth because of the increased burden of indebtedness. **271**

default A situation in which the party issuing a debt instrument is unable to make interest payments or pay off the amount owed when the instrument matures. **28, 116**

default-free bonds Bonds with no default risk, such as U.S. government bonds. **117**

defensive open market operations Open market operations intended to offset movements in other factors that affect the monetary base (such as changes in Treasury deposits with the Fed or changes in float). **348**

deleveraging Occurs when financial institutions cut back on their lending because they have less capital. **268**

demand curve The curve depicting the relationship between quantity demanded and price when all other economic variables are held constant. **88**

demand for money The quantity of money that people want to hold. **458**

demand shocks Shocks that can shift the aggregate demand curve, including changes in the money supply, changes in government expenditure and taxes, changes in net exports, changes in consumer and business spending, and financial frictions. **511**

demand-pull inflation Inflation that results when policymakers pursue policies that shift the aggregate demand curve. **564**

deposit facility The European Central Bank's standing facility, in which banks are paid a fixed interest rate 100 basis points below the target financing rate. **362**

deposit outflows Losses of deposits when depositors make withdrawals or demand payment. **193**

deposit rate ceiling A restriction on the maximum interest rate payable on deposits. **244**

depreciation A decrease in a currency's value. **402**

devaluation The resetting of the fixed value of a currency to a lower level. **436**

discount bond A credit market instrument that is bought at a price below its face value and whose face value is repaid at the maturity date; it does not make any interest payments. Also called a *zero-coupon bond*. **67**

discount loans A bank's borrowings from the Federal Reserve System; also known as *advances*. **188**

discount rate The interest rate that the Federal Reserve charges banks on discount loans. **195, 327**

discount window The Federal Reserve facility at which discount loans are made to banks. **349**

discretion When policymakers make decisions that they believe are the best policies to address a given situation at a given point in time. **584**

disintermediation A reduction in the flow of funds into the banking system that causes the amount of financial intermediation to decline. **244**

disposable income Total income available for spending, equal to aggregate income minus taxes. **475**

diversification Investing in a collection (portfolio) of assets whose returns do not always move together, with the result that the overall risk is lower than that on the individual assets. **36**

dividends Periodic payments made by equities to shareholders. **25, 141**

divine coincidence A phrase coined by Olivier Blanchard, referring to the situation in which a policy meant to stabilize inflation is also the best policy for stabilizing economic activity. **556**

dollarization The adoption of a sound currency, like the U.S. dollar, as a country's money. **451**

dominated assets Assets such as currency and checkable assets, which earn lower returns than other assets that are just as safe. **467**

dual banking system The banking system in place in the United States, in which banks supervised by the federal government and banks supervised by the states operate side by side. **236**

dual mandate A central bank mandate that features two co-equal objectives: price stability and maximum employment. **371**

duration analysis A measurement of the sensitivity of the market value of a bank's assets and liabilities to changes in interest rates. **207**

dynamic open market operations Open market operations that are intended to change the level of reserves and the monetary base. **348**

e-cash Electronic money that is used on the Internet to purchase goods or services. **54**

e-finance A new means of delivering financial services electronically. **6**

easing of monetary policy The lowering of the federal funds rate. **301**

economies of scale The reduction in transaction costs per dollar of transaction as the size (scale) of transactions increases. **35**

economies of scope The ability to use one resource to provide many different products and services. **38, 253**

Edge Act corporation A special subsidiary of a U.S. bank that is engaged primarily in international banking. **262**

effective exchange rate index An index reflecting the value of a basket of representative foreign currencies. **417**

effectiveness lag The time it takes for a policy to actually have an impact on the economy. **562**

efficient market hypothesis The application of the theory of rational expectations to financial markets. Also called the *theory of efficient capital markets*. **148**

electronic money (e-money) Money that exists only in electronic form and substitutes for cash as well. **54**

emerging market countries Countries that have recently opened up to flows of goods, services, and capital from the rest of the world. **442**

equation of exchange The equation $MV = PY$, which relates nominal income to the quantity of money. **457**

equities Claims to share in the net income and assets of a corporation (such as common stock). **25**

equity capital See *net worth*. **172**

equity multiplier (EM) The amount of assets per dollar of equity capital. **199**

Eurobonds Bonds denominated in a currency other than that of the country in which they are sold. **33**

Eurocurrencies A variant of the Eurobond; foreign currencies deposited in banks outside the home country. **33**

Eurodollars U.S. dollars that are deposited in foreign banks outside the United States or in foreign branches of U.S. banks. **33**

excess demand A situation in which the quantity demanded is greater than the quantity supplied. **90**

excess reserves Reserves in excess of required reserves. **189, 318, 327**

excess supply A situation in which the quantity supplied is greater than the quantity demanded. **90**

exchange rate The price of one currency stated in terms of another currency. **419, 478**

exchange-rate peg The fixing of the value of the domestic currency to the value of another currency, so that the exchange rate is fixed. Also called *exchange-rate targeting*. **445**

exchange-rate targeting See *exchange-rate peg*. **445**

exchanges Secondary markets in which buyers and sellers of securities (or their agents or brokers) meet in one central location to conduct trades. **26**

exogenous Independent of variables in the model. **475**

expectations theory The proposition that the interest rate on a long-term bond will equal the average of the short-term interest rates that people expect to occur over the life of the long-term bond. **126**

expected return The return on an asset expected over the next period. **86**

face value A specified final amount paid to the owner of a coupon bond at the maturity date. Also called *par value*. **67**

fair-value accounting See *mark-to-market accounting*. **225**

federal funds rate The interest rate on overnight loans of deposits at the Federal Reserve. **29, 314, 341**

Federal Open Market Committee (FOMC) The committee that makes decisions regarding the conduct of open market operations; composed of the seven members of the Board of Governors of the Federal Reserve System, the president of the Federal Reserve Bank of New York, and the presidents of four other Federal Reserve banks (on a rotating basis). **293**

Federal Reserve Banks The 12 district banks in the Federal Reserve System. **293**

Federal Reserve System (the Fed) The central banking authority responsible for monetary policy in the United States. **10**

fiat money Paper currency decreed by a government as legal tender but not convertible into coins or precious metal. **53**

financial crisis   A major disruption in financial markets that is characterized by sharp declines in asset prices and the failures of many financial and nonfinancial firms. 7, **268**

financial derivatives   Instruments that have payoffs that are linked to previously issued securities; used as risk reduction tools. **239, 275**

financial engineering   The process of researching and developing new financial products and services that will meet customer needs and also prove profitable. **237**

financial frictions   Asymmetric information problems that act as barriers to the efficient allocation of capital. **268, 478**

financial innovation   The introduction of new types of financial products in an economy. 6, **268**

financial intermediaries   Institutions (such as banks, insurance companies, mutual funds, pension funds, and finance companies) that borrow funds from people who have saved and then make loans to others. **6**

financial intermediation   The process of indirect finance whereby financial intermediaries link lender-savers with borrower-spenders. **34**

financial liberalization   The elimination of restrictions on financial markets. **268**

financial markets   Markets in which funds are transferred from people who have a surplus of available funds to people who have a shortage of available funds. **2**

financial panic   The widespread collapse of financial markets and intermediaries in an economy. **43**

financial supervision (prudential supervision)   The oversight of financial institutions and their operations. **223**

fire sales   Forced, rapid sales of assets to raise needed funds. **271**

fiscal policy   Policy that involves decisions about government spending and taxation. **11**

Fisher effect   Describes the rise in interest rates that occurs when inflation is at the level of expected inflation; named after economist Irving Fisher. **98**

fixed exchange rate regime   A regime in which central banks buy and sell their own currencies to keep their exchange rates fixed at a certain level. **433**

fixed investment   Spending by firms on equipment (computers, airplanes) and structures (factories, office buildings), and planned spending on residential housing. **476**

fixed-payment loan   A credit market instrument that provides the borrower with an amount of money that is repaid through fixed periodic (usually monthly) payments made over a set number of years. **67**

float   Cash items in process of collection at the Fed minus deferred-availability cash items. **322**

floating exchange rate regime   An exchange rate regime in which the values of currencies are allowed to fluctuate against one another. **433**

foreign bonds   Bonds sold in a foreign country and denominated in that country's currency. **32**

foreign exchange intervention   An international financial transaction in which a central bank buys or sells currency to influence foreign exchange rates. **427**

foreign exchange market   The market in which exchange rates are determined. 13, **400**

foreign exchange rate   See *exchange rate*. **13**

forward exchange rate   The exchange rate for a forward transaction. **401**

forward guidance   A central bank commitment to a future path of the policy interest rate. **360**

forward transaction   A transaction that involves the exchange of bank deposits denominated in different currencies at some specified future date. **401**

free-rider problem   The problem that occurs when people who do not pay for information take advantage of the information that other people have paid for. **169**

fully amortized loan   See *fixed-payment loan*. **67**

fundamental economic values   Values of assets based on realistic expectations of their future income streams. **269**

futures contract   A contract in which the seller agrees to provide a certain standardized commodity to the buyer on a specific future date at an agreed-on price. **239**

gap analysis   A measurement of the sensitivity of bank profits to changes in interest rates, calculated by subtracting the amount of rate-sensitive liabilities from the amount of rate-sensitive assets. **206**

general equilibrium   Occurs when all markets are simultaneously in equilibrium, at the point where the quantity of aggregate output demanded equals the quantity of aggregate output supplied. **521**

generalized dividend model   A model in which the price of a stock is determined only by the present value of the dividends. **142**

goal independence   The ability of the central bank to set the goals of monetary policy. **303**

gold standard   A fixed exchange rate regime under which a currency is directly convertible into gold. **433**

Gordon growth model   A simplified model used to compute the value of a stock by assuming constant dividend growth. **142**

government budget constraint   The requirement that the government budget deficit must equal the sum of the change in the monetary base and the change in government bonds held by the public. **463**

government purchases   Spending by all levels of government (federal, state, and local) on goods and services. **475, 509**

gross domestic product (GDP)   The value of all final goods and services produced in the economy during the course of a year. **11**

haircuts   The excess amount of collateral above the amount of a loan. **278**

hedge   To protect oneself against risk. **239**

hierarchical mandate   A central bank mandate in which the goal of price stability comes first; once price stability has been achieved, other goals can be pursued. **370**

high-powered money   The monetary base. **317**

hyperinflation   An extreme inflation in which the inflation rate exceeds 50% per month. **52, 464**

implementation lag   The time it takes for policymakers to change policy instruments once they have decided on a new policy. **562**

impossible trinity   Another term for the policy trilemma, in which a country cannot pursue the following three policies at the same time: free capital mobility, a fixed exchange rate, and an independent monetary policy. **439**

incentive-compatible   Used to describe a contract in which the incentives of both parties to the contract are in alignment. **177**

income   The flow of earnings. **50**

inflation   The economic condition of a continually rising price level. **8**

inflation gap   The difference between inflation and the inflation target. **553**

inflation hedges   Alternative assets whose real returns are less affected than that of money when inflation varies. **467**

inflation rate   The rate of change of the price level, usually measured as a percentage change per year. **8**

inflation shocks   Shifts in inflation that are independent of the amount of slack in the economy or expected inflation. **516**

inflation target   A central bank target for the inflation rate. **553**

inflation targeting   A monetary policy strategy that involves the public announcement of a medium-term numerical target for inflation. **371**

instrument independence   The ability of the central bank to set monetary policy instruments. **303**

interest parity condition   The observation that the domestic interest rate equals the foreign interest rate plus the expected appreciation in the foreign currency. **425**

interest rate   The cost of borrowing or the price paid for the rental of funds (usually expressed as a percentage per year). **3**

interest-rate risk   The possible reduction in returns associated with changes in interest rates. **78, 193**

intermediate target   Any of a number of variables, such as monetary aggregates or interest rates, that have a direct effect on employment and the price level and that the Fed seeks to influence. **387**

intermediate-term   With reference to a debt instrument, having a maturity of between one and ten years. **25**

international banking facilities (IBFs)   Banking establishments in the United States that can accept time deposits from foreigners but are not subject to reserve requirements or restrictions on interest payments. **262**

International Monetary Fund (IMF)   The international organization created by the Bretton Woods agreement whose objective it is to promote the growth of world trade by making loans to countries experiencing balance-of-payments difficulties. **434**

international reserves   Central bank holdings of assets denominated in foreign currencies. **427**

inventory investment   Spending by firms on additional holdings of raw materials, parts, and finished goods. **476**

inverted yield curve   A yield curve that is downward-sloping. **125**

investment banks   Firms that assist in the initial sale of securities in the primary market. **26**

IS curve   The relationship that describes the combinations of aggregate output and interest rates for which the total quantity of goods produced equals the total quantity demanded (goods market equilibrium). **481**

junk bonds   Bonds with ratings below Baa (or BBB) that have a high default risk. **120**

Keynesian   A follower of John Maynard Keynes who believes that movements in the price level and aggregate output are driven by changes not only in the money supply but also in government spending and fiscal policy, and who does not regard the economy as inherently stable. **561**

law of one price   The principle that if two countries produce an identical good, the price of this good should be the same throughout the world, no matter which country produces it. **403**

legislative lag   The time it takes to pass legislation to implement a particular policy. **561**

lender of last resort   A lender that provides reserves to financial institutions when no one else is willing to do so; such lending is usually done to prevent a financial crisis. **351**

leverage cycle   A feedback loop in which a boom in the issuance of credit leads to higher asset prices, which results in higher capital buffers at financial institutions, which supports further lending, which raises prices further, etc.; during the subsequent bust, asset prices fall, leading to cuts in lending, declines in asset prices, and so on. **284**

leverage ratio   A bank's capital divided by its assets. **221**

liabilities   IOUs or debts. **23**

liability management   The acquisition of funds at low cost to increase profits. **193**

liquid   Easily converted into cash. **26**

liquidity   The relative ease and speed with which an asset can be converted into cash. **52, 86**

liquidity management   The decisions made by a bank in order to maintain enough liquid assets to meet the bank's obligations to depositors. **193**

liquidity preference framework   A model developed by John Maynard Keynes that predicts the equilibrium interest rate on the basis of the supply of and demand for money. **101**

liquidity preference theory   John Maynard Keynes's theory of the demand for money. **465**

liquidity premium theory   The theory that the interest rate on a long-term bond will equal an average of the short-term interest rates expected to occur over the life of the long-term bond, plus a positive term (liquidity) premium. **130**

liquidity services   Services that financial intermediaries provide to their customers to make it easier for the customers to conduct their transactions. **35**

liquidity trap   A case of ultrasensitivity of the demand for money to interest rates, in which conventional monetary policy has no direct effect on aggregate spending because a change in the money supply has no effect on the interest rate. **469**

loan commitment   A bank's commitment to provide a firm with loans (for a specified period of time) up to a given amount at an interest rate that is tied to some market interest rate. **204**

loan sale   The sale through a contract (also called a *secondary loan participation*) of all or part of the cash stream from a specific loan, thereby removing the loan from the bank's balance sheet. **208**

long-term   With reference to a debt instrument, having a maturity of ten years or more. **25**

longer-term refinancing operations   A category of open market operations conducted by the European Central Bank; similar to the Fed's outright purchases or sales of securities. **362**

M1   A measure of money that includes currency, traveler's checks, and checkable deposits. **56**

M2   A measure of money that includes M1 plus the following: money market deposit accounts, money market mutual fund shares, small-denomination time deposits, savings deposits, overnight repurchase agreements, and overnight Eurodollars. **58**

macroeconometric models   Models used to forecast the effects of policy on economic activity; macroeconometric models use collections of equations that describe statistical relationships among many economic variables. **582**

macroprudential regulation   Regulatory policy that affects the credit markets in the aggregate. **386**

macroprudential supervision   Supervision that focuses on the safety and soundness of the financial system in the aggregate. **284**

main refinancing operations   Weekly reverse transactions (purchases or sales of eligible assets through repurchase agreements or credit operations, with eligible assets as collateral) that are reversed within two weeks and are the primary monetary policy tool of the European Central Bank. **361**

managed float regime   An exchange rate regime in which countries attempt to influence their exchange rates by buying and selling currencies (also called a *dirty float*). **433**

management of expectations   A term coined by Michael Woodford that refers to a commitment by the Fed to keep the federal funds rate at zero for an extended period in order to generate a fall in the long-term interest rate. **360**

marginal lending facility   The European Central Bank's standing lending facility, in which banks can borrow (against eligible collateral) overnight loans from the national central bank at a rate that is 100 basis points above the target financing rate. **362**

marginal lending rate   The interest rate charged by the European Central Bank for borrowing at its marginal lending facility. **362**

marginal propensity to consume   The slope of the consumption function line that measures the change in consumer expenditure that results from an additional dollar of disposable income. **476**

mark-to-market accounting   An accounting method in which assets are valued on the balance sheets at the price at which they would sell in the market. Also called *fair-value accounting*. **225**

market equilibrium   Occurs in an economy when the quantity that people are willing to buy (demand) is equal to the quantity that people are willing to sell (supply). **90**

market fundamentals   Items that have a direct impact on the future income streams of a security. **155**

matched sale–purchase transaction   An arrangement whereby the Fed sells securities and the buyer agrees to sell them back to the Fed in the near future; sometimes called a *reverse repo*. **349**

maturity   The time to the expiration date (maturity date) of a debt instrument. **25**

medium of exchange   Anything that is used to pay for goods and services. **50**

microprudential supervision   Supervision that focuses on the safety and soundness of individual financial institutions. **283**

monetarist   A follower of Milton Friedman who sees changes in the money supply as the primary source of movements in the price level and aggregate output, and who views the economy as inherently stable. **585**

monetary aggregates   The measures of the money supply (M1 and M2) used by the Federal Reserve System. **56**

monetary base   The sum of the Fed's monetary liabilities (currency in circulation and reserves) and the U.S. Treasury's monetary liabilities (Treasury currency in circulation, primarily coins). **317**

monetary policy   The management of the money supply and interest rates. **10**

monetary policy (*MP*) curve   The curve showing the relationship between the real interest rate set by the central bank and the inflation rate. **495**

monetary theory   The theory that relates changes in the quantity of money to changes in economic activity. **7, 456**

monetary (currency) union   A group of countries that decides to adopt a common currency, thereby fixing the countries' exchange rates in relation to each other. **440**

monetizing the debt   A method of financing government spending whereby the government debt issued to finance government spending is removed from the hands of the public and is replaced by high-powered money instead. Also called *printing money*. **463**

money (money supply)   Anything that is generally accepted as payment for goods or services or in the repayment of debts. **7**

money center banks   Large banks in key financial centers (New York, Chicago, San Francisco). **197**

money market   A financial market in which only short-term debt instruments (generally those with original maturities of less than one year) are traded. **27**

money multiplier   A ratio that relates the change in the money supply to a given change in the monetary base. **331**

money supply   The quantity of money. **7**

moral hazard   The risk that one party to a transaction will engage in behavior that is undesirable from the other party's point of view. **37**

mortgage-backed securities   Securities that cheaply bundle and quantify the default risk of the underlying high-risk mortgages. **30**

mortgages   Loans to households or firms that wish to purchase housing, land, or other real structures; the structure or land itself serves as collateral for the loan. **30**

multiple deposit creation   The process whereby, when the Fed supplies the banking system with $1 of additional reserves, deposits increase by a multiple of this amount. **323**

national banks   Federally chartered banks. **236**

natural rate of output   The level of aggregate output produced at the natural rate of unemployment—the rate at which there is no tendency for wages or prices to change. **369, 515**

natural rate of unemployment   The rate of unemployment consistent with full employment; the rate at which the demand for labor equals the supply of labor. **368, 515**

net exports   Net foreign spending on domestic goods and services, equal to exports minus imports. **475, 509**

net worth   The difference between a firm's assets (what it owns or is owed) and its liabilities (what it owes). Also called *equity capital*. **172**

nominal anchor   A nominal variable, such as the inflation rate, an exchange rate, or the money supply, that monetary policymakers use to tie down the price level. **367**

nominal GDP targeting   A monetary policy strategy in which the central bank announces an objective of hitting a particular level of nominal GDP (real GDP times the price level) that grows over time. **597**

nominal interest rate   An interest rate that does not take inflation into account. **79**

nonaccelerating inflation rate of unemployment (NAIRU)   The rate of unemployment at which there is no tendency for inflation to change. **392**

nonactivists   Economists who believe that wages and prices are very flexible and so the self-correcting mechanism works very rapidly; nonactivists do not see the need to pursue policies to return the economy to full employment. **561**

nonborrowed monetary base   The monetary base minus discount loans (borrowed reserves). **322**

nonconventional monetary policy tools   The non-interest-rate tools used by central banks to stimulate the economy: liquidity provision, asset purchases, and commitments to future monetary policy actions. **355**

off-balance-sheet activities   Bank activities that involve the trading of financial instruments and the generation of income from fees and loan sales, all of which affect bank profits but are not visible on bank balance sheets. **208, 221**

official reserve transactions balance   The current account balance plus items in the capital account. **432**

open market operations   The Fed's buying or selling of bonds in the open market. **297, 319**

open market purchase   A purchase of bonds by the Fed. **319**

open market sale   A sale of bonds by the Fed. **319**

operating instrument   A variable that is very responsive to the central bank's tools and indicates the stance of monetary policy (also called a *policy instrument*). **387**

opportunity cost   The amount of interest (expected return) sacrificed by not holding an alternative asset. **102**

optimal forecast   The best guess of future conditions, made using all available information. **146**

originate-to-distribute model   A business model in which a mortgage is originated by a separate party, typically a mortgage broker, and then distributed to an investor as an underlying asset in a security. **243**

output gap   The difference between aggregate output and potential output. **515**

over-the-counter (OTC) market   A secondary market in which dealers at different locations who have an inventory of securities stand ready to buy and sell securities "over the counter" to anyone who comes to them and is willing to accept their prices. **26**

overnight cash rate   The interest rate for very-short-term interbank loans in the euro area. **361**

par value   See *face value*. **67**

payment technology   Methods of payment that include credit cards and electronic payments. **465**

payments system The method of conducting transactions in an economy. **53**

perpetuity See *consol*. **73**

Phillips curve theory A theory suggesting that changes in inflation are influenced by the state of the economy relative to its production capacity, as well as other factors. **391**

planned expenditure The total amount that households, businesses, the government, and foreigners want to spend on domestically produced goods and services. **447**

planned investment spending Total planned spending by businesses on new physical capital (e.g., machines, computers, apartment buildings) plus planned spending on new homes. **475, 509**

policy instrument A variable that is very responsive to the central bank's tools and that indicates the stance of monetary policy (also called an *operating instrument*). **387**

policy trilemma The idea that a country cannot pursue the following three policies at the same time: free capital mobility, a fixed exchange rate, and an independent monetary policy. **439**

political business cycle A business cycle caused by expansionary policies that are pursued prior to an election. **305, 586**

portfolio A collection or group of assets. **36**

potential output The level of aggregate output produced at the natural rate of unemployment (also called the *natural rate of output*). **369, 515**

preferred habitat theory A theory that holds that the interest rate on a long-term bond is equal to an average of the short-term interest rates expected to occur over the life of the long-term bond, plus a positive term premium. Closely related to the liquidity premium theory. **130**

present discounted value See *present value*. **64**

present value Today's value of a payment to be received in the future, when the interest rate is *i*. Also called *present discounted value*. **64**

price stability Low and stable inflation. **366**

primary dealers Government securities dealers, operating out of private firms or commercial banks, with whom the Fed's open market desk trades. **319, 349**

primary market A financial market in which new issues of a security are sold to initial buyers. **25**

principal–agent problem A moral hazard problem that occurs when the managers in control (the agents) act in their own interest rather than in the interest of the owners (the principals), due to differing sets of incentives. **173**

printing money See *monetizing the debt*. **463**

prudential supervision See *financial supervision*. **223**

quantity theory of money The theory that nominal income is determined solely by movements in the quantity of money. **458**

quantitative easing An expansion of the Federal Reserve's balance sheet. **358**

quotas Restrictions on the quantity of foreign goods that can be imported. **406**

random walk Movements of a variable whose future values cannot be predicted (are random) because, given today's value, the value of the variable is just as likely to fall as it is to rise. **151**

rate of capital gain The change in a security's price relative to its initial purchase price. **76**

rate of return See *return*. **75**

rational expectations Expectations that reflect optimal forecasts (the best guess of future conditions) made using all available information. **146**

real business cycle theory A theory that views real shocks to tastes and technology as the major driving force behind short-run business cycle fluctuations. **533**

real exchange rate The rate at which domestic goods can be exchanged for foreign goods; i.e., the price of domestic goods relative to foreign goods denominated in domestic currency. **404**

real interest rate The interest rate adjusted for expected changes in the price level (inflation) so that it more accurately reflects the true cost of borrowing. **79**

real money balances The quantity of money in real terms. **465**

real terms Terms that reflect the actual amount of goods and services that one can buy. **80**

recession A period during which aggregate output is declining. **7**

recognition lag The time it takes for policymakers to feel confident about the signals the data are sending regarding the future course of the economy. **561**

regulatory arbitrage A process in which banks keep on their books assets that are relatively risky, such as a loan to a company with a very low credit rating, while taking off their books low-risk assets, such as a loan to a company with a very high credit rating. In regulatory arbitrage, the risky and low-risk assets have the same risk-based capital requirements. **221**

repurchase agreement (repo) An arrangement whereby the Fed or another party purchases securities with the understanding that the seller will repurchase them in a short period of time, usually less than a week. **278, 348**

required reserve ratio The fraction of deposits that the Fed requires be kept as reserves. **189, 318**

required reserves Reserves that are held to meet the Fed's requirement that for every dollar of deposits at a bank, a certain fraction must be kept as reserves. **189**

reserve currency A currency, such as the U.S. dollar, that is used by other countries to denominate the assets they hold as international reserves. **434**

reserve requirements   Regulations that oblige depository institutions to keep a certain fraction of their deposits in accounts with the Fed. **189**

reserves   Banks' holding of deposits in accounts with the Fed plus currency that is physically held by banks (vault cash). **189, 318**

residual claimant   A stockholder's right to receive whatever remains after all other claims against a firm's assets have been satisfied. **140**

restrictive covenants   Provisions that restrict and specify certain activities that a borrower can engage in. **165**

return   The payments to the owner of a security plus the change in the security's value, expressed as a fraction of its purchase price. More precisely called the *rate of return*. **75**

return on assets (ROA)   Net profit after taxes per dollar of assets. **199**

return on equity (ROE)   Net profit after taxes per dollar of equity capital. **199**

revaluation   The resetting of the fixed value of a currency at a higher level. **436**

reverse transactions   Purchases or sales of eligible assets by the European Central Bank under repurchase agreements or credit operations, with eligible assets as collateral, that are reversed within two weeks. **361**

risk   The degree of uncertainty associated with the return on an asset. **36, 86**

risk premium   The spread between the interest rate on bonds with default risk and the interest rate on default-free bonds. **117**

risk sharing   The process of creating and selling assets with risk characteristics that people are comfortable with and then using the funds acquired by selling these assets to purchase other assets that have far more risk. **36**

risk structure of interest rates   The relationships among the interest rates on various bonds with the same term to maturity. **116**

rules   Binding plans that specify how policy will respond (or not respond) to particular data, such as data on unemployment and inflation. **584**

secondary market   A financial market in which securities that have previously been issued (and are thus second-hand) can be resold. **25**

secondary reserves   Short-term U.S. government and agency securities held by banks. **189**

secured debt   Debt guaranteed by collateral. **165**

securitization   The process of transforming illiquid financial assets into marketable capital market instruments. **242**

security   A claim on a borrower's future income that is sold by the borrower to the lender. Also called a *financial instrument*. **3**

segmented markets theory   A theory of term structure that sees the markets for different-maturity bonds as completely separated and segmented, so that the interest rate on bonds of a given maturity is determined solely by supply of and demand for bonds of that maturity. **129**

seignorage   The revenue that a government receives by issuing money. **451**

self-correcting mechanism   A characteristic of the economy that causes output to return eventually to the natural rate level, regardless of where it lies initially. **525**

shadow banking system   A system in which bank lending is replaced by lending via the securities market. **237**

short sales   Borrowing stock from brokers and then selling the stock in the market, with the hope that a profit will be earned by buying the stock back again ("covering the short") after it has fallen in price. **157**

short-term   With reference to a debt instrument, having a maturity of one year or less. **25**

simple deposit multiplier   The multiple increase in deposits generated by an increase in the banking system's reserves. The behavior of depositors and banks plays no role in this simple model. **326**

simple loan   A credit market instrument that provides the borrower with an amount of funds that must be repaid to the lender at the maturity date, along with an additional payment (interest). **65**

smart card   A stored-value card that contains a computer chip that allows the card to be loaded with digital cash from the owner's bank account whenever needed. **54**

speculative attack   Involves massive sales of a weak currency or purchases of a strong currency that can cause a sharp change in the exchange rate. **436**

spot exchange rate   The exchange rate for a spot transaction. **401**

spot transaction   The predominant type of exchange rate transaction, involving the immediate exchange of bank deposits denominated in different currencies. **401**

stagflation   A situation of rising inflation but a falling level of aggregate output. **530**

standing lending facility   A lending facility in which healthy banks are allowed to borrow all they want from a central bank. **351**

state banks   State-chartered banks. **236**

state-owned banks   Banks that are owned by governments. **181**

sterilized foreign exchange intervention   A foreign exchange intervention that is accompanied by an offsetting open market operation that leaves the monetary base unchanged. **430**

stock   A security that is a claim on the earnings and assets of a company. **3**

stockholders   Those who hold stock in a corporation. **140**

store of value   A repository of purchasing power over time. **52**

stress tests Tests used by financial institutions to calculate potential losses and capital needs under fictional dire scenarios. **225**

structured credit products Securities that are derived from the cash flows of underlying assets and are tailored to have particular risk characteristics that appeal to investors with different preferences. **274**

subprime mortgages Mortgages made to borrowers with less-than-stellar credit records. **243**

superregional banks Bank holding companies that are similar in size to money center banks but whose headquarters are not based in one of the money center cities (New York, Chicago, San Francisco). **253**

supply curve A curve depicting the relationship between quantity supplied and price when all other economic variables are held constant. **89**

supply shock Any change in technology or the supply of raw materials that can shift the aggregate supply curve. **516**

sweep account An arrangement whereby any balances above a certain amount that remain in a corporation's checking account at the end of the business day are "swept out" of the account and invested in overnight repos that pay the corporation interest. **245**

systemically important financial institutions (SIFIs) Firms that are designated by the Financial Stability Oversight Council as systemically important and so are subject to additional oversight and regulation by the Federal Reserve. **285**

T-account A simplified balance sheet with lines in the form of a T that lists only the changes that occur in balance sheet items starting from some initial balance sheet position. **190**

target financing rate The European Central Bank's target for the overnight cash rate, the interest rate for very-short-term interbank loans in the euro area. **361**

tariffs Taxes on imported goods. **406**

Taylor principle The principle that the monetary authorities should raise nominal interest rates by more than the increase in the inflation rate. **391, 495**

Taylor rule Economist John Taylor's monetary policy rule that explains how the federal funds rate target is set. **391**

term structure of interest rates The relationships among interest rates on bonds with different terms to maturity. **116**

theory of efficient capital markets See *efficient market hypothesis*. **148**

theory of portfolio choice A theory that outlines how much of an asset people will want to hold in their portfolios, as determined by wealth, expected returns, risk, and liquidity. **87**

theory of purchasing power parity (PPP) The theory that exchange rates between any two currencies will adjust to reflect changes in the price levels of the two countries. **404**

thrift institutions (thrifts) Savings and loan associations, mutual savings banks, and credit unions. **38**

tightening of monetary policy An increase in the federal funds rate. **301**

time-inconsistency problem The problem that occurs when monetary policymakers conduct monetary policy in a discretionary way and pursue expansionary policies that are attractive in the short run but lead to poor long-run outcomes. **367**

too-big-to-fail problem Problem in which regulators are reluctant to close down large financial institutions because doing so might precipitate a financial crisis. **218**

trade balance The difference between merchandise exports and imports. **432**

transaction costs The time and money spent trying to exchange financial assets, goods, or services. **34**

transmission mechanisms of monetary policy The channels through which the money supply affects economic activity. **602**

Troubled Asset Relief Plan (TARP) A provision of the Bush administration's Economic Recovery Act of 2008 that authorized the Treasury to spend $700 billion on purchases of subprime mortgage assets from troubled financial institutions or on injections of capital into these institutions. **282**

underwrite To purchase securities from a corporation at a predetermined price and then resell them in the market. **42**

underwriting Guaranteeing the price for a corporation's securities and then selling them to the public. **26**

unemployment rate The percentage of the labor force not working. **7**

unexploited profit opportunity A situation in which an investor can earn a higher-than-normal return. **150**

unit of account Anything used to measure value in an economy. **51**

unsecured debt Debt not guaranteed by collateral. **165**

unsterilized foreign exchange intervention A foreign exchange intervention in which a central bank allows the purchase or sale of domestic currency to affect the monetary base. **429**

value at risk (VaR) Calculations that measure the size of the loss on a trading portfolio that might happen 1% of the time over a short period—say, 2 weeks. **225**

vault cash Currency that is physically held by banks and stored in vaults overnight. **189**

velocity of money The rate of turnover of money; the average number of times per year that a dollar is spent in buying the total amount of final goods and services produced in the economy. **457**

venture capital firm A financial intermediary that pools the resources of its partners and uses the funds to help entrepreneurs start up new businesses. **175**

virtual bank A bank that has no building but rather exists only in cyberspace. **240**

wealth All resources owned by an individual, including all assets. **50, 86**

World Bank The International Bank for Reconstruction and Development, an international organization that provides long-term loans to assist developing countries in building dams, roads, and other physical capital that will contribute to their economic development. **434**

World Trade Organization (WTO) An organization headquartered in Geneva, Switzerland, that monitors rules for the conduct of trade between countries (tariffs and quotas). **434**

yield curve A plot of the interest rates on particular types of bonds with different terms to maturity. **124**

yield to maturity The interest rate that equates the present value of payments received from a credit market instrument with its value today. **68**

zero-coupon bond See *discount bond*. **67**

zero-lower-bound problem A situation in which the central bank is unable to lower short-term interest rates further because they have hit a floor of zero. **355**

Index

GUIDE TO COMMONLY USED SYMBOLS

Symbol	Term	Symbol	Term
Δ	change in a variable	M	money supply
π	inflation rate	M^d	demand for money
π^e	expected inflation	M^s	supply of money
π^T	inflation target	$M1$	M1 monetary aggregate
AD	aggregate demand curve	$M2$	M2 monetary aggregate
AS	aggregate supply curve	MB	monetary base (high-powered money)
B^d	demand for bonds	MB_n	nonborrowed monetary base
B^s	supply of bonds	MP	monetary policy curve
BR	borrowed reserves	mpc	marginal propensity to consume
c	currency ratio	NBR	nonborrowed reserves
C	yearly coupon payment	NX	net exports
C	currency	P	price level
C	consumption expenditure	P_s	stock prices
D	demand curve	P_t	price of a security at time t
D	checkable deposits	ρ	price shock
DL	discount loans	r	real interest rate
e	excess reserves ratio	rr	required reserve ratio for checkable deposits
E_t	exchange (spot) rate		
E_{par}	par (fixed) exchange rate	R	reserves
$(E^e_{t+1} - E_t)/E_t$	expected appreciation of domestic currency	R	return
		R^e	expected return
EM	equity multiplier	R^D	expected return on domestic deposits
ER	excess reserves		
$\bar{f}$	for financial frictions	R^F	expected return on foreign deposits
G	government purchases	ROA	return on assets
i	interest rate (yield to maturity)	ROE	return on equity
i_d	discount rate	RR	required reserves
i^D	interest rate on domestic assets	S	supply curve
i^F	interest rate on foreign assets	T	taxes
i_{or}	interest rate paid on reserves	V	velocity of money
I	planned investment spending	Y	aggregate output (national income)
IS	IS curve	Y^{ad}	aggregate demand
m	money multiplier	Y^P	potential (natural rate level of) output

APPLYING THEORY TO THE REAL WORLD: APPLICATIONS AND BOXES

Applications

Following the Financial News Boxes